Letter-key reaches

Figure- and symbol-key reaches

Reach techniques

Basic techniques

Typewriter parts and functions

Special operations

Business letters

Other types of correspondence

Executive office forms

Professional and technical forms

Envelopes

Manuscripts or reports

Business forms

List of illustrations

List of drills and timed writings

Alphabetic sentences [1]
Figure sentences [2]
Figure/symbol sentences [3]
Fluency (speed) sentences [4]

[1] An alphabetic sentence appears in each Preparatory Practice beginning with page 27.

[2] A figure sentence appears in most Preparatory Practices beginning with page 34.

[3] A figure/symbol sentence appears in most Preparatory Practices beginning with page 51.

[4] Beginning on page 18, an easy sentence, designed for fluency and speed, appears in every Preparatory Practice, except on page 21.

Reach concentration drills

a, 8, 9, 10, 11, 13, 15, 45; **b**, 19, 20, 25; **c**, 17, 18, 21; **d**, 8, 9, 10, 11, 13, 15, 43; **e**, 8, 10, 11, 15, 16, 37, 46; **f**, 8, 9, 10, 11, 13, 15; **g**, 18, 20; **h**, 12, 13, 15, 16; **i**, 11, 13, 15, 16, 35, 46; **j**, 8, 9, 10, 11, 15; **k**, 8, 9, 10, 11, 13, 15; **l**, 8, 9, 10, 11, 15; **m**, 18, 20, 32; **n**, 16, 18, 21, 25, 32, 74; **o**, 8, 10, 11, 15, 16, 35; **p**, 19, 20, 25, 31; **q**, 23, 25, 28, 31; **r**, 13, 15, 16, 32, 37; **s**, 8, 9, 10, 11, 13, 15, 43, 45; **t**, 11, 13, 15, 16, 32; **u**, 17, 18, 21; **v**, 21, 29, 31; **w**, 14, 15; **x**, 16, 18, 21, 25, 31; **y**, 21, 25, 31; **z**, 24, 25, 27; **ce**, 74; **un**, 74; **gr**, 74; **um**, 74; **br**, 68; **min**, 219; **l**, 32; **2**, 37; **3**, 34; **4**, 32; **5**, 36; **6**, 37; **7**, 34; **8**, 32; **9**, 36; **0**, 34; **apostrophe**, 47, 78; **colon**, 24; **comma**, 22, 183; **dash**, 37, 93; **degrees**, 85; **diagonal**, 36; **exclamation point**, 47, 184; **feet**, 85; **hyphen**, 37, 66, 81, 85, 89, 93, 105, 165, 243, 282; **inches**, 85; **italics**, 48; **math signs**, 85; **minutes**, 85; **period**, 13, 47, 182; **question mark**, 23, 25, 28, 29, 180; **quotation marks**, 48, 89, 187; **seconds**, 85; **semicolon**, 8, 9, 10, 11, 13, 15; **underline**, 48; **$**, 43; **#**, 43; **%**, 45; **&**, 43; **( )**, 45, 187

Guided writing copy

Paragraphs: 21, 24, 25, 29, 30, 31, 33, 34, 35, 36, 38, 40, 41, 42, 44, 45, 46, 47, 49, 52, 54, 120

Sentences: 18, 20, 28, 42, 46, 49, 52

Metric activities

84, 156, 172, 284, 285, 286, 287, 288

Preapplication manipulative drills

Addressing envelopes, large, 69, 71, 106; small, 69, 106
Aligning Arabic numerals, 78; Roman numerals, 112
Aligning/typing over words, 81
Assembling/inserting carbon pack, 70
Attention line, 124
Automatic line finder (ratchet release), 85, 180
Backspacer/margin release, 26
Bell cue, 56
Bibliography, 186, 187
Blind carbon copy notation, 129, 236
Boxed tables, 161, 162
Carbon pack assembly, 70
Carbon copy notation, 129
Carriage return, 18
Centering, columns, 76-77, 154, 155; horizontal, column headings, 80, 155; lines, 57; over line of writing, 183; reading position, 59; vertical, 59
Centering on special-size paper, 60
Centering main headings in leftbound reports, 183
Company name in closing lines of letter, 127
Correcting errors, 64
Dollar signs in columns, 79, 157
Drawing lines on the typewriter, 173
Enclosure notation in letters, 127
Erasing, 64; on carbon copies, 70
Footnotes, 86, 182
Headings, outline, 83; report, 87-88, 181
Leaders, typing, 140
Mailing notations in letters, 106, 124
Margin release, 26
Margin stops, 5
Proofreader's marks, 44, 98, 208
Postscript, 129
Ratchet release, 85, 180
Reference citations, 184
Reply reference notation in letter, 125
Rulings (single and double), 160; drawing, 173
Second-page headings, interoffice communication, 135; letters, 131
Shift lock, 22
Spacing a tabulation, 29, 100, 112, 172, 176
Special characters and symbols, 85
Special-size paper, centering on, 60
Spread headings, 85, 254
Squeezing/expanding letters, 109
Subject line in letters, 125
Superscripts/subscripts, 85, 180
Tab clear key, 19
Tab mechanism, 19, 23, 29, 30, 31, 53, 75, 76
Tab set key, 19
Variable line spacer, 81
Word division, 58, 100

Problems in rough draft and script

Rough draft: 44, 46, 49, 52, 60, 122, 123, 128, 137, 140, 143, 158, 159, 168, 185, 186, 197, 212, 213, 223, 230, 231, 233, 235, 238, 239, 240, 241, 242, 249, 250, 252, 256, 258, 259, 263, 267, 268, 277, 279, 280, 285, 286, 287, 288, 295, 297, 299, 300

Script: 35, 38, 39, 52, 53, 55, 57, 60, 71, 102, 122, 123, 129, 137, 142, 155, 156, 162, 173, 178, 179, 184, 195, 196, 221, 222, 229, 231, 232, 233, 234, 237, 248, 250, 251, 257, 262, 266, 276, 278, 282, 294, 298, 299

Related learning activities

Capitalization guides, 177, 191
Composing at the typewriter, 62, 65, 66, 82, 87, 107, 114, 115, 123, 125, 127, 134, 135, 137, 138, 139, 141, 142, 156, 158, 177, 182, 183, 184, 187, 189, 190, 191, 215, 221, 222, 237, 240
Leaders, 140, 210
Misseplled words, 64
Partially filled page with footnotes, 88, 182
Proofreader's marks, 44, 98, 208
Proofreading, 33, 36, 138, 170
Punctuation guides, 102, 114, 115, 123, 125, 127, 134, 138, 141, 142, 156, 158, 177, 187, 191
Second-page heading of interoffice memo, 135; of letter, 131
Spacing after punctuation, 8, 13, 23, 40, 47
Spread headings, 85, 254
Underlining, 48
Word division, 58, 66, 100

Rough-draft timed writings

1′: 52, 55, 98, 122, 167, 203, 224
3′: 55, 75, 89, 90, 208, 244, 269
5′: 75, 90, 98, 122, 148, 167, 203, 208, 224, 269

Script timed writings

1′: 39, 52, 121, 166, 201, 289
2′: 55, 166
3′: 206, 243, 289
5′: 121, 166, 201, 206

Statistical timed writings

1′: 99, 120, 150, 168, 204, 226, 291
2′: 33, 34, 38, 46
3′: 36, 41, 44, 45, 47, 49, 54, 61, 89, 93, 245, 271, 291
5′: 61, 93, 99, 120, 150, 168, 204, 226, 245, 271

Straight-copy timed writings

1′: 20, 28, 44, 97, 110, 117, 119, 132, 144, 146, 165, 169, 170, 207, 209, 225, 227, 270, 272, 290
2′: 21, 24, 25, 29, 30, 31, 33, 35, 67, 79, 84, 120, 202
3′: 35, 38, 40, 42, 44, 49, 52, 61, 72, 95, 244, 246, 290, 292
5′: 61, 72, 95, 97, 110, 117, 119, 132, 144, 146, 165, 169, 170, 193, 207, 209, 225, 227, 244, 246, 247, 270, 272, 290, 292, 293, 296

Technique drills

Keystroking: 9, 10, 11, 12, 13, 14, 15, 16, 17, 18, 19, 20, 21, 22, 23, 24, 27, 28, 32, 34, 36, 37, 39, 43, 45, 47, 48, 51, 54, 74, 89, 119, 126, 165, 167, 169, 202, 203, 204, 226, 243, 245, 269, 271, 291

Machine parts:

backspacer, 26, 30, 42, 53
carriage (carrier) return, 18, 23, 30, 31, 42, 53
margin release, 26, 42, 53
shift keys, 15, 23, 26, 30, 31, 42, 70, 75, 89, 104, 129, 172, 206, 212, 224, 229, 237, 249, 298
shift lock, 22, 23, 30, 31, 53, 75, 174
space bar, 15, 23, 30, 31, 75, 176
tabulator, 19, 23, 29, 30, 31, 42, 53, 75, 76, 171, 173, 177

Response patterns:

letter (stroke), 37, 41, 51, 55, 74, 121, 125, 269, 271
word, 37, 41, 51, 55, 74, 121, 125, 226, 269, 271
combination, 37, 41, 51, 55, 74, 121, 125, 269, 271, 291

Intensive Course • Tenth Edition

College Typewriting

S. J. Wanous
Professor of Education, Emeritus
University of California, L. A.

Charles H. Duncan
Professor of Business Education
Eastern Michigan University

S. ElVon Warner
Head, Business Education
and Office Administration Department
University of Northern Iowa

Thomas E. Langford
President, Bradford/Zorn
School of Business
Houston

ISBN: 0-538-20200-9

Library of Congress Catalog Card Number: 80-50161

1 2 3 4 5 6 7 8 9 10 11 12 13 14 H 7 6 5 4 3 2 1

Printed in U.S.A.

T20

Published by
SOUTH-WESTERN PUBLISHING CO.

CINCINNATI   WEST CHICAGO, ILL.   DALLAS   PELHAM MANOR, N.Y.   PALO ALTO, CALIF.

Contents

Division 3

Advanced Typewritten Communications

Preface

COLLEGE TYPEWRITING, Intensive Course, Tenth Edition, is the new revision of a series of learning materials, first published in 1930, designed exclusively for college students. The learning materials and procedures in this new Tenth Edition have thus gone through 50 years of testing, evaluating, writing, rewriting, selecting, and polishing. With each edition, the less effective materials have been eliminated or improved and new classroom-tested materials have been added. This new edition, therefore, combines the best of the old with the best of the new.

Organization of the Book

This book is organized into three divisions of 50 well-planned lessons each plus a Reference Guide of useful typing information strategically placed.

Division 1 is divided into two Levels of closely related material. Level 1 (Lessons 1-26) is designed to develop manipulative skills. Stressed are keyboard mastery, use of correct techniques, and other manipulative operations—the essential foundation for all successfully applied typewriting activities. Level 2 (Lessons 27-50) emphasizes centering and copy-arrangement concepts and procedures as they apply to such commonly used business papers as letters, tables, outlines, and reports. Composing and communication skills are also stressed. Supplemental skill-building practices are interspersed to reinforce basic skills.

Division 2 also consists of two Levels of closely related activities. Prior to Level 3, a series of activities are provided to inventory levels of basic and problem skills. Level 3 (Lessons 51-74) extends problem and production skills on basic letter styles, letters with special features, simplified forms of business correspondence, and administrative communications. Level 4 (Lessons 75-100) emphasizes statistical communications: tables with special features, business forms, technical and statistical reports, and employment communications.

Throughout Division 2, emphasis is placed on integrating spelling, punctuating, capitalizing, and number expression with typewriting, not only to make these skills more useful in real-life settings but also to lay the foundation for effective composing and careful proofreading. Supplemental skill-building practices are also interspersed to refine basic skills.

The two Levels of Division 3 are organized as office job simulations. These simulations integrate the knowledge and skills developed in earlier levels by putting the typist in realistic office-like settings to perform related job assignments as they would be performed by an office typist in a variety of job situations.

Following Level 1 in which the major emphasis is on the development of manipulative skills, basic skills are refined through a series of speed/control sections interspersed among the application sections. These sections may be used in order of occurrence; they may be grouped; or they may be selected from to provide the basic skill emphasis student performance indicates is needed at specific points in the program.

Midway through Divisions 2 and 3 and again at the end of each division there are sections of lessons which focus on measurement of achievement in basic skill and production power. Thus, ample opportunities are provided in the textbook to evaluate intensively a student's overall growth in skill, work habits, production know-how, proofreading, and other attributes of a typist.

Special Features of the Book

1. The scientifically structured keyboard learning and basic skill-building materials are based on the letter-combination and word-frequency studies of Lessenberry, Robinson, and others and on the response pattern ("chaining") research of Langford, Robinson, and Shell. Students are thus assured that they are practicing what they *will* eventually type, not merely what they *may* type.
2. Basic skill-building and measurement paragraph copy is triple-controlled for difficulty, using the difficulty indexes established by Robinson with over 2,500 students. The three difficulty factors—syllable intensity, average word length, and percentage of high-frequency words—are simultaneously controlled to assure valid and reliable measures of demonstrated skill.
3. Learning goals are supplied at the beginning of each section of lessons to orient and motivate the student.
4. Each basic typing operation (letters, reports, tables, and the like) occurs repeatedly in cycles of emphasis to provide spaced reviews, to assure long-time retention, and to maximize transfer.
5. Heavy emphasis, especially in Division 3, is placed on typing from script and rough-draft copy to provide the realism of office typing as identified by the research of Erickson, Frisch, Ober and Perkins.
6. Complete directions and visual models are used liberally in presenting new learnings. Thereafter, students are given a sense of direction but fewer directions so that they learn to make most of the decisions on matters of style, placement, and procedure.
7. A directions-left/copy-right format aids students in distinguishing typing directions from the copy to be typed.
8. From cover to cover, the text includes the most current conventions of typewritten communication and the most up-to-date business and government office procedures.

Special Acknowledgment

In addition to acknowledging the many contributions made by the thousands of teachers who have used prior editions of *College Typewriting*, special recognition is given to Dr. D. D. Lessenberry, the original author who for 50 years set the pattern and pace of typewriting instruction throughout the United States.

S. J. Wanous • C. H. Duncan
S. E. Warner • T. E. Langford

The diagram above shows the parts of an electric typewriter. Page 2 shows a diagram of the parts of a nonelectric typewriter.

You should be able to locate the parts of your typewriter from one of these diagrams; but if you have the instructional booklet that comes with your typewriter, use it to identify exact locations of these parts.

1 Carriage return lever (not on electric)

2 Left platen knob: used to insert paper or (with left carriage release 4) to move carriage right or left (except with single–element typewriters)

3 Variable line spacer; used to change writing line setting permanently

4 Left carriage release: used to release carriage so it moves freely to left or right (except on single element typewriters, such as the one shown)

5 Line–space selector: sets typewriter to advance (using carriage return lever 1) 1, 2, or (on some machines) 3 lines for single, double, or triple spacing

6 Automatic line finder: used to change line spacing temporarily, then refind the line

7 Paper guide: used as a guide for inserting paper

8 Paper guide scale: used to set paper guide at desired position

9 Left margin set: used to set left margin stop

10/14 Paper bail rolls: used to hold paper against platen

11 Paper bail: used to hold paper against platen

12 Card/envelope holders: used to hold cards, labels, and envelopes against platen

13 Printing point indicator: used to position carriage at desired point to set margins and tab stops and for horizontal centering

14 (See 10)

15 Right margin set: used to set right margin stop

16 Paper table: supports paper when it is in typewriter

17 Platen (cylinder): provides a hard surface against which type element or bars strike

18 Paper release lever: used to allow paper to be removed or aligned

19 Right carriage release: used to release carriage so it moves freely to left or right (except on single element typewriters)

20 Right platen knob: used to turn platen as paper is being inserted or (with right carriage release lever 19) to move carriage to the right or left

21 Aligning scale: used to align copy that has been reinserted

22 Line–of–writing (margin) scale: used to check margins, tab stops, and other settings

23 Ribbon carrier: positions and controls ribbon at printing point (not shown—under the cover)

24 Tabulator: used to move carriage (carrier) to tab stops

25 Tab set: used to set tabulator stops

26 Backspace key: used to move printing point to left one space at a time

27 Right shift key: used to type capitals of letter keys controlled by left hand

28 Space bar: used to move printing point to right, one space at a time

29 Left shift key: used to type capitals of letter keys controlled by right hand

30 Shift lock: used to lock shift mechanism so that all letters are capitalized

31 Ribbon control: used to select ribbon typing position (not shown—under cover)

32 Margin release key: used to move carriage (carrier) beyond margin stops

33 Tab clear: used to clear tab stops

34 Carriage return key: used to return carriage to left margin and to advance paper up

35 ON/OFF control: used to turn electric typewriters on or off

Job 1, continued

words

Introduction 145

The materials, and manufacture, and the mechanical requirements 145
of high-strength structural bolts used in structural steel joints will 157
be discussed in this report. 172

Materials and Manufacture 177

The bolts wire shall be made from steel produced by open- 188
hearth, electric-furnace, or basic-oxygen process. All bolts 198
will shall be heat treated in a liquid medium and then tempered by rehaet- 210
ing at temperatures of to at least 427° C. (800° F.). The threads of the bolts 224
may be either rolled or cut. All galvanized bolts will be 239
hot-dip zinc coated or, when specified, mechanically zinc coated. All work performed 251
by subcontractors must should be returned to the manufacturer for 268
further testing. 279

Mechanical Requirements 281

All bolts shall meet the hardness specifications shown 291
in the following table. 302

Hardness Requirements 307

	Birnell		Rockwell C	
Bolt Size	Min.*	Max.*	Min.*	Max.*
DS 1/2 to 1 in., incl.	248	331	24	35
1 1/8 to 1 1/2 in., incl.	223	293	19	31

311 333 336 347 354 365 371 379 390

* Hardness number 394

All galvanized boults with nuts (bolt/nut assembly) will be tested in an as- 409
sembled joint. After full tightening, the bolt/nut assembly shall show 423
no signs of fatigue. 428

Conclusion 432

DS All bolts to be used in structural steel joints will be 443
tested both as to the materials and the manufacture process 455
and the mechanical requirements before becoming certified safe 468
for use in structural steel joints. 475

478

Source: 1979 Annual Book of ASTM Standards. 494

Job 2
If time permits, retype Job 1.

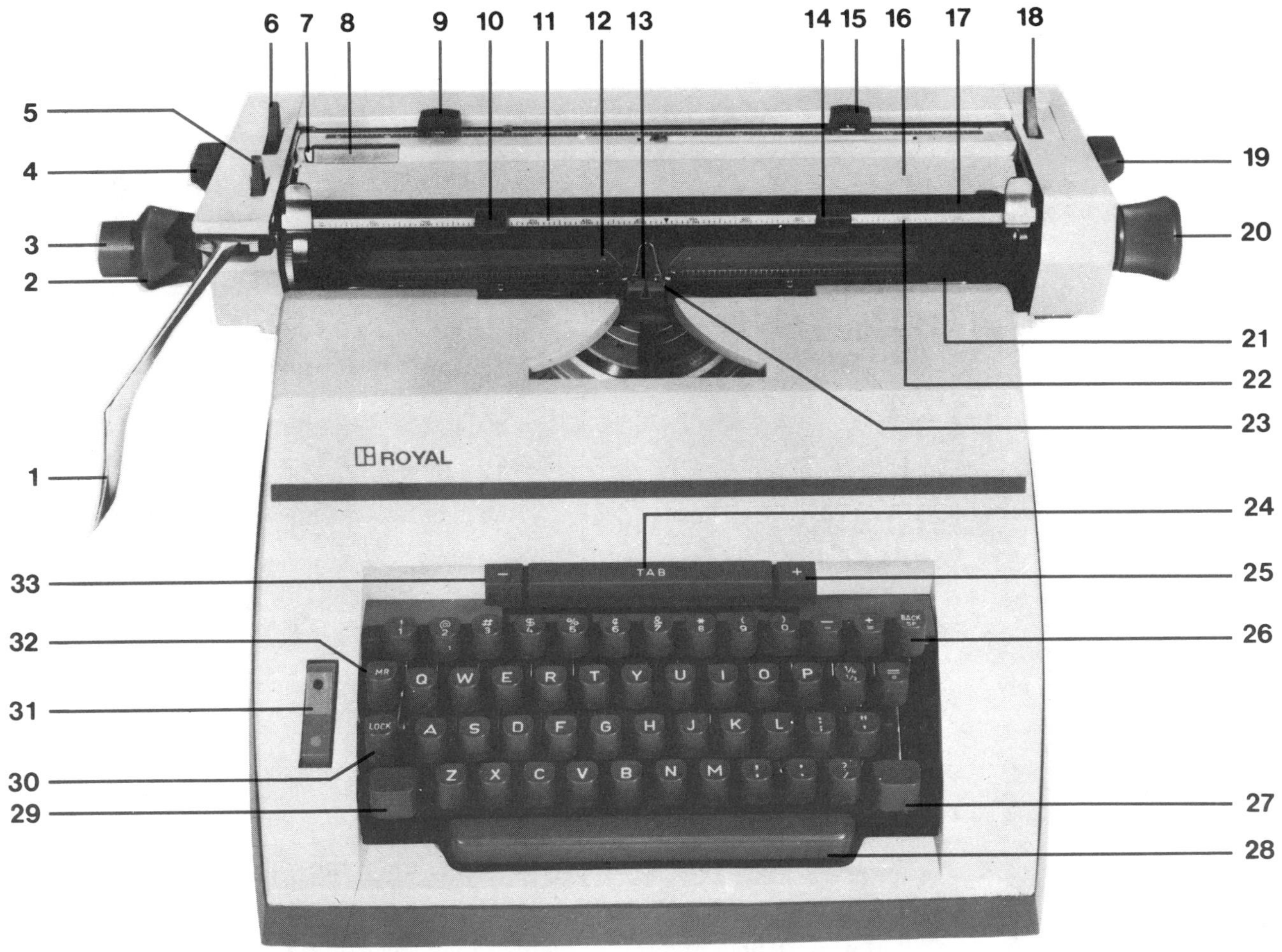

The diagram above shows the parts of a nonelectric typewriter. Page 1 shows a diagram of the parts of an electric typewriter.

You should be able to locate the parts of your typewriter from one of these diagrams; but if you have the instructional booklet that comes with your typewriter, use it to identify exact locations of these parts.

1 Carriage return lever: used to return carriage to left margin and to advance paper

2 Left platen knob: used to position paper or (with left carriage release 4) to move carriage to right or left

3 Variable line spacer: used to change writing line setting permanently.

4 Left carriage release: used to release carriage so it moves freely to left or right

5 Line-space selector: sets typewriter to advance (using carriage return lever 1) 1, 2, or (on some machines) 3 lines for single, double, or triple spacing

6 Automatic line finder: used to change line spacing temporarily, then refind the line

7 Paper guide: used as a guide for inserting paper

8 Paper guide scale: used to set paper guide at desired position

9 Left margin set: used to set left margin stop

10/14 Paper bail rolls: used to hold paper against platen

11 Paper bail: used to hold paper against platen

12 Card/envelope holders: used to hold cards, labels, and envelopes against platen

13 Printing point indicator: used to position carriage at desired point to set margin and tab stops and for horizontal centering

14 (See 10)

15 Right margin set: used to set right margin stop

16 Paper table: supports paper when it is in typewriter

17 Platen (cylinder): provides a hard surface against which typebars strike

18 Paper release lever: used to allow paper to be removed or aligned

19 Right carriage release: used to release carriage so it moves freely to left or right

20 Right platen knob: used to turn platen as paper is being inserted or (with right carriage release lever 19) to move carriage to the right or left

21 Aligning scale: used to align copy that has been reinserted

22 Line-of-writing (margin) scale: used to check margins, tab stops, and other settings

23 Ribbon carrier: positions and controls ribbon

24 Tabulator: used to move carriage to tab stops that have been set

25 Tab set: used to set tabulator stops

26 Backspace key: used to move printing point to left one space at a time

27 Right shift key: used to type capitals of letter keys controlled by left hand

28 Space bar: used to move printing point to right, one space at a time

29 Left shift key: used to type capitals of letter keys controlled by right hand

30 Shift lock: used to lock shift mechanism so that all letters are capped

31 Ribbon control: used to select ribbon typing position

32 Margin release key: used to move carriage beyond margin stops

33 Tab clear: used to clear tabulator stops

149b, continued

words

Job 3
Boxed table with braced heading

Type and center the table DS on a full sheet. Use exact vertical centering.

SANDERS BUSINESS EQUIPMENT 5

(Quarterly Sales) 9

Branch	Sales Volume			Year to Date	words
	April	May	June		36 39 48 49 54 68
Boston	$165,200	$ 170,900	$ 182,100	$1,001,200	79
Cincinnati	86,100	90,200	89,100	530,500	87
Denver	62,800	65,100	66,700	420,300	95
Kansas City	141,900	148,600	147,200	910,700	103
Los Angeles	300,100	299,700	308,500	1,900,200	113
New York City	201,300	209,100	205,800	1,245,500	123
Seattle	30,800	35,100	40,600	192,100	131
					144
Totals	$988,200	$1,018,700	$1,040,000	$6,200,500	155
					169

150

150a ▶ 5

Preparatory practice

each line 3 times SS (slowly, faster, still faster); retype selected lines as time permits

alphabet Q. R. King was very zealous; he completed the job and excused himself.

fig/sym The $10,000 bond (#231-A-7469) at 8.5% interest earned $850 this year.

long words Wilhelmina Rhodenbaugh's tremendous professional creativity is superb.

fluency A flame's height is a result of the quantity of fuel that is consumed.

| 1 | 2 | 3 | 4 | 5 | 6 | 7 | 8 | 9 | 10 | 11 | 12 | 13 | 14 |

150b ▶ 45

Production measurement:

special reports [plain sheets]

Time schedule
Assembling materials .... 3′
Timed production ....35′
Final check; compute *n-pram* .... 7′

Job 1
Leftbound technical report

Type this report according to the technical report format (See page 281, if necessary)

words

Page 1 1
Report No. BO-143 5

STANDARDS FOR BOLTS IN STRUCTURAL STEEL JOINTS 31

Summary 35

(quenched and tempered)

The three types of steel bolts (commonly referred to as 50
high-strength structural bolts) covered by these standards 62
are: Type 1--bolts (made) of medium-carbon steel (in) sizes 1/2 to 1 1/2 76
inches (inclusive,) in diameter; Type 2--bolts made from low-carbon mar- 90
tensite steel in sizes 1/2 to 1 1/2 inches, inclusive, in di- 102
ameter; and type 3 bolts that have (atmospheric) corrosion resistance and 117
weathering characteristics (two times the atomospheric cor- 128
rosion reisstance of carbon structural steel) (with copper). 140

(continued on page 300)

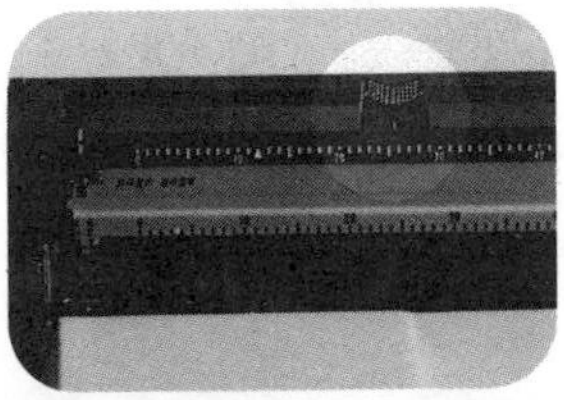

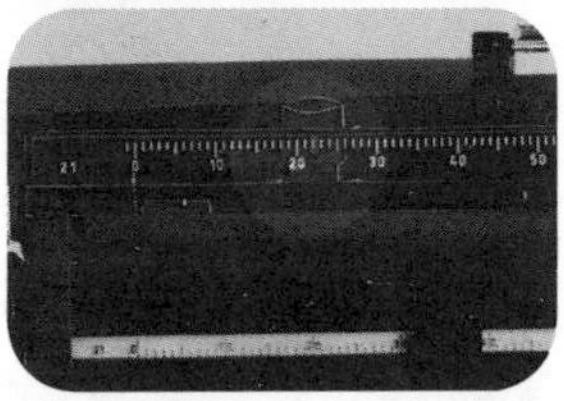

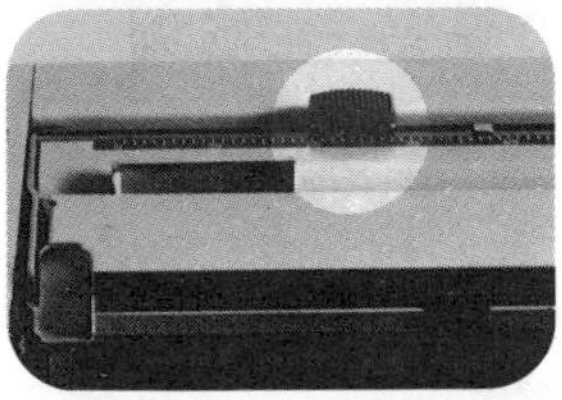

Type A

Push-button set

Adler, Olympia, Remington, Royal 700/870 manuals, Smith–Corona

1. Press down on the left margin set button.

2. Slide it to desired position on the line–of–writing (margin) scale.

3. Release the margin set button.

4. Using the right margin set button, set the right margin stop in the same way.

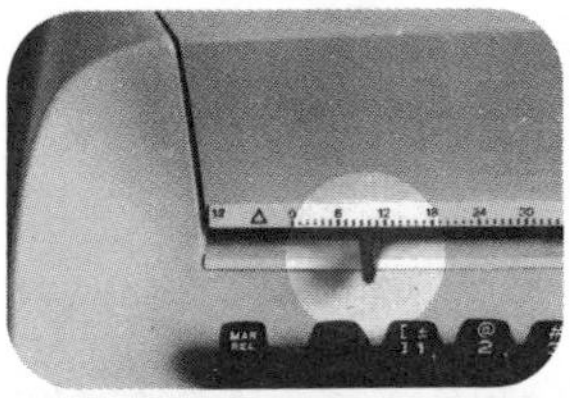

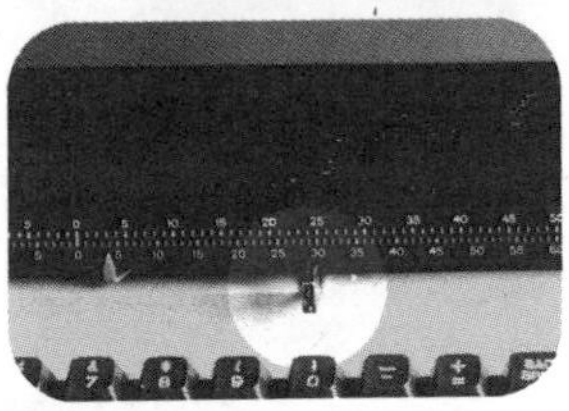

Type B

Push-lever set

Single element typewriters, such as Adler, Olivetti, Royal, Selectric, Sperry/Remington

1. Push in on the left margin set lever.

2. Slide it to desired position on the line–of–writing (margin) scale.

3. Release the margin set lever.

4. Using the right margin set lever, set the right margin stop in the same way.

Type C

Magic margin set

Royal 470/560/970

1. Pull left magic margin lever forward.

2. Move carriage to desired position on the line–of–writing (margin) scale.

3. Release the left margin lever.

4. Using the right magic margin lever, set the right margin stop in the same way.

Type D

Key set

IBM typebar, Olivetti electric

1. Move carriage to the left margin stop by depressing the return key.

2. Depress and hold down the margin set (IBM reset) key as you move carriage to desired left margin stop position.

3. Release the margin set (IBM reset) key.

4. Move carriage to the right margin stop.

5. Depress and hold down the margin set (IBM reset) key as you move carriage to desired right margin stop position.

6. Release the margin set (IBM reset) key.

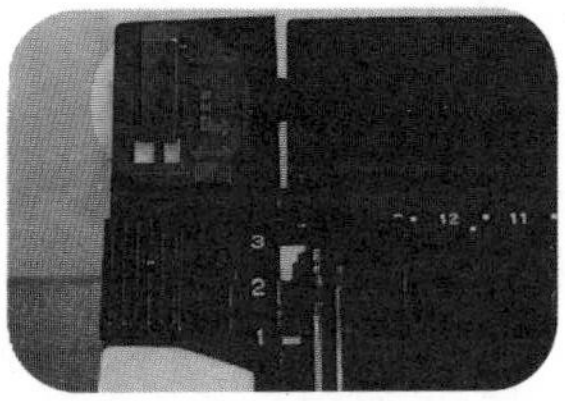

Type E

Lever-arrow set

Olivetti manual

If margin stop is to be moved inward:

1. Move carriage to desired position.

2. Pull appropriate margin lever forward.

If margin stop is to be moved outward:

1. Move carriage to existing margin stop.

2. Move appropriate margin lever forward and hold it in the forward position.

3. Depress carriage release button and move the carriage to desired position.

4. Release margin lever.

General information for setting margin stops is given here. If you have the manufacturer's booklet for your typewriter, however, use it; the procedure for your particular model may be slightly different.

149

149a ▶ 5

Preparatory practice

each line 3 times SS (slowly, faster, still faster); retype selected lines as time permits

alphabet Both maneuvers require good maps with exact keys of the Zulu's jungle.

fig/sym An auto sold for $8,450 in 1976; four years later it was worth $2,300.

shift keys John Rust works at Macy's in either Buffalo, New York City, or Albany.

fluency The panel has a new theory that half of all fuel costs are very rigid.

| 1 | 2 | 3 | 4 | 5 | 6 | 7 | 8 | 9 | 10 | 11 | 12 | 13 | 14 |

149b ▶ 45

Production measurement:

forms and tables [LM p. 175]

Time schedule
Assembling materials .... 3′
Timed production ....35′
Final check; compute *n-pram* .... 7′

Job 1
X-ray report

Type the form with 1 cc.

Job 2

Retype Job 1 on a plain full sheet with 1 cc. Type all necessary headings and captions; SS; DS between items.

Add 24 words to Job 1 word count for the additional words typed for the heading and the captions.

GRANTLAND COUNTY HOSPITAL

words

X-RAY REPORT

Name Cynthia A. Robinson Hospital No. 54930 5

Age 23 X-ray No. 1824 7

Sex Female Room No. Emergency Room 11

Attending Physician Anna Hurlbut, M.D. Date April 12, 19-- 18

EXAMINATION REQUESTED: X-rays of Chest, Left Arm, Left Wrist, and 31
Abdomen 33

Portable x-ray of the chest reveals bilateral pneumothorax 45
and fractures of the sixth, seventh, and eighth ribs. The 57
pneumothorax in the left lung is on the facies costalis of the 69
middle lobe. The base of the right lung has either a 80
pulmonary contusion or atelectasis. The mediastinum and 91
heart are normal. 95

X-rays of the left arm reveal a Colles' fracture of the radius. 108

X-rays of the left wrist reveal an impacted fracture of the 120
lunate bone and dislocation of the navicular bone. 131

X-rays of the abdomen reveal well defined psoas and renal 142
outlines. The pelvis contains an oblique fracture of the left 155
iliac crest extending to the level of the inferior margin of 167
the sacroiliac joint. The symphysis pubis contains three 179
transverse fractures bilaterally. 186

IMPRESSION: Bilateral pneumothorax, Colles' fracture of the left 199
radius, impacted fracture of the lunate and dislocation of 211
the navicular in the left wrist, and fractures of the iliac 222
crest and symphysis pubis of the pelvis. 231

Radiologist: Silvio Fuentes, M.D. 235

1
Arrange work area

Begin each lesson by arranging your desk or table as shown.

- Typing paper at left of typewriter
- Front frame of typewriter even with front edge of desk
- Book at right of typewriter and elevated for easy reading
- Rest of desk clear of unneeded books and other materials

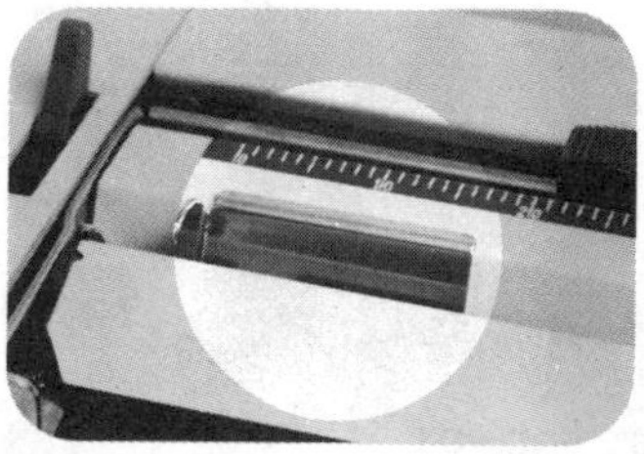

2
Adjust paper guide

Move **paper guide (7)** left or right so that it lines up with 0 (zero) on the **paper-bail scale (11)** or the **line-of-writing** or **margin scale (22).**

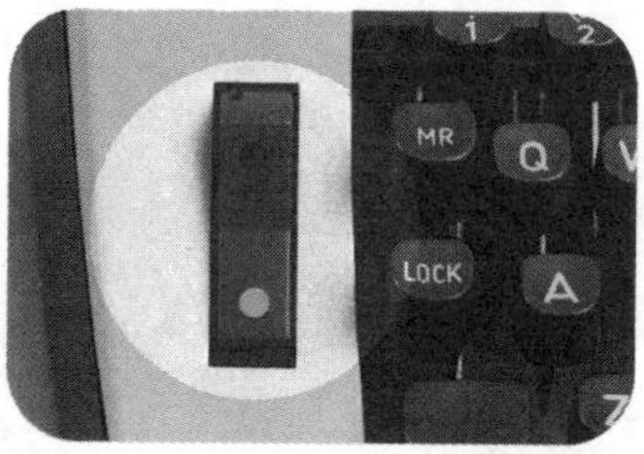

3
Adjust ribbon control

Set **ribbon control (31)** on black to type on upper part of ribbon.

4
Insert typing paper

Take a sheet of paper in your left hand and follow the directions and illustrations at the right and below.

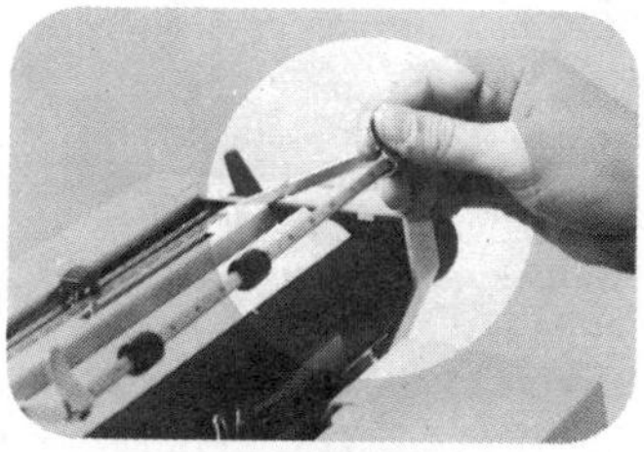

1. Pull **paper bail (11)** forward (or up on some machines).

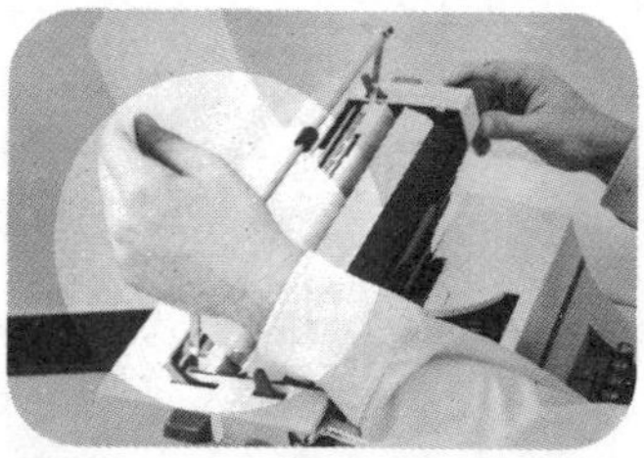

2. Place paper against paper guide, behind the **platen (17).**

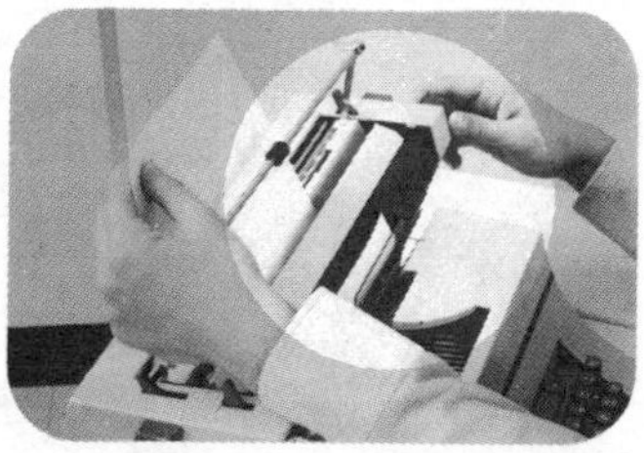

3. Twirl paper into machine, using **right platen knob (20).**

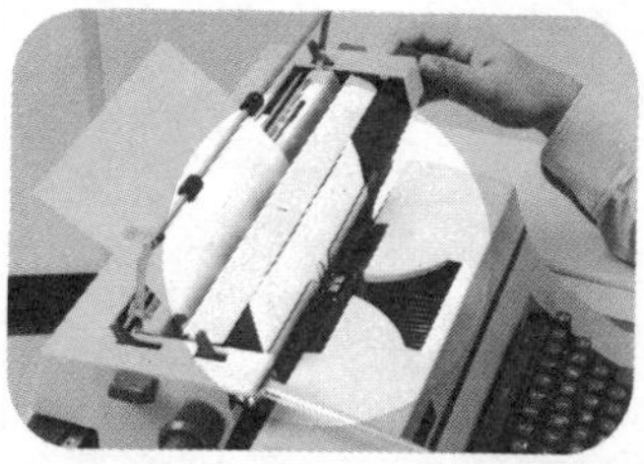

4. Stop when paper is about 1½ inches above **aligning scale (21).**

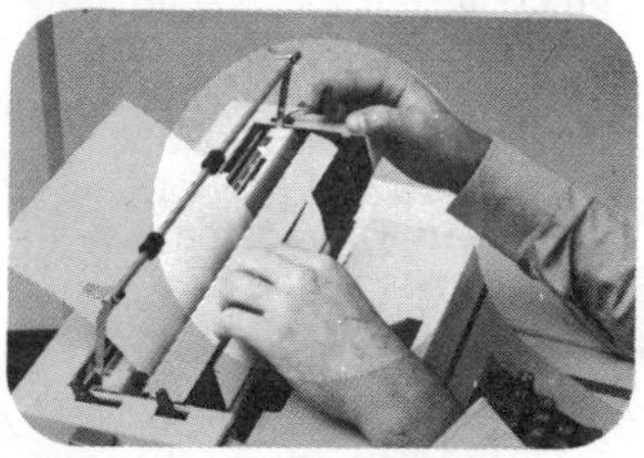

5. If paper is not straight, pull **paper release lever (18)** forward.

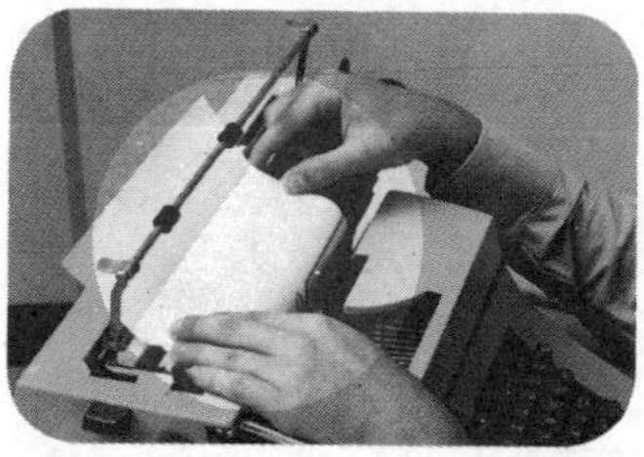

6. Straighten paper, then push paper release lever back.

7. Push paper bail back so that it holds paper against platen.

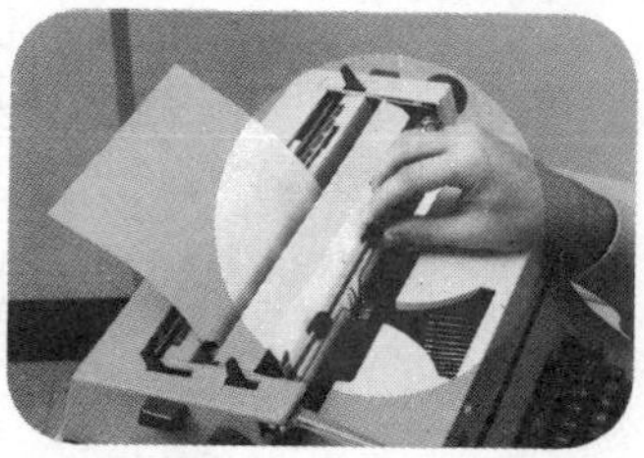

8. Slide **paper bail rolls (10/14)** into position, dividing paper into thirds.

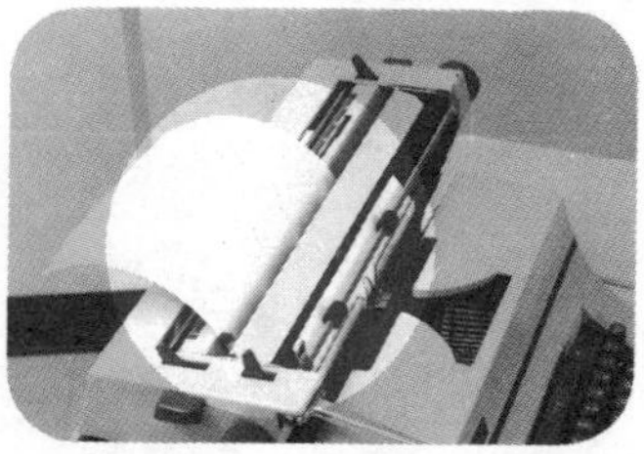

9. Properly inserted paper.

148c ▶ 37
Production measurement:

legal documents [LM pp. 171–174]

Timed schedule

Assembling supplies ..... 2′
Timed production ....30′
Final check; compute *n-pram* .... 5′

Job 1
Warranty deed

Type the warranty deed and an endorsement on the back. The attorney who prepared this legal document is:

Andrea J. Pickmann
Attorney-at-Law
Suite 367
Du Pont Building
169 East Flagler Street
Miami, FL 33131

Job 2

Type another warranty deed and endorsement using the basic form of Job 1. Substitute the following data:

Cheryl Lomis is selling the real property to Georgian K. Thurman. The property is located in the City of Homestead, County of Dade, State of Florida.

Description of property:
Lot 126-C4-2, Tract 3-B, as per recorded in Book 421, pages 348-349, in the records of the Dade County Recorder's Office.

The document was prepared and signed by both the maker and the Notary Public on July 10, 19—, in Miami, County of Dade, State of Florida. The same attorney prepared this document as in Job 1.

words

W A R R A N T Y   D E E D 5

FOR A VALUABLE CONSIDERATION, I, Carlos 13
Vegas, do hereby acknowledge the receipt of such con- 23
sideration and grant, with general warranty covenants, to 35
Stephano V. Ricardo all the real property situated in 45
the City of Opa-Locka, County of Dade, State of 55
Florida, described as follows: 61

Lot 438-B2-5, Tract 8-C, as per re- 68
corded in Book 312, pages 628- 74
629, in the records of the Dade 80
County Recorder's Office. 85

IN WITNESS WHEREOF, I hereby covenant with 94
Stephano V. Ricardo that I am in possession of a fee 104
simple title to that above described property, and that 116
the property is completely free from any and all encum- 126
brances, liens, and attachments. 133

WITNESS my hand this 10th day of July, 19--. 142
148
151
________________________(L.S.) 154
Carlos Vegas 156

STATE OF FLORIDA) 159
: ss. 169
County of Dade) 180

Before me, a Notary Public in and for the County 191
and State aforesaid, personally appeared the above-named 203
person and acknowledged the signing of the foregoing in- 209
strument to be his/~~her~~ voluntary act and deed for the uses 219
and purposes therein stated. 231

In testimony whereof, I have hereunto subscribed 237
my name at Miami, Florida, this 10th day of July, 19--. 239

____
Notary Public 247

My commission expires on June 30, 1989. 268

5
Set line-space selector

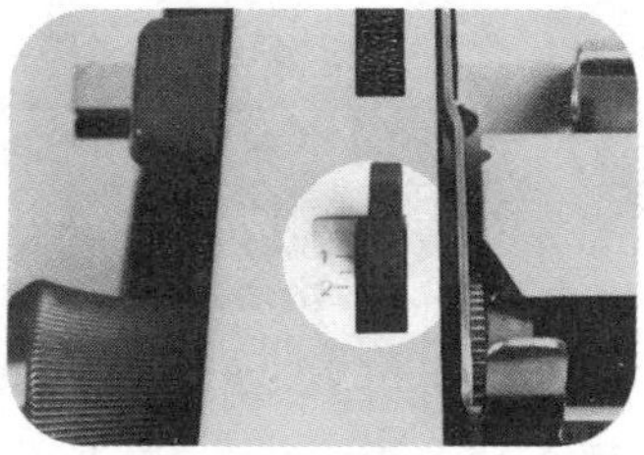

Set **line-space selector (5)** on "1" to single-space (SS) the lines you are to type in Phase 1 lessons.

When so directed, set on "2" to double-space (DS) or on "3" to triple-space (TS).

Single-spaced (SS) copy has no blank line space between lines; double-spaced (DS) copy has 1 blank line space between lines; triple-spaced (TS) copy has 2 blank line spaces between lines.

```
1 Lines 1 and 2 are single-spaced (SS).
2 A double space (DS) separates Lines 2 and 4.
3                 1 blank line space
4 A triple space (TS) separates Lines 4 and 7.
5
                  2 blank line spaces
6
7 Set the selector on "1" for single spacing.
```

6
Plan and set margin stops

Study the following information, then set margin stops for a 50-space line as directed on page 3 for your typewriter.

Typewriters have at least one **line-of-writing scale (22)** that reads from 0 to *at least* 110 for machines with *elite* type, from 0 to *at least* 90 for machines with *pica* type.

The spaces on the line-of-writing scale are matched to the spacing of the letters on the typewriter—elite or pica, as shown above right.

When 8½- by 11-inch paper is inserted into the typewriter (short side up) with left edge of paper at 0 on the line-of-writing scale, the exact center point is 51 for elite, 42½ for pica machines. Use 42 for pica center.

To have typed material centered horizontally, set left and right margin stops the same number of spaces from center point of paper (51, elite center; 42, pica center).

A warning bell on the typewriter rings 6 to 11 or more spaces before the right margin stop is reached, so add 3 to 7 spaces (usually 5) before setting right margin stop.

The diagrams at right indicate margin stop settings for 50-, 60-, and 70-space lines, assuming the paper is inserted with the left edge at 0 on the line-of-writing scale and that 5 spaces are added to right margin for ringing of the bell.

You can type 12 elite characters in a horizontal inch. (2.54 centimeters)

You can type 10 pica characters in a horizontal inch.

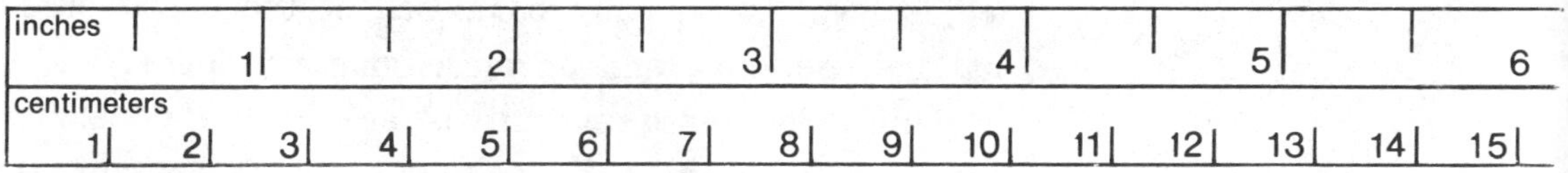

Elite type is smaller than pica type. As a result, there are 12 elite spaces but only 10 pica spaces to an inch.

Elite center

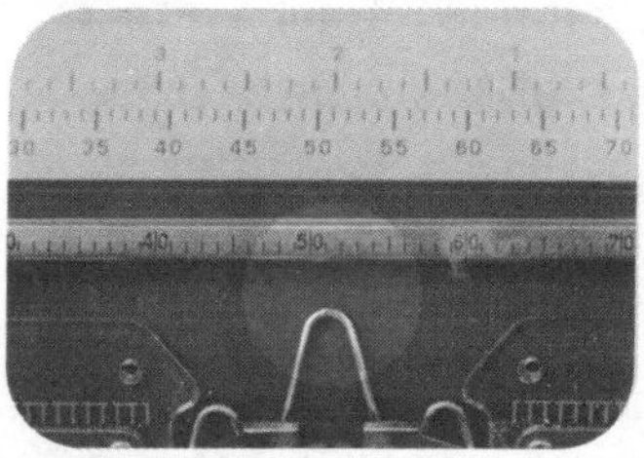

Pica center

Elite

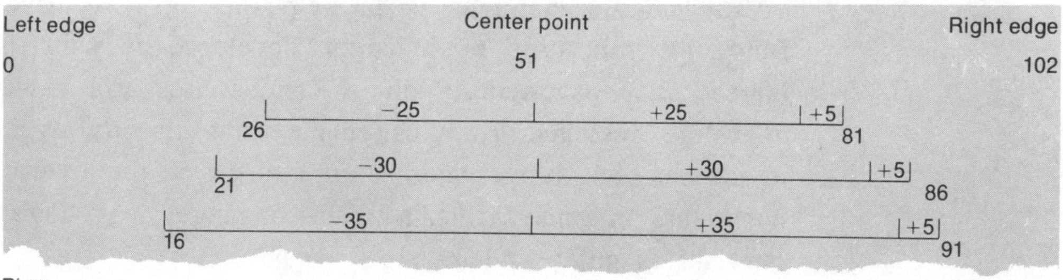

Pica

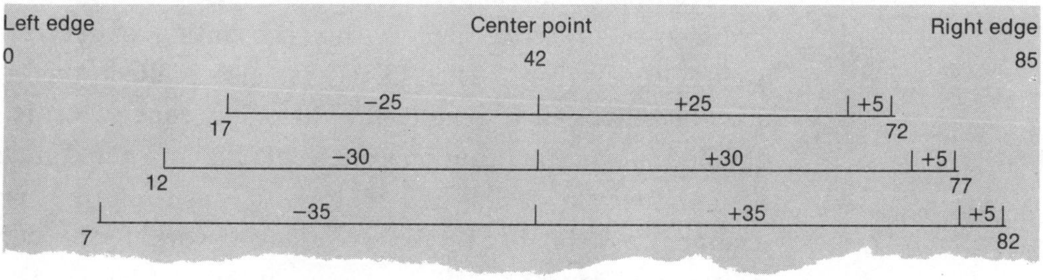

148

148a ▶ 5 Preparatory practice

each line 3 times SS (slowly, faster, still faster); retype selected lines as time permits

alphabet Jabez Q. Maxim was prepared for anything; he was a very skilled scout.

fig/sym They delivered 3,480# of potatoes, 1,650# of peas, and 2,579# of corn.

direct reaches My brother and uncle brought the amount they collected for the center.

fluency A visitor may want to visit the ancient burial chapel in the old city.

| 1 | 2 | 3 | 4 | 5 | 6 | 7 | 8 | 9 | 10 | 11 | 12 | 13 | 14 |

148b ▶ 8 Straight-copy measurement

one 5′ writing; record *gwam* and number of errors

Difficulty index

all letters used

A	1.5 si	5.7 awl	80% hfw

gwam 5′

Most of the large firms have three levels of management. These 3 85
three levels of management are known as top, middle, and supervisory. 5 88
The top level is typically composed of the board of directors, the presi- 8 91
dent, and, perhaps, one or more vice presidents. The key areas of re- 11 93
sponsibility for these executives are in the development of long-range 14 96
plans for the firm and in the establishment of the firm's policies. 17 99
Also, the top management is charged with the task of selecting and evalu- 20 102
ating the key executives of the firm. For the most part, people who 22 105
attain the top-level jobs are hard workers; they have climbed the ladder 25 107
of success in their own firm, from a supervisor to a manager, then from 28 110
a manager to an executive. 29 111

At the middle management level, a person might discover a variety 32 114
of job titles such as the controller, sales manager, treasurer, and 35 117
office manager. In some firms, the actual number of these jobs may be 37 120
much larger, and in other firms, much smaller. In each case, the role 40 123
of the middle manager is to help the top executives in the planning 43 125
functions; this type of manager develops the short-range plans, estab- 46 129
lishes the departmental policies, and writes and reviews the day-to-day 49 131
operating systems. A manager may not directly oversee the day-to-day 51 134
operations, but a manager is in charge of the overall results of a de- 54 137
partment. In some firms, a middle manager may have more than one su- 57 139
pervisor to guide and manage. 58 141

A few of the supervisory titles that a person may discover in some 61 143
firms are the office supervisor, accounting supervisor, and word proc- 64 146
essing supervisor. This level is also called the operating level of 67 149
management. As a result, the first-line supervisor is required to make 69 152
detailed plans for the operation of his or her functional area and to 72 154
assign specific tasks and duties to each of the workers supervised. 75 157
Another task is to analyze each day's work to be certain that the area 78 160
is running smoothly. If a person wants to be on the front line of ac- 81 163
tion, a supervisor is what one should be. 82 164

gwam 5′ | 1 | 2 | 3 |

level **1**

Learning to type

lessons 1–26

Typists have certain special advantages that work for them. Probably the most important of these is the ability to put thoughts on paper more rapidly and in a form more easily read than is possible with other methods of writing. In addition, typists often develop greater awareness of words and word usage, of ways to give structure and unity to their thoughts, and of the various procedures used in the world of business.

The activities in Level 1 are designed to help you take the important first steps toward typewriting competence—making keyreaches that are executed speedily and with accurate results. You will also learn how to use the various manipulative parts of the typewriter and to position material on the page attractively. Ample opportunities for practice and for measuring skill growth are also included.

For best results, remember this: There are no shortcuts to skill acquisition. You must read and listen to directions carefully, observe all demonstrations and illustrations closely, and practice meaningfully what is to be perfected. Discipline yourself to learn—and you will learn to type.

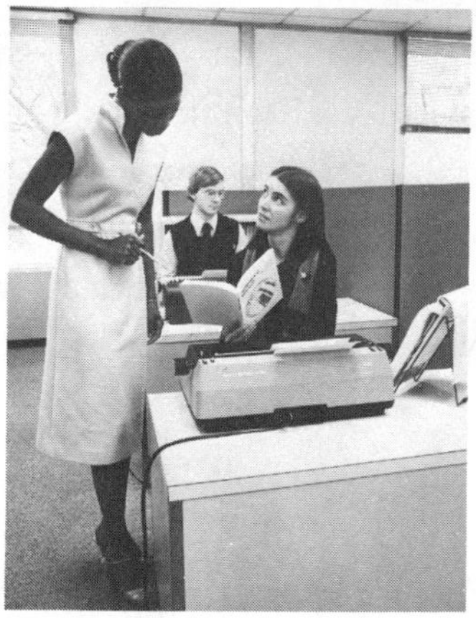

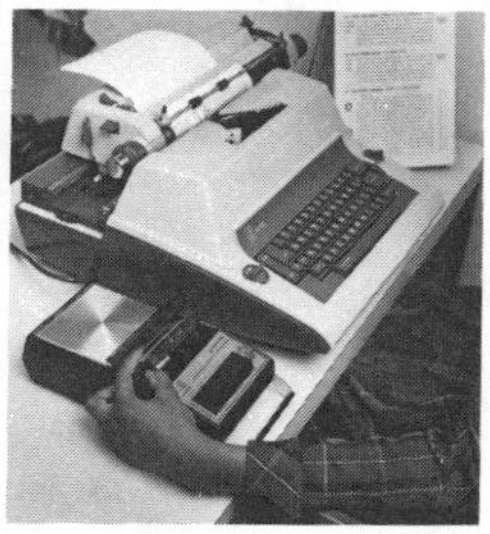

section **1**

Learning letter-key reaches

lessons 1–11

In Lessons 1-11 you will learn the keystroking technique for each of the alphabetic keys (both lowercase and capital). In addition, you will learn to use the parts of the typewriter that will enable you, among other things, to type copy in paragraph form. Lessons 2, 5, and 8 provide opportunities for reviewing and reinforcing learning.

Performance goals

By the time you complete Lesson 11, you should have the ability to type easy paragraph copy at least 14 words a minute. As you type, your eyes should be on the material from which you are copying; your feet should be on the floor for balance; and your hands, arms, and body should be in proper position. Your keyreaches should be very similar to those illustrated in the textbook.

Machine adjustments

1. If desk and chair adjustments are possible, adjust them to a height comfortable and appropriate for you.

2. Set the left margin stop for a 50-space line and the right margin stop at the end of the carriage scale.

3. Set the line-space selector for single spacing.

4. Place your book where it can be read easily; put paper and other supplies where you can reach them easily.

147c, continued

Job 2
Informal government letter

words

DATE: July 9, 19-- 3
REPLY TO
ATTN OF: AFAW 4
SUBJECT: Flexi time work schedule 8
TO: All federal supply service employees 16

We have had numerous request concerning the posibility of im- 30
plementing a flexi time schedule. In order to guage the amount 48
of support for such a schedule, a survy was conducted of all 62
employees. The results of the survey idnicate that a majority 78
would like to try some form of a flextime schedule. Beginning 86
on August 1, 19--, all employees that wuould like to have a 98
flexitime schedule may do so. 105
The following rules and regulations will govern the new flexi- 118
time program in FSS. 126

a. The lucnh break will continue to be observed from 12 196
noon to 1:00 p.m. Employees may choose a half-hour lunch 211
break. 212

b. All employees must be to work between the hours of 138
10:00 a.m. and 2:00 p.m. This is known as the core period. 152

c. The supervisor of each area must make certain that at 165
least two people are at work during the hours of 8:00 a.m. to 178
10:00 a.m. and 2:00 p.m. and 4:00 p.m. 183

d. A maximum of eight hours may be worked during one day 220
at regular pay; hours beyond eight will be at the overtime 227
rate. 236

Each supervisor will have a flexitime work schedule to com- 251
plete. Any conflict in scheduling between two employees will 267
be resolved by the supervisor according to seniority. No em- 284
ployee will be required to come to work before 8:00 a.m. or 298
stay at work past 4:30 p.m. Also, any employee may opt to be- 312
gin work as early as 7:00 a.m. and stay as late as 6:00 p.m. 314

JEROLD K. DRUMMOND 318
Chief, Federal Supply Service 324

cc: 325
Official File--AFAW 329

AFAW:RGDunn:xx 7-9--- 334

Job 3
Formal government letter for window envelope

Retype Job 1 as a formal government letter. Include a subject line, an appropriate salutation, and complimentary close. Add 4 extra words to word count if you type through the salutation before time is called. If you type the complimentary close, add 2 more words to your word count.

1

1a
Preparing to type (see pages 1-5)

(see pages 1-5)

1. Arrange work area (p. 4).
2. Adjust paper guide (p. 4).
3. Adjust ribbon control (p. 4).
4. Insert typing paper (p. 4).
5. Set line-space selector (p. 5).
6. Set left margin stop (p. 5).

1b
Taking typing position

1. Study the models demonstrating proper typing position shown below.

2. Observe each posture point as you take good position at your typewriter.

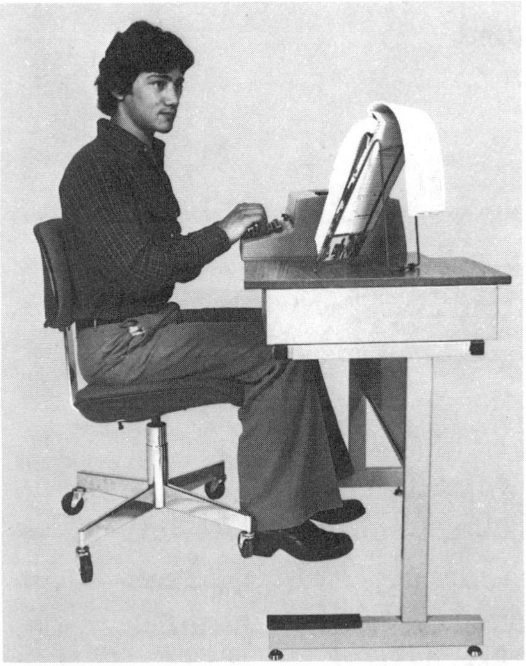

eyes on copy

fingers curved and upright; wrists low

forearms parallel to slant of keyboard

sit back in chair; body erect

textbook at right of machine and elevated for easy reading

table free of unneeded books

feet on floor for balance

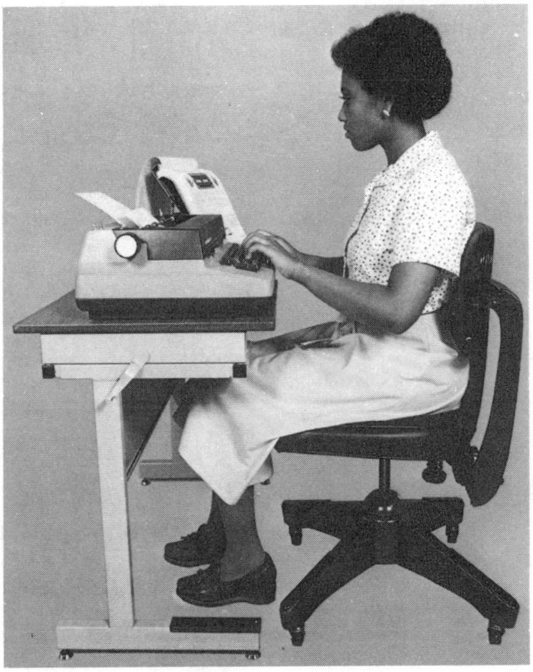

1c
Positioning your fingers

1. Let your hands hang loosely at your sides. Your fingers will relax in curved position.

2. With fingers curved in this relaxed position, lightly place fingertips of your left hand on keys f d s a (*home keys*).

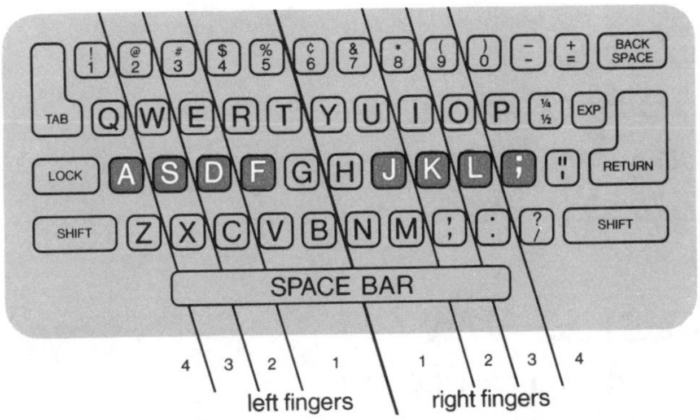

3. Similarly, lightly place the fingertips of your right hand on keys j k l ; (*home keys*).

4. Repeat steps 1, 2, 3. Learn to keep fingers curved and upright (not slanting). Only the fingertips should touch the typewriter—and they, lightly!

Production measurement procedure

For each production measurement activity in this section, follow the procedure given at the right.

1. Remove whatever stationery is supplied in the laboratory material (LM); have plain sheets and carbon sheets available.
2. Arrange stationery and plain paper in the order of need in completing the jobs.
3. Place correction supplies in a convenient location.
4. When the signal to begin is given, insert paper and make machine adjustments for the first job. Type as many jobs as you can in the time allowed.
5. Proofread each job and make needed corrections before removing it from the typewriter.
6. When time is called, proofread the final job and circle any uncorrected errors.
7. Compute *n-pram*.

147c ▶ 37

Production measurement:

letters and memos [LM pp. 165–170]

Time schedule

Assembling materials ... 2′
Timed production ....30′
Final check; compute *n-pram* .... 5′
(SS; 1 cc for each job)

Job 1
Informal government letter for window envelope

Words

DATE: July 9, 19-- 3
REPLY TO ATTN OF: AFAW 4
SUBJECT: Notification of fourth-quarter supplies bid deadline 14
TO: Ms. Phoebe A. Zrostlik, President 21
Alabama Wholesale Distributors, Inc. 28
5450 Bear Fork Road 32
Mobile, AL 36608 36
(¶1) A notification of bid, a set of bidding regulations, and a 48
specification sheet were mailed to you on June 1, 19--. As of today, 62
we have not received a bid from your company. If you do plan to 75
submit a bid on the fourth-quarter supplies, your bid must be 87
postmarked no later than July 31, 19--. 95
(¶2) The bids will be opened on August 8, 19--, and the supplier 107
chosen will be notified immediately by registered mail. 119
(¶3) Any bids that do not comply with our bidding regulations 130
will be disqualified and will not be considered; therefore, please 143
be sure to comply with all bidding regulations. Under separate 156
cover, we are forwarding to you another complete set of bid- 168
ding materials. 171
JEROLD K. DRUMMOND 175
Chief, Federal Supply Service 181

3 Enclosures: 184
Notification of Bid 188
Bidding Regulations 192
Specification Sheet 196

cc: 196
Official File--AFAW 200
AFAW: RGDunn: xx 7-9--- 205

Jobs 2–3 appear on next page

1d
Striking home keys and space bar

Study the keystroking and spacing illustrations.

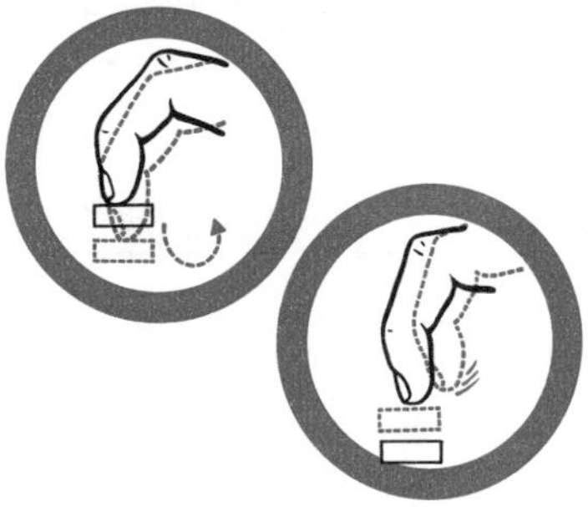

Strike key with a quick, sharp finger stroke; snap finger toward palm of hand as keystroke is made. *On electrics, strike keys as on manual typewriters, except with less force.*

Strike space bar with down-and-in (toward palm) motion of right thumb. Avoid pauses before and after spacing.

1. Type first line of drill at right; read and follow directions for 1e below before you return carriage (carrier).

2. After studying 1e, return and finish 1d.

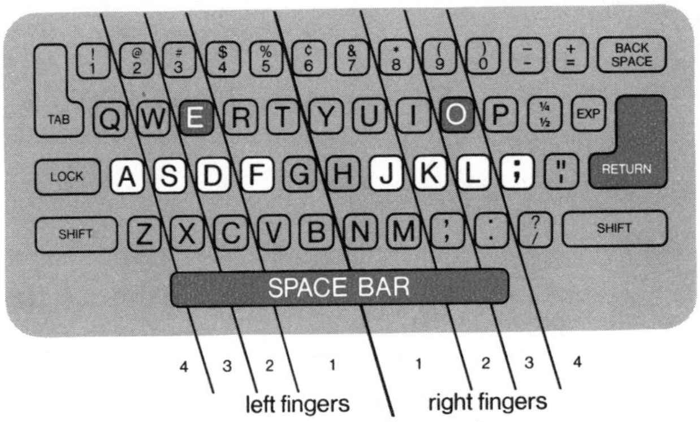

space once

```
fdsa fdsa jkl; jkl; fdsa jkl; fj a;
ff jj dd kk ss ll aa ;; ff jj dd kk
fj fj dk dk sl sl a; a; sl sl dk dk
ad sad as add jak; a fad; ask a lad
```

1e
Learning to return carriage (carrier)

The **return lever (1)** on a manual typewriter or the **return key (34)** on an electric is used to space the paper up and make the return to the beginning of the new line.

Study the illustrations at the right; then make the return *3* times (triple-space) at the end of each typed line in 1d.

Electric return
Reach with the little finger of the right hand to the return key, tap the key, and return the finger quickly to its typing position.

Manual return
Move the left hand, fingers bracing one another, to the carriage return lever and move the lever inward to take up the slack;

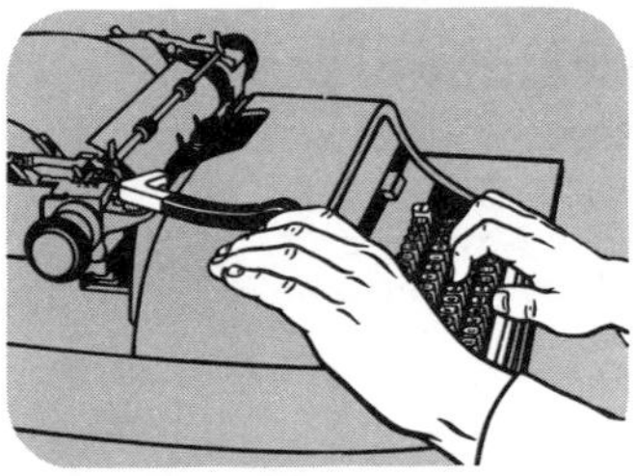

then return the carriage with a quick inward flick-of-the-hand motion. Drop the hand quickly to typing position without letting it follow carriage across.

1f
Learning new keyreaches: E and O

1. Find new key on keyboard chart at top of page; then find it on your typewriter.

2. Study carefully the reach-technique shown for the key.

3. Watch your finger make reach to new key a few times.

4. Type reach-technique drill for the key.

Reach technique for e

Reach technique for o

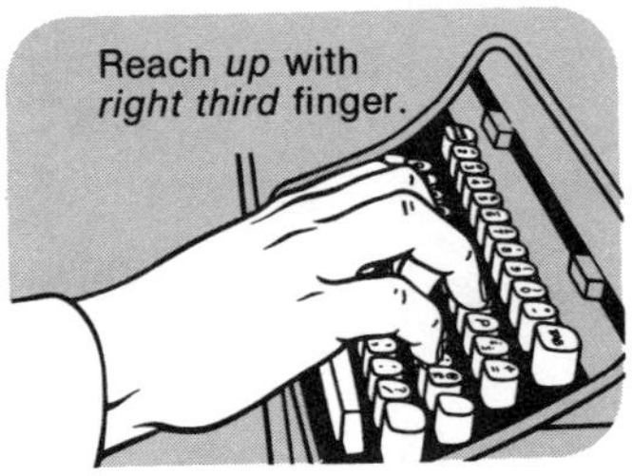


```
e    1 d ed ed led fled ale sale kale fake lake sled desk
     2 e el elf self see seek sell jell jade sea seal led
                                        DS (double space)
o    3 l ol old sold fold odd sod oak loss load loaf soak
     4 o of of do do so off fool food soda also oaks folk
                                                       DS
e/o  5 ode lode lose doe does foe sole aloe joke sloe led
     6 dole food see dose foes ode odes also else doe sod
                                        TS (triple space)
```

section

35

Measuring basic/production skills

lessons 147–150

This section is designed to measure your knowledge and skill in performing various typing operations: straight copy, letters, reports, forms, tables, and special reports.

Measurement goals

1. To select and organize all needed materials and supplies quickly for efficient use.
2. To plan your work and make machine adjustments carefully and efficiently.
3. To type a maximum number of jobs acceptably (errors neatly corrected) in the production time allowed.

Machine adjustments

1. Set paper guide at *0*.
2. Set ribbon control on black.
3. Margins: 70-space line for drills and ¶ writings; as directed (or appropriate) for problems.
4. SS drill lines; DS ¶s; space jobs as directed (or appropriate).

147

147a ▶ 5

Preparatory practice

each line 3 times SS (slowly, faster, still faster); retype selected lines as time permits

alphabet	The Venezuelan lexicographer jotted down two zany quips from the book.
fig/sym	The interest on Note #H7358 for $40,900 for 12 months at 9% is $3,681.
double letters	The cannoneer will shoot the cannonballs across the Mississippi River.
fluency	The auditor's amendment is to suspend the endowment fund as a penalty.

| 1 | 2 | 3 | 4 | 5 | 6 | 7 | 8 | 9 | 10 | 11 | 12 | 13 | 14 |

147b ▶ 8

Straight-copy measurement

one 5′ writing; record *gwam* and number of errors

Difficulty index

all letters used | A | 1.5 si | 5.7 awl | 80% hfw |

	gwam 5′	
The development and expanded use of the computer has not caused the	3	66
large number of jobs to be lost that so many people expected about twenty-	6	69
five years ago. In fact, the total number of people in the work force	8	72
has increased during the past twenty-five years, and the computer has	11	75
had the effect of creating many of the new jobs. While it is indeed	14	78
true that the development of the computer has made many of the routine,	17	81
less-skilled jobs unnecessary, it has also created many other highly	20	83
skilled jobs which call for employees who are trained for such fields	22	86
as data-entry and computer operations, programing, and system analysis.	25	89
In short, the occupations that call for specialized training, judgment,	28	92
and knowledge have increased in number; and thus, the computer has, in	31	95
fact, helped to create even more jobs and, in turn, to increase wages.	34	98
There are many people who insist that the computer has not had a	37	100
positive effect on the worker. They assert that many firms are more	39	103
concerned with net profit than they are with satisfied workers. In	42	106
many firms, the telephone calls, the invoices, the letters, and the	45	108
reports can all be done with the aid of a computer. Some firms are now	48	111
to the point where they can see how negative the impact of technology is	51	114
on their employees, and these firms are beginning job enrichment pro-	53	117
grams that will help their employees gain greater personal satisfaction	56	120
from their jobs. Perhaps the development of the computer may, in the	59	123
end, force firms to do what should have been done earlier--create pleas-	62	126
ant and satisfying jobs for all workers.	64	127

gwam 5′ | 1 | 2 | 3 |

1g
Practicing keystroking technique

each pair of lines twice SS (first slowly, then faster); DS between pairs of lines

Goals

- quick, snap strokes
- down-and-in space bar motion
- fingers curved, upright

home row

asdf jkl; aj sk dl f; as ask fad all fall lad lass
as a lass; ask a lad; a fall ad; as all ask; a fad

DS (double space)

e/o

ed ol do eel doe foes ode lode joke lead load dole
do see; sold jade; oak sales; also does; do a solo

DS

all reaches learned

see a doe; a sled does sell; also seek a safe deal
jade does sell; a desk sale; oak sled; sell a sofa

TS (triple space)

1h
Ending the lessons
(standard procedure for all lessons)

1. Raise **paper bail (11)** or pull it toward you. Pull **paper release lever (18)** toward you.

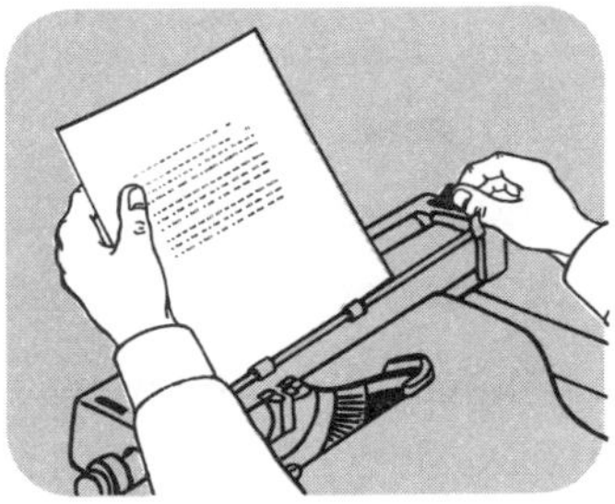

2. Remove paper with your left hand. Push paper release lever back to its normal position.

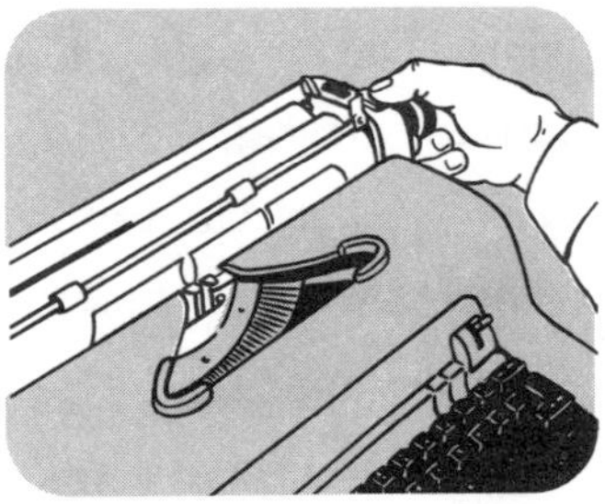

3. *(for carriage-type machines only)* Depress **right carriage release (19)**; hold **right platen knob (20)** firmly and move carriage so that it is approxi-mately centered.

4. Turn *electrics* **off.**

2

2a
Preparing to type

1. Study "Know Your Typewriter" on pages 1–3.

2. Follow "Daily Get Ready to Type" on pages 4–5.

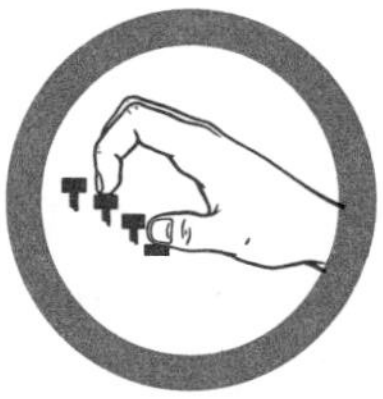

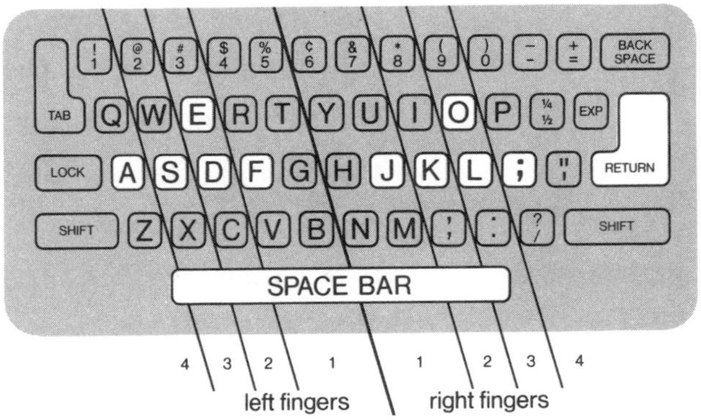

2b
Preparatory practice

each line twice SS (slowly, then faster); DS between 2-line groups

▶ Visually check hands and fingers only when they feel "lost."

home row

aa ff jj dd kk ss ll aa ;; fj jf dk kd sl ls a; ;a

DS

e/o

e ed ded deed desk seed fee o ol old fold sold doe

DS

all reaches learned

as do foe ale sad old ask eel oak lea so off joke;

TS

146d ▶ 20
Measuring straight-copy typing skill

1. A 3′ speed writing; determine *gwam*.
2. Two 5′ control writings; record *gwam* and number of errors for the more accurate writing.

Difficulty index

all letters used | A | 1.5 si | 5.7 awl | 80% hfw

gwam 3′ | 5′

On display at several of the offices in our city is a small sign 4 3
showing what is surely a very important message. The sign says quite 9 5
simply "Think." Busy workers and customers hastily look at the sign, 14 8
and it is interesting to conjecture that maybe the message says some- 18 11
thing a little bit different to every one who reads it. To some, for 23 14
example, it might portend that they should exercise greater caution in 28 17
their work; to others, it could offer encouragement to attack a pressing 32 19
problem that needs solving; while a third group might interpret it to be 37 22
a note of stimulation toward expanded creativity. That a five-letter 42 25
word printed on a sign should, like a tiny, mystical beacon, flash an 47 28
individualized message to those who read it, is itself thought provoking. 52 31

Every person can think. In the kingdom of animals, anthropologists 56 34
tell us, the power to reason is a distinctive characteristic of humans. 61 37
Although there appears to be little unanimity about why people can think, 66 40
it seems evident that we do our best job of it when faced with the pos- 71 42
sibility of making a mistake. At such times, we feel quite forced to 75 45
"act wisely," to "make a basic decision," to "use good judgment"--in 80 48
other words, to "think." The ability to think, therefore, is a valuable 85 51
prize to us; and, we will, ideally speaking, take advantage of any chance 90 54
to improve our capacity for it if in so doing we can develop our abil- 94 57
ity to avoid dangerous and expensive errors that could affect our family, 99 59
our friends, our city, our employer--and us. 102 61

The act of thinking is not an end in itself. It also needs to be 106 64
purposeful; that is, thinking should look for a solution to a problem, 111 67
explore phenomena, or even provide for our own amusement. In its best 116 70
form, thinking is a very efficient act. Merely wondering about things 121 72
does little; it is, as one individual has put it, a kind of "intellec- 125 75
tual vagrancy." Freed of routine duties, the mind can engage itself in 130 78
seeking, sorting, and assembling data; make basic decisions; and plan 135 81
positive action. It is thus that the act of thinking is elevated to its 140 84
loftiest plane--the conception of human action based on a well-analyzed 144 87
foundation of philosophy. It is the way of human beings to so conduct 149 89
themselves and their activities for their own and their neighbor's good. 154 92

gwam 3′ | 1 | 2 | 3 | 4 | 5 |
5′ | 1 | 2 | 3 |

2c
Practicing keystroking technique

Type these often-used letter combinations and words once as shown.

Correct finger curvature

Correct finger alignment

Correct keystroke

Goal

Try to type the words and combinations without pausing. Don't let doubt hold your fingers back; let them go.

▶ Keep your eyes on copy as much as you can; look only when you feel "lost."

home row
1 as al ll ld ad aj ss sa ff da ak fa ja ds a; d; k;
2 as ask all sad fad jak ads add lads lass sass fall
DS

e
3 es ed le ea de ee el ej fe ef eo ek oe je fe ke ed
4 el eel els led lea ade sea see fee eke doe fed joe
DS

o
5 fo so os lo oo ol do od ok eo oa jo oe of ko oj ao
6 so sod sol doe ado loa odd oak oaf foe off koa ode
DS

all reaches learned
7 all eas ase ess ese sed ose lea ake off los see ;;
8 fall ease less dose leak lake doff loss seek jade;
TS

2d
Typing words/phrases

Practice Lines 1, 2, and 3 until you type them at a pace that feels comfortable to you; repeat with 4, 5, and 6; then finish with 7, 8, and 9.

Successful typing depends on self-confidence. Follow directions carefully as you proceed. Do not try to force speed now. Be patient; gain confidence first.

Space down and in

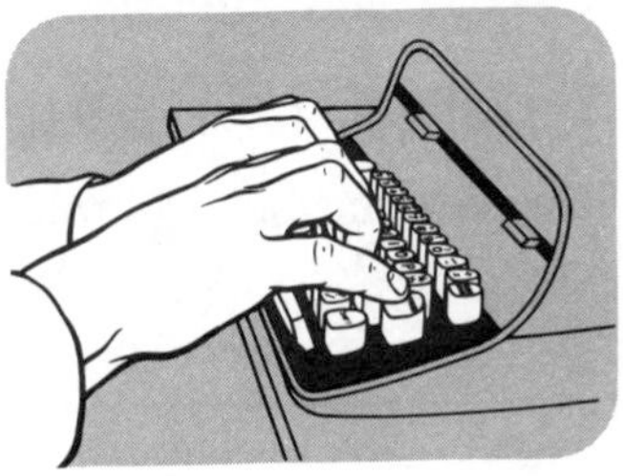

Electric return

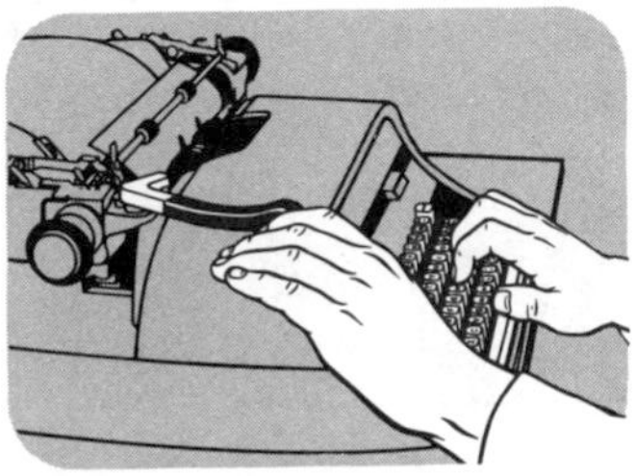

Manual return

all reaches learned

words 1 see led doe eel old sod ask sad oak ade sea fee ;;
words 2 ads fad off joe all kea oaf ode ale jak foe lee ;;
phrases 3 see a sad lad; all of; ask a fee; old oak; all ads
DS

words 4 joke does seed feel sold soda asks soak jade feed;
words 5 fads fade doff fall dead loaf sale leaf foal leak;
phrases 6 all fads fade; do a deed; see a sad doll; old jade
DS

words 7 folk falls lasso salad fell flake leads deals joke
words 8 dose lease flask aloof seed loose eases deals leak
phrases 9 sells jade; a faded leaf falls; loses a sales deal

2e
Ending the lessons (see page 9, if necessary)

Remove paper

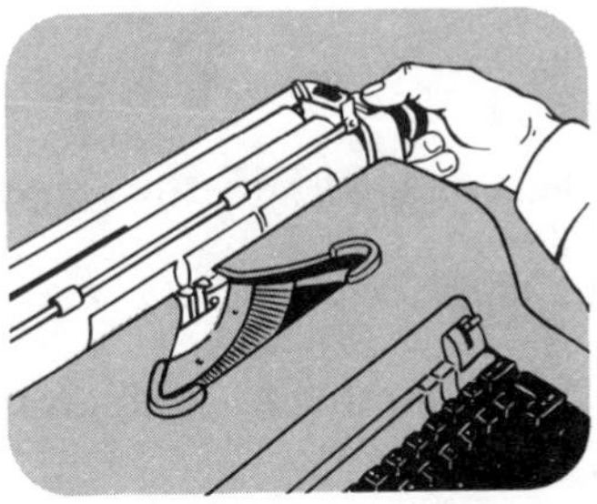

Center carriage

Turn electric off

146

146a ▶ 5
Preparatory practice

each line 3 times SS (slowly, faster, slowly); retype selected lines as time permits

alphabet	Genevieve just accepted the quick excuse which Elizabeth made for Ivy.
fig/sym	Is the new rate on our #694 note for $5,370 (dated May 21) to be 8.5%?
double letters	A bookkeeper will tell the association to settle all accounts in full.
fluency	They will not get very far until they have learned to make time count.

| 1 | 2 | 3 | 4 | 5 | 6 | 7 | 8 | 9 | 10 | 11 | 12 | 13 | 14 |

146b ▶ 10
Improving keystroking technique

each line at least 3 times without error

direct reaches	If June Ceece is hungry, she must try Min's grape sherbet for dessert.
right hand	John, he pointed out, found a lump of molybdenum on our mountain.
left hand	They read that tax rates on traded cars are now swerving upward again.
balanced hand	A sense of contentment comes with our knowing that work is done right.
balanced hand	If they qualify, special aid may be given to the citizens of the city.
combination	The regulation of television is of particular importance to all of us.

| 1 | 2 | 3 | 4 | 5 | 6 | 7 | 8 | 9 | 10 | 11 | 12 | 13 | 14 |

146c ▶ 15
Building statistical-copy-typing skill

1. Two 1′ speed writings on each ¶; determine *gwam*.
2. Two 3′ speed writings on both ¶s combined; determine *gwam* on each.

Difficulty index

all letters used | A | 1.5 si | 5.7 awl | 80% hfw |

	gwam 1′	3′	
After analyzing the 1978 records, the total income of the clinic	13	4	55
was $3,895,000; this was an increase of nearly 47% over last year's	27	9	60
income of $2,650,000. Quite a substantial amount of this tremendous	40	14	65
increase was due to the increase of clinic size and to the hiring of sev-	55	18	69
eral key doctors. The actual increase in revenue per physician was	69	23	74
just 13.9%.	71	24	75
The 1979 financial picture of the clinic showed that a sizable in-	13	28	79
crease in revenues was a direct result of obtaining 2,895 new patients.	28	33	84
Revenue for 1979 was $4,533,500 (10.6% more than the 1978 revenue), even	42	38	89
though the capacity of the physicians, equipment, and building was ex-	56	42	94
pected to have just an 86% use factor at the end of the 1979 fiscal year.	71	47	99
Revenue is expected to keep up this pace for next year.	82	51	102

gwam 1′ | 1 | 2 | 3 | 4 | 5 | 6 | 7 | 8 | 9 | 10 | 11 | 12 | 13 | 14 |
3′ | 1 | 2 | 3 | 4 | 5 |

3

3a
Preparing to type

1. Does the paper guide need adjustment?

2. Is the line–space regulator set for single spacing?

3. Is the ribbon control set for typing on the black (upper) part of the ribbon?

4. Is the left margin stop set 25 spaces to the left of center for a 50–space line?

5. Did you adjust your chair and desk to a height that is correct for you?

6. Should the right margin stop be moved to the extreme right?

3b
Preparatory practice

each line 3 times SS (slowly, faster, still faster); DS between 3-line groups

home row	`a; sl dk fj a;sl dkfj ad as all ask fads adds asks`
e/o	`ol ol old sold fold ed ed fed lead feel so so solo`
all reaches learned	`all ale; a fall ad; as a lad; a lass; seeks a joke`

DS

3c
Learning new keyreaches: T and I

Standard plan (use daily)

1. Find new key on keyboard chart at right.

2. Study carefully the reach technique shown at right.

3. Watch your finger make reach to a new key a few times.

4. Type reach–technique drill for the key.

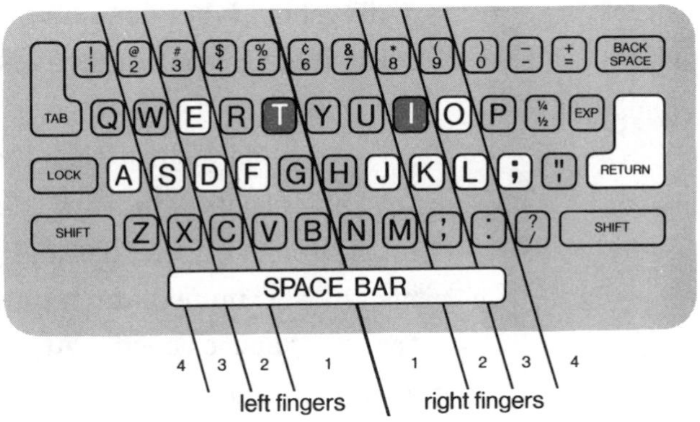

Reach technique for t

Goal: Smooth, continuous typing; avoid pauses. Space quickly with down–and–in motion of right thumb.

Reach technique for i

▶ Keep keystroking action in the fingers.

t	1	`tf tf to to to let let lot lot tall jest last late`
	2	`at date fate eat seat feat lest to tot toast total`
i	3	`ik ik if if is is did did like dike file fill kids`
	4	`aid said laid ill fill sills ails fails sails jail`
t/i	5	`list it tilt edit diet site sit tie lilt toil till`
	6	`kit lit fit tail silt jilt its kite tied tile diet`
phrases	7	`as is|to do it|if it is|did it|at a date|if it did`
	8	`to let|to let it|is to do|to see it|if so|as it is`

145c ▶ 25
Building straight-copy typing skill

1. A 1′ speed writing on each ¶; determine *gwam*.

2. Two 3′ speed writings on all ¶s combined; determine *gwam*.

3. A 5′ control writing on all ¶s combined; record *gwam* and number of errors.

Difficulty index

all letters used	A	1.5 si	5.7 awl	80% hfw

	gwam 1′	3′	5′
You can safely consider that poor stroking habits are generally the	14	5	3
cause of failure to achieve high typing speeds and are the major reasons	28	9	6
for plateaus; but you can find material especially designed to help de-	42	14	8
velop quick, easy stroking. Use a part of the drill period each day to	57	19	11
work on these special drill exercises. You may not notice an immediate	71	24	14
change, but it will come if you work for it and if you analyze your	85	28	17
stroking habits very carefully.	91	30	18
Among other specific ideas to keep before you is the advice that	13	35	21
all drills must be practiced with a definite goal in mind. Unless you	27	39	24
know what you are trying to attain, you can't hope to achieve any par-	41	44	26
ticular degree of success. It is useless to pound away at the keyboard	55	49	30
day after day, hoping that practice will make your typing perfect. Your	70	54	32
drills should be done with very specific objectives in mind. Ask your-	84	58	35
self about your objectives to determine if your exercises are right	98	63	38
for you.	99	63	38
A good course has long-term goals, or at least desired outcomes,	13	68	41
for all of its students. In order to reach these goals, each student	27	72	43
must decide upon the daily practice objectives that are appropriate to	41	77	46
his or her immediate requirements. There should be a specific objective	56	82	49
for a specific need. At times, a student will need to increase speed;	70	87	52
at other times, a student will require a reduction in speed in order to	84	91	55
eliminate error. At still other times, the goal may be to improve a	98	96	58
vital technique: keystroking, spacing, shifting, and the like.	111	100	60
Very little is accomplished in the world by mere accident. Any	13	105	63
major achievement is realized by following a good plan of attack. Many	27	109	66
people have an unlimited amount of luck "going for them," but relying	41	114	68
too heavily on luck is just foolish. If your typewriting skill needs	55	119	71
to be improved, learn what you need to practice; then you can expect	69	123	74
quality improvement. Use any aids available to you; but, above all,	83	128	77
take the responsibility for your own growth--and take pride in it, too.	97	133	80

gwam														
1′	1	2	3	4	5	6	7	8	9	10	11	12	13	14
3′		1			2			3			4			5
5′			1					2				3		

3d
Learning new keyreaches: H and Left Shift

Follow Standard Plan of 3c, p. 11.

Reach technique for h

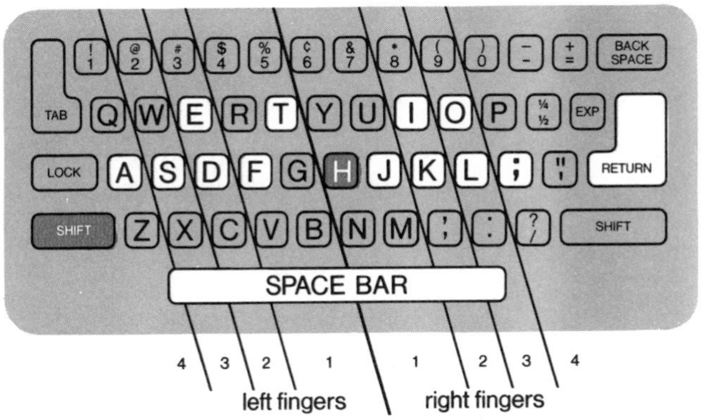

Control of left shift key

Reach *down* with *left little* finger; shift, type, release.

▶ Fingers curved and upright; stretch to left shift.

all reaches learned

```
h             1 hj hj ha has hash lash dash halts hall shall shell
              2 h oh oh she the hit had hat that his this hot shot
                                                                DS
left shift    3 Ja Ja Jake Jakes Oa Oa Oake Oakes La La Lake Lakes
              4 Joe Lee Oats Lila Kale Lisa Otto Leda Kit Jess Jed
                                                                DS
h/left shift  5 Kate Olds had a doll hat; Hal Hale looks like Lee;
              6 Jill Kale is head of Hill Hall; Jo has had a sale;
                                                                DS
phrases       7 has had|that is|if it had|of the|is the|if she did
              8 as Kit had it|Lee has it|if Hal had|as Jess did it
```

3e
Typing words/phrases

1. Type Lines 1–3 at an even pace as you read from the book.

2. When you feel you can type these lines with confidence, practice Lines 4–6; then, when you can type these lines with confidence, practice Lines 7–9.

all reaches learned

```
words     1 oh hot his has had the ash hat she hoe hod hit hid
words     2 his he ash the she hit hot has had the ash hat she
phrases   3 Hal has his hat; Joe hid his hoe; Kit hit the ash;

words     4 head hash shed dish jets host shoe hill hose dash;
words     5 held loaf that halt hall this half sash lash hole;
phrases   6 He had this half; hold this dish; she has the hoe;

words     7 shall shell shelf least leash lease those these ;;
words     8 shoes shots shoot sheet heads heats heals hides ;;
phrases   9 Lee shall hold the lease; Kit Leeds has the shoes;
```

section

34

Improving basic skills

lessons 145–146

Learning goals

Since accuracy is a major goal of basic skill development, you should be able to type at one of the following rates on a 5-minute straight-copy timing of average difficulty with 8 errors or fewer: 60 *gwam*, excellent; 54-59, good; 45-53, acceptable.

The minimum goal in this section should be between 45-53 *gwam* with 8 or fewer errors.

Machine adjustments

1. Set paper guide at *0*.
2. Set ribbon control on black.
3. Use a 70-space line and single spacing (SS) for drill lines.
4. Use a 70-space line, double spacing (DS) and 5-space ¶ indentions for paragraph copy.

145

145a ▶ 5

Preparatory Practice

each line 3 times SS (slowly, faster, slowly); retype selected lines as time permits

alphabet	Jacque Kelley wrote a very exciting play about Zeus, god of mythology.
fig/sym	Rick hoped to purchase 24 dozen at $.79/dozen ($18.96) plus 3.50% tax.
left hand	After the wet December weather, Eve's crabgrass grew excessively fast.
fluency	The firm must show signs of vigor if it is to make a profit this time.

| 1 | 2 | 3 | 4 | 5 | 6 | 7 | 8 | 9 | 10 | 11 | 12 | 13 | 14 |

145b ▶ 20

Building script typing skill

1. Two 1′ speed writings on each ¶; determine *gwam*.
2. Three 3′ speed writings on the 2 ¶s combined; determine *gwam* on each.

Difficulty index

all letters used | HA | 1.7 si | 6.0 awl | 75% hfw |

	gwam 1′	3′
The accounting profession is divided into three basic	11	4
divisions: public, private, and governmental sectors. If a	23	8
woman wants the job of a public accountant, she will dis-	35	12
cover that she will be expected to perform an annual audit and to	47	16
analyze her clients' books. She is charged with the responsi-	60	20
bility of saying that the records and financial statements do or	73	24
do not adequately reflect a true financial picture of the firm.	85	28
Those who enter the private accounting sector are loyal	11	32
to a private organization; in other words, a woman who becomes	24	36
this type of an accountant is in the employ of a firm for the	36	40
explicit purpose of handling or supervising that firm's finan-	48	45
cial records. A governmental accountant is a civil servant	60	49
equal to all other civil servants. Therefore, one must satis-	73	53
factorily pass a civil service examination to qualify for the	85	57
position. If a woman is interested in governmental accounting,	98	61
she will be able to choose from among a broad variety of jobs.	110	65

4

4a
Preparing to type

Check: paper guide
line-space regulator
ribbon control
margin stops
desk and chair

4b
Preparatory practice

each line 3 times SS (slowly, faster, slowly); DS between 3-line groups

home row jk fd jkfd sa l; sal; as lass ad dad joke fad fads

t/i/h ft tf ki ik jh hj fit hit its his sit hot the this

all reaches learned Jodi has the file; Keith led the list; look at it;

4c
Learning new keyreaches: R and . (Period)

Reach technique for r

Reach *up* with *left first* finger.

Reach technique for . (period)

Reach *down* with *right third* finger; space twice after . at end of sentence.

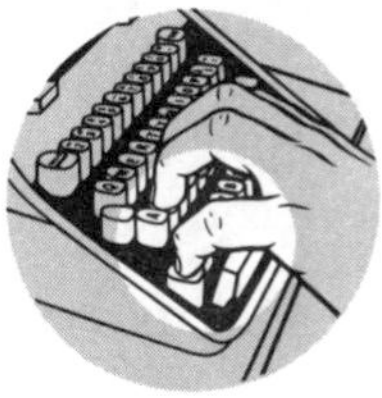

▶ Keep your wrists low, but do not allow them to touch the typewriter frame.

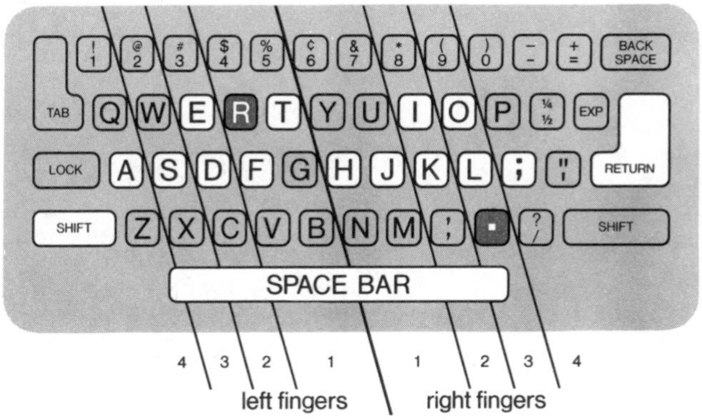

Note: Space once after period following an abbreviation, twice after period at end of sentence. However, do not space after a period at the end of a line.

r
1 rf rf rid ride read or ore for fore sore tore rear
2 ire fire dire tire sir oar soar roar ear hear hers

.
3 .l .l l.l adj. alt. La. Ill. Hale leads all sales.
4 Lt. Lee left. He had a lease. It is at the file.

r/.
5 He rode a sorrel horse. It reared. He is afraid.
6 Lori tried to sell the roses ordered for Lt. Kirk.

all reaches learned
7 Lil tried to tell her joke; she tells it too fast.
8 Jake Loth has had three hits; he is safe at first.

141b-144b, continued

Job 7
Rough-draft letter
[LM p. 149]

Dr. Fernandes has given you this rough-draft letter to retype and send to Ms. Washington. The letter is to be dated October 16, 19— and it is to be addressed to: Ms. Constance V. Washington, Executive Director, American Society for Testing and Materials, 916 Race Street, Philadelphia, PA 19103. Send a pc to Mr. Karl R. Mrzlak.

Dear ~~Connie~~ Ms. Washington

¶ Thank you for sending the information I requested for our Electrical manual. The ~~data~~ about magnetizing makes a handy reference for our Electrical ~~test~~ engineers. The information about ~~SI~~ and the conversion tables ~~are~~ also of great use to us. We have been using the mksa system for years, but we understand that the inter national System of units is a modern version of the mksa system.

¶ Our engineers have suggested that we include such current items as IS Measurements ~~to~~ our companys testing manual. Many manufactrurers of components are now converting to metrics and our research and testing ~~areas need~~ the metric conversion ~~data~~.
With metric conversion tables, our engineers will not waste time calculating the equivalents.

¶ If we need any additional information, we shall not hesitate to call. Again, thanks for your help.

sincerely

Marcos Fernandes
Cheif test engineer

¶ Your suggestion to read the article on metric practice in the latest Annual Book of ASTM Standards was certainly appreciated. This article contains a wealth of information about the use of metrics and the International System of Units (SI).

4d
Learning new keyreaches: W and Right Shift

Reach technique for w

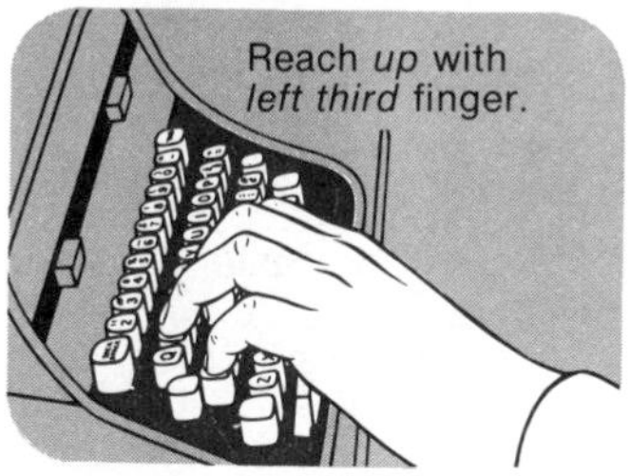

Control of right shift key

Reach *down* with *right little* finger; shift, type, release.

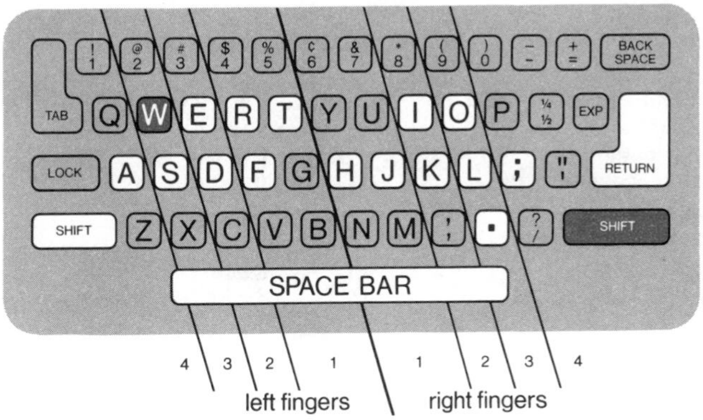

▶ Fingers curved and upright; stretch the little *finger* to right shift; do not move the hand.

w
```
1 ws ws we wit with how show low slow flows we wells
2 wish wise was saw wall walk work word wore owe jaw
```

right shift
```
3 Do Do Dora Dori Ford Dirk Flo Flora First Aid Tess
4 Sol or Sid Todd; Sir Dolf Sojak; Ella or Rod Rosso
```

right shift/w
```
5 Wade has the wood.  Wes Fisk said it.  Sal saw it.
6 We shall wait; Ella saw her; Walt saw Flo or Wilf.
```

all reaches learned
```
7 Sara said that we failed to hear Jake; he is late.
8 Jodie Falk walked to the store; I walked with her.
```

4e
Typing words/sentences

1. Can you type a complete line in a minute? If you can, you are off to a good start.

2. If you type less than a line in a minute, don't be discouraged. Keep working; each good practice builds skill, but sometimes, slowly.

all reaches learned

```
1 raw was how jaw saw eke owe war rid wit the for or
2 wed red rod tow jak was oar ire low law row off to
3 Dr. Loo saw the red oar.  Flo saw Sid row for Rio.

4 here were hear word flow show joke well fort there
5 east roar walk work road wall rows ward wire jerks
6 Dora will ride to work.  Jodi said she saw a show.

7 rolled worked jokers wills sword rowed words sawed
8 writes wrote toward forts fires trades slows draws
9 Their horse reared; it threw a shoe.  Dale saw it.
```

141b-144b, continued

Job 5
Table (plain full sheet)
Ms. Washington has sent the conversion table at the right to Dr. Hernandes, to which he has added the material in script. The table is to be retyped by you as a separate sheet insert in the *Electrical Testing Manual*. You are to use 1½" top margin and side margins for a leftbound report. Use the mathematical method to determine intercolumn spacing.
The heading for this table is: METRIC CONVERSION TABLE
The subheading is: (Weight, Length, Area)

Type	Multiply	By	To Obtain
Weight	kilograms (kg)	2.2046	pounds
	grams (gm)	0.0022046	pounds
	pounds (lbs.)	0.45359	kilograms
	pounds	453.59	grams
Length	meters (m)	39.370	inches
	inches (in.)	0.0254	meters
	centimeters (cm)	0.3937	inches
	centimeters	0.032808	feet
	inches	2.54	centimeters
	feet (ft.)	30.48	centimeters
Area	sq. meters	10^4	sq. centimeters
	sq. centimeters	10^{-4}	sq. meters
	sq. meters	1.5500×10^3	sq. inches
	sq. inches	6.4516×10^{-4}	sq. meters
	sq. centimeters	0.155	sq. inches
	sq. centimeters	1.0764×10^{-3}	sq. feet
	sq. inches	6.4516	sq. centimeters
	sq. feet	929.04	sq. centimeters

Source: <u>1979 Annual Book of ASTM Standards</u>

Job 6
Table (plain full sheet)
This table was also received from Ms. Washington. The table will also be a separate sheet insert in the *Electrical Testing Manual* and thus will have the same margin settings as for Job 5. However, since the table is shorter, DS the body of the table.
The heading for this table is: MAGNETIZING FORCE CONVERSION TABLE

Multiply	By	To Obtain
ampere-turns/meter	0.0254	ampere-turns/inch
ampere-turns/meter	10^{-2}	ampere-turns/centimeter
ampere-turns/meter	0.012566	oersteds
ampere-turns/inch	39.37	ampere-turns/meter
ampere-turns/inch	0.3937	ampere-turns/centimeter
ampere-turns/inch	0.49474	oersteds
ampere-turns/centimeter	100.00	ampere-turns/meter
ampere-turns/centimeter	2.54	ampere-turns/inch
ampere-turns/centimeter	1.2566	oersteds
oersteds	79.577	ampere-turns/meter
oersteds	0.79577	ampere-turns/centimeter
oersteds	2.0213	ampere-turns/inch

Source: <u>1979 Annual Book of ASTM Standards</u>

5

5a
Preparing to type

1. Review the Know-Your-Typewriter information, pp. 1-3.
2. Follow the Get-Ready-To-Type steps, pp. 4-5.

5b
Preparatory practice

each line twice SS (once slowly, once faster); DS between 2-line groups

home row a as jak ask add sad fad lass asks lad fall falls;

e/o/t/i so at ell is off sat jell aid load lake lids deals

h/r/w ah far jaw had war walk hash ark saw; Do her work.

sentence Jo saw a sad lad trade the rare old wok for a saw.

5c
Practicing keystroking technique

each set of 3 lines twice SS (once slowly, once faster); DS between 6-line groups

Goals

Lines 1-3: curved, upright fingers; fingers close to home keys

Lines 4-6: quick, snappy keystrokes; snap the finger toward the palm of the hand as the keystroke is completed

Lines 7-9: fluency—steady, continuous keystroking; no pauses between letters or words; space quickly

words
1 or ore tore; he her hers; at ate late; is his this
2 ho how show; or for fort; we wed weed; l. il. ail.
3 it sit site; to tow stow; hi hid hide; w. ow. low.

phrases
4 or is | or is the | or is it | if it is the | if I had the
5 if he | if he is | if she | if she is | if he had the work
6 I had | we had | she has had | he has had it | she had the

sentences
7 We see that he has the old file. She had it last.
8 Jill had a list. She has lost the list at a lake.
9 We had the food for the fair. Leo heard the talk.

5d
Practicing spacing and shifting

each set of lines 3 times SS; DS between 9 line groups

Goals

Lines 1-3: down-and-in motion of spacing thumb

Lines 4-6: shift-type-release in a quick 1–2–3 count; no pauses

Lines 7-9: quiet hands; no pauses before or after spacing or shifting

all reaches learned

spacing
1 to do it at we as if he oh so or ad do hi is ho of
2 the row for did law all lot led dot sat oil ark or
3 all we did | or of the | if she is ill | it will | to file

shifting
4 Al Alf Lee Leo Dee Rosa Rose Jill Joe Jodi Sal Sid
5 We shall see Lee Walls. Osa joked with Dr. Drews.
6 Dr. Ida Fee is the Head of Staff at Old Fell Hall.

spacing and shifting
7 Dr. Rader had it; Dr. Jae lost it; Dr. Lei has it.
8 I was ill. Sara Law was well. Fred did the work.
9 J. Ore had the deed. H. Lee is here; he filed it.

$\omega = v/(r\pi)$ (angular velocity)

Where: ω = angular velocity (radians a second)
v = linear velocity (in. per second or cm per second)
r = radius (in. or cm)

$T = J(\omega/t)$ (relationship between torwue and rotary motion)

where: T = torque (ounce-inches or newton-meters)
J = moment of inertia (ounce-inch-seconds^2 or newton-meter-seconds^2)
ω = angular velocity (radians per second)
t = time (seconds)

To use the torque/rotary motion equation with J in units of ounce-inches^2, use the following formula:

$T = J(\omega/t)\ (1/384)$

Where: 1/384 = ounce-inches^2

$J = Wr^2/2$ (moment of inertia for rotating disk)

Where: J = moment of inertia (ounce-inch-seconds^2 or newton-meter-seconds^2)
r = radius of disk
W = weight of disk

<u>Conclusion</u>

A Series of tests at different speeds will determine maximum torque ponit, maximum speed with no torque, and resonance points of any given motor.

---

*Stepping motors are obtained from the following manufacturers: Superior Electric Co., Middle Street, Bristol, CT 06010; Sigma Instrucents, Inc., Motion Control Division, 170 Pearl Street, Braintree, MA 02184; North American Phillips Control Corp., Cheshire Industrial Park: Cheshire, CT 06410; Warner Electric Brake, MCS Division, Beloit, WI 53511; Computer Devices of California, 11901 Burke Street, Santa Fe Springs, CA 90670; Singer Company, Kearfott Division, 1150 McBride Avenue, Little Falls, NJ 07424; Berger-Lahr Co., Jaffrey, NH 03452; and AST/Servo Systems, Inc., 930 Broadway, Newark, NJ 07104

6

6a ▶ 2
Preparing to type

Check: desk and chair
line–space regulator
ribbon control
margin stops
paper guide

Note: Beginning with Lesson 6, each lesson part will include in its heading a suggested number of minutes for practicing that activity.

6b ▶ 8
Preparatory practice

each line 3 times SS (slowly, faster, slowly); DS between 3-line groups

t/h/i	This is the hat that she had with her at the fair.
r/e/o	He has the tools there; those are her other tools.
all reaches learned	Alf Klei wore the hat as a joke; he later sold it.

6c ▶ 10
Learning new keyreaches: N and X

Reach technique for n

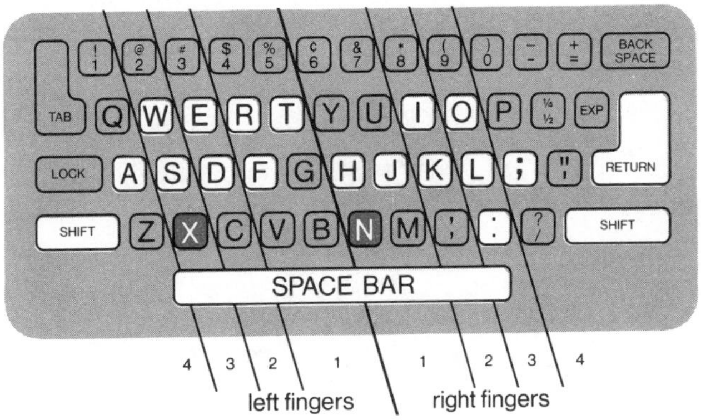

Reach technique for x

▶ Sit in an erect position; eyes on copy in book.

n	1	nj nj an an and land than then hand not fan fanned
	2	in an ran tan and sand den dent rent fin find kind
x	3	xs xs ax ax axe axle tax taxed six sixth wax waxed
	4	six fix fox lox lax text axis flax flex fixed axes
n/x	5	Lex X. Knox owns six of those next nine tax texts.
	6	Rex Jax sold six tons of sand to Nan Foxx at noon.
all reaches learned	7	Lex knows Frieda well; he did not ask her to join.
	8	Jake sat next to Rolf; his radio was on that seat.

141b-144b, continued

Job 4
Leftbound technical report
(plain full sheets)

Dr. Fernandes has compiled the stepping motor calculation formulas at the right for inclusion in the *Electrical Testing Manual*. The title of the report is "COMMONLY USED STEPPING MOTOR CALCULATION FORMULAS," the report number is SC-58, and the report begins on page 492.

The footnote indicated by * appears at the end of the report, but you should type it on the page on which its reference symbol appears.

Note: The symbol for angular velocity must be inserted into the report in ink thus: ω

"Pi" must also be inserted into the report in ink.

Summary

A stepping motor should be checked for ~~both~~ speed and torque. The speed versus torque curve will provide an accurate ~~one~~ measurement of the actual response of the stepping motor. This report provides the calculation formulas needed to test the final performance of a stepping motor. In addition, ~~Also,~~ several other stepping motor calculation formulas are illustrated ~~listed~~.

Introduction

The compilation of these commonly used stepping motor calculation formulas was undertaken to provide a ready reference guide for the newly created motor testing research facility.*

Calculation Formulas

RPM = ω60/N (speed in revolutions per minute)

Where: ω = angular velocity in steps per second
N = number of steps per revolution

T = Fd (torque)

Where: d = radius from pivot point to force
F = force applied or restraining force; i.e., friction, weight, load (ounce or newton)

$s = 1/2at^2 + v_0t + c$ (distance)

Where: s = distance (in. or cm)
a = acceleration (in. or cm per second^2)
t = time (seconds)
v_0 = velocity, initial (ft. per second or m per second)
c = constant

$v = at + v_0$ (linear velocity)

Where: v = velocity (in. per second or m per second)
a = acceleration (in. or cm per second)
t = time (seconds)
v_0 = velocity, initial (ft. per second or m per second)

ω = (RPM) N/60 (angular velocity in steps per second)

Where: N = number of steps per revolution
ω = angular velocity in steps per second
RPM = revolutions per minute

(continued on page 286)

6d ▶ 10
Learning new keyreaches: C and U

Reach technique for c

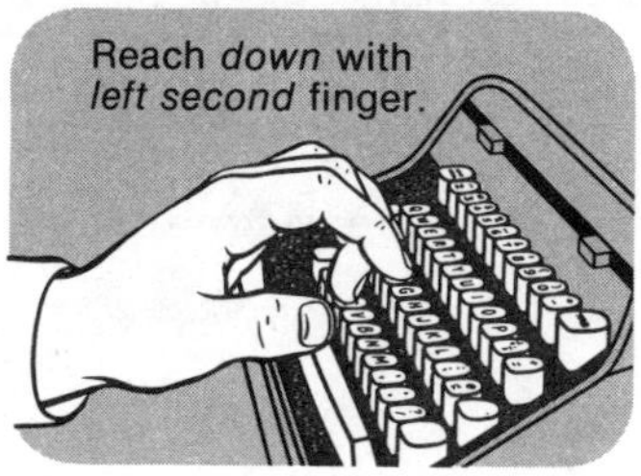

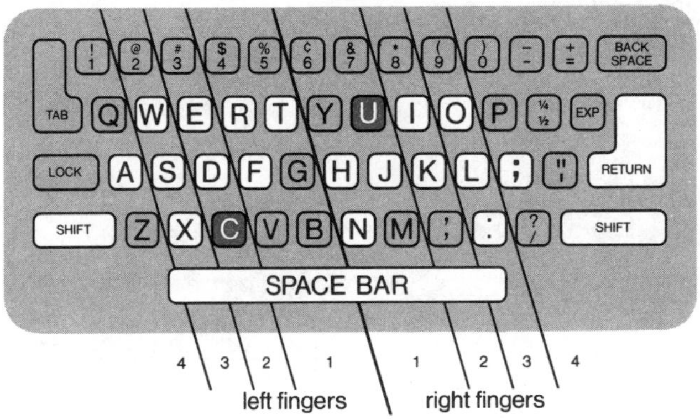

▶ Type at a relaxed, steady pace; avoid pauses between letters and words.

Reach technique for u

c
1 cd cd cod code coda cola colder ice dice rice nice
2 con cone cane cake call sick check clad lacks jack

u
3 uj uj us us use due sue hut hurt fun sun nut nurse
4 fuse ruse four sure just turn thus would surf unit

c/u
5 Curt could cut cold fruit for his lunch with Luci.
6 Aunt Cat could cure an ache with just fruit juice.

all reaches learned
7 Lex knew she had joined the course; it was French.
8 Jill could ask Felix to read next; he knows Latin.

6e ▶ 20
Typing words/phrases/sentences

1. Type each line twice SS (slowly, faster) for practice; DS between 6–line groups.

2. Type each of Lines 3, 6, and 9 as a 1–minute writing. Determine *gwam* (gross words a minute).

Counting typewritten words

Five strokes are counted as 1 standard typewritten word. The figures in the scale beneath the copy show the word–by–word count (5 strokes a word) for each line.

all reaches learned

words 1 nut cue hut sun fun us six cut her axe wan fox run
phrases 2 out of the sun|cut the action|a fox den|fun at six
sentence 3 That car is not junk; it can run in the next race.

words 4 etc. tax nick cure lack flex walls uncle clad hurt
phrases 5 lack the cash|not just luck|next in line|just once
sentence 6 June Dunn can send that next tax case to Rex Knox.

words 7 would counts fruit lances ounce juice chunks fixed
phrases 8 sixth annual dinner|fixed and waxed|no extra taxes
sentence 9 Lucie said she could fix the cracked axle for Tex.

| 1 | 2 | 3 | 4 | 5 | 6 | 7 | 8 | 9 | 10 |

To determine words-a-minute rate

1. List the figure 10 for each complete line typed during a writing.

2. For a partial line, note from the scale the figure directly below the point at which you stopped typing.

3. Add these two figures to determine the total gross words typed (the same as *gwam* for a 1' writing).

MAGNETIZING FORCES

Page 277
Report No. MF-5

Magnetizing Force--Incremental

A magnetic material that is subjected simultaneously to a symmetrical, periodically varying, magnetizing force and to a biasing magnetizing force has a magnetizing force that is one half the algebraic difference of the maximum and minimum values of the magnetizing force during a cycle.

Magnetizing Force--Instantaneous

A magnetic substance in an SCM flux-current loop--with the exciting voltage at zero--is assumed to be all magnetizing current; therefore, the formula is:

$H_t = 0.4\pi N_1 I/l_1$

Magnetizing Force--Maximum

There are two values of H in the maximum variation. They are:

a. H_m, which is the maximum value of H in a hysteresis loop;

b. H_{max}, which is the maximum value of H in a flux-current loop.

Job 3
Table (plain sheet)
Ms. Washington has also sent this table of the International System of Units at Dr. Fernandes' request. He has given you the table to type for insertion into the *Electrical Testing Manual*. Because the table is a separate sheet insert, you decide to use a 1½" top margin. Further, because the table must fit within the line length of the leftbound report, you decide to use the mathematical method for determining intercolumn spaces as given in the "Manual for Technical Typists."

1. Count the number of characters in the longest item in each column.

2. Add these figures.

3. Subtract the sum from the number of spaces in the line of writing (the right margin setting minus the left margin setting).

4. Divide the result by the number of intercolumns.

center 54

65.34

INTERNATIONAL SYSTEM OF UNITS (SI)* 17

Quantity 4	Unit 2	Symbol 3
acceleration	meter/second squared	m/s^2
angular acceleration	radian/second squared 10	rad/s^2
angular velocity	radian/second	rad/s
area	square meter	m^2
current density	ampere/square meter	A/m^2
electric charge density 11	coulomb/cubic meter	C/m^3
electric field strength	volt/meter	V/m
electric flux density	coulomb/square meter	C/m^2
energy density	joule/cubic meter	J/m^3
magnetic field strength	ampere/meter	A/m
molar heat capacity	joule/mole kelvin	J/(mol·K)
moment of force	newton meter	N·m
permeability	henry/meter	H/m
radiance	watt/square meter stradian	$W/(m^2 \cdot sr)$ 4
specific energy	joule/kilogram	J/kg
specific volume	cubic meter/kilogram	m^3/kg
thermal conductivity	watt/meter kelvin	W/(m·K)
velocity	meter/second	m/s
volume	cubic meter	m^3

*Source: 1979 Annual Book of ASTM Standards

7

7a ▶ 8 Preparatory practice

each line twice SS (slowly, faster); DS between 2-line groups

all reaches learned Jack worked with Ceil and Fred Caulde; so did Rex.

n/x Anne can send a ton of flax seed to Tex next June.

c/u Una Custer could cut our curls in just four hours.

easy sentence Ella Cox can find the tour she wants in that list.

7b ▶ 12 Developing carriage (carrier) return technique

1. Type each line once untimed.
Goal: to return with-out pausing at line endings or beginnings

2. Type two 30″ writings on each line.
Goal: to reach end of each line as "return" is called

3. Type a 1′ writing on each line without the call to "return."
Goal: at least 10 gross words a minute *(gwam)*

	words in line	gwam 30″
1 Jan sent the cake to the fair.	6	12
2 We know that we want to work there.	7	14
3 Kit tried until six to do that next one.	8	16
4 Candie did the final drills in an hour or so.	9	18
5 Jake takes a jet at six; find a road to the field.	10	20

| 1 | 2 | 3 | 4 | 5 | 6 | 7 | 8 | 9 | 10 |

7c ▶ 10 Learning new keyreaches: M and G

Reach technique for m

▶ • eyes on copy in book
• curved, upright fingers
• finger-action keystrokes
• down-and-in motion of thumb to space
• shift—type capital—release quickly

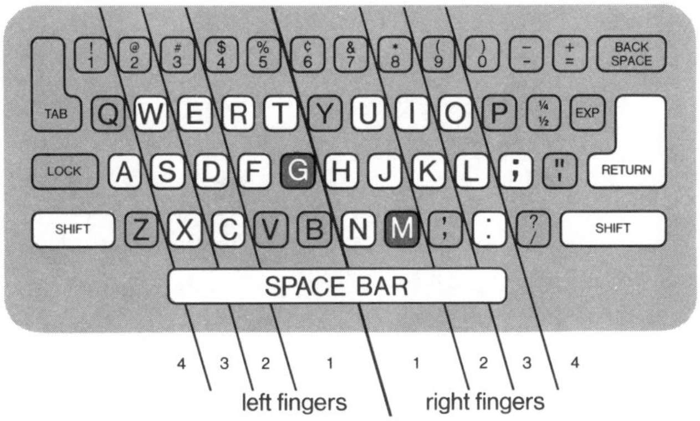

Reach technique for g

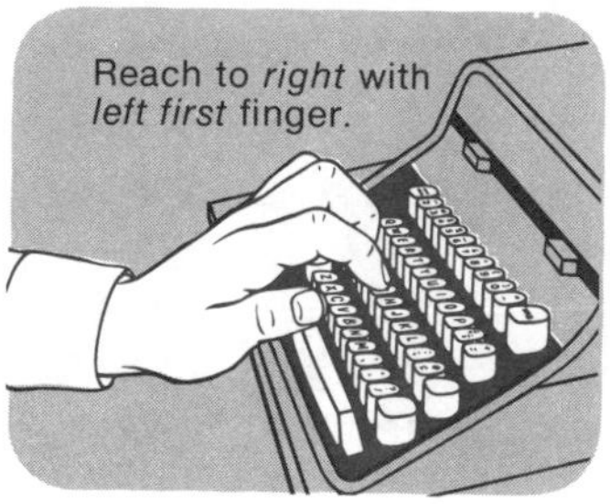

m
1 mj mj me met mit mist miss firm form harm come sum
2 am dam ram me met lame tame fame arm harm farm mix

g
3 gf gf go got tog fog log dog rug dug tug lags wing
4 rig gag cog rag flag drag snag nag wig dig jig egg

m/g
5 Sam Muggs made a shag mat from his gold game flag.
6 Grace met Greg some time ago; Meg met him in Rome.

all reaches learned
7 Judd is coming next week; Rachel left him at home.
8 Kit will sing at six in the Fuji Room; do come in.

| 1 | 2 | 3 | 4 | 5 | 6 | 7 | 8 | 9 | 10 |

Job 2
Leftbound technical report
(plain full sheets)

Dr. Fernandes has requested information about magnetizing forces from the American Society of Testing and Materials. Ms. Washington, Executive Director of the American Society of Testing and Materials, has responded by sending an abstract from the *1979 Annual Book of ASTM Standards*. This report must now be typed in leftbound style for insertion in the *Electrical Testing Manual*. The report begins on page 276 of the *Electrical Testing Manual* and is numbered MF-57.

Note:

The formula for Magnetizing Force—Instantaneous contains the symbol "pi." This symbol must be inserted into the report in ink thus: π

Page 276
Report No. MF-57

MAGNETIZING FORCES* 9

Summary 3

There are five basic variations of the magnetizing force: (1) magnetizing force--a-c, (2) magnetizing force--biasing, (3) magnetizing force--incremental, (4) magnetizing force--instantaneous, and (5) magnetizing force--maximum. This report provides a brief summary of these five variations in the magnetizing force.

Introduction 6

A magnetizing force is the magnetic-field strength of a given substance. It is that magnetic-vector quantity located at a specific point in a magnetic field which measures the inherent ability of magnetized substances or electrical currents to develop magnetic induction at the specified location.

The formula for calculating the magnetizing force (H) is as follows:

$H = C(NI/l)$

Where: H = magnetizing force
C = constant whose value depends on the system of units
N = number of units
I = current
l = axial length of the coil

The variations in the magnetizing force will be presented in the remainder of this report.

Magnetizing Force--a-c

There are three different values of dynamic magnetizing force parameters in common use today. They are:

a. H_L, which is an assumed peak value that is computed in terms of peak magnetizing current;

b. H_Z, which is an assumed peak value that is computed in terms of measured rms exciting current;

c. H_p, which is computed in terms of a measured peak value of exciting current and is generally equated with the value H'_{max}.

Magnetizing Force--Biasing

Magnetic substance that is subjected simultaneously to a periodically varying magnetizing force and to a constant magnetizing force has a magnetizing force that is the algebraic mean value of the two forces. The symbol for the magnetizing force--biasing is H_b.

---

*Source: 1979 Annual Book of ASTM Standards

(continued on page 284)

7d ▶ 10
Learning new keyreaches: P and B

Reach technique for p

Reach technique for b

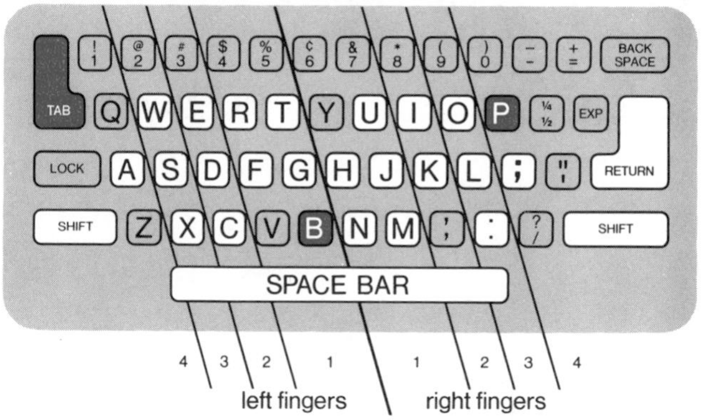

▶ Reach down to the bottom row and up to the third row with the *fingers*, not with the hands.

p
1 p; p; pal pad paid pen open pan span pane pun spun
2 up up sup sip sap lip slip lips pep prep trip trap

b
3 bf bf bid rib fib fob job rob robe bobs lobs lobes
4 be bell bill bore born bond bus but burn subs buns

b/p
5 Bob Pabst paid Barb for a pen; Paula will keep it.
6 Bob Robb has pep and push; Barb Rapp boasts pluck.

all reaches learned
7 Mark and she left Pecos in June; Bob will go next.
8 Judge Caben must stop work; she flew there at six.

| 1 | 2 | 3 | 4 | 5 | 6 | 7 | 8 | 9 | 10 |

7e ▶ 10
Learning to operate the tabulator

To clear tab stops

1. Move carriage to extreme *left* (or carrier to extreme *right*).

2. Depress **tab clear (33)** and hold it down as you return carriage to extreme right (or carrier to extreme left) to remove all tab stops.

To set tab stops

Move the carriage (carrier) to the desired position; then depress the **tab set (25)**. Repeat this procedure for each stop needed.

Tabulating technique

Electric (and some manuals): Tap lightly the **tab key (24)** [nearer little finger] or **bar** [index finger]; return the finger to home-key position at once.

Manual: Depress and hold down the **tabulator bar (24)** [right index finger] or **key** [nearer little finger] until the carriage has stopped.

Drill procedure

1. Clear all tab stops, as directed above.

2. Begin Line 1 at the left margin.

3. Set tab stop for Line 2 five spaces to the right of left margin stop.

4. Set tab stop for Line 3 five spaces to right of first tab stop; and so on for Line 4.

5. Type the drill once DS as shown.

Margin ▼

Now is the time for me to gain the use of the tab.

Indent 5 — Tab once → First I clear all the tab stops as I am told.

Indent 10 — Tab twice → I next set three stops from left margin.

Indent 15 — Tab three times → I shall then use the tab to indent.

141-144

141a-144a ▶ 5

Preparatory practice

type as many times as you can in 5′

alphabet	That Juarez Plaza was extremely quiet and dark for an October evening.
fig/sym	The correct formula for page 23 of your report is P (5.76) × Y (14.908).
hyphen	My son-in-law won the first-place award in the coast-to-coast contest.
fluency	A neighbor owns the sorority dormitory, but now she wishes she didn't.
	| 1 | 2 | 3 | 4 | 5 | 6 | 7 | 8 | 9 | 10 | 11 | 12 | 13 | 14 |

141b-144b ▶ 45

Office work simulation

Job 1

Memorandum [LM p. 147]

Dr. Fernandes has asked you to type the handwritten memo he has prepared for the test engineers in his department. The required number of copies will be made on the photocopy machine.

To: All Test Engineers

From: Marcos Fernandes, Chief Test Engineer

Date: October 15, 19--

Subject: Additions to Electrical Testing Manual

Many of you have requested that we continue to update our Electrical Testing Manual. We have received some excellent suggestions for new material to be included in our manual. As a result of your interest and suggestions, we have located some new items which are being prepared for distribution to you.

The following items are now being processed:

1. Magnetizing Forces
2. International System of Units (SI)
3. Commonly Used Stepping Motor Calculation Formulas
4. Metric Conversion Table
5. Magnetizing Force Conversion Table

These new inserts should be ready within a few days. If you need more than one copy of each insert, please let us know and we shall send you extra copies.

8

8a ▶8

Preparatory practice

each line 3 times SS (slowly, faster, slowly); DS between 3-line groups

all reaches learned	Tab and Jo Camp worked for six hours; so did Gale.
b/p/m/g	Bob and Greg might camp at Boom Gap or Maple Park.
easy	to be | to be the | it might be | and be sure | and is due

| 1 | 2 | 3 | 4 | 5 | 6 | 7 | 8 | 9 | 10 |

8b ▶ 15

Practicing keystroking technique

twice as shown (once slowly, then faster)

Goals

Lines 1-3: Make direct reaches for such sequences as *ce*, *br*, and *un* without returning the controlling finger to home row.

Lines 4-6: Make adjacent-key reaches (such as *re*, *rt*, and *oi*) evenly, without pauses.

Lines 7-9: Do not hurry the repeat stroking of a key.

all reaches learned

direct reaches	1 once deck herb unit bunt gun pump hum ice gum cede 2 Brad decided at lunch to jump from the cedar deck. 3 I found an unfed brown junco near the barbed wire.
adjacent reaches	4 are art toil germ has stop extra point lions polls 5 We were to ask for free oil for her fast red auto. 6 Marg has a new tire for sale; it has a trim tread.
double letters	7 room upper pepper inn been tell doom ebb mass seen 8 Lee will look to see who has been at the inn door. 9 Megg will cross the creek at the foot of the hill.

| 1 | 2 | 3 | 4 | 5 | 6 | 7 | 8 | 9 | 10 |

8c ▶12

Reaching for new goals

1. Type each line once for practice.

Goal: to increase speed

2. Type two 30″ writings on each line.

Goal: to reach the end of the line as "return" is called

all reaches learned

	words in line	gwam 30″
1 Jo read six pages of the book.	6	12
2 Greg will work at the bank on Guam.	7	14
3 Joseph showed me the stables last March.	8	16
4 We knew she bought four of these brown lamps.	9	18
5 Gale has the new job; Peg sells paint in the mall.	10	20

| 1 | 2 | 3 | 4 | 5 | 6 | 7 | 8 | 9 | 10 |

8d ▶ 15

Typing paragraphs

1. Review clearing and setting tab stops (p. 19).

2. Clear tab stops; set a stop 5 spaces to right of left margin.

3. Type each ¶ DS, indenting the first line.

4. Type two 1′ writings on each ¶ to build speed and continuity. If you complete a ¶ before time is called, start it again.

all letters learned — Difficulty index: E | 1.2 si | 5.1 awl | 90% hfw

	gwam 1′
It stands to reason that most people like to	9
do their best in order to further their own goals.	19
It also seems to stand to reason that people	9
will exercise their hands and minds in the effort.	19
Sometimes we do a great job; sometimes we do	9
less. We can accept failures when we do our best.	19

| 1 | 2 | 3 | 4 | 5 | 6 | 7 | 8 | 9 | 10 |

section

33

Typing in a technical office

lessons 141–144

Section 33 is designed to provide you with a variety of typing problems that you would normally encounter when working in a technical office.

Supplies needed:
letterhead and memo forms [LM pp. 147-150] or plain full sheets; appropriate envelopes

Machine adjustments

1. Check chair and desk adjustments and placement of copy for easy reading.
2. Set paper guide at *0*.
3. Set ribbon control on black.
4. Margins: 70-space line for drills; as directed (or appropriate) for problems.
5. SS line drills; space problems as directed (or appropriate).

Daily practice plan

Preparatory practice ...... 5′
Office work simulation .... 45′

Learning goals

1. To become familiar with the type of work performed in a technical office.
2. To follow directions carefully and completely.
3. To use your production skills effectively on a technical job.

Office Job Simulation

Read carefully the material at the right before you begin the work in Section 33. Make notes of any standard or unusual procedures that you think will save you time during the completion of the production activities of this section.

Introduction

You have been hired as a technical typist by Gemini International, Inc., 1355 Highland Avenue, Durham, NC 27704. Your immediate supervisor is Dr. Marcos Fernandes, the Chief Test Engineer in the Materials Testing Department.

Technical office typing does not always conform to generally accepted business styles and formats. Some technical reports may vary considerably from the traditional business format; therefore, you will be expected to follow all instructions pertaining to each job. You will note, however, that most letters and memorandums are typed in the standard business styles. Gemini International prefers its letters to be typed in the block style with open punctuation. All copies are made on the photocopy machine. As a technical typist, you will be given adequate instructions for each job you type. In addition, the specifications for preparing a technical report are given in the "Excerpts from the Manual for Technical Typists."

Excerpts from the Manual for Technical Typists

Technical reports prepared for Gemini International adhere to the following format guidelines:

Margins. All pages of a technical report are typed in leftbound report style. The top margin of the first page is 2″; of all subsequent pages, 1″.

Top Margin Headings. All pages of a technical report contain the same basic information in the top margin area. All pages have the page numbered on Line 4 and the report number typed on Line 5. Begin the page number and the report number at points that will result in the longer of the lines ending flush with the right margin (see illustration at right).

The report title is centered and typed on Line 13 (2″ from the top) on the first page; on Line 7 (1″ from the top) on all subsequent pages as illustrated below.

Other Headings. First order subheadings are centered on the line of writing, typed in caps and lowercase, and underlined. They are preceded and followed by a TS. Second order subheadings are typed flush left in caps and lowercase, underlined, and preceded by a TS and followed by a DS.

Spacing. DS the ¶s in the report. Formulas and tables may be SS.

Footnotes. A footnote is typed at the bottom of the page on which its reference figure appears. Use standard footnote form for a report.

Page 2
Report No. RC-386

UNIT REACTOR HEAT EXCHANGER FOULING RATE CORRELATION TESTS

much higher heat fluxes for sustained periods of time than before. Data have been collected from hydroclone Runs 1 through 3 and a portion of Run 4.[1]

Correlation Tests

The fouling rate data coll
clone runs and the data of the
four reactor coolers have been
ing equations:

Reactor Coolers 1-3:

dR/d O = K1(Q/A)2 + K

Reactor Cooler 4:

dR/d O = K1(Q/A)2 + K

Where:

dR/d O + Rate of chan

Q/A = Heat flux in in
Btu/(

Q1-4 = Heat transfer
throu

1One run is considered tha
reactor coolers are cleaned unt
to be cleaned again.

Page 1
Report No. RC-386

UNIT REACTOR HEAT EXCHANGER FOULING RATE CORRELATION TESTS

Summary

The fouling rates of the reactor coolers can be reduced significantly by adequate control of the heat flux. The statistical analysis of the data collected for this report is inconclusive beyond the high correlation between the heat flux and the fouling rates.

Other items undoubtedly have an effect on the fouling rates; i.e., solid particle size, particle growth from one cooler mixer circuit to another, and the % solids in the reactor system. As soon as more empirical data concerning the fouling system can be generated, better corrections will be possible.

Introduction

This statistical evaluation of the fouling rates of the reactor coolers was undertaken to determine whether the significant factor relating to the fouling of the reactor coolers was due to heat flux.

Procedures

Since the hydroclone solids recycle system was started up on June 15, reactor heat exchanger operation has been at

Two pages of a technical report

9

9a ▶ 8
Preparatory practice

each line 3 times SS (slowly, faster, slowly); DS between 3-line groups

all reaches learned	Burl took a few cases; Jan hid six pages from Max.
n/x/c/u	Luci Cox can wax and fix our next units after six.
phrases	if it|if it is|if it is to be|if it is to be there

| 1 | 2 | 3 | 4 | 5 | 6 | 7 | 8 | 9 | 10 |

9b ▶ 12
Typing paragraphs

1. Clear tab stops; set a stop for a 5-space ¶ indention; DS.

2. Type the ¶s as shown; then type at least two 1′ writings on each ¶, striving for speed.

Goal: at least 13 words a minute

Difficulty index

all letters learned | E | 1.2 si | 5.1 awl | 90% hfw |

gwam 2′

We must be able to express our thoughts with 5
ease if we desire to find success in the world of 10
business. It is there that sound ideas earn cash. 15

It makes good sense to decide that we should 19
stop to get our thoughts in order before we begin 24
to talk. Talk before thought is often just noise. 29

gwam 2′ | 1 | 2 | 3 | 4 | 5 |

9c ▶ 10
Learning new keyreaches: Y and V

Reach technique for y

Reach technique for v

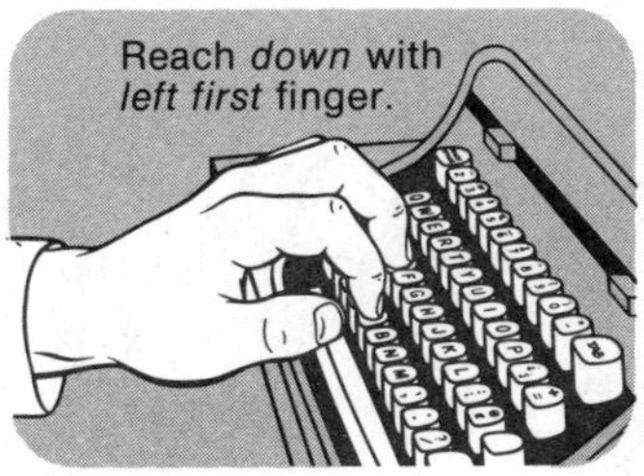

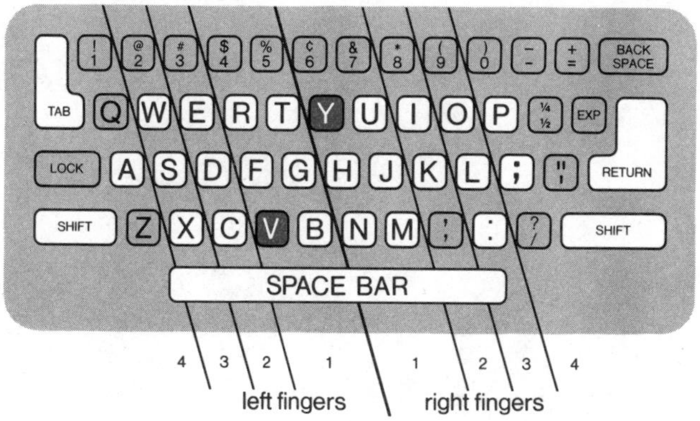

▶ Look at what you have typed or at your fingers only when it is necessary. Type as you read.

y
1 yj yj jay jay lay fly day say way your year yearly
2 sky dry cry try boy joy toy you yen away tray yard

v
3 vf vf vie view vow save rave love dove cove events
4 live jive five vain vane have cave vice vest sieve

y/v
5 You say Viv Yost served over five days on my jury.
6 Val Yung says you may have saved money for my van.

all reaches learned
7 Six heavy trucks jammed Bona Road; Peg flew north.
8 Judy Vixon spoke frankly; chewing gum bothers her.

| 1 | 2 | 3 | 4 | 5 | 6 | 7 | 8 | 9 | 10 |

Mrs. Wyn J. Renaldi 2

In connection with FSS, I understand the practice ~~before~~ & prior to the Combined United Fund Campaign was to split receipts among the various united fund areas. There does not seem to be any basis for changing this practice as a result ~~because~~ of the Combined United Fund Campaign. In addition, it is my understanding that FSS officials representing the employees ~~workers~~ at the installation have asked to have the opportunity for the employees to pledge to the fund covering the area in which they live. Under such circumstances, it seems desirable to accede to ~~agree with~~ the wishes of the employees ~~workers~~ if a successful campaign is to ~~result~~ be conducted.

The problem you raise is one that can best be worked out by the local united funds involved along with officials ~~ers~~ of the particular agency in which you are raising funds. I was under the impression that you had agreed with the United Fund of the District of Columbia ~~D.C.~~ on the arrangement covering the proceeds from last ~~the~~ fall's CUFC at Federal Supply Service.

We would like to see any type of arrangement carried out that is agreeable to the local united funds. I see no basis for the FSS trying to make a decision ~~ruling~~ in connection with the distribution of receipts. If FSS management and employees wish the opportunity to designate their ~~re~~ contributions to the area in which they live, ~~reside~~ I would want this option to continue from the standpoint of a successful campaign in the agency. ~~service~~

Sincerely,

JEROLD K. DRUMMOND
Chief, Federal Supply Service

cc:
Ms. Monica Fuentes
Mr. Louis C. Berger
Mr. Alonzo J. Watson

AFAW:BCDukowicz:xx 8-15---

9d ▶ 10
Learning new keyreaches: , (Comma) and Shift Lock

Reach technique for , (comma)

Reach *down* with *right second* finger; space once after , used as punctuation.

Reach technique for shift lock

Reach *left* with *left little* finger.

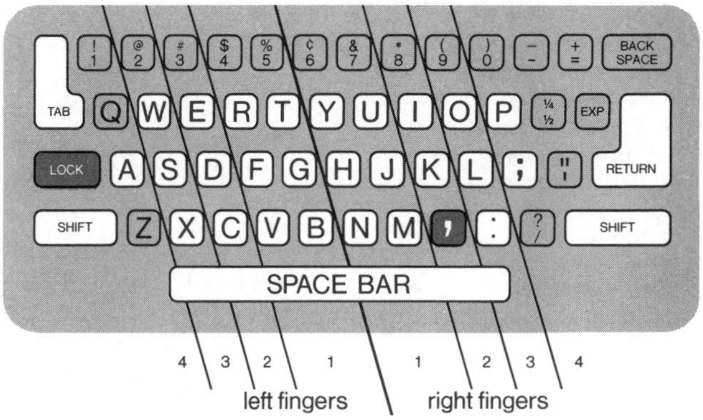

Shift lock
Depress the shift lock and leave it down until you have typed the combination to be capitalized. To release the lock, operate the shift key. The comma and the period may be typed with the shift lock depressed.

,	1 ,k ,k Rick, Jack, and Lee left; Dale will go, too.
	2 to be, we can be, on the job, be sure, but it can,
shift lock	3 She joined the NEA or OEA. She works for the IRS.
	4 The class read A TALE OF TWO CITIES and JANE EYRE.
,/shift lock	5 He saw each of the new shows on NBC, ABC, and CBS.
	6 For the state she wrote ME, MS, MI, MO, MT, or MD.
all reaches learned	7 After lunch, Judge Byrne spoke on WRVX; I saw him.
	8 Jud, we have a copy of SIX KINGS; ours is by Tilm.

| 1 | 2 | 3 | 4 | 5 | 6 | 7 | 8 | 9 | 10 |

9e ▶ 10
Building typing speed

▶ Keep wrists low, arms relaxed.

Type each line of 10a below as two 1′ writings. Try to complete a line *at least* once in the 1′ timing. Keep the carriage (carrier) moving–avoid pauses or stops.

10

10a ▶ 8
Preparatory practice

each line 3 times SS (slowly, faster, slowly); DS between 3-line groups

Curve your fingers and position them upright (not slanting) on home keys. Keep your wrists low and relaxed.

all reaches learned	Max Waver sang before her party; Lu Jack did, too.
y/v	Yves may have heavy vans; yet, Evelyn drives them.
shift keys and lock	Ken, Rex, and Eva did not read GONE WITH THE WIND.
easy	That man has the time to fix the light on the bus.

| 1 | 2 | 3 | 4 | 5 | 6 | 7 | 8 | 9 | 10 |

137b-140b, continued

Job 8 [LM p. 145]
Two-page formal government letter with window envelope

B. C. Dukowicz has drafted a letter for Mr. Drummond's correction and signature.

Mr. Drummond asks that you type the rough draft in final form as a two-page formal government letter. Use a plain sheet for the second page of the letter.

August ~~12~~ *15*, 19--

Mrs. Wyn J. Rinaldi, *Chairperson*
Northeastern Virginia United *Fund* ~~Appeal~~
2361 Jefferson Davis Highway
Arlington, ~~Virginia~~ *VA* 22202

Dear Mrs. Renaldi:

~~In reply~~ *Let me react* to some of the questions *you* raised in your leter to Monica Fuentes, Chairperson of the Federal Supply Service Combined United Fun*d* concerning the arrangements between the United Fund of Northeastern Virginia and the United ~~Givers~~ Fund of the District of Columbia involving Combined United Fund Campaign receipts from employees of the federal supply service.

In ~~starting~~ *establishing* a Combined United Fund Campaign, the campaign *area* is ordinarily the same as the area of the local united fund which is involved in the campign. However, the Fund-*Raising* Manual does not provide any hard-and-fast rules on this and there are some variations dependøng onthe local ditruation. The opportunity of giving where the employee works is *fully* recognized.

The situation in ~~the federal supply servive~~ *FSS, however,* is different. Most employees do not reside in one area but are split *among* several separate united fund ~~centers.~~ *areas.* This is also the case with other agencies where the United Fund of Arlington/Fairfax counties is involved. Because of the large number of workers *who* resid~~ing~~*e* outside the campaign area in which thye work, a provision is made to ~~permit~~ *enable* them to give to the fund representing the area in which they ~~reside.~~ *live.* In an agency where 35-50 percent of the employees live in a united fund area other, than the one in which the agencyis located it just does*n't* appear desirable to try to force them to contribute *to* the fund covering the area in which ~~they are employed.~~ *the agency is located.*

For example, employees located in agencies in downtown Washington are covered by the United Fund of the District of Columbia.

(continued on page 280)

10b ▶ 12
Developing machine parts control

1. Clear all tab stops.

2. Set a tab stop at center (42, pica; 51, elite).

3. Type the drill once as shown; repeat if time permits.

Goals

Lines 1-2: to tab and return with eyes on book

Lines 3-5: to use space bar efficiently and to maintain fluency

Lines 6-8: to shift rhythmically and keep letters on line

Lines 9-11: to lock and unlock shift smoothly

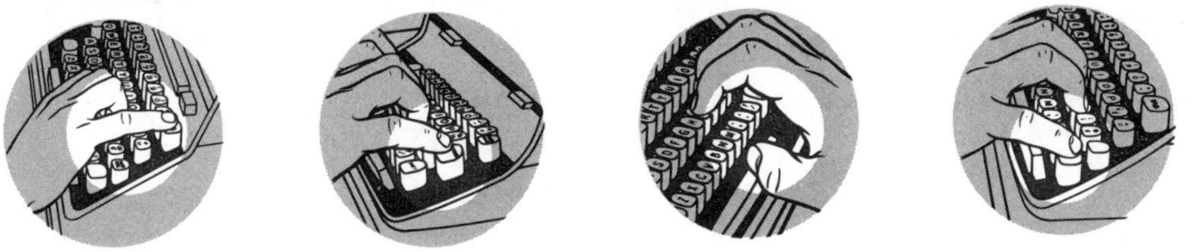

all reaches learned

▼ Center

tab and return
```
 1 Tab ————————————————→ She said that this is the
 2 lot to be sent; I agreed.
```

space bar
```
 3 it is the|for it is|to do|to do it|and to do|do so
 4 If I am not to do the job, I do not need this hat.
 5 She is the one who is to be in the cab when we go.
```

shift keys
```
 6 Lex Vance saw Cyd Burn at the New Trent Book Fair.
 7 LeRoy Hale asked Jill Yee to visit Old Home Manor.
 8 The Ace Card Co. will hire Jim McGee or Lois Holt.
```

shift lock
```
 9 Use ALL CAPS for items such as NASA, NHA, and HEW.
10 Our team will play NYU, UCLA, and UTEP this month.
11 Each day I read THE FREE PRESS and THE DAILY NEWS.
```

| 1 | 2 | 3 | 4 | 5 | 6 | 7 | 8 | 9 | 10 |

10c ▶ 10
Learning new keyreaches: Q and ?

Reach technique for q

▶ While making a reach-stroke with the little finger, keep the tips of other fingers close to home-row position.

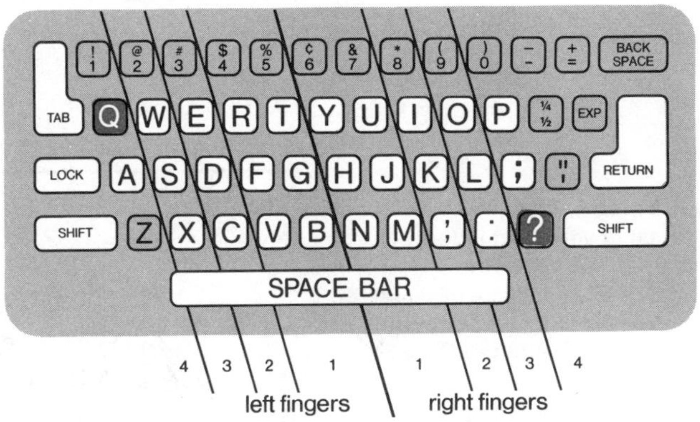

Question mark

Hold the left shift key in depressed position as you strike the question mark.

Reach technique for ? (question)

q
```
1 qa qa qu quit quite quiet quire quires quirt quilt
2 qu qu quay quack quail quake quart qualm quip quid
```

?
```
3 ?; ?; Is she?  Is he next?  Did I meet Jo?  Where?
4 Is Peg right?  May Doug and I go?  May I see Jean?
```

q/?
```
5 Did Marq Quor make a quick quest in Quarte Square?
6 Did Squire Quigg quote the quiet queen?  Did Quin?
```

all letters learned
```
7 Has Quin, Tex, or Clay joined GPFV?  Has Kim Webb?
8 Will Drex enjoy his copy of my book QUIET SAVAGES?
```

| 1 | 2 | 3 | 4 | 5 | 6 | 7 | 8 | 9 | 10 |

137b-140b, continued

Job 6 [LM p. 141]
Informal government letter
(no envelope needed)

Mr. Drummond asks that you type a usable copy of the letter for his signature.

DATE: August 12, 19--
REPLY TO
ATTN OF: AFAW

SUBJECT: Bids for electronic computer components

TO: Barbara Wexford, Purchasing Officer

(¶) Enclosed are the 25 bids that we received as of the close of the bidding date, August 10, 19--. Will you please acknowledge receipt of these bids by notifying each bidder by return mail.
(¶) The bids are to be opened at 1:00 p.m. on August 20. Will you therefore please make the necessary arrangements for this bid-opening session and notify all concerned individuals of the time, date, and location.
(¶) I would recommend that, in addition to the regular procurement officers, we invite Dr. Russell I. Reed to assist us in evaluating the bids.

Jerold K. Drummond, Chief

Job 7 [LM p. 143]
Formal government letter with window envelope

Mr. Drummond wants this letter to be typed for his signature on August 12. Address the letter to:

Carolina Paper Company
ATTN: Miss O. D. Reynolds
2105 Carver Street
Durham, NC 27705

Ladies and Gentlemen
(¶) Because of the accumulated effect of several recent design changes, we request that you increase the height and width of the No. 24 container that we procure from your company. (¶) The new specifications are as follows:

	Present	Requested
Height	44.5 cm	48.0 cm
Width	30.5 cm	32.0 cm
Length	77.5 cm	77.5 cm

(¶) Please acknowledge this change and confirm the earliest date that we shall be able to procure the new containers. Sincerely

cc: Mrs. Karen M. Silva
AFAW:RLDiaz:xx 8-12---

10d ▶ 10
Learning new keyreaches: Z and : (Colon)

Reach technique for z

Reach *down* with *left little* finger.

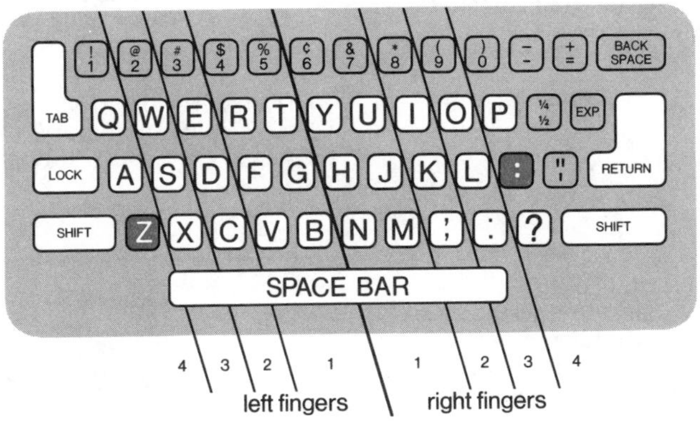

Reach technique for : (colon)

Left shift and strike ; key; space twice after : used as punctuation.

▶ While making a reach–stroke with the little finger, keep the tips of other fingers close to home–row position.

z
1 za za zany zed zeal zero zest zip zinc zing zigzag
2 raze faze gaze zoom haze jazz size doze froze ooze

:
3 ;: :; :; : Read: Date: Send: Type: From: See:
4 Space twice after a colon, thus: To: No.: Time:

z/:
5 Type these words: haze, blaze, maze, maize, zinc.
6 Type: zoo, zoom, zed. Now type: zip, zing, adz.

all letters used
7 Jaz gave Quin two books: PROXY FIGHT and BE CALM.
8 If Mark Zolby quits, what can Jude expect to give?

| 1 | 2 | 3 | 4 | 5 | 6 | 7 | 8 | 9 | 10 |

10e ▶ 10
Checking keystroking skill

1. Type each ¶ once for practice, then type any troublesome words 2 or 3 times.

2. Type a 1′ writing on each ¶. Calculate gross words a minute (*gwam*) using the superior figures.

3. Type two 2′ writings, using both ¶s; calculate *gwam*.

Goal: at least 13 *gwam*

Difficulty index

all letters learned	E	1.2 si	5.1 awl	90% hfw

gwam 2′

If you think about words that have been used 5
in your effort to learn to type, you might wisely 10
prize those that place a high value on your labor. 15

Ask this question of yourself: If tenseness 19
can cause an error, how can I type better? Relax 24
as you do each job; make your skills work for you. 29

gwam 2′ | 1 | 2 | 3 | 4 | 5 |

137b-140b, continued

Job 4 [LM p. 137]
Formal government letter with window envelope

On August 10, Mr. Drummond asks you to prepare for his signature a letter to:

Mr. Juan M. Rios, President
Office Interiors, Inc.
14688 East Bannister Road
Kansas City, MO 64139

Use the 3 paragraphs of the letter typed in Job 3. Supply an appropriate salutation and complimentary close. Compose a final paragraph to say that one of our Federal Supply Service officials, Miss Juanita Rivera, will be in Kansas City on September 8 and will be available on September 9 or 10 to discuss bid requirements with appropriate staff members. Indicate that arrangements for such discussions can be made by contacting Mr. Drummond's office prior to Miss Rivera's departure for Kansas City on September 8.

Job 5 [LM p. 139]
Informal government letter
(no envelope required)
Mr. Drummond has drafted a letter to all employees that he wants you to type in final form for duplication and distribution. Because no envelope is required, he suggests that you begin the body a triple-space below the "To:" caption.

DATE: August 10, 19--
REPLY TO ATTN OF: AFAW
SUBJECT: The 19-- Savings Bond Campaign
TO: All Federal Supply Service Employees

The 19-- [Savings] Bond Campaign is now underway throughout the Federal Government. Savings bonds are a safe, sound invest ment. they are risk free, loss proof, and theft proof; they can be converted to cash quickly to meet emergencies.

No ¶ There is no easier way to accumulate savings than through the payroll savings plan. It is automatic and effortless. Your key person, who will be contact[ing] you shortly, will explain all of the advantages of investing in bonds regularly though the payroll savings plan. ¶ If you already buy bonds [regularly] and can increase your allotment, I recommend that you do so. By buying bonds today [now], you will be helping yourself at ain your personal goals; [and] You will be help[ing] our country. ¶ Of course, when you buy savings bonds, you do more than invest in your own fugure; you invest inthe future of our Country, and you demonstrate your faith in America.

No ¶ Many Americans have seen small savings bond allotments help finance a college education or a new home.

AFAW:JKDrummond:XX 8-10---

11

11a ▶ 8
Preparatory practice

each line 3 times SS (slowly, faster, slowly); DS between 3-line groups

all letters learned Roz Groves just now packed my box with five quail.

q/? Did Marq Quin go? Did Quent Quin go? Did Quincy?

z Note: Liz Zahl saw Zoe feed the zebra in the zoo.

easy She can do the job, but she must go with them now.

| 1 | 2 | 3 | 4 | 5 | 6 | 7 | 8 | 9 | 10 |

11b ▶ 6
Practicing difficult reaches

1. Type each line once. Checkmark lines that seem difficult for you.
2. Type at least twice each line that you checked.

b 1 Barb, not Bob, will buy the new bonds at the bank.

x 2 Tex Cox waxed that next box for Jinx and Rex Knox.

p 3 Pat Pratt can help pay for part of the prize plan.

y 4 Kaye said you should stay with Fay for sixty days.

n 5 Nan Connor danced many times; now Donna can dance.

| 1 | 2 | 3 | 4 | 5 | 6 | 7 | 8 | 9 | 10 |

11c ▶ 11
Reaching for new goals

1. Type each ¶ once for practice; then type any troublesome words 2 or 3 times.
2. Type a 1′ writing on each ¶. Calculate gross words a minute (*gwam*) using the superior figures.
3. Type two 2′ writings, using both ¶s; calculate *gwam*.

▶ Work for smooth, continuous typing to increase your speed.

Goal: at least 14 *gwam*

Difficulty index

all letters learned	E	1.2 si	5.1 awl	90% hfw

gwam 2′

You might not like change, but changes often 5
can become great values. Soon you will be typing 10
many items you formerly had to write by hand, and 15
this is just one of the prizes of a typing course. 20

To many folks, it seems, the main motive for 24
learning to type is the fact that they want to be 29
able to write while thinking or, next to that, to 34
write faster than they can using other techniques. 39

gwam 2′ | 1 | 2 | 3 | 4 | 5 |

137b-140b, continued

Job 2 [LM p. 129]
Formal government letter with window envelope

August 10, 19-- REGISTERED Subject: Contract A-579436-00-69 Ms. Amanda J. Washington Vice President Midwestern Manufacturing Co. 5304 North Askew Avenue Kansas City, MO 64119 Dear Ms. Washington:

(¶ 1) Four copies of Contract A-579436-00-69 are enclosed with this letter. They are complete in all details except for additional provisions listed as required on page 474 of the Manual of Form for Government Contracts.

(¶ 2) In order to expedite completion of this contract, we have typed and signed as an addendum the required provisions on page 8. Our legal office informs us that these addenda items must now be signed by the officers of your company.

(¶ 3) All other terms of the contract are agreeable to our office; and with the return of our copies of the signed contract, we can accept delivery of our preliminary order entered with you when contract negotiations began.

Sincerely, JEROLD K. DRUMMOND Chief, Federal Supply Service 5 Enclosures: 4 copies of Contract A-579436-00-69 Manual of Form for Government Contracts cc: Official File--AFAW GSS Legal Officer AFAW:JHGaley:xx 8-10---

Job 3 [LM pp. 131–136]
Formal government letters with window envelopes

Today, August 10, Mr. Drummond hands you the 3 file cards and the handwritten letter shown here. He asks you to type the letter to each addressee, adding an appropriate salutation and complimentary close.

Dixon, Clyde M. (Mr.)

Mr. Clyde M. Dixon, Manager
Star Office Equipment Company
145 North Mill Street
Lexington, KY 40507

Escobar, Beatriz (Ms.)

Ms. Beatriz Escobar, Manager
Apex Office Furniture Corp.
6319 Bradbury Avenue
Ft. Wayne, IN 46809

Glabman, Rona (Mrs.)

Mrs. Rona Glabman, President
Illinois Desk and Chair, Inc.
2599 South Faraday Street
Peoria, IL 61607

Your bid has been received, but it was not in compliance with our bidding regulations. Will you please review the bid requirements that were sent to you and make sure that you have complied with all specific items referred to under the section titled "Bid Requirements."

Perhaps you were using last year's bidding regulations. Please check to make certain that you are following the current regulations for the submission of bids.

If you need further clarification about any specific bid requirement, please contact us immediately. We have extended the bid closing date until September 30 to allow sufficient time for your bid to be adjusted.

11d ▶ 10

Learning new keyreaches: Backspacer and Margin Release

exact 50-space line
(center −25; center +25)

Line 1: backspacer—(26)

1. Type the first incomplete word in Line 1 (including comma).

2. Backspace and fill in the missing letter *n*.

3. Repeat 1 and 2 with the other incomplete words in Line 1.

Line 2: margin release—(32)

1. Depress margin release and backspace 5 spaces into left margin.

2. Type Line 2 twice. If the carriage locks, depress the margin release and complete the line.

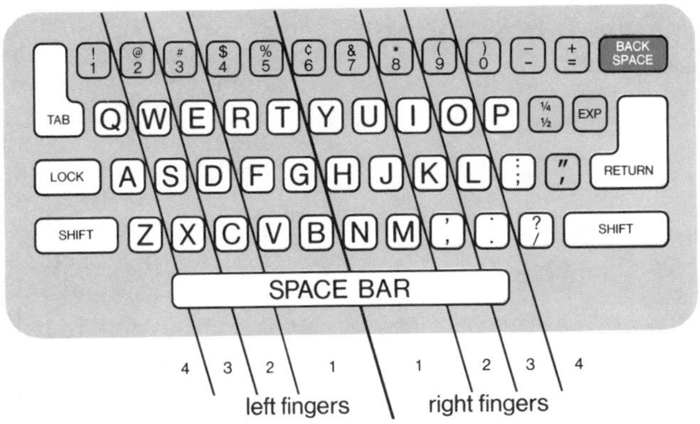

Backspacer
Use the backspace key (26) to position the carriage to type a missing letter.

Electric: Make a light, quick stroke with the appropriate little finger. Depress the key firmly if you want repeated back-space action.

Nonelectric: Reach to the backspace key with the appropriate little finger. Depress the key firmly.

1 ofte , faste , thi g, dri k, ve dor, pe cil, u til

2 My work may be judged many times. I must be its best judge.

11e ▶ 15

Keystroking review

1. Read goals below for the line or lines before typing them.

2. Type each line at least once.

3. Repeat lines that seem difficult to you.

Goals

Lines 1-3: Keep unneeded fingers still and in home-row position.

Lines 4-6: Keep wrists low; do not rest palm on typewriter.

Line 7: Use a distinct repeat stroke.

Line 8: Read letter-by-letter as you type.

Line 9: Read word-by-word as you type.

Lines 10-12: Use shift-strike-release for typing capitals.

1st fingers	1	June Grove may yet try to buy a toy horn for them.
2d fingers	2	Dick, not Dee, said the ice cracked on Keck Creek.
3d/4th fingers	3	You will write quickly: Zeus, Apollo, and Xerxes.
1st (bottom) row	4	Did Nan get a comb from the extra box in the cave?
2d (home) row	5	Jack Hall held a sale; Alf shall add half a glass.
3d row	6	Betty wrote to Troy Trapp. He did not quote Ruth.
double letters	7	Will Anne and Poll take three books to the troops?
one hand	8	Milo acted on only a few tax rebate cases in July.
balanced hand	9	If they wish, she may make the form for the disks.
left shift	10	Kate Long and Jan Hunt will join Lois in New York.
right shift	11	Suzi, Don, Cyd, and Rod will go to Green Bay soon.
both shifts	12	Josh Wertz will see Lyle Branch in Oak Creek Park.

Office Job Simulation, continued

Distribution of Copies. A carbon copy notation is shown only on the file copy. Type the notation a double space below the last line of the signer's title or the enclosure notation or the separate cover listing. List the names of the recipients one below the other with office symbols when appropriate:

```
cc:
Official File--BRAR
Reading File--BRA
```

Identification of Office, Writer, and Typist. Type the office symbol of the preparing office, the writer's initials and surname, the typist's initials, and the date on the file copies only. In some cases the writer of the letter is not the same as the signer; therefore, the name of the writer appears in the identification line. Type this line flush with the left margin a double space below the last line used. Example:

```
FMSX:MJRodriguez:dp 2-26-81
```

Formal government letters

Stationery. Standard 8½″ × 11″ letterheads (without heading captions) are used for formal government letters.

Style and Margins. Block style and 1-inch side margins are used. A salutation and a complimentary close may be included, with mixed punctuation. All other aspects are the same as those of the informal letter.

Date. Type the date on Line 7 at left margin.

Special Mailing Instructions. Type on Line 9 at the left margin.

Subject. Type on Line 11 at the left margin.

Address. Begin the address on Line 14 at the left margin.

137-140

137a-140a ▶ 5
Preparatory practice

each line 3 times SS (slowly, faster, slowly); retype selected lines as time permits

alphabet	Jack will ship by express the quantity of goods that we have itemized.
fig/sym	The large jewelry box--19″ × 24″ × 37″--sells for $136.58, less 10.5%.
long words	Management has preferred the qualitative to the quantitative approach.
fluency	If they amend the audit forms, eight clerks may handle the usual work.

| 1 | 2 | 3 | 4 | 5 | 6 | 7 | 8 | 9 | 10 | 11 | 12 | 13 | 14 |

137b-140b ▶ 45
Office work simulation

Be sure to study "Excerpts from *Correspondence Manual* before you begin work.

Prepare 2 carbon copies of each job on plain paper; correct all errors neatly before submitting your work for approval.

Job 1 [LM p. 127]
Informal government letter with window envelope

Date: **July 9, 19--** Reply to Attn of: **AFAW** Subject: **Substandard shipment returned** To: **Mr. Alan B. Randolph, President Michigan Tool and Die Corporation 5000 Imperial Highway Detroit, MI 48240**

(¶ 1) Tests on items selected at random from your most recent shipment indicate that standards as specified in our contract with your firm have not been met. The entire shipment, therefore, has been returned to you.

(¶ 2) A copy of the report on our laboratory tests will be forwarded to you under separate cover. If after studying the report you believe it to be in error, you may file an exception (Form B-801/33) with our office.

(¶ 3) As you know, our contract with you specifies that any failure to maintain minimum-standard requirements must be remedied within 90 days or the contract becomes subject to review. We encourage you, therefore, to take prompt action in this matter.

JEROLD K. DRUMMOND Chief, Federal Supply Service Separate cover: Laboratory Test Report cc: Official File--AFAW AFAW:RDGunn:xx 7-9---

section

2

Developing basic skills

lessons 12–15

Learning goals

1. To type with smoother keystroking.
2. To improve use of auxiliary typewriter parts.
3. To relax and type with greater confidence.
4. To improve keystroking speed.

Machine adjustments

1. Set paper guide at *0*.
2. Set ribbon control on black.
3. Set the left margin stop for a 50-space line (center −25) and the right margin stop at the end of the carriage scale.
4. Single-space (SS) drills; double-space (DS) paragraphs.

12

12a ▶8 Preparatory practice

each line 3 times SS (slowly, faster, slowly); DS between 3-line groups

alphabet One judge saw five boys quickly fix the prize elm.

z/: TO: Zelda Mazzo, Yuma, AZ. FROM: Noel Z. Rizzo.

easy They may pay the firm the price for the new forms.

| 1 | 2 | 3 | 4 | 5 | 6 | 7 | 8 | 9 | 10 |

12b ▶12 Developing keystroking technique

Type as shown (without numbers).

▶ **Lines 1-2:** Reach with *fingers*; keep hand movement to a minimum.

Lines 3-4: Curve fingers over home row.

Lines 5-6: Reach *fingers* to third-row keys without moving hands.

all letters used

1st row
1 Did Ben, the cabby, have extra puzzles? Yes, one.
2 Do they, Mr. Zack, expect a number of brave women?

2d row
3 Gale Hill had a sale; Jake has a sale in the fall.
4 Jacky was sad; she had just lost a gold golf ball.

3d row
5 There were three poor points in your quiet speech.
6 Trent quietly puts her whole heart into her words.

| 1 | 2 | 3 | 4 | 5 | 6 | 7 | 8 | 9 | 10 |

12c ▶8 Developing space-bar control

each line 3 times SS (slowly, faster, still faster); DS between 3-line groups

▶ Use down-inward thumb motion; space immediately after each word.

Spacing cue: Space once after . following an initial. Abbreviations such as M.D., Ph.D., U.S., N.Y., C.O.D., f.o.b., a.m., and p.m. may be typed solid (without internal spacing).

to am in no at on of it as up he be we us or so do

Get set. Ask her. I pay him. Try one. You can.

I left; Jo did, too. Is it true? TO: M. W. Kitz

| 1 | 2 | 3 | 4 | 5 | 6 | 7 | 8 | 9 | 10 |

12d ▶7 Gaining shift key/shift lock control

each line twice SS (slowly, faster); DS between 2-line groups

K. W. Hinze lives on Ada Street; he works for RCA.

Sammy Drews will read OUTLOOK before joining ISBE.

Liza Storm left for USC; she wants to get her M.D.

| 1 | 2 | 3 | 4 | 5 | 6 | 7 | 8 | 9 | 10 |

FEDERAL SUPPLY SERVICE
WASHINGTON, DC 20406

DATE: February 25, 19--
REPLY TO ATTN OF: AFAW CERTIFIED
SUBJECT: Format for the Informal Letter

TO: Federal Supply Service (AFAS)
ATTN: Ms. Kayoka Tanaka
1889 Inverson Street
San Francisco, CA 94102

This letter shows the format for preparing letters throughout the United States Government. This format will expedite the preparation of correspondence and save effort, time, and materials.

The following features of this format should please typists.

a. All elements except the first line of lettered items are blocked along the left margin. This block style minimizes the use of the space bar, tabulator set key, and the tabulator bar or key.

b. Salutations and complimentary closes are omitted in most letters. They may be included in formal letters to any individual on a personal or private matter (letters of condolence, notices of serious illness, where a warm and personal feeling is paramount, etc.), or where protocol or tradition dictates. See the enclosed copy of a formal letter.

c. The address is positioned for use in a window envelope, eliminating the need for typing an envelope.

JEROLD K. DRUMMOND
Chief, Federal Supply Service

2 Enclosures:
Copy of Formal Letter
United States Government Correspondence Manual, 1977

cc:
Official File--AFAW

AFAW:RGDunn:xx 2-25--- ← Not shown on original copy

Informal government letter; window envelope to be used

FEDERAL SUPPLY SERVICE
WASHINGTON, DC 20406

February 25, 19--

CERTIFIED

Subject: Format for the Formal Letter

Ms. Kayoko Tanaka
Assistant Director
Federal Supply Service
1889 Inverson Street
San Francisco, CA 94102

Dear Ms. Tanaka:

This letter shows the format for preparing formal letters throughout the United States Government. This format will expedite the preparation of formal correspondence and save effort, time, and materials.

The following features of this format should please typists.

a. All elements except the first line of lettered items are blocked along the left margin. This block style minimizes the use of the space bar, tabulator set key, and the tabulator bar or key. Formal stationery omits the printed captions in the upper-left margin (see enclosed copy of an informal letter.)

b. Salutations and complimentary closes may be used with mixed punctuation in most formal letters. Formal letters include letters to any individual on a personal or private matter or where protocol or tradition dictates.

c. The address is positioned for use in a window envelope, eliminating the need for typing an envelope.

Sincerely,

JEROLD K. DRUMMOND
Chief, Federal Supply Service

Enclosure

cc:
Official File--AFAW

AFAW: REDunn:xx 2-25--- ← Not shown on original copy

Formal government letter; window envelope to be used

Office Job Simulation, continued

about Line 20. Begin each main paragraph flush with the left margin. If a paragraph is broken into subparagraphs, indent 4 spaces the first line of each subparagraph; type the second and succeeding lines flush with the left margin.

Succeeding Pages. Type the name of the addressee at the left margin on the 7th line from the top of the page, the page number on the same line flush with the right margin. Continue typing the body of the letter a double space below the name and page number.

Signature Element. Type the name of the signer of the letter in all capital letters on the 4th line space below the last line of the body, flush with the left margin. Type the title of the signer on the next line, flush with the name. If more than 1 line is needed for the signer's title, type succeeding lines flush with the left margin. The entire signature block (name and title) should not exceed 4 lines.

Enclosures. Type the word "Enclosure," when needed, a double space below the signer's title. For more than 1 enclosure, use the plural form and indicate the number of enclosures, as "5 Enclosures." If the enclosure(s) is not identified in the body of the letter, list each enclosure on a separate line below the word "Enclosure(s)" flush with the left margin.

Material Sent Under Separate Cover. If material mentioned in the letter is to be sent under separate cover, type the words "Separate cover:" flush with the left margin, a double space below the signer's title or the enclosure notation, if there is one. List material to be sent under separate cover, whether or not it is identified in the body of the letter. Send a copy of the letter with the material sent under separate cover.

```
Separate cover:
Form Letters Handbook
Plain Letters Pamphlet
```

Information Not Shown on Original Copy. To exclude information from the original copy, turn the cylinder (platen) knob toward you, rolling the carbon pack backward. Insert a half sheet of fairly transparent paper in front of the original to cover the area where notations are to be typed. Then, turn the pack back to typing position and type the notations in proper position.

12e ▶15

Reaching for new goals

Type each sentence as a 1′ writing, typing the sentence as many times as you can until time is called.

Goals

- 14 *gwam*, good
- 17 *gwam*, very good
- 20 *gwam*, excellent

all letters used

	Sentence	words in line	gwam 30″
1	Is there a job for all of us to do?	7	14
2	Shoes in my size are quite hard to find.	8	16
3	Maud just saw that car. Did it stop in time?	9	18
4	If he is to do this work for us, he can do it now.	10	20
5	They all know they have to put first things first.	10	20
6	Bo knows they can fix the old auto they left here.	10	20
7	A worker with push can pass a worker who has pull.	10	20

| 1 | 2 | 3 | 4 | 5 | 6 | 7 | 8 | 9 | 10 |

13

13a ▶8

Preparatory practice

each line 3 times SS (slowly, faster, slowly); DS between 3-line groups

alphabet Mavis Zeff worked quickly on the next big project.

q/? Can you spell queue? quay? aqua? quavered? acquit?

easy Do the clerks take bids for work on the city dock?

| 1 | 2 | 3 | 4 | 5 | 6 | 7 | 8 | 9 | 10 |

13b ▶8

Reaching for new goals

Retype 12e above. Beginning with Line 1, type each sentence with a guide called every 30 seconds. Try to reach the end of the line as "Return" is called.

13c ▶12

Developing keystroking technique

Type each line as shown; then repeat.

▶ Keep wrists low, elbows and arms relaxed.

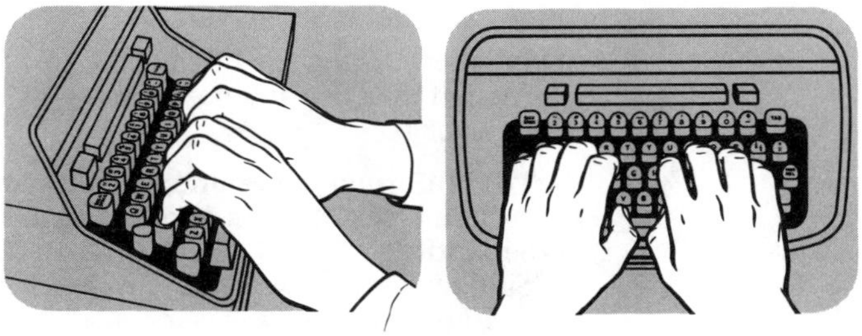

all letters used

1st finger
1 John hit the bright green turf with his five iron.
2 Bob Hughs hunted for five minutes for your number.

2d finger
3 Kind, decent acts can decidedly reduce skepticism.
4 As he kicked, I decided he needed to diet quickly.

3d finger
5 Who saw Polly? Max Zoe saw her; she is quiet now.
6 Who has wax? Zoe Roq has wax; she will polish it.

| 1 | 2 | 3 | 4 | 5 | 6 | 7 | 8 | 9 | 10 |

section

32

Typing in a government office

lessons 137–140

Section 32 is designed to provide you with the opportunity to type correspondence in the two styles generally used by government agencies.

Supplies needed

Informal and formal government letter forms and letterheads [LM pp. 127-146] carbon sheets; second sheets; appropriate envelopes

Machine adjustments

1. Check chair and desk adjustments; check copy placement for easy reading.
2. Set paper guide at *0*.
3. Set ribbon control on black.
4. Set line-space selector on *1* for single spacing.
5. Margins: 70-space line for preparatory practice; 1″ side margins for government letters.

Daily practice plan

Preparatory practice ...... 5′
Office work simulation .... 45′

Learning goals

1. To develop knowledge and skill in typing government correspondence.
2. To plan your work and complete it correctly and efficiently.

Office Job Simulation

Read carefully the material at the right and on pages 274–75 before you begin the work of Section 32. Note any standard procedures that you think will save you time during the completion of the government office job activities.

Introduction

You have been hired as a senior typist by the General Services Administration of the U.S. Government in Washington, D.C. You are to work for Jerold K. Drummond, Chief of the Federal Supply Service.

Your primary responsibility is to prepare Mr. Drummond's correspondence according to the requirements specified in the official *Correspondence Manual*, excerpts of which are given here for quick reference.

Excerpts from the Correspondence Manual

The Federal Supply Service uses both the informal and the formal government letter styles. The informal style is typed on a special form similar to the interoffice memo form used by business. The formal style is typed on a special letterhead. Both the informal and the formal letters are essentially "block styles *with exceptions*." Their features are illustrated on page 274 and are described in the paragraphs which follow.

Informal government letters

Stationery. Agencies of the U.S. Government now use standard 8½″ × 11″ stationery.

Style. Informal government letters are typed in block style on a form which has the captions "Date:," "Reply to Attn of:," "Subject:," and "To:" printed in the left margin. Type the necessary headings opposite these captions. Type the main paragraphs flush with the left margin. Indent 4 spaces the first line of subparagraphs (either numbered or lettered). Single-space paragraphs, but double-space between them. A letter consisting of a single paragraph of fewer than 10 lines should, however, be double-spaced.

Margins. Government correspondence is typed with 1-inch side margins. Because the heading captions are printed in the left margin, a 1-inch left margin places the typed headings about 2 spaces to the right of the captions. The bottom margin on any page should not be less than 1 inch.

Sender's Reference. Type the official symbol of the sender flush with the left margin in line with the "Reply to Attn of:" caption (a double space below the date). An office that does not have an official symbol uses the abbreviated name of the office.

Special Mailing Instructions. Type special mailing instructions such as SPECIAL DELIVERY, CERTIFIED, or REGISTERED on the same line as the sender's reference, starting at the horizontal center of the letterhead. These instructions are typed on the letter only when special mailing is required and the typist does not prepare the envelope. If the reference element extends to or beyond the center of the line, begin the special mailing instruction 3 spaces to the right of it.

Subject. Capitalize only the first letter of the first word and all proper nouns. If more than 1 line is required for the subject, begin each succeeding line flush with the first line.

Address. Begin the address at the left margin in line with the "To:" caption. Arrange the lines in block style single-spaced. When a window envelope is to be used, no line of the address may be longer than 4 inches. If a line must be divided, begin the second line 2 spaces from the left margin. No address should exceed 5 lines.

Attention Line. If an attention line is needed, type it as the second line of the address. Type "ATTN:" followed by the name of the person to whose attention the letter is called.

Body (Message). Begin the message *at least* 2 lines below the last line of the address. When a window envelope is to be used, start the body of the letter at least 6 lines below the "To:" caption--

13d ▶7

Developing tabulator control

Clear tab stops; set one stop 5 spaces, one 10 spaces, and one 15 spaces to the right of the left margin. Type the lines twice.

▶ Tab; release; type quickly.

```
               Liz sent cash to the bank; the bank wants a check.
tab once ——————→ Ted will face the fact that a job takes work.
tab twice ——————————→ He took the old truck route to the fair.
tab three times ———————————→ Lex can be there for the fall show.
```

13e ▶15

Developing typing continuity

1. Clear tab stops; set tab stop for 5-space ¶ indention.
2. Type the ¶s as shown for orientation.
3. Type two 1′ writings on each ¶ and two 2′ writings on both ¶s combined.

Goal: 16 *gwam* on 2′ writing

Difficulty index

all letters used | E | 1.2 si | 5.1 awl | 90% hfw |

	gwam 2′
Whether you plan to sell luxury cars, take a	5
drive in space, write good books, serve dinner in	10
a restaurant, or get any one of a number of jobs,	15
take the job that will require some mental effort.	20
When you are ready to go to work, you should	24
be able to use your mental skills as well as your	29
muscles. Size up each job offer with care. Does	34
the job demand your finest production? It should.	39

gwam 2′ | 1 | 2 | 3 | 4 | 5 |

14

14a ▶8

Preparatory practice

each line 3 times SS (slowly, faster, slowly); DS between 3-line groups

```
alphabet  Kim Janby gave six prizes to qualified white cats.
v/?       Did Viv vote? Can Vance move it? Could Van dive?
easy      Who ran the dirty red auto down the old post road?
          | 1 | 2 | 3 | 4 | 5 | 6 | 7 | 8 | 9 | 10 |
```

14b ▶6

Developing response patterns

once as shown

▶ **Lines 1-2:** Type one-hand words letter by letter; avoid pauses.

Lines 3-4: Speed up stroking on the balanced-hand words.

Lines 5-6: Use high speed for easy words, low for difficult ones.

```
one-hand       1 were loin treated hum fret join sadder jumpy craft
               2 Sara erected extra seats; Jimmy sat in only a few.

balanced-hand  3 if they go|with them|they did|their work|the forms
               4 Did they mend the torn right half of their ensign?

combination    5 fade corn join lend read rock mill make draw theme
               6 My act forms a base for a tax case with the state.
                 | 1 | 2 | 3 | 4 | 5 | 6 | 7 | 8 | 9 | 10 |
```

136d ▶ 15

Measuring straight-copy typing skill

two 5′ writings for *accuracy*; determine *gwam* and errors; record the better writing

Difficulty index

all letters used | A | 1.5 si | 5.7 awl | 80% hfw |

	gwam 1′	5′
An exciting typing job can be found in the professional office for	13	3
the zealous typist. In order to succeed, a person must be able to type	28	6
all the work in a very efficient way. This means typing rapidly with a	42	8
very high degree of accuracy. Also, the typist must be able to think	56	11
and make the decisions required in the normal day-to-day assignments.	70	14
Some of the offices that hire good typists are legal, medical, and sci-	85	17
entific offices. These professional offices can provide a typist with	99	20
a broad range of typing activities every day.	108	22
A typist in a legal office must exhibit the ability to type all	13	24
kinds of reports and documents. A large portion of the typing requires	27	27
the typist to arrange the material so that it will be acceptable in our	42	30
courts of law. Legal style is not the same as regular manuscript style;	56	33
a person must learn this very special format and type all legal documents	71	36
using this style. Although erasures are not wanted on any legal docu-	85	39
ment, proper corrections do not jeopardize the document. A person can	99	41
learn how to make good corrections.	106	43
A medical typist will discover the job to be extremely challenging	13	46
and demanding. The vocabulary a doctor uses in reports and letters may	28	49
not be common, routine terms to the neophyte typist. An occasional quiz	42	51
on the more difficult and strange words would help the typist be more	56	54
alert to check the spelling of any word that is not familiar. The basic	71	57
formats used in medical offices are similar to those used in most busi-	85	60
ness offices. However, as in any office, typists may be required to	99	63
learn a special format that may be used only in that one office.	112	68
An individual who obtains a job as a typist in a scientific organi-	13	65
zation may find that there is a need to learn, in addition to new terms,	28	71
new formats for reports. A typist must also become proficient in the use	43	74
of scientific symbols. Most offices use typewriters that are equipped	57	77
with special keys for the most commonly used scientific symbols; but at	72	80
times a person may be required to insert something in ink. A person in	86	83
this kind of office must be able to accept and to meet these challenges	100	85
without too much extra frustration.	107	87

gwam 1′ | 1 | 2 | 3 | 4 | 5 | 6 | 7 | 8 | 9 | 10 | 11 | 12 | 13 | 14 |
5′ | 1 | 2 | 3 |

14c ▶14
Controlling machine parts

once as shown; repeat

Lines 1-2: Set 2 tab stops at 20–space intervals; tab for second and third sentences.

Lines 3-4: Space correctly after punctuation marks.

Lines 5-6: Use shift key or lock as appropriate.

Lines 7-8: Use margin release, then backspace 5 times into left margin.

```
tab/return     1 He can. ——Tab——> He will. ——Tab——> He thinks.
               2 She is.          She was.          She could.

space bar      3 I know.  This is it.  We saw it.  She is?  I have.
               4 Was it here?  I saw it; June saw it, too.  We did.

shift/lock     5 The USS Sam Simon sent an SOS; USS McVey heard it.
               6 STUDY:  THE GOOD EARTH by Buck and ILIAD by Homer.

backspace/   7 A light touch is the right touch to use to build skill.
margin release 8 Quent is not quite sure he can take my next major quiz.
```

14d ▶ 8
Mastering difficult reaches

once as shown

▶ Keep typing pace smooth and continuous; avoid pauses.

```
direct reaches     1 why lace once branch debt hunt lunch brisk aft nut
                   2 Herb Brice must hunt for my checks; he is in debt.

adjacent reaches   3 has poor suit buy oil cards talk prior three treat
                   4 Theresa answered her question; order was restored.

repeat strokes     5 pool jazz roll off pass need adds feel loss jarred
                   6 Anne stopped off at school to see Bill Wiggs cook.
                     | 1 | 2 | 3 | 4 | 5 | 6 | 7 | 8 | 9 | 10 |
```

14e ▶14
Developing typing continuity

1. Clear tab stops; set tab stop for 5–space ¶ indention.

2. Type the ¶s as shown for orientation.

3. Type two 1′ writings on each ¶ and two 2′ writings on both ¶s combined.

Goal: 16 *gwam*

▶ Pace yourself. Do not press for speed; work for continuous typing.

Difficulty index

all letters used	E	1.2 si	5.1 awl	90% hfw

```
                                                         gwam 2'
                       .       4       .       8
     One major goal of this course is to help you           5
 .       12      .       16      .
learn to type, and another is to help you improve          10
    20      .       24      .       28
your writing quality.  You must do more than copy          15
 .       32      .       36      .
word for word; learn to compose at the typewriter.         20
                       .       4       .       8
     As you learn to type, you can also fine tune          24
 .       12      .       16      .
your writing skills.  The next time you are asked          29
    20      .       24      .       28
to write anything, size up the job and compose it          34
 .       32      .       36      .
on your machine.  Slow work?  Maybe, but worth it.         39
gwam 2' |    1    |    2    |    3    |    4    |    5    |
```

15

15a ▶8
Preparatory practice

Repeat 14d above. Type each line once as shown.

136

136a ▶ 5

Preparatory practice

each line 3 times SS (slowly, faster, slowly); retype selected lines as time permits

alphabet	After June bought the zinnias, Wade quickly put them in an extra vase.
fig/sym	The price of Item #4526 changed from 10 for $276.97 to 12 for $418.39.
long words	Procedures announced yesterday include regulations regarding absences.
fluency	A good habit can rust with disuse; keep it workable with methodic use.

| 1 | 2 | 3 | 4 | 5 | 6 | 7 | 8 | 9 | 10 | 11 | 12 | 13 | 14 |

136b ▶ 10

Technique emphasis

each line at least 4 times with not more than 1 error for each set of 4 lines

letter response	In effect, Jo treated my opinion of a great oil monopoly with reserve.
word response	The problem is that the firm paid for title to half of the big island.
combination	They were down at the dock to set the stage for the great new regatta.
adjacent-key reaches	Were we to open a new development as a retirement village last season?
direct reaches	My choice of music on a bright sunny day can doubtless bring me cheer.

| 1 | 2 | 3 | 4 | 5 | 6 | 7 | 8 | 9 | 10 | 11 | 12 | 13 | 14 |

136c ▶ 20

Building statistical typing skill

two 3′ writings for *speed* and two 5′ writings for *accuracy*

Difficulty index

all letters/figures used | A | 1.5 si | 5.7 awl | 80% hfw |

	gwam 3′	5′	
In 1978 our firm invested over $2.8 million in secured indentures;	4	3	35
this was over 23% of our accumulated surplus. This year we shall invest	9	6	38
nearly $3.7 million at a sizable return of 8.2% per year. Our total	14	8	41
investments will be in excess of $5.1 million, which is about 9.25% of	19	11	44
our total assets of $55.14 million. We have been requested by the board	23	14	46
members to keep our investments adjusted to 10.5% of assets.	28	17	49
All prospective investments are given a good review; if they do not	32	19	52
meet positive analysis, they are rejected. The size of the offering is	37	22	55
not a factor if it meets SEC rules. A check of the prospectus will iden-	42	25	57
tify those that qualify. Only about 5% of all stock offerings will meet	47	28	60
our exacting requirements. An expected return of at least 6.5% per year	52	32	65
must be evident; 7 to 8% is better.	54	31	63

gwam 3′ | 1 | 2 | 3 | 4 | 5 |
5′ | 1 | 2 | 3 |

15b ▶16
Controlling machine parts

exact 50-space line; each 3-line group twice

Lines 1-3: Set a tab stop 27 spaces from left margin. Type with eyes on copy.

Line 10: Depress margin release; backspace 5 spaces into left margin. Use margin release again if needed to complete sentence.

```
           1 ———————— Tab ————————▶ Curve your fingers over
tab/return 2 the home keys.  Keep your wrists down.  Reach with
           3 each finger.

           4 we on so as in or be no an ax up me at my am do oh
 space bar 5 may coy say joy cry pay why day shy sky any fry my
           6 Have you a pen?  If so, write:  Free; pay no cash.

           7 Our HANDBOOK says you use either AC or DC current.
shift/lock 8 Mary and Lee Herz wrote THE PIGEON WING as a team.
           9 LeRoy DeLoris, a member of the USMC, visited Dale.

margin release/
backspace     WRITE:  Price does not include shipping charge or insurance.
```

15c ▶12
Mastering difficult reaches

each line 3 times SS (slowly, faster, slowly); DS between 3-line groups

▶ Type at a smooth, steady pace; hold hands and arms quiet.

```
y 1 Roy Clay may pay Fay Kyle for any enjoyable plays.
x 2 Knox can relax; Alex gets a box of flax next week.
v 3 Eve and Vera drive the heavy vans every five days.
p 4 Pat happily plans to pay Pepper in copper pennies.
q 5 Raquel Squire quietly quilted her antique squares.
    | 1 | 2 | 3 | 4 | 5 | 6 | 7 | 8 | 9 | 10 |
```

15d ▶14
Measuring straight-copy skill

1. Type the ¶s as shown for orientation.

2. Type a 1′ writing on each ¶; determine *gwam*.

3. Type two 2′ writings on both ¶s combined; determine *gwam*.

▶ Do not push for high speed; type evenly at a pace that is comfortable for you.

Difficulty index

all letters used	E	1.2 si	5.1 awl	90% hfw

```
                                                        gwam 2′
     After you write a letter, read it.  Then ask          5
yourself these questions:  Does it have life?  Is         10
it able to move naturally and take you along with         15
it?  Or is it just a haze of tired old words with         20
no strength to excite action from you?  It should.        25
     Remember this as you write:  You must relate         29
to your reader as if the two of you were speaking         34
face to face.  Try it; your style may become much         39
more free and natural.  If your style is cold and         44
dreary, you cannot expect to hold the reader long.        49
gwam 2′ |    1    |    2    |    3    |    4    |    5    |
```

135d ▶ 15 Building straight-copy typing skill

two 5′ writings for *accuracy*; determine *gwam* and errors; record the better writing

Difficulty index

all letters used | A | 1.5 si | 5.7 awl | 80% hfw |

	gwam 1′	5′
A typist for an accounting firm is expected to be one who can type	13	3
a great quantity of numbers and symbols quickly and accurately. Some-	28	6
times the job is almost entirely quantitative, which means that the	42	8
typist must be alert to see that no errors are allowed to remain uncor-	56	11
rected. A wrong number or symbol can't be recognized like a misspelled	71	14
word, so a typist must make sure that the number or symbol has been	86	17
typed correctly. Accuracy is very important.	91	19
The preparation of charts and tables will just naturally become a	13	21
considerable part of the work-load arrangement when you become a typist	27	24
in an accounting office. Since so much accounting work is quantitative,	42	27
it stands to reason that some parts of longer reports can be presented	56	30
best in graphic or tabulated form, such as charts or tables. It is not	71	33
unusual for a longer report to have, perhaps, as many as a dozen displays	85	36
in its appendix.	89	37
A typist in an accounting office may not journalize but will type	13	39
many letters and memorandums. When a change in procedure is to be ef-	27	42
fected, a memo is typed and sent to all concerned. A typist will need	42	45
to know the exact number of copies to make before starting to type. This	57	48
ensures that all people affected will be sure to receive the notice of	71	51
change. Most internal communication queries between the accounting of-	85	53
fice and other locations within the business are done by memo.	99	56
Just as with any other typing job, the typist in an accounting	13	58
office must be very good at the job of proofreading. A typist must be	27	61
able to recognize and correct all errors. Accounting reports and records	42	64
are perhaps equal to legal papers in regard to the need for absolute	55	67
accuracy of content. Many typists use the "verifying" method of checking	70	70
their work. Verifying is a term used to refer to the proofreading pro-	84	73
cess when one person reads aloud the text of the source document while	99	76
the other person checks the new copy.	106	77

gwam 1′ | 1 | 2 | 3 | 4 | 5 | 6 | 7 | 8 | 9 | 10 | 11 | 12 | 13 | 14 |
5′ | 1 | 2 | 3 |

section

3

Learning figure-key reaches

lessons 16–19

Learning goals

1. To master number reaches.
2. To learn to proofread and verify copy.
3. To learn to type statistical copy.
4. To learn to type handwritten copy (script).
5. To improve keystroking speed.

Machine adjustments

1. Set paper guide at *0*.
2. Set a 60-space line (center – 30; center + 30).
3. Set ribbon control on black.
4. Single-space (SS) drills; double-space (DS) paragraphs.

16

16a ▶7
Preparatory practice

each line 3 times SS (slowly, faster, slowly); DS between 3-line groups

alphabet Jenny Quarry packed the zinnias in twelve large, firm boxes.

n/m Name a man or woman who can manage the Marine Manor in Nome.

t/r Terry had trouble starting his trip to Terrytown in a truck.

easy Surely the auditor can handle the fuel problems in the city.

| 1 | 2 | 3 | 4 | 5 | 6 | 7 | 8 | 9 | 10 | 11 | 12 |

16b ▶12
Learning new keyreaches: 1 8 4

1. Find new key on keyboard chart at the right.

2. Study carefully the reach technique shown for the key.

3. Watch your finger make reach to new key a few times.

4. Type technique drill for key.

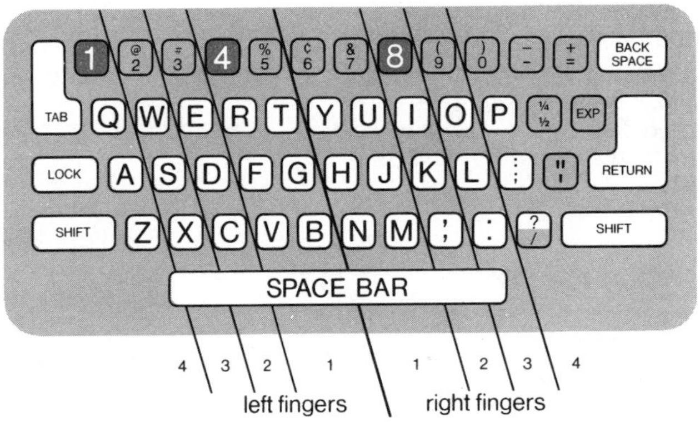
SPACE BAR
left fingers
right fingers

Reach technique for 1

Reach *up* with *left little* finger.

If your typewriter has a special key for 1, reach up to it with the left fourth (little) finger. If your typewriter does not have such a key, use the small letter l to type 1.

Reach technique for 8

Reach *up* with *right second* finger.

Reach technique for 4

Reach *up* with *left first* finger.

▶ Stretch the appropriate finger to the top row; let the other fingers curl under. Do not move entire hand to the top row.

1 1 a1 a1 11 111 11 houses, 111 tons, 1 pint, 11 months, 1 day
The 11 members met at 1 p.m. at 11 West 11th Drive in Minot.

8 8 8k 8k 8 kits, 88 keys, pack 8 kites, cook 8 kinds, 8 knots
The 8 scouts mailed 8 kits to the 88 doctors in 8 hospitals.

4 4 f4 f4 4 figs, 4 films, off 4 feet, gaff 4 fish, if 44 fans
Tour 4 leaves at 4 p.m. to see 4 bays in 4 lakes in 4 hours.

1/8/4 Car 4 hauls 84 tons of coal 48 miles in 8 hours, 41 minutes.
Is it Channel 4, 8, or 11? Was the score 4 to 8? or 8 to 1?

all figures learned Four of the 148 scouts are late; the other 144 arrived at 8.
I need 18 file cabinets, 41 desk chairs, and 84 typewriters.
The Essex left Pier 841 with 481 tourists and a crew of 148.

| 1 | 2 | 3 | 4 | 5 | 6 | 7 | 8 | 9 | 10 | 11 | 12 |

section

31 Improving basic skills

lessons 135–136

Learning goals

Since accuracy is a major goal of basic skill development, you should be able to type at one of the following rates on a 5-minute straight-copy timing of average difficulty with 8 or fewer errors: 57 *gwam*, excellent; 52-56, good; 44-51, acceptable. The minimum acceptable goal in this section should be between 44-51 *gwam* with no more than 8 errors.

Machine adjustments

1. Set paper guide at *0*.
2. Set ribbon control on black.
3. Set a 70-space line.
4. SS drill lines; DS paragraphs with 5-space ¶ indentions.

135

135a ▶ 5 Preparatory practice

each line 3 times SS (slowly, faster, slowly); retype selected lines as time permits

alphabet Zephina requested five tax blanks in May; the wrong ones came in June.

fig/sym Your Invoice #9758 for $341.02 is subject to a 6% discount in 10 days.

long words They organized symposiums for the programming of electronic computers.

fluency The quality of the work done is more significant than is the quantity.

| 1 | 2 | 3 | 4 | 5 | 6 | 7 | 8 | 9 | 10 | 11 | 12 | 13 | 14 |

135b ▶ 10 Technique emphasis

each line at least 4 times with not more than 1 error for each set of 4 lines

letter response That opinion was read by a million readers; taxes serve our interests.

word response The giant flakes did not melt, so they kept their usual size and form.

combination Average water height was eight feet when the streams became a problem.

continuity Keep your book at the right side so you can see it well when you type.

| 1 | 2 | 3 | 4 | 5 | 6 | 7 | 8 | 9 | 10 | 11 | 12 | 13 | 14 |

135c ▶ 20 Building rough-draft typing skill

two 3′ writings for *speed* and two 5′ writings for *accuracy*

Difficulty index

all letters used | HA | 1.7 si | 6.0 awl | 75% hfw |

	gwam 3′	5′	
An individual who questions anopinion is canny; ~~but~~ one who	4	2	31
quaels with facts maybe just a plain fool; But any one who can	8	5	34
recognize differ ences between reliable facts and shear opinions	12	7	36
is liekly to have perception. ~~Some~~ individuals are ~~really~~ open-	17	10	39
minded; they can usually perceive stwo points of view in a situa-	21	13	41
tion--the ~~right~~ one and theirs.	23	14	43
For every individual who exhibits a ~~small~~ spark of genius,	27	16	45
one can easily identify a ~~few~~ others who ~~must be~~ experiencing	31	19	47
quite serious iginition trouble. If you associate with the latter	35	21	50
groups, ~~stop~~ looking for easy solutoins to your problems. Adjust	40	24	53
your coarse action and begin liiking for the right solutions.	44	26	55
Happiness is a gift; it is earned through work.	48	29	57

16c ▶7

Learning to proofread

There are two ways to check completed work: (1) by *proofreading* and (2) by *verifying*.

Proofreading. Con–scientious typists always check carefully what they have typed. Paragraphs are *proofread*; that is, they are read for *meaning*, as if they had not been read before. Figures, proper names, and uncertain spellings are double–checked against the original or some other source.

Verifying. One person reads aloud from the original while another checks the new copy. Tricky words are spelled; punctuation marks are indicated. This procedure, called *verifying*, is especially recommended for statistical copy.

Proofread the ¶ for meaning. Note how errors become apparent.

Learning to typewrite mean laerning to type right. Do now allow what you wnat to say to get last in the way you might have said it. Be alert. Find your mistakes befere somebody else does.

Ask someone to help you *verify* that List 1 is the same as List 2 by reading one list as you check the other. Note how discrepancies can be found.

List 1

was	141	art	481	ask
not	844	way	418	two
mat	118	eat	114	ram
zoo	884	don	848	got

List 2

was	141	art	418	ask
ton	488	way	184	two
mat	118	ate	114	ram
zoo	848	don	848	got

16d ▶12

Building statistical-copy skill

two 1′ writings; then two 2′ writings; ask someone to help you *verify* each writing; circle errors

Goal: at least 12 *gwam*

Difficulty index

all figures learned | E | 1.2 si | 5.1 awl | 90% hfw | gwam 2′

On May 1 they purchased 8 of the 11 electric fans they 6 | 29
now own. These 8 new fans were sent on May 4 to their home 12 | 35
address at 148 East 41st Avenue. On May 14 they paid their 18 | 41
bill with Check No. 4848. They are looking for 8 more fans. 24 | 47

gwam 2′ | 1 | 2 | 3 | 4 | 5 | 6 |

16e ▶12

Building straight-copy skill

two 1′ writings; then two 2′ writings; proof-read each writing; circle errors

Goal: at least 16 *gwam*

Difficulty index

all letters used | E | 1.2 si | 5.1 awl | 90% hfw | gwam 2′

Study this helpful note: Work to learn the top row of 6 | 29
your machine. Whether you type as an expert or just do the 12 | 35
work you need for your own use, you will prize that control 18 | 41
you have of the top row. Begin acquiring the control today. 24 | 47

gwam 2′ | 1 | 2 | 3 | 4 | 5 | 6 |

131b-134b, continued

Job 7
Clinical resumé [LM p. 111]

Dr. Davenport has dictated the following resumé of Samuel Thornton on a dictation machine. You typed a first draft of the clinical resumé and returned it to Dr. Davenport for his comments. The resulting rough-draft has been returned to you to type a final copy for the patient's files.

COLUMBUS MEDICAL ARTS CLINIC 14

CLINICAL RESUMÉ

Name Samuel C. Thornton **Date** 6/23/19--

Outpatient No. 368425 **Age** 66

Attending Physician Roger V. Davenport, M.D. **Sex** Male

Diagnosis Abrasions and contusions, neck and lower back

Special Procedures None

Consultations Marjorie Hahn, M.D.

Thornton first came to the clinic on June 18 complaining of severe headaches and lower back pain. The complaint was caused by an accident 2 days before onset of symptoms when th tripped and fell, striking his head and back on concrete porch steps.

The latissimus dorsi and sternocleidomastoid were found to be pantiful and spastic upon manipultation. No evidence of concussion was found, but the patient complained of ringing in his ears. Urinalysis showed a trace of blood.

He was send to Mercy Hospital for brain and renal scans, which were negative. He was given 10cc robaxin injectible I.M. and 1 tab of robaxin 750 q. 4h. and darvon p.r.n. for pain. An appointment was made for June 22 at the clinic.

On June 22 the patient felt much better. He was no longer taking the darvon for pain. The latissimus dorsi and sternocleidomastoid are tender but no longer spastic to manipulation. Examination revealed some damage to the greater occipital nerve, but she feels this will heal naturally during the healing process. No other nerve dammge was found. The paitent was told to remain on the robaxin until all the pills are taken and to refrain from heavy lifting or hard labor for at least 2 months. The patient need not return unless complications arise.

His past history is essentially negative. He has been in good health. He had a routine physical examination 1 year ago including EKG which was normal.

17

17a ▶7
Preparatory practice
each line 3 times SS (slowly, faster, slowly); DS between 3-line groups

alphabet Did Evelyn Wellington quiz Peter Jackson about his tax form?

difficult reaches Beverly sneezed even though she ate a dozen square lozenges.

figures The numbers on the 4 lockers in Room 8 are 4, 8, 14, and 18.

easy Did he stop to notice how the worker rakes hay in the field?

17b ▶12
Learning new keyreaches: 7 3 0
(follow directions of 16b, p. 32)

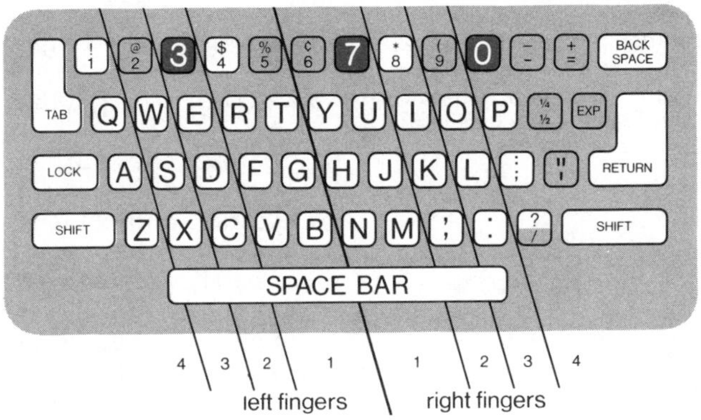

SPACE BAR
4 3 2 1 1 2 3 4
left fingers
right fingers

▶ Do not pause before making a reach to the top row; once the finger has learned the move, it will reach automatically if you will let it go.

Be sure of yourself. Lack of confidence will hold back your responses.

▶ Do not space after a colon used to separate hours from minutes or ratios stated in figures.

Reach technique for 7

Reach *up* with *right first* finger.

Reach technique for 3

Reach *up* with *left second* finger.

Reach technique for 0

Reach *up* with *right little* finger.

7
7 j7 j7 7 7 7 jays, 7 jars, 7 jugs, 77 jets, 7 June, 7 jumps
Old No. 777 pulled 7 cars filled with 77 tons of No. 7 sand.

3
3 d3 d3 33 had 3 dates, fed 3 dogs, add 3 days, paid 3 debts
At 3:33 p.m. on May 3, 3 cars left; they returned on June 3.

0
0 ;0 ;0 00 10 pins, 300 points, 700 pines, 800 pans, 40 pies
I know the lot at 10100 Ford Street is 100 feet by 100 feet.

7/3/0
Read pages 3, 37, and 73; copy lines 3, 7, and 30 on page 7.
Take No. 730 for 307 miles; then follow No. 70 for 30 miles.

all figures learned
On June 14 we sent Check 478 to either 130 or 780 Lynn Lane.
On May 18, 1847, at 7:30 p.m., the 147 new settlers arrived.
Jerry weighs 108 pounds; Lee, 174; Dale, 103; and Knox, 137.

17c ▶12
Building statistical-copy skill
two 1′ writings; then two 2′ writings; *proofread* and *verify* each writing

Goal: at least 12 *gwam*

▶ Keep wrists low for reaches to numbers. Stretch fingers.

Difficulty index

all figures learned | E | 1.2 si | 5.1 awl | 90% hfw |

	gwam 2′	
The record was set 37 years ago. In the past 4 years,	6	29
18 people almost broke it. But it was not until the May 10	12	35
meet, with 40 teams and 170 people running, that the record	18	41
fell; and it was broken 4 times in the 10 days of that meet.	24	47

Job 5
Radiology report [LM p. 107]

Dr. Davenport ordered a brain and renal scan to be done on Mr. Thompson "stat"–meaning at once, on an emergency basis–at Mercy Hospital. The tests were done by Dr. Reyes and the results were called to the Clinic and left on the automatic answering recorder. You typed the material from the recording in rough-draft form, and now you are to type a final draft for the patient's file.

COLUMBUS MEDICAL ARTS CLINIC 14

X-RAY REPORT

Name Samuel C. Thornton **Outpatient No.** 368425

Age 66 **X-ray No.** 8512

Sex Male **Date** 6/18/19--

Attending Physician Roger V. Davenport, M.D.

EXAMINATION REQUESTED: Brain and Renal Scan

Becaubse the patient was having btoh brain and renal scan, it was elected to use Technetium 99 DPTA. He was injected with 5.6 millicuries, and films weretaken of the neck vasculature. This proved to be normal in all respects. ¶ Static study of the brain through four views demonstrated equal concentration of the isotope through the entire area. No areas of increased or decreased concentration were detected. ¶ Four hours later the patient was returned to the x-ray department where a scan of both kidneys was done. The scan showed normal appearing kidneys, without evidence of hot or cold sopts, and having normal contours.

IMPRESSION:

The brain scan, both dynamic and static studies, is within normal limits. The renal scan is within normal limits.

Radiologist: /s/ Hortencia Reyes, M.D.
Department of Radiology, Mercy Hospital

Job 6
Letter [LM p. 109]

Dr. Davenport has asked Dr. Marjorie Hahn, a neurologist, to consult with him on the Thompson case. He discussed the case earlier with Dr. Hahn by telephone, and he is now sending her a letter updating the case and giving her the time of the next appointment with the patient. The letter is to be dated June 18, 19--, and is to be addressed to:

Marjorie Hahn, M.D.
Neurological Institute
710 West 168th Street
New York, NY 10032

I *just* received the results of the *brain and renal* scans that I ordered on *Samuel Thornton,* the patient I called you about this morning. Both ~~were~~ *are* negative.

Now I want to ~~check~~ *assess* the extent of nerve damage*, if any,* in his back and neck. I ~~made~~ *have scheduled* an appointment with ~~him here~~ *Mr. Thornton at the Clinic* for noon on June 22.

Today I gave ~~him~~ *Mr. Thornton* 10cc of Robaxin *Injectible* and placed him on *1 tablet of* Robaxin 750 q.4h. and Darvon p.r.n. *for pain.* I feel *his* present muscular spaticity should be sufficiently *under* control~~led~~ by ~~then~~ *June 22* to allow neurologic testing. *Would you* ~~S~~stop by a few minutes early to review the case. *Since you will be in town that day for the conference of the Columbus Medical Association, I would appreciate your consultation on this case.*

17d ▶8
Developing keystroking skill

each line twice (slowly, faster); DS between 2-line groups

▶ Do not allow your reading skill to get ahead of your typing skill. Read only slightly ahead of what you are typing.

Trip 148 to France is set to depart at 1 p.m. on October 30.

Whether you are 10 or 80, our workday is from 10:10 until 4.

The 17 girls picked 130 cases of peas in 4 hours, 4 minutes.

Try Model 373 or 4870 with 34 fittings or Model 178 with 18.

Pay the May 13 bill for 3 racks; date Check No. 138 June 14.

Group 7 arrived on Flight 88; they leave on Flight 33 at 10.

17e ▶11
Building straight-copy skill

two 1′ writings; then two 2′ writings; *proofread* each writing

Goal: at least 17 *gwam*

all letters used — Difficulty index: E | 1.2 si | 5.1 awl | 90% hfw

	gwam 2′	
You must realize that if you want to type well, expert	6	29
form will be required. Your fingers must be held just over	12	35
your keys, and your eyes and mind must be occupied with the	18	41
job of reading. Then let it go; let yourself begin to type.	24	47

gwam 2′ | 1 | 2 | 3 | 4 | 5 | 6 |

18

18a ▶7
Preparatory practice

each line 3 times SS (slowly, faster, slowly); DS between 3-line groups

alphabet Fire hazards of the job were quickly explained by Ms. Novig.

o/i We take action from our position to avoid spoiling our soil.

figures The 14 men on Shift 8 had 7 days to make 80 No. 4738 wagons.

easy Their work is done, so they can go by the end of the period.

| 1 | 2 | 3 | 4 | 5 | 6 | 7 | 8 | 9 | 10 | 11 | 12 |

18b ▶11
Building straight-copy speed

one 1′ writing; then two 3′ writings; *proofread* each writing

▶ Relax and type. Don't try to force speed. It will happen if you just keep trying.

Goal: at least 17 *gwam*

all letters used — Difficulty index: E | 1.2 si | 5.1 awl | 90% hfw

	gwam 3′	
As you begin to write, try to organize your ideas. If	4	23
you plan ahead before you start work, you might not have to	8	27
fret over a style; just put the fresh, exciting thoughts of	12	31
yours to use. If you do not find a subject to write about,	16	35
stop right there; it is quality, not quantity, that matters.	20	39

gwam 3′ | 1 | 2 | 3 | 4 |

131b-134b, continued

Job 4
Medical history
(plain sheet)

Patricia Cromwell has been examined by Dr. Rivera. He has given you her medical history to type and file in the patients' file.

1"

MEDICAL HISTORY

NAME *Patricia R. Cromwell* DATE *June 15, 19--*

ADDRESS *4930 Castlegate Road, Columbus, OH 43209*

DATE OF BIRTH *8/22/53* OCCUPATION *Engineer* SEX *Female*

ATTENDING PHYSICIAN *Dr. Julio Rivera*

CHIEF COMPLAINT *Severe sore throat and enlargement of glands on both sides of the neck.*

HISTORY OF ILLNESS *The patient is a 27-year-old woman complaining of sore throat of 4 days' duration. Prior to the development of the sore throat, she did not feel well for about a week, complaining of slight fever and general malaise. She noticed swelling of the glands in both sides of her neck 2 days ago.*

PAST HISTORY *Patient is gravida 1, para 1, ab 0. Normal childhood diseases. Tonsillectomy at age 7. Broken right ankle at age 14. No other serious illnesses or injuries.*

1" SYSTEMS REVIEW 1"

General. Fever of 100.2. No chills or weight loss.

Head and Neck. Eyes, ears, and nose not remarkable. Throat swollen, injected, with no pustules noted. Enlargement of lymph glands on both sides of neck.

Cardiorespiratory. Normal.

Gastrointestinal. No food intolerance, nausea, vomiting, diarrhea, or abdominal pain.

Genitourinary. No dysuria, hematuria, or frequency of urination. No vaginal discharge or dysmenorrhea.

Back and extremities. Not remarkable.

Neurologic. No numbness, tingling, or paralysis; patient complains of general weakness.

FAMILY HISTORY *Mother and father are living and in good health. She has two brothers and one sister; all are living and in good health.*

1"

18c ▶12

Learning new keyreaches: 9 5 / (diagonal)

Reach technique for 9

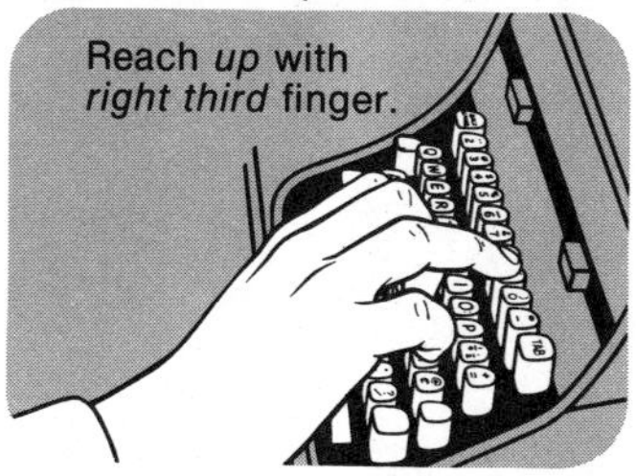

Reach *up* with *right third* finger.

Reach technique for 5

Reach *up* with *left first* finger.

Reach technique for /

Reach *down* to / with *right little* finger.

▶ For downward reaches, stretch the finger down from the palm, touching first-row keys with the very tip and part of the fingernail of the operating finger. Keep other fingers close to their homerow stations.

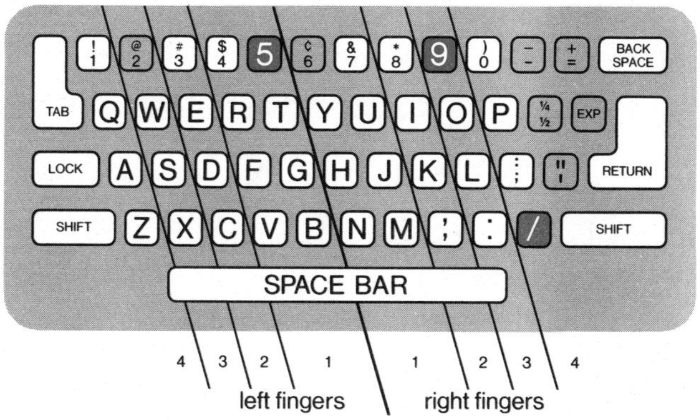

9 — 9 91 91 9 99 less, call 99 lads, mail 9 letters, seal 9 lids
On 99th Street, 9 doves, 9 wrens, and 9 robins ate 99 seeds.

5 — 5 5f 5f 55 flats, if 5 fans, of 5 forms, off 5 feet, 5 flags
At 5:55, 5 cars, 5 trucks, and 5 bicycles began the 5 races.

/ — / /; /; /; 1/5 or 1/9 or 1/7; Type this copy: 3 1/3, 8 1/8.
Now type these fractions: 1/3, 5/7, 4/9, 3/8, 1/7, and 1/9.

9/5/ / — Memo 559 requests 59 5/9 feet of No. 5995 carpet by April 9.
On 5/9/59, 559 tourists hiked 9 5/9 miles to tour this city.

all figures learned — Enter his/her name on pages 40 and 135 and date them 1/9/78.
Gina proudly entered her high scores: 5/17, 180; 5/19, 143.
Terms for Invoice 7598 were 3/10, n/30. It was paid May 14.

| 1 | 2 | 3 | 4 | 5 | 6 | 7 | 8 | 9 | 10 | 11 | 12 |

18d ▶12

Building statistical-copy skill

one 1′ writing; then two 3′ writings; *proofread* and *verify* each writing

Goal: at least 12 *gwam*

all letters/figures learned

Difficulty index

E	1.2 si	5.1 awl	90% hfw

	gwam 3′	
I know of a text, written in 1975, which declares that	4	23
job quality has almost no link with the age or education of	8	27
the worker. As I read page 40, I realize that neither age,	12	31
whether it is 18 or 81, nor years of school, 13 or 19, make	16	35
the real difference; factors such as our drive and pride do.	20	39

gwam 3′ | 1 | 2 | 3 | 4 |

18e ▶8

Improving proofreading skills

each line twice

Read each sentence before you type it. As you type each sentence, correct the circled errors.

The camera is so snall that you can slip it into your pruse.

I thing you can espect the prices to drop is she is elected.

Iam pleased to get ex tra copies of opposing ponits of view.

We hope to read TO RACE THE wind and TIME OUTFOR H APPINESS.

Major cities are Rich with problems but p9or with solution.s

/7 Loss of function of an organ______________________________
____

/7 Loss of function of a limb (or part of a limb)______________
____

/7 Disfiguring scars ______________________________________
____

/7 Other ____
____

The doctor has explained to me the most likely complications or undesired results that might occur in this surgical or medical procedure and I understand them. The doctor has offered to detail the less likely complications or undesired results which, even if rare, could occur.

I do_____/I do not_____ wish to have a full description of all the possible complications given to me.

I hereby authorize and direct the above-named physician, with his or her associates or assistants, to provide such additional services as they might deem reasonable and necessary including, but not limited to, the administration of any anesthetic agent, or the services of the X-ray department or laboratories, and I consent thereto.

I hereby state that I have read and understand this consent and that all blanks were filled prior to my signature.

Date__________________________ Time________________a.m. or p.m.

Signature of Patient______________________________________

Signature of Relative or Guardian (where required)

____

Witness____

I certify that I have personally completed all blanks in this form and explained to the patient or the patient's representative all pertinent information relating to the contemplated surgical or medical procedure before asking the patient or the patient's representative to sign the form.

Signature of Physician____________________________________

19

19a ▶7
Preparatory practice

each line 3 times SS (slowly, faster, slowly); DS between 3-line groups

alphabet James quickly helped fix a latch to be given to Zora Wilson.

e/r We were reserving every reader there for members. We erred.

figures What are the sums of 5 1/3 and 30; 57 and 93; 48 and 14 1/8?

easy If our approach is hit or miss, we miss as surely as we hit.

| 1 | 2 | 3 | 4 | 5 | 6 | 7 | 8 | 9 | 10 | 11 | 12 |

19b ▶12
Learning new keyreaches: 2 6 - (hyphen) -- (dash)

Reach technique for 2

Note: The *hyphen* is a symbol that is used to join closely related words or word parts.

Striking the hyphen twice results in a *dash*--a symbol that shows sharp separation or interruption of thoughts.

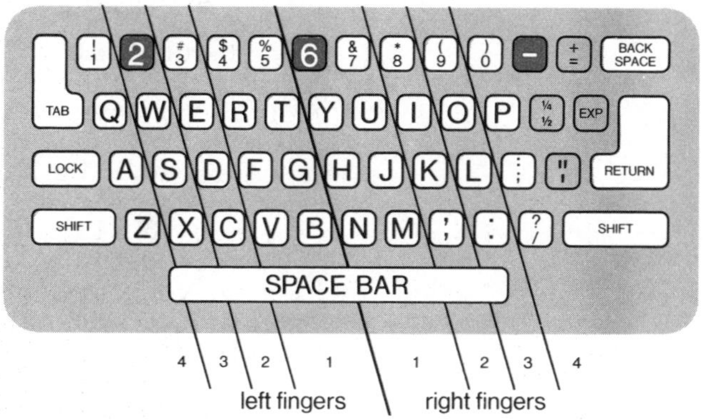

Reach technique for 6

2 2 2s 2s 2 sets, has 2 sips, buys 2 skis, uses 2 saws, 2 seas
At 2:22 on August 22, 22 boys and 22 girls entered Room 222.

6 6 6j 6j 6 juncos, 6 jokes, 6 jumps, 666 Jones Street, 6 July
In 6 days, on June 6, the 6 oaks and 6 elms will be planted.

Reach technique for -

-/-- - -; -; -; -- co-op, up-to-date books, first-class newspaper
Use a 6-inch line--60 pica spaces--for your past-due papers.

2/6/- We--all of us--have read pages 2, 26, 62, 226, 262, and 266.
Buy 2- and 6-yard lengths--not those that are 22 or 66 feet.

all figures learned We entered these file codes: 378/29-1, 507/140, and 344/06.
Of 2,534 ex-students polled, 7/8 had jobs in 169 industries.
Bin 87-9 is 3/4 full. Move Car 125 to Track 60 and load it.

| 1 | 2 | 3 | 4 | 5 | 6 | 7 | 8 | 9 | 10 | 11 | 12 |

19c ▶5
Improving response patterns

once as shown; repeat

word response the right form | they may go | it is due | go to work | for that pen
Is it the duty or the wish of men or women to make a profit?

letter response only you | after my | you saw | my tax case | refer to our | were ever
As you are aware, my estate tax case was, in fact, deferred.

combination response if they look | when the facts | if they imply | they also serve to
He treated the data with care; he stated my case with vigor.

| 1 | 2 | 3 | 4 | 5 | 6 | 7 | 8 | 9 | 10 | 11 | 12 |

131b-134b, continued

Job 3
Consent form (plain sheets)

Dr. Davenport has asked you to type this temporary consent form to be used by the doctors until the printed supply can be obtained from the printer. Type one clean copy from which the temporary supply can be duplicated.

CONSENT FOR SURGICAL OR MEDICAL PROCEDURE AND ACKNOWLEDGMENT OF RECEIPT OF RISK INFORMATION 15 30

State law requires us to obtain your consent before we can perform any surgical or medical procedure on you. What you are being asked to sign is simply a confirmation that we have discussed your contemplated surgical or medical procedure. We have given you sufficient information that you, of your own free will, can make a decision whether to have the surgical or medical procedure, and that you can make any choice necessary of the type of technique that will be employed. We have already discussed with you the common problems or undesired results that sometimes occur. We wish to inform you, not to alarm you. If you wish, however, we can go into more elaborate details or more unlikely problems. If you do not, that is also your privilege. Please read the form carefully. Ask about anything you do not understand; we will be pleased to answer your questions.

I hereby authorize and direct ______________________________, with associates or assistants of his or her choice, to perform the following surgical, diagnostic, or medical procedure: __________
____,
as we have previously agreed.

I further authorize the above-named physician to perform any other procedure that, in his or her judgment, is advisable for my well-being. Details of this surgical or medical procedure have been explained to me. Alternative methods of treatment, if any, have also been explained to me as have the advantages and disadvantages of each. I am advised that, though good results are expected, the possibility and nature of complications cannot be accurately anticipated and that, therefore, there can be no guarantee as expressed or implied either as to the result of the surgical or medical procedure or as to cure.

The degrees and kinds of risks known to be associated with this procedure, including anesthesia, are listed below. Each marked box indicates some risk that is to be associated with the above named procedure.

/_7 Death____
____

/_7 Brain Damage____
____

/_7 Paralysis (state degree, such as quadriplegia)______________
____

/_7 Loss of an organ____
____

/_7 Loss of a limb (or part of a limb)_________________________
____

(continued on page 265)

19d ▶10 Building statistical-copy skill

three 2′ writings; *verify* each writing; circle errors

Goal: at least 12 *gwam*

Difficulty index

all figures used | E | 1.2 si | 5.1 awl | 90% hfw | — gwam 2′

Think about the cars of 24 to 26 years from now. Will 6
we use fast 250-mile-an-hour cars, or will they have become 12
part of history? Although we have designed models--this is 18
on the record--to travel at 3 7/8 miles or better a minute, 24
we legally drive cars now at only about 9/10 miles a minute. 30

gwam 2′ | 1 | 2 | 3 | 4 | 5 | 6 |

19e ▶5 Developing keystroking skill

each line once DS

▶ Think the figures as you type them.

The rods came in these sizes: 14 3/8 inches and 6 1/5 feet.

In just 6 years, we made 10 changes in Models 3829 and 5748.

They can also use Items 39, 46, 201, 578, and 292 very soon.

She ordered 27 pens, 63 notebooks, 185 maps, and 490 rulers.

His speed--50 mph--was not excessive; he made 476 3/8 miles.

FOR SALE: 8-room, 3-bath house--4/5 acre at 290 Pine Drive.

19f ▶11 Measuring straight-copy skill

one 1′ writing on each ¶; then two 3′ writings on all ¶s combined; *proofread* carefully; circle errors

▶ Type with ease and control. Drop back in rate and type on the *control* level.

Difficulty index

all letters used | E | 1.2 si | 5.1 awl | 90% hfw | — gwam 3′

Often we must work very hard trying to master a course 4
that we have decided has an important place in the plans we 8
have made for our lives and the work we see ourselves doing. 12

Any plan worth the name will place great demands on us 15
to excel in some skill, art, or other quality that can help 19
open the door to success; but for most people the plan must 23
include lots of hard work to get that door open wide enough. 27

We each, as we dream of the future, should account for 31
the ways we will use our time. First, of course, we should 35
realize that a job will have initial claim on our time. In 39
addition, we should account for our leisure time; for it is 43
with wise use of this time that we add variety to our lives. 47

gwam 3′ | 1 | 2 | 3 | 4 |

Job 2
Outline (plain sheet)

Dr. Davenport has made a rough-draft outline of a speech he will deliver to the senior medical school class at Ohio State University. He has asked you to type a master copy of the outline to be duplicated and distributed to the students for their notebooks. Type the outline in unbound manuscript style. Dr. Davenport prefers that his outlines be typed in a simplified style; therefore, only the main heading need be typed in ALL CAPS and all other entries can be typed with an initial CAP only.

Doctrine of Informed Consent*

I. Required disclosures in lay terminology

A. Alternatives to the suggested treatment.

B. Problems in recuperatoin that are anticipated.

C. Description of the proposed treatment.

D. Inherent risks of death or seriously bodily injury in the porposed treatment.

II. Exceptions to dis closure

A. In an emergency.

B. If the procedure is simple and the damage is remote and commonly recognized as remote.

C. If the patient does not want to be told.

D. If in the phusicians judgment it is not in the patients best interest to know; e.g., when the information would so seriously distract the patient that he could not make a reasonable decision.

III. Penalties for failure to acquire informed consent

A. Possibility of reprimand from the medical association if failure to acquire incormed consent can be proven to be for unethical reasons or through gross negligence.

B. Possibility of being named in a malpractiace suit if the patient can prove that he or she was not informed of serious risks in the proposed treatment when he or she wished to be informed and was capable of understanding the information with out becoming unduly hysterical.

C. Loss of confidence of patients and resulting decline of practice.

D. Other possible penalties.

E. Any additional information other physicians would disclose in similar circumstances

---

*Legal precedent:

Cobbs vs. Grant, 8 Cal. 3d 229,502 P. 2d 1 (1972)

Canterbury vs. Spence, 464 F. 2d 772,789 (DC Cir. 1972)

section

4

Developing basic skills

lessons 20–22

Learning goals

1. To type with continuous, fluid motions.
2. To improve proofreading and verification skills.
3. To develop greater facility with figure reaches.
4. To develop smoother typing from script copy.
5. To improve keystroking speed.

Machine adjustments

1. Check chair and desk adjustments.
2. Set paper guide at *0*.
3. Set 60-space line.
4. Set ribbon control on black.
5. Single-space (SS) drills; double-space (DS) paragraphs.

20

20a ▶ 7 Preparatory practice

each line 3 times SS (slowly, faster, slowly); DS between 3-line groups

alphabet Bob realized very quickly that jumping was excellent for us.

direct reaches Grace grew hungry; she served a number of rolls from Greece.

figure Of the 13 numbers, these 4 were chosen: 29, 56, 78, and 90.

easy They want to go downtown and view the shows we talked about.

| 1 | 2 | 3 | 4 | 5 | 6 | 7 | 8 | 9 | 10 | 11 | 12 |

20b ▶ 7 Improving keystroking technique

1. Type each line twice SS (slowly, faster); DS between 2-line groups.
2. Retype lines that seem most difficult for you.

1st row May Ms. Xavier ask Bob, Zona, and/or Marc to climb Mt. Zemb?

2d row Sada and Jake had a dish of salad; Fran had a glass of soda.

3d row At our party, we quietly poured the tea from an antique pot.

4th row Buy 147 fish, 25 geese, 10 ponies, 39 lambs, and 68 kittens.

| 1 | 2 | 3 | 4 | 5 | 6 | 7 | 8 | 9 | 10 | 11 | 12 |

20c ▶ 9 Typing from script

1. Type the ¶ once for practice.
2. Type three 1′ writings on the ¶.
3. Proofread each writing.

▶ Keep your eyes on the book copy while you type.

Difficulty index

all letters used

E	1.2 si	5.1 awl	90% hfw

gwam 1′

Some of us fret so much about our writing style that we 11
fail to get the job under way. Remember this about style: 23
Once you realize what you have to say, your words will seem 35
to flow in a simple, direct way. Style requires knowing the 47
idea you want to express. 52

20d ▶ 7 Improving space-bar technique

1. Type a 1′ writing on each line.
2. Retype the line on which you scored least speed.

Note special spacing in Lines 3 and 4.

▶ Space once after ? within a sentence.

1 no be it do in we of am my be me an up as if to oh ad on and

2 ham pan icy lap hem own lay map hum yon lip him inn only mop

3 Notice: Mr. Riley left at 5:16 p.m.; the train was on time.

4 Was it Mary? Helen? Pam? It was a woman; I saw one of them.

| 1 | 2 | 3 | 4 | 5 | 6 | 7 | 8 | 9 | 10 | 11 | 12 |

131-134

131a-134a ▶ 5
Preparatory practice

Type as many times as you can in 5'.

alphabet The experts moved quickly to adjust ten gauges before the water froze.
fig/sym Herb & Diane (974 Fir Drive) can't pay their $368.25 bill by April 10.
one-hand Only Edward Linny saw Lou Street win the awards at the bazaar in Lyon.
fluency Any individual who puts his or her talents to work can surely prosper.
| 1 | 2 | 3 | 4 | 5 | 6 | 7 | 8 | 9 | 10 | 11 | 12 | 13 | 14 |

131b-134b ▶ 45
Office work simulation

Job 1
Memorandum [LM p. 105]

Dr. Davenport has written a memo and left it for you to type and distribute to all doctors at the Clinic. Type one master copy to be duplicated and distributed to the doctors.

To: All Staff Physicians
From: Roger V. Davenport, Director
Date: June 12, 19--
Subject: New Consent Form To Be Used in Our Clinic

¶ Since the Ohio Legislature has included a model consent form in its statute, I would like us to begin using this form in our clinic. The intent of the statute is to create a consent form that, when used properly, will assure the validity of consent of any patient receiving medical treatment from a qualified physician in Ohio. Therefore, beginning immediately, this new consent form will be used in our clinic.

¶ A temporary supply of these forms is now available at the clinic's business office. Please pick up your forms within the next day or so.

20e ▶ 7
Controlling number reaches

Type 1′ writings on each line.

Goal: at least 12 *gwam* on Line 3

1234 2345 3456 5678 7890 1223 2334 3445 4556 6778 8990 9001

2343 7906 4532 6067 5132 8098 5453 7066 2335 7868 3244 9000

1492 5036 4728 9120 6583 7475 3850 1462 3947 6574 3920 1357

| 1 | 2 | 3 | 4 | 5 | 6 | 7 | 8 | 9 | 10 | 11 | 12 |

20f ▶ 13
Improving keystroking continuity

1. Type two 1′ writings. Proofread; circle errors.

2. Type two 3′ writings. Proofread; circle errors.

Goals: 1′—at least 17 *gwam*
3′—at least 13 *gwam*

Alternate procedure
See inside cover for Guided (Paced) Writings procedures.

Difficulty index

all letters used | E | 1.2 si | 5.1 awl | 90% hfw |

	gwam 3′	
Did you realize it can pay to advertise when you start (4, 8)	4	23
looking for a job? That does not really mean putting an ad (12, 16, 20)	8	27
in the paper; it does mean getting the word to everyone you (24, 28, 32)	12	31
know. Some inquiries show that an excellent way to turn up (36, 40, 44)	16	35
leads for a top job is just to talk with friends and others. (48, 52, 56)	20	39

gwam 3′ | 1 | 2 | 3 | 4 |

21

21a ▶ 7
Preparatory practice

each line twice SS (slowly, faster); DS between 2-line groups

alphabet Zora and Dwight Quick flew over Byrd Peak six times in July.

adjacent reaches Bert quickly pointed to where asters grew in the sandy soil.

figure Your 3:15 p.m. show drew 49 men, 72 women, and 680 children.

easy Why did he ask me how I got a job for a girl I did not know?

| 1 | 2 | 3 | 4 | 5 | 6 | 7 | 8 | 9 | 10 | 11 | 12 |

21b ▶ 13
Improving keystroking continuity

Repeat 20f above. **Goals:** 1′—at least 19 *gwam*
3′—at least 14 *gwam*

21c ▶ 10
Proofreading: identifying errors

Type the ¶ twice, making needed corrections as you type. Proofread and verify.

How many GWAM canyou type to day: 18, 20, 22 24, or more? You should by able to addd some worda to your rate by stressing the correct knds of typin habits. Do not freeze as you tyep. Instead, space ver quickly and begin teh next word at once? Type with out puasing.

section

30

Typing in a medical office

lessons 131–134

Section 30 is designed to provide you with ample opportunity to type the kinds of problems that you would normally expect to encounter when working in a medical office.

Supplies needed

letterheads, memorandum forms, and medical forms [LM pp. 105-112] or plain full sheets
carbon sheets; second sheets; envelopes

Machine adjustments

1. Check chair and desk adjustments and placement of copy for easy reading.
2. Set paper guide at *0*.
3. Set ribbon control on black.
4. Margins: 70-space line for drills and ¶ writings; as directed (or appropriate) for problems.
5. SS line drills; DS ¶s; space problems as directed (or appropriate).

Daily practice plan

Preparatory practice ...... 5′
Office work simulation .... 45′

Learning goals

1. To develop above average skill in medical typing.
2. To become familiar with many clerical and administrative functions of an efficient medical office.

Office Job Simulation

Read carefully the material at the right before you begin work on Section 30. Note any standard procedures that you think will save you time during the completion of the production activities.

Introduction

You have been hired as the medical office assistant for the physicians and the director of the Columbus Medical Arts Clinic, 3501 Indianola Avenue, Columbus, OH 43214. You will work under the direction of Roger V. Davenport, M.D., director of the Clinic.

Use COLLEGE TYPEWRITING as a guide for matters of style and placement. When a job requires unusual specifications, the Columbus Medical Arts Clinic provides them in "Excerpts from the Medical Office Manual." Proofread all work carefully before removing it from your typewriter; correct all detected errors.

Excerpts from the Medical Office Manual

Letters. All letters are to be typed in modified block style with open punctuation and indented paragraphs. The closing lines of all letters should include the typed name of the person for whom the letters are typed, followed on the next line by that person's official title. All letters and memorandums require *one* carbon copy for the file. Address appropriate envelopes for all letters typed.

Medical reports. Type medical reports on either a preprinted form (where provided) or on plain sheets. If typed on plain sheets, use the illustration below as a guide for the general style of a medical report.

For medical reports typed on plain sheets, leave 1″ top and side margins for all pages. Leave an approximate 1″ bottom margin for a full page. For the main heading of a report, type in ALL CAPS the title of the report. Triple-space below the title; double-space the personal information about the patient, including the name, the address, current date, date of birth, sex, occupation, and the name of the attending physician.

For preprinted forms and plain sheets, type the body of a medical report single-spaced with a double-space between paragraphs. Side headings introduce general topics or areas of examination. Paragraph headings introduce specific items or areas examined.

Other reports. Type reports that will become a part of a patient's record as a regular report, using the standard rules for unbound, topbound, or sidebound reports.

1″

MEDICAL HISTORY

NAME George M. Fulbright DATE 6/5/19--

ADDRESS 3432 Trabue Road, Columbus, OH 43204

1″ DATE OF BIRTH 7/23/38 OCCUPATION Teacher SEX Male 1″

ATTENDING PHYSICIAN Rosemarie A. Hardy, M.D.

CHIEF COMPLAINT

The patient complains of severe pain in his right side of approximately 24 hours duration that radiates into the groin.

21d ▶ 7
Controlling number reaches

1′ writings on each line

Goal: at least 12 *gwam* on Line 3

1212 1313 1414 1515 2626 2727 2828 2929 8282 8383 8484 8585
2390 3489 4578 4567 4309 5498 5487 2845 3458 7892 2340 6785
1247 3847 5674 2938 1010 2093 4983 5874 6547 3820 3290 9032

| 1 | 2 | 3 | 4 | 5 | 6 | 7 | 8 | 9 | 10 | 11 | 12 |

21e ▶ 5
Improving shift-key/-lock technique

each line twice SS (slowly, faster); DS between 2-line groups

Ella McGowan, Karl Oates, Willie Leeds, Jane Dorn, Alex Nynn
Sam joined the USMC, Lois attends UCLA, and Nel goes to IUP.
Ready to cross the North Sea, Captain Nox boarded HMS Henry.
Lily read BLITHE SPIRIT by Noel Coward. I read VANITY FAIR.

| 1 | 2 | 3 | 4 | 5 | 6 | 7 | 8 | 9 | 10 | 11 | 12 |

21f ▶ 8
Improving response patterns

Line 1: Read and type each word as a *word*.
Line 2: Read each word letter by letter as you type it.
Lines 3-4: Type short, easy words as words; type others letter by letter.

word 1 Suzy makes the forms for the firm to use for its field work.
letter 2 As you are aware, I look upon Lynn Savage as a great trader.
combination 3 When I agreed to the rates, he signed the proxy you gave me.
4 Think of the time you would lose without an intercom system.

| 1 | 2 | 3 | 4 | 5 | 6 | 7 | 8 | 9 | 10 | 11 | 12 |

22

22a ▶ 7
Preparatory practice

each line twice SS (slowly, faster); DS between 2-line groups

alphabet Dick Webster hopes Zoe Quigley can leave for Mexico in June.
adjacent reaches He said that poised talk has triumphed over violent actions.
figure The 9 clerks checked Items 27, 10, 36, 48, and 15 on page 7.
easy If she does not want to move, why does she not pay the rent?

| 1 | 2 | 3 | 4 | 5 | 6 | 7 | 8 | 9 | 10 | 11 | 12 |

22b ▶ 10
Building statistical-copy skill

one 1′ writing; then two 3′ writings; proofread and verify each writing; circle errors

Goals: 1′—13 *gwam*
3′— 9 *gwam*

all figures used

Difficulty index

E	1.2 si	5.1 awl	90% hfw

gwam 3′

Do you realize you could add 2, 3, or 4 words a minute 4 | 23
to your typing speed during each of the 8 to 10 weeks often 8 | 27
required to learn to type by touch? A few people, however, 12 | 31
gain 5 or 6 words a week; it is not uncommon to find people 16 | 35
who record 38 or 39 words a minute after the first 10 weeks. 20 | 39

gwam 3′ | 1 | 2 | 3 | 4 |

126b-130b, continued

Job 5 [LM pp. 101–104]
Last will and testament

Mr. Clayton has typed a draft of the Last Will and Testament of Anita K. Martinez. He now wants you to prepare it in final form complete with an appropriate endorsement.

Miss Martinez will come into the office next week to sign the will.

LAST WILL AND TESTAMENT
OF ANITA K. MARTINEZ

I, ANITA K. MARTINEZ, being a single woman, residing in the City of Waterloo, State of Iowa, do make, publish, and declare this instrument to be my Last Will and Testament, hereby revoking and canceling all former Wills and Codicils by me at any time made.

FIRST: I direct that all of my just debts, including the expenses of my last illness and funeral, shall be paid out of my estate by my executrix hereinafter named.

SECOND: I give and bequeath my complete art collection and the sum of Fifty Thousand Dollars ($50,000) to my nephew, LUIS R. MARTINEZ, if living at the time of my death, otherwise to his wife and children equally.

THIRD: I give and bequeath my house at 1593 Prospect Circle and the sum of Fifty Thousand Dollars ($50,000) to my niece, TERESA ANN SOMMERFELT, if living at the time of my death, otherwise to her husband and children equally.

FOURTH: All articles of household furniture and furnishings, books, silverware, my automobiles, all of my clothing and jewelry, not otherwise disposed of, all similar articles of household use and wearing apparel, which I may own at the time of my death, and the residue of my estate, I give and bequeath to my brother, JORGE M. MARTINEZ, if living at the time of my death, otherwise to his wife and children equally.

FIFTH: I direct my executrix to pay all estate and inheritance taxes, and succession duties assessed by the United States, any state thereof, or any foreign government, against my estate predicated upon my death as the taxable event.

SIXTH: I hereby nominate, constitute, and appoint MARTA L. COPELAND as executrix of my Last Will and Testament.

IN WITNESS WHEREOF, I have hereunto subscribed my hand and seal to this my Last Will and Testament, at the City of Waterloo, State of Iowa, this 31st day of January, 19--.

____
Anita K. Martinez

We, the undersigned, do hereby certify that ANITA K. MARTINEZ, the above-named testator, on the day and year above written, signed the foregoing instrument in our presence, and published and declared the same to be her Last Will and Testament, and we, at the same time, at her request, in her presence, and in the presence of one another, have hereunto set our hands as subscribing witnesses; and we further certify that at such time she was of sound and disposing mind and memory.

______________________________ residing at ______________________

______________________________ residing at ______________________

______________________________ residing at ______________________

22c ▶ 10
Improving machine parts control

Lines 1-4: Set tab stop 10 spaces to right of center. Tab and type.
Line 5: Type each word, including comma, as shown; backspace and insert missing *r*.
Line 6: Use shift keys and shift lock as needed.
Line 7: Depress margin release; backspace 3 spaces into left margin. Type sentence. When carriage locks at right margin, depress margin release and complete sentence.

tab and return
1 ——— Tab ———► Reach the finger to
2 the tabulator key or bar.——— Tab ———►Depress it quickly;
3 then move back to home position.— Tab ►Reach to the return
4 lever or key quickly, too.

backspacer 5 rive , sta t, ca ve, c isp, ea ns, clea est, fla es, ma ket,

shift 6 Peg and Neil LoPresti appeared on NBC on a Tuesday in April.

margin release 7 This is a helpful hint: Put things away as you finish with them.

22d ▶ 13
Building keystroking speed

Type each line as two 1′ writings with the call of the guide each 15″, 20″, or 30″, depending upon your speed goal.

	gwam per line 30″	20″	15″
In 1978, 45 of us sold 32 Model 60 cars.	16	24	32
Buy 19 or 20 each of Series 78, 135, and 146.	18	27	36
The 68 women and 49 men met at 10:35 on August 27.	20	30	40
From 5:30 until 6:17 p.m. on May 24, 9 to 18 cars left.	22	33	44
Flight 986 should leave in 15 or 20 minutes, about 7:34 a.m.	24	36	48

| 1 | 2 | 3 | 4 | 5 | 6 | 7 | 8 | 9 | 10 | 11 | 12 |

22e ▶ 10
Measuring straight-copy skill

1. Type a 1′ writing on each ¶; determine *gwam* on each.
2. Type a 3′ writing on all the ¶s combined. Determine *gwam* and compare with *gwam* on 1′ writings.

► Relax. Do not try to force speed. Measure your best efforts.

Difficulty index

all letters used | E | 1.2 si | 5.1 awl | 90% hfw |

gwam 3′

It seems that people in business can be put into three 4
classes. In the first class is the worker who must be told 8
everything in detail. This worker is a great burden to the 12
company. What is missing is a mind that can work by itself. 16

The worker in the next class is never much better, for 19
this one does just the work required. He or she has skills 23
but slight interest in the job. The interested worker will 27
size up every job, decide what must be done, and then do it. 31

Now, in the third class are the workers who do the job 35
assigned to them. These do not need constant scrutiny, for 39
you know they will do good work. They are devoted to their 43
jobs and will work to find new, interesting ways to do them. 47

gwam 3′ | 1 | 2 | 3 | 4 |

126b-130b, continued

Job 4 [LM pp. 97–100]
Partnership agreement

Mr. Clayton asks you to type this 2-page partnership agreement in standard double-spaced legal format, inserting the handwritten information at appropriate points.

He reminds you to type an appropriate endorsement on the back of the second sheet of the document.

P A R T N E R S H I P   A G R E E M E N T 20

THIS AGREEMENT, made January 15, 19--, between SAMUEL E. COWENS, of 1643 Kimball Avenue, City of Waterloo, County of Black Hawk, State of Iowa, and RITA M. EDWARDS, of 1494 West Fourth Street, City of Cedar Falls, County of Black Hawk, State of Iowa, herein referred to as partners.

WHEREIN IT IS MUTUALLY AGREED AS FOLLOWS:

1. That the partnership name shall be GIFTS + SUCH. The partnership shall be conducted for the purpose of selling gifts and novelties. The principal place # of business shall be at College Square Mall, unless relocated by mutual consent of the partners.

2. That the term of this agreement shall be for five (5) years, commencing on March 1, 19--, and terminating on February 28, 19--, unless sooner terminated by mutual consent of the parties or by operation of the provisions of this agreement.

3. That each partner shall contribute Ten Thousand Dollars ($10,000) on or before March 1, 19--, to be used by the partnership to establish its capital position. Any additional contribution required of partners shall be determined and established in accordance with capital requirements in order to meet expenses.

4. That each partner shall be entitled to fifty percent (50%) of the net profits of the business, and all losses occurring in the course of the business shall be borne in the same proportion, unless the losses are occasioned by the willful neglect or default, and not mere mistake or error, of either of the partners, in which case the loss so incurred shall be made good by the partner through whose neglect or default the losses shall arise. Distribution of profits shall be made on the 28th day of February of each year.

5. That no partner shall receive any salary from the partnership, but that each partner shall be at liberty to draw out of the business in anticipation of the expected profits a maximum of Eight Hundred Dollars ($800) per month. The total sum of the advanced draw for each partner shall be deducted from the sum that partner is entitled to under the distribution of profits as provided in Item 4 herein.

IN WITNESS WHEREOF, the parties have executed this agreement at Waterloo, Iowa, on the date first above written.

Samuel E. Cowens

Rita M. Edwards

Signed and delivered
in the presence of

section

5 Learning symbol-key reaches

lessons 23–26

Learning goals

1. To learn symbol reaches.
2. To improve proofreading and verification skills.
3. To develop greater facility with figure reaches.
4. To learn meaning and use of proofreader's marks.
5. To improve keystroking speed.

Machine adjustments

1. Check chair and desk adjustments.
2. Set paper guide at *0*.
3. Set 60-space line.
4. Set ribbon control on black.
5. Single-space (SS) drills; double-space (DS) paragraphs.

23

23a ▶ 7 Preparatory practice

each line 3 times SS (slowly, faster, slowly); DS between 3-line groups

alphabet Freda Jencks will have money to buy six quite large topazes.

s/d Denis Dase sold daisy seeds to a student from Sedan, France.

figure On June 24, Flight 89 left at 1:30 with 47 women and 65 men.

easy Do the job the way it ought to be done; do it the right way.

| 1 | 2 | 3 | 4 | 5 | 6 | 7 | 8 | 9 | 10 | 11 | 12 |

23b ▶ 12 Learning new keyreaches: $ # &

1. Find new key on keyboard chart at the right.
2. Study carefully the reach technique shown for the key.
3. Watch your finger make reach to new key a few times.
4. Type technique drills for the key.

$ = dollars
# = number/pounds
& = ampersand

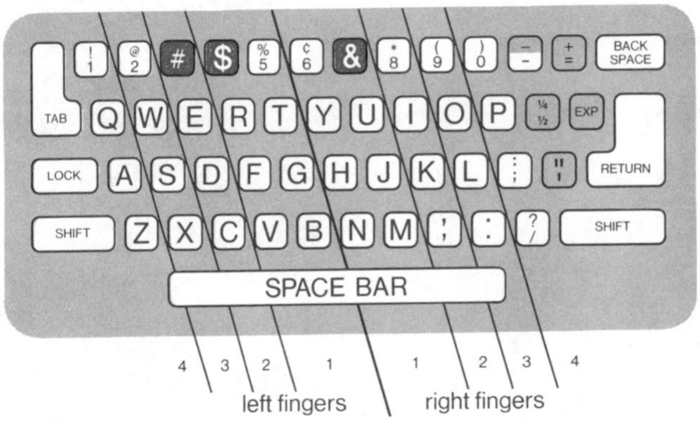

Reach technique for $

Shift; then reach *up* to $ with *left first* finger.

Reach technique for #

Shift; then reach *up* to # with *left second* finger.

Reach technique for &

Shift; then reach *up* to & with *right first* finger.

▶ Hold the shift key down until you have struck the desired symbol; then release it.

$
$ $f $4 $44, half of $4, $44 fee, 4 for $44, off $4, $44 fan
We cashed the 4 checks; they were for $45, $54, $34, and $4.

#
#d #3 #33, Period #3, Card #33, Grid #3, Herd #33, #3 dish
Check Card #32 and Card #34 to find Load #13 of #33 decking.

&
& &j &7, Jones & Onroj & James, Raj & Jana, J & B, F & F Co.
Bye & Johns, Unruh & Junlo, and J & N Co. have offices here.

$/#/&
M & J Co. paid $485 for 400# of Grade #3, Size #3/17 gravel.
Item #29 says J & H owes Car & Car $740, plus $17 for taxes.
This $9.35 item from Day & Combs is from their List #178-22.

all symbols learned
The large Nuel & Harvy catalog lists #3 beams at $4.38 each.
Memo #47 from Argo & Grill shows $56 due on our May 27 bill.

| 1 | 2 | 3 | 4 | 5 | 6 | 7 | 8 | 9 | 10 | 11 | 12 |

126b-130b, continued

Job 3 [LM p. 95]
Power of attorney

For his convenience, Mr. Clayton has prepared rough–draft copies of certain forms that he can fill in to adapt to specific persons and situations. He hands you the accompanying draft and asks you to type it in final form, properly endorsed.

POWER OF ATTORNEY 16

Know all men by these presnents, that I, Joel K. Moser, of the city of Waterloo, County of Black Hawk State of Iowa, do make, constitute and appoint CAROL V. MOSER , of the city of Cedar Falls, County of Black Hawk, State of Iowa, as my lawful and legal attorney, to act for me and in my name, place and stead, for all matters relating to both my personal and business transactions for the period of time, April 1, 19--, through and including March 31, 19--,

and I hereby ratify and confirm all transactions that my said agent or attorney my do lawfully in connection with my personal and business transcations during the above-stated period of time.

IN WITNESS WHEREOF, I have hereby signed and sealed this Power of Attorney on this the 10th day of January , 19--.

Joel K. Moser

STATE OF IOWA)
: ss.
County of Black Hawk)

On the 20th day of January, 19--, Joel K. Moser personally appeared before me, a Notary Public, in and for the said County and State, and acknowledged that he had executed the above document and that he was the person whose name is ~~sub~~ subscribed to the above document. DS

In testimony whereof, I have hereunto subscribed my name at Waterloo, Iowa, this 20th day of January, 19--.

Notary Public

My commission expires on June 30, 1989.

23c ▶ 12
Building statistical-copy skill

two 1′ writings; then two 3′ writings; proofread and verify each writing; circle errors

Goals: 1′—at least 17 *gwam*
3′—at least 13 *gwam*

Difficulty index

all figures used | E | 1.2 si | 5.1 awl | 90% hfw |

	gwam 3′	
At last--on May 17, I believe--the large blue box from	4	23
North & Page came. The meet was just 30 days away, and the	8	27
before-meet party would be on May 19. The box cost $65 and	12	31
held a small official present for every member of the other	16	35
side--48 club shirts; and written on each shirt: WE ARE #2.	20	39

gwam 3′ | 1 | 2 | 3 | 4 |

23d ▶ 7
Typing from corrected copy

Errors are often circled in copy that is to be retyped; or, perhaps more frequently, the copy is marked with special symbols called "proofreader's marks," which indicate changes desired by the editor. Some commonly used proofreader's marks are shown at the right.

Study the proofreader's marks; then type each drill line at least twice.

Symbol	Meaning	Symbol	Meaning
Cap or ≡	Capitalize	#	Add horizontal space
^	Insert	/ lc	Lowercase letters
⸙	Delete (take out)	⁀	Close up space
⊏	Move to left	∿	Transpose

1 the hand writing wall is oftten huneeded by must of su.

2 it is to decide ona risd then is it wo life with i t.

3 With out question, theworst Bos can we have bad habit.

4 Thus, faceing thetruth can altar the diretion ofour life.

5 our prblem that they day begans with first half hour.

6 Use quick, light, sur strikes tobuild useable skill.

23e ▶ 12
Developing keystroking continuity

two 1′ writings; then two 3′ writings; proofread each writing and circle errors

Goals: 1′—at least 24 *gwam*
3′—at least 19 *gwam*

Difficulty index

all letters used | E | 1.2 si | 5.1 awl | 90% hfw |

	gwam 3′	
We are on a quest for success; and to find it, we have	4	23
fixed our sights on some goal that we believe will bring it	8	27
to us. But where is success? Men and women who get things	12	31
done rarely claim success just because they work with zeal;	16	35
they are a success at many things. They are special people.	20	39

gwam 3′ | 1 | 2 | 3 | 4 |

126b-130b, continued

Job 2 [LM p. 93]
Bill of sale

Mr. Clayton has drawn up the accompanying bill of sale which he asks you to type while Miss Milroy waits. She will sign the document with you and Mr. Clayton as witnesses.

Mr. Clayton also asks you to type an appropriate endorsement on the reverse side and to make 3 photocopies of the document.

BILL OF SALE

KNOW ALL MEN BY THESE PRESENTS, that I, RAMONA C. MILROY, of Evansdale, in the County of Black Hawk, and the State of Iowa, in consideration of Two Thousand Five Hundred Dollars ($2,500) to me paid by MARY LOU ALDRICH of Waterloo, Iowa, the receipt whereof is hereby acknowledged, do hereby grant, sell, transfer, and deliver unto MARY LOU ALDRICH the following goods and chattels, ~~namely~~, one service for twelve, solid sterling ^silver tableware (72 pieces).

TO HAVE AND TO HOLD all and singular the goods and chattels to MARY ^LOU ALDRICH and her executors, administrators, and assigns, to their own use ^and behoof forever.

AND I HEREBY COVENANT with the grantee that I am the ~~true and~~ lawful owner of said goods and chattels; that they are free from all encumbrances; that I will warrant and defend the same against the lawful claims and demands of all persons.

IN WITNESS WHEREOF, I, RAMONA C. MILROY, hereunto set my hand, this 20th day of January, 19--.

____
Ramona C. Milroy

Signed and delivered
in the presence of

____

____

24

24a ▶ 7
Preparatory practice

each line 3 times SS (slowly, faster, slowly); DS between 3-line groups

alphabet	Baxter Fork requested my help in covering the Iwo Jima zone.
a/s	This essay says it is easy to save us from disaster in Asia.
figure	The box is 6 5/8 by 9 1/2 feet and weighs 375 to 400 pounds.
easy	We can always use those antique chairs at our downtown mall.

| 1 | 2 | 3 | 4 | 5 | 6 | 7 | 8 | 9 | 10 | 11 | 12 |

24b ▶ 12
Learning new keyreaches: ( ) %

(follow directions for 23b, p. 43)

(= left parenthesis
) = right parenthesis
% = percent

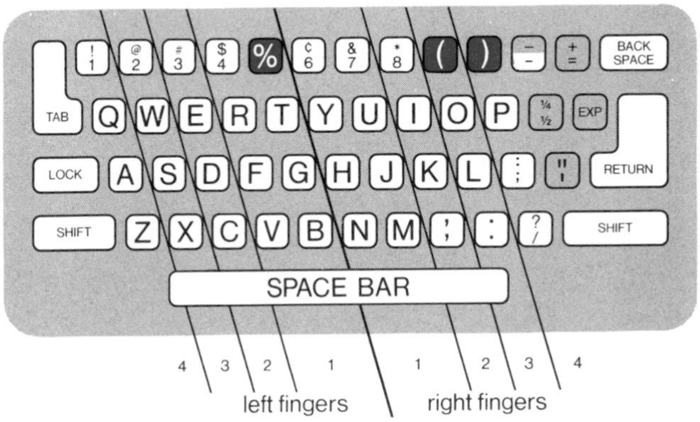

Reach technique for (

Shift; then reach *up* to (with *right third* finger.

Reach technique for)

Shift; then reach *up* to) with *right little* finger.

Reach technique for %

Shift; then reach *up* to % with *left first* finger.

( ) — ((1 (1;));); (1) (91) (10) (01) (109) (9100) (1090) (19)
Ann (my aunt) and Charles (my cousin) are the same age (23).

% — % %f %f 5% 15% 25%, forfeit 15%, 25% off, 5% tax, 15% profit
Note our discounts: coats, 50%; hats, 25%; and gloves, 20%.

( ) / % — We (Jess and I) paid interest twice (6% and 7%) on one loan.
Our profits (up 25%) are studied in the report (see page 9).
Now (July) the rate (7%) is higher than it was in June (6%).

all symbols learned — Brent got 3% more ($78) with Myles & Brynn at their #8 mill.
Barrymore & Hume spent 2% more ($7,775) for six #189 chairs.

| 1 | 2 | 3 | 4 | 5 | 6 | 7 | 8 | 9 | 10 | 11 | 12 |

24c ▶ 14
Building statistical-copy skill

two 1′ writings; then three 3′ writings; proofread and verify each writing; circle errors

Goals: 1′—at least 19 *gwam*
3′—at least 15 *gwam*

Difficulty index

all figures used | E | 1.2 si | 5.1 awl | 90% hfw |

	gwam 3′	
Reports from the Ameo Savings & Loan (city branch) say	4	23
that one day this spring (April 8) the bank made 7 loans to	8	27
young (under 23) people in the local area. Of these loans,	12	31
coming to a total of $6,900, 4 (57%) were paid back in less	16	35
than a month; one loan (listed #13) was paid back in 2 days.	20	39

gwam 3′ | 1 | 2 | 3 | 4 |

126-130

126a-130a ▶ 5

Preparatory practice

each line 3 times SS (slowly, faster, slowly); retype selected lines as time permits

alphabet Jacqueline Kase led the expedition down the foggy river to Mozambique.

fig/sym Please pay Bill #48012 for $1,671.98, but first add 3.5% to the total.

double letters I feel that good manners are essential to success in business affairs.

fluency It is my wish to amend my will by codicil to make the change he wants.

| 1 | 2 | 3 | 4 | 5 | 6 | 7 | 8 | 9 | 10 | 11 | 12 | 13 | 14 |

126b-130b ▶ 45

Office work simulation

Be sure to study the "Excerpts from the Legal Document Format Manual" on pages 254–255 before you begin the jobs.

Job 1 [LM p. 91]
Warranty deed

Mr. Clayton hands you the accompanying rough draft to type in final form. He suggests that you study the illustrated warranty deed in the "Excerpts" (p. 255) for guidance.

WARRANTY DEED 6 TS

Indent 10

SUSAN R. PROCHASKA, being single, of 1816 Pinoak Drive, City of Cedar Falls, County of Black Hawk, State of Iowa, for valuable consideration paid, grants, with general warranty covenants, to ARTHUR S. BLUHM, whose tax-mailing address is 1705 Minnetonka Drive, City of Cedar Falls, county of Black Hawk, State of Iowa, the following described real property in the County of Black Hawk, State of Iowa:

SS

Lot 633 of Tract 2976, as per map recorded in Book 2875, at pages 495-497 of Maps, in the records of the country recorder of said County.

PRIOR instrument reference: Volume 21, page 295, January 23, 1958. JUSTIN PHILLIP PROCHASKA, father of dower therein.

WITNESS my hand this 15th day of January, 19--.

_______________________________ (L.S.)
Susan R. Prochaska

STATE OF IOWA)
: ss.
County of Black Hawk) DS

Before me, a Notary Public in and for the County and State aforesaid, personally appeared the above-named person and acknowledged the signing of the foregoing instrument to be her voluntary act and deed for the uses and purposes therein mentioned. DS

In testimony whereof, I have hereunto subscribed my name at Waterloo, Iowa, this 20th day of January, 19--.

____
Notary Public

My commission expires on June 30, 1989.

24d ▶ 17 Reaching for new goals

1. Type the first line of each 2-line group as a 1′ writing, with the call of the guide each 15″, 20″, or 30″. Then try to type the second line of the group at the same rate.

2. As time permits, type 1′ writings on the second line of each group.

	gwam 30″	20″	15″
1 Did Rex see Eva and Max at the new pool?	16	24	32
2 Lee & Baye shipped 28 coats to J & J Co.	16	24	32
3 Joan Marquis may be the mayor of Troy in May.	18	27	36
4 Order #16 asks that we ship a dozen #17 taps.	18	27	36
5 She can live in luxury at the Lei Hotel in Hawaii.	20	30	40
6 Blair will be here (at home) on Friday (March 30).	20	30	40
7 He may eat in the dining room and simply sign the bill.	22	33	44
8 The $450 repair bill was $29 less than we had expected.	22	33	44
9 To learn more about this unique car, visit your dealer soon.	24	36	48
10 A 5% discount is not enough; we need to deduct at least 15%.	24	36	48

| 1 | 2 | 3 | 4 | 5 | 6 | 7 | 8 | 9 | 10 | 11 | 12 |

25

25a ▶ 7 Preparatory practice

each line 3 times SS (slowly, faster, slowly); DS between 3-line groups

alphabet June Quirk believes the campaign frenzy will excite Douglas.

i/e Neither friend believes she receives benefits from the diet.

figure The 26 clerks checked Items 37 and 189 on pages 145 and 150.

easy These health benefits are ours to use for the medical chair.

| 1 | 2 | 3 | 4 | 5 | 6 | 7 | 8 | 9 | 10 | 11 | 12 |

25b ▶ 12 Building statistical-copy skill

two 1′ writings; then two 2′ writings; proofread and verify each writing; circle errors; determine *gwam*

Goals: 1′—at least 20 *gwam*; 2′—at least 17 *gwam*

Difficulty index

all figures used | E | 1.2 si | 5.1 awl | 90% hfw |

	gwam 2′	
The Ray & Enis Auto Report--Issue #6--indicated that a	6	35
record number of late-model cars will go on sale soon. The	12	41
figures (up 2.8%) will mean more (1.9 million) new autos on	18	47
our roads; but--good news--many of them will cost less than	24	53
$5,400. Prices could be down as much as 1.73% by next fall.	30	59

gwam 2′ | 1 | 2 | 3 | 4 | 5 | 6 |

25c ▶ 9 Typing from corrected copy

Type twice, making needed corrections as you type.

[move to right] [stet leave as originally written]

Some wirters thinks that it is essential to use complez [x]

terms to ~~really~~ impress ~~others~~ [us]; but it is the [correct] choice of wor [ds,]

not the[#]size of the work [d] that is ~~important~~ [of importance]. Be ~~as concise as~~ [direct]

~~possible~~ in your [crucial] quest to ~~improve~~ [stet] your w riting. use as many

words as you need--but only that many--to state your points. [stet]

Warranty deed

Approximate 2" top margin

Heading centered between ruled lines

WARRANTY DEED

10 space ¶ indention; DS except quoted copy and land descriptions; all typing within marginal rules; names in body of instrument in all caps

SUSAN R. PROCHASKA, being single, of 1816 Pinoak Drive, City of Cedar Falls, County of Black Hawk, State of Iowa, for valuable consideration paid, grants, with general warranty covenants, to ARTHUR S. BLUHM, whose tax-mailing address is 1705 Minnetonka Drive, City of Cedar Falls, County of Black Hawk, State of Iowa, the following described real property in the County of Black Hawk, State of Iowa:

Land description

Lot 633 of Tract 2976, as per map recorded in
Book 2875, at pages 495-497 of Maps, in the
records of the County Recorder of said County.

PRIOR instrument reference: Volume 21, page 295, January 23, 1958. JUSTIN PHILLIP PROCHASKA, father of dower therein.

WITNESS my hand this 15th day of January, 19--.

_________________________(L.S.)
Susan R. Prochaska

Acknowledgment SS

STATE OF IOWA)
: ss.
County of Black Hawk)

Before me, a Notary Public in and for the County and State aforesaid, personally appeared the above-named person and acknowledged the signing of the foregoing instrument to be her voluntary act and deed for the uses and purposes therein mentioned.

In testimony whereof, I have hereunto subscribed my name at Waterloo, Iowa, this 20th day of January 19--.

____
Notary Public

My commission expires on June 30, 1989.

One-page instrument does not need a page number

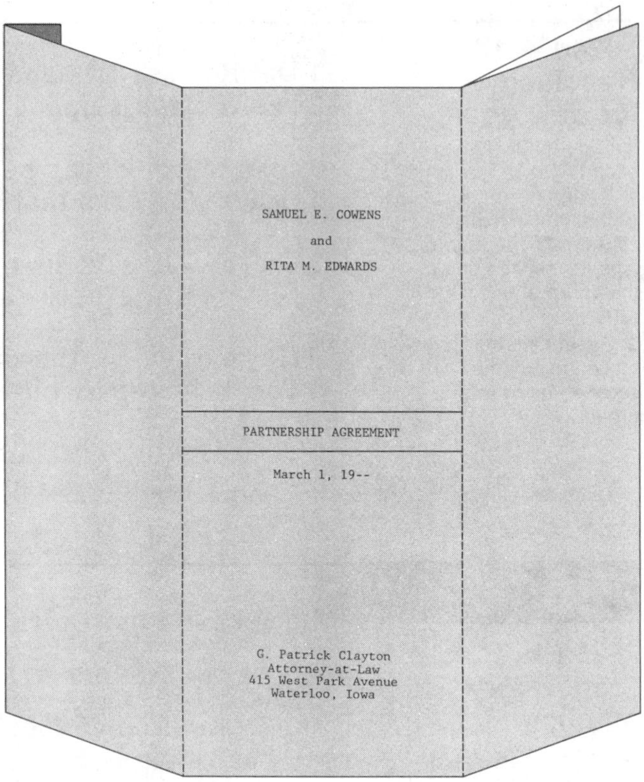

Endorsement on a legal back

Office Job Simulation, continued

Correcting Errors. Any important item such as numbers, names, or sums of money should not be erased unless (1) all parties concerned initial each erasure or (2) the double writing of numbers in both figures and words provides positive identification of the correct amount. Probably no legal question would be raised if one digit or letter were erased and corrected provided verification could be made by the double writing.

If the final signed copies of the legal document are to be reproduced on a photocopy machine, the original copy from which the photocopies are to be made may be corrected by neat erasures, liquid paper, or lift-off tape because such corrections will not be detected on the photocopies.

Proofreading. Use the verifying method to proofread all legal documents. In this method, one person reads from the original copy while another person (preferably not the typist) checks the new copy. Tricky words are spelled; punctuation marks are also indicated by the person reading aloud.

Copies. Photocopies are used in lieu of both original and carbon copies in many law offices today thereby reducing or eliminating the need for carbon copies.

Latin Abbreviations. When a legal document is "under seal," the signature on the document is followed by "L.S." which refers to the Latin phrase *locus sigilli*. The abbreviation "ss." is used for the Latin word *scilicet*, meaning "to wit."

Legal Backs and Endorsements. A legal document may be bound in a cover (a *legal back*) that is somewhat heavier and larger than the paper on which the document is typed. The names of the parties, the title of the document, the date, and the name and address of the attorney or legal firm are typed on the middle fold for 8½" x 11" paper (see illustration above) or on the outer fold for longer legal sheets. The information typed on the legal back is called the *endorsement*.

To prepare an endorsement on a legal back for 11" paper:

1. Fold down the top ½" and crease it; this fold will later be used to bind the legal document.*

2. Fold the remainder into equal thirds (as in folding a business letter).

3. Type the endorsement within the middle section.

*** Omit this step for Mr. Clayton's work.**

25d ▶ 10 Learning new keyreaches: apostrophe ('); exclamation point (!)

Apostrophe

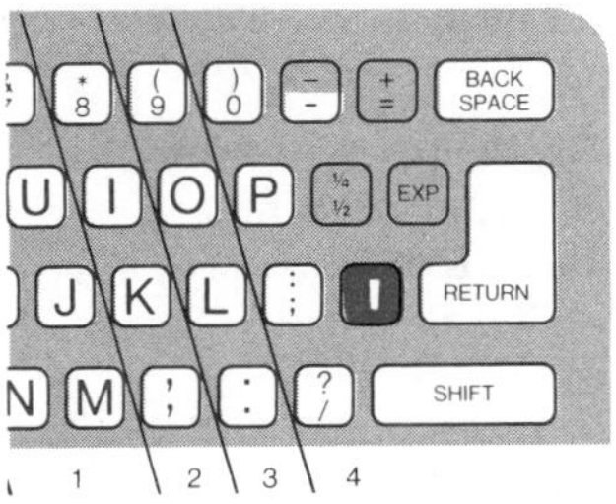

Electric
The **'** is to the right of the **;** and is controlled by the *right fourth finger*.

`;'; ;'; ;' it's`

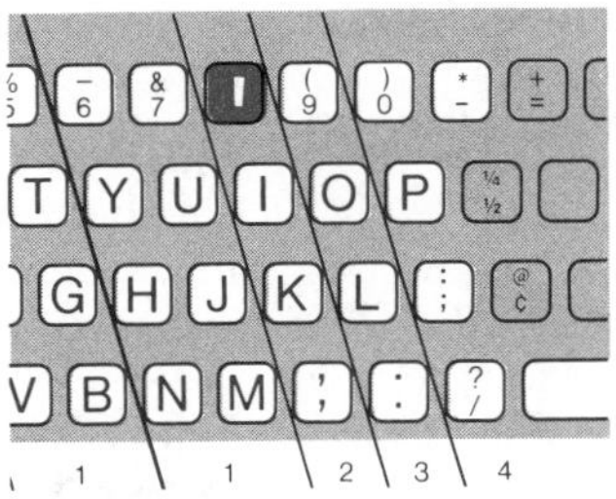

Nonelectric
The **'** is the shift of 8. Shift; then reach for it with the *right second finger*.

`k'k k'k k' it's`

Exclamation Point

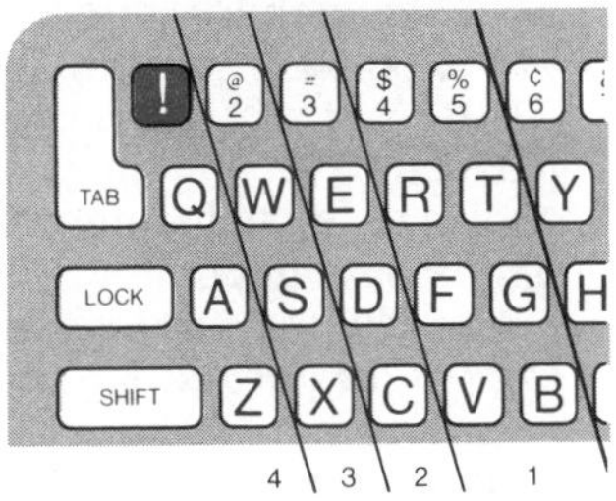

Electric (and some nonelectric)
If your typewriter has a **!** key, reach for it with the appropriate finger. If not, use the same procedure as given for nonelectric.

`a!a a!a a! Wow!`

Nonelectric
Type apostrophe, backspace, and type a period under it; thus, **!**

`k!k k!k k! Wow!`

▶ Space twice after an exclamation point at the end of a sentence.

' It's here. I'm ready. It's four o'clock. It's Nan's book.
It's Bill's bat and Lil's ball. We can't find Glen's glove.

! On your mark! Get set! Go! Watch them! You won! Hurrah!
Jump! Hold tight! Great! Catch the pole! You won a trip!

'/! Cooper's tour couldn't be more enjoyable--when it's on time!
Don't leave now! It's Sue's opportunity to top Vic's score.

all symbols learned A & B's Order #3 (for $95 at 9% discount) must be sent rush!
Here's B & M's Order #6 ($985); send 50% by air express now!

| 1 | 2 | 3 | 4 | 5 | 6 | 7 | 8 | 9 | 10 | 11 | 12 |

25e ▶ 12 Measuring statistical-copy skill

two 1' writings on each paragraph; then two 3' writings on both paragraphs combined; proofread and verify each writing; circle errors; determine *gwam*

Goals: 1'—23 *gwam*
3'—18 *gwam*

Difficulty index

all figures used

E	1.2 si	5.1 awl	90% hfw

gwam 3'

Thank you for your request of May 29. We are sorry we 4 39
could not reply to it before now, but the letter was mailed 7 43
to 3478 Western Drive, not 658 West Drive (which is now our 12 47
mailing address). We did not get your letter until June 10. 16 51
We are pleased to reserve for you a single room (#794) 19 55
for July 26 to 30. If you believe you might get here after 22 59
4, won't you please forward a 50% deposit of $18.50 to hold 27 63
the room. We shall be happy to serve you and hope you will 31 67
enjoy your 5-day visit with us here at the Hotel Washington. 35 71

gwam 3' | 1 | 2 | 3 | 4 |

Office Job Simulation

Before you begin to type any of the jobs in Section 29, study carefully the material at the right and on page 255. Make notes of all standard procedures you think will save you time as you complete the legal office typing activities.

Introduction

You have been employed as a legal typist by G. Patrick Clayton, Attorney-at-Law, 415 West Park Avenue, Waterloo, IA 50701. You will not be required to prepare any carbon copies because all copies of legal documents are made on a photocopy machine.

Mr. Clayton has available a *Legal Document Format Manual* to assist you in preparing legal documents. For your convenience, excerpts from this manual are given here for quick reference.

Excerpts from the Legal Document Format Manual

Paper. Printed forms are available for many legal documents; however, if you do not have a printed form, use standard-size paper (8½" x 11") or special legal-size paper (8½" x 13" or 14") *with ruled left and right margins.*

Ruled paper has a double ruling down the left side 1⅜" from the left side of the paper, and a single ruling down the right side ⅜" from the right edge of the paper. Paper ruled in this way permits you to set the machine for a 1½" left margin and a ½" right margin and type within the rulings.

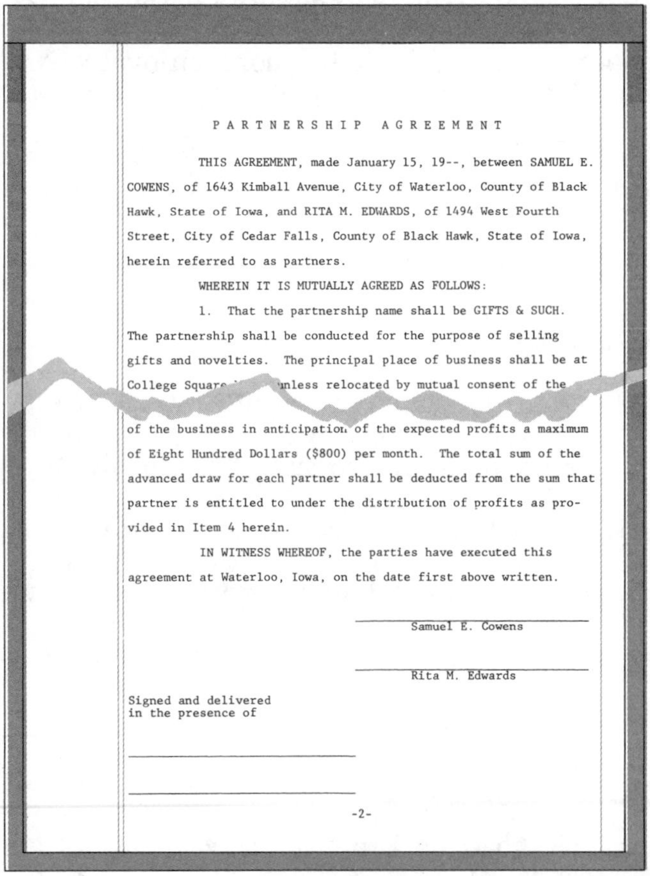

PARTNERSHIP AGREEMENT

THIS AGREEMENT, made January 15, 19--, between SAMUEL E. COWENS, of 1643 Kimball Avenue, City of Waterloo, County of Black Hawk, State of Iowa, and RITA M. EDWARDS, of 1494 West Fourth Street, City of Cedar Falls, County of Black Hawk, State of Iowa, herein referred to as partners.

WHEREIN IT IS MUTUALLY AGREED AS FOLLOWS:

1. That the partnership name shall be GIFTS & SUCH. The partnership shall be conducted for the purpose of selling gifts and novelties. The principal place of business shall be at College Square ... unless relocated by mutual consent of the ...

of the business in anticipation of the expected profits a maximum of Eight Hundred Dollars ($800) per month. The total sum of the advanced draw for each partner shall be deducted from the sum that partner is entitled to under the distribution of profits as provided in Item 4 herein.

IN WITNESS WHEREOF, the parties have executed this agreement at Waterloo, Iowa, on the date first above written.

Samuel E. Cowens

Rita M. Edwards

Signed and delivered
in the presence of

-2-

Partial pages of partnership agreement

Titles on Legal Documents. Center the title between the vertical rulings. Type titles in all capital letters. Titles for legal documents are often *s p r e a d.*

To spread a title or heading:

1. Backspace from the horizontal center point *one backspace for each stroke* (letter, space, and character) in the title *except* the last.

2. Type the title (in all capital letters) with one blank space between letters (or other characters) and 3 blank spaces between words in the title.

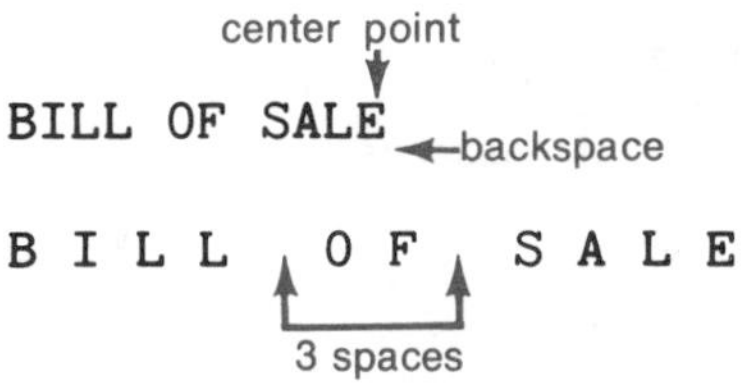

Margins and Spacing. On ruled paper, type within the ruled lines; leave one or two spaces between the ruling at the left and the beginning of the typing line. Set the margin stops for a 1½" left and a ½" right margin. Indent paragraphs 10 spaces. Double-space the copy *except* land descriptions and quoted matter which should be single-spaced and indented 10 spaces from both margins. The notary statement and the witness statement, when used, should also be single-spaced.

On each page, leave a top margin of about 2" (12 blank lines) and, on a full page, a bottom margin of about 1".

Page Numbers. The first page is not usually numbered, *except* in a will. Numbers of subsequent pages are centered between the margins 3 blank lines from the bottom of the page. Type a hyphen before and after the page number; for example, -5-

Signature Lines. The maker or makers of a legal document sign on the right side of the page, and the witnesses, if any, sign on the left side. Signature lines are about 3" long, and 2 or 3 blank lines are left between two signature lines.

The page containing the signatures of the maker and any witnesses must contain at least 2 typewritten lines of the body of the document.

26

26a ▶ 7
Preparatory practice

each line 3 times SS (slowly, faster, slowly); DS between 3-line groups

alphabet Roxy waved as she did quick flying jumps on the trapeze bar.

b/v Bev Bovar waved to a bevy of brave Bavarians in the bivouac.

figure Do Problems 6 to 19 on page 275 before class at 8:30, May 4.

easy If we do this job when we ought, it might not delay us long.

| 1 | 2 | 3 | 4 | 5 | 6 | 7 | 8 | 9 | 10 | 11 | 12 |

26b ▶ 10
Learning new keyreaches: quotation marks ("); underline (_)

Quotation Marks

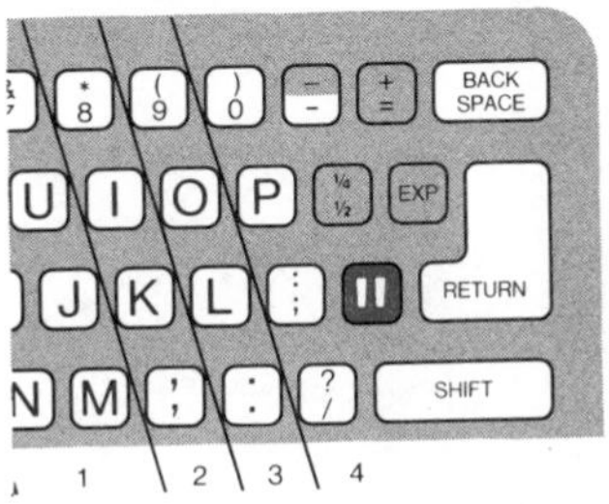

Electric

Type " (the shift of ') with the *right little finger* as you shift with the left little finger.

;"; ;"; ;" "so"

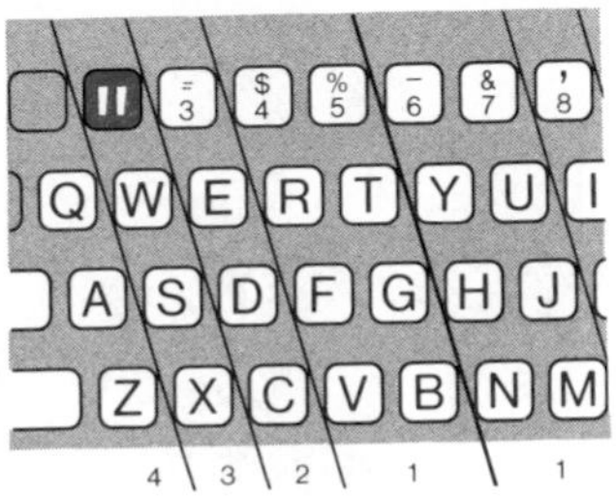

Nonelectric

Type " (the shift of 2) with the *left third finger* as you shift with the right little finger.

s"s s"s s" "so"

Underline

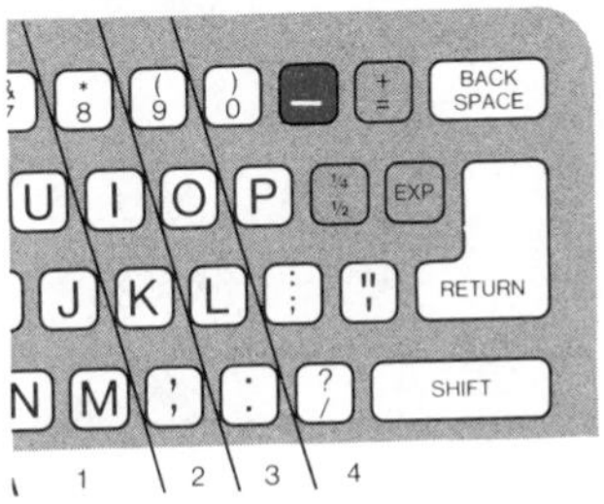

Electric

Type _ (the shift of the hyphen) with the *right little finger* as you shift with the left little finger.

' ' ' ' ' Now.

Nonelectric

Type _ (the shift of 6) with the *right first finger* as you shift with the left little finger.

j j j j j Now.

" In his hurry, he typed "not" for "knot" and "see" for "sea."
"I must," he said, "go now." "Please," I said, "come back."

_ Use a quick stroke. Please think as you type; try to relax.
That is the way to do this job. It is easy if you know how.

"/_ "This," she said, "is the one right way to make a decision."
She said, "Having talent is fine, but wasting it is tragic."

all symbols learned D & D says, "Here's Check #23 ($95); ship 50% of order now!"
Hynes & Abt's Report #7 ($25) says, "Raise fees 5% at once!"

| 1 | 2 | 3 | 4 | 5 | 6 | 7 | 8 | 9 | 10 | 11 | 12 |

▶ To underline, backspace (or move carriage by hand) to the first letter of the word; then type the underline once for each letter in the word.

Typewritten words are underlined to indicate that they should be in *italic* when typeset.

26c ▶ 5
Controlling number reaches

Type 1′ writings on each line.

Goal: at least 12 *gwam* on Line 3

3826 4015 1520 4627 5938 1028 3647 5940 1837 2936 1740 5829

2003 3994 5881 9338 6220 4771 7440 8227 1550 0116 4775 9337

4937 5124 2830 5738 5049 2139 4758 6051 2938 3047 2851 6930

| 1 | 2 | 3 | 4 | 5 | 6 | 7 | 8 | 9 | 10 | 11 | 12 |

level

6

Service office simulations

lessons 126–150

The primary purpose of Level 6 is to provide the opportunity for you to develop your production skills in a variety of office situations that are commonly found in legal, medical, governmental, and technical offices.

A secondary but important purpose, however, is to help you further improve your basic speed and accuracy skills. In addition to the daily Preparatory Practice, two sections of lessons are devoted entirely to speed/accuracy skill development.

The final section of Level 6 is a measurement section in which you will be asked to demonstrate your best performance on both basic and production typing materials.

Your two major goals for the remainder of the course are:

- To develop a keen sense of responsibility for producing high-quality typewritten work in minimum time.
- To develop the ability to make decisions without direct supervision.

In this level you will spend about 20 percent of your classroom time developing basic skills and about 80 percent on production work.

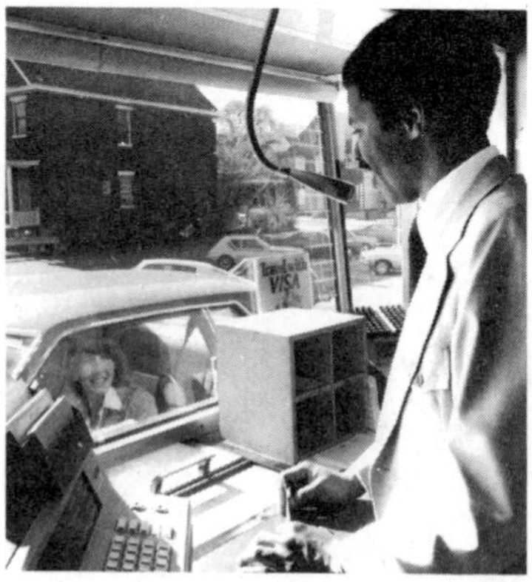

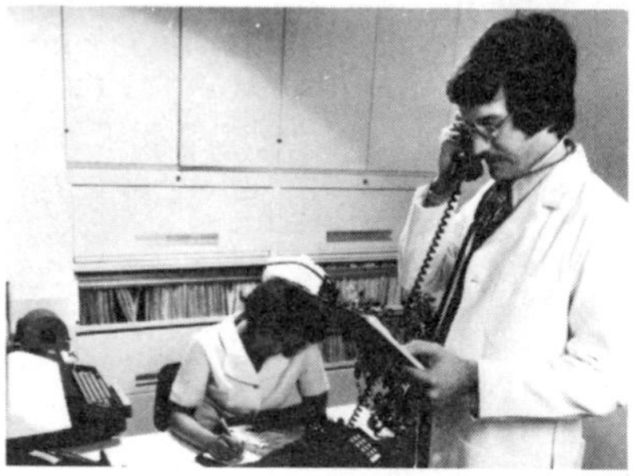

section

29

Typing in a legal office

lessons 126–130

Section 29 is designed to provide practice on the kinds of jobs you would expect to encounter as a typist in a legal office.

Supplies needed

ruled legal paper (8½" x 11")
[LM pp. 91-104]
or plain full sheets

Machine adjustments

1. Check chair and desk adjustments; check copy placement for easy reading.
2. Set paper guide at *0*.
3. Set ribbon control on black.
4. Set line-space selector on *1* for single spacing for drills; on *2* for double spacing when required for jobs.
5. Margins: 70-space line for drills; 1½" left and 1" right for legal documents.

Daily practice plan

Preparatory practice .... 5′
Office work simulation .....45′

Learning goals

1. To develop knowledge and skill in typing legal documents.
2. To plan your work carefully.
3. To complete your work correctly and efficiently.
4. To proofread all work carefully and to make needed corrections neatly.

26d ▶ 10
Building statistical-copy skill

1. Type the ¶ once for practice.
2. Type two 3′ writings. Proofread and verify carefully; circle errors; determine *gwam*.

Difficulty index

all figures used	E	1.2 si	5.1 awl	90% hfw

gwam 3′

As you may know, our hotel is run by Far & Far, a firm 4 | 27
well known for group service. We're able, for instance, to 8 | 31
set up meeting rooms for small groups--5, 10, or 20--or for 12 | 35
large groups of 250 to 300. Our dining areas can serve 638 16 | 39
persons at a time. We're able to offer discounts to groups 20 | 43
this year: up to 4% for small groups and 9% for large ones. 24 | 47

gwam 3′ | 1 | 2 | 3 | 4 |

26e ▶ 6
Typing from corrected copy

Type the ¶, making corrections as you type. If time permits, type the ¶ again.

One writer say that ~~pretty~~ music improves the way we work
with others. another wirter says ~~it~~ helps get ~~increased~~
donewith less effort. Ot hers say that ~~it~~ will take ~~of~~ our
minds awa from work ~~Still another~~ says it helsp us thing.

26f ▶ 12
Measuring straight-copy skill

1. Type a 3′ writing. Proofread; circle errors; determine *gwam*.
2. Type a 1′ writing on each ¶. Type at a comfortable rate.
3. Type a second 3′ writing. Proofread; circle errors; determine *gwam*.
Goal: at least 20 *gwam* on last 3′ writing

Difficulty index

all letters used	E	1.2 si	5.1 awl	90% hfw

gwam 3′

Men or women who are a success will give the best that 4
they can give. They do not do this just because their egos 8
order it. They do it because they are oriented to succeed; 12
they fail to recognize that they could put forth any effort 16
that is not first class. They just expect to do their best. 20

The top men and women in their fields seem to realize, 23
though, that success has to mean a lot more than just doing 27
quality work. To be a real success, they say, we must look 31
at the work we do and rate it against our own standards for 35
excellence. Success is bound up with a belief in ourselves. 39

gwam 3′ | 1 | 2 | 3 | 4 |

125b, continued

Job 4
Financial report with table

Type DS a final copy of the report in standard leftbound form for binding. SS items in the table.

words

DEBLIN INDUSTRIES, INC. 5
Comparative Sales Report by Business Area, 1981 } DS 14

Industries
Deblin is engaged primarily in the purchase, manufacture, 28
processing, and distribution of a broad range of food and 40
chemical products, both domestically and in foreign countries. 53
Internally, Deblin Industries is organized into four operating 65
divisions: Deblin Foods, Deblin Dairy and Services, Deblin 77
Chemical, and Deblin International. A three-year summary of 89
sales by the four operating divisions is presented below. 101
(The data are in millions of dollars.) 109

Division	1981	1980	1979	words
Foods	$1,067,836	$1,027,823	$1,030,924	126
Dairy and Services	1,061,564	982,781	970,657	135
Chemical	923,808	876,189	833,563	142
International	749,351	594,485	545,931	154
Total	$3,802,559	$3,481,278	$3,381,075	175

(Heading row: 118)

The foods division's sales imvroved 3.9% in 1981 as com- 186
compared to 1980, and divisoinal operating income increased 198
6.9%. Operating income as a prcent of sales was 5.3% in 1981 210
compared to 5.1% in 1980. 216

The Dairy and Service Division's sales in 1981 increased 228
8.9% over 1980, and operating income increased 3.1%. The gain 240
in sales generally reflected higher selling prices on moder- 252
ately higher volume in fluid milk, beverages, cream, and cer- 266
tain of the division's specialty operations. 275

The Chemical Division's 1981 sales in creased 5.4% over 286
1980, while income for the same period decreased 6.6%. The 301
improvement over 1980 did result in increased profit in 1981 314
because selling prices could not keep pace with cost increased. 327

The International Division's sales increased 25.1% in 338
1981 as compared with 1980, and oerating income increased by 350
12.4%. Both the foods and chemical segments of this Division 363
contributed to the growth in sales and operating income. 374
In the chemical segment, strong increases in sales and 385
operating income in the European chemical operations andthe 398
Latin American chemical operations more than off set the re- 410
duction in exports of chemicals and fertilizers. The reduc- 422
tion in chemical and fertilizer exports can be attributed to 433
lessoned demand and lower prices. 440

Job 5

If time permits, retype the report of Job 4 in unbound form.

level

2

Typing letters, tables, and reports

lessons 27–50

By successfully completing Level 1, you have established your ability to type material by touch and to center it attractively on a page. Now you are ready to begin a new level of instruction, one in which you will learn to put these basic skills to practical use.

The most important element of Level 2 for you will be its emphasis on the development of your skill for use in a variety of personal and business applications. You will learn, for example, to prepare personal and business correspondence, tables of various kinds, topical outlines, and professional-looking reports.

As you type the problems of Level 2, your operational skill will continue to grow. Speed should increase. Emphasis will be placed on control of skill, on increased accuracy of typewritten work, and on the correction of typographical errors.

Additional opportunity will be provided for you to improve your ability to type from different kinds of copy and to work from rough draft and corrected materials.

The final three lessons of Level 2 are composed of copy that will measure (1) your problem-solving ability and (2) the improvement of your basic typewriting skills.

A final note. Learning to operate a typewriter skillfully is a genuine accomplishment. However, the typewriter is only a machine; you must recognize that, from now on, what comes *out* of that machine is just as important as what happens *at* the machine.

section

6

Developing/measuring basic skills

lessons 27–29

Learning goals

1. To type with smooth, continuous stroking.

2. To improve proofreading and verification skills.

3. To make figure/symbol reaches with greater ease and with increased speed.

4. To type script/rough-draft copy smoothly.

Machine adjustments

1. Check chair and desk adjustment and placement of copy for ease of reading.

2. Set paper guide at *0*.

3. Set 60-space line.

4. Set ribbon control on black.

5. Single-space (SS) drills; double-space (DS) paragraphs.

125b, continued

Job 2
Purchase order

Type the purchase order given at the right. Prepare 2 cc's on plain half sheets. Proofread carefully; correct errors neatly.

DONALDSON ENTERPRISES, INC.
30 North Michigan Avenue
Chicago, IL 60602 (312) 821-4200

PURCHASE ORDER

		words
Purchase order No.	D-403-M-2775	3
Pickering Office Supplies	Date July 12, 19--	10
4949 Golf Road	Terms 2/10, net 30	16
Skokie, IL 60077		19
	Ship Via Intercity Parcel	23

Quantity	Cat. No.	Description	Price	Total	words
50	L2-38617	Pressboard 3-ring binders	1.80 ea.	90.00	34
50	L6-NP2-14U	Pressboard data processing binders	1.97 ea.	98.50	47
4 bx.	L6-N6P	Nylon posts/threaded heads	11.25 bx.	45.00	58
5	L6-DT-350	Data tote zipper cases	10.95 ea.	54.75	68
2	M3-1606	Auto-stop electric sharpeners	59.50 ea.	119.00	81
				407.25	82

By________________________ Purchasing Agent

Job 3
Invoice

Type the invoice given at the right. Prepare 2 cc's on plain half sheets. Proofread carefully; correct errors neatly.

DONALDSON ENTERPRISES, INC.
30 North Michigan Avenue
Chicago, IL 60602 (312) 821-4200

Invoice

		words
		3
Song Ki House of Gifts	Date July 12, 19--	7
625-57th Street	Our Order No. M-5692-487	10
Kenosha, WI 53141	Cust. Order No. P-274631-K	13
		19
Terms 2/10, n/30	Shipped Via Lakeshore Delivery	25

Quantity	Description	Unit Price	Total	words
				31
8	Kamura hand-painted tea sets	15.00	120.00	37
	(assorted designs)			47
36	Kohler crystal animals (assorted)	15.00	540.00	55
12	D'Orlac lead crystal flower vases	27.50	330.00	63
	(assorted shapes and cuts)			69
24	Stand-mounted butterflies with	12.50	300.00	76
	plastic encasements			86
72	Alabaster eggs (assorted colors)	1.50	108.00	92
72	Egg stands (assorted designs	1.25	90.00	98
	and finishes)		1,488.00	100

Jobs 4–5 appear on next page.

27

27a ▶ 7 Preparatory practice

each line 3 times SS (slowly, faster, still faster); DS between 3-line groups

alphabet	Jill Wargey put a dozen quarts of jam in the box for Vickie.
double letters	Will Buzz and Lee carry the supplies across the street soon?
figure/symbol	Bob's 5% note (dated May 23, 1978) was lost at 4690 J Drive.
easy	Helen pays for the forms; ask her to write the usual checks.

| 1 | 2 | 3 | 4 | 5 | 6 | 7 | 8 | 9 | 10 | 11 | 12 |

27b ▶ 10 Improving response patterns

each 2-line group 2 times (slowly, faster); DS between 2-line groups

Easy: Read these lines word by word as you type.

Difficult: Read these lines letter by letter as you type.

Combination: Vary your rate according to the word being typed.

easy
1 and the, and then, if they, they did, to them, when they did
2 It is right for them to sign the forms; Jan may do so, also.

difficult
3 we see, we see him, as you, as you are, we only, we only saw
4 After the new rate was set, we detected a decrease in taxes.

combination
5 if the grade, with the only case, for the mill, if the vases
6 She agreed to get the draft for the treasurer if it is here.

combination
7 were not safe, jump the gun, gear for profit, asserts a fact
8 I will not desert the stand I have taken for several months.

| 1 | 2 | 3 | 4 | 5 | 6 | 7 | 8 | 9 | 10 | 11 | 12 |

27c ▶ 10 Improving keystroking technique

1. Type each line once.

2. Place a checkmark next to lines that seemed difficult for you.

3. Type again those lines you checked.

▶ • fingers curved
• wrists low
• eyes on copy

home row
1 glad flag dash half shall salad ask flask gash had gall lash
2 Dallas said: "Jay's flag fell; Karl's lashing didn't hold."

1st row
3 can zany zinc cave nimble box examine cab bank van verb comb
4 Can Bev and/or Max excavate the six caves? If not, Zeb may.

3d row
5 too tower rope you quote power write trout rewrite trip pert
6 Terry wrote two reports to Quint on the proper way to quilt.

1st fingers
7 hurry hunt burnt jury buff tub try bunt thumb brunt grunt TV
8 The truth of the matter is that Jeb Vaughan was very hungry.

2d fingers
9 kick cede deck kid dike dice ice deed did decide iced kicked
10 Dick and Edie decided to be kind to Cedric, Enid, and Kitti.

3d/4th fingers
11 plow pass zoos ox was loop squall wax wallop lollipops plaza
12 A lazy ox pulls a plow as wasps buzz past a squawking squab.

short words
13 in AC so we or it by up do of go he OK me TV ox el my at zoo
14 If it is up to us to do it, let us try to do it in two days.

long words
15 amplifiers deliberate transparent re-emphasize redevelopment
16 Several hundred people suddenly jammed Kensington Boulevard.

| 1 | 2 | 3 | 4 | 5 | 6 | 7 | 8 | 9 | 10 | 11 | 12 |

124b, continued

Job 3
Boxed table with braced heading
After typing the table, draw the vertical rules with a pen.

			words
CARBONELL INSURANCE COMPANY			6
Depreciation Comparison			10
(Cost: $10,000; Life: 5 years; Salvage: $500)			20
			43
	Depreciation Method		47 57
Year	*Declining-Balance*	*Sum-of-the-Years-Digits*	61 67 78
1	$4,507	$3,167	81
2	2,476	2,533	84
3	1,360	1,900	87
4	747	1,267	89
5	410	633	91 103
Totals	$9,500	$9,500	107 119

125

125a ▶ 5
Preparatory practice
each line 3 times SS (slowly, faster, still faster); retype selected lines as time permits

alphabet **Judge Zerb will not acquit the expert; the key witness may have proof.**

fig/sym **The total of the 327 checks was $6,054.81 (or 94% of the May payroll).**

long reaches **My aunt displayed her nerve by jumping her bicycle over the high curb.**

fluency **All of us can profit by keeping our hands and arms quiet when we type.**

| 1 | 2 | 3 | 4 | 5 | 6 | 7 | 8 | 9 | 10 | 11 | 12 | 13 | 14 |

125b ▶ 45
Production measurement: special reports and business forms
[LM p. 89]

Time schedule
Assembling materials ... 3′
Timed production ...... 35′
Final check; compute *n-pram* .... 7′

Job 1
Agenda for meeting
[plain sheet]
Prepare for left binding along with the minutes of the meeting.

Jobs 2–3 appear on next page.

```
                         DEBLIN INDUSTRIES, INC.                  } ds      5
             Agenda for Meeting of the Board of Directors         }        14
                              May 20, 19--                                 16

1.  Call to order . . . . . . . . . . . . .        Claressa Bowen          28
                                                       Robert
2.  Minutes of last Meeting . . . . . . . .         J. Re Dullea           39
                                                  e
3.  Special Reports                                                        43
       Foods Division . . . . . . . . . . .        Cilina Marquez          53
       Dairy and Service Division . . . .     Delbert M. Jackson           64
       Chemical Division . . . . . . . . .     Dallas K. Dahlman           74
ds     International Division . . . . . .          Akemi Iwasaki           84
4.  Discussion of Special Reports . . . .         Claressa Bowen           95

5.  Current Business            d            Leonard C. Ruthvan            99
    Declaration of Divident . . . . . .       J. Robert Dulleas           110
       Annual Forecast Report . . . . .     Michael F. Lasalle            120

6.  Discussion of Current Business . . .       Gordon S. Deblin           132

7.  Adjournment                                                           135
```

27d ▶ 11 Building keystroking speed

1. Type Line 1 as a 1′ writing with the call of the guide at 30″, 20″, or 15″; then try to type Line 2 at the same rate.

2. Type Lines 3 and 4 in the same manner; then Lines 5 and 6, 7 and 8.

		gwam 30″	20″	15″
1	How well can you read? How well do you type?	18	27	36
2	A relationship exist tewteen the skills. (handwritten corrections: s, b, two)	18	27	36
3	Train your eyes to transmit words to your fingers.	20	30	40
4	Don't just copy it. read for meaning; type thoughts.	20	30	40
5	They saw the movie June 2; they sat in Seats 40 and 68.	22	33	44
6	Please ship 19 coats, 135 hats, and 17 pairs of gloves. (handwritten: s are, #, them)	22	33	44
7	Try to read slightly ahead of words your fingers are typing.	24	36	48
8	Your hands will tell you when to spede up or sl ow down. (handwritten: fingers, to)	24	36	48

27e ▶ 12 Measuring straight-copy skill

1. Type a 1′ writing on each ¶. Proofread and circle any errors; determine *gwam*.

2. Type two 3′ writings, using both ¶s. Proofread and circle any errors; determine *gwam*.

Goals: 1′—at least 25 *gwam*
3′—at least 21 *gwam*

Difficulty index

all letters used | LA | 1.4 si | 5.4 awl | 85% hfw

gwam 3′

If you think success in an office job is a viable part 4 39
of your future objective, you must realize how essential it 8 43
is to learn to work well with others. With most positions, 12 47
new workers are required to become part of the team swiftly. 16 51

One way to become part of the team, for example, is by 19 55
helping fellow workers with their jobs after finishing your 23 59
own. Helping others in this way works to build the kind of 27 63
group effort that pays off in several ways: in better work 31 67
in your office and in improved chance for promotion for you. 35 71

gwam 3′ | 1 | 2 | 3 | 4 |

28

28a ▶ 7 Preparatory practice

each line 3 times SS (slowly, faster, slowly); DS between 3-line groups

alphabet: Jan Kamen expects to fly to Quebec to visit with Doug Zerba.

adjacent reaches: We sat talking by ruined columns prior to an opera overture.

figure/symbol: Veronica bought 16 7/8 yards of #240 cotton at $3.59 a yard.

easy: Doris always has problems with shorthand, science, and math.

| 1 | 2 | 3 | 4 | 5 | 6 | 7 | 8 | 9 | 10 | 11 | 12 |

124

124a ▶ 5

Preparatory practice

each line 3 times SS (slowly, faster, still faster); retype selected lines as time permits

alphabet	Quivering and almost frozen, the six boys crawled over a jutting peak.
fig/sym	Torres & Sheng paid Invoice #9863 totaling $742.50, less 15% discount.
shift keys	Wally Partins and Janice Appleby went to the Memorial Day Speed Races.
fluency	It is the right and the duty of all citizens to vote in the elections.

| 1 | 2 | 3 | 4 | 5 | 6 | 7 | 8 | 9 | 10 | 11 | 12 | 13 | 14 |

124b ▶ 45

Production measurement: tables

[plain sheets]

Time schedule

Assembling materials ... 3′
Timed production ...... 35′
Final check; compute *n*–*pram* .... 7′

Job 1
Unruled table

Center and type the table DS in cap-and-lowercase form on a full sheet in *reading position*. In the date column, use the last two digits of the current year.

CARBONELL INSURANCE COMPANY — 6
New Policies for Week of July 8-12 — 13

Insured	Date	Policy No.	words
			17/22
DOLORES L. CASTILLO	7/08/--	C-489-B-3905	30
TIEN CHANG	7/10/--	B-644-T-1137	37
MICHI HARADA	7/12/--	A-404-N-8302	43
GLENDOLA L. JUSTIN	7/09/--	B-644-T-1149	51
MARVIN C. KOMOSKI	7/08/--	C-489-B-3905	59
FRANK M. LOCKWOOD	7/11/--	C-489-B-3984	67
SONIA E. NAVARRO	7/10/--	A-404-N-8289	75
EDWARD K. ORLANDO	7/09/--	D-855-M-4450	82
JOSE L. QUINTERO	7/12/--	B-644-T-1205	90
CEOLA J. WASHINGTON	7/11/--	A-404-N-8295	98

Job 2
Ruled table

Center and type the table in double-spaced form on a full sheet in exact vertical center.

LIFE INSURANCE OWNERSHIP IN THE U.S. — 7
(In Millions of Dollars) — 12

Year	Ordinary	Group	Industrial	Total	words
					29
					45
					53
1977	242,842	117,960	6,533	367,335	69
1976	213,784	104,683	6,382	324,849	76
1975	207,052	102,659	6,714	316,452	83
1973	175,629	67,703	7,224	250,556	90
1965	89,643	52,867	7,302	149,812	97
1960	56,183	15,328	6,906	78,417	103
					110
					126

Source: American Council of Life Insurance. 135

Job 3 appears on next page.

28b ▶ 12

Building keystroking speed

1. Type Line 1 for 30″; note the *number* of times you completed the line.

2. Type Line 2 for 30″. Try to complete the line the same *number* of times as Line 1.

3. Retype Line 2 for an additional 30″.

4. Repeat steps 1–3 with Lines 3 and 4, 5 and 6, 7 and 8.

1 We can send this order to our plant in Azusa.
2 Read Items #7, 8, and 9 to me.

3 The bananas, if ripe, can be trucked from Florida.
4 Pay the 6% note on June 3 with $25.

5 Our quotation will exclude freight rates and insurance.
6 She paid J & D's $1,400 note (Check #8).

7 Surely he wants to know much more about those lovely plants.
8 She said that "Old No. 173" left at 6:49 p.m.

| 1 | 2 | 3 | 4 | 5 | 6 | 7 | 8 | 9 | 10 | 11 | 12 |

28c ▶ 8

Typing from script and rough-draft copy

1. Type each ¶. Proofread; mark errors with appropriate proofreader's marks.

2. Type each ¶ from your marked copy. Proofread; circle errors.

Without question, we live in an age of numbers. Ask a question; some number is likely to be the answer. A number is used with a license, student ID, catalog, telephone, etc.

Numbers are ~~often~~ assigned to a good, many other such things, as a street address, a da te, time, or a zip code. When you shop in a story, a number ^often^ detremines your turn to by food. Some day we mighty be using a nubmer instead of a name.

28d ▶ 10

Improving machine parts control

Lines 1-4: Clear all tab stops; set a tab at centerpoint of page (51 for elite, 42 for pica); tab and type as shown.

Line 5: Type word, including comma; backspace, insert any missing *t*; repeat with next word.

Lines 6-8: Use the shift and shift-lock as appropriate. Check each line to make sure that capitals sit on writing line.

Line 9: Depress margin release; backspace 3 spaces into the left margin; type the line. Use the margin release again if needed to complete the line.

tab and return
1 ——————————tab→Reach to the tabulator key or
2 bar without looking up.——tab→Keep your eyes on the book or
3 other source materials.——tab→When you tab without looking,
4 you are learning to type.

backspacer
5 trea , sla e, af er, s ars, s ar er, brigh es , s ree , i em

shift and shift lock
6 In June, the NCAA finals (UCLA vs. MSU) were played in Utah.
7 Myrv and Zelda sang lead roles in CARMEN on Station WRNC-TV.
8 Did Joan Hartig, Lilly Derr, and Lee Dobka join CRTA in May?

margin release
9 Jobs worth doing and friends worth having make life worth living.

Production measurement procedure

For each production measurement activity in this section, follow the procedure given at the right.

1. Remove whatever stationery is supplied in the laboratory material (LM); have plain full sheets available, also.
2. Arrange stationery and plain paper in the order of need in completing the jobs.
3. Place correction supplies in a convenient location.
4. When the signal to begin is given, insert paper and make machine adjustments for the first job. Type as many jobs as you can in the time allowed.
5. Proofread each job and make needed corrections before removing it from the typewriter.
6. When time is called, proofread the final job and circle any uncorrected errors.
7. Compute *n-pram*.

123c ▶ 37 Production measurement: letters

[LM pp. 83–88]

Time schedule

Assembling materials ... 2′
Timed production ...... 30′
Final check; compute *n-pram* .... 5′

Job 1

Executive-size stationery; 1 cc; AMS style; envelope

words

September 5, 19-- Mrs. Joanna Jordan Jordan-Frazier Associates 84 13
West Santa Clara Street San Jose, CA 95113 INVITATION TO ADDRESS 26
AICPA IN DENVER (¶ 1) Mrs. Jordan, one of my business associates 38
heard you speak recently in San Francisco on the topic "Accounting and 52
Tax Reform." He was impressed by both your message and your delivery. 67
(¶ 2) As program director for the next annual convention of the Ameri- 79
can Institute of Certified Public Accountants, I am wondering if you 93
might have the time and inclination to address the Institute on the 107
same topic. The convention is to be held in Denver on April 18-21 at 121
the Denver Hilton Hotel. (¶ 3) If your schedule will permit you to 133
participate in our program, let me know which of the dates is most 146
suitable for you. As a member of AICPA, you know that our honorariums 161
are modest; but they do cover travel expenses with a bit to spare. 174
(¶ 4) May I hear from you soon regarding your availability. ALAN J. 187
WEST--AICPA PROGRAM DIRECTOR xx 193/**209**

Job 2

Standard-size stationery; 1 cc; modified block style, open punctuation; envelope

Job 3

Using Job 2 directions, type a copy of the Job 2 letter to:

Miss Cecilia Mendosa, Director
Pan-American Industries, Inc.
120 Red Jacket Parkway
Buffalo, NY 14220

Delivery date: September 30
Auditors: Miss Georgia Gibbs
Mr. Lu Shen
Office manager: Miss Sue Eads

Job 4

If time permits, retype the letter of Job 1 on a full-size plain sheet.

words

Sept. 5, 19-- Mr. Kenneth J. Rosen, General Agent Rosen 12
& Blackburn Insurance Agency 50 Chestnut Street 22
Rochester, NY 14604 Dear Mr. Rosen (¶1) We are cur- 31
rently in the process of completing the audit that 41
was made of your financial records for the fiscal 51
year ended June 30, 19--. The final audit report 61
should be delivered to your office no later than 71
Sept. 18. (¶2) Our two auditors, Miss Denise Devereaux 82
and Mr. Earl Johnson, reported that their audit 91
procedures were greatly simplified because of the 101
excellent cooperation and courtesy that were ex- 111
tended to them by your office manager, Ms. Lovella 121
Jones. She is to be commended for the professional 132
manner in which she conducted your office during 141
our audit. (¶3) Mr. Rosen, as soon as you have 150
received our audit report, I shall call to make an 160
appointment with you to discuss the audit, our 170
recommendations, and the final billing of the 179
audit fee. Sincerely yours Mrs. Joanna Jordan, 185
CPA Senior Partner 192/**278**

28e ▶ 13
Measuring statistical-copy skill

1. Type a 1′ writing on each ¶. Proofread and circle any errors; determine *gwam*.

2. Type two 3′ writings on both ¶s. Proofread and circle any errors; determine *gwam*.

Goals: 1′—at least 19 *gwam*
3′—at least 14 *gwam*

Difficulty index

all figures used | LA | 1.4 si | 5.4 awl | 85% hfw |

	gwam 3′	
My memo #67-8 mentioned the manager of the Surf & Turf	4	39
(a nightclub at 1139 Zodiac Avenue), who said that her food	8	43
costs are "up 12.4% this year." Her usual <u>daily</u> food bill,	12	48
she said, was $275 last year. She said it's $309 this year.	16	52
Memo #67-8 says on page 3 that a family can save $7 to	20	55
$8 a month by buying bigger quantities of needed goods. To	24	59
buy 12 of something, rather than 4 or 5, can save 9% to 10%	28	63
on food bills (over the months). Another good "tip" to the	32	67
thrifty consumer says, "Buy when things are in high supply."	36	71

gwam 3′ | 1 | 2 | 3 | 4 |

29

29a ▶ 7
Preparatory practice

each line 3 times SS (slowly, faster, still faster); DS between 3-line groups

alphabet Max Jurez worked to improve the quality of his basic typing.

direct reaches Will Ervyn Cerbus agree to bring the check to Brech & Trump?

figure/symbol I said, "My check for $739.50 (#184) is not dated March 26."

easy Claudia has the authority to hire most of the city auditors.

| 1 | 2 | 3 | 4 | 5 | 6 | 7 | 8 | 9 | 10 | 11 | 12 |

29b ▶ 10
Improving keystroking technique

1. Type each line once. Place a checkmark next to lines that seemed difficult or which you could not type without looking for key locations.

2. Retype the lines you checked; work for touch typing.

▶ • eyes on copy
• wrists low
• smooth, continuous typing rate

1 Was Rhyn & Gordon's check (or was it Mr. Jalo's) for $2,500?

2 Wixom & Vee, Inc., gave checks of $350 and $275 to the club.

3 The 10% discount on Bill #1592 for cassettes comes to $7.25.

4 O'Malley doesn't know the difference between "to" and "two."

5 Bev's father said, "Might won't make right!" He's so right.

6 <u>The Master Spy</u> and <u>Decision at Sea</u> are on your reading list.

7 The Sr/C Club walked and/or ran 15 1/2 miles in 6 3/4 hours.

8 My $45 first-class ticket entitles me to an up-to-date room.

| 1 | 2 | 3 | 4 | 5 | 6 | 7 | 8 | 9 | 10 | 11 | 12 |

section

28

Measuring basic/production skills

lessons 123–125

This section is designed to measure your knowledge and skill in performing various typewriting operations: straight copy, letters, reports, business forms, tables, and letters and reports including tables.

Measurement goals

1. To select and organize all needed materials and supplies quickly for efficient use.
2. To plan your work and make machine adjustments efficiently.
3. To type a maximum number of jobs acceptably (errors neatly corrected) in the production time allowed.

Machine adjustments

1. Set paper guide at *0*.
2. Set ribbon control on black.
3. Margins: 70-space line for drills and ¶ writings; as directed (or appropriate) for problems.
4. SS drill lines; DS ¶s; space jobs as directed (or appropriate).

123

123a ▶ 5 Preparatory practice

each line 3 times SS (slowly, faster, still faster); retype selected lines as time permits

alphabet My half dozen flavorful new soup mixes are in big, quick-to-open jars.

fig/sym The only fee for a 52-week course covering 104 basic areas is $987.36.

long reaches She will doubtless receive the five brown carved servers from my aunt.

fluency A profit can come from any problem if the problem is handled properly.

| 1 | 2 | 3 | 4 | 5 | 6 | 7 | 8 | 9 | 10 | 11 | 12 | 13 | 14 |

123b ▶ 8 Straight-copy measurement

one 5′ writing; record *gwam* and number of errors

Difficulty index

all letters used	A	1.5 si	5.7 awl	80% hfw

gwam 5′

What factors determine if an employee will be a success? The three 3 58
basic factors of success on the job are: good technical skills, good 6 61
human relations skills, and a good work attitude. A person must be able 8 64
to exhibit the required technical skills in order to perform in an ade- 11 67
quate manner. Also, the need to get along with other people is equal 14 70
in importance to technical skills. And, even if a person builds good 17 73
technical skills and good human relations skills, a positive feeling 20 75
about the job is still essential in order to be a success. Cognizance 22 78
of these factors plays an important part in attaining success; if any 25 81
one of them is not realized, an employee may feel unsuccessful. 28 84

A person needs to prepare adequately in order to succeed on a job. 31 86
Preparation for a job must start long before the first day at work. A 33 89
part of this preparation is building a job entry-level skill. Also, an 36 92
employee must learn to develop a good, positive interpersonal relation- 39 95
ship with others. This ability to get along well with others is not an 42 98
instinct--much time and effort must be devoted to achieving good human 45 101
relations skills. Finally, an employee should look forward to work with 48 104
pleasure; therefore, a positive attitude towards work must be developed 51 106
if the job is to be rewarding. Remember, anyone can learn to succeed as 54 109
an employee; all it takes is a real desire and work. 56 112

gwam 5′ | 1 | 2 | 3 |

29c ▶ 10
Typing from script

1. Type the ¶ once for practice; proofread; circle errors.

2. Type two 2′ writings; proofread; circle errors. Determine *gwam*.

▶ Read just a bit ahead of what you are typing.

Difficulty index

all figures used	LA	1.4 si	5.4 awl	85% hfw

gwam 2′

The claims seem highly improbable, but you can believe 6 | 35
most of what you hear about the rapid speed of the 9 newest 12 | 41
copiers on the market. Claims for them range from 30 up to 18 | 47
75 or more copies per minute. The new 1284 makes 65 sharp, 24 | 53
uniform copies a minute; and it works for days without stop. 30 | 59

29d ▶ 10
Improving response patterns

each line 3 times: easy lines word by word; difficult lines letter by letter; combination lines with both approaches

▶ Let your eyes tell your fingers to read by word response or letter by letter.

easy
if he is to go with she did the work he may show to show the
Dixie may go to the firm to pay for the forms that Kent got.

difficult
only states jolly daze plump verve join extra upon great him
You exceeded the stated rate; only the street guard saw you.

combination
to do my and the date it is only and they care if he saw the
Dave may look for work as an executive secretary for a firm.

| 1 | 2 | 3 | 4 | 5 | 6 | 7 | 8 | 9 | 10 | 11 | 12 |

29e ▶ 13
Measuring rough-draft skill

1. Type a 1′ writing on each ¶. Proofread and circle any errors; determine *gwam*.

2. Type two 3′ writings, using both ¶s. Proofread and circle any errors; determine *gwam*.

Goals: 1′—at least 20 *gwam*
3′—at least 17 *gwam*

Difficulty index

all letters used	LA	1.4 si	5.4 awl	85% hfw

gwam 1′ | 3′

Having new pro ducts is prized perhaps too much, as a 11 | 4
end in it self. This is a quest for ways to express out 23 | 8
personality inobjects I own. Hardly. We don't like feeling 35 | 12
we are not for real". Our identity is mo st value to us. 47 | 16
Consider autos, for instnance. They are made up by using 11 | 19
facotry method to kep their cost low; but we can get them 23 | 23
ni more than one color, sizes, style or other features that 35 | 27
aim to make an auto Ours. can our jobs pass a similiar test 48 | 32
by giving us the c hance toex press ourself as we are. 59 | 35

122d ▶ 20
Measuring straight-copy typing skill

two 3′ writings for speed and two 5′ writings for accuracy; record *gwam* and number of errors for the more accurate 5′ writing

Difficulty index				
all letters used	A	1.5 si	5.7 awl	80% hfw

gwam 3′ | 5′

A business firm may use one of many letter formats that are in 5 3
use today; but, most companies are using one of the following styles: 9 6
block, modified block, and modified block with paragraphs indented. 14 8
Some companies have now decided to use a letter style that helps them 19 11
to avoid sex bias in their letter writing. That style is a simplified 23 14
letter style, which does not include a salutation, and, therefore, 28 17
does not show the bias against women that was found in the usual salu- 32 19
tations of the past. 34 20

The block style and the simplified style are quite easy to type be- 38 23
cause all parts of both styles begin at the left margin. The major 43 26
difference between the block style and the simplified style is that the 47 28
salutation and the complimentary close are included in the block style 52 31
but are excluded from the simplified format. In addition, the simpli- 57 34
fied letter style always has a subject line; the block style may or 61 37
may not include one. According to one study, the block style is used in 66 40
about a fourth of business firms. The simplified style, however, enjoys 71 43
only limited use. 73 45

The modified block style differs from the block and the simplified 77 46
styles in that the date and the closing lines in the former begin at 81 49
the horizontal center of the paper rather than at the left margin. 86 51
The modified block style--which may use paragraph indention, but more 90 54
often does not--is the most generally used letter style. It results in 95 57
a well-balanced, attractive letter with only a limited amount of time 100 60
spent in operating the tab control to indent the date and closing lines. 105 63

In addition to letter styles, one must make a choice between two 109 65
major styles of punctuating letters--mixed and open. Learn to recognize 114 68
each style. In mixed punctuation style, only a colon after the saluta- 119 71
tion and a comma after the complimentary close are required at the end 123 74
of the lines in the opening and closing parts of the letter. All other 128 77
parts require no end-of-line punctuation. In open style, no end-of-line 133 80
punctuation is used in the opening and closing parts except when a line 138 83
ends with an abbreviation. 140 84

gwam 3′ | 1 | 2 | 3 | 4 | 5 |
5′ | 1 | 2 | 3 |

section **7**

Learning to center data

lessons 30–33

Learning goals

1. To center copy horizontally/vertically.
2. To determine line endings using warning bell.
3. To divide words at line endings.
4. To type announcements and short reports.

Machine adjustments

1. Check chair and desk adjustments and placement of copy for easy reading.
2. Set paper guide at *0*.
3. Set 70-space line (center −35; center +35).
4. Single-space (SS) drills; double-space (DS) paragraphs.

30

30a ▶ 7

Preparatory practice

each line 3 times SS (slowly, faster, still faster); DS between 3-line groups

alphabet Ben Jackson will save the money required for your next big cash prize.

figure Leona Torres moved from 479 East 125th Street to 238 West 60th Street.

adjacent reaches We condemned her notion that power in the past excuses present policy.

easy It is true that the road to the top has many side roads that tempt us.

| 1 | 2 | 3 | 4 | 5 | 6 | 7 | 8 | 9 | 10 | 11 | 12 | 13 | 14 |

30b ▶ 15

Setting the right margin/using the warning bell

full page; exact 70-space line (center − 35; center + 35); DS; 5-space ¶ indention

1. Set margin stops for exact 70-space line.

2. Slowly type the sentence. As soon as the bell rings, type consecutive numbers—1234, etc.—until the carriage locks. The last number typed is the number of spaces between the bell and lock, called the *carriage return area*.

3. Adjust the right margin so the bell will give adequate warning to return. Many typists want the bell to ring 5 spaces before the line ends. To determine your adjustment: Subtract the desired warning (5) from the number counted as your *carriage return area*. Move the right margin farther to the right the resulting number of spaces.

4. Type the ¶s. When bell rings, finish the word you are typing; then return. If the carriage locks, depress the margin release and complete the word.

Sentence

To get a bell cue, add your adjustment figure to the exact-margin figure.

Note
Your line endings will not be the same as those shown below.

Paragraphs

Set the right margin stop to allow for as much framing space on the right as appears on the left, thus centering the line of writing.

When the warning bell sounds, you must decide when to return the carriage and begin a new line. Usually, if the word you are typing can be finished with 5 or fewer additional strokes, finish it; if it can't, the word should be divided. You will learn later to divide words at line endings.

122

122a ▶ 5
Preparatory practice

each line 3 times SS (slowly, faster, slowly); retype selected lines as time permits

alphabet	A good zone trap will quickly exhibit a defensive judgment of players.
fig/sym	I shipped 1,395# of supplies and was billed $2.46/cwt. ($34.32 total).
long reaches	My uncle undoubtedly hunted for hundreds of unknown uniforms annually.
fluency	We should take pride in our work if we have sincerely done our utmost.
	| 1 | 2 | 3 | 4 | 5 | 6 | 7 | 8 | 9 | 10 | 11 | 12 | 13 | 14 |

122b ▶ 10
Improving keystroking precision

each line at least twice without error

direct reaches	I am unable to make any progress on the service contract for my truck.
one-hand	In Kim's opinion, the wages in our trade are in excess of the average.
3d, 4th fingers	We saw at least six fellows who were watching our opening performance.
long words	Please offer your suggestions concerning bibliographic materials used.
	| 1 | 2 | 3 | 4 | 5 | 6 | 7 | 8 | 9 | 10 | 11 | 12 | 13 | 14 |

122c ▶ 15
Building statistical-copy typing skill

two 3′writings for speed and one 5′ writing for accuracy; record *gwam* and number of errors for the 5′ writing

Difficulty index

all letters used	A	1.5 si	5.7 awl	80% hfw

	gwam 3′	5′
The exports to our distributors last year were $1,230,495 as com-	4	3
pared with $356,780 for the last calendar year. This increase of 246.3%,	9	6
or $878,715, was just more than double what had been anticipated. Why	14	9
have our exports gone up so dramatically the past two years? The answer	19	11
is that we work to produce quality goods at very competitive prices.	23	14
We are expecting a sizeable increase next year--perhaps as much as 150%	28	17
above this year's level.	30	18
Just three years ago our profit margin was a mere 8.9%. We decided	34	21
to take a 30% reduction in that margin and at the same time to increase	39	23
the quality of the goods. The decision resulted in an amazing increase	44	26
in our export orders--exports increased 50% in the first quarter alone.	49	29
With this swift increase in demand, our manufacturing costs fell by 13%;	54	32
therefore, we were able to cut our prices by 10%, which made our goods	58	35
more competitive in the export market.	61	37

gwam 3′ | 1 | 2 | 3 | 4 | 5 |
5′ | 1 | 2 | 3 |

30c ▶ 28
Centering lines horizontally

Drill 1

half sheet; DS; begin on Line 12

1. Insert paper with left edge at *0*.

2. Move both margin stops to ends of the scale. Clear all tab stops; set a new stop at center point of the page.

3. From the center point, backspace *once* for each *2* letters, figures, spaces, or punctuation marks in the line.

4. Do not backspace for an odd or leftover stroke at the end of the line.

5. Begin to type where you complete the backspacing.

6. Tab to center point and center each subsequent line.

DR. LARRY SHAVER

TS

announces the relocation of his

DENTAL PRACTICE

in the Briarwoode Medical Center

1775 College Road

742-0662

Drill 2

half sheet; DS; begin on Line 11, center each line; proofread and circle errors

THE MUSICAL ARTS ASSOCIATION

TS

proudly presents

Sergio de la Costa

in concert

Friday evening, March 27, at eight o'clock

Guild Hall

31

31a ▶ 7
Preparatory practice

each line twice SS (slowly, faster); DS between 2-line groups

alphabet	The explorer questioned Jack's amazing story about unknown lava flows.
fig/sym	Chi's Policy #718426 for $49,300 has been renewed for another 5 years.
3d row	We try to treat the young workers as we treat the others in this firm.
easy	The auto firms may ask for my formal audit of their financial records.
	| 1 | 2 | 3 | 4 | 5 | 6 | 7 | 8 | 9 | 10 | 11 | 12 | 13 | 14 |

31b ▶ 10
Using the warning bell/ dividing words

2 half sheets; 60-space line; DS; begin on Line 11

1. Type the ¶. Listen for the bell; divide words as necessary.

2. Before typing the ¶ again, examine the right margin of your finished copy and make any necessary adjustments.

Once you have decided to divide a word, leave as much of that word as you can on the first line; that way, a minimum of guesswork is required of the reader. Hyphened compounds (such as <u>first-class</u> or <u>son-in-law</u>) should be divided only at the point of the hyphen. Compound words written without the hyphen are best divided between the elements of the compound; as, <u>sun-light</u>.

121d ▶ 10
Building rough-draft typing skill

two 3′ speed writings; determine *gwam* on each

Difficulty index

all letters used	A	1.5 si	5.7 awl	80% hfw

gwam 3′

The [free] enter prise system ~~w~~[h]as created much of our ~~present~~ high 4 | 40
standard~~s~~ of living~~s~~. Through competition, consumers have been 8 | 44
given a [prize--a better] ~~good~~ selection of ~~extremely good and~~ high-quality [goods.] ~~mer-~~ 12 | 48
~~chandise.~~ It has [also kept] ~~been able to keep~~ the cost of [most goods and] services well 16 | 52
within the reach of the majority of us. 18 | 55

The market~~'s~~ ~~supply and demand~~ has a large effect on [two of] the 21 | 58
[basic] economic factors[--supply and demand.] nevertheless, just a [quasi-] ~~semi- or partially~~ con- 26 | 63
trolled market may distort ~~or cause changes in~~ [both of] these curves and 30 | 66
~~as a~~ [may] result [in] ~~create~~ an inflexible or frozen market. Of course, 34 | 70
the ~~ideal solution~~ [best situation] is an uncontrolled market. 37 | 73

121e ▶ 20
Measuring straight-copy typing skill

three 5′ writings for accuracy; record *gwam* and number of errors for the most accurate writing

Difficulty index

all letters used	A	1.5 si	5.7 awl	80% hfw

gwam 3′ | 5′

Most people want to make sure their own welfare is being taken 5 | 3
care of properly. This need will embrace such items as job security, 9 | 6
fringe benefits, and final retirement. There are dozens of other items 14 | 8
that could be grouped under personal welfare; but, people can cope with 19 | 11
these other items if the basic three are covered. For most people, per- 24 | 14
sonal welfare means more than acquiring the mere basics of life--food, 28 | 17
clothing, and shelter; they want to be able to afford a few luxuries. 33 | 20

Job security, to some, is recognized as the single most critical 37 | 22
category of these items. If you do not possess good job security, you 42 | 25
may not have adequate fringe benefits and a good retirement program. If 47 | 28
you are like most people, you expect a job that is pleasant and finan- 52 | 31
cially rewarding as well; however, a good environment is ofttimes of more 56 | 34
importance than wages to some people. Your whole outlook on life can be 61 | 37
more positive when there is no significant concern about your job security. 66 | 40

The next category that is of big concern to most workers is fringe 71 | 42
benefits. Some of the most common fringe benefits that we now tend to 75 | 45
expect are health and major medical insurance, sick leave, retirement 80 | 48
paid for by the employer, and adequate vacation and holidays. Even 85 | 51
though wages are often the center of concern for most people, the single 90 | 54
largest item of controversy between workers and employers is the size of 94 | 57
the fringe benefits package that will be paid for by the firm. 99 | 59

Retirement should be a major item of concern to all individuals. 103 | 62
Today, more than ever, the need for well-planned and well-financed 107 | 64
retirement programs is essential. Most of us can expect to spend many 112 | 67
years in retirement; hence, we should begin planning for retirement the 117 | 70
day we begin our very first job. After we have arranged the financial 122 | 73
part of our retirement, we must be just as eager to organize the kinds 126 | 76
of activities in which we can participate when we finally quit working. 131 | 79

gwam 3′ | 1 | 2 | 3 | 4 | 5
5′ | 1 | 2 | 3

31c ▶ 33
Problem typing

full sheet; SS; line: 60; begin on Line 12; DS between items; proofread; circle errors

1. Read the report.

2. Center the main heading; TS; then type first ¶.

3. After typing the first line of the first numbered item, reset the left margin stop 4 spaces to the right. To type subsequent numbers, depress the margin release and backspace 4 spaces. Move the margin stop back to its original position to type the last ¶.

words

DIVIDING WORDS 3

TS

A word is divided at the end of a line in order to keep the 15
lines as nearly equal in length as possible. Divided words, 27
however, tend to be more difficult to read than undivided 39
words; so good judgment is needed. The following guides can 51
help you make decisions about word division. 60

2 spaces ↓ Reset margin

1. When a word is to be divided, it should be divided only 72
between syllables; as, friend-ship. 82

Use margin release; backspace 4 spaces

2. A word such as through that has only one syllable cannot 95
be divided. Words of five or fewer letters with two or 107
more syllables, such as prior or ideal, are not divided. 120

3. Regardless of the length of the word, do not divide a one- 133
letter syllable from the first part of a word; as, e-vent 145
or i-dentify. A two-letter syllable occurring at the end 159
of a word should not be separated from the rest of the 170
word; as, identi-fy or poor-ly. The hyphen itself occu- 184
pies one of the spaces to be saved. 192

4. Words that contain double consonants are usually divided 204
between consonants; as, mil-lion. If a final consonant is 217
doubled to add a suffix, divide between the double letters; 229
as, begin-ning or stop-ping. On the other hand, if a word 245
ending in double letters has a suffix attached, divide 256
after the double letters; as, press-ing. 266

5. Words containing an internal single vowel which is a syl- 278
lable should be divided after that syllable; as, sepa-rate. 292
However, if the single letter syllables a, i, and u are 303
followed by the ending syllables bly, ble, cle, or cal, 315
divide before those syllables; as, flex-ible. 326

6. When two one-letter syllables occur together within a word, 339
divide between the one-letter syllables; as, gradu-ation. 352

Reset margin

Word division demands discretion as well as know-how. When 364
you have doubts about how to divide a word (and you will), a 376
good dictionary or word-division manual can help you solve the 389
problem quickly. 392

32

32a ▶ 7
Preparatory practice

each line twice SS (slowly, faster); DS between 2-line groups

alphabet Gladys and John quickly won several prizes at the Foxburgh track meet.

figure The test on March 26 will cover the contents of pages 14-59 and 70-83.

1st row Max and Mona Bench expect to be in breezy Vera Cruz, Mexico, next May.

easy They may find that one element of the problem is difficult to analyze.

| 1 | 2 | 3 | 4 | 5 | 6 | 7 | 8 | 9 | 10 | 11 | 12 | 13 | 14 |

section

27

Improving basic skills

lessons 121–122

Learning goals

Because accuracy is a major goal of basic skill development, you should be able to type at one of the following rates on a 5-minute straight-copy timing of average difficulty with 8 errors or fewer: 56 *gwam*, excellent: 51-55 *gwam*, good; 43-50 *gwam*, acceptable.

The minimum goal in this section should be between 43-50 *gwam* with fewer than 8 errors.

Machine adjustments

1. Set paper guide at *0*.
2. Set ribbon control on black.
3. Use a 70-space line and single spacing (SS) for drills.
4. Use a 70-space line, double spacing (DS), and 5-space ¶ indentions for paragraph copy.

121

121a ▶ 5
Preparatory practice

each line 3 times SS (slowly, faster, slowly); retype selected lines as time permits

alphabet	Jodie Quinwall packages frozen vegetables for shipment by REA Express.
fig/sym	Order #425719 from Frank & Robb for 3,600 pens was filled on August 8.
hyphen	Submit an up-to-date account of your mother-in-law's May transactions.
fluency	If our work is worth doing, it is worth doing as well as we can do it.

| 1 | 2 | 3 | 4 | 5 | 6 | 7 | 8 | 9 | 10 | 11 | 12 | 13 | 14 |

121b ▶ 5
Improving keystroking precision

each line at least once without error

left hand	The best rewards at a drag race are for the fast cars and eager crews.
right hand	In my opinion, no nylon from our nonunion mills was used in my kimono.
bottom row	Zebras can be made to run very quickly when frightened by loud noises.
third row	You tried to wire your sister yesterday; perhaps you should try today.

| 1 | 2 | 3 | 4 | 5 | 6 | 7 | 8 | 9 | 10 | 11 | 12 | 13 | 14 |

121c ▶ 10
Building script-copy typing skill

two 3′ writings for speed; determine *gwam* on each

Difficulty index

all letters used | A | 1.5 si | 5.7 awl | 80% hfw |

gwam 3′

If the earth is to stay a beautiful and productive 3 37
globe, we must do our part to protect its environment. 7 41
With the increased population, conservation must be the 11 45
key word for just about every citizen if we are to con- 14 48
tinue to experience a quality life. 17 51
We are in a world of technology. Rather than being 20 54
independent, we are quickly becoming more and more depen- 24 58
dent upon one another and the environment. We are not 28 62
generalists; we are now exceedingly specialized -- most of 31 65
us are trained to do but one major job. 34 68

32b ▶ 10
Using the warning bell/ dividing words

2 half sheets; DS; begin on Line 11

Type the ¶ twice, dividing words as necessary. Proofread and circle errors after each writing.

There are more guides to word division that you should keep in mind. For example, do not divide abbreviations, numbers, or contractions. Avoid dividing proper names or dates whenever possible. If this type of division becomes unavoidable, do divide the name before the surname and the date between the day and year. Also, do not divide the last word on a page.

32c ▶ 13
Centering problems vertically

half sheet; DS

1. Count all typed and blank lines used for the copy at right.

2. Subtract these lines from 33, which is the number of lines on a half sheet. (Paper 11" long can accommodate 66 lines.) The result is unused lines.

3. Divide unused lines by 2 to distribute them as top and bottom margins. Disregard fractions.

4. To leave the exact blank space, space down from the top edge of the paper 1 more line than the number of lines figured for the top margin. (This centers material in *exact vertical center*.)

5. Center each line horizontally.

words

VERTICAL CENTERING 4

TS

Count the lines to be centered. 10

DS

Count 2 for the triple space after the heading. 20

Count 1 for each blank line space for double-spaced lines. 32

Subtract total lines from 66 (full sheet) or 33 (half sheet). 45

Divide the result by 2 for top margin. 53

If a fraction results, disregard it. 60

Space down that number plus 1. 66

32d ▶ 20
Problem typing

Problem 1

On a half sheet, type the announcement at the right DS. Center each line horizontally and the entire announcement vertically. Proofread; circle errors.

Problem 2

On a full sheet, type the announcement at the right DS. Center each line horizontally and the entire announcement vertically in reading position. Proofread; circle errors.

Reading Position

For *reading position*, which is positioned 2 lines higher than exact vertical center, subtract 2 from the exact top margin. Reading position is used only for full sheets (or half sheets with long edge at the left).

words

THE LEON ABRUZZI GALLERY 5

TS

takes great pleasure in announcing 12

as its Spring Gala showing 17

an exhibition of paintings 23

by the eminent American artist 29

Elaine Collingwood 33

Monday, April third, two until ten 40

One Elgard Place 43

Addis Ababa (Ethiopia) Project.

The current Project Director, Mr. Frank P. Condi, will be leaving his position as of May 15, 19--. The Addis Ababa project is well ahead of schedule, perhaps as much as two months. The Ethiopian Customs Division has been extremely pleased with the progress that has been made during the past two years. ~~Our new~~ but his replacement as Project Director, Mr. Carlos V. Rosini, is an expert at implementation of customs procedures for developing countries. Mr. Rosini is expected to arrive in Addis Ababa on May 11, 19--.

Blantyre (Malawi) Project. The Blantyre project is responsible for reorganization of the Malawi Ministry of Agriculture; the project is in its final phase. The last month's project report indicated that the four-month extension would be sufficient to complete the project. Unless some unforeseen circumstance occurs, this project should be completed by June 1, 19--. Miss Koski thinks that the Malawi Ministry of agriculture will propose another project as soon as the current project is completed.

Cario (Egypt) Project. The Cario project was started ~~only~~ two weeks ago; therefore, only the initial orientation of team members has taken place.

Nairobi (Kenya) Project. The Nairobi Project ended during this past month. All project team members have departed Kenya, and the final report has been delivered to the Kenyan Ministry of Health. A final courtesy visit will be made to the Minister of Health on May 17, 19--.

Lusaka (Zambia) Project. Phase I of the Lusaka project has been completed, and Phase II has had a very encouraging start. Phase II is the development of a five-year plan for the National Railroad System; and our new transportation engineer, Mrs. Sophia Gonzales, is making good progress toward the completion of this project.

Pending Project

The Riyadh (Saudi Arabia) Project will ~~be finished when~~ start after the contrat is signed in Riyadh on May 5, 19--. This project will be a five-year public administration project; it is scheduled to begin September 1.

33

33a ▶ 7

Preparatory practice

each line twice SS (slowly, faster); DS between 2-line groups

alphabet	Maxwell Jacks gave the lovely box as a prize to our "Queen for a Day."
fig/sym	Interest accumulated to $240.56 in 1978 when the rate increased by 3%.
home row	Did Dale Flagg laugh after Sally asked that she look at the joke book?
easy	The auditors said a generous gift had been sent to the endowment fund.

| 1 | 2 | 3 | 4 | 5 | 6 | 7 | 8 | 9 | 10 | 11 | 12 | 13 | 14 |

33b ▶ 10

Vertical centering: backspace-from-center method

half sheet; DS; center each line horizontally; center invitation vertically

1. The vertical center of a full sheet (66 lines) is Line 34; of a half sheet (33 lines), Line 17.

2. From the vertical center of the paper, roll the platen (cylinder) back one line for each two lines, either typed or blank, in the problem. Disregard a leftover line.

	words
THE QUICK STOP SHOP	4
TS	
announces	6
it's Grand Opening	10
Friday, May 27th	13
4190 South Leonard Drive	18
Quincy	19
gifts, refreshments, prizes	24

33c ▶ 10

Centering data on special-size paper

half sheet, short side up (long side at paper guide); DS; begin on Line 22; center information requested on each line

To find the horizontal center of special-size paper or cards

1. Insert the paper or card into the machine. From the line-of-writing scale, add the numbers at the left and right edges of the paper.

2. Divide this sum by 2. The result is the horizontal center point for that size paper.

The name of your college (all caps)

The street address

The city and state address

Your name

Today's date

33d ▶ 23

Problem typing

1. Center the problem vertically and horizontally on a 5" x 3" card (Laboratory Materials [LM] p. 13); proofread; circle errors.

2. Type the problem again, this time on a 6" x 4" card [LM p. 13].

3. Type 33c above on a 6" x 4" card [LM p. 13].

Reminder: There are 6 horizontal lines to a vertical inch. A 3" card, therefore, holds 18 lines.

	words
It's that time again!	6
TS	
THE NINTH ANNUAL MEDWIN BOOSTER CLUB	13
ox roast and barbecue	18
Friday, October 27	22
Medwin Memorial Field	26

117b-120b, continued

Job 7
Three-page report

Mr. Gabre-Mariam made a pasteup of his monthly status report. Type this report as a leftbound manuscript. The photocopy machine is not working today; therefore, prepare 1 cc for the file.

½"

DS> Monthly Status Report 10
on Middle East and East Africa Projects 19 >all Capitals

This report includes the eight current projects in the Middle East and East Africa. There are three projects in the Middle East and five projects in East Africa.

Middle Eastern Projects

~~There are~~ The three projects are located ~~currently in progress~~ in the Middle East ~~"one each"~~ in Jordan, Syria, and Lebanon.

Amman (Jordan) Project.

This project is now in its final phase. The final report to the Jordanian Government will be completed and ready for submission by July 1, 19--.

Damascus (Syria) Project. Progress at the Damascus project site has been impeded by a major problem during the past month; the subcontractor (R.P. Conrad Co.) for the civil service wage and salary classification study has had difficulty obtaining ~~current~~ data about the current government wage and salary classification system. The subcontractor indicates that this part of the project may require two additional months to complete because of "red tape."

1½" 1"

The urban planning phase of the project is on schedule. The preliminary specifications for a five-year urban plan have been completed, and the actual writing of the document should take about ~~one~~ a month to complete. The rural planning phase has just begun and appears to be progressing according to our plan.

Beirut (Lebanon) Project. The Beirut project with the Lebanese Tourist Agency is nearly 50 percent completed. All of the planning has been done, and the new tourist strategies have been formulated. Next month the project team will begin assisting the Lebanese Tourist Agency with the implementation of the new plan.

East African Projects

The five projects ~~were~~ in progress during the past month in East Africa are located ~~"one each"~~ in Ethiopia, Malawi, Egypt, Kenya, and Zambia.

1"

Job 7 continued on page 242

Supplemental skill-building practice

Measuring statistical-copy skill

one 3′ and one 5′ writing; determine *gwam*; proofread and verify; circle errors

all letters, figures, symbols used

Difficulty index

LA	1.4 si	5.4 awl	85% hfw

gwam 3′ | 5′

On April 24, last year, I purchased a new Bell & Graf motor and boat 5 | 3
from you. According to our agreement, I paid $2,500 for the motor and 9 | 6
boat, less 12% cash discount. While I like this equipment, I want to 14 | 8
trade the motor for one with more power (perhaps a 75-horsepower motor 19 | 11
would meet my needs). The service number of my motor is #876/A/93. It 24 | 14
is important to me, however, that I make this exchange--at once. 28 | 17

Time is important because I plan to move from this immediate area 32 | 19
within the next 60 days and hope to have a larger motor before I leave. 37 | 22
To expedite the matter, I have checked Justin's Boating Guide; and I 42 | 25
find it shows (as Item #98) a 75-horsepower "Blue King" motor priced at 47 | 28
$1,300 that I like. Do you have that size motor in stock? If we can 51 | 31
reach agreement on a trade, will you allow me a 12% discount if I pay 56 | 33
any difference in cash? 57 | 34

gwam 3′ | 1 | 2 | 3 | 4 | 5 |
5′ | 1 | 2 | 3 |

Measuring straight-copy skill

one 3′ and one 5′ writing; determine *gwam*; proofread; circle errors

all letters used

Difficulty index

LA	1.4 si	5.4 awl	85% hfw

gwam 3′ | 5′

Let's talk about hard work. There appears to be an area of our 4 | 3
culture that says: Work hard, and you will in time be rewarded with 9 | 5
something known as success. When we are young, therefore, we set out to 14 | 8
find success by educating ourselves for a career. After that, we seek 18 | 11
for just the right opportunity in which to expend our efforts. Then, the 23 | 14
best advice seems to be: Work hard. If the plot turns out right, 27 | 16
success is ours. 29 | 17

There is no question about the value of hard work, and we should 33 | 20
expect to do our share of it. Rather, the important question is: What 38 | 23
shall we work hard to gain? Ultimately, each of us must arrive at her 43 | 26
or his own definition of success; and when we do, we shall realize what 48 | 29
is important in our lives. Failing to define what success means to us 52 | 31
allows others to define it for us. When that happens, we find ourselves 57 | 34
working hard to meet other people's standards of success. 61 | 37

gwam 3′ | 1 | 2 | 3 | 4 | 5 |
5′ | 1 | 2 | 3 |

117b-120b, continued

Job 5
Composing a letter on executive-size stationery
[LM p. 73]

Mr. Gabre-Mariam asks you to compose for his signature a letter to Mr. Nabil Toubassy, our Lebanese Project Director. Inform Mr. Toubassy that our Controller, George Franklin, wired a fund transfer of $125,000 on March 21, 19—, from the City National Bank in New York to his project account at the City National Bank of Beirut.

Ask him to acknowledge receipt of this fund transfer. Also, tell him that Mr. Gabre-Mariam is tentatively scheduled to arrive in Beirut on April 25; you will confirm the date later. Use a P.S. to tell Mr. Toubassy that Mr. Gabre-Mariam received his monthly report on time.

Toubassy, Nabil (Mr.)

Mr. Nabil Toubassy
Project Director
International Management, Inc.
114 Hamra Street
Hamra P.O. Box 379
Beirut, Lebanon

Job 6
Rough-draft letter on executive-size stationery with bpc notation
[LM p. 75]

You are to type the edited copy of a letter that you typed in rough-draft form for Mr. Gabre-Mariam. He has made all the necessary corrections. Send a bpc to Miss Carin Young.

Dugaither, Fahad (Mr.)

Mr. Fahad Dugaither
Director General
Institute of Public
  Administration
Ministry of Finance
P.O. Box 928
Riyadh, Saudi Arabia

Dear Mr. Dugaither:

I was ~~indeed~~ pleased to receive your letter and *to* learn that the contract *for the Public Administration Project* is ready to be signed. ¶ I will be in the middle east the first part of ~~April~~ *May*; therefore, your suggestion that I come to *Riyadh* ~~Saudi Arabia~~ to sign the contract *on May 5, 19--,* is acceptable to me. I shall make reservations at the Sahara Palace hotel. ¶ The project *team* ~~members~~ will arrive in Riyadh by ~~the first of~~ September *1* to begin the *preliminary review* ~~project~~. This *initial* team will consist of 15 people: a project director, two assistant directors, and 12 management consultants. In order for the project to progress *smoothly* ~~on schedule~~, office space should be provided in the Institute Building. We will need a suite of offices with a private office for the project director, a reception area, and adjoining space to accommodate the two assistant directors and the *in staff of* 12 consultants. I can take care of these *arrangements* ~~matters~~ when I come to Riyadh in May.

Sincerely,

section

8 Typing business correspondence

lessons 34–39

Learning goals

1. To type business letters in block and modified block styles.
2. To align typewritten characters and type over them.
3. To address envelopes.
4. To improve composing skill.
5. To type carbon copies.

Machine adjustments

1. Check chair and desk adjustment and placement of copy for ease of reading.
2. Set paper guide at *0*.
3. Set 70-space line.
4. Set ribbon control on black.
5. Single-space (SS) drills; double-space (DS) paragraphs.

34

34a ▶ 7 Preparatory practice

each line twice SS (slowly, faster); DS between 2-line groups

alphabet Gwendolyn Austin lives in a quiet area six blocks from the Jasper zoo.

fig/sym Wang & Dwyer's $623.75 check (Check 1489) was delivered on January 10.

1st/2d fingers As Frederick Vertman hinted, they were regarded as tame but untrained.

easy He may work for many days on the eight forms for the city light panel.

| 1 | 2 | 3 | 4 | 5 | 6 | 7 | 8 | 9 | 10 | 11 | 12 | 13 | 14 |

34b ▶ 10 Composing and typing

2 half sheets; 1″ top margin; 50-space line; DS; 5-space ¶ indention

1. Type the sentences in ¶ form, inserting the needed information. Line endings will differ from those in the copy. Do not correct errors.

2. When you have completed the ¶s, remove the paper, make pencil corrections, and retype the ¶s. Proofread; correct errors.

(¶ 1) My name is (your name). My home address is (street number and name or P.O. box, city, state, and ZIP Code). I am a student at (name of your school) in (city and state). I am now living at (street address, dormitory, or other).

(¶ 2) The brand name of the typewriter I use is (type the brand name). I type at approximately (state the rate in figures) gwam. My greatest difficulty seems to be (name one, as: too many errors, not enough speed, poor techniques, lack of confidence).

34c ▶ 33 Typing problems: business letters in block style

1 letterhead [LM p. 19]

1. Study Style Letter 1 on page 63.

2. Type a copy of the letter, following directions given on the letter; proofread; circle errors.

3. Type three 2′ writings on opening lines and ¶1 on plain paper. Begin with the paper out of the machine. Estimate placement of the date; move quickly from part to part to improve your speed.

Business letter placement information

Good letter placement results from an acquired ability to make responsible decisions based on the length of the letter, style of stationery, and size of type.

All business letters in Section 8 are full size (8½″ x 11″) and of average length. Average-length letters fit well on a 60-space line; and the date line usually begins on Line 15, which is 2½″ from the top of the page. This placement is recommended for letters in Section 8.

It is standard procedure to return the carriage 4 times (leaving 3 blank lines) below the date and above the letter address. This procedure is repeated after the complimentary close, leaving 3 blank line spaces where the signature is to be written. These placement procedures should be followed with all letters.

The initials of the typist may be shown at the left margin DS below the title. In Section 8 problems, reference initials are indicated by *xx*; you should substitute your own initials.

Remember that an attractive appearance is an essential aspect of business letters. All proofreading and correcting must be expertly done if a letter is to have the desired effect. Remember, too, that every letter you type must have a return address. Most business letters have a printed return address, or *letterhead*; and a return address is not typed on the lines preceding the data, as is the case with most personal letters. If plain paper is used to type practice letters, it should be assumed to have a letterhead.

117b-120b, continued

Job 4
Employment agreement

Mr. Gabre-Mariam filled in the necessary information on the standard employment agreement form. Use 1" top and side margins. You will need to prepare 3 copies—an original and 2 copies. The original and one copy will be enclosed with the letter to Mr. Rosini. The extra copy will be attached to the file copy of Mr. Rosini's letter.

↓ 1"

EMPLOYMENT AGREEMENT 10

This is an employment agreement between INTERNATIONAL MANAGEMENT, INC., New York City, and Carlos V. Rosini, Denver, Colorado, who has been hired as Ethiopian Project Director, on the contract project between INTERNATIONAL MANAGEMENT, INC., and the Ethiopian Tourist Organization. Employment shall be for two years, but may be extended by mutual consent of both parties.

INTERNATIONAL MANAGEMENT agrees to pay Carlos V. Rosini a net annual salary of $ 36,000 (after all Ethiopian and U.S. taxes have been paid). On the first day of each month, $ 3,000 will be deposited in his/~~her~~ U.S. bank account.

INTERNATIONAL MANAGEMENT agrees to pay or provide the following fringe benefits for Carlos V. Rosini while employed in Ethiopia:

1. A furnished ~~apartment~~/house.
2. Utility costs for the ~~apartment~~/house.
3. A/~~An~~ new automobile.
4. Educational expenses for dependent children through the 12th grade.
5. Full coverage, non-deductible medical insurance coverage for accompanying family members. ← 1"
6. A $ 200,000 life insurance policy on Carlos V. Rosini.
7. Tourist-class air transportation to and from Addis Ababa, Ethiopia for immediate family members.
8. A $ 150 per diem for 4 days to and from Ethiopia.
9. Storage of personal/household goods to 10,000 kg.
10. Professional packing of personal/household goods stored and shipped to and from Addis Ababa, Ethiopia.
11. Shipping of personal/household goods to and from Addis Ababa, Ethiopia, not to exceed 1,000 kg of airfreight and 5,000 kg of surface freight.
12. A four-week rest period outside Ethiopia for all members of the family as follows:
    a. Tourist-class air transportation to and from Athens, Greece, or equivalent expenses.
    b. A $ 150 per diem for family expenses.
13. Reimbursement for any emergency travel expenses related to the death of any member of the immediate family--including the parents of Mr. or Mrs. Carlos V. Rosini.

Carlos V. Rosini agrees to report as the Project Director of the Ethiopian Project on May 1, 19__, in Addis Ababa, Ethiopia.

Carlos V. Rosini	Yosef Gabre-Mariam Executive Vice President
Date:	Date: March 20, 19--

SMS
the society of management specialists
24 EAST BROADWAY
SALT LAKE CITY, UT 84111
(801) 221-3212

		gwam 2'	total words
Dateline	January 24, 19-- Line 15	2	3
	Operate return 4 times		
	Mr. Grady M. Decker	4	7
Letter	AFT Laboratories	5	11
address	407 Groton Street	7	14
	Hartford, CT 06106	9	18
	DS		
Salutation	Dear Mr. Decker	11	21
	DS		
Body of	Because I have worked previously with a company similar to	17	33
letter	yours, Mr. Lehman asked me to respond to your inquiry about	23	45
	typing letters in the block style.	26	52
	This letter, Mr. Decker, is an example of one that has been	6	64
	typed in block style. Notice that <u>all</u> lines, including the	12	76
	date, have been "blocked"; that is, they begin at the left	18	88
	margin. Because it requires fewer machine manipulations, this	24	101
	style is considered very efficient and economical.	29	111
	The spacing between parts of business letters is standard and	36	123
	should be carefully observed. Notice the placement of this	42	135
	average length letter. For a short or long letter, the date	48	148
	is raised or lowered and the length of writing line changed.	54	160
	I am happy to enclose our booklet on the subject of letter	6	172
	styles and special features of business letters.	11	181
	DS		
Complimentary close	Sincerely yours	12	185
	Operate return 4 times		
	June Hayman		
Typed name	Ms. June Hayman	14	188
Official title	Consultant	15	190
	DS		
Reference initials	abt	15	191
	DS		
Enclosure notation	Enclosure	16	193

Shown in pica type

Style letter 1: business letter in block style, open punctuation

117b-120b, continued

Job 3
Two-page letter
[LM pp. 67–70]

Mr. Gabre–Mariam dictated a letter to you and asked that you type a rough-draft copy so that he could edit it and make changes, if necessary. Now, he has edited the letter and has asked that you prepare the final copy for his signature on executive-size stationery with enclosures.

Mr. Rosini's personal calling card is shown below:

CARLOS V. ROSINI
4809 Syracuse Street
Denver, CO 80216

303-241-3075

March 20, 19--

Dear Mr. Rosini:

Thank you for coming to New York to ~~meet~~ *visit* with us ~~in regards to~~ *about* the project director's position in ~~Addis Ababa,~~ Ethiopia. ~~As soon as we receive your~~ *If you will send us a statement of* expenses for your New York trip, *we shall send you* a reimbursement check ~~will be sent to you~~ immediately. ¶ Our Executive Committee has reviewed your applications and has authorized me to offer you this position at an annual *net* salary of $36,000. (Our firm will guarantee your *net* salary to be $36,000 after the payment of all *Ethiopian and U.S.* taxes.) In addition to the annual salary, the fringe benefits *package* includes comples *tely* furnished housing, ~~all~~ utilities, ~~an~~ automobile, educational allowances for your ~~kids,~~ *children* and *medical and* life insurance protection. ¶ If you accept this offer, you should plan to report for work in Addis Ababa on May 1, 19--. Please sign *and date* both copies of the enclosed employment agreement; keep the duplicate copy for your files and return the original copy to me *within five days by certified mail.* ¶ We hope that you will accept this offer and that we may have a long and successful association with you as the Project Director of our Ethiopian project.

Sincerely,

Also, once each year your entire family will be entitled to four weeks of vacation outside Ethiopia. This four-week rest period will include payment of the round-trip air transportation from Addis Ababa to Athens (or some other city of equivalent distance) and a $150 per diem for family expenses. Any additional expenses incurred during this four-week rest period will be assumed by you.

35

35a ▶ 7

Preparatory practice

each line 3 times SS (slowly, faster, slowly); DS between 3-line groups

alphabet With a fixed goal in mind, quickly size up a job before making a move.

figure Our latest inventory includes 958 rings, 3,064 pins, and 172 brooches.

shift keys Send Marshall & Filarb ten copies of THE NEW LOOK by Hahn and Santana.

easy Of those major elements, I knew which one had the most value for Rosa.

| 1 | 2 | 3 | 4 | 5 | 6 | 7 | 8 | 9 | 10 | 11 | 12 | 13 | 14 |

35b ▶ 15

Correcting errors

1. Read the information at the right about error correction.

2. Type the lines below the information as they appear DS; correct the errors after you have typed each line.

An error should be corrected as soon as it has occurred, and typists often know at once when they have mistyped. To be absolutely certain that no error goes uncorrected, however, the typist should proofread all typewritten material before it is removed from the typewriter. Correcting errors while the paper is still in the typewriter is easier than reinserting the paper and realigning the typing line to do so.

There are a number of ways that typographical errors can be corrected, and several of the more common procedures are explained below. Whichever method is used should be used with the following points in mind:

Evidence that an error was made must be removed without damaging either the paper or any other typed material.

The remedy must be skillfully used; a correction should not be obvious.

If a rubber eraser is used, abrasive bits of rubber must be kept out of the typewriter mechanism.

Rubber Eraser

1. Use a plastic shield (to protect surrounding type) and a typewriter (hard) eraser.

2. Turn the paper forward or backward in the typewriter to position the error for easy correction.

3. Move the carriage far enough to the right or left that rubber particles will not fall into the machine. If the typewriter has an element instead of a carriage, space the carrier away from the error so that crumbs will not fall on the element.

4. Return to the typing line; make the correction.

Correction Paper

1. Backspace to the error.

2. Place the correction paper in front of the error, coated side toward the paper.

3. Retype the error. The substance on the correction paper will cover the error.

4. Backspace; type the correction.

Correction Fluid

1. Be sure the color of the fluid matches the color of the paper.

2. Turn the paper forward or backward to ease the correction process.

3. Brush the fluid on sparingly; cover only the error, and it lightly.

4. The fluid dries quickly. Return to typing position and type the correction.

1 Sometimrs your fingers can tell you when you have make a typing error.

2 Whenever thst happens, stop ty;ing immediately and correct your error.

3 It is not always wise ot trust the fongers to tell you about mistakes.

4 Proofread all work carefilly before you remobe it from the typewriter.

5 The accuracy of your typing will reflict the accuracy of your messate.

117-120

117a-120a ▶ 5

Preparatory practice

Type as many times as you can in 5′ at the beginning of each practice session during this section.

alphabet Max Zwick--a very quiet, friendly person--joined the new jogging club.

fig/sym The total of 5 clocks at $94.39 and 10 chairs at $167.80 is $2,149.95.

shift key Sam Moser drove to Salt Lake City, Utah, from Ottumwa, Iowa, in April.

fluency The sale of the antique chairs is a problem of profit for the auditor.

| 1 | 2 | 3 | 4 | 5 | 6 | 7 | 8 | 9 | 10 | 11 | 12 | 13 | 14 |

117b-120b ▶ 45

Office work simulation

Job 1

Memorandum [LM p. 63]

Mr. Gabre–Mariam hands you a sheet of note paper on which he has written a memo. He asks you to type the memo to Sarah Jones, Personnel Director. Today is March 20. The subject of the memo is: Affirmative Action Program. Remember, Mr. Gabre–Mariam prefers to have his title typed after his name on all memos for which the business title is typed after the name of the addressee.

The Executive Committee met this morning to consider the new affirmative action program that you submitted. The Executive Committee was pleased with this new program and approved it with only a few minor changes.

I was asked by the Executive Committee to congratulate you for the outstanding work you did in developing the new affirmative action program. The Committee is confident that our firm will be able to accomplish significant improvement in our future efforts to achieve positive results in the recruitment of individuals from protected classes.

Mrs. Franco will make an appointment with you to explain the Committee's rationale for making a few changes in the program.

Again, Congratulations!

(Note: Send pc to Mrs. Julia Franco)

Job 2

Composing a memorandum [LM p. 65]

Mr. Gabre–Mariam asks you to compose a memorandum to all administrative heads. The content of the memo is given to you in sketchy outline form. The required number of copies will be made on the photocopy machine. Date the memo March 20, 19—.

1. Administrative heads staff meeting, March 27, 3 p.m.
2. Purpose of meeting: Present and discuss the new affirmative action program.
3. Inform all heads that they will receive copies of the new program on Mar. 23.
4. If anyone has questions that need to be answered before the March 27 meeting, talk with ~~Julia~~ Sarah Jones.
5. Sarah Jones, Personnel Director, will give the formal presentation at the meeting.

35c ▶ 8
Composing and typing

2 full sheets; 2″ top margin; 50-space line; DS

1. Center your name horizontally; then TS.

2. Type complete sentences to answer the questions.

3. Make pencil corrections on your composition; then retype it. Proofread; correct errors.

1. How long have you been studying at your school?
2. What is major? and your minor?
3. When do you plan to finish your formal schooling?
4. What plans have you made for your professional future after you finish college?

35d ▶ 20
Problem typing: business letters in block style

2 letterheads [LM pp. 21–24] see page 62 for letter placement directions; use current date

Problem 1

Type the letter; proofread and correct your copy before removing it from the typewriter.

words

(Current date) | Mr. Paul V. Castillo | Rugby & Company | 11934 Barrington 14
Avenue | Cleveland, OH 44108 | Dear Mr. Castillo (¶ 1) I am happy to send 26
you the following information about using personal and professional titles in 42
business letters. (¶ 2) When writing a business letter, it is a matter of cour- 57
tesy always to precede the name of the addressee with a personal title, such 72
as Mr. or Miss, in the letter address and in the salutation when it contains a 89
surname. Such professional titles as Doctor, Professor, and Reverend may be 109
used instead of the personal titles. (¶ 3) In letter closings, a personal or pro- 124
fessional title should not precede a man's name in the signature. When re- 139
sponding to such a letter and doubt exists about the man's exact title, it is 155
well to remember that Mr. is usually correct and is, in fact, preferred over 170
an incorrect guess. (¶ 4) A personal or professional title isn't required with a 186
woman's name in the closing lines of a letter. A woman writer, however, 200
shows consideration for the reader when she types her title before her typed 216
name or when she writes it (in parentheses) before her signature to indicate 231
her preference. Sincerely yours | Ms. June Hayman | Consultant | xx 243

Problem 2

Follow directions given for Problem 1.

words

(Current date) | Miss Grace Ashmyer | Office Manager | Aymes-Erb-Fargo 13
Company | 6711 Garvin Street | Orlando, FL 32803 | Dear Grace (¶ 1) Your 25
question about using abbreviations in letter addresses is quite an interesting 41
one; and you are right, I do have an opinion on the subject. (¶ 2) Personal and 56
professional titles (Mrs., Dr.) are almost always abbreviated. A directional 73
word, on the other hand, is spelled in full when it precedes the noun 86
(15 North Hume Street) unless full spelling makes the line unduly long. If the 103
directional word follows the noun, however, it is typically abbreviated 118
(127 Hazel Street, N.). (¶ 3) The U.S. Postal Service encourages the use of the 133
two-letter ZIP abbreviations (without periods or spaces) for state names. 148
These abbreviations, however, may be used only with ZIP Codes. If the ZIP 163
abbreviation is unknown, the standard abbreviation may be used. (¶ 4) I en- 177
joyed receiving your letter from Florida, Grace. I hope my opinions are 191
helpful. | Sincerely | Ms. June Hayman | Consultant | xx 201

section

26

Typing in an executive office

lessons 117–120

Section 26 is designed to provide the kinds of typing activities you would expect to encounter when working in an executive office.

Supplies needed

memorandum forms [LM pp. 63-66]
or plain full sheets
letterheads [LM pp. 67-76]
or plain full sheets
full sheets; second sheets; carbon sheets; envelopes of appropriate size

Machine adjustments

1. Check chair and desk adjustments and placement of copy for easy reading.
2. Set paper guide at *0*.
3. Set ribbon control on black.
4. Margins: 70-space line for drills and ¶ writings; as directed (or appropriate) for problems.
5. SS line drills; DS ¶s; space problems as directed (or appropriate).

Daily practice plan

Preparatory practice ...... 5′
Office work simulation ... 45′

Learning goals

1. To become familiar with the work in an executive office.
2. To plan and organize your work in an efficient manner.
3. To complete your work neatly and correctly.
4. To integrate your skills and knowledge.

Office Job Simulation

Read carefully the material at the right before you begin the work in Section 26. Make notes of any procedures that you think will save you time during the completion of the production activities of this section.

Introduction

You have been employed as an executive typist for International Management, Inc. (a management consulting firm), Suite 6832, World Trade Center, New York, NY 10048. You are to work for Mr. Yosef Gabre-Mariam, Executive Vice President.

Mr. Gabre-Mariam is directly responsible for all consulting projects in the Middle East and East Africa.

The firm's office manual specifies that all company letters are to be typed in the modified block style with mixed punctuation. The closing lines of all letters should include the typed name of the person for whom the letters are typed followed on the next line by that person's business title. All letters and memorandums require *one* photocopy (pc) for the file. Some letters require a blind photocopy (bpc) or a blind carbon copy (bcc). Address appropriate envelopes for all letters typed.

Proofread all work carefully before removing it from your typewriter; correct all detected errors. All typed work that is to leave the firm should be "mailable." All typed work to be used *within* the company should be "usable."

When specific job instructions are given, follow them carefully; but when specific instructions are not given, make appropriate decisions on the basis of your knowledge and experience. If your employer (your teacher) considers some of your decisions unacceptable, learn from her or his suggestions.

International Management, Inc., has based its office manual on COLLEGE TYPEWRITING, so use the Reference Guide and the index of your textbook to check matters of style and placement when you are in doubt. When a job requires unusual specifications, International Management, Inc., provides them in "Excerpts from the Office Manual."

Excerpts from the Office Manual

Executive-size stationery. The size of the paper is 7¼″ by 10½″. When you use stationery that is narrower than the standard 8½″, use 1″ side margins. The placement of the dateline will vary depending on the length of the letter.

Blind carbon copy notation. The originator of a letter may wish to send a copy of the letter to someone without disclosing that fact to the addressee of the letter. When such a copy is sent, a notation is omitted from the original copy of the letter; however, a notation--called a *blind carbon copy notation*--is typed at the left margin a double space below the last typed line on all carbon copies requiring the notation. To type the blind carbon copy notation, insert a heavy piece of paper between the ribbon and the original (first) sheet; type the notation, for example; bcc Miss Su Wong.

The original typing will appear on the piece of inserted paper and will not appear on the original copy; however, the notation will appear on the carbon copies.

If any carbon copy should not have the blind carbon copy notation, follow the same procedure as that used for eliminating it from the original: Insert a piece of paper behind the carbon sheet and in front of the carbon copy; type the notation; it will not appear on the original or any copy for which you inserted a piece of paper.

Blind photocopy notation. If you want to send a photocopy of a letter to someone without disclosing that fact to the addressee of the letter, type a notation on the photocopy but not on the original. This notation, called a *blind photocopy notation* (bpc), is typed at the left margin a double space below the last typed line, for example: bpc Miss Su Wong.

The bpc notation is *not* typed on the original, but should be typed on the file copy.

36

36a ▶ 7
Preparatory practice

each line 3 times SS (slowly, faster, still faster); DS between 3-line groups

alphabet Dixie Vaughn acquired the prize job with a large firm just like yours.

fig/sym Arroyo & Ford's catalog lists Item #92376 at $845 (less 10% for cash).

hyphen Nan thinks we have an up-to-the-minute plan for our out-of-town sales.

easy They did not include in the report the profits due the firm in August.

| 1 | 2 | 3 | 4 | 5 | 6 | 7 | 8 | 9 | 10 | 11 | 12 | 13 | 14 |

36b ▶ 10
Composing and typing

2 full sheets

1. Compose at your typewriter a ¶ describing how and why you might resolve the situation presented at the right.

2. Study your first draft; make pencil corrections.

3. Make placement decisions to center copy on page; type a final copy of your ¶.

Composing Situation

You are the credit manager of an area department store. One of the store's best credit customers has returned a new chain saw purchased two weeks previously explaining, "I bought this saw as a gift for my brother, but he already has one." The saw looks unused, but a quick examination inside the cover reveals an accumulation of sawdust. What do you recommend? Refuse the return? Issue a credit memorandum in full? Issue a reduced credit memorandum? Why do you make your recommendation?

36c ▶ 8
Dividing words

2 half sheets, long side up; 60-space line; divide words as needed; proofread; correct errors

1. Beginning on Line 12, type ¶ DS with 5-space indention.

2. Beginning on Line 14, type ¶ SS, blocked.

See 30b, page 56, if necessary for proper use of warning bell.

When you compose at the typewriter, try simply to concentrate on the subject and let your thoughts flow onto the page. Ignore errors temporarily. Use double spacing so that typewritten and pencil notations can be inserted easily. Rewrite your composition as many times as necessary to make you confident that it is your best effort.

36d ▶ 25
Typing problems: business letters in modified block style

2 letterheads [LM pp. 25-28]· 60-space line; date on Line 15

1. Study Style Letter 2, page 67. Note especially the placement of the date and closing lines.

2. Type a copy of the letter; proofread; circle errors.

3. Type three 2' writings on the date and opening lines. Begin with paper out of machine.

4. Type another copy of letter.

Business letter placement information

The modified block is probably the most popular letter style in use today. It is considered a "conservative style" that does not attract undue attention to itself.

As you study Style Letter 2, page 67, note that the basic block style has been "modified" by moving the dateline and the closing lines from block position at the left margin. In the modified block style, these lines begin at the center point of the page.

Because stationery with printed letterhead is either used or assumed, the dateline will be the first item typed in these letters. As all letters in Section 8 are average-length letters, it is correct to type the dateline on Line 15 and to use a 60-space line for all of them. Spacing between letter parts is the same as was used with the block style. This spacing is standard for all business letters.

113b-116b, continued

Job 11
Table with horizontal and vertical rulings and braced headings

Ms. Jackson asks you to type the weekly employee earnings report for Department C and gives these instructions:

full sheet sideways
center vert. & horiz.
DS body; 3 sp. bet. cols.

JACKSON, BROWN & FINK

Employee Earnings in Department C

Week Ending August 5, 19--

Employee	Employee Number	Gross Earnings	Deductions (center) F.I.T.	F.I.C.A.	Other	Net Pay
Kevin Celarek	201	$ 320.90	$ 43.20	$ 19.67	$16.05	$ 241.98
Lydia Gonzalez	187	265.75	44.20	16.29	13.30	191.96
Alpha Hutchins	204	298.60	52.10	18.30	14.95	213.25
Jerry Kennedy	159	287.40	49.40	17.62	14.35	206.03
Celia Puente	216	301.25	55.10	18.47	15.05	212.63
Mimi Trufant	135	315.75	41.10	19.35	15.80	239.50
Totals		$1,789.65	$285.10	$109.70	$89.50	$1,305.35

Job 12
Itinerary with rulings and braced headings

Ms. Jackson asks you to type her European itinerary. She hands you these instructions:

full sheet sideways
Center vert. & horiz.
DS body; 4 sp. bet. cols.

11 x 8½ — begin on line 14 — 65.48

CECILIA K. JACKSON

European Itinerary

Departure: Date	Departure: City	Departure: Time	Flight: Airline	Flight: No.	Arrival: City	Arrival: Time	Accommodations: Hotel	Accommodations: Phone
Sept. 11	Miami	17:15	National	2	London	7:00	Embassy	229 1212
Sept. 16	London	12:00	BEA	044	Paris	13:55	Sofitel	657-11-43
Sept. 21	Paris	15:45	Air France	636	Rome	18:35	Excelsior	424 483
Sept. 27	Rome	13:15	Alitalia	480	Athens	16:00	Bretagne	215 346
Oct. 4	Athens	12:00	Olympic	411	New York	15:20	Empire	265-7400
Oct. 10	New York	9:20	Eastern	7	Miami	12:01	--	--

SMS

the society of management specialists

24 EAST BROADWAY
SALT LAKE CITY, UT 84111
(801) 221-3212

Tab to center to type date and closing lines

		gwam 2'	total words
Dateline	Line 15 December 14, 19--	2	4
	Operate return 4 times		
Letter address	Mr. John M. Montgomery	4	8
	Office Supervisor	6	12
	Noyes, Banhart & Bruce	8	17
	2532 Marshall Avenue, E.	11	22
	Tacoma, WA 98421	13	25
Salutation	Dear Mr. Montgomery	14	29
Body of letter	You have done a fine job with your first draft of a new office	6	41
	manual. I suggest only one change: Add a page to your first	13	54
	chapter to explain to the staff how important business letters	19	66
	are to the firm. Explain that the success of a letter must be	25	79
	measured in terms of the effect on the reader, that its goal	31	91
	is to gain a response--a positive response.	36	100
	Explain that the process begins with the creation of a favor-	42	112
	able first impression. A letter that is well placed on a page,	48	125
	typed with clean type, and free of poor corrections and smudges	55	138
	helps to create that impression. Correct punctuation, grammar,	61	151
	and spelling (especially of names) help to sustain it.	67	162
	Finally, Mr. Montgomery, emphasize to your typists that their	6	175
	skill, combined with their ability to use language well, makes	13	187
	them a vital link in the company's chain of communications.	18	199
Complimentary close	Sincerely yours	20	202
	Operate return 4 times		
	June Hayman		
Typed name	Ms. June Hayman	22	205
Official title	Consultant	23	208
Reference initials	abt	23	208

Shown in pica type

Style letter 2: modified block style, block paragraphs, open punctuation

113b-116b, continued

Job 8
Statement of changes in financial position

Jerry Kennedy, an accounting clerk, has prepared the accompanying statement of changes in financial position. Mrs. Fink has verified the accuracy of the data and asks you to type the final copy for inclusion in the audit report.

FLORIDA EQUIPMENT MANUFACTURING, INC. 18

Statement of Changes in Financial Position--Working Capital 39

For the Year Ended June 30, 19-- 16

Sources of working capital:			
Operations during the year:			
Net income	$218,948		
Add depreciation	102,500	$321,448	
Issuance of common stock at par for land		20,500	$341,948
Applications of working capital:			
Purchase of equipment		$130,700	
Purchase of land by issuance of common stock at par		20,500	
Declaration of cash dividends . .		162,500	313,700
Increase in working capital . . .			$28,248

Job 9
Duplicating and binding copies of audit report

Now that the eight statements for the audit report are done, Mrs. Fink asks you to make 2 photocopies of each statement and to assemble the copies for binding in the order of completion.

Using a paper punch, punch each of the 3 copies of the complete report for binding in a looseleaf clasp binder. Bind the report at the left.

Job 10
Typing binder labels

[LM p. 61]

Mrs. Fink asks you to type a 5" x 3" binder label for each of the bound copies of the report just completed. She supplies appropriate copy.

FLORIDA EQUIPMENT MANUFACTURING, INC.

ANNUAL FINANCIAL REPORT

June 30, 19--

Prepared by
Jackson, Brown & Fink
Certified Public Accountants

37

37a ▶ 6
Preparatory practice
each line 3 times SS (slowly, faster, still faster); DS between 3-line groups

alphabet Except on Friday, Jan works all day at that big aquarium in Vera Cruz.
figure We are sending 2,795 of the 4,680 sets now and the balance on June 13.
br Brad's brother, Bruce, broke my bronze brooches and other bric-a-brac.
easy She can find a park just by making a sharp right turn by the big lake.
| 1 | 2 | 3 | 4 | 5 | 6 | 7 | 8 | 9 | 10 | 11 | 12 | 13 | 14 |

37b ▶ 25
Typing problems: business letters in modified block style
2 letterheads [LM pp. 29-32]; see page 66 for letter placement directions

Problem 1

Type a copy of the letter; proofread and correct your copy before removing it from typewriter.

words

January 4, 19-- | Mrs. Antonia Quintero, Manager | Quintero Direct Mail 14
Service | Box 285, Church Road | Schenectady, NY 12306 | Dear Mrs. 26
Quintero (¶ 1) Thank you for telephoning this morning to inquire about the 39
possibility of our providing you with temporary office help next month. We 55
shall be glad to work with you. (¶ 2) We can furnish on short notice typists, 69
stenographers, and bookkeepers who are capable of using standard equip- 83
ment. If you need operators for specialized equipment, we shall make every 99
effort to provide them. (¶ 3) The enclosed brochure describes our functions 113
and briefly outlines our methods of operation. The table of pay rates for 128
various job classifications will give you a good idea of the cost of the work 143
you want to have done. (¶ 4) Ms. Mary Ragona, one of our work-relations 157
coordinators, will call you early next week to arrange an appointment to dis- 172
cuss your work needs in detail. You will find her helpful in matching the 187
worker to the job. | Sincerely yours | Marvin D. Atgood | Sales Manager | xx | 201
Enclosure 203

Problem 2

Follow directions given for Problem 1.

words

October 12, 19-- | Miss April Rigby, Sales Manager | O'Grady Office Machines 15
| 4600 Bachman Place | San Diego, CA 92130 | Dear Miss Rigby (¶ 1) Thank 27
you for taking time last evening to talk with me on the telephone about our 42
need for business machines. We shall be grateful to you if you will send us 57
your catalog and the price lists for machines you have ready for sale at the 73
present time. (¶ 2) We are particularly interested in printing calculators, 87
either new or used. The calculators must be in excellent running condition, 102
however. (¶ 3) Let us hear about the machines you have in stock; and keep us 117
in mind when additional printing or nonprinting electronic calculators, copy- 132
ing machines, or editing typewriters become available. We rent such 146
machines to offices that we service and have a heavy demand for them. | Sin- 161
cerely | Yoshikazu Eto | Purchasing Department | xx 170

113b-116b, continued

Job 6
Schedule of accounts and notes payable

Lydia Gonzalez, an accounts payable clerk, has drawn up a schedule of accounts and notes payable. Mrs. Fink has verified the data, and she asks you to prepare a typed copy of the schedule, adding an appropriate heading and alphabetizing the names under *Accounts payable*.

Creditor	Amount	Total
Accounts payable:		
West Florida Suppliers	$60,000	
Franklin Brothers, Inc.	16,500	
Toledo Fixtures	39,000	
Delgado Contractors	8,500	
Southern Freight Lines	19,640	
DS Total accounts payable		$143,640
Notes payable:		
Florida National Bank	$100,000	
Jacksonville State Bank	50,000	
DS Total notes payable		150,000
Total accounts and notes payable		$293,640

Job 7
Schedule of landholdings

Mrs. Fink has prepared the accompanying schedule of landholdings. She asks you to type the table for inclusion in the audit report. For ease of reading, she asks you to DS the items.

FLORIDA EQUIPMENT MANUFACTURING, INC.
Schedule of Landholdings*
June 30, 19--

Location	Current Market Value	Original Purchase Price	% Increase in Value
120 South Olive Avenue	$200,000	$ 50,000	300.00
1200 Island Road	100,000	30,000	233.33
2950 Florida Avenue	150,000	50,000	200.00
750 Palmetto Road	35,000	25,000	40.00
1500 Silver Beach Road	50,500	15,995	215.72
1200 Sunset Road	49,000	20,500	139.02
1550 Summit Boulevard	5,500	3,505	56.92
Totals	$590,000	$195,000	

*Exclusive of buildings.

37c ▶ 10
Addressing envelopes for letters

1. Study the information at the right and the illustrations below.

Envelope placement information

Small or large envelopes are commonly used for one-page business letters and for personal letters. Although exact placement data is given below for addressing small and large envelopes, train your eye to estimate placement of both the return address and the envelope address.

Return address: Type writer's name and address SS in block style in upper left corner. Start about 3 spaces from left edge on Line 2.

Envelope address: Placement depends upon envelope size. Set a tab stop 2½" from left edge of a small envelope, 4" for a large envelope. Space down 2" from top edge of small envelope, 2½" for a large envelope. Begin address at the tab stop position.

Large envelope (No. 10) 9½" x 4⅛"

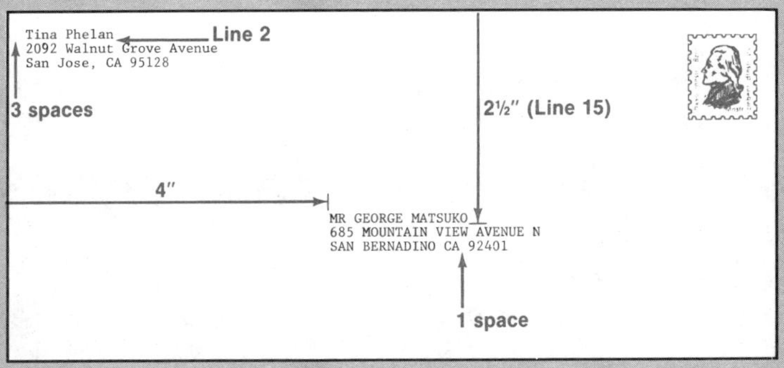

Small envelope (No. 6¾) 6½" x 3⅝"

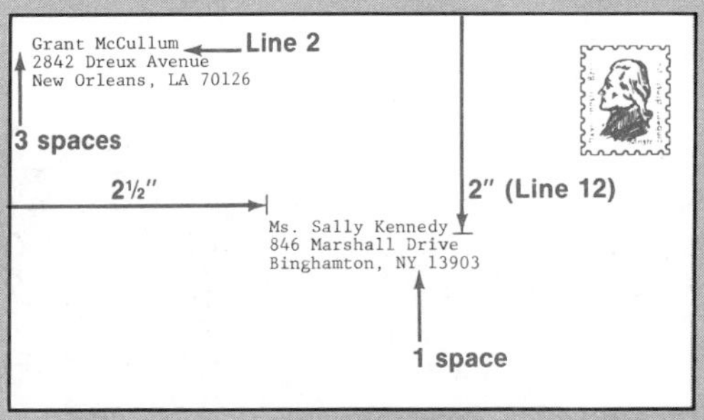

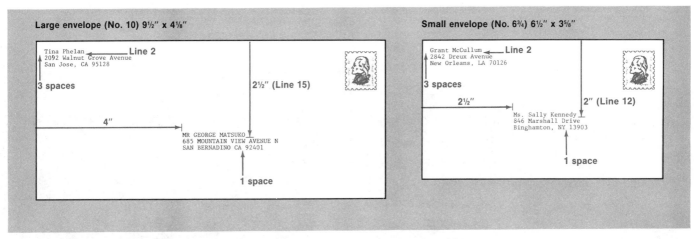

Notice that the envelope above is typed in ALL CAPS with no punctuation, which is the form recommended by the U.S. Postal Service.

2. Type in U.S.P.S. style a large (No. 10) and in standard style a small (No. 6¾) envelope for each address [LM pp. 33–38]. Use your own return address; proofread; circle errors.

Miss Juanita Hyatt
38 Lenox Drive
Norman, OK 73069

Mr. Grant Wymore
111 Greer Avenue
Covina, CA 91724

Mrs. Barbara Abt
981 Rita Place
El Paso, TX 79907

37d ▶ 8
Folding and inserting letters

Study the illustrations below. Practice folding 8½" x 11" paper for large envelopes and for small ones.

Folding and inserting letters into large envelopes

Step 1
With letter face up, fold slightly less than ⅓ of sheet up toward top.

Step 2
Fold down top of sheet to within ½ inch of bottom fold.

Step 3
Insert letter into envelope with last crease toward bottom of envelope.

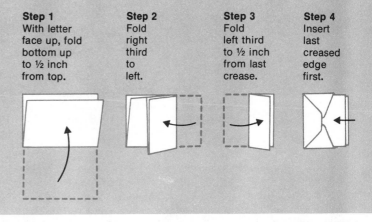

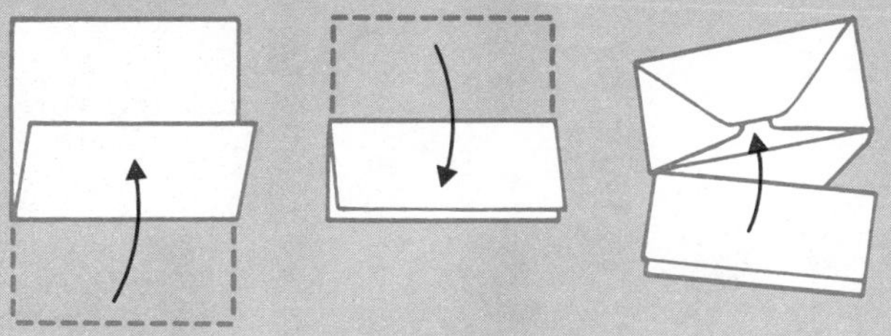

Folding and inserting letters into small envelopes

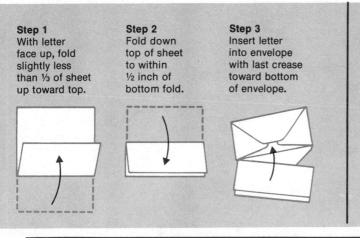

Step 1
With letter face up, fold bottom up to ½ inch from top.

Step 2
Fold right third to left.

Step 3
Fold left third to ½ inch from last crease.

Step 4
Insert last creased edge first.

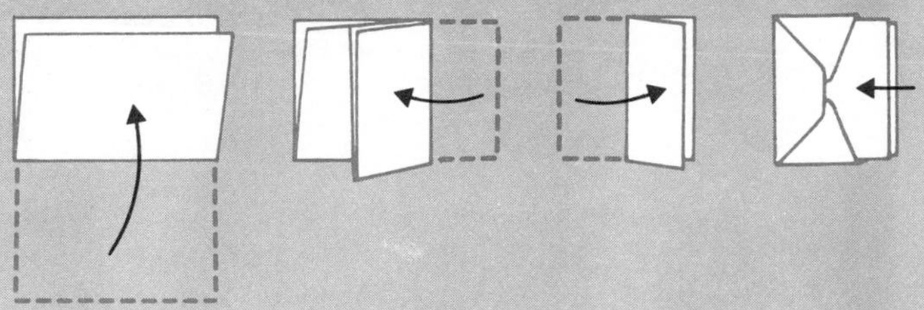

113b-116b, continued

Job 5
Schedule of accounts and notes receivable

Kevin Celarek, an accounts receivable clerk, has prepared a handwritten draft of a schedule of accounts and notes receivable. Mrs. Fink has verified the data and asks you to type it in double-spaced form to become part of the audit report.

FLORIDA EQUIPMENT MANUFACTURING, INC.
Schedule of Accounts and Notes Receivable
June 30, 19--

Debtor	Amount Due	Original Amount	Age (Months)
Aikens Equipment Sales	$ 4,300	$ 20,900	16
Berman Associates, Inc.	12,855	12,855	1
Columbia Enterprises	8,900	20,000	1
Daisuke Exporters, Inc.	50,000*	50,000	6
Espino Sales Company	1,000	1,000	1
Farmers' Co-op Group	25,000	25,000	1
Giant Industries, Inc.	2,000	5,000	1
Holiday Farms	30,000	75,900	18
Iowa Producers, Inc.	8,500	10,000	1
Jeffers Supply Co.	10,120	10,120	1
Long Row Implement, Inc.	5,000	20,000	2
Machinery & Tools, Inc.	30,000	60,000	3
Manufacturers Unlimited	13,200	13,200	1
O'Brien and Associates	500	2,500	4
Robeson & Lee, Inc.	2,500	5,000	1
Valdivia Products Corp.	4,500	10,000	2
Waltz Distributors, Inc.	12,000	60,000	20
Xavier Transport Co.	2,400	6,000	2
Zwick and Zwick, Inc.	15,000	50,000	4
Total accounts and notes receivable	$ 237,775		

*Notes receivable

38

38a ▶ 6
Preparatory practice

each line 3 times SS (slowly, faster, still faster); DS between 3-line groups

alphabet Tex queried Kip and Vinny about jewel boxes for the many huge zircons.

fig/sym The 7 1/2% interest of $18.68 on my $249.05 note (dated May 3) is due.

shift keys Heda and Pablo spent April in Mexico City and June and July in Brazil.

easy The six authentic lamps from an ancient land came with this endowment.

| 1 | 2 | 3 | 4 | 5 | 6 | 7 | 8 | 9 | 10 | 11 | 12 | 13 | 14 |

38b ▶ 14
Using carbon paper

Materials needed:
- 2 original sheets
- 4 second sheets
- 2 carbon paper sheets
- 1 firm (5″ × 3″) card

60-space line; DS; 2½″ top margin; correct errors

1. Study the information and illustrations at the right.

2. Using the "desk-top method," type an original and 2 carbon copies of the ¶ shown below the illustration.

3. Using the "machine method," type an original and 2 carbon copies of the ¶.

Desk-top assembly method

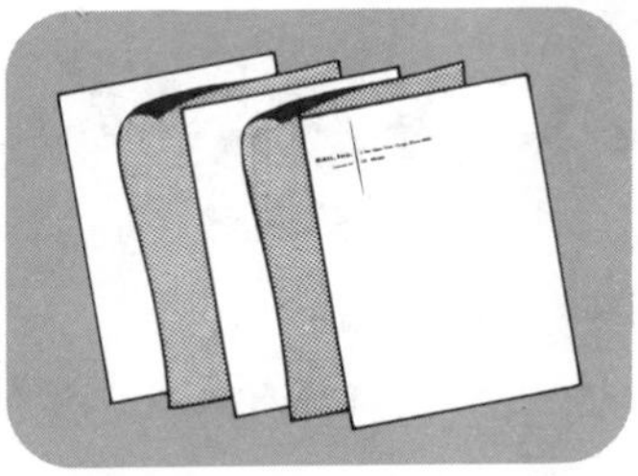

1 Assemble letterhead, carbon sheets (uncarboned side up), and second sheets as illustrated above. *Use one carbon and one second sheet for each copy desired.*

2 Grasp the carbon pack at the sides, turn it so that the *letterhead faces away from you, the carbon sides of the carbon paper are toward you, and the top edge of the pack is face down*. Tap the sheets gently on the desk to straighten.

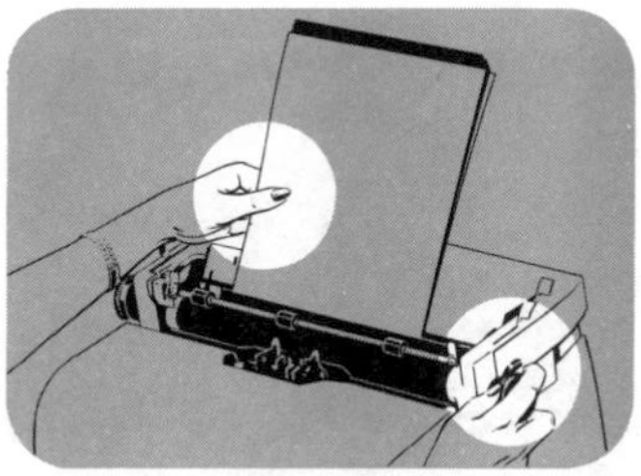

3 Hold the sheets firmly to prevent slipping; insert pack into typewriter. Hold pack with one hand; turn platen with the other.

Machine assembly method

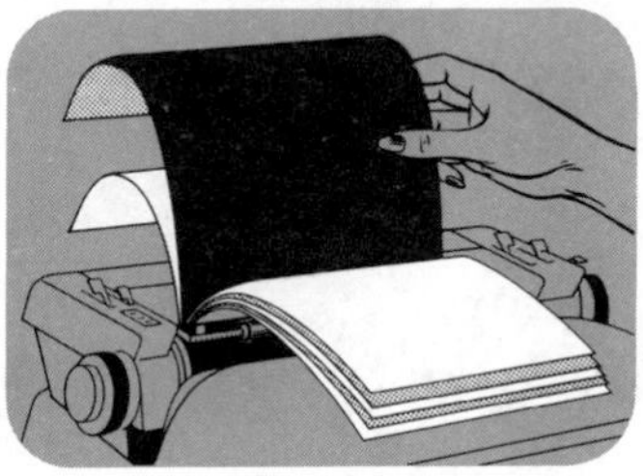

1 Assemble paper for insertion (original on top; second sheets beneath). Turn the "pack" so *original faces away from you* and the *top edge faces down*.

2 Insert sheets until the tops are gripped by the feed rolls; then pull the bottom of all sheets except the last over the top (front) of the typewriter.

3 Place carbon paper between sheets, *carboned side toward you*. Flip each sheet back (away from you) as you add each carbon sheet.

4 Roll pack into typing position.

To erase errors when using a carbon pack, pull the original sheet forward and place a card (such as a 5″ x 3″ card) in front of the carbon sheet. Erase the error on the original with a hard (typewriter) eraser. With a soft (pencil) eraser, erase the error on the second sheet. If there are several carbon sheets to erase, use the card to protect them by placing it between the sheet being erased and the next sheet of carbon paper.

113b-116b, continued

Job 3
Income statement

Celia Puente, an accounting clerk, prepared for Mrs. Fink a rough draft of the accompanying income statement. Mrs. Fink has approved the work as marked and asks you to type it to become part of the audit report.

FLORIDA EQUIPMENT MANUFACTURING, INC. 18

~~Statement of Earnings~~ Income Statement 8

For Year Ending June 30, 19-- 14

TS

Revenues:		
Sales (net)	$2,945,294	
Less cost of good^s sold	1,761,325	
Gross profit on sales		$1,183,969
Expenses:		
Accounting	$ 21,750	
Collection expenses (add leaders)	8,650	
Depreciation	102,500	
Insurance	16,000	
Interest paid	172,580	
Legal retainer	25,000	
Miscellaneous	19,240	
Office supplies	6,328	
Operating supplies	12,782	
Property taxes	16,892	
Repairs	8,925	
Salaries	289,640	
Telephone	18,620	
Transportation	49,230	$ 768,137
Income from operations before income taxes		$ 415,832
Estimated income taxes		196,884
Net income		$ 218,948

SS (expenses); TS

Job 4
Statement of retained earnings

Mrs. Fink asks you to use the same heading as for the income statement except that the second line should read: Statement of Retained Earnings

DS

Balance, July 1, 19-- $110,625
Net income after taxes . . 218,948
Balance, June 30, 19-- . . $329,573

38c ▶ 9
Addressing envelopes

4 large (No. 10) envelopes [LM pp. 39-42]

1. Acceptable address placement on large envelopes can be quickly determined by judgment. Visualize a horizontal line drawn through the vertical center of the envelope, a vertical line through the horizontal center (as illustrated). Begin the address near the point where the two imaginary lines intersect. (A tab stop set at the center of the letterhead can also be used as the horizontal beginning point for the letter address on large envelopes.)

2. Using the first address below and your own return address, type a large envelope. Estimate placement for both addresses.

3. Compare your typed envelope with the one illustrated. Make adjustments if necessary as you type the other 3 envelopes; proofread; circle errors.

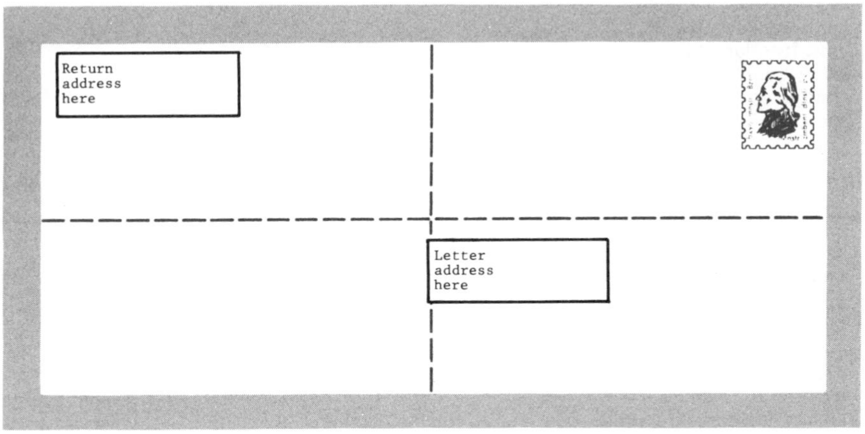

Mr. Myles Boehm	Mr. Hubert Beck	Mrs. Muriel Cosby	Miss Laura Wilke
8167 Edgar Street	3572 Grand Avenue	1234 Brown Street	3221 Erwin Road
Houston, TX 77051	Reading, PA 19605	Akron, OH 44301	Durham, NC 27705

38d ▶ 20
Typing problem: business letter

1 letterhead [LM p. 43]; 1 sheet plain paper; 1 copy sheet; carbon paper; 1 large envelope

Type a copy of the letter; 1 cc; address a large envelope. Make all decisions about placement and style; proofread; correct errors.

words

November 29, 19-- | Miss Kathryn Lee-Sangtree | Personnel Director | 13
Barnhart & Herbst, Inc. | 1428 Essex Drive | Sioux Falls, SD 57106 | Dear 26
Miss Lee-Sangtree (¶ 1) Our company plans to publish next year a booklet 40
called (DS and center) RIGHT STEPS TO RIGHT JOBS (DS) This booklet, 49
which will be distributed to college students, will attempt to focus on 63
factors of employment that are most important to people with hiring re- 78
sponsibilities. (¶ 2) In order to identify accurately those factors, we are 92
asking selected personnel directors like you from different parts of the 106
country to identify just five factors that they consider the best indicators 122
of a good employee. (¶ 3) Will you take a few minutes from your busy day 135
to share with us the top five factors that influence your decision to em- 150
ploy? After all results have been compiled and the booklet published, we 165
shall send you a copy; you will be listed as a contributor. (¶ 4) Thank you, 179
Mrs. Lee-Sangtree. We hope to hear from you soon. | Very truly yours | L. 194
David Ratgliff | Vice President | xx 200/**221**

113b-116b, continued

The next seven job assignments (2–8) are accounting statements and schedules to be bound into the audit report mentioned in Job 1. For all these jobs, use a 1½" left margin and 1' top and right margins.

Job 2
Balance sheet

Masami Komuro, one of the junior accountants, has prepared a rough draft of a balance sheet (sometimes called a statement of financial condition) for Mrs. Fink's approval or correction. She approves the work as corrected and includes it among the jobs you are to type for the preliminary audit report.

FLORIDA EQUIPMENT MANUFACTURING, INC. 18
Balance Sheet 6
~~Statement of Financial Position~~ S
June 30, 19-- 6 DS

Assets 3

Current ~~Assets~~ assets:		
Cash	$ 241,896	
Accounts and notes receivable (net)	237,775	
Inventories	2,336,500	
Prepaid ~~accounts~~ expenses	83,192	
Total current assets		$2,899,363
Property, plant, and equipment:		
Land	$ 195,000	
Buildings (net)	1,250,000	
Furniture and equipment (net) . . .	2,948,200	
Total property, plant, and equipment		$4,393,200
Total assets		$7,292,563

Liabilities and ~~Capital~~ Stockholders' Equity 18

Current liabilities:		
Accounts and notes payable	$ 293,640	
Taxes payable	189,350	
Total current liabilities . . .		$ 482,990
Long-term debt:		
Bonds payable	$1,500,000	
Mortgages payable	980,000	
Total long-term debt		$2,480,000
Total ~~Liabilities~~ liabilities		$2,962,990
~~Capital:~~ Stockholders' equity:		
Preferred stock, $100 par (15,000 shares authorized and issued)	$1,500,000	
Common stock, $100 par (25,000 shares authorized and issued)	2,500,000	
Retained earnings	329,573	
Total stockholders' equity . .		$4,329,573
Total liabilities and stockholders' equity		$7,292,563

39

39a ▶ 6
Preparatory practice

each line 3 times SS (slowly, faster, still faster); DS between 3-line groups

alphabet	Paddy Quigley worked very hard to minimize the fixed costs of the job.
figure	The 1980 edition of this book has 5 parts, 34 chapters, and 672 pages.
double letters	Three little batters slugged a ball across the deep and narrow valley.
easy	I ought to do quite well if I try one of those fine pens for the work.

| 1 | 2 | 3 | 4 | 5 | 6 | 7 | 8 | 9 | 10 | 11 | 12 | 13 | 14 |

39b ▶ 11
Measuring straight-copy skill

a 3′ and a 5′ writing; determine *gwam*; proofread and circle errors

Difficulty index

all letters used | A | 1.5 si | 5.7 awl | 80% hfw |

gwam 3′ | 5′

There is no question about my plan. Some bright afternoon in the 4 3
imminent future, I shall enter an office somewhere to be interviewed 9 5
for an important job that I intend shall be the first in my long and 14 8
successful career. It stands to reason that I shall be nervous and a 18 11
little apprehensive, but I shall face every contingency zealously. 23 14

I envision myself awaiting the interview. I am not alone in the 27 16
immense waiting room, for there are scores of other people who apparently 32 19
have made plans for the same job. But I have anticipated their presence; 37 22
I have prepared myself for competition. After all, I have been doing 42 25
my planning for a long time. 43 26

I must assure the employment officer that my qualities are truly 48 29
unique ones. I explain about the special skills I have acquired through 53 32
training; they will be valuable to the company. I point with pride, 57 34
too, to my references; for they say that I have a pleasant, friendly, 62 37
cooperative personality--that I am team material. I talk about all the 67 40
experience I shall likely have had by that time. 70 42

My plan always turns out the same way. I get the desired position 74 45
without undue difficulty. Eventually I become president of the company. 79 48
At least I have planned it that way. 82 49

gwam 3′ | 1 | 2 | 3 | 4 | 5 |
5′ | 1 | 2 | 3 |

39c ▶ 33
Measuring skill application

Time schedule

Assembling materials ... 2′
Timed production ...... 25′
Final check; proofread; compute *g–pram* ..... 6′

Materials needed:
3 letterheads [LM pp. 45–50] or plain paper and 2 envelopes

When the signal to begin is given, insert paper and begin typing Problem 1. Type the problems in sequence until the signal to stop is given. Type Problem 1 again if you have finished Problem 3 and time has not been called. Proofread all problems; circle errors. Calculate *g–pram*.

$$g\text{–}pram = \frac{\text{total words typed}}{\text{time } (25')}$$

113-116

113a-116a ▶ 5
Preparatory practice

each line 3 times SS (slowly, faster, slowly); retype selected lines as time permits

alphabet Excited voices kept buzzing as qualified members of the jury withdrew.
fig/sym Flight #807 leaving here at 12:45 is scheduled to reach Cairo at 6:39.
shift keys Paul and Iris DeWitt live on West Newton Street, Salt Lake City, Utah.
fluency I did ask the auditor to amend the statement to show the right profit.

| 1 | 2 | 3 | 4 | 5 | 6 | 7 | 8 | 9 | 10 | 11 | 12 | 13 | 14 |

113b-116b ▶ 45
Office work simulation

The partners of Jackson, Brown & Fink have agreed that you must complete Jobs 1–10 before being given any other work to type. The audit of Florida Equipment Manufacturing, Inc., has just been completed, and the preliminary audit report must be finished within the next few days.

Mrs. Fink, the partner in charge of this audit, has given you the ten jobs to type. She asks you to place Jobs 1–8 in looseleaf clasp binders to be submitted to the client as a preliminary report. She says that when you are ready to prepare the binders, she will give you needed help.

Job 1 [LM p. 59]
Auditor's statement

Mrs. Fink has prepared the auditor's statement in the form of a letter. Because it is to be bound into the full leftbound report, she asks that you use a 1½" left margin and a 1" right margin. Mrs. Fink's customary signature is KAREN T. FINK, CPA. No envelope is required, of course, because the letter is a part of the report.

July 31, 19--

Ms. Rosa C. Ubaldo, President
Florida Equipment Manufacturing, Inc.
5809 Belvedere Road
West Palm Beach, FL 33406

AUDITOR'S STATEMENT

(¶1) We have examined the balance sheet of Florida Equipment Manufacturing, Inc., as of June 30, 19--, and the related statements of income and of retained earnings for the year then ended. Our examination was made in accordance with generally accepted auditing standards and accordingly included such tests of the accounting records and such other auditing procedures as we considered necessary under the circumstances. (¶2) It is our opinion that the accompanying balance sheet and statements of income and of retained earnings present fairly the financial condition of Florida Equipment Manufacturing, Inc., on June 30, 19--, and the results of its operations for the year then ended in conformity with generally accepted accounting principles applied on a basis consistent with that of the preceding year.

39c, continued

words

Problem 1
block style;
large envelope

April 17, 19-- | Mrs. Myrle Cretchmer | 4378 Bynum Avenue | Baton Rouge, LA 14
70802 | Dear Mrs. Cretchmer (¶ 1) I want to introduce myself. I am Jack 27
Heckman. I work at Higbee's; in fact, I'm the new head of the carpet depart- 42
ment. (¶ 2) So why do I intrude on your day? I want you to have copies of 56
two excellent booklets about carpeting. One, published by the United States 72
Carpet Institute, has over 20 pages of valuable information about judging 87
price, fabric, color, texture, and pattern. The other, a Consumer Bureau 101
booklet, presents little-known facts about carpet and rug care. (¶ 3) Bring my 116
enclosed business card with you the next time you shop at Higbee's. It will 132
remind you to come to the carpet area and ask for me. I shall be happy to 147
give you the two booklets I am saving for you and answer your questions 161
about carpeting. Our coffee is good, too; have a cup with us. (¶ 4) A final 175
note: The big Higbee's Holiday Sale begins next week. Don't miss the great 191
bargains that will be available throughout the entire store. Cordially | Jack 206
Heckman | Carpet Department | xx | Enclosure 214/**226**

Problem 2
modified block style;
large envelope

May 5, 19-- | Mr. and Mrs. John Murdoch | 1821 Grove Court | Far Rockaway, 14
NY 11691 | Dear Mr. and Mrs. Murdoch 21
(¶ 1) Our truck and automobile tires are priced lower than those of any other 35
tire dealer in this area. We know. We have checked our competitors' prices. 51
(¶ 2) What is wrong with buying tires at the lowest possible price? Absolutely 66
nothing if: 68
(¶ 3) --the tires you buy are built to give you extra miles of safe, problem-free 83
driving 85
(¶ 4) --you can obtain local service quickly and reasonably when you feel you 99
need it 101
(¶ 5) Satisfying these requirements--low price, high-quality tires, and prompt 116
service cheerfully rendered--forms the foundation of our business efforts. 131
(¶ 6) Enclosed is our latest catalog. When you next have a question about 145
tires, call us for a personal appointment. If you prefer, one of our represen- 160
tatives will come to see you. 167
Sincerely | Bob Greenhammer | Manager | xx | Enclosure 176/**189**

Problem 3
style of your choice;
no envelope

September 14, 19-- | Mr. E. Samuel Hughes | Keystone Business Academy | 13
9327 Darby Place | Harrisburg, PA 17109 | Dear Mr. Hughes (¶ 1) In response 26
to your request, we are very happy to send you a complimentary copy of our 41
communications layout guide (DS and center) LETTER PERFECT (DS) This little 52
booklet has become a popular item on the shelves of many college 65
bookstores. (¶ 2) After you have used this guide as a reference for a few 79
days, you are sure to want each of your students to have one. It is available 95
at $2.25 a copy from Mr. Tomas Nieves, Copyhouse Books, Inc., 29 Barberry 110
Hill Road, Providence, RI 02906. (¶ 3) Thank you for your interest in our 124
communications materials. We shall be pleased to receive any comments or 138
suggestions you may have for their improvement. | Very truly yours | Ms. 152
Marge E. Irvine | Assistant Editor | xx | Enclosure 161

section

25

Typing in an accounting office

lessons 113–116

Section 25 is designed to provide the opportunity for you to type the kinds of accounting papers and reports that are typical of those prepared by workers in accounting offices.

Supplies needed

letterhead form [LM p. 59]
 or plain full sheet
5″ x 3″ labels [LM p. 61]
 error correction supplies
 3 looseleaf binders

Machine adjustments

1. Check chair and desk adjustments; check placement of copy for easy reading.
2. Set paper guide at *0*.
3. Set ribbon control on black.
4. Set line-space selector on *1* for single spacing except when otherwise directed.
5. Margins: 70-space line for preparatory practice; as directed (or appropriate) for typing jobs.

Daily practice plan

Preparatory practice ...... 5′
Office work simulation ... 45′

Learning goals

1. To develop knowledge and skill in typing accounting papers, reports, and tables.
2. To plan your work and complete it correctly and efficiently.

Office Job Simulation

Read carefully the material at the right before you begin the work of Section 25. Note any standard procedures that you think will save you time during the completion of the accounting office job activities.

Introduction

You have been hired as a statistical typist by the firm of Jackson, Brown & Fink (a public accounting partnership), Suite 1600, Guaranty Building, 120 South Olive Avenue, West Palm Beach, FL 33401. The three partners are: Ms. Cecilia K. Jackson, CPA; Mr. Washington I. Brown, CPA; and Mrs. Karen T. Fink, CPA.

Jackson, Brown & Fink have selected the AMS Simplified letter style. Because photocopy equipment is used, no carbon copies are required of any work. Error corrections must be made with utmost care. Proofread all work carefully and correct all detected errors neatly before you remove each sheet from the typewriter.

Jackson, Brown & Fink have based their office procedures and job instructions manual on COLLEGE TYPEWRITING; therefore, use the Reference Guide and the index of your textbook to look up matters of style and placement when in doubt. When a job requires unusual specifications, the firm provides them in "Excerpts from the Job Instructions Manual."

When specific job instructions are given, follow them carefully. When specific instructions are not given, make appropriate decisions on the basis of your knowledge and experience. If one of the partners (your teacher) considers some of your decisions unacceptable, learn from her or his suggestions—just as you should do in any business office.

Excerpts from the Job Instructions Manual

Braced Headings. A braced heading is a heading which is centered over 2 or more columns. Although braced headings can be used in simple tables and ruled tables, they are found primarily in tables that have both horizontal and vertical rulings. In a table with horizontal rulings, all braced headings are located between the double horizontal ruling below the main heading and above the single ruling below the column headings. Braced headings are separated from other braced headings and/or the column headings by horizontal rulings. Double-space (DS) above and below the double horizontal ruling which follows the main heading. Single-space (SS) above all other horizontal rulings in the table, but DS below them. Study the illustration of a braced heading shown below.

QUARTERLY SALES REPORT
DS

	DS Sales Volume* SS			
Area	April	May	DS June SS	Year to Date

* **Braced heading**

Typing Labels. Study the illustration of a label shown below. To type a label, insert a sheet of paper into the typewriter until the top edge is ½″ above the ribbon. Place the label behind the top edge of the paper and against the platen or cylinder. Roll the cylinder toward you until the label is in position for typing the first line; type the information.

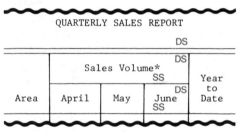

CARBRERA TEMPORARIES, INC.
ANNUAL FINANCIAL REPORT
June 30, 19--

Prepared by
Jackson, Brown & Fink
Certified Public Accountants

Supplemental skill-building practice

Using the warning bell

2 half sheets; DS; line: 60; begin on Line 10

Type the ¶ twice, listening for the bell to return carriage. Proofread and circle errors after each writing.

Take time to evaluate your work. Study carefully what you have typed; then, from your observations, you can make decisions about the effect your work will have on a reader. Convince yourself that the content of your work is accurate, that you have chosen the proper form to present it, and that the reader will be impressed with what is said and the form in which it appears. If you can't convince yourself, you won't convince anyone else.

Improving keystroking technique

each line twice SS (slowly, faster); DS between 2-line groups

1st row Calvin Bixman became excited when Anna Mae McVan zoomed over the line.
2d row Gladys Falk had a fall as she made a gallant dash to lash Jack's flag.
3d row Is it true that you were the one who quoted an expert on party policy?
top row Their 1982 sales projection is for 460 Model 7359 heavy-duty tractors.
1st fingers Jeff Brough may travel with my brother rather than fly alone at night.
2d fingers Edie Cedrick kidded Dick King, for he decided not to debate the edict.
3d/4th fingers Six qualified players overlooked opportunities to win valuable prizes.

| 1 | 2 | 3 | 4 | 5 | 6 | 7 | 8 | 9 | 10 | 11 | 12 | 13 | 14 |

Building keystroking control

each line 3 times SS; DS between 3-line groups

ce 1 Cecelia Brice's hat once had a trace of lace in place of a cerise bow.
un 2 Unfortunately, my uncle and aunt waited until June to lunch at the UN.
gr 3 Greta Gros agrees my grass is greener and regrets hers has grown gray.
ny 4 Can anyone deny that Lenny Snyder, of Albany, has many tiny onyx gems?
um 5 I assume Lum read a number of humdrum resumes on humanism this summer.

| 1 | 2 | 3 | 4 | 5 | 6 | 7 | 8 | 9 | 10 | 11 | 12 | 13 | 14 |

Improving response patterns

each line twice; then a 1′ writing on Lines 3 and 4

letter 1 We were regarded as the team to beat after winning only three debates.
word 2 They can handle their profit problem if they do their work with vigor.
combination 3 Our crafts display at the civic arts center show was observed by many.
4 A great many workers in today's world could benefit from a faith lift.

| 1 | 2 | 3 | 4 | 5 | 6 | 7 | 8 | 9 | 10 | 11 | 12 | 13 | 14 |

112d ▶20
Measuring straight-copy typing skill

1. Two 5′ writings for *accuracy* on ¶s 1–3 combined. Record *gwam* and number of errors for the more accurate writing.

2. As time permits, type a 1″ writing for *speed* on each ¶.

Difficulty index

all letters used	A	1.5 si	5.7 awl	80% hfw

gwam 1′ | 5′

Three standard report formats used by almost every major business 13 3
organization are the topbound, leftbound, and unbound. The right and 27 5
bottom margins are approximately the same on all three of the standard 41 8
formats; however, the left or top margin changes with the individual 55 11
style used. Unbound and leftbound reports have the same top margin; 69 14
however, the topbound increases the top margin by a half inch. In addi- 83 17
tion, the topbound and unbound have the same left margin, but the left- 98 20
bound increases the width of the left margin by a half inch. The addi- 112 22
tional half inch of space in either the left or the top margin of a 125 25
report is to allow for the easy binding of the report. 136 27

A business organization may use one of many individual letter for- 13 30
mats; however, most companies use one of the following: block, modified 28 33
block, or modified block with paragraphs indented. The block style is 42 36
easy to type quickly because only the margin stops on the machine need 56 38
to be set, and all parts of the letter begin at the left margin. The 70 41
modified block style is different from the block style only in that the 85 44
date and closing lines begin at the center point of the paper. The 98 47
modified block with paragraphs indented is very similar, but this style 113 50
has one major difference in that the first line of text in each para- 126 53
graph is indented. 130 53

Most companies require a typist who is able to type many different 13 56
types of tables; therefore, a good typist should know the tabulation 27 59
process thoroughly. As a rule, most tabulation problems in a firm will 42 62
use one of the three basic tables: simple, ruled, or boxed. The simple 56 64
table usually has only a heading and one-line column headings above the 71 67
body of the table. The ruled table may be more difficult than the simple 85 70
table, but the major difference is that the ruled table has horizontal 100 73
rulings above and below the column headings and below the body of the 114 76
table. The boxed table will have vertical rulings in addition to hori- 128 79
zontal ones. 130 79

gwam 1′ | 1 | 2 | 3 | 4 | 5 | 6 | 7 | 8 | 9 | 10 | 11 | 12 | 13 | 14 |
5′ | 1 | 2 | 3 |

Improving machine parts control

each line once SS; set tab at center point for typing Lines 3-7

Technique cues

Lines 1-2: quick down-and-in thumb motion

Lines 3-7: set tab at center; tab and type with eyes on copy

Lines 8-9: keep other fingers in typing position as you reach to shift key/lock

space bar

1 She wrote: Mrs. Reza left at 2:17 p.m.; Marta left at that time, too.
2 Who sent Order 590 for 3 1/2 dozen locks? Was it Jim? or Jan? or Lou?

tab key/bar

3 ——— Tab ———→ When you tabulate, do you make the
4 necessary reach correctly?— Tab → Do you use the appropriate finger,
5 not the whole hand? —— Tab ——→ Do you look at your keyboard every
6 time you tab? ——— Tab ———→ Think about the difference between
7 DO YOU and CAN YOU. ——— Tab ——→ You CAN tabulate properly. DO you?

shift key/lock

8 "Get speed AND accuracy," wrote Mr. Fox, "for REAL typewriting power."
9 Both Bob Lenz and Lana Cowon work at WIDB-TV; Ella Marx works at WMAC.

Measuring rough-draft skill

one 3′ and one 5′ writing; determine *gwam*; proofread; circle errors

Difficulty index

all letters used	LA	1.4 si	5.4 awl	85% hfw

gwam 3′ | 5′

Their is an old saying that informs us: It is the little 4 | 3
things that count. This adage would have us believe and it is 9 | 5
probably ture, that there are no big things in life; the big 14 | 8
things in life, it tiles to say, are just acumulations of alot 18 | 11
of little things. There is one more old saying that recommends: 23 | 14
take care ofthe pennies and dollars will take care ofthemselves. 28 | 17
This is very good advice for handling dollars, and it can also 32 | 19
be applied quite directly to other phases of life. 33 | 20
If you learn, for instance, to submit to or conquer each of your 38 | 23
little frustrations asthey occur day day, you will develop in 42 | 25
the process ability to face your personal crisis if and when 47 | 28
they areise. You will also learn to main tain a clear head and 52 | 31
not be panicked by the size of the next majer problem that may 56 | 34
block your progress. An ability to take cdae of little things 61 | 37
the details is a sire sign of an educated person. 63 | 38

112

112a ▶5

Preparatory practice

each line 3 times SS (slowly, faster, slowly); retype selected lines as time permits

alphabet	With a fixed goal in mind, quickly size up a job before making a move.
fig/sym	B & Q will send #9076-X tacks in these sizes: 1/4, 3/8, 1/2, and 3/5.
long words	The morning speaker outlined the characteristics of digital computers.
fluency	The past is of use to us only as it can make fuller the life of today.
	| 1 | 2 | 3 | 4 | 5 | 6 | 7 | 8 | 9 | 10 | 11 | 12 | 13 | 14 |

112b ▶10

Improving keystroking precision

each line at least 2 times without an error

word response	When he finds that he has to pay on time, he will find a way to do it.
left-hand	After a date was set for the meeting, a secretary addressed the cards.
right-hand	In my opinion, you must give up not only the oil but your leases, too.
direct reaches	Many of the mementos my brother collected were brought to Grady Thumb.
	| 1 | 2 | 3 | 4 | 5 | 6 | 7 | 8 | 9 | 10 | 11 | 12 | 13 | 14 |

112c ▶15

Building statistical typing skill

1. Two 1′ writings for *speed* on each ¶.

2. One 5′ writing for *accuracy on* ¶ 1 and 2 combined. Determine *gwam*; circle errors.

Difficulty index

all letters/figures used | HA | 1.7 si | 6.0 awl | 75% hfw |

	gwam 1′	5′	
In 1980, the firm was in a very good financial position. Total	13	3	43
adjusted assets were $49,250,000; these assets were composed of $890,000	27	5	46
in cash, $350,500 in current receivables, $25,000,000 in investments,	41	8	49
$15,250,000 in fixed assets, and $7,759,500 in land and buildings. The	56	11	52
liabilities and equity side of the balance sheet was as follows: Current	71	14	55
liabilities were $1,250,000; long-term debt was $10,350,000; capital	99	17	57
stock was $35,000,000; and retained earnings were a sizable $2,650,000.	99	20	60
In 1980, the company had an exceptionally profitable year. The	13	22	63
gross revenue for the 12 months was equal to the gross revenue in 1979	27	25	66
at $69,800,000. The total expenditure deduction was, after deducting	41	28	69
taxes, $68,100,000. A surprising profit after taxes was $1,700,000;	55	31	71
this was a 4.8% return on investments in the firm. In 1979, the net	69	34	74
earnings were just 2.75%. Direct costs were decreased by 12.5%, and	82	36	77
the indirect costs decreased by 9.5%. With work we anticipate a sizable	97	39	80
increase in profits next year.	103	40	81

gwam 1′ | 1 | 2 | 3 | 4 | 5 | 6 | 7 | 8 | 9 | 10 | 11 | 12 | 13 | 14 |
5′ | 1 | 2 | 3 |

section

9

Typing tables and reports

lessons 40–47

Learning goals

1. To type two-, three-, and four-column tables in exact center and in reading position.
2. To type main, secondary, and column headings.
3. To align figures in columns; to align dollar signs and decimals.
4. To develop greater awareness of copy content.
5. To type outlines with headings and subheadings of first and second order.
6. To type unbound and left-bound reports.
7. To type spread headings.

Machine adjustments

1. Check chair and desk adjustment and placement of copy for easy reading.
2. Set paper guide at *0*; remove tab stops.
3. Set a 70-space line.
4. Set ribbon control on black.
5. SS drills; DS paragraphs.

40

40a ▶ 6
Preparatory Practice

each line 3 times SS (slowly, faster, slowly); DS between 3-line groups

alphabet	The wizard quickly converted six pert frogs into small bags of jewels.
figure	Flight 973 will leave at 6:40 and arrive in Philadelphia at 12:58 p.m.
direct reaches	No doubt my brother Marvin saw service as an umpire on that sunny day.
easy	Eight girls and Bud may bicycle to the lake for a trip to six islands.

| 1 | 2 | 3 | 4 | 5 | 6 | 7 | 8 | 9 | 10 | 11 | 12 | 13 | 14 |

40b ▶ 9
Preapplication drill

70-space line, SS

1. Remove all tab stops. Set a tab stop at center point.

2. Type the drill 3 times as shown; DS between drills. Keep your eyes on the book while you type.

——— tab ———► Typing a table is quite similar to
centering a horizontal line. ——— tab ———► View a line in a table the same as
a continuous line of type. ——— tab ———► Backspace for blank spaces just as
for typed characters. ——— tab ———► Backspace for the whole line, then
set the left margin stop. ——— tab ———► Backspace one for two; set margin;
space forward one for one. ——— tab ———► Set tab stops as needed.

40c ▶ 35
Typing problems: two-column tables

3 half sheets

Steps in horizontal centering of columns

1. Preparatory steps
a. Move margin stops to ends of scale. Clear all tabulator stops.
b. Move carriage (carrier) to center of page.
c. If spacing is not specified, decide spaces for intercolumns (area between columns)—preferably an even number of spaces (4, 6, 8, 10, 12, etc.).

2. To set left margin stop
From center of paper, backspace once for each 2 characters and spaces in longest line of each column, then for each 2 spaces to be left between columns. Set the left margin stop at this point.
If the longest line in one column has an extra letter or number, combine that letter or number with the first letter or number in the next column when backspacing by 2's; as in *ruler* (6) *ink*.

1 1 1 1 1 1 1
ru | le | ri | nk | 1-2 | 3-4 | 5-6

If one stroke is left over after backspacing for all columnar items, disregard it.

3. To set tabulator stops
From the left margin, space forward once for each letter, figure, symbol, and space in longest line in the first column and for each space to be left between first and second columns. *Set tab stop at this point for second column.* Follow similar procedure for additional columns to be typed.

111c ▶25
Building straight-copy typing skill

1. Two 1′ writings for *speed* on each ¶.
2. Two 5′ writings for *accuracy* on ¶s 1–3 combined. Record *gwam* and number of errors for the more accurate writing.

Difficulty index

all letters used	A	1.5 si	5.7 awl	80% hfw

gwam 1′ | 5′

Every administrator should try to cut the cost of preparing letters 14 3
and memos. There are many ways that an organization can reduce the cost 28 6
of correspondence; a few of these ways will be discussed at this time. 43 9
Perhaps the most efficient way to reduce correspondence costs is just to 57 11
write shorter letters. A shorter letter is more effective and takes less 72 14
time to prepare. Another way to trim costs is to ask executives to do 86 17
all of their dictation at one time; this should be accomplished quite 100 20
early in the day, if at all possible. If a secretary is utilized to take 115 23
the dictation, time used during dictation is a dual expenditure--a cost 129 26
of both the executive's and secretary's time. 138 28

Form letters can play quite a major part in cutting the cost of 13 30
preparing letters and memos. Care needs to be taken to insure that all 27 33
form letters are properly prepared and utilized only when needed. Not 41 36
only do form letters save the time of the executive, but the speed with 56 39
which a typist can produce a form letter is faster than transcribing a 70 42
dictated letter. Of course, many form letters can be typed on an auto- 84 45
matic typewriter, which will not only type the letters faster than a typ- 99 47
ist but will also type them more accurately. The use of preprinted 112 50
forms or postal cards for routine replies will cut costs considerably. 127 53
The office manager should determine which method of preparing letters 141 56
should be used. 144 66

There are many other ways of cutting costs in an office. When it 13 59
is appropriate, a secretary should be allowed to compose replies to rou- 28 62
tine requests and correspondence; just this one item will save a great 42 65
deal of the executive's time and will result in a significant cost sav- 56 68
ings. The key to cost reduction is planning and reorganizing; if done 70 70
properly, a lot of time and effort can be saved. All mail should be 98 76
answered the same day as received, if possible; but overtime costs should 84 73
not be incurred just to answer routine mail. Whenever a better procedure 113 79
is discovered, a long-range cost reduction will result, even if an immedi- 128 82
ate cost increase is incurred while the new way is learned. 140 84

gwam 1′ | 1 | 2 | 3 | 4 | 5 | 6 | 7 | 8 | 9 | 10 | 11 | 12 | 13 | 14 |
5′ | 1 | 2 | 3 |

			words
	ZEBRON COMPANY EXECUTIVE BOARD		6
		TS	
Margin stop ↓		Tab stop ↓	
	Rosa T. Washington	President	12
	Peter J. Vreede	Vice President	18
	Veda A. Angbier	Secretary	23
	M. L. Ortiz	Treasurer	28
	Louise R. Krobte	Member	33
	Taylor V. Reece	Member	37
Longest item in column	*Rosa T. Washington*	*10*	*Vice President*		

Center the tables vertically and horizontally on half sheets. (See page 59 for a review of vertical centering.)

Problem 1

Study the information on page 76 and the illustration above; then type the illustrated problem on a half sheet, long side up, SS; exact center; 10-space intercolumn.

Problem 2

Type the illustrated problem again. Use same directions as for Problem 1, but change SS to DS.

Problem 3

Type the problem at the right on a half sheet, long side up; SS; exact center; 10-space intercolumn.

▶ As standard procedure, triple-space between main or secondary headings and columns.

		words
ZEBRON COMPANY BRANCH MANAGERS		6
	TS	
J. Donald Husker	Albany	11
D. K. Stargill	Beaumont	16
Laurel A. Runcimun	Berkley	21
Mary Kipp Leahy	Canton	26
Paul K. Harvey	Milwaukee	31
Wayne D. McNulty, Jr.	St. Petersburg	38
Consuelo K. Bayh	Savannah	43
Elizabeth Reymer	Spokane	48
Wayne D. McNulty, Jr.	*10*	*St. Petersburg*		

section

24 Improving basic skills

lessons 111–112

Learning goals

Section 24 is designed to help you improve your typing speed and accuracy.

You should be able to type at one of the following rates on a 5-minute straight-copy timing of average difficulty with 8 or fewer errors: 54 *gwam*, excellent; 49-53 *gwam*, good; 42-48 *gwam*, acceptable.

The minimum goal in this section should be 42-48 *gwam*.

Machine adjustments

1. Set paper guide at *0*.
2. Set ribbon control on black.
3. Use a 70-space line and single spacing (SS) for drill lines.
4. Use a 70-space line, double spacing (DS), and 5-space ¶ indentions for paragraph copy.

111

111a ▶5 Preparatory practice

each line 3 times SS (slowly, faster, top speed); retype selected lines as time permits

alphabet	When judging books and movies, she frequently awarded exciting prizes.
fig/sym	Invoice #9863104, due on January 27, gave the discount for cash at 5%.
shift keys	J. T. Kane will visit Binford, N.D.; Altoona, Pa.; and Lake Shore, Md.
fluency	They told both of us to send the original form to the downtown office.

| 1 | 2 | 3 | 4 | 5 | 6 | 7 | 8 | 9 | 10 | 11 | 12 | 13 | 14 |

111b ▶20 Building rough-draft typing skill

1. A 1′ writing for *speed* on each ¶.

2. Two 5′ writings for *accuracy* on ¶s 1 and 2 combined. Record *gwam* and number of errors for the more accurate writing.

Difficulty index

all letters used | HA | 1.7 si | 6.0 awl | 75% hfw |

	gwam 1′	5′	
Educated ~~men~~ have learned that they can ~~uneover~~ important	12	2	42
details through the simple act of ~~hearing.~~ The secret, how-	26	5	45
ever, is well known, is to listen with discretion. Our usaul	39	8	47
ability to hearforces us to hear many thousands of noises,	51	10	50
while our amazing ability lets us select only what is important	65	13	53
what is minutae. often our only contribution is a question	79	16	55
and if our listening ~~sport~~ is an exciting program, we are	93	19	58
required to reply.	97	19	59
The class room is useful even if we have may finished the	13	22	62
formal part of our education. Advanced degrees are desirable	23	24	64
and possible. For the individual who does wish to enter a	38	27	67
degree program yet needs ~~for~~ some additional, perhaps specail-	53	30	70
ized, ~~training,~~ classes are ~~often~~ offered. adult classes ni	66	33	72
a locality, for example have been know to run from interior	79	35	75
design to judo, from philately to art. some of these classes	91	38	77
are fun for learning can be fun ~~and~~ useful.	101	40	79

41

41a ▶ 6 Preparatory practice

each line 3 times SS (slowly, faster, slowly); DS between 3-line groups

alphabet	The queen and king brought dozens of expensive jewels from the colony.
fig/sym	Order #7849-0 (dated 3/16) must be shipped by May 25 to Silva & Perez.
shift	THE LAKER BULLETIN, published in Dayton, Ohio, will be issued in July.
easy	Did the auditors say the visit of the legislator helped this endowment?

| 1 | 2 | 3 | 4 | 5 | 6 | 7 | 8 | 9 | 10 | 11 | 12 | 13 | 14 |

41b ▶ 9 Aligning figures in columns

twice as shown DS

1. Note the longest item in each column. Backspace from center once for each 2 strokes in the longest items and for an intercolumn of 14 spaces. Set the left margin.

2. Space forward once for each digit in the longest item in the first column; space forward one space for each space in the intercolumn; set a tab for the second column.

Since spacing forward and backward will be needed to align items at the right, adjust the margin and tab settings for the digit that requires the least forward and backward spacing. Thus, the left margin should be moved 2 spaces to the right (after typing first item), and the tab stop should be moved one space to the right.

	margin	tab
	4106	726
	37	space once → 26
	32	315
space once →	8	backspace once → 8448
	59	990
margin release; backspace →	115	70

4106	*14*	*8448*

41c ▶ 35 Typing problems: two-column tables with figures and headings

Problem 1

full sheet; DS; reading position; 20-space intercolumn

After setting the margin and tab stops as usual, adjust the left margin 2 spaces to the right to accommodate the most common word length. Use the margin release and backspacer to type longer lines. Similarly, adjust the tab stop one space to the right, then space forward and backward for shorter and longer lines.

		words
BARRYMORE PARK TREE CENSUS		5
TS		
Broad-leaf trees		9
Elm	3	11
Maple	227	13
Oak	129	15
Sycamore	42	17
Needle-leaf trees		21
Arborvitae	72	24
Cedar	90	26
Hemlock	74	28
Spruce	7	30
Yew	305	32
Fruit trees		34
Apple	4	36
Cherry	51	38
Pear	7	40

Needle-leaf trees	*20*	*227*

1 2 3 4 5 6 7 8 9 10 11 12 13 14 15 16 17 18 19 20

Continue with Problem 2, page 79.

107b-110b, continued

Job 10
Form letter [LM pp. 43–50]

Mr. LaFayette is Chairperson for a Business Equipment Show sponsored by the local chapter of the Administrative Management Society. The show is to be held in New Orleans. He has prepared a rough-draft letter of invitation to exhibit. You are to type the letter to each of the four persons whose names appear on the cards below. Date the letter May 10, 19—.

Stover, Katherine R. (Dr.)

Dr. Katherine R. Stover
Research Director
Advanced Systems, Inc.
133 Audubon Boulevard
New Orleans, LA 70118

Johnston, Frank C. (Mr.)

Mr. Frank C. Johnston
General Manager
Duplication, Inc.
1834 Bayou Road
New Orleans, LA 70116

Freestone, Sophia V. (Ms.)

Ms. Sophia V. Freestone
Vice President--Services
Business Machines, Inc.
1108 Pere Marquette
150 Baronne Street
New Orleans, LA 70112

DuPont, Carlton X. (Mr.)

Mr. Carlton X. DuPont
Executive Vice President
Louisiana Equipment Company
1504 International Trade Mart
2 Canal Street
New Orleans, LA 70130

Dear

The new Orleans and Baton Rouge chapters of the Administrative Management Society ~~AMS~~ extend a cordial ~~an~~ invitation to your company to exhibit your latest ~~newest~~ business equipment ~~machines~~ at the thirteenth Annual business equip ment show. ¶ This event will ~~even is to~~ be held at the new Hyatt Regency in New Orleans on June 21, 22, and 23. ~~Baton Rouge.~~ If the past business ~~e~~equipment shows are an indication ~~a true measure~~ of what we can ~~to~~ expect, this ~~year's~~ show will be the best ever. Last year, ~~T~~the number of people attending the sow h was 50 percent more than we had expected. our preliminary estimates are that this show ~~exhibit~~ will be even better. ¶ Remember, this is the only Business Equipment ~~Machines~~ Show of its kind in Louisiana. ~~the state.~~ If you will be one of the exhibitors, we know it will be a most ~~very~~ successful event.

Sincerely

Charles LaFayette, Chair~~man~~person
Business Equipment Show

¶ A layout of the available exhibit booths is enclosed; the booths are priced at $300, $350, and $400. Please complete and return the enclosed form within the next three weeks. The earlier your application is sent, the better will be your chance of being assigned your first choice.

TYPIST: Don't forget the enclosure notation.

41c, continued

Problem 2

full sheet; DS; reading position; 18-space intercolumn

A TS usually separates a main heading from a table; when a secondary heading is used, DS after the main heading and TS after the secondary heading.

For money columns, use the dollar sign only with the top figure and the total (when one is shown). Type it one space to the left of horizontal beginning point of the longest line in the column. It should be typed again in the same position when total line appears in the table.

main heading → ZEBRON COMPANY (words: 3)

DS

secondary heading → Branch Office Sales for January (words: 9)

tab stop → TS

		words
Albany	$127,325	13
Beaumont	14,295	16
Berkley	8,270	19
Canton	69,134	22
Milwaukee	28,400	25
St. Petersburg	9,356	29
Savannah	6,207	33
Spokane	14,375	37
	$277,362	39

18

42

42a ▶ 6 Preparatory practice

each line 3 times SS (slowly, faster, slowly); DS between 3-line groups

alphabet Qualified judges will have to analyze our club performances next week.

fig/sym Our #30865 pens will cost Moya & Brady $12.97 each (less 4% discount).

one hand In my opinion, Kim Loy based wages on average rates in affected areas.

easy The title to the land is now in the hands of the auditors of the firm.

| 1 | 2 | 3 | 4 | 5 | 6 | 7 | 8 | 9 | 10 | 11 | 12 | 13 | 14 |

42b ▶ 9 Developing alertness

twice untimed from book copy; DS; proofread and circle errors; then two 2′ writings from book copy

The ¶ has certain words that are scrambled. Keep the sense of the ¶ in mind as you type it, and these words will suggest themselves to you as you type. Work to avoid pauses. Concentrate on the copy.

Difficulty index

all letters used | LA | 1.4 si | 5.4 awl | 85% hfw |

gwam 2′

What is wrod processing? It is a new term that symbolizes the 6
effort currently being edam to permit an executive to turn his or her 13
thoughts toni letters and reports at top speed, with high accuracy, 20
with the least krow, and at the lowest soct. The machine that plays 27
the most vital arpt in this process is the automatic typewriter, and 34
competent experts say hatt the frequency of the use of this new process 41
for writing papers will increase by moer than four times in tsuj the 48
next few years. 50

gwam 2′ | 1 | 2 | 3 | 4 | 5 | 6 | 7 |

107b-110b, continued

Job 8
Approval copy of tabulation

Mr. LaFayette wants all typists in the company to have a copy of the two-letter ZIP abbreviations for ready reference at their desks. You have been asked to prepare an approval copy of this table for direct-copy duplication. Arrange the table attractively on the page. The main heading is: TWO-LETTER ZIP ABBREVIATIONS. The subheading is: For Use with ZIP Code.

2 sp. 14 sp. 2 sp.

AL	Alabama	MT	Montana
AK	Alaska	NE	Nebraska
AZ	Arizona	NV	Nevada
AR	Arkansas	NH	New Hampshire
CA	California	NJ	New Jersey
CZ	Canal Zone	NM	New Mexico
CO	Colorado	NY	New York
CT	Connecticut	NC	North Carolina
DE	Delaware	ND	North Dakota
DC	District of Columbia	OH	Ohio
FL	Florida	OK	Oklahoma
GA	Georgia	OR	Oregon
GU	Guam	PA	Pennsylvania
HI	Hawaii	PR	Puerto Rico
ID	Idaho	RI	Rhode Island
IL	Illinois	SC	South Carolina
IN	Indiana	SD	South Dakota
IA	Iowa	TN	Tennessee
KS	Kansas	TX	Texas
KY	Kentucky	UT	Utah
LA	Louisiana	VT	Vermont
ME	Maine	VI	Virgin Islands
MD	Maryland	VA	Virginia
MA	Massachusetts	WA	Washington
MI	Michigan	WV	West Virginia
MN	Minnesota	WI	Wisconsin
MS	Mississippi	WY	Wyoming
MO	Missouri		

Job 9
Composing a letter [LM p. 41]

Mr. LaFayette has asked you to prepare a reply to a letter that was received from an associate of his. The body of the letter is shown at the right. Date your letter May 9, 19—. Address the letter to Ms. Carol S. Wang who is Office Manager of Wang & Wang Consultants, 4034 Alpine Avenue, Memphis, TN 38108.

Dear Charles:

We are preparing a new Office Procedures Manual for our employees. I remember discussing some of our mutual problems last May when we were at the International AMS Conference.

I recall that your company had decided to use justified right margins for all in-house publications. Could you give me a brief summary of the procedures that a typist should follow when preparing copy with the right margin justified. Perhaps a statement of rationale (at least the major advantage) for using the procedure would also be of help to me.

Sincerely,

42c ▶ 10
Centering column headings

1. Read the information about centering column headings.

2. Type the drill at right; center headings over the columns. Underline the headings.

Centering column headings

1. A column heading should be centered over a column as represented by the longest item in the column.

2. To determine the center point of the longest item in a column, space forward from the starting point of the column once for every two strokes or spaces in the longest item. Disregard a leftover stroke.

3. The point where the forward spacing stops is the center of the column. Backspace once for each two strokes in the heading. Disregard a leftover stroke. Starting at the place where backspacing ended, type the heading.

half sheet; DS; 10 spaces between columns

Painting	Artist
The Blue Boy	Gainsborough
Mona Lisa	Da Vinci
View of Toledo	El Greco
The Starry Night	Van Gogh

The Starry Night	*10*	*Gainsborough*

42d ▶ 25
Typing problems: three-column tables with main and column headings

Problem 1

full sheet; DS; reading position; 6-space intercolumns

OFFICIAL INSECTS AND FLOWERS OF SELECTED STATES — words 10

State	Insect	Flower	words
			17
Arkansas	honeybee	apple blossom	24
Connecticut	praying mantis	mountain laurel	32
Delaware	ladybug	peach blossom	39
Illinois	monarch butterfly	native violet	47
Maryland	checkerspot butterfly	black-eyed susan	56
Massachusetts	ladybug	mayflower	63
Nebraska	honeybee	goldenrod	69
New Jersey	honeybee	purple violet	76
North Carolina	honeybee	dogwood	82
Pennsylvania	firefly	mountain laurel	90

North Carolina	*6*	*checkerspot butterfly*	*6*	*black-eyed susan*

Problem 2

half sheet, long side up; SS; exact center; 8-space intercolumns

For Column 2, use the column heading *Place* as the longest item in the line. After typing the heading, adjust the tab stop 2 spaces to the right.

CHARLESTON YACHT CLUB RACE RESULTS — 7

Boat	Place	Time	
			13
Challenger	4	2:58	17
Chieftain	6	3:00	20
Dora's Dream	1	:58	24
Lottaluck	9	10:08	28
Ocean Era	5	2:59	31
Aberdeen Rolling Stone	2	:59	37
Saucy	7	3:17	40
Stalwart	8	4:24	43
Trident Three	3	2:35	47

Aberdeen Rolling Stone	*8*	*Place*	*8*	*10:08*

107b-110b, continued

Job 5
Letter [LM p. 35]

Today, May 2, Mr. LaFayette wrote a letter to the Kansas Supply Company, 535 South Broadway, Wichita, KS 67202. He has given you the letter to type. The letter should be called to the attention of Ms. Wilma Crenshaw, Manager. You are to supply an appropriate salutation and a complimentary close for the letter.

Subject: Our Purchase Order No. B-80321

(¶) I sent an order to you three weeks ago; and as of today, I have not received an acknowledgment from you. (¶) Because our present stock of paper is very low, this order must be received within two weeks. If you cannot expect to deliver at least a partial shipment within two weeks, we shall have to cancel this order and place it with another supplier. (¶) Our association with your firm has been excellent during the past five years, and I hope we can continue to do business with you for many years to come. However, we must receive an acknowledgment of our orders within ten days or we shall be forced to find a new supplier for our paper requirements. (¶) On the assumption that our order has been accidentally lost or misplaced, I am enclosing a duplicate copy of the original order. Please acknowledge by return mail and inform me of the exact status of this order.

Job 6
Composing a memo [LM p. 37]

Mr. LaFayette has asked you to compose a memo for him to send to Mr. Sven Jorgensen, Purchasing Agent, on May 8. Inform Mr. Jorgensen that you (Mr. LaFayette) just received an acknowledgment from Kansas Supply Company stating that our order for paper will arrive within 10 days. Ms. Crenshaw explained that the order had been misplaced; she apologized for the inconvenience. Try to be thorough and give ample information to Mr. Jorgensen. Include the fact that you had written about the delay on May 2.

Job 7
Typing index cards [LM p. 39]

Mr. LaFayette maintains a current file of all approved suppliers. The name of each supplier is typed on a 5″ × 3″ index card. You will notice on the sample card that the first typed line contains the transposed name of the individual if an individual's name is the first line of the supplier's name.

Mr. LaFayette has given you the names of 4 new suppliers to be added to the file. (See the list below.) You are to type an index card for each supplier and arrange the cards in alphabetical order.

```
                              TS
Franklin, Henry I. (Mr.)
                              TS
Mr. Henry I. Franklin
3500 Drennen Road
Colorado Springs, CO 80911
```

1. **Miss Phyllis Santi**
   2104 Dillingham Street
   Shreveport, LA 71104
2. **New Orleans Paper, Inc.**
   415 Bolivar Street
   New Orleans, LA 70112
3. **Baton Rouge Stationers**
   7899 Jefferson Highway
   Baton Rouge, LA 70809
4. **Mr. Frank S. Longfellow**
   8130 Beechnut Street
   Houston, TX 77036

43

43a ▶ 6 Preparatory practice

each line 3 times SS (slowly, faster, slowly); DS between 3-line groups

alphabet	Julie began to study the six chapters on vitamins for her weekly quiz.
fig/sym	The 2% discount on Rob & Bond's Bill 34019 amounted to exactly $78.65.
adjacent reaches	As Klu Amneus said, few exceed the points asserted by Portia Trewspon.
easy	Problems in math that involve right angles or triangles are difficult.

| 1 | 2 | 3 | 4 | 5 | 6 | 7 | 8 | 9 | 10 | 11 | 12 | 13 | 14 |

43b ▶ 9 Developing alertness

twice untimed from book copy; DS; proofread and circle errors; then two 2′ writings from book copy

Keep the sense of the ¶ in mind as you type so that the scrambled words will suggest themselves to you. Avoid pauses; concentrate.

Difficulty index

all letters used | A | 1.4 si | 5.4 awl | 85% hfw | gwam 2′

The automatic typewriter has long bene used to type form letters. 7
Because the letters are typed instead of printed, they vahe a personal- 14
ized look about them. Another way in which this machine can be sude 21
is to record on tape copy htat is to be typed on paper. The pocy is 28
then edited, and changes are made by checking the places to be changed 35
and adjusting for the new copy. The final copy, which can hent be made 42
quickly romf the tape, is exactly as edited. 46

gwam 2′ | 1 | 2 | 3 | 4 | 5 | 6 | 7 |

43c ▶ 10 Aligning and typing over words

It is sometimes necessary to reinsert the paper to correct an error. The following steps will help you learn to do so correctly.

1. Type this sentence, but do not make the return:

`I can align this copy.`

2. Locate aligning scale (21) and variable line spacer (3) on your typewriter.

3. Move carriage (carrier) so that a word containing an *i* (such as *align*) is above the aligning scale. Note that a vertical line points to the center of *i*.

4. Study the relation between top of aligning scale and bottoms of letters with downstems (*g, p, y*).

Get an exact eye picture of the relation of typed line to top of scale so you will be able to adjust the paper correctly to type over a word with exactness.

5. Remove paper; reinsert it. Gauge the line so bottoms of letters are in correct relation to top of aligning scale. Operate the *variable line spacer*, if necessary, to move paper up or down. Operate *paper release lever* to move paper left or right, if necessary, when centering the letter *i* over one of the lines on the aligning scale.

6. Check accuracy of alignment by setting the *ribbon control* in stencil position and typing over one of the letters. If necessary, make further alignment adjustments.

7. Return ribbon control to normal position (to type on black).

8. Type over the words in the sentence, moving paper up or down, to left or right, as necessary to correct alignment.

43d ▶ 25 Typing problems: four-column tables with main, secondary, and column headings

Problem 1

half sheet, long side up; SS; exact center; 6-space intercolumns

▶ Reminder: When main and secondary headings are used, DS after the main heading and TS after the secondary heading.

AMERICA'S TALL BUILDINGS (DS) — words 5

Construction Completed (TS) — 10

Building	City	Feet	Stories	words
				20
Sears Tower	Chicago	1,454	110	26
World Trade Center	New York	1,350	110	33
Empire State	New York	1,250	102	40
Standard Oil (Indiana)	Chicago	1,136	80	48
John Hancock Center	Chicago	1,127	100	56
Chrysler	New York	1,046	77	61
60 Wall Tower	New York	950	67	68

Standard Oil (Indiana)	6	New York	6	1,454	6	Stories

123456

107b-110b, continued

Job 2
Approval copy of memo to be duplicated [LM p. 33]

Mr. LaFayette has asked you to type an approval copy of a memo he will send to all typists. Date the memo May 1, 19—. The subject of the memo is: Justifying the Right Margin.

Because the memo is about justifying the right margin, Mr. LaFayette wants the memo typed with the right margin justified. Therefore, you will need to type the memo twice as indicated in the "Excerpts from the Office Procedures Manual" on page 217.

In the body of the memo, there are two 4-line examples of material to be justified on a 46-space line; be sure to center the 46-space line when typing these two examples.

If a direct-copy machine is available, make 2 good copies.

(¶ 1) All publications of the Andersen-Jones Manufacturing Co. will be prepared and duplicated within our own office. Because we want all our publications to have the appearance of a printed page, you should become experts in justifying the right margin. (¶ 2) As you can see from this memorandum, an even right-hand margin has a very professional-looking effect. Even though this process of justifying the right margin is time-consuming, we feel that the improved public relations image is worth the additional time and expense incurred. (¶ 3) As you type a line to be justified, come as close to the right margin as possible (avoid extending beyond the desired margin). As a procedure for determining how many extra spaces will be needed in the line, type a diagonal (/) in every space remaining to the right margin. As an example, the following material is typed on a 46-space line:

```
All the cards in a card index file should be //
typed in the same form.  Uniformity of style //
facilitates the filing and finding operations.
Individual and company names should be typed //
```

(¶ 4) After you have typed the material the first time, retype the material and evenly distribute the extra blank spaces throughout the line. For example, the illustration above would be retyped as follows:

```
All the cards in a card  index  file should be
typed  in  the same form.  Uniformity of style
facilitates the filing and finding operations.
Individual and company names  should  be typed
```

(¶ 5) Please read thoroughly the procedures as outlined in the new Office Procedures Manual.

Job 3
Typing a spirit master

After Mr. LaFayette (your teacher-supervisor) has approved the copy of the memo you typed in Job 2, you are to prepare a spirit master of this approval copy. Because the memo will be duplicated on plain paper, you will need to type the memo headings TO:, FROM:, DATE:, and SUBJECT: on the spirit master. (Refer to pages 218–219 if necessary.) Remember to proofread carefully and correct all errors.

If a spirit duplicator is available, run 10 good copies.

Job 4
Typing a stencil

Mr. LaFayette later decided that the demand for copies of the memo in Job 2 will require the preparation of a stencil; therefore, he has asked you to prepare a stencil of the approval copy of that memo. Be sure to type the memo headings on the stencil. (If necessary, refer to pages 217–218.) Proofread carefully and correct all errors.

If a stencil duplicator is available, run 10 good copies.

43d, continued

Problem 2
half sheet, long side up; make all decisions for placement of copy

				words
	ZEBRON COMPANY			3
	Savannah Branch Salespersons			9
Salesperson	Address	ZIP	Telephone	22
Boehm, Marvyne	645 Senauki Lane	31411	397-3569	31
Higbee, Toni Jay	One Columbia Avenue	31405	394-6677	42
Hughes, Elizabeth	4123 Lawton Avenue	31404	394-1235	52
Jiminez, Andres	375 Caithness Street	31405	394-8975	63
Lobthaler, Martyn	5082 Frazier Drive	31405	394-7611	72
Po-ling, Lu-yin	509 Wellington Court	31410	397-8590	83
Rayhontz, Faye P.	384 Burbank Boulevard	31406	397-1020	94
St. Johns, Frank O.	666 Byck Avenue	31408	384-5408	104

44

44a ▶ 6
Preparatory practice
each line 3 times SS (concentrate on copy); DS between 3-line groups

alphabet The audience was amazed by the report Joan F. Maxwell gave so quickly.

fig/sym Kauffman's Invoice #2378 for $461.50 (less 2%) was paid on November 9.

adjacent reaches Last Wednesday, Drew Poins inquired about transportation for Sam Polk.

easy The aid we got from them did much to help us all get this paper typed.

| 1 | 2 | 3 | 4 | 5 | 6 | 7 | 8 | 9 | 10 | 11 | 12 | 13 | 14 |

44b ▶ 9
Composing and typing
1. Type a ¶ describing what you think your reaction would be to the situation described.

2. Correct your draft; type a final copy. Use full sheet; 70-space line; begin on Line 13.

A new car? Help the family? Savings certificate? Las Vegas? These are just a few of the thoughts that zing through your mind as you receive in the mail a $1 million prize winner's check for a contest you entered. Describe how you think your life would be changed (or would it?) immediately and in the long run now that you are a millionaire What will you do with all that money?

44c ▶ 35
Typing problems: outlines and reports
Study the information at the right, then type the problems on page 83.

Information for typing outlines and reports

It is important that typists, especially students who type, be familiar with standard procedures for typing outlines and reports. (The term *report* also refers to *term papers, themes, manuscripts,* and other forms of reporting).

The lessons in Section 9 contain examples of problems that arise while typing outlines and reports, and their solutions are illustrated often in the problems themselves. Read the suggested standard guides in the following paragraphs; then study the form of each problem visually, read it for comprehension, and type it for practice.

Outlines. Notice that outlines separate subject matter into divisions and subdivisions. As data is divided, it is typed farther to the right in 4-space stages. For margin settings, use the same placement guides as are suggested for typing reports.

Reports. In the absence of more specific instructions, the following guides are usually acceptable and should be followed for typing the problems in Section 9.

Use double spacing. For the second and subsequent pages, allow 1" margins on all four sides. However, if the report is to be bound, stapled, or clipped at the top or left, add an extra ½" to that margin. Read carefully Problem 2, page 83, for more information about placement.

When 1" side margins are used, 10 pica or 12 elite spaces should be allowed. Set the left margin 1" from the left edge. Set the right margin 1" from the right edge, then adjust it to the right to accommodate the bell warning desired. Six lines constitute one vertical inch for either elite or pica type.

Office Job Simulation, continued

In preparing materials for copy machines, follow these guides:

1. Clean the type; use a good ribbon.
2. Type the material to be copied on plain paper, letterhead, or special form.
3. Erase or correct all errors neatly before making the additional copies.

Memo Headings on Plain Paper. If a printed memo form is not available, or if a memo is to be typed for duplication on a spirit master or a stencil, the memo headings TO:, FROM:, DATE:, and SUBJECT: must be typed as a part of the memo. Note the placement of the headings in the illustration below.

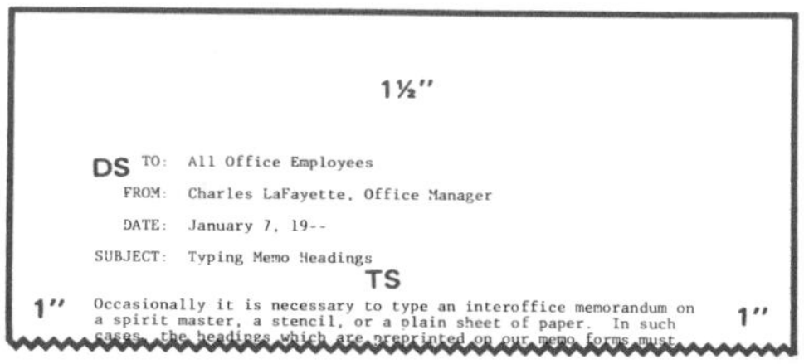

1½"

DS TO: All Office Employees
FROM: Charles LaFayette, Office Manager
DATE: January 7, 19--
SUBJECT: Typing Memo Headings

TS

1" Occasionally it is necessary to type an interoffice memorandum on a spirit master, a stencil, or a plain sheet of paper. In such cases, the headings which are preprinted on our memo forms must 1"

107-110

107a-110a ▶ 5 Preparatory practice

Type as many times as you can in 5'.

alphabet	The queer caves in Arizona were explored by Jackie Morgan before dawn.
fig/sym	Use two dollar signs in such expressions: $169 to $530; $720 or $840.
min	The minister was mindful that the minor ate a minimum of twenty mints.
fluency	Eight of us signed the amendment to change the title to the lake land.
	| 1 | 2 | 3 | 4 | 5 | 6 | 7 | 8 | 9 | 10 | 11 | 12 | 13 | 14 |

107b-110b ▶ 45 Office work simulation

Job 1: Interoffice Memorandum [LM p. 31]

Mr. LaFayette has asked you to prepare this memorandum for direct-copy duplication. It will be sent to all office employees. Date the memo May 1, 19—. The subject of the memo is: Preparing Material for Duplication.

Proofread, then correct any errors before you remove the memo from your typewriter.

The Executive Council of the Company has approved our new Office Procedures Manual; therefore, all materials to be duplicated should follow the guidelines listed on pages 68 through 75 of the Manual.

All office employees are encouraged to review the complete Manual and become very familiar with all sections. As office manager, I shall periodically prepare a memo about a specific section of the Manual in order to help everyone keep current and up to date. This memo is designed to call your attention to the guidelines for preparing material for duplication.

Generally, it is recommended that an approval copy of material to be duplicated be prepared, especially if the material is to be stenciled. Be sure to double-check the copy--once for accuracy of typing and once for accuracy of style.

To insure that you will get the best results from the duplication process, clean the type on your typewriter. All errors must be corrected properly; the Manual contains a step-by-step procedure for correcting errors on stencils, on spirit masters, and on copy to be used in the direct-copy process--see pages 69, 72, and 75.

If you have any questions concerning the proper procedures for preparing materials for duplication, please ask me for assistance. It is much better to ask for assistance than it is to follow the wrong procedure and waste valuable time in redoing a job. Be sure to take the time necessary to learn the correct procedures before proceeding with the job. Remember the old adage, "Haste makes waste."

xx

44c, continued

Problem 1

full sheet; 2" top margin; center heading; 1" side margins; space as directed

		words
	TOPIC OUTLINE	3
	TS	
Space forward twice from margin (2 spaces)	I. IDENTIFYING DIVISIONS OF AN OUTLINE	11
	DS	
Reset margin (2 spaces)	A. Roman Numerals for Major Divisions	19
	B. Capital Letters for First-Order Subheadings	29
	C. Arabic Numerals for Second-Order Subheadings	38
	D. Lowercase Letters for Third-Order Subheadings	48
	DS	
Backspace 5 times	II. CAPITALIZATION OF HEADINGS IN AN OUTLINE	57
	DS	
	A. Major Headings in All Caps	65
	B. First-Order Subheadings with Important Words Capped	76
	C. Second-Order Subheadings with Only First Word Capped	87
	D. Third-Order Subheadings with Only First Word Capped	99
	DS	
Backspace 6 times	III. SPACING AND PUNCTUATION IN AN OUTLINE	109
	DS	
	A. Spacing	111
1st tab	1. Horizontal spacing	116
2d tab	a. Title typed either solid or as spread heading	126
	b. Other headings typed solid	133
	c. Two spaces after identifying designation	142
	2. Vertical spacing as indicated in this outline	152
	B. Punctuation	157
	1. Except for abbreviations, no end-of-line punctua-	166
	tion in topic outlines	171
	2. Appropriate end-of-line punctuation in sentence	182
	outlines	184

Problem 2

follow Problem 1 directions

	words
UNBOUND REPORTS	3
I. MARGINS FOR UNBOUND REPORT	10
A. Top Margin	13
1. First page: pica, 1 1/2"; elite, 2"	21
2. Other pages: 1"	25
B. Side and Bottom Margins (All Pages)	33
1. Left and right margins: 1"	40
2. Bottom margins: 1"	45
II. SPACING	49
A. Manuscripts for Publication, School Reports, Formal	60
Reports Double-Spaced	64
B. Business Reports Often Single-Spaced	73
C. Quoted Material of Four or More Lines Single-Spaced	84
1. Indented 5 spaces from both margins	92
2. Quotation marks permissible but not required	102
D. Enumerations	105
1. Indented 5 spaces from both margins; blocked lines	117
2. Single-spaced with a double space between items	127

Office Job Simulation, continued

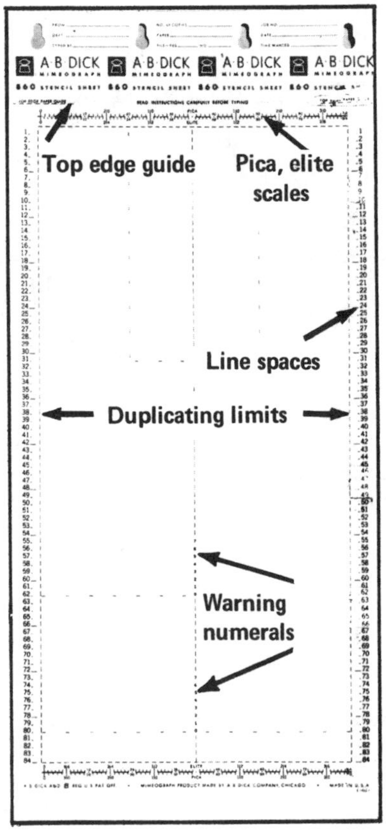

The following steps should be followed when typing a stencil:

1. Type a model copy of the material. Check it for accuracy of form and typing.
2. Clean the type thoroughly.
3. Move the ribbon-control lever to the stencil position.
4. Insert the cushion sheet between the stencil sheet and the backing sheet.
5. Set the touch control at the point that will insure the sharpest outlines without cutting out the characters.
6. Push the paper-bail rollers to the extreme left and right sides of the bail so that they will not roll on the stencil sheet.
7. Place the top edge of the model copy at the corner marks of the stencil to see where to type the first line of copy.

Use a firm, uniform, staccato touch as you type. Correct all errors with correction fluid. Use a glass burnisher or a paper clip to rub the surface of the error; apply a light coat of correction fluid over the error. Let it dry and make the necessary correction, using a light touch.

Spirit Duplication. The spirit process is generally used for runs of 10 to 100 copies, although up to 300 can be made from a single spirit master. The spirit master set consists of two basic parts: a master sheet and a sheet of special carbon. See illustration below. The use of a backing sheet will improve the consistency of the type impression. As you type, the carbon copy will be on the *back* of the master sheet.

The following steps should be followed when typing a spirit master:

1. Prepare a model copy of the material to be typed on the master. Check the copy for accuracy of form and typing.
2. Clean the type. The ribbon should be light-weight to prevent broad impressions and filled-in characters.
3. Use a firm, even stroke on a nonelectric typewriter. On an electric typewriter, one of the lower pressure settings is better.
4. If you make an error, scrape off the letter or word on the back of the master sheet with a knife or razor blade. Rub the scraped area with a correction pencil. Then, place a small piece of carbon (torn from an unused section of the spirit master) under the area to be retyped; place the glossy side toward you. Type over the incorrect letter or word. Remove the piece of carbon as soon as you have corrected the error.

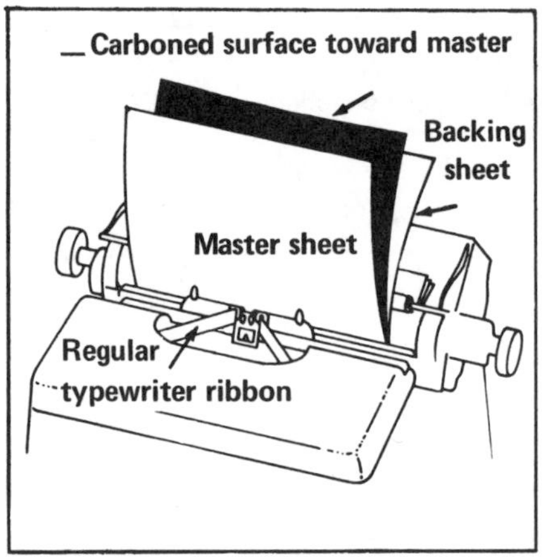

Direct-Copy Duplication. The direct-copy process is used primarily for making from one to ten copies. Copy machines are especially useful in making additional copies of incoming documents such as customers' orders and bills of lading. They may also be used when a few copies of correspondence are needed.

45

45a ▶ 6
Preparatory practice

each line 3 times SS (concentrate on copy); DS between 3-line groups

alphabet They expected to solve the jigsaw puzzle more quickly than Deb Franks.
fig/sym Did Ned pay $4.81 to $4.95 (less 6% discount) for 37 feet of #02 wire?
one-hand Several facets of test data, based on our abstracts, detected a trend.
easy Dorothy informed the firms of the total value of her stocks and bonds.

| 1 | 2 | 3 | 4 | 5 | 6 | 7 | 8 | 9 | 10 | 11 | 12 | 13 | 14 |

45b ▶ 9
Developing awareness

twice untimed and two 2′ timed writings from book copy; DS; proofread and circle errors after each typing

Concentrate on copy as you type, supplying as many of the missing 4-stroke words as you can without pausing. Work for accuracy.

Missing words
best when
good will
need your (or down)
read

Difficulty index

all letters used | LA | 1.3 si | 5.4 awl | 85% hfw |

gwam 2′

When you compose your reports, you _____ discover that the first 6
writing is rarely your _____ one. Your work may be readable all right, 14
but usually there are some areas that _____ polish. An excellent first 21
step, therefore, is to jot _____ ideas on paper as quickly as possible, 28
then edit and revise as needed. _____ your paper aloud; if it sounds 35
good to you, it will likely sound _____ to your readers. Realize that 42
time will not permit you to be too fussy. Know when to polish--and 48
_____ to finish. 50

gwam 2′ | 1 | 2 | 3 | 4 | 5 | 6 | 7 |

45c ▶ 35
Typing problems: unbound reports/spread headings

Problem 1
full sheet

Margins
top: 2″ elite
1½″ pica
sides: 1″

Type the report DS; 5-space ¶ indentions; heading solid as shown.

METRIC EQUIVALENTS

	Centimeters (cm)
1 inch	2.5
1½ inches	3.75
2 inches	5.0
10 pica spaces	2.5
12 elite spaces	2.5
6 vertical line spaces	2.5
8½ by 11-inch paper	21.5 by 28

Continue with Problem 2, page 85.

words

SIMPLE REPORT STYLE 4
TS

You have typed most of your work up to this time with a specified line 18
length of 60 or 70 spaces, regardless of whether your typewriter had pica- or 34
elite-size type. Now you will be asked to prepare formal reports (manuscripts), 50
using generally accepted procedures for typing them. These procedures 64
establish placement according to the number of inches in margins instead 79
of by the number of spaces in writing lines. 88

When these standard procedures are followed, pica and elite solutions 102
will differ somewhat. If 1-inch side margins are used, for example, an elite 118
line will contain 78 spaces; but a pica line will contain only 65 spaces. As a 134
result, more copy will fit on a page of elite type. 144

When side margins of 1 inch are desired, 10 pica spaces should be 158
allowed in each margin. On the other hand, users of elite type should allow 173
12 spaces. 175

section **23**

Typing in a general office

lessons 107–110

Section 23 is designed to provide you with ample opportunity to type the kinds of problems that you would normally expect to encounter when working in a general office.

Supplies needed

letterheads and memorandum forms [LM pp. 31-38, 41-50] or plain full sheets
index cards [LM p. 39]
spirit masters; stencil; carbon sheets; second sheets; envelopes of appropriate size

Machine adjustments

1. Check chair and desk adjustments and placement of copy for easy reading.
2. Set paper guide at *0*.
3. Set ribbon control on black except when typing a stencil.
4. Margins: 70-space line for drills and ¶ writings; as directed (or appropriate) for problems.
5. SS line drills; DS ¶s; space problems as directed (or appropriate).

Daily practice plan

Preparatory practice ...... 5′
Office work simulation .... 45′

Learning goals

1. To become familiar with the work of a general office.
2. To plan your work and complete it efficiently.
3. To integrate your knowledge and skills in completing office work acceptably.

Office Job Simulation

Read carefully the material at the right, on page 218, and at the top of page 219 before you begin the work of Section 23. Note any standard procedures that you think will save you time during the completion of the office job production activities.

Introduction

You have been hired as an employee of the Andersen-Jones Manufacturing Co., 2434 Highland Road, Baton Rouge, LA 70802. You will be the typist for Mr. Charles LaFayette, Office Manager.

The company style manual specifies that all company letters are to be typed in block style with open punctuation. The closing lines of all letters should include the typed name of the person for whom the letters are typed followed on the next line by that person's business title. All letters and memorandums require *one* carbon copy for the file. Address appropriate envelopes for all letters typed.

Proofread all work carefully before removing it from your typewriter; correct all detected errors. All typed work that is to leave the company should be "mailable"--technically correct with all errors corrected neatly. All typed work to be used *within* the company should be "usable"--content correct but with *minor* "flaws" in format and placement permitted.

When specific job instructions are given, follow them carefully. When specific instructions are not given, make appropriate decisions on the basis of knowledge and experience. If your supervisor (your teacher) considers some of your decisions unacceptable, learn from her or his suggestions--just as you would do in a business office.

The Andersen-Jones Manufacturing Co. has based its office manual and job instruction booklets on COLLEGE TYPEWRITING, so use the Reference Guide and the index of your textbook to look up matters of style and placement when in doubt. When a job requires unusual specifications, Andersen-Jones Manufacturing Co. provides them in "Excerpts from the Office Procedures Manual."

Excerpts from the Office Procedures Manual

Justifying the Right Margin. The process of justifying the right margin gives the finished copy the appearance of a printed page with the right margin evenly aligned. Except for the last line of a paragraph, the words in each line are carefully spaced so that the right margin will be even. All material must be typed twice. The first typing is used to determine how many extra spaces must be added to each line during the final or second typing. The normal procedure is to type as close to the end of the line as possible and then fill the remaining spaces with diagonals.

First typing:

```
It is human nature to resist///
change.  A hundred years ago,//
for example, many people said//
that the invention of the cot-/
```

Second typing:

```
It is  human  nature  to resist
change.  A hundred  years  ago,
for example,  many people  said
that  the invention of the cot-
```

When typing the material in final form, you must use good judgment in distributing the unused spaces throughout the line so they are least noticeable.

Stencil Duplication. The stencil duplication process can be used to reproduce more than a thousand clear, dark copies. A stencil, as illustrated on page 218, consists of three basic parts: a stencil sheet, a backing sheet, and a cushion sheet. The cushion sheet is placed between the stencil and the backing sheet to absorb the impact of the striking keys. A typing film may be placed over the stencil if darker copies are desired. This film also protects the stencil sheet from letter cutout when the typeface is extremely sharp.

45c, continued

Problem 2

half sheet; 2" top margin; DS; center each heading at the far right as a spread heading, as shown in the first heading

> **Centering spread headings**
> **1.** To center a spread heading, backspace from the center point once for each letter, character, and space except for the last letter or character in the heading.
> **2.** From this point, type the heading, spacing once after each letter or character and 3 times between words.

S P R E A D   H E A D I N G S 14

PREPARING REPORTS 16

PREPARING TERM PAPERS AND THEMES 31

TYPING AN OUTLINE 16

Problem 3

full sheet; top margin of 2" (pica) or 2½" (elite); side margins of 1"; DS; 5-space ¶ indention

Retype the report in Problem 1, page 84. Use a spread heading.

46

46a ▶ 6
Preparatory practice

each line 3 times SS (work for fewer than 3 errors per group); DS between 3 line groups

alphabet	**Mrs. Brown was dazzled by the quick jumps of five or six gymnasts.**
fig/sym	**Baxter & Moore's check for $946.20 (Check #1385) was cashed on July 7.**
double letter	**Will Ginny Feeser discuss Miss Bell's brilliant book, HAWAIIAN SUMMER?**
easy	**A worker ought to want sufficient work to do and the muscles to do it.**

| 1 | 2 | 3 | 4 | 5 | 6 | 7 | 8 | 9 | 10 | 11 | 12 | 13 | 14 |

46b ▶ 9
Typing special characters

each line at least twice

Special characters and symbols are useful when space for typing is restricted (typing forms, for example) or in certain problem situations. Use them sparingly, if at all, in prose material.

addition	+	diagonal; backspace; hyphen
multiplication	x	lowercase x
insert (omission)	/	made a/symbol
minus	-	hyphen (leave a space on each side)
second/inches	"	quotation marks
minutes/feet	'	apostrophe
division	÷	colon; backspace; hyphen
superscript	32°	roll platen backward ½ space
subscript	H_2O	roll platen forward ½ space
equals	=	hyphen; backspace; roll platen forward slightly; hyphen

```
The 2' speed range, typed with the 15" call of the guide, is 30 to 46.
A rug 15'6" x 18'9" will be just right for a room that is 20'6" x 25'.
His problem is 27 x 89 - 364 ÷ 2.  What is the sum of 157 + 509 - 263?
Type:  15 x 90 - 62 + 136 ÷ 2 = 712 and 7 x 284 - 965 + 301 ÷ 2 = 662.
If 32 x 564 - 897 + 109 equals 17,260, what would 57 + 590 - 63 equal?
```

The boiling point of H_2O is 212° F., and 32° F. is its freezing point.

T. W. Birch and P. Gyorgy[1] isolated/vitamin B_6 in experiments on rats.

103b-106b, continued

Job 10
Quotation [LM p. 27]

The Request for Quotation shown at the right was received today, April 12. Prepare a Quotation for Gurnick and Hershey.

1. Date the Quotation April 13.

2. Use the quantity and description from the Request for Quotation.

3. In the *Description* column, type:

$36.00 per gross list price
  10% quantity discount
Net price
Quoted price good for 60 days from the above date of issue.

Anthony V. Zellinski
Assistant Sales Manager

4. In the *Price* column, record these figures:

gross list price	$540.00
10% quantity discount	54.00
net price	$486.00

Request for Quotation - - This is not an order.

Gurnick & Hershey Enterprises

12703 Benham Road
Florissant, MO 63034
(314) 721-2121

To: A and K Wholesale Distributors, Inc.
Suite 1295
International Office Building
722 Chestnut Street
St. Louis, MO 63101

Date Issued: April 10, 19--   Date Required: April 30, 19--

Quantity	Description
15 gross	XL 150 Hard-tip pens (black)

Job 11
Invoice [LM p. 29]

You have received a Purchase Order (shown at right) from Gurnick & Hershey. The pens have been shipped; therefore, you need to type the invoice. If you need an example, use the illustration of an invoice on page 211. The additional data you will need are as follows:

Date: April 22, 19--
Our Order No.: S-31228
Cust. Order No.: K-36482
Shipped Via: UPS

Gurnick & Hershey Enterprises   PURCHASE ORDER

12703 Benham Road Florissant, MO 63034 (314) 721-2121

Purchase order No. K-36482

A and K Wholesale Distributors, Inc.
Suite 1295
International Office Building
722 Chestnut Street
St. Louis, MO 63101

Date April 20, 19--
Terms 2/10, n/30
Ship Via Parcel post

Quantity	Cat. No.	Description	Price	Total
15 gross	XL 150	Hard-tip pens (black)	36.00/gross	540.00
		10% quantity discount		54.00
		Net price		486.00

By______________________________ Purchasing Agent

46c ▶ 5
Typing the * (asterisk)

The * (asterisk) may be used to refer to a footnote. Find the location of the * on your typewriter; watch as your finger practices the reach; then type the appropriate drill line twice.

Electric typewriter: The * is the shift of **8**. Type it with the **8** finger.

```
k8k k*k k*k My first * refers to page 129, ** refers to page 307.
```

Nonelectric typewriter: The * is the shift of –. Type it with the ; finger.

```
;–; ;*; ;*; My first * refers to page 129, ** refers to page 307.
```

46d ▶ 30
Typing problems: unbound report with footnote

full sheet

Margins

top: 2″ elite
1½″ pica
side: 1″
bottom: approx. 1″

1. Read the information in the unbound report at the right before inserting paper into the typewriter.

2. Type the report DS. Indent listed items 5 spaces from both margins; SS individual items; DS between items.

words

TYPING FOOTNOTES 3

TS

In formal reports, sources for all opinions or statements of fact of some- 18
one not the writer and all direct quotations taken from books and articles must 34
be shown with footnotes. Also, Keithley and Schreiner say, "Footnotes provide 50
the most versatile method of referring the reader to information outside the 65
text material."* 69

Footnotes are typed at the foot of the page on which their reference num- 84
bers appear or at the end of the report. They are single-spaced with a blank line 100
space between them. When footnotes are numbered, the numbers run in 114
sequence throughout a report or begin anew on each page. Reference numbers 129
or symbols are typed a half space above the line at the end of a quotation. 145

The following procedure for positioning footnotes works well: 157

1. Before putting paper into the machine, pencil a light line to 171
mark space needed for a 1-inch bottom margin. 180

2. Insert paper into the machine to the pencil mark. Roll the 193
platen up three lines for the footnote plus one more line 205
for the space between footnotes. Make a new pencil line. 217

3. Repeat the procedure for each additional footnote on same page, 239
allowing an extra line space for double-spacing between foot- 242
notes. Make a new pencil line for each footnote and another 254
pencil line two line spaces above the uppermost footnote for the 267
divider line. Erase all pencil marks after you have finished page. 281

4. After typing the last line of text (to top pencil line), single-space 296
and type an underline 1 1/2″ long, double-space, indent five 308
spaces, and type the raised footnote number or symbol and the 320
footnote. 322

_______________ 325

DS

*Erwin M. Keithley and Philip J. Schreiner, A Manual of Style for the 344
Preparation of Papers & Reports (2d ed.; Cincinnati: South-Western Publishing 366
Co., 1971), p. 38. 370

103b-106b, continued

Job 7
Form letters [LM pp. 17–22]

Ms. Hernandes has prepared a draft of a letter that you are to type; send an original letter to each of the three divisional managers. The address cards are shown below. Date the letters April 11, 19—.

Zancenella, Ralph P. (Mr.)

Mr. Ralph P. Zancenella
Western Division Manager
5309 Washington Boulevard, W.
Los Angeles, CA 90016

Ott, Virginia B. (Ms.)

Ms. Virginia B. Ott
Central Division Manager
950 North Michigan Avenue
Chicago, IL 60611

Loomis, Rebecca I. (Mrs.)

Mrs. Rebecca I. Loomis
Eastern Division Manager
Room 8401
World Trade Center
New York, NY 10048

SUBJECT: Sales Forecast for Next Year

According to our Sales Forecast Report, we shall experience a net growth in total sales of roughly 8 percent.

All indicators point to a rather slow year in the United States; however, our foreign markets appear to be excellent. In fact, we are anticipating that our foreign sales will more than double next year.

Because our foreign sales will represent only 10 percent of our total sales, we must continue to develop our domestic market or face the possibility of a reduction in total sales. We are forecasting that our sales in the United States will increase only a modest 2.4 percent. The expert opinion of our marketing department is that we must work even harder next year than we have this year to achieve this modest increase in domestic sales.

Will you please keep us informed of any unusual happenings in your division.

Sincerely

Ms. Juanita F. Hernandes
Executive Vice President
and Sales Manager

Job 8
Composing a letter [LM p. 23]

You are to compose for Ms. Hernandes' signature a letter to Mr. Adolf R. Oesterle, our Foreign Sales Representative in Europe. Address the letter to:

Mr. Adolf R. Oesterle
German Imports, AG
Gerhofstrasse 32
D-2000 Hamburg 36
WEST GERMANY

Date the letter April 11, 19—. Indicate that his appraisal of conditions in the European market was correct. Other items you should include are: Sales should more than double next year; a majority of our marketing personnel will be assigned to work with him; Ms. Janice Frogley, Assistant Vice President—Marketing, will be contacting him soon; and Mr. Oesterle may contact Ms. Frogley at our office in St. Louis, if necessary. You are to send a carbon copy of this letter to Ms. Janice Frogley.

Job 9
Composing a letter [LM p. 25]

You are to compose a letter to our Foreign Sales Representative in Asia and the Far East. This letter, to be signed by Ms. Hernandes, is to be addressed to:

Mr. Sing Lu Fung
Fung & Son Importers
508 Waterloo Road
KOWLOON, HONG KONG

Date the letter April 11, 19—. You are to use the basic letter that you composed in Job 10. Be sure to substitute "Asian and Far East market" for the "European market" mentioned in Job 10.

Ms. Janice Frogley will also be working directly with Mr. Fung; therefore, send her a carbon copy of this letter.

47

47a ▶ 6
Preparatory practice

each line 3 times SS (work for fewer than 3 errors per group); DS between 3-line groups

alphabet Can the judge quiz the lawyer from Iowa about extensive profit-taking?

fig/sym Are those last-minute reports on Bill #3657-48 due on August 19 or 20?

one-hand Lyn saw Jimmy Polk pull oily junk up a hill; Lu Dax dragged junk, too.

easy If I can do all the little jobs well, the big jobs will be no problem.

| 1 | 2 | 3 | 4 | 5 | 6 | 7 | 8 | 9 | 10 | 11 | 12 | 13 | 14 |

47b ▶ 9
Composing and typing

2 full sheets

1. Read copy at right. Compose on your typewriter a ¶ or two in which you state your two choices and why you think they are good ones.

2. Remove your first draft from the typewriter and make corrections.

3. Compose a heading for the corrected ¶; then type a final copy of your ¶ as the first ¶ of an unbound report.

The Great Legume visits you in your sleep one night. "I have decided," it intones, "to grant you one wish." "Hey, great!" says you. "How about making me a person who is truly admired." "Can do," says the Great L., "but you must tell me what you want to be admired for. Here is a list of attributes over which I have some control. Choose two and, presto, you will be admired for them." You glance at the list. It says:

athletic ability
intellect
good looks
sense of humor
friendliness

Which two do you choose? and why?

47c ▶ 35
Typing problems: leftbound report with footnotes and headings

Problem 1
report

two full sheets; type copy as second and third page of leftbound report; type footnote at bottom of page on which reference appears

Spacing reminders

1. Leftbound reports require an extra half inch for left margins.

2. The center of the line of writing for leftbound reports is 54 for elite and 45 for pica.

3. TS below main headings.

4. TS above side headings; DS below them.

5. Indent long quotes and listed items 5 spaces from each margin and type SS.

words

Spacing 3

Reports such as school papers, formal reports, and manuscripts to be 17
submitted for publication should be double-spaced. Business reports, how- 32
ever, are often single-spaced. 38

Margins 41

Leave a bottom margin of about one inch. Leave one-inch top and side 55
margins on all pages, with the following exceptions: 66

1. For the first page of an unbound or leftbound report, leave a top 80
margin of 1 1/2 inches for pica type or 2 inches for elite type. 93

2. On all pages of a leftbound report, leave a left margin of 1 1/2 107
inches to allow for binding. 113

3. For the first page of a topbound report, leave a top margin of 2 127
inches for pica type or 2 1/2 inches for elite type for binding. 140
All subsequent pages should have top margins of 1 1/2 inches. 153

Indent the first line of a paragraph five or ten spaces. For quoted matter 168
of four or more lines, use single spacing and indent the quotation five spaces 184
from the left and right margins. Precede and follow the quotation with one 199
blank line space. 203

Headings 206

Main headings. The main heading is typed in all capitals and centered 223
over the line of writing. A secondary heading, when used, is typed a double 238
space below the main heading in capitals and lowercase, followed by a triple 253
space. When no secondary heading is used, triple-space after the main heading. 269

(continued on page 88)

103b-106b, continued

Job 5

Revised agenda

(plain sheet)

Ms. Hernandes has given you the following changes to be made on the agenda you prepared in Job 2. Center the agenda as you did in Job 2 and use the same date. Make the following changes in the revised agenda:

Subheading: delete the word "Tentative"

Item #2: delete the word "board"

Item #3: place "Domestic Suppliers," to be presented by Karl W. Handorf, first

Item #4: change the discussion leader to Andrea Jenkins

Item #5: after "Sales Forecast Report," add "Quarterly Sales Report" to be presented by Phillip B. Brown

Item #6: change the discussion leader to Juanita F. Hernandes

Job 6

Sales forecast report

(plain sheets)

Ms. Hernandes has asked you to type the Sales Forecast Report that was prepared by Mr. Zellinski. Use unbound manuscript style and appropriate spacing between parts.

SALES FORECAST REPORT

April 15, 19--

The total anticipated sales for the next fiscal year will be approximately $17,777,000; this represents an 8 percent increase over the current-year sales.

Domestic Sales

All reports received from the field representatives indicate that next year our sales will only increase slightly--a modest 2.4 percent. The primary reason for this low growth rate is due to the uncertainty of the economy. The domestic sales are expected to be about $15,977,000; this is an increase of $377,000 in sales when compared to the current year. All indications are that the best market conditions will be during the first six months and then taper off to a near zero increase during the last quarter of the year.

Foreign Sales

The data that were collected from our foreign representatives indicate that the demand for our products will more than double during the next year. The sales for the current year will be about $860,000; the forecast for foreign sales next year should be approximately $1,800,000. This increase of $940,000 in sales represents an increase in foreign sales of 109.3 percent. The economic indicators in the developing countries of the world appear to be very positive. Our sales should increase throughout the entire year.

Conclusion

Since the foreign market will result in the largest share of our increase for next year, every effort must be made to insure that foreign orders are secured as soon as possible. Our promotion efforts will be expanded substantially in those foreign markets where indicators point to good sales potential. In order to capture our share of these markets, a majority of the marketing personnel will be assigned to support our foreign field representatives. If the foreign sales have not reached 70 percent of the estimated sales for the first six months, a total reassessment of our sales promotions will be made and adjustments made accordingly.

47c, continued

Side headings. Side headings (like Spacing, Margins, Headings, and Page 293
Numbers in this report) are typed at the left margin with no terminal punctua- 310
tion and are underlined. Begin main words with a capital letter. Two blank line 326
spaces are left above and one blank line space is left below a side heading. 342

Paragraph headings. You have just typed a paragraph heading. It is 359
indented, followed by a period, and underlined. Generally, only the first word 375
or proper nouns are capitalized. 382

Page Numbers 387

Note: If a page with a footnote is only partially filled, leave the resulting blank space between the last text line typed and the footnote divider line so that the bottom margin below the footnote will be approximately 1" (6 lines) deep.

The first page need not be numbered; if it is, the number is centered 401
1/2 inch from the bottom edge. On leftbound and unbound reports, the second 416
and subsequent pages are numbered on Line 4 at the right margin. On 430
topbound reports, all pages are numbered in first-page position. If a title 445
page is used, it is not numbered; but it is counted in the pagination.[1] 459

__________________ 462

[1] Kate L. Turabian, A Manual for Writers of Term Papers, Theses, and 485
Dissertations (4th ed.; Chicago: The University of Chicago Press, 1973), p. 199. 504

Problem 2
outline

full sheet; make decisions about placement; add designation numerals and letters for each order; use correct capitalization and spacing

procedures for data handling

recording data
- using original source documents
- preparing punched cards and tape
- preparing magnetic cards and tape

classifying data
- using alphabetic code
- using numeric code
- using alphanumeric code

sorting data

creating new data
- programming to manipulate data
- performing arithmetic operations
    - addition
    - subtraction
    - multiplication
    - division

summarizing data
- consolidating data
- providing for information retrieval

103b-106b, continued

Job 3

Quarterly Sales Report (plain sheet)

You have been asked by Ms. Hernandes to type the Quarterly Sales Report. This report will be bound with other documents; therefore, you should use the leftbound manuscript style. In addition to the report heading—QUARTERLY SALES REPORT—center and type a DS below the report heading the following subheading: For the Three-Month Period Ending March 31, 19—.

The total quarterly have increased from $4,011,944 last year to $4,435,666 for this year. This isan increase of 10.6 per cent.

Eastern Division

The eastern division includes one third of the country. Sales for this area is up 4.5 percent when it's compared with the same period last year and sales for last year were $1,345,876; for this year, $1,406,440. We had 15 field representatives last uear; This year we have only 12.

Central Division

Central division includes the middle of the United States. Quarterly sales for this division is up 8.9 percent when compared with the same time last year. The sales for year were $589,853; for this year, $642,350. We had 4 field representatives last year; this year we have 5.

Western Division

Western Division includes the western third of the country. quarterly sales for this division is up 15 percent when compared with same period a year ago. Sales for last year were $2,076,215; for this year, $2,386,876. We had 15 representatives last year; this year we have 19.

Job 4

Table (plain sheet)

Ms. Hernandes has requested that you prepare a table from the data provided in the manuscript in Job 3. The heading for the table is: A AND K WHOLESALE DISTRIBUTORS, INC.

The subheading is: Quarterly Sales. You are to begin the table 1½" from top of page and center it horizontally. DS the body and provide appropriate totals for each column.

Ms. Hernandes wants you to use the following 4-column headings:

Division	Sales This Year	Sales Last Year	Percent Increase
Eastern	1,406,440	1,345,876	4.5
Central	642,350	589,853	8.9
Western	2,386,876	2,076,215	15

Supplemental skill-building practice

Improving keystroking control

each line twice SS; proofread and circle errors before typing the next line; DS between 2-line groups

Type at a steady rate; concentrate on the copy.

shift	1	Lori West left for Greece, but Pedro Rivera went to Hungary with Carl.
double letters	2	To accommodate us, Ella Furrmann took a bigger pepper from the cooler.
hyphen	3	She has made her out-of-town trips to avoid any last-minute traveling.
Roman numerals	4	Type Roman numerals in ALL CAPS: one, I; three, III; five, V; ten, X.
long words	5	On TV, frequent consultations are necessary to accomplish spontaneity.
direct reaches	6	I doubt if June Breck will hunt for a number of curved cedar brackets.
quotations	7	"I know," she said, "it's a 'hard back' crab." "It's not," he argued.

Improving basic skill: rough-draft

three 3′ writings; proofread; circle errors

Goal: at least 27 *gwam* with fewer than 6 errors

Difficulty index

all letters used | A | 1.5 si | 5.7 awl | 80% hfw |

gwam 3′

The typical person ~~will~~ hurries. Nothing that really merit *s* attention 4
gets enough time. Capable *people* ~~persons~~, contrariwise, do not race. They 8
sat an easy pace, but they continue working steadily. ~~Also, the typ-~~ *stet* 13
ical person tried to do a dozen tasks at once. As a result, he *or* she 18
does not have adequate time for many of the activities that should be 22
dome. If one *obligation is not met,* ~~duty must be slighted,~~ *the entire program can collapse.* 27
As often as not, exigenceis--not people--make decisions. Genreally, 32
this tactic does not pay; for enough time is not spent on each element 36
of a decision. Theable person avoids this trap, by doing first things 41
first, one at a time. 43

Improving basic skill: statistical copy

three 3′ writings; proofread carefully; circle errors

Goal: at least 28 *gwam* with fewer than 6 errors

Difficulty index

all letters used | A | 1.5 si | 5.7 awl | 80% hfw |

gwam 3′

As an interesting addition to the news, a big city paper recently 4
carried an article (#3 of a series) that presented a panorama of the 9
city in figures. According to the article, the area baseball club won 14
a game 11 to 2. For the evening, known in the area as "family night," 18
31,309 people turned out to attend an event that took 2 hours and 58 min- 23
utes to play. The happy customers, the article said, purchased 23,000 28
Soria & Soria (a local firm) hot dogs, 12,000 ice cream bars, and 4,200 33
bags of peanuts; and they were served 29,000 soft drinks and 30,000 37
other beverages. Food expenses: <u>more</u> than $76,000. They saw 4 pitchers 42
turn 322 pitches into 191 strikes (59.3%) and 131 other pitches as the 47
teams turned 26 hits into 13 runs. The number of baseballs used: 15. 52

gwam 3′ | 1 | 2 | 3 | 4 | 5 |

103–106

103a-106a ▶ 5

Preparatory practice

Type as many times as you can in 5 minutes.

alphabet	June and Max Zachary saw an aquatic show in Gibbsville Park on Friday.
fig/sym	Report #20 was not correct; I saw errors on pages 36, 84, 91, and 157.
shift keys	Ask Helen if she has seen Tom, Jan, Andy, Ruth, Peter, Brian, or Mike.
fluency	I may profit more from my work if I form the habit of using time well.

| 1 | 2 | 3 | 4 | 5 | 6 | 7 | 8 | 9 | 10 | 11 | 12 | 13 | 14 |

103b-106b ▶ 45

Office work simulation

Job 1

Memorandum [LM p. 15]

Please send this memo to Mr. Anthony V. Zellinski, Assistant Sales Manager. Date the memo April 5, 19—. The subject of the memo is: Sales Forecast for Next Year.

Tony, we need to complete our Sales Forecast report within the [next] week in order to meet the deadline for the next Board of directors' meeting. Jim called [me] today and indicated that the Chair~~man~~[person] of the Board, Andrea Jenkins, would like to have a copy of our Sales Forecast report at least 3 [sp] days before the Board meeting.

Since Joan [and Kent] will not be back in the office until the middle of next week, will you analyze our situation and decide whom we should assign to this task so that the bulk of the work can be ~~finished~~ [accomplished] before Joan [and Kent] gets back?

I think that next year should be [an] excellent [year] if the reports from our [field] representatives show an accurate picture of the demands. I am very anxious to see the ~~first~~ [preliminary] draft of the Sales Forecast.

Job 2

Tentative agenda

(plain sheet)

Ms. Hernandes has asked that you type the tentative agenda for the next board meeting. You are to use a 2" top margin, center the agenda horizontally, and leave 10 spaces between columns. Also, use leaders between columns.

DS and center each line

A and K Wholesale Distributors, Inc. ← all caps
~~Tentative~~ Agenda for Meeting of the Board of Directors
April 15, 19--

TS

1. Call to Order	Andrea Jenkins
2. Minutes of Last ~~Board~~ Meeting	Phillip B. Brown
3. Special Reports	
Foreign Suppliers	Karen M. Swenson
Domestic Suppliers	Karl W. Handorf
4. Discussion of Special Reports	Juanita F. Hernandes
5. Current Business	
Sales Forecast Report	Anthony V. Zellinski
Foreign Bank Transfers	LuAnn J. Klepfer
6. Discussion of Current Business	Andrea Jenkins
7. Adjournment	

section

10

Measuring skill growth

lessons 48–50

Measurement goals

1. To demonstrate your ability to type average-difficulty writings in straight copy, rough-draft, and statistical copy for 3′ and 5′.
2. To demonstrate your ability to type letters, tables, and reports in proper format from semi-arranged copy according to specific directions.

Machine adjustments

1. Check chair and desk adjustments and placement of copy for ease of reading.
2. Set paper guide at *0*.
3. Set 70-space line.
4. Set ribbon control on black.

Materials: Letterheads, full and half sheets, carbon paper, copy sheets, and large and small envelopes.

48

48a ▶ 5 Preparatory practice

each line 3 times SS (slowly, faster, still faster); DS between 3-line groups

alphabet	Packard Grewe may yet fly to Zanesville to inquire about his next job.
figure	On January 29 they ordered 186 books, 370 pens, and 45 reams of paper.
3d row	Where were you when they typed their themes on Quint's red typewriter?
easy	Five or six clerks may work for the shoe firm for eight nights in May.

| 1 | 2 | 3 | 4 | 5 | 6 | 7 | 8 | 9 | 10 | 11 | 12 | 13 | 14 |

48b ▶ 11 Measuring skill growth: rough-draft copy

a 3′ and a 5′ writing; determine *gwam*

Difficulty index

all letters used | A | 1.5 si | 5.7 awl | 80% hfw |

	gwam 3′	5′
Many people believe that dreams have realistic results. ~~Maybe~~ it was	4	3
Thoreau who said that fi people move mentaly in the direction of their	9	5
dreams and ~~actually~~ try to live the lives they imagine they can meet	14	8
with unexpected success. dreams make the impossible impossible; but you	19	11
must if you want to make your dreams come true be active.	22	13
A Idea--a dream--consciously and persistently held in mind tends	27	16
to be fulfilled. Frequently, ime is needed to allow ideas to develop;	32	19
but they can be realized--of that you can be certain. The ~~amount~~ of	36	22
positive thought is more than just ~~a clever slogan~~. It is latent pow	41	25
that can make the unusual happening. It results from concentration	45	27
Noone is justified in beleiving that opportunity comes only by	49	30
change. The things that happen to me are consequences not coincidences.	54	33
If I beleive that circumstances ~~and~~ be controled by learning to apply	59	36
positive thinking, such factors as "luck" and "fat" lost a lof of the	64	38
importance. Iam the sum of what I beleive. This principal has ~~often~~	69	41
been followed fir years by men and women of every nation.	73	44

A AND K WHOLESALE DISTRIBUTORS, INC.

Agenda for Meeting of the Board of Directors

April 15, 19--

1. Call to Order . . . . Andrea Jenkins
2. Minutes of Last Meeting . . . . Phillip B. Brown
3. Special Reports
   - Domestic Suppliers . . . . Karl W. Handorf
   - Foreign Suppliers . . . . Karen M. Swenson
4. Discussion of Special Reports . . . . . Andrea Jenkins
5. Current Business
   - Sales Forecast Report . . . . Anthony V. Zellinski
   - Quarterly Sales Report . . . . Phillip B. Brown
   - Foreign Bank Transfers . . . . LuAnn J. Klepfer
6. Discussion of Current Business . . . . Juanita F. Hernandes
7. Adjournment

Leaders in *justified* copy

Business Forms. Business forms such as purchase requisitions, purchase orders, and invoices can be typed quickly and efficiently if the following procedures are observed by the typist.

1. Set the left margin stop for typing the name and address block.

2. Set a tab stop for aligning the items in the information section to the right of the address block.

3. Set additional tab stops for aligning and typing the columnar entries.

Note: Well-designed business forms permit the left margin stop to be used for positioning both the address and one column of entries beneath the address block (usually the first column). Often, too, the tab stop set for the information section may be used to position the items in one of the columns beneath the information section.

4. Position columnar entries (except Description items) so that they are in the approximate horizontal center of their respective columns. Begin the Description items 2 spaces to the right of the vertical rule.

5. SS the columnar entries when there are 4 or more single-line items. DS the items in the body of the form when there are 3 or fewer single-line items.

6. If an item in the body of the form requires more than 1 line, SS the item and indent the second and succeeding lines 3 spaces.

7. Underline the last figure in the Total column; then DS before typing the total amount.

8. Tabulate and type *across* the form rather than typing all items in the first column.

Properly arranged and typed business forms are illustrated at the right.

Phillips Secretarial College
509 South Boston Avenue Tulsa, OK 74103 (918) 251-3020

PURCHASE ORDER

A and K Wholesale Distributors, Inc.
Suite 1295
International Office Building
722 Chestnut Street
St. Louis, MO 63101

Purchase order No. NO-421-6
Date March 26, 19--
Terms 2/10, n/30
Ship Via Allied Transport

Quantity	Cat. No.	Description	Price	Total
3	F1-S2-A	Secretarial posture chair	45.00	135.00
3	F1-63-TX	Single pedestal desk	201.00	603.00
3	D3-4D-GY	Desk organizer	45.00	135.00
				873.00

By ______________________ Purchasing Agent

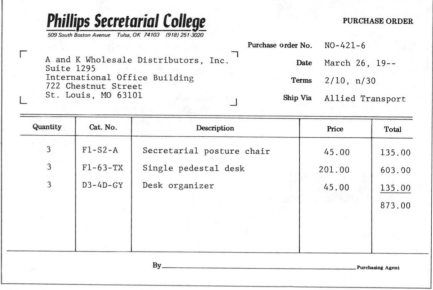

Properly typed purchase order

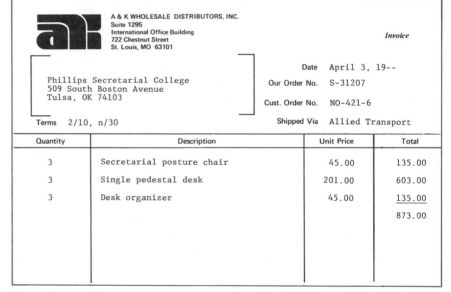

A & K WHOLESALE DISTRIBUTORS, INC.
Suite 1295
International Office Building
722 Chestnut Street
St. Louis, MO 63101

Invoice

Phillips Secretarial College
509 South Boston Avenue
Tulsa, OK 74103

Date April 3, 19--
Our Order No. S-31207
Cust. Order No. NO-421-6
Shipped Via Allied Transport

Terms 2/10, n/30

Quantity	Description	Unit Price	Total
3	Secretarial posture chair	45.00	135.00
3	Single pedestal desk	201.00	603.00
3	Desk organizer	45.00	135.00
			873.00

Properly typed invoice

48c ▶ 34
Measuring skill application: reports

Time schedule

Assembling materials .... 3′
Timed production .... 25′
Final check; compute
g–pram .... 6′

Materials needed:
3 full sheets

When the signal to begin is given, insert paper and begin typing Problem 1 as directed. Type the problems in sequence until the signal to stop is given. Type Problem 1 again if you finish Problem 2 before time is called. Proofread all problems; circle errors. Compute *g–pram*.

Problem 1

Type the problem as a 2–page unbound report. Center the heading; type the foot–note on the same page as its reference.

words

THE CHANGING COMPUTER 4

Processing information with computers is hardly new. The theory has 18
been around for years; we simply had to wait for the right parts to be invented. 35
The history of computers actually stretches back to the original digital com- 50
puters (our fingers and toes), progresses through the hand-held abacus, the 65
simple mechanical adding machine, and the electric calculator to the 78
modern electronic computer. 85

In 1950, there were at most 15 electronic computers in use in the United 99
States (but the prime computer manufacturers are still found in this country). 115
Since then, the electronic computer has become one of the most important 130
technological developments of this century. There are approximately 800,000 145
computers, valued at $160 billion, operating in various parts of the world. 161
They provide work for thousands of people--and they do the work it would 175
take thousands more to do if time were available. 186

Computers were originally developed by scientists and engineers to solve 200
problems involving large amounts of computation (hence "computers"). Com- 215
puters now touch the lives of virtually everyone. Computer installations have 231
moved beyond the walls of business and science buildings into government 245
and education structures; and computers at home--even at the local pinball 260
arcade--are a matter of fact. 267

The uses to which computers have been adapted have also changed 279
dramatically. Originally they were intended to solve difficult mathematical 295
equations (and they still do), but now they have also become depositories for 310
various forms of data that can be recalled to provide us with information, 325
entertainment, and even protection. 333

A recent magazine article describes how some of these data can be used 351
via "computer graphics," which is the ability of a computer to present infor- 362
mation in picture form. The article contains the following illustration: 377

> The congressman sits down at the computer terminal and, 388
> by pressing a series of keys, fires off a barrage of commands: 401
> draw a map of the percentage of people in Florida with four years 414
> of high-school education, the number of persons employed in manu- 427
> facturing in Iowa, the percentage of the civilian labor force 440
> employed in New York City. On a screen the display pops up in 452

(continued on page 92)

section

22

Typing in a sales office

lessons 103–106

Section 22 is designed to provide you with ample opportunity to type the kinds of problems that you would normally expect to encounter when working in a sales office.

Supplies needed

letterheads [LM pp. 15-26] or plain full sheets
business forms [LM pp. 27, 29]
carbon sheets; second sheets;
envelopes of appropriate size

Machine adjustments

1. Check chair and desk adjustments and placement of copy for easy reading.
2. Set paper guide at *0*.
3. Set ribbon control on black.
4. Margins: 70-space line for drills and ¶ writings; as directed (or appropriate) for problems.
5. SS line drills; DS ¶s; space problems as directed (or appropriate).

Daily practice plan

Preparatory practice ...... 5′
Office work simulation .... 45′

Learning goals

1. To become familiar with the work in a sales office.
2. To plan your work and complete it efficiently.
3. To integrate your knowledge and skills in completing office work acceptably.

Office Job Simulation

Before you begin the work in Section 22, read carefully the material at the right and on page 211. Make any notes of standard procedures that you think will save you time during the completion of the production activities.

Introduction

You have been hired as a typist by A and K Wholesale Distributors, Inc., Suite 1295, International Office Building, 722 Chestnut Street, St. Louis, MO 63101. You will work under the direction of Ms. Juanita F. Hernandes, Executive Vice President and Sales Manager.

The company style manual specifies that all company letters are to be typed in modified block style with mixed punctuation. The closing lines of all letters should include the typed name of the person for whom the letters are typed followed on the next line by that person's business title. All letters, memorandums, and forms require *one* carbon copy for the file. Address appropriate envelopes for all letters typed.

Proofread all work carefully before removing it from your typewriter; correct all detected errors. All typed work that is to leave the company should be "mailable"--technically correct with all errors corrected neatly. All typed work to be used *within* the company should be "usable"--content correct but with *minor* "flaws" in format and placement permitted.

When specific job instructions are given, follow them carefully. When specific instructions are not given, make appropriate decisions on the basis of your knowledge and experience. If your supervisor (your teacher) considers some of your decisions unacceptable, learn from her or his suggestions--just as you would do in a business office.

A and K Wholesale Distributors has based its office manual and job instruction booklets on COLLEGE TYPEWRITING, so use the Reference Guide and the index of your textbook to look up matters of style and placement when in doubt. When a job requires unusual specifications, A and K provides them in "Excerpts from the Office Procedures Manual."

Excerpts from the Office Procedures Manual

Leaders. Leaders are a series of periods (. . . .) that are typed between two items in tabular material. The purpose of leaders is to aid reading by "leading the reader's eye" from one columnar item to another. They are used primarily when the distance between certain items in two columns is so great that matching columnar items is difficult.

Leaders are made by alternating the period (.) and a space. Lines of leaders should be aligned in vertical rows and should end at the same point at the right. To align leaders, type all periods on either the odd or the even numbers on the line-of-writing scale guided by their position in the first line of leaders. Begin the first line of leaders on the second space after the first item in the column and end the leaders 2 or 3 spaces to the left of the beginning of the next column.

When the last column is *justified* at the right, end the leaders 2 or 3 spaces to the left of the longest item in such a column.

Study carefully the following illustrations of leaders in *nonjustified* and *justified* tabular reports.

```
                A AND K WHOLESALE DISTRIBUTORS, INC.

             Agenda for Meeting of the Board of Directors

                          April 15, 19--

1.  Call to Order . . . . . . . . . . . . .  Andrea Jenkins

2.  Minutes of Last Meeting . . . . . . . .  Phillip B. Brown

3.  Special Reports
       Domestic Suppliers . . . . . . . . .  Karl W. Handorf
       Foreign Suppliers  . . . . . . . . .  Karen M. Swenson

4.  Discussion of Special Reports . . . . .  Andrea Jenkins

5.  Current Business
       Sales Forecast Report  . . . . . . .  Anthony V. Zellinski
       Quarterly Sales Report . . . . . . .  Phillip B. Brown
       Foreign Bank Transfers . . . . . . .  LuAnn J. Klepfer

6.  Discussion of Current Business  . . . .  Juanita F. Hernandes

7.  Adjournment
```

Leaders in *nonjustified* copy

48c, continued

words

seconds, illustrated in color and matched on the map with similar 465
statistics from across the country.[1] 473

This portrayal emphasizes the extent of the computer trip from our fingers and 489
toes to our present keyed consoles. Yet maximum utilization of computer 503
technology is still perhaps a decade or more away. 513

Can we even speculate on its form? 521

——————————— 524

[1]"Mapping With a Computer," Newsweek, Vol. XCII, No. 11, (Septem- 539
ber 11, 1978), p. 87. 543

Problem 2
Type the problem as a leftbound–report. Center the heading; indent the enumerated items.

words

INVESTING IN BUSINESS LETTERS 6

Despite many technological advances in recent times, the ordinary letter 21
is still probably the most effective form of external communication for busi- 36
ness use. Say Keeling et al., "Even in the age of automation when telephone and 52
computer communications receive increasing attention, the popularity of the 67
business letter remains."[1] 73

Unfortunately, however, the ordinary business letter is an expensive form 88
of communication--a typical business letter, all things considered, costs be- 103
tween $4 and $5 to produce. It is vital, therefore, that each letter written should 120
have maximum potential for accomplishing its mission. 131

To write business letters effectively, the following guides should be kept 146
in mind: 148

1. Make the purpose of the letter immediately clear. Get to the 161
point, state it, then stop when the case has been made. 173
2. Remember the reader's point of view. 181
3. Be wary of humor. Avoid attempts at cleverness. Don't use 194
slang. 196
4. Be yourself--sincere, friendly, courteous, warm, and human. 209

An effective business letter has three important items to sell: the writer, 224
the company, and the subject of the letter. If it does not do that, it has been an 241
expensive letter indeed. 246

——————————— 249

[1]B. Lewis Keeling, Norman F. Kallaus, and John J. W. Neuner, Adminis- 264
trative Office Management (Cincinnati: South-Western Publishing Co., 1978), 285
p. 164. 286

102d ▶ 15
Measuring straight-copy typing skill

1. Two 5′ writings for *accuracy* on ¶s 1–3 combined. Record *gwam* and number of errors for the more accurate writing.

Difficulty index

all letters used	A	1.5 si	5.7 awl	80% hfw

	gwam 1′	5′
We are now living in an era of great and dynamic change. We are in	14	3
the middle of a revolution in the business world which was brought about	28	6
by the implementation of computer systems. The value of the computer	42	8
lies in its capacity to process information at amazingly high speeds. It	57	11
is no problem whatever for a computer to process up to a billion bits of	72	14
information per second. The computer can handle a wide variety of prob-	86	17
lems, ranging from the very simple to the most complex. The importance	100	20
of the computer is growing; therefore, many people are quite certain that	115	23
the use of the computer will cause a great number of office workers to	129	26
lose their jobs.	133	27
The computer has the ability to execute many of the routine jobs	13	29
done in an office; therefore, the need for office clerks who can perform	28	32
only repetitive jobs has declined. The computer can type orders, com-	42	35
pute invoices, and file records. It can even type a full-page letter in	56	38
less than three seconds. Despite the extensive use of the computer, the	71	41
need for skilled office workers has grown steadily during the past ten	85	44
years. Even though it is true that the use of the computer has not re-	99	46
duced the need for office personnel, it has had a decided effect on the	114	49
quality of office workers hired. It appears that the need for office	128	52
workers will continue to grow notwithstanding the increased utilization	142	55
of the computer.	145	56
The demand for the worker with managerial skills has grown very	13	58
rapidly during the past decade. This is true of individuals who work	27	61
in professional offices. Therefore, the professional secretary is one	41	64
of the highest paid employees in an office. To attain one of these high-	56	67
paying jobs, a person must know how to type, take notes, file, use the	70	70
phone, and do other office tasks. Also, you must be adept in the skills	84	72
of office administration. You must know how to think, how to make wise	99	75
decisions, how to solve problems, and how to organize and plan your work	113	78
properly. These are some of the extra qualities that make the difference	128	81
between hiring a qualified secretary and a typical typist.	140	84

gwam 1′	1	2	3	4	5	6	7	8	9	10	11	12	13	14
5′			1					2				3		

49

49a ▶ 5
Preparatory practice

each line 3 times SS (work for smooth, continuous rhythm); DS between 3-line groups

alphabet Joan and Ezra Voigt played a number of quiet games with Clark Boxmann.

fig/sym Add the 4% sales tax of $7.22 (on $180.56) to Webb & Orr's Bill #8390.

one-hand The union referred only a few of my cases to a referee to be assessed.

easy Good word sense is vital to writers, for words give wings to thoughts.

| 1 | 2 | 3 | 4 | 5 | 6 | 7 | 8 | 9 | 10 | 11 | 12 | 13 | 14 |

49b ▶ 11
Measuring skill growth: statistical copy

a 3′ and a 5′ writing; determine *gwam*

Difficulty index

all figures used | A | 1.5 si | 5.7 awl | 80% hfw |

gwam 3′ | 5′

It was just another quite warm day in a large Midwestern town. 4 3
Certainly nothing unusual seemed to be happening. It's very easy to 9 5
forget, isn't it, that the "ordinary day" might not be so ordinary after 14 8
all. For cities move. 15 9

On that particular day, for example, the local city bus company 19 12
collected $90,075 in cash (approximately 80% in small change) from about 24 15
175,000 people who read their Dun & Bradstreet reports on the way to 29 17
work. These buses, by the way, went 94,714 miles on 21,295 gallons of 34 20
gas--about 4.5 miles to a gallon; 51 of them broke down, and 6 were igno- 39 23
miniously hit by other vehicles while they--the buses--were motionless. 43 26

While a total of 639,000 people went to work in the city by any 47 28
means that would get them there, 10,432 took Buses #14, 38, 39, or 42 52 31
to the various city and county recreational areas. At the local airport, 57 34
689 planes (mostly commercial carriers) landed and took off. The largest 62 37
cab company sent 1,232 cars to answer calls for service. Nobody tried 67 40
to count the million or so private automobiles on the streets. 71 43

This was simply another warm summer day in a large city in the 75 45
Middle West. Certainly nothing much seemed to be happening. 79 47

gwam 3′ | 1 | 2 | 3 | 4 | 5 |
5′ | 1 | 2 | 3 |

49c ▶ 34
Measuring skill application: tables

Time schedule

Assembling materials ..... 3′
Timed production .... 25′
Final check; compute *g-pram* .... 6′

Materials needed:

full sheet, 2 half sheets

When the signal to begin is given, insert paper and begin typing Problem 1 as directed. Type the problems in sequence until the signal to stop is given. Type Problem 1 again if you finish Problem 3 before time is called. Proofread all problems; circle errors. Compute *g-pram*.

102

102a ▶5 Preparatory practice

each line 3 times SS (slowly, faster, top speed); retype selected lines as time permits

alphabet — Mona Hazer just displayed a fashionable, exquisite black evening gown.

fig/sym — During your term (1975 to 1980), sales increased by $4,329,795 (466%).

double letters — If you succeed in applying a wood filler, see them tomorrow afternoon.

fluency — A visitor may want to visit the ancient burial chapel in the old city.

| 1 | 2 | 3 | 4 | 5 | 6 | 7 | 8 | 9 | 10 | 11 | 12 | 13 | 14 |

102b ▶10 Communication aid: proofreader's symbols

half sheet, long side up; begin on Line 10; DS; 6 strokes for blank lines; 4 spaces between columns

Center and type the two columns at the right. Remove the problem from the typewriter and, using the list of proofreader's symbols, write the correct symbol to the left of its appropriate meaning. (See RG page ix.)

Symbols

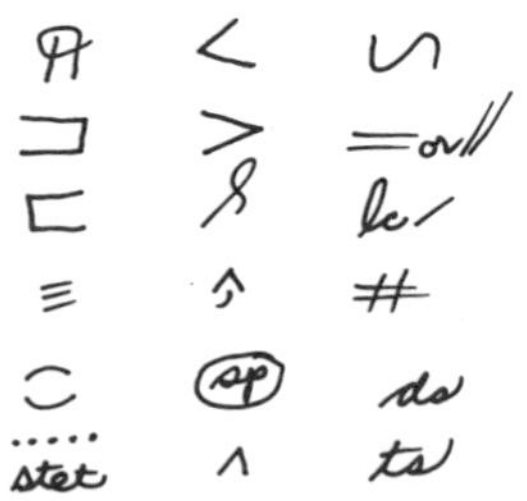

____ Align type	____ Capitalize
____ Use lowercase	____ Close up horizontal space
____ Close up vertical space	____ Insert horizontal space
____ Insert vertical space	____ Delete
____ Transpose	____ Insert copy shown
____ Spell out	____ Move left
____ Paragraph	____ Let it stand; ignore the correction

102c ▶20 Building rough-draft typing skill

two 3′ writings for *speed* and two 5′ writings for *accuracy*; record *gwam* and number of errors for the more accurate 5′ writing

Difficulty index

all letters used | A | 1.5 si | 5.7 awl | 80% hfw |

gwam 3′ | 5′

A typist is real ly an artist. The typist must be able to 4 3
see the appearanceof the finished job before the work is ~~begun.~~ 9 6
~~When~~ although a person may laern the basic rules and procedures 13 8
for production work, a ~~person~~ will be amazed at the extent of 18 11
creativity needed in the actual typingprocess. at times the 22 13
typist must quickly act, and the final product is the direct 26 16
result developing a fine sense of placement and balance. If 30 18
you ~~want~~ to become a typist, you must ~~want to~~ develop an artis- 34 21
tiac ability that results in attractive, neat, and ~~good~~ type- 39 23
written work. 39 24

A typist begins to learn the ~~science~~ of production typing by 43 26
first recongizing some ~~sound~~ rules for the placement balance of 48 29
letters ~~and~~ manuscripts. A person may later discard the place- 53 32
ment rules, but the beginning typist must have something ~~solid~~ 57 34
upon which to ~~start~~ a sound production skill. A typist improves 62 37
in time, and is able to type a job without the exact adherence 65 39
to any set of "hard and fast" rules. ~~It will be~~ the final evalu- 69 41
ation of a job ~~that~~ is based on it's appearance and accuracy. If 73 44
the end product is correct and ~~it~~ is quite within the acceptable 77 46
form, the appearance will be accepted. 81 48

49c, continued

words

Problem 1
half sheet, long side up
Center and type (SS) the table in exact vertical and horizontal center; allow 12 spaces between columns.

FIRST SEMESTER ENROLLMENTS		5
By Colleges and Schools		10
Art	208	12
Business Administration	1,606	18
Education	980	21
Engineering	453	24
Graduate	633	26
Letters and Science	5,225	32
Library Science	91	36
Music	174	38
Public Health	47	42
Theater Arts	117	45

Problem 2
full sheet
Center and type (DS) the table in reading position; decide intercolumn spacing.

NORTH PALMER STATE COLLEGE			5
Football Schedule			9
Date	Opponent	Place	16
September 9	East Grenada	Home	22
September 16	Allegheny	Home	28
September 23	Morrowsburg Tech	Away	35
September 30	East Swainton	Away	42
October 7	Alberton	Home	46
October 14	Leesburg	Home	51
October 21	Davis A & M	Away	57
October 28	Western State	Away	63
November 4	Browning	Home	68
November 11	Northern State	Away	74

Problem 3
half sheet, long side up
Center and type (SS) the table in exact vertical and horizontal center; decide intercolumn spacing.

LONG-RUN BROADWAY PLAYS				5
Play	Type	Opened	Times	13
Fiddler on the Roof	Musical	1964	3,242	21
Life with Father	Comedy	1939	3,224	28
Tobacco Road	Drama	1933	3,182	34
Hello, Dolly!	Musical	1964	2,844	41
My Fair Lady	Musical	1956	2,717	47
Man of La Mancha	Musical	1965	2,329	54
Abie's Irish Rose	Comedy	1922	2,327	61
Grease	Musical	1972	2,284	67
Oklahoma!	Musical	1943	2,212	72
Pippin	Musical	1972	1,944	77
South Pacific	Musical	1949	1,925	84
Harvey	Comedy	1944	1,775	89

101d ▶15
Building straight-copy typing skill

1. A 1′ writing for *speed* on each ¶.

2. A 5′ writing for *accuracy* on all ¶s combined. Determine *gwam*; circle errors.

Difficulty index

all letters used	A	1.5 si	5.7 awl	80% hfw

	gwam 1′	5′
Most businesses of today offer a great many job opportunites for	13	3
people who are ready to accept the unique challenge of helping to solve	28	6
the many problems that are found in modern business. There are	40	8
jobs available in the areas of chemicals, insurance, finance, sales,	54	11
medicine, and law, just to name a few. The scope of a modern business	68	14
is second only to its wide variety of existing jobs that must be filled	83	17
by good, willing, and zealous workers. The demand for those who are well	98	20
trained ranges from a basic entry-level typist to the manager who sets	112	22
the goals and directs the workers at all levels of the company.	124	25
In choosing a career from among the many opportunities available,	13	28
there are a number of factors you must analyze. Your inherent talent	27	30
and your education, of course, are two primary factors. You cannot hope	42	33
to gain success in an area for which you have little ability or no train-	58	36
ing. Most of the experts in personnel will agree that your interests will	71	39
play a significant role in determining your success on the job. Success	86	42
comes more easily to those who like the work they do than it does to	100	45
those people who dislike or merely tolerate their jobs. Before you look	114	48
for a rewarding career, do your utmost to equip yourself for success by	129	51
obtaining a good education.	134	52
When it is time to choose a position within a specific business	13	54
organization, there are also a number of factors that must be explored	27	57
in minute detail. The primary factor is the starting salary; this is,	41	59
of course, a very vital aspect. In the long run, however, there may be	56	62
many other factors that may be more significant than the initial salary.	70	65
The scale of wages must be looked at as well as the chances for promo-	84	68
tion. Another important factor is the on-the-job training that is avail-	99	71
able to new employees. In addition to the above factors, you must inquire	114	74
about the fringe benefits that are granted to all workers. After you	128	77
have taken all these factors into consideration, you will then have an	142	80
overall estimate of the real worth of the job.	151	82

gwam	1′	1	2	3	4	5	6	7	8	9	10	11	12	13	14
	5′			1					2				3		

50

50a ▶ 5 Preparatory practice

each line 3 times SS (slowly, faster, slowly); DS between 3-line groups

alphabet	Lori Cox and Sam Jay puzzled over the workbook required for geography.
fig/sym	Dial 649-5718 or 649-5709 to obtain your copy of this 32-page booklet.
direct reaches	The subtle humor of Cecil Ervyn was undoubtedly funny to the audience.
easy	For cleaner towns and cities, depend on the citizens who live in them.
	| 1 | 2 | 3 | 4 | 5 | 6 | 7 | 8 | 9 | 10 | 11 | 12 | 13 | 14 |

50b ▶ 11 Measuring skill growth: straight copy

a 3′ and a 5′ writing; determine *gwam*

Difficulty index

all letters used | A | 1.5 si | 5.7 awl | 80% hfw |

	gwam 3′	5′
A noted philosopher said that the mind is a very unusual invention.	5	3
It starts operating the instant we are born and never stops until we get	9	6
up to talk publicly. Generally, nobody questions that practice makes	14	8
perfect--nor that we can learn and apply rules on which to base that	19	11
practice according to our needs.	21	13
While we can memorize rules, the essence of making an excellent	25	15
speech may still elude us. Truthfully, the kind of eloquence that will	30	18
excite the imagination of listeners may be impossible to acquire. We	35	21
can learn many things by the rules, but a feeling for what will really	39	24
move people is apparently an inborn trait.	42	25
A talk about nothing--however eloquent--can become rather tedious.	47	28
The speaker must believe in the subject and know it very well. Listeners	52	31
can spot a phony a mile away. A good talk is a short talk. Some say	56	34
that speakers who get to their feet, skip over the introduction, and make	61	37
a concluding statement always get the heartiest approval.	65	39

gwam 3′ | 1 | 2 | 3 | 4 | 5 |
5′ | 1 | 2 | 3 |

50c ▶ 34 Measuring skill application: letters

Assembling materials . . . 3′
Timed production . . . . . . 25′
Final check; compute *g-pram* . . . . 6′

Materials needed: letterheads [LM pp. 59–64], copy sheets, carbon paper, large and small envelopes

Type as many problems as you can in 25′. Type Problem 1 again if you finish Problem 3 before time has been called. Proofread all problems; circle errors.

101

101a ▶5 Preparatory practice

each line 3 times SS (slowly, faster, slowly); retype selected lines as time permits

alphabet	Judy explained the law requiring the man to have his back fence razed.
fig/sym	Order 112 gross of #2 pencils at $7.89/gross; 360 pens at $4.85/gross.
shift keys	David, Ruth, Fred, and Zelmo ate at San Francisco's Fisherman's Wharf.
fluency	The auditor's amendment is to suspend the endowment fund as a penalty.

| 1 | 2 | 3 | 4 | 5 | 6 | 7 | 8 | 9 | 10 | 11 | 12 | 13 | 14 |

101b ▶10 Communication aid: capitalization/punctuation

1. Read the ¶ at the right. Type it with correct capitalization and punctuation.
2. Check your corrected ¶ with your instructor. Use your corrected copy to type two 1′ writings.
3. Use the textbook copy to type two 1′ writings.

	gwam 1′
of the total number who started on the well reported trip of may	13
second to the estuary of the amazon three were natives of quayaquil	27
ecuador five had been at one time or another in rio de janeiro eight	40
were bostonians and one although few of the others actually believed	54
him indicated reykjavik was his exact birthplace and hometown.	67

| 1 | 2 | 3 | 4 | 5 | 6 | 7 | 8 | 9 | 10 | 11 | 12 | 13 | 14 |

101c ▶20 Building script-typing skill

two 3′ writings for *speed* and two 5′ writings for *accuracy*; record *gwam* and number of errors for the more accurate 5′ writing

Difficulty index

all letters used | A | 1.5 si | 5.7 awl | 80% hfw |

	gwam 3′	5′	
We are living in a wonderful period of history--	3	2	38
a time when historians are recording many excit-	6	4	40
ing changes in our world. The past two decades	10	6	42
have shown that the people of this planet must learn	13	8	44
to exist together. We no longer are able to isolate	17	10	46
ourselves from other countries. The action of one	20	12	48
nation has a direct effect on nearly every	23	14	50
other nation in the world. We must quickly rec-	26	16	52
ognize and adjust to peaceful solutions.	29	17	54
The time of ignoring what is happening in	32	19	55
other countries has passed. We must now be	35	21	57
consciously aware of what is happening in all parts	38	23	59
of the world. Our key modes of communication	41	25	61
have improved to the point that we can now be-	44	26	63
come acquainted with almost any event either live	47	28	65
and directly or within just a few minutes of	50	30	67
the actual happening. With few exceptions, the peoples	54	32	69
of the earth are no longer strangers. The world has	58	35	71
diminished in size; we are now really neighbors.	61	36	73

50c, continued

Problem 1
Personal letter
[full sheet]
modified block style, large envelope; 50–space line; begin on about Line 15

Problem 1

words

September 18, 19-- | Ms. Tanya Onedeer | 15 Mountain View Boulevard | Billings, 15
MT 59101 | Dear Ms. Onedeer (¶ 1) What is a cotter pin? "Easy question," a 28
friend answered me not long ago. "A cotter pin is a dofus that holds a gremmer 44
to a zoomican." Ah, well, ask a silly question. (¶ 2) Actually, a cotter pin is a bit 61
of split metal that is inserted through an opening; by separating the ends, it 77
holds two parts together. But we have found an altogether new use for cotter 92
pins. (¶ 3) We have fashioned cotter pins into attractive costume jewelry that 107
can be worn as a pin or on a chain; and we have one of these attractive pieces for 124
you when you come in to look at the new Fitzjohn Duraliner--the battery-driven 139
automobile of the future. (¶ 4) That's all I can tell you about the Duraliner. You 155
must see the rest to believe it. I can tell you, though, that there are 11 more 171
cotter pins in a Duraliner; before the day is over, you could be the happy owner 188
of an even dozen of them. Very truly yours | Eva L. Brynoff | Manager | xx 201
215

Problem 2
Business letter [full sheet]
modified block style, 1 carbon copy, large envelope; 60–space line; begin on about Line 15

Problem 2

June 4, 19-- | Dr. Samuel Hunsecker, Head | Business Education 12
Department | Westside Community College | 5075 Newburg 22
Avenue | Baltimore, MD 21228 | Dear Dr. Hunsecker (¶ 1) We are 33
processing the employment application of Mr. Julian Reyes, who 45
has applied for a job with us as assistant office manager. Mr. Reyes 59
lists you as one of his references, and we should like to have your 73
personal assessment of him. (¶ 2) The job requires someone who 84
is competent in the use of the typewriter, can file, knows and can 98
use language well, and is adept with arithmetic. As assistant of- 111
fice manager, Mr. Reyes would need to be the kind of person who 124
works well with others; adapts to different situations with ease; 137
remains calm under pressure; and, of course, helps manage a busy 150
office. (¶ 3) In your opinion, would Mr. Reyes be able to handle this 163
job? We shall appreciate your giving us this information either on 177
the enclosed form or by letter. Sincerely yours | Mrs. Rosetta 189
Lee-Wells | Personnel Officer | xx | Enclosure 197
222

Problem 3
Business letter [full sheet]
block style, 2 carbon copies, small envelope; 60–space line; begin on about Line 15; indent enumerated items 5 spaces from margins; DS between enumerated items

Problem 3

June 21, 19-- | Mr. Julian Reyes | 63 Normount Avenue | Baltimore, 12
MD 21216 | Dear Mr. Reyes (¶ 1) Mrs. Lee-Wells has asked me 22
to send you the following payroll record forms to be completed 35
before you report for work on the first of next month: 1. Em- 48
ployee's Withholding Exemption Certificate 2. Health insurance 60
application 3. Personal data card (¶ 2) We are pleased that you 72
have decided to join our company as its assistant office manager. 86
Those of us here in the main office shall do whatever we can to 98
make your adjustment to new surroundings as smooth and pleas- 111
ant as possible. Please let us know how we can help. Cordially 124
yours | Miss Barbara McBurnum | Chief Payroll Clerk | xx | Enclo- 134
sures 135
146

level

5

Staff office simulations

lessons 101–125

This level of Advanced Typewritten Communications is designed to provide you with ample opportunity to develop your typewriting skills in a variety of situations that are commonly found in sales offices, general offices, accounting offices, and executive offices.

Although the primary emphasis in Level 5 is on the development of your production typewriting skills, you should continue to improve your basic speed and accuracy skills. This level of the textbook provides you with three sections that are devoted entirely to speed and accuracy development.

In addition, the final section is a measurement section that tests both your production typing skills and your speed and accuracy skills. Two major performance goals for you in Division 3 are:

- To develop a keen responsibility for high-quality typewritten work.
- To develop the ability to make decisions without direct supervision.

This level provides for about 28 percent of your classroom time to be devoted to basic speed and accuracy development and 72 percent to production activities.

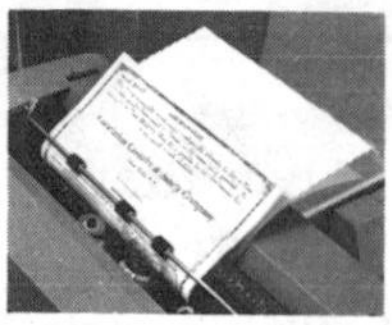

section

21

Improving basic skills

lessons 101–102

Learning goals

Because accuracy is a major goal of basic skill development, you should be able to type at one of the following rates on a 5-minute straight-copy timing of average difficulty with 8 errors or fewer:

51 *gwam*, excellent; 46-50 *gwam*, good; 41-45 *gwam*, acceptable.

The minimum goal in this section should be 41-45 *gwam*.

Machine adjustments

1. Set paper guide at *0*.

2. Set ribbon control on black.

3. Use a 70-space line and single spacing (SS) for drill lines.

4. Use a 70-space line, double spacing (DS), and 5-space ¶ indentions for paragraph copy.

Skills inventory: basic/problem skills

The purpose of the following inventory is to check your ability to:

1. Type from straight copy and rough draft.
2. Apply word-division rules.
3. Type unbound and leftbound reports.
4. Type block and modified block letters.
5. Express numbers correctly.
6. Apply related communication skills.

Straight-copy skill inventory

two 5′ writings; determine *gwam*; proofread and circle errors

To determine words-a-minute rate

1. List the figure at the end of the last complete line typed.

2. For a partial line, note from the scale the figure directly below the point at which you stopped typing.

3. Add these two figures to determine gross words a minute (*gwam*).

Difficulty index

all letters used | A | 1.5 si | 5.7 awl | 80% hfw |

	gwam 1′	5′
A business letter is uniquely representative of its writer. It	13	3
should be neat and well centered on a page, or it will seem that it has	27	5
been typed with little care. Any error should be repaired so that it	41	8
cannot be seen. Accurate spelling and grammar are also important to a	55	11
letter. A good dictionary is a correspondent's best friend.	67	13
The letters we write are extensions of our own personalities, so	13	16
each one should say to the reader that we are capable of acting in a	27	19
judicious and businesslike way. A letter that is well done is one good	41	22
indication of our ability. The importance of proofreading is apparent;	56	25
all errors must be found before a business letter is mailed.	68	27
There are a few specific guides and tables that can be useful in	13	30
typing a business letter. Such guides indicate how a letter can be	27	32
placed attractively on a page and how its special lines can be punctu-	41	35
ated. If the guides are followed, letter forms become standardized;	54	38
and a reader is less likely to be distracted by vagaries of style.	68	40
A touch of class is a statement heard frequently in reference to an	14	43
intelligent performance. A kicker who consistently makes field goals	28	46
is said to have a touch of class. An actor or actress who always gives	42	49
an outstanding performance is said to have it. So it is that a typist	56	52
who consistently turns out letters that are correct in wording and dig-	70	55
nified in appearance is said to have a touch of class. The remark de-	84	57
scribes ability, not promise. It means consistent performance on the	98	60
job.	99	60

gwam 1′ | 1 | 2 | 3 | 4 | 5 | 6 | 7 | 8 | 9 | 10 | 11 | 12 | 13 | 14 |
5′ | 1 | 2 | 3 |

Technique improvement: keystroking

each line 3 times SS (slowly, top speed, in-between rate)

fig/sym 1 The payments of $386.75 and $142.90 ($529.65 total) were 30 days late.

fig/sym 2 Model #407 created by Wang & Lee, Inc., has sold 39,582 units--up 61%.

fig/sym 3 Guy & Lee, Inc., 870 Main (Suite #4), lowered their bid 5% to $13,926.

figure 4 These 64 rooms house up-to-date files for a 127-year span (1853-1980).

Technique emphasis: tabulating

SS body; type drill 3 times; DS between drills; 10 spaces between columns

			words
12,608	coax	200-30-5752	5
52,573	a.m.	899-25-0934	10
96,001	know	173-25-7732	14
79,080	area	293-64-5020	19
32,463	keep	070-53-1020	24

Building/measuring statistical-copy skill

1. Two 1' *speed* writings on each ¶; determine *gwam* on each.

2. One 5' *control* writing on all ¶s combined; determine *gwam*; circle errors.

all letters/figures used

Difficulty index			
A	1.5 si	5.7 awl	80% hfw

	gwam 1'	5'	
The proper use of energy and new sources of power are two of the	13	3	61
major problems that we face as a country. The United States is the	27	5	64
largest energy consumer in the world. With roughly 6 percent of the	40	8	67
people on earth, we use about 35 percent of all the energy that is pro-	55	11	70
duced. Although our basic energy resources continue to be oil, 45.9	68	14	72
percent; coal, 18.8 percent; and natural gas, 28.4 percent; much greater	83	17	75
use of nuclear power and solar energy are in the future.	94	19	77
The sun is a future source of greater power because it provides a	13	21	80
limitless supply of nonpolluting energy. Although not a large star, it	28	24	83
is about 864,900 miles in diameter or a little more than 109 times the	42	27	86
size of earth. The surface temperature of the sun is 11,000 degrees	56	30	89
Fahrenheit, and it increases to approximately 27 million degrees at its	70	33	91
center. The process of fusion on its surface creates a great amount	84	36	94
of energy which is sent 93 million miles to the earth in the form of	98	38	97
sunlight.	99	39	97
In 1975 this country had 56 nuclear power plants in operation, with	14	41	100
63 more being constructed and another 100 on order. These 56 plants	27	44	103
provided us with slightly more than 5 percent of our total electricity	42	47	106
needs. Data such as these make it very plain that we are going to be in	56	50	109
an energy squeeze for a number of years. But with a vast amount of hard	71	53	111
work between now and the late 1980's, plus improved technologies, new	85	56	114
mineral sources, and a wiser use of energy, we can overcome this problem.	99	59	117

gwam 1' | 1 | 2 | 3 | 4 | 5 | 6 | 7 | 8 | 9 | 10 | 11 | 12 | 13 | 14 |
5' | 1 | 2 | 3 |

Proofreader's marks

Standardized proofreading marks are illustrated at the right. They indicate the types of corrections to be made when retyping rough-draft copy.

In practice, spelling, punctuation, word usage, and some typing errors are merely circled. The typist is expected to make the needed corrections.

PROOFREADER'S MARKS

Mark	Example	Mark	Example
∧ Insert	to study my problem	Close up vertical space	1. The items that / 2. Several of the
Delete	all of my money	lc / Use lowercase	the Secretary
Transpose	to rapidly type	≡ Capitalize	east; East; east
Close up horizontal space	in as much as	Move to left	When I first saw
# Add horizontal space	a fine job	Move to right	it was clear that
> Add vertical space	1. The items that / 2. Several of the	¶ New paragraph	many years. ¶ In the

Rough-draft copy skill inventory

two 5′ writings; determine *gwam*; proofread and circle errors

Difficulty index

all letters used | A | 1.5 si | 5.7 awl | 80% hfw |

	gwam 1′	5′
If you are planing to enter hte busimess world after you	12	2
have completed school, you should utilize your school year to	24	5
develop and improve all the qualities, basic skill, and know-how	35	7
that are demanded of those who wish wish to derive a sense of	49	10
satisfaction from their jobs. in preparing your self, you can	61	12
Recognize the improtance of neat, suitable cloghing and good	73	15
grooming. You just also know that fi you wish very far in an	87	17
office job, you real must be abel to dresswell--even on a	98	20
budget that is very limited.	101	20
You must learn when you should express in a clear, appro-	12	23
priate language. The ability is usualy place near top of the	25	25
reports of those most need ed by graduates. Consequently, you	38	28
must try to improve your wrod power by learning of the estab-	51	30
lishment or agency for whichyou Are working. If you are a grad-	64	33
uate your employer will expect you to know how to compose	76	35
refined, logical, answer to an inguiry.	85	37
Almost all office jobs require the skill to type. Usually this	13	40
taken for granted. An of fice position demands that you also	25	42
ack as will as look the part. A neat apperance is very import-	39	45
ant, so are good posture, the correct attitude, and pleasant	51	47
foice. Few employers select an attractive package	61	50
that has little value in it. The more ability you have	72	52
to offer, the better your chances will be of getting the job	85	54
you want.	86	55

Technique improvement: keystroking

each line 3 times SS (slowly, top speed, in-between rate)

direct reaches	1	The company decided to grant a bonus after payment of long-term debts.
1st/2d fingers	2	Five Navy tugs tried to enter the harbor before fog ruined visibility.
3d/4th fingers	3	Paula appeared puzzled as Pat chose six lovely purple azaleas to show.
long reaches	4	Many bankers come to back my move to become a member of the committee.
1st row	5	Were you or Roy required to write about our trip in your prior report?
3d row	6	All his possessions have been transferred to an office in Tallahassee.
long words	7	If an additional air-conditioning duct is needed, it can be installed.
fluency	8	Capable workers take more notice of what they do than of who they are.
numbers	9	Call 875-0529 on May 9 to purchase Volume #4 at a discount of 33 1/3%.

Rough-draft skill building

1. Two 1' *speed* writings on each ¶; determine *gwam*.
2. One 5' *control* writing on all ¶s combined; determine *gwam*; circle errors.

all letters used

Difficulty index			
A	1.5 si	5.7 awl	80% hfw

	gwam 1'	5'	
All of us ~~are aware of~~ many individuals who we ~~felt~~ would be	13	3	50
very sucesfull in life. When we talk about them we speak ~~highly~~	26	5	53
of there ~~personalities~~, their intelligence, and innate abilities.	40	8	55
On the other ~~hand~~, there are those who while not nearly so ~~smart~~	53	11	58
or alluring have gone farther and achieved much more, eventhough	67	13	61
no one expected the to rise so high.	74	15	62
This ~~takes~~ us to a very unique and often-discussed ~~point.~~	12	17	65
why do so many people who are judged most likely to succeed be-	24	20	67
come such failure too their friends and to them selves while	36	22	69
other who appeared to be average ~~type people~~ more than made the	49	25	72
grade. In most cases the answer is simple: success is not de-	63	27	75
termined soley by one's abilities ~~to work,~~ but also by ones	74	30	77
attitude.	78	30	78
ability in itself is meaningless; It must be ~~realized~~ befor	12	33	80
it developes any value. We have all potential regardless of	24	35	83
whom we are or what we do. Granted some of us posses greater	37	38	85
potenital than others; but the important thing is how well we	49	40	88
use the dynamics we have. Take the time to analyze your	62	43	90
achievements and ~~attempt~~ to determine your future goals; poten-	74	45	93
tial for success can be as infinite as you make it.	84	47	95

Statistical-copy skill inventory

1. Two 1′ *speed* writings on each ¶; determine *gwam*.
2. One 5′ *control* writing on all ¶s combined; determine *gwam*; circle errors.

	gwam 1′	5′	
The Fair Labor Standards Act of 1938 set a minimum wage that cov-	13	3	49
ered most American workers. The act set a minimum rate of 25 percent	27	5	52
per hour with raises that went to 40 cents per hour by 1945. Subsequent	42	8	55
changes have increased the minimum wage over the past years. In May,	56	11	57
1974, the minimum wage had reached $2.00 per hour and the January, 1981,	70	14	60
rate is set at $3.35 per hour. The 1981 minimum represents an increase	85	17	63
of over 1200 percent of the original minimum of 25 cents per hour. There	99	20	66
have been many arguments stated both pro and con each time increases in	114	23	69
the minimum wage have been suggested.	121	24	70
For example, organized labor fought hard recently for raises in	13	27	73
the minimum wage. At the same time, many opponents were after a lower	27	30	76
wage for teenage workers than for adult workers. This plan would enable	42	33	79
employers to pay persons from 16 to 19 years of age about 15 percent less	56	36	82
than the adult minimum. One reason for making this argument is the fact	71	38	85
that the postwar baby boom has swelled the supply of this age group to	85	41	87
about 9.5 percent of the total labor force. In the middle 1950's, the	99	44	90
labor pool for this age group was about 6.5 percent.	110	46	92

gwam														
1′	1	2	3	4	5	6	7	8	9	10	11	12	13	14
5′			1					2					3	

Report typing skill inventory

Leftbound report on number usage
full sheet; DS, but SS multiline rules; indent numbered items 5 spaces from left and right margins

Use NUMBER USAGE for heading.

When a choice between expressing numbers in figures or words is necessary, the following guidelines and examples will assist you in making the proper selections:

1. Spell out numbers ten and under except when used with numbers above ten.

   Examples: All six members of the family will go.
   The 7 chairs and 15 tables came May 2.

2. Numbers with abbreviations such as in., ft., a.m. are typed as figures; isolated fractions or indefinite amounts in a sentence are typed as words.

   Examples: About fifty or sixty items are lost.
   One of the desks was 5 ft. by 30 in.

3. House numbers except house number One are typed as figures; small-numbered streets and avenues are typed as words.

   Examples: Tom moved to 88 Third Street.
   The office is at One Fifth Avenue.

4. When two numbers are used together, spell out the shorter number and type the longer one in figures.

   Examples: The six 50-gallon drums have come.
   All 100 six-ounce bottles were sold.

Technique improvement: keystroking

each line 3 times SS at a controlled rate

double letters	Unnecessary commissions allocated to Mrs. Babb were usually corrected.
3d/4th fingers	Six antique shops in an old piazza ask low prices for small clay pots.
long reaches	Bunny Bruce, my niece, brought many excerpts from my column on Brazil.
adjacent keys	Sam Powers added a hundred points to the total made by Roberta Saxton.

| 1 | 2 | 3 | 4 | 5 | 6 | 7 | 8 | 9 | 10 | 11 | 12 | 13 | 14 |

Skill-comparison: progressive straight copy

1. One 2′ writing on ¶ 1 to set base rate.

2. Two 2′ writings on ¶ 2. Try to maintain ¶ 1 rate.

3. Two 2′ writings on ¶ 3. Try to maintain ¶ 1 rate.

4. Two additional writings on the slowest ¶. Work to meet or exceed ¶ 1 rate.

¶ 1 Difficulty index

E	1.2 si	5.1 awl	90% hfw

¶ 2 Difficulty index

A	1.5 si	5.7 awl	80% hfw

¶ 3 Difficulty index

D	1.8 si	6.3 awl	70% hfw

	gwam 2′	
Most lines of work have some factors that are unique to that field.	5	51
Those who want to be good at their work must be prepared to handle such	12	58
factors. For example, few office workers work in a vacuum. Office work	19	65
requires people who work with each other. They will find that they must	27	73
listen to what others say to them, and they must provide data to co-	34	80
workers in a form that is easily understood. At other times, they may	41	87
be called upon to work in groups in order to do a job.	46	92
Accuracy is one of those factors that is vital to office work. Mis-	7	53
takes mean time and time means money. Only work that is error free is	14	60
useful. That is why office workers must give constant attention to the	21	68
quality of the work they do. In addition to making few mistakes, an	28	75
alert employee is able to recognize a mistake made and rectify it in the	35	82
most efficient way. Quality work must be produced within a reasonable	42	89
period of time and according to deadlines.	47	93
To accomplish priorities, efficiency experts recommend planning	4	51
work and then following that plan to discharge a variety of assignments	12	58
that will be encountered. There are various ways of organizing work	19	65
schedules; however, one very critical factor to remember is to remain	26	72
flexible. Develop a plan that permits you to perform at maximum effi-	33	79
ciency, tackle the most pressing or vital job first, and then continue	40	86
adjusting that plan so that you are able to meet any reasonable deadline.	47	94

gwam 2′ | 1 | 2 | 3 | 4 | 5 | 6 | 7 |

Word-division inventory

Type the copy at the right in unbound manuscript style: top margin 2″; side margins 1″; DS the first ¶; SS and indent numbered ¶s 5 spaces from both margins; reset the margins; DS between numbered items.

words

DIVIDING WORDS AND SENTENCE PARTS 5

TS

A word may be divided at the end of a line in order to keep the 18
right margin as even (and attractive) as possible. When in doubt about 32
the proper division of a word, consult a dictionary or a word-division 46
guide. With very few exceptions, the word divisions indicated by these 61
references are acceptable in typewriting. The following guides will be 75
helpful. 77

1. If you decide to divide a word, divide it between syllables, 90
as your-self, con-flict, dif-fer-ent. 104

2. Words of one syllable cannot be divided, as thought, 116
trained, straight. 124

3. Divide words between two vowels if each is a separate syl- 136
lable, as situ-ations, evalu-ation. 148

4. Hyphened compounds should be divided only at the point of 160
the hyphen, as know-how, cross-file, son-in-law. 176

5. Words should not be divided before the single letter syl- 189
lables a, i, and u, unless they are followed by the 199
ending syllables bly, ble, cle, or cal, as gradu-ate, flex- 217
ible. 219

6. Regardless of a word's length, don't divide a one-letter 231
syllable at the beginning of it, as e-nough, or a one- or 244
two-letter syllable at the end of a word, as read-y, or 257
ghast-ly. 260

7. Even though they may have two or more syllables, never 272
divide words of five or fewer letters, as offer, onto. 285

8. Divide words after a prefix or before a suffix if possi- 297
ble, as pre-scribe. 303

9. Words should be divided between double consonants unless 316
the root word ends in a double letter, as strip-ping, pro- 330
cess-ing. 334

Word-division skill

half sheet, long side up; 1½″ top margin; center heading; DS body of table; 8 spaces between columns

1. Follow the steps at the right for horizontal placement of columns.

2. Checked words are the longest in each column.

3. Type the hyphen to show word divisions, as in Line 1. If necessary, consult the word-division guides or a dictionary.

4. Correct errors.

Guides for horizontal placement of columns (backspace-from-center method)

1. Move margin stops to ends of scale. Clear all tabulator stops. Move carriage (carrier) to center of paper.

2. From center of paper, backspace once for each 2 strokes in the longest line of each column and for each 2 spaces to be left between columns.

3. Set left margin stop at the point where you complete the backspacing.

4. From the left margin, space forward once for each stroke in the longest line of the first column and for each space to be left between the first and second columns.

5. Set a tab stop at this point for the second column.

6. Follow this procedure for each additional column.

WORD DIVISION

TS

√year-book	blan-ket	news-room	√dis-tur-bance
freedom	skillful	√knowledge	frequence
passed	√self-direct	separate	judgment
losing	thought	mixture	masterful
missile	modifying	janitor	often

Script-copy skill building

1. Two 1′ *speed* writings on each ¶; determine *gwam*.

2. One 5′ *control* writing on all ¶s combined; determine *gwam*; circle errors.

Difficulty index

all letters used	A	1.5 si	5.7 awl	80% hfw

	gwam 1′	5′	
People have many theories on how workers are	9	2	52
motivated to produce on the job. Some people feel that	20	4	55
workers motivate themselves in the work environment. Others	32	6	57
say motivation comes from the supervisor, an incentive	43	9	59
award, or the task itself. You will find that you get	54	11	61
more out of life if you can find ways to inspire	64	13	63
yourself to do a better-than-average job despite any	75	15	65
obstacles that may be thrown in your path.	83	17	67
One substantial theory centers around the notion	10	19	69
that, in order to be properly motivated, a person must	21	21	71
first recognize the need for a positive self-image.	31	23	73
How you feel about yourself as a person determines	42	25	75
how others feel about you. In other words, the	51	27	77
way a person thinks he or she looks can be more	61	29	79
important than the way he or she actually looks to	71	31	81
others. Begin now to picture yourself in a more	81	33	83
complimentary light.	85	34	84
Nourish your ego by quietly feeding it self-	9	35	86
respect and see how quickly it grows. And as it	19	37	88
develops, watch those around you respect you more	29	39	90
and more. Go out of your way if necessary to	38	41	92
observe and meet successful people with your	47	43	94
background and learn what makes them excel. By	56	45	95
believing that you are a talented, educated, and	66	47	97
informed individual, you present this image to	76	49	99
those who meet you; and they believe it, too.	84	51	101

Letter style inventory

1. Study the general format of the two letters below.

2. For standard spacing of letter parts, read both problems below before typing them.

3. Proofread; correct errors

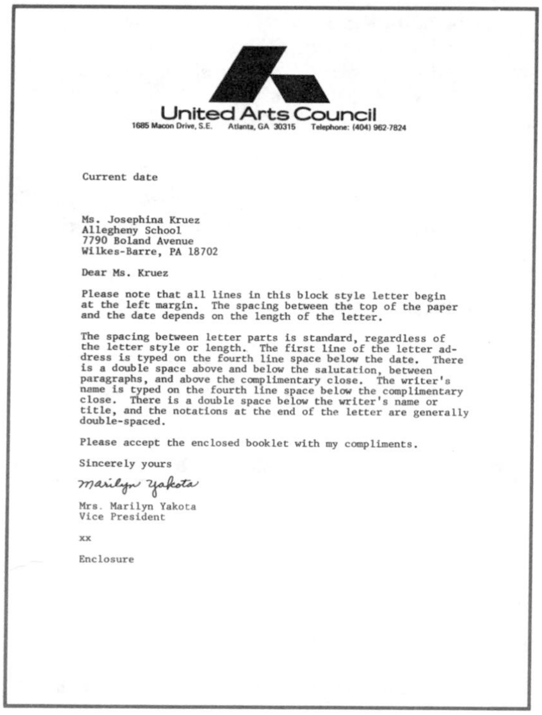
United Arts Council
1685 Macon Drive, S.E. Atlanta, GA 30315 Telephone: (404) 962-7824

Current date

Ms. Josephina Kruez
Allegheny School
7790 Boland Avenue
Wilkes-Barre, PA 18702

Dear Ms. Kruez

Please note that all lines in this block style letter begin at the left margin. The spacing between the top of the paper and the date depends on the length of the letter.

The spacing between letter parts is standard, regardless of the letter style or length. The first line of the letter address is typed on the fourth line space below the date. There is a double space above and below the salutation, between paragraphs, and above the complimentary close. The writer's name is typed on the fourth line space below the complimentary close. There is a double space below the writer's name or title, and the notations at the end of the letter are generally double-spaced.

Please accept the enclosed booklet with my compliments.

Sincerely yours

Marilyn Yakota

Mrs. Marilyn Yakota
Vice President

xx

Enclosure

Block style, open punctuation: All lines start at the left margin. No punctuation after the salutation or complimentary close.

Modified block style with block paragraphs, open punctuation: Dateline and complimentary close start at horizontal center. No punctuation after the salutation or complimentary close.

When using either style for a personal business letter on stationery without a letterhead, type your return address on the two lines above the dateline.

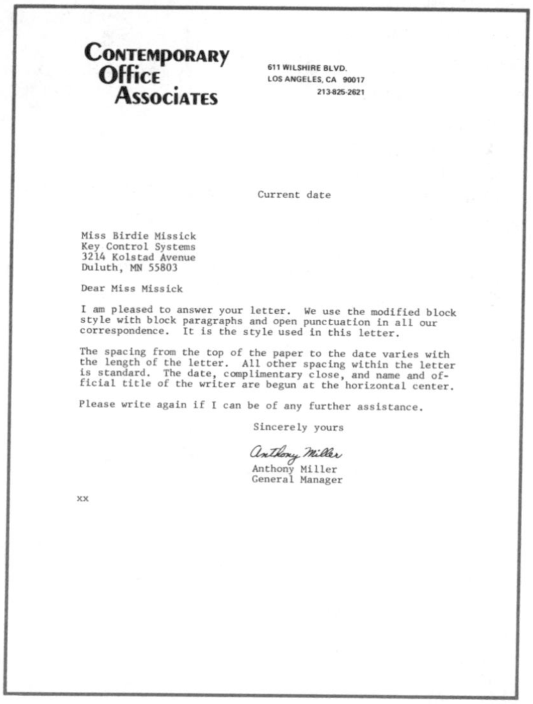
Contemporary Office Associates
611 WILSHIRE BLVD.
LOS ANGELES, CA 90017
213-825-2621

Current date

Miss Birdie Missick
Key Control Systems
3214 Kolstad Avenue
Duluth, MN 55803

Dear Miss Missick

I am pleased to answer your letter. We use the modified block style with block paragraphs and open punctuation in all our correspondence. It is the style used in this letter.

The spacing from the top of the paper to the date varies with the length of the letter. All other spacing within the letter is standard. The date, complimentary close, and name and official title of the writer are begun at the horizontal center.

Please write again if I can be of any further assistance.

Sincerely yours

Anthony Miller

Anthony Miller
General Manager

xx

Problem 1
Block style, open punctuation

plain sheet; 60-space line; date on Line 16

words

Current date | Ms. Josephina Kruez | Allegheny School | 7790 Boland Ave- 14
nue | Wilkes-Barre, PA 18702 | Dear Ms. Kruez 22
(¶ 1) Please note that all lines in this block style letter begin at the left 37
margin. The spacing between the top of the paper and the date depends on 52
the length of the letter. (¶ 2) The spacing between letter parts is standard, 66
regardless of the letter style or length. The first line of the letter address is 83
typed on the fourth line space below the date. There is a double space above 98
and below the salutation, between paragraphs, and above the complimentary 113
close. The writer's name is typed on the fourth line space below the compli- 128
mentary close. There is a double space below the writer's name or title, and 142
the notations at the end of the letter are generally double-spaced. (¶ 3) 156
Please accept the enclosed booklet with my compliments. 167
Sincerely yours | Mrs. Marilyn Yakota || Vice President | xx | Enclosure 180

Problem 2
Modified block style, block paragraphs, open punctuation

plain sheet; 60-space line; date on Line 18

words

Current date | Miss Birdie Missick | Key Control Systems | 3214 Kolstad 14
Avenue | Duluth, MN 55803 | Dear Miss Missick 22
(¶ 1) I am pleased to answer your letter. We use the modified block style 36
with block paragraphs and open punctuation in all our correspondence. It is 52
the style used in this letter. (¶ 2) The spacing from the top of the paper to 66
the date varies with the length of the letter. All other spacing within the 82
letter is standard. The date, complimentary close, and name and official title 98
of the writer are begun at the horizontal center. (¶ 3) Please write again if I 113
can be of any further assistance. 120
Sincerely yours | Anthony Miller | General Manager | xx 130

Supplemental skill-building practice

Technique improvement: response patterns

1. Each line at least twice SS.

2. A 1′ writing on Line 2, then on Line 4, then Line 6.

3. Determine *gwam* on each writing; compare speed scores.

Letter Response: See, think, and type difficult combinations letter by letter.

Word Response: See, think, and type short, easy words as word wholes.

Combination Response: Type short, easy words as word wholes. Type difficult combinations letter by letter. Blend the two responses into a smooth typing rhythm.

letter response	Berez was requested to decrease the minimum number of pollution tests.
	Decision-making capability demands considerable insight and foresight.
word response	We must all learn that this is a right time and a right place to grow.
	There are but few signs on the road to mark the way to the old bridge.
combination response	In all lines of work, thought without any action can become a disease.
	The way you type what you type determines the kind of skill you build.

| 1 | 2 | 3 | 4 | 5 | 6 | 7 | 8 | 9 | 10 | 11 | 12 | 13 | 14 |

Straight-copy skill building/measurement

1. Type a 5′ writing; determine *gwam*; circle errors.

2. Type two 1′ writings on each ¶; circle errors. **Goal:** not more than 1 error in each writing.

3. Type another 5′ writing; determine *gwam*; circle errors. Compare *gwam* and number of errors with first writing.

Difficulty index

all letters used | A | 1.5 si | 5.7 awl | 80% hfw |

	gwam 1′	5′	
Whenever you write a business letter (or any letter), write it	13	3	61
as if you were speaking directly to the person to whom you are writing.	27	5	64
Express your ideas clearly enough that there is scant reason for a re-	41	8	66
cipient to be confused. Whether or not the recipient agrees with you	55	11	69
is usually important, but rest assured that there will be no meeting	69	14	72
of minds if the reader does not recognize what you are talking about.	83	17	75
Whenever you have doubts about clarity, ask someone to scan the let-	97	19	77
ter before you mail it.	101	20	78
When we receive a reply that doesn't seem sensible, it could be	13	23	81
that our own original message is at the root of the difficulty. Did we,	27	26	84
for example, try to be more impressive than expressive? Plain words,	41	29	87
nicely chosen, usually allow little room for confusion. It is true,	55	31	89
of course, that words are imperfect tools for conveying our ideas; how-	69	34	92
ever, we just don't have anything else that works quite so well. We	83	37	95
can't mail a gesture, a look, or an attitude. We must use words.	96	40	98
However, the fact must be realized that words are meaningful only	13	42	100
when they are put together in sentences. Generally, short sentences are	28	45	103
better than long ones. We must be brief without being miserly with	41	48	106
facts. We must remember that we are writing to someone with likes	55	50	109
and dislikes similar to ours. We can use a bit of psychology here and	69	53	111
there to add appeal and conviction to our letters. Above all, we	82	56	114
should write the kinds of messages we like to receive.	93	58	116

gwam 1′ | 1 | 2 | 3 | 4 | 5 | 6 | 7 | 8 | 9 | 10 | 11 | 12 | 13 | 14 |
5′ | 1 | 2 | 3 |

Communication aids checkup

half sheet; 1" top margin; 1" side margin; DS; add an appropriate title for each paragraph.

Terminal punctuation and capitalization

Test your knowledge of punctuation, capitalization, etc., by making the necessary corrections in these paragraphs. Use the following directions for each paragraph.

What a tremendous feat Congratulations Did you hear that our sales department which is made up of branch offices in Boston New York Philadelphia etc. leads all regions in increased sales this year Mrs Jefferson the regional vice president for marketing will present an award at the annual sales conference Individuals who met or exceeded their sales quotas will receive individual recognition The job is done and we are proud The work was hard but it was worth the effort Thank you Ms. Blessing for your leadership Will you please relay my congratulations to the members of your staff

Numbers

If necessary, refer to the report on number usage, page 99.

10 members of the 15-member committee attended the 6-hour session held at the corporate office located at 10 5th Avenue. All 9 of the major items contained in Report No. 96 were discussed in detail. The remaining 15 items were briefly reviewed and will be handled at our next meeting on June 29. Almost 1/3 of the project is completed, and we should meet the deadline we set at our 1st meeting eleven months ago.

Quotation marks

Did you read Jack's article entitled Life in the Suburbs? In it he told the story of the city lady who said to the farmer, What is the strange odor in your garden? That, said the farmer, is fertlizer. For the land's sake! exclaimed the lady. Yes, said the farmer.

Punctuation, capitalization, spelling

If time permits, compose a second ¶ that exhibits your understanding and knowledge of the communication skills emphasized in prior lessons.

you met your deadline congratulations your report was precise timely and accurate therefore mayor browns staff will submit the report to the governor in boise idaho on june 30 1981 my plan is to emphasize 1 innovation 2 unity 3 communications as joan stated earlier in the communication journal now is the time for action

100b, continued

Problem 3
Invoice
Type invoice at right.
Make 1 cc.

				words
SOLD TO	Brooks Hardware, Inc.	DATE	August 13, 19--	3
	401 N. Michigan Avenue	OUR ORDER NO.	A13-1579	8
	Chicago, IL 60611	CUST. ORDER NO.	39570-3	14
				18
				19
TERMS	2/10, n/30	SHIPPED VIA	Penn Central RR	25

QUANTITY	DESCRIPTION	UNIT PRICE	TOTAL	
10	C-rated fire extinguisher	9.99	99.90	33
100	AC-powered smoke detector	14.99	1,499.00	42
75	1/3-HP variable speed drill	39.99	2,999.25	51
10	2-HP air compressor	299.99	2,999.90	59
25	1-HP belt sander	55.49	1,312.25	68
10	Super Stor/Drawer	11.95	119.50	74
20	12-pc. auger bit set	18.95	379.00	84
			9,408.80	85

Problem 4
full sheet; reading position; DS body; 6 spaces between columns

words

CAMPUS INTERVIEWS FOR MARKETING POSITIONS 8

(Week Ending June 3, 19--) 14

Date	Company	Representative	Room	26
May 30	Leesona Corporation	Marvin Barnes	120	35
May 31	A. T. Cross	Colleen Coleman	236	43
June 1	Textron, Inc.	Wayne Carrington	157	51
June 1	American Airlines	Louis Marzilli	853	60
June 2	IBM Corporation	Julie Serydnyski	904	69
June 2	B. B. Greenberg Co.	Patricia Thacker	748	78
June 3	Brite Industries, Inc.	Robert Bailey	961	88
June 3	Telecom Systems, Inc.	Elizabeth Washington	370	99
June 3	National Insurance	Floyd Sheffield	849	108

level

3

Business correspondence

lessons 51–74

Now that you have achieved basic typing skill and have learned how to type a number of business papers, you are ready to use these skills as a foundation to make your typing more valuable as a business tool.

Level 3 is devoted primarily to developing your expertise in solving a wide variety of communication problems. Letter styles, including many commonly used special features, are illustrated and explained. Word choice, punctuation, grammar, and writing style are stressed to help you better express in typewritten form your own thoughts and to help others in presenting theirs.

The directions and sample solutions included in the lessons will acquaint you with the standard procedures to be followed. Study the directions carefully. Apply them to the unarranged problems included.

Know, however, that style directions are not laws. They are general guides to be followed or changed as needs arise. Learn to recognize those needs.

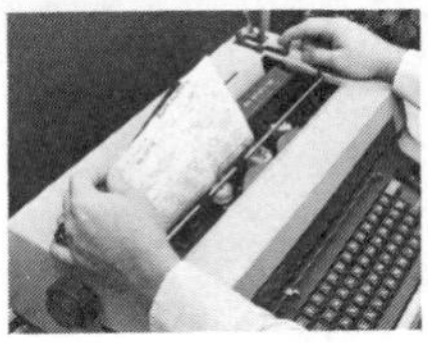

section

11

Typing letters in basic styles

lessons 51–55

Learning goals

1. To type business letters in two acceptable styles, centered attractively on letterhead or plain paper, and under pressure of time for an extended period.

2. To manage efficiently the forms and supplies needed in letter production.

3. To improve basic typing and proofreading skills.

Machine adjustments

1. Paper guide at *0*.

2. 70-space line for drills and timed writings.

3. SS drill sentences; DS ¶s and indent 5 spaces; space problems as directed.

100b ▶ 45

Production measurement: tables and an invoice

Time schedule

Assembling materials . . . 5′
Timed production . . . . . . 30′
Final check; compute *n-pram* . . . . 10′

1. Arrange plain sheets, the invoice form [LM p. 229], and supplies.

2. Type for 30′ from the problems provided here; correct errors as you type.

3. Circle uncorrected errors found in final check; compute *n-pram* (see p. 110).

Problem 1

full sheet; reading position; DS body; 10 spaces between Columns 1 and 2; 6 spaces between Columns 2, 3, and 4

INCREASING COST OF AN AVERAGE BUSINESS LETTER

(Estimates by Dartnell Institute of Business Research)

Cost Factors	1973	1975	words
Dictator's Time	$ .72	$ .88	38
Secretarial Time	.99	1.07	44
Nonproductive Labor	.26	.29	51
Fixed Charges	.86	.96	56
Materials Cost	.10	.14	62
Mailing	.21	.25	67
Filing	.17	.20	71
Totals	$3.31	$3.79	78

(words: title 9; subtitle 20; column heads 31)

Problem 2

full sheet; reading position; DS body; 8 spaces between columns

TIME WORKED TO PAY BASIC LIVING COSTS* (words 8)

Expense	Portion of Workday	Percent of Workday	words
			10, 25
Taxes	2 hours, 45 minutes	34	30
Housing	1 hour, 28 minutes	18	36
Food	1 hour, 4 minutes	13	42
Transportation	30 minutes	6	47
Medical	30 minutes	6	52
Clothing	23 minutes	5	56
Recreation	19 minutes	4	61
Electric/gas service	11 minutes	2	68
All other	50 minutes	11	77
Total	8 hours	99	80

_______________ 84

* The Tax Foundation estimates of the average U.S. taxpayer. 96

Problems 3 and 4 are on the next page.

51

51a ▶ 5
Preparatory practice
as many times as possible in time available

alphabet Eliza quit both her jobs, packed six bags, and moved far away to Nome.

fig/sym Exactly 25 7/16 of the solids (384 pounds) must be added at 10:29 a.m.

shift keys Bob and Kim Murry visited the Hillsdale County Fair in July or August.

fluency Our problem is that there is a right and a wrong way with any problem.

| 1 | 2 | 3 | 4 | 5 | 6 | 7 | 8 | 9 | 10 | 11 | 12 | 13 | 14 |

51b ▶ 10
Production typing information: business letter placement

LETTER PLACEMENT TABLE

5-Stroke Words in Body of Letter	Letter Length	Side Margins	Dateline from Top Edge	Placement of Second Page Heading
Up to 100 words	Short	2" 50sp.	Line 20 25·80	Type the first line
101 to 150 words	Short–average	1½" 60sp.	Line 17 20·85	of second and follow–
151 to 200 words	Average	1½" 60sp.	Line 15 20·85	ing page headings on
201 to 250 words	Long–average	1½" 60sp.	Line 14 20·85	7th line from top edge.
251 to 325 words	Long	1" 70sp	Line 12 15·90	TS below the heading,
More than 325 words	Two–page	1" 70sp.	Line 12 15·90	then continue the letter.

Stationery
Business letters are usually typed on 8½" × 11" letterhead paper. For a multipage letter, plain paper of the same size, color, and quality as the letterhead is used after page 1. Onionskin or manifold paper is used for carbon copies.

Margins/vertical placement
Some offices use a set line length for all letters. Others vary the margins according to the letter length.

The placement table given here will help you place letters properly. Use the table as an aid; discontinue using it as soon as possible.

Estimate letter length, and place letters by judgment. Your ability to judge will be vital.

Adjustment guides
As you learn to judge letter placement, consider two factors: (1) Is your type size pica or elite and (2) does the letter contain extra opening and closing lines, a table, or a list? Allow for these extra lines by raising the dateline from 1 to 3 lines.

If the letterhead prevents typing the date on the designated line, type it on the second line below the last letterhead line.

51c ▶ 30
Problem typing: business letters

plain paper, 8½" × 11"

Type the three letters following the directions given for each. (Letter styles illustrated on page 101.) Use your initials as the reference initials. Determine placement from the table above. The number of 5–stroke words in the body of the letter is indicated by the number in parentheses at the end of each letter. Correct all errors.

▶ In *mixed* punctuation, use a colon after the salutation and a comma after the complimentary close. In *open* punctuation, no punctuation follows the salutation or the complimentary close.

Problem 1
Block, open punctuation

words

Current date | Mr. Ira Whitmore | 5578 Crestview Drive | Pasadena, CA 13
91107 | Dear Mr. Whitmore 18
(¶ 1) A neighbor of yours has recently installed a Firestone Security System. 33
You may have seen one of our signs indicating that their home is protected 48
by Firestone. (¶ 2) Most people install a security system only after experienc- 63
ing a burglary, holdup, fire, or some other emergency in their home. We'd like 79
to be there first for a change. (¶ 3) If you are interested in knowing why 93
more families are installing Firestone Home Security Systems, please call me 108
or simply return the enclosed card today. Sincerely yours | Ms. Rose M. 122
Washington | Sales Representative | xx | Enclosure (101) 131

99b, continued

Problem 2
Leftbound report
Use the following heading: CHANGING JOB HOURS

words

Among the various types of experiments being undertaken to improve 13
working conditions, perhaps none has greater implications than those involving 29
alteration of working hours. Not only are these alterations relevant to leisure- 45
time use, energy consumption, and labor force participation; but to the extent 61
that if they attract more married women into the labor force, they may change 77
sex and family roles as well. 83

Several different types of arrangements in working hours, including fixed 98
working time, rational working hours, variable working hours, and flexi-time, 113
have been noted in research evaluations by Albert Glickman and Zenia Brown.[1] 129

1. Fixed working time is best represented by the 5-day, 40-hour 142
week, but with variations such as the compact or 4-day work- 154
week. 155
2. Rational working hours provide for more hours to be worked in 169
some contract periods than others, or on particular days. 180
3. Variable working hours give each employee complete freedom 193
in the selection of time he or she decides to work, subject to his 206
or her responsibility for completing the total hours contracted. 220
4. Flexi-time, wherein each employee is allowed to start and 232
finish the workday within certain limits, when he or she 243
pleases. 245

Only time and additional research will provide us with significant find- 260
ings regarding the impact various time patterns have had on either job satis- 275
faction or family roles. 280

__________ 284

[1] Albert Glickman and Zenia Brown, Changing Schedules of Work (Wash- 303
ington, D.C.: American Institute for Research, 1973), pp. 21-22. 316

Problem 3
Second page of unbound report

words

What happens in the future depends on males as well as women. 14
If men are willing to accept an equal share of household re- 26
sponsibilities and to respect wives occupational activities, 38
family life will stay stabel. If they are not we may see a 50
sharpe increase in divorce rates later and fewer marriages 62
and more childless couples. 68
Regardless of our past feelings, beliefs, or value the 79
year ahead offer a time of meaning and oppotunity to come to 92
terms with human relations. in any case, it will be exciting 106
because their has never been a time with so many options, 121
alternative, varieties of roles. 132

100

100a ▶ 5
Preparatory practice
each line 3 times SS; DS between 3-line groups; retype selected lines as time permits

alphabet Jake saw a herd of playful zebras quietly relaxing near the main cove.

fig/sym The payments of $386.75 and $142.90 ($529.65 total) were 30 days late.

3rd/4th fingers Perhaps an opposite response may have expressed it more appropriately.

fluency A problem may ensue if they make a formal amendment to end the panels.

| 1 | 2 | 3 | 4 | 5 | 6 | 7 | 8 | 9 | 10 | 11 | 12 | 13 | 14 |

words

Problem 2
Block style, mixed punctuation

Current date | Ms. Delia Ramos | Apartment 12 | 1417 Simeon Avenue | Brockton, 15
MA 02402 | Dear Ms. Ramos: (¶ 1) Welcome to the rather special circle of 27
DELIGHT readers, and thank you for accepting our subscription invitation. Your 43
first issue of our magazine should arrive momentarily--if it has not already been 60
delivered. (¶ 2) We strive for pictorial excellence as well as informed and lively 75
writing about exciting places and people. I hope our efforts will please you. 91
Again, welcome. Sincerely yours, | Andre Lazarof | Editor and Publisher | xx (75) 105

words

Problem 3
Modified block style, block paragraphs, open punctuation

Current date | Dr. Telford Wurtele | 5002 Longfellow Street | Wichita, KS 67207 | 15
Dear Dr. Wurtele (¶ 1) If you were to ask Jack Parren what he was doing all alone 31
in the classroom after all the students had left, he'd probably say, "Thinking." 47
(¶ 2) Jack Parren teaches at Nancy Hastings School because he likes to think. He 62
couldn't stand using last year's notes for this year's class. He has to find new 79
ways to communicate with adolescent students, because adolescent students are 94
different every day. (¶ 3) He has to get students thinking about what to expect of 110
themselves in the way of leadership and involvement; what their particular 125
talents are and how they intend to develop them; and what it takes not only to be 141
understood, but also to understand. (¶ 4) Perceiving and analyzing and 154
communicating are what grown people have to do. Growing people have to learn 170
how. (¶ 5) Jack Parren teaches communications at Nancy Hastings School 183
because he wants to. Write for a detailed catalog describing all courses offered 200
by our school. Sincerely yours | Miss Susan Purcell, Principal | xx (182) 213

51d ▶ 5

Evaluate your work

Examine the 3 letters you have typed. Did you proofread each letter while it was still in the typewriter to find any uncorrected errors? Were all corrections neatly made? Did you remember to type your reference initials in the proper position? If you were a supervisor, would you be pleased with the appearance of the letters? Be critical of your work; you know that others will be.

52

52a ▶5

Preparatory practice

as many times as possible in the time available

alphabet Brazilian Judge Frank Wavo is quietly confirming the risk of smallpox.

fig/sym Lau & Lehan's office, 3547 Cord Street, opened May 26, 1980, at 8 a.m.

hyphen I re-covered a second-rate sofa for my son-in-law with on-sale fabric.

fluency Many elements must be combined to produce work in which we take pride.

| 1 | 2 | 3 | 4 | 5 | 6 | 7 | 8 | 9 | 10 | 11 | 12 | 13 | 14 |

99

99a ▶ 5
Preparatory practice

each line 3 times SS; DS between 3-line groups; retype selected lines as time permits

alphabet	The judges realized the six quick verdicts would benefit my plaintiff.
fig/sym	Of the 2,760 dispensers made by Employee #2984, 135 could not be OK'd.
3rd/4th fingers	Perhaps I shall push soon for someone to help us work on the old plan.
fluency	To the dismay of the city auditor, an audit of the fuel profit is due.

| 1 | 2 | 3 | 4 | 5 | 6 | 7 | 8 | 9 | 10 | 11 | 12 | 13 | 14 |

99b ▶ 45
Production measurement: reports

Time schedule

Assembling materials ...... 3′
Timed production .... 35′
Final check; compute
n–pram .... 7′

1. Arrange plain paper and supplies for easy handling.

2. When directed to begin, type for 35′ from the problems on this page and page 197. If you complete the problems in less than 35′, start over with Problem 1.

3. Correct errors neatly as you type.

4. Proofread and circle any uncorrected errors found in final check.

5. Compute n–pram (see p. 110).

Problem 1
Unbound report

words

TODAY'S COLLEGE WOMEN 5

During the past decade, the number of individuals, 15
organizations, and educational programs concerned with 26
defining and redefining traditional and nontraditional sex roles 39
has skyrocketed. Young women especially have been encouraged to 52
raise their educational and career aspirations and also to demand 65
equality both in and out of the home. 72

Current Trends 78

Recent findings reflect a national trend on the part of 89
women to project a more positive image and attitude toward their 102
roles. In general, women now possess a greater confidence than at 115
any time in the past regarding their right to compete with men, their 129
abilities, and their expectation of an equal division of domestic duties. 144

Marriage and Motherhood 154

Interestingly enough, however, such increased activism does not 166
extend to a rejection of material or maternal roles. Instead, surveys 181
reveal the continuing existence of a strong interest in marriage and 194
motherhood. Today's college women are determined to have both a 207
career and family. The women of earlier generations felt compelled to 222
keep career and family separate: They were expected to leave their jobs 236
for childbearing, and to carry the full burden of household duties while 251
working. Today's women have found that they can work while their chil- 265
dren are small, and that it is not unreasonable to assume that their hus- 280
bands will take on a major share of the child-rearing and domestic duties. 294

Problems 2 and 3 are on page 197.

52b ▶ 10
Problem typing information: addressing envelopes

To hasten the sorting of mail, the U.S. Postal Service is using an automatic scanning device at more and more regional mail sorting centers. The Postal Service asks that the following directions be observed.

Postal recommendations

1. Type the address lines in block style (even left margin) in the area on the envelope that the scanner is programmed to read.

2. For a large (No. 10) envelope, type the address about 2½ inches from the top (Line 15) and 4 inches from the left edge.

3. For a small (No. 6¾) envelope, type the address about 2 inches (Line 12) from the top and 2½ inches from the left edge of the envelope.

4. Capitalize everything; eliminate all punctuation in the address.

5. Use the standard 2-letter ZIP Code abbreviation for the state. State abbreviations for use with ZIP Codes appear on page iv of the Reference Guide (RG).

6. Type the name of the city, 2-letter state abbreviation, and ZIP Code on the last line of the address. The space below the address must be completely clear.

7. The last line must not exceed 22 digits. If necessary, long city names and street designators may be abbreviated, using the abbreviations found in the *National ZIP Code Directory* or *Customer Service Publication 59* (both available from the U.S. Postal Service).

Recommended placement of additional information

1. When an address contains such notations as *Personal* or *Confidential*, underline them or type them in all capital letters 3 lines below the return address and aligned with the left edge of the address.

2. Type mailing directions such as SPECIAL DELIVERY or REGISTERED MAIL in all capital letters below the space for the stamp.

3. When an address contains an *attention line*, type it as the second line of the address.

General information

1. If the ZIP Code of an address is not available, type the state name in full or use the traditional abbreviation. Typing may be in capital and lowercase or all capitals.

2. As a mark of courtesy, always use an appropriate personal title on a letter, envelope, or card addressed to an individual. When a woman's preferred title is unknown, use Ms. as the personal title.

3. Some companies use No. 10 envelopes as a standard practice. Others use No. 10 envelopes for all original copies on 8½" × 11" stationery and No. 6¾ envelopes for half-size stationery or onionskin sheets.

4. Although the U.S. Postal Service recommends the use of ALL CAPS and no punctuation in envelope addresses, many companies continue to use cap and lowercase style with punctuation as illustrated on the No. 6¾ envelope below.

Examples

MR WENDELL OGDEN
BOX 158
GARDEN CITY NY 11530

MISS GINA MOORE
SCOTT SHOE COMPANY
3561 SHOSHONE ROAD
ST PAUL MN 55109

MOLLOY PRODUCTS CO
ATTENTION MR E S MOLINO
999 CUMBERLAND STREET
WACO TX 76707

Mrs. Carol Mincer
RR 3 Box 193-B
Challenge, Calif.
(When ZIP Code is not available)

Style of addressing envelope used below is recommended by U.S. Postal Service to aid mechanical mail sorting.

Large envelope (No. 10) 9½" × 4⅛"

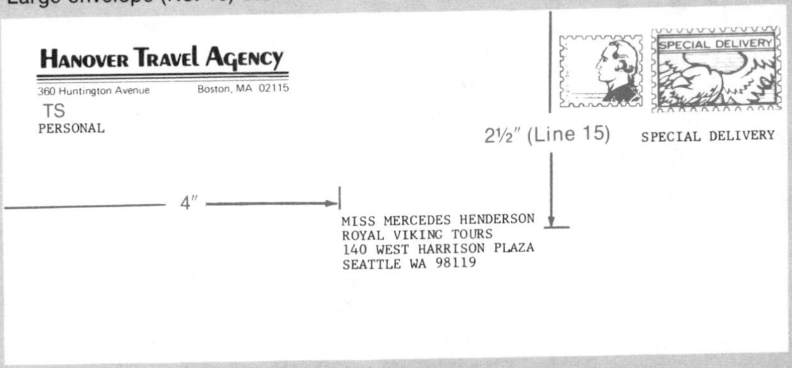

Small envelope (No. 6¾) 6½" × 3⅝"

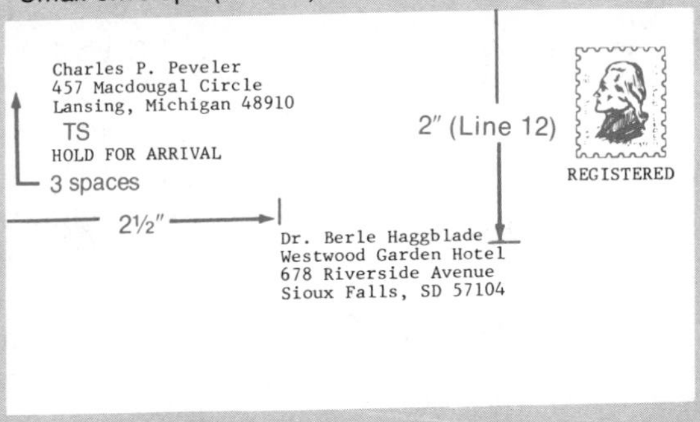

98b ▶ 45

Production measurement: communications

Time schedule

Assembling materials . . . 3′
Timed production . . . . . . 35′
Final check;
compute *n-pram* . . . . . 7′

1. Arrange forms [LM pp. 223–228] and supplies for easy handling.

2. When directed to begin, type for 35′ from the problems at the right. If you complete the problems in less than 35′, start over on plain paper.

3. Correct errors neatly as you type. Proofread and circle errors found in final check.

4. Compute *n-pram* (see p. 110).

5. If necessary, refer to pp. 112–115 for review of business forms.

Problem 1
Full-size interoffice memo

	words: Problems 1	3
TO: Cynthia Pankiewicz, Admissions Director	8	8
FROM: George Fong, Academic Dean	13	13
DATE: December 13, 19--	17	17
SUBJECT: Continued Compliance with Civil Rights Act	26	26
Title VI of the Civil Rights Act provides that no person shall,	38	
on the grounds of race, color, or national origin, be excluded	51	
from participation, be denied the benefits of, or be subjected to	64	
discrimination under any program or activity receiving	75	
federal financial assistance. Please check to see	85	30
that all new and continuing admissions counselors	95	40
are familiar with these regulations. The following	106	50
points are to be emphasized:	112	56
1. Facilities are to maintain records of each enrollee	123	67
uniformly and without discrimination.	131	75
2. Recipients may implement procedures which will	141	85
provide statistically accurate data on racial	151	95
and ethnic composition.	156	100
3. Racial and ethnic identification will be volun-	166	
tary on the part of applicants or enrollees.	175	
3. 4. Any housing maintained by the facility for its	185	111
enrollees is to be open to all enrollees on a	194	120
nondiscriminatory basis.	200	125
Arrangements have been made for a meeting with	209	
your staff on Tuesday, January 15, at 9:00 a.m.	219	
to outline our plan for compliance with the new	228	
state regulations dealing with the handicapped.	238	

Problem 2
Two-way communication on message/reply form

Type the two-way communication at right. Make 1 cc.

(Message for Problem 2)	words
TO: Miss Ellen Batastini Person-	6
nel Director 337 Corporate Annex	12
DATE: June 30, 19-- (¶ 1) Recent	16
feedback from customers who	22
deal with our office has raised	28
some concern about the image and	35
impact our office staff projects to	42
the outside world. (¶ 2) We all	48
agree it is vital that each of us un-	55
derstand the powers of effective	62
telephone communications.	67
Therefore, I suggest you initiate a	74
program with all office employees	81
to develop and improve our tele-	87
phone power. BY: Manuel Lopes,	93
Public Relations	96

(Reply for Problem 2)	words
DATE: July 14, 19-- (¶ 1) I have re-	5
quested a series of four one-hour	12
meetings with all office em-	17
ployees to discuss and develop our	24
telephone techniques. The first	31
meeting is scheduled for 8 a.m.,	37
Tuesday, July 14.(¶ 2) Topics to be	44
discussed include: placing, an-	50
swering, and transferring calls;	57
handling complaints; taking mes-	63
sages accurately; giving and get-	70
ting information; and terminating	76
calls. (¶ 3) Feel free to attend and	83
participate in any of the sessions. I	91
shall report the results of our	97
training sessions to you. SIGNED:	102
Ellen Batastini	105

Problem 3
Interoffice memo

Retype Problem 1 making the following changes:

1. Delete sentence one of ¶ 1.

2. Delete enumerated item 3; change item 4 to 3.

3. Delete ¶ 2.

52c ▶35
Problem typing: envelopes and business letters

Problem 1

three each of No. 10 and No. 6¾ envelopes [LM pp. 65–70] or paper cut to size

Type the addresses at the right on both size envelopes. Follow the directions on page 106 and make any needed changes to make the addresses agree with the U.S. Postal Service recommendations.

Ms. Madge Schmidt, Buyer
Garman Department Store
7401 Melrose Street
Portland, Maine 04101
(Registered Mail)

Harold L. Haydock
1896 Bonanza Street
El Paso, Texas 79925
(Confidential)

Old World Antiques, Inc.
4784 Adair Avenue
Richmond, Virginia
(Attention Mrs. Jamie Hall)

▶ From this point, LM page references refer to the *Laboratory Materials*.

Problem 2

Modified block, block ¶s, open punctuation

1 letterhead and envelope [LM p. 71]

1. Use the Letter Placement Table, page 104.
2. Type PERSONAL notation on envelope.
3. Correct all errors.

▶ The total word count is shown as 166/189: the first figure, the letter count; the second, the letter plus the envelope.

words

Current date| Ms. Winifred M. Sager| Executive Secretary| Knoxville Chamber 15
of Commerce| 4478 Aralia Lane, N.E.| Knoxville, TN 37918| Dear Ms. Sager 29
(¶ 1) I am pleased to tell you that you have been unanimously elected a mem- 43
ber of the Board of Directors of the Clean Air Council of Knoxville. (¶ 2) The first 59
meeting of the year will be held on the first Friday of next month at three in the 76
afternoon in the Board offices at 1750 Allen Avenue, S.E. The election of officers 93
will be the main item of business on that day. A complete agenda and portfolio 109
for the meeting will be mailed to you this afternoon. (¶ 3) Please accept my 123
sincere congratulations. I am happy to welcome you as a Board member and look 139
forward with pleasure to the opportunity of working with you during the coming 155
year. Very truly yours| Oscar K. Vandergoot| President| xx (126) 166/**189**

Problem 3

plain paper

1. Compose and type a response to the letter in Problem 2 using current date. Assume the letter was addressed to you as executive secretary of the Knoxville Chamber of Commerce.
2. Express your interest in the work of the Council, accept the directorship, and indicate your intention to attend the first meeting.
3. Correct errors as you type.
4. Type the letter in modified block style, block ¶ s, and open punctuation. Mr. Vandergoot's address is: Clean Air Council of Knoxville, 1750 Allen Avenue, Knoxville, TN 37912.

53

53a ▶5
Preparatory practice

as many times as possible in the time available

alphabet	Grif Bass quickly explained why we don't have zero weather in Jamaica.
fig/sym	Invoices 332-56 and 745-98 were sent to us by Diehl & Co. on 10/23/79.
double letters	Annette can tell her zoology class that the 22 books will arrive soon.
fluency	The more one tends to rely on chance, the more chance one has to fail.

| 1 | 2 | 3 | 4 | 5 | 6 | 7 | 8 | 9 | 10 | 11 | 12 | 13 | 14 |

53b ▶10
Problem orientation

plain paper; 1½" margins

1. Using Style Letter 3, page 108, type the dateline through the first line of the body. Leave proper spacing between parts.
2. Type the last line of the body and remaining letter parts, leaving proper spacing between them.
3. On another sheet of paper, type a 1′ writing on the opening lines and ¶ 1; a 1′ writing on ¶s 2, 3, and 4; and 1′ writing on the last ¶ and closing lines.

53c ▶35
Problem typing: business letters

Problem 1

plain paper

Type the letter (237 words) on page 108 at rough-draft speed. Strike over any errors you make.

Proofread; use standard proofreader's marks to indicate the needed corrections.

Problem 2

[LM p. 73]

Using your corrected copy, retype the letter making the corrections indicated in your copy. Correct errors as you type. Address an envelope.

Problem 3

plain paper

If time permits, type a 5′ writing on the letter.

97c ▶ 30
Production measurement: business letters

Time schedule

Assembling materials .. 3′
Timed production ......20′
Final check;
compute *n-pram* .... 7′

1. Arrange letterheads and envelopes [LM pp. 217–222] and supplies for easy handling.

2. When directed to begin, type for 20′ from the problems. Start over on plain paper if you complete the problems in less than 20′.

3. Correct your errors neatly as you type.

4. Address envelopes.

5. Proofread and circle uncorrected errors found in final check.

6. Compute *n-pram* (see p. 110).

Problem 1
block; open punctuation

words

June 1, 19-- Mr. Spencer J. Martin 221 State Street New London, CT 06320 Dear 15
Mr. Martin (¶ 1) As a citizen deeply concerned about the future generations, 30
you are acutely aware of the potential hardships they face because of the fuel 45
crisis. (¶ 2) Within the next 12 years, our demands for electricity may double. 61
With gas and oil in short supply, other sources of energy must be found. All 76
Americans must share some of the responsibility for this problem. Equally 91
important is the responsibility all Americans must feel to help solve this prob- 107
lem. (¶ 3) One alternative receiving much attention lately is nuclear energy. It 123
has been suggested that a thimbleful of nuclear fuel can provide as much 137
energy as 330 gallons of fuel oil. (¶ 4) Learn more about this valuable potential 153
energy source. You are invited to attend the lecture being sponsored by the 168
Concerned Citizens of New London, Wednesday, June 16, at 7:30 in the evening. 184
The meeting will be held at the Neighborhood Guild House, Kingston Road, New 199
London. (¶ 5) Show your concern for the future by attending this informative 214
lecture, "Planning for the Future with Nuclear Energy." Sincerely yours Ms. 229
Marilyn Plunckett, Director xx (207) 237/**247**

Problem 2
modified block; mixed punctuation; indented ¶s

words

May 3, 19-- Mr. Joseph L. Calihan 128 South Drive Pittsburgh, PA 15238 Dear 15
Joe: (¶ 1) Congratulations on your nomination to the Honor Association of 29
School Directors. You have worked long, hard years and are a most deserving 44
nominee. (¶ 2) Remember when we started teaching 35 years ago? I'm sure 58
that neither of us will ever forget some of the mistakes we shared as novices in 74
the educational system of Liverpool! (¶ 3) Get those golf clubs out of storage, 89
polish them up, and enjoy your well-earned vacation. You and Brenda can now 105
enjoy all those activities for which you could find little or no time in the past. 121
(¶ 4) Congratulations again, Joe, to the most recent member of the Honor As- 135
sociation of School Directors. Sincerely, John C. Welter, Principal xx (125) 150/**162**

Problem 3
block; mixed punctuation
Retype the letter in Problem 2 but substitute ¶ 3, ¶ 4, and the closing at the right.

words

(¶ 3) You will be returning from Bermuda just in time to be the featured speaker 97
at our Honors Colloquium. We will be pleased if you can accept this invitation. 113
The choice of topic is open; you may choose something of interest to you. Can 129
we count on you to be the guest speaker on May 29? (¶ 4) Again, Joe, con- 143
gratulations on your most recent award. Sincerely yours, Ms. Agnes Schantz 158
Director, Honors Colloquium xx (134) 164/**176**

98

98a ▶ 5
Preparatory practice

each line 3 times SS; DS between 3-line groups; retype selected lines as time permits

alphabet	The four very rhythmic and quietly relaxing jazz bands were kept busy.
fig/sym	An out-of-court settlement made May 2, 1980, gave our firm $43,608.75.
2d finger	I definitely remember receiving the second dividend check in December.
fluency	Both of the firms may fight the big penalty if their auditor is right.

| 1 | 2 | 3 | 4 | 5 | 6 | 7 | 8 | 9 | 10 | 11 | 12 | 13 | 14 |

REPUBLIC COMMUNICATION COMPANY
3903 WESTER AVE., FT. WORTH, TX 76133 • 817-358-4411

		words in parts	total words
	Start at center point of paper ↓		
Dateline	September 30, 19--	4	4
	4 line spaces (3 blank lines)		
Letter address	Mr. Albert G. Heisten	8	8
	Attorney-at-Law	11	11
	National Bank Building	16	16
	76930 Kaskaskia Street	21	21
	Springfield, IL 62702	25	25
Salutation	Dear Mr. Heisten:	28	28
Body of letter	When you switch to Republic's Automatic Dialer 26,	38	38
	you will have the wonderful sensation of clearing your	49	49
	memory of many annoying facts. Your mind will have room	61	61
	for more important information.	67	67
	With Republic's Automatic Dialer 26, those phone	10	77
	numbers you frequently dial are at your fingertips instead	22	88
	of on the tip of your tongue. There are 30 buttons for	33	100
	your prerecorded numbers, including 4 colored ones for	44	110
	emergencies. Next to each button there is a place for	55	121
	the name. When you want to make a call, you just point	66	138
	to the name you want, and push the button.	74	141
	The 31st button is a "last number dialed" button.	84	151
	It automatically records your last manually-dialed number.	96	163
	So, if you get a busy signal, you can call back without	108	174
	redialing. You merely push the 31st button.	116	183
	The Automatic Dialer 26 is just one of the services	127	194
	we offer to save you time and money. Our consultants con-	138	205
	tinually analyze your telephone system to make sure that	150	217
	you are using it as efficiently as possible.	159	225
	Getting in touch with us, however, does take a little	11	236
	effort. You will have to dial all the digits of your	22	247
	Republic Communication Company's office or visit the	32	258
	nearest Republic Phone Mart.	38	263
Complimentary close	Yours very truly,	41	267
Signature	4 line spaces (3 blank lines) *Joseph Sierra, Jr.*		
Typed name and official title	Joseph Sierra, Jr.	45	271
	Assistant Sales Manager	50	275
Reference initials	xx	50	276
			297

In *mixed punctuation*, a colon follows the salutation and a comma follows the complimentary close.

Style letter 3: modified block with indented paragraphs and mixed punctuation

section

20

Employment testing

lessons 97–100

Measurement goals

1. To demonstrate your best straight-copy typing skill.
2. To demonstrate your best letter-typing skill.
3. To demonstrate your best skill in typing business forms.
4. To demonstrate your best report- and table-typing skill.

Machine adjustments

1. Paper guide on *0*.
2. Margins: 70-space line for drills and ¶s; as directed for problems and business forms.

97

97a ▶ 5
Preparatory practice

each line 3 times SS; DS between 3-line groups; retype selected lines as time permits

alphabet The jumpy gazelle often runs off quickly when excited by human voices.

fig/sym Paula handled 530 new accounts in 1980 with sales totaling $44,798.26.

1st finger You may remember that Mary gave great amounts of time and money to us.

fluency Did they also land a bid for the giant fish when they got to the dock?

| 1 | 2 | 3 | 4 | 5 | 6 | 6 | 7 | 8 | 9 | 10 | 11 | 12 | 13 | 14 |

97b ▶ 15
Measuring straight-copy typing skill

two 5′ writings for *accuracy*; determine *gwam* and errors; record the better writing

Difficulty index

all letters used | A | 1.5 si | 5.7 awl | 80% hfw |

gwam 5′

You communicate by your actions as well as by your language. Any 3 | 62
move you make may be used to indicate your mood, attitudes, thoughts, 5 | 64
and even the state of your psychological condition. You may not always 8 | 67
realize it, but your body sends out hundreds of signals to other people; 11 | 70
and you receive just as many from them. Your facial expressions, hand 14 | 73
gestures, body motions, and even how far you stand from a person that 17 | 76
you are talking with are all a part of your nonverbal messages. 19 | 78

A nodding head, raised brows, misty eyes, folded arms, trembling 22 | 81
hands, or patting another person on the back are typical reactions to 25 | 84
what is being said or heard. Some of the signals that you send and 28 | 87
receive may amaze you. For example, studies have shown that a feeling 30 | 89
of pleasure can cause the pupils of your eyes to enlarge to double their 33 | 92
normal size. Any of these indicators may tell you more about the person 36 | 95
or ideas under discussion than the actual words that are being spoken. 39 | 98

Be alert for any sign that can help you to find out whether a person 42 | 101
is receptive to what you are saying or is refusing to accept it. A 45 | 104
closed body position often means disagreement. Folding the arms, avoid- 47 | 106
ing eye contact with others, or leaning back from others all tend to 50 | 109
set up a barrier against what others are saying. If you can learn to 53 | 112
interpret quickly the signals others send you and also control the sig- 56 | 115
nals you send out, your ability to communicate with others will improve 59 | 118
greatly. 59 | 118

gwam 5′ | 1 | 2 | 3 |

54

54a ▶5 Preparatory practice

as many times as possible in the time available

alphabet The buzzing, jumping insects quieted; for it was exactly five o'clock.

fig/sym How can Thomas, Inc., meet accounts of $27,463 and $85,900 by March 1?

1st row Can Victor Zorn cleverly recover much extra evidence and deceive them?

fluency Eight or ten big firms may make a profit from the sale of the islands.

| 1 | 2 | 3 | 4 | 5 | 6 | 7 | 8 | 9 | 10 | 11 | 12 | 13 | 14 |

54b ▶15 Correcting copy by squeezing and expanding

Some errors can be corrected by squeezing omitted letters into half spaces or spreading letters to fill out spaces.

Type the first phrase at the right exactly as it is; then follow the solution to make the correction. Compare your corrected line with the one that follows the solution. Repeat the line if needed. Follow the same procedure for 2–5.

1 Omitted letter at end of word

lette at end

Solution

Move carriage to letter *e*; then depending upon typewriter:

a Depress and hold down space bar; strike letter *r*;

b use the half-space mechanism; or

c hold the carriage by hand at the half-space point.

letterat end

2 Omitted letter at beginning of word

beginning etter at

Solution

Move carriage to space before error; then depending upon typewriter:

a Depress and hold down space bar; strike letter *l*;

b use the half-space mechanism; or

c hold the carriage by hand at the half-space point.

beginning letter at

3 Omitted space between words

omittedspace at

Solution

Erase last letter of first word and first letter of next word; then using solutions described for 1 and 2, make the correction.

omitted space at

4 Omitted letter within word

omitted leter in

Solution

Erase incorrect word, position carriage at space after the letter *d*; then depending upon typewriter:

a Depress and hold down space bar; strike letter *l*;

b repeat process for remaining letters, or

c use half-space mechanism.

omitted letter in

5 Addition of letter within word

added lettter in

Solution

Erase incorrect word, position carriage at space for *l*; then depending on typewriter:

a Depress and hold down space bar; strike letter *l*;

b repeat process for remaining letters; or

c use half-space mechanism.

added letter in

54c ▶30 Sustained production typing: business letters

Time schedule

Assembling materials .... 3′
Timed production .... 20′
Final check; compute *n-pram* .... 7′

1. Arrange letterheads and No. 10 envelopes [LM pp. 75–78], plain paper, and supplies for easy handling.

2. Make a penciled list of the following problems to be typed:
page 105, 51c, Problem 2
(To be typed on plain paper.)
page 107, 52c, Problem 2
page 108, Style letter 3

3. When directed to begin, type for 20′. Follow directions given for each problem. Move from one problem to the next quickly. As you type, correct all errors neatly. Proofread carefully each letter and envelope before removing from the typewriter. If you finish all problems before time is called, retype the first problem.

4. Compute *n-pram* according to the directions given at the top of page 110.

APPLICATION FOR EMPLOYMENT

PLEASE PRINT WITH BLACK INK OR USE TYPEWRITER

AN EQUAL OPPORTUNITY EMPLOYER

NAME (LAST, FIRST, MIDDLE INITIAL)	SOCIAL SECURITY NUMBER	CURRENT DATE
Crane, Joseph M.	200-30-8794	July 25, 19--

ADDRESS (NUMBER, STREET, CITY, STATE, ZIP CODE): 2200 Lafayette Avenue, Kansas City, KS 66104

HOME PHONE NO. 834-0564
REACH PHONE NO. 792-2157

MARITAL STATUS: Single
U.S. CITIZEN? YES X NO
DATE YOU CAN START: August 1, 19--

ARE YOU EMPLOYED NOW? Yes
IF SO, MAY WE INQUIRE OF YOUR PRESENT EMPLOYER? Yes

TYPE OF WORK DESIRED: Accounting
REFERRED BY: Newspaper advertisement
SALARY DESIRED: $ open

IF RELATED TO ANYONE IN OUR EMPLOY, STATE NAME AND POSITION: None

DO YOU HAVE ANY PHYSICAL CONDITION THAT MAY PREVENT YOU FROM PERFORMING CERTAIN KINDS OF WORK? YES NO X IF YES, EXPLAIN

HAVE YOU EVER BEEN CONVICTED OF A CRIME (OTHER THAN TRAFFIC VIOLATIONS)? YES NO X IF YES, EXPLAIN

EDUCATION

	EDUCATIONAL INSTITUTION	LOCATION (CITY, STATE)	DATES ATTENDED FROM MO.	FROM YR.	TO MO.	TO YR.	DIPLOMA, DEGREE, OR CREDITS EARNED	CLASS STANDING (CHK QUARTER) 1	2	3	4	MAJOR SUBJECTS STUDIED
COLLEGE	Univ. of Kansas	Lawrence, KS	9	75	5	80	B.A.	X				Math, Eng. business
HIGH SCHOOL	Central High School	Kansas City, KS	9	71	6	75	Diploma	X				Accounting
GRADE SCHOOL	Taft Elementary	Kansas City, KS	9	63	6	71						
OTHER												

LIST BELOW THE POSITIONS THAT YOU HAVE HELD (LAST POSITION FIRST)

1. NAME AND ADDRESS OF FIRM
Gayle & Gompers Insurance Agency
1414 Junction Road
Kansas City, KS 66106

DESCRIBE POSITION RESPONSIBILITIES
Accounts receivable, payroll preparation, routine accounting, telephone sales, and technical manual editing

NAME OF SUPERVISOR
Mr. George Heddleston

EMPLOYED (MO-YR) FROM: June, 1979 TO: Present

REASON FOR LEAVING
To secure permanent position

2. NAME AND ADDRESS OF FIRM
(Same as above)

DESCRIBE POSITION RESPONSIBILITIES
(Same as above)

NAME OF SUPERVISOR
(Same as above)

EMPLOYED (MO-YR) FROM: June, 1978 TO: September, 1978

REASON FOR LEAVING
To return to school

3. NAME AND ADDRESS OF FIRM

DESCRIBE POSITION RESPONSIBILITIES

NAME OF SUPERVISOR

EMPLOYED (MO-YR) FROM: TO:

REASON FOR LEAVING

I UNDERSTAND THAT I SHALL NOT BECOME AN EMPLOYEE UNTIL I HAVE SIGNED AN EMPLOYMENT AGREEMENT WITH THE FINAL APPROVAL OF THE EMPLOYER AND THAT SUCH EMPLOYMENT WILL BE SUBJECT TO VERIFICATION OF PREVIOUS EMPLOYMENT, DATA PROVIDED IN THIS APPLICATION, ANY RELATED DOCUMENTS, OR RESUME. I KNOW THAT A REPORT MAY BE MADE THAT WILL INCLUDE INFORMATION CONCERNING ANY FACTOR THE EMPLOYER MIGHT FIND RELEVANT TO THE POSITION FOR WHICH I AM APPLYING, AND THAT I CAN MAKE A WRITTEN REQUEST FOR ADDITIONAL INFORMATION AS TO THE NATURE AND SCOPE OF THE REPORT IF ONE IS MADE.

Joseph M. Crane
SIGNATURE OF APPLICANT

54c, continued

N-PRAM (net production rate a minute)

N–pram refers to the rate on production copy when a number of items are to be typed and when errors are to be erased and corrected. *N–pram* measures both typing and nontyping activities; therefore, it is good procedure to have all supplies ready before beginning to type.

Penalty: Deduct 10 words for each unerased error if no carbon copies are typed. Deduct 15 if carbon copies are called for.

$$n\text{–}pram = \frac{\text{Gross (total) words} - \text{penalties}}{\text{Length (in minutes) of writing}}$$

55

55a ▶5 Preparatory practice

as many times as possible in the time available

alphabet	Explain quietly how Dickens vilified Ebenezer Scrooge or Jacob Marley.
fig/sym	In 1948, A & E Company's net sales were $273,590; in 1978, $6,309,471.
adjacent keys	We were assured Polk Power Saws were proper saws to cut sides 32 x 45.
fluency	It can be an amazing experience to find that work can be a lot of fun.

| 1 | 2 | 3 | 4 | 5 | 6 | 7 | 8 | 9 | 10 | 11 | 12 | 13 | 14 |

55b ▶10 Straight-copy skill measurement

one 5′ writing on control level; determine *gwam*; proofread and circle errors

Difficulty index

all letters used | A | 1.5 si | 5.7 awl | 80% hfw |

	gwam 1′	5′
The computer performs so many miracles that we quite often regard	13	3
it as a brain that can think. A computer cannot think, but it does	27	5
give us data that improves our judgments. It makes us think better.	41	8
Computers perform what seems like magic. The only magic is their fast	55	11
speed and their ability to sort out and make available jewels of helpful	70	14
information.	72	14
There are three principal elements on which a computer operates.	13	17
One is data--lots of it. The second is a set of instructions called a	27	20
program developed by people. The program tells the computer how to	41	23
process the data, step by nit-picking step. The third is displaying	55	25
the information obtained in a form most convenient to the user. The	69	28
form can be a graph, table, or report--just about anything that may	82	31
be required. These elements are the nuts and bolts of data processing.	96	34
The computer helps us develop plans, and plans mean that we can	13	36
predict the future. But can we? We all know that significant decisions	27	39
based on these plans cannot be divorced from some form of crystal gazing.	42	42
The inclination to plan a future that will happen for us instead of to	57	45
us is delightful to contemplate, but it does not come on today's blue	71	48
plate special. The future is not static. The computer does not give	85	51
us perfect foresight. Its forte is to make available more information	99	53
than we have ever had before. Consequently, we can only make better	113	56
guesses about what the future will hold for us.	122	58

gwam 1′ | 1 | 2 | 3 | 4 | 5 | 6 | 7 | 8 | 9 | 10 | 11 | 12 | 13 | 14 |
5′ | 1 | 2 | 3 |

96b ▶ 35

Problem typing: application and follow-up letters

Problem 1 [LM p. 211]
Application form
Type the application for employment shown on page 192.

Problem 2
Follow-up letter
Type the letter at the right on plain paper. Choose your own letter and punctuation styles.

P.O. Box 379 Lawrence, KS 66044 July 31, 19-- Ms. Joan Swenson, Senior Accountant Kansas City Mutual Insurance Company P.O. Box 6066 Kansas City, KS 66109 Dear Ms. Swenson (¶ 1) Thank you for the opportunity to discuss your need for a junior accountant. Thank you, too, for discussing with me my qualifications for this position. (¶ 2) Kansas City Mutual is everything that I've heard and read about and more. What an exciting feeling to see such a dynamic, progressive firm in action! I know now why you have earned the enviable reputation as a leader in the field of insurance. (¶ 3) The accounting position you have available is just the kind of position for which I have been preparing during my studies in college. Ms. Swenson, I look forward to the opportunity of becoming a part of Kansas City Mutual in the position of junior accountant. Sincerely Joseph M. Crane (132)

Problem 3
Composing a follow-up letter
Compose and type in rough-draft form a follow-up letter using the information provided at the right. If time permits, retype the letter in final copy.

1. Prepare a follow-up letter to an interview held yesterday.
2. Address the letter to Mr. Ralph Washington, Affirmative Action Officer, Discount Fabrics, Inc., 38 Cochrane Street, Newbury, MA 01950.
3. Thank Mr. Washington for the interview and for discussing your qualifications for the position of management trainee.
4. Indicate your impressions of the company and of any individuals you may have met during the interview.
5. Provide a courteous, goodwill ending for your letter.
6. Prepare the letter for your signature.

96c ▶ 10

Report on capitalization

plain paper; 2" top margin; 1" side margins; DS, but SS multiline rules and example sentences

1. Use CAPITALIZATION for the heading.
2. Type each rule and example; compose and type a second sentence to illustrate further the rule.
3. Proofread; correct errors.
4. If time permits, retype the fourth Communication aids checkup, page 102. Check your corrections with your instructor.

1. Capitalize the proper names of things such as the names of businesses, buildings, hotels, rooms, etc.

   The new office of the Masey Company is in Room 263 of the Warmkey Building adjacent to the Grand Hotel.
   (Compose a sentence.)

2. Capitalize the days of the week, months of the year, holidays, and religious days.

   Have you noticed that both Thanksgiving Day and Christmas Day fall on a Thursday this calendar year?
   (Compose a sentence.)

3. Capitalize a title that refers to a specific person; however, a title not referring to a specific person is not capitalized unless it is a title of high distinction.

   The presidents of several student groups met with Governor Jackson to discuss the removal of President Newman.
   (Compose a sentence.)

55c ▶35
Production measurement: business letters

Time schedule
Assembling materials .... 3′
Timed production .... 25′
Final check; compute *n–pram* .... 7′

1. Arrange letterheads [LM pp. 79–84] or plain paper and supplies for easy handling.
2. Address a No. 10 envelope for each letter.

3. Type each problem; correct errors; circle uncorrected errors found in final check.
4. Compute *n–pram* (see p. 110).

Problem 1
Block style; open punctuation

words

Current date | Mr. Benjamin McShane | Assistant to the President | Sunset 14
Industries, Inc.| 2249 E. Devon Avenue| Des Plaines, IL 60018| Dear Mr. 28
McShane (¶ 1) The Comp Word Processor is an expandable typing system that 42
grows as your word processing needs grow. If you purchased one of the original 58
units, you have mag card compatibility and 500 wpm speed. By adding the 72
telecommunication option, your processor can "talk" to computers and other 87
communicating word processors. (¶ 2) Something new has been added. Now 101
there is a math capability that can handle repetitive numerical jobs. Soon you 117
will be able to add even more to your processor. (¶ 3) Our "building block" 131
concept is an important feature to keep in mind when you consider a word 145
processing system. The options you consider a luxury today may be a necessity 161
tomorrow. (¶ 4) For further information, call your nearest Comp Word 174
Processor dealer, or write us. Very truly yours | Ms. Bertha L. Kogan| 188
Assistant Sales Manager| xx (149) 193/**216**

Problem 2
Modified block style; block ¶s; mixed punctuation

words

Current date| Miss Blanche Wisdom| 7632 Recovery Road| Niagara Falls, NY 15
14304| Dear Miss Wisdom: (¶ 1) Before you buy, drive. Before you drive, read. 29
Obviously a motor home is not something you buy every day. So, before you do, 45
some preparation is in order. (¶ 2) A thorough test-drive, for example, is a must. 61
We will admit that our motives for recommending this drive are purely selfish, 77
but it is the only true way to appreciate the features of our motor home. 92
Features include the front-wheel drive, tandem rear wheels, and self-leveling 107
air suspension. (¶ 3) Before you take the wheel, however, we would like you to 122
read our booklet, "The Pleasures of a SKALD Motor Home." It has answers for 138
such questions as, What's it like to drive? to have serviced? to store? to live in? 155
All in all, we hope the booklet is an enlightening introduction to a big subject. It 172
is entertaining and educational. Best of all, it's free. Just ask for it at your 188
SKALD dealer. Sincerely yours,| Nicolas M. Winslade, Director| Advertising 202
Department| xx (184) 205/**217**

Problem 3
Modified block style; indented ¶s; mixed punctuation

words

April 10, 19-- | Mr. and Mrs. Stanley Cantwell | Box 67 | Stillwater, OH 13
44679 | Dear Mr. and Mrs. Cantwell: (¶ 1) Thank you for calling us for 26
reservations. I am pleased to confirm your participation on a tour of Austrian 42
castles departing from Boston on May 8. (¶ 2) I have also extended your trip to 57
leave the tour on May 29 in Lisbon and to arrive in London on the same day. 72
Departure from London for Boston has been set for June 25. A complete 86
itinerary will be sent to you soon. (¶ 3) Again, thank you for calling. Sincerely 102
yours,| Floyd A. Plotts| xx (71) 107/**117**

95

95a ▶ 5

Preparatory practice

each line 3 times SS; DS between 3-line groups; retype selected lines as time permits

alphabet	Any size jukebox that fragile will be quite difficult to pack or move.
fig/sym	Invoice No. 90612 for 785 lbs. of beef at $3.45 per lb. has been paid.
long number patterns	54545 or 45455; #152087; 250,921; 1990-200; 325-98-274; (701) 253-7536
fluency	Ruth may sign the work audit for the city so the firm may do the work.
	| 1 | 2 | 3 | 4 | 5 | 6 | 7 | 8 | 9 | 10 | 11 | 12 | 13 | 14 |

95b ▶ 45

Problem typing: applying for employment

Problem 1
Letter of application
Type the letter at the right on plain paper. Decide letter style and punctuation.

Problem 2
Help wanted ad
Compose and type a help wanted ad similar to the one shown at the right. Prepare the ad for a position for which you feel you are qualified.

Problem 3
Composing letter of application
Compose and type on plain paper a letter of application in response to the help wanted ad you prepared in Problem 2. Decide letter and punctuation styles. Proofread and edit your first draft; type a final copy.

303—HELP WANTED

Accountant, Junior--For local highly respected insurance company. Experience preferred. Responsible for office management, budgets, and billing. Ability to plan work and assume responsibilities. Send resumé to: Ms. Joan Swenson, Senior Accountant, Kansas City Mutual Insurance Co., P.O. Box 6066, Kansas City, KS 66109

P.O. Box 379 Lawrence, KS 66044 July 24, 19-- Ms. Joan Swenson, Senior Accountant Kansas City Mutual Insurance Company P.O. Box 6066 Kansas City, KS 66109 Dear Ms. Swenson (¶ 1) Please accept this letter as the initial step in my application for the accounting position in your firm which was advertised in the Kansas City Journal on Friday, July 24, 19--. (¶ 2) You can see on the enclosed personal data sheet how I have prepared myself for the position you have available. The courses listed have provided me with an excellent background. In addition, my work experience with Gayle & Gompers has served to broaden my understanding of the goals and functions of insurance companies and of the work of the accountant in them. This experience has helped to reaffirm my desire to become a successful accountant. (¶ 3) Please give me an opportunity to discuss my training, qualifications, and experience with you as they relate to the position you have available. You may call me at (913) 792-2157 to suggest a convenient time for an interview, or you may write to me at the address shown above. Sincerely Joseph M. Crane Enclosure (181)

96

96a ▶ 5

Preparatory practice

each line 3 times SS; DS between 3-line groups; retype selected lines as time permits

alphabet	The bold offering made for the seized explosives was quickly rejected.
fig/sym	Invoice No. 5397-P for $3,482.16 (less 10%) was mailed to Cole & Able.
long number patterns	1982 and 1985; 609,528; 765-3530; 200-84-5735, (203) 824-0624, 1982-85
fluency	Dori is an auditor and may lend them a hand with their usual problems.
	| 1 | 2 | 3 | 4 | 5 | 6 | 7 | 8 | 9 | 10 | 11 | 12 | 13 | 14 |

section

12

Simplified forms of business correspondence

lessons 56–59

Learning goals

In the lessons of this section, you will learn to type three simplified communication forms as they are typed in the business office.

In doing so, keep these goals in mind:

1. To improve your basic proofreading skills.
2. To improve efficiency in handling the materials needed for each job.
3. To type each problem in the format recommended.

Machine adjustments

1. Paper guide at *0*.
2. Margins: 70-space line for drills and ¶s; as directed for problems.
3. SS line drills; DS ¶s; as directed for problems.

56

56a ▶5 Preparatory practice

as many times as possible in the time available

alphabet	The exultant jockey had won five bronze plaques and seven gold medals.
fig/sym	In 1977, Luis Gomez paid $2,438.65 for a boat and $150.92 for a motor.
long words	Secretary Blanchard's noncommittal responses delighted her detractors.
fluency	The future is not with a job; it is with the worker who does that job.

| 1 | 2 | 3 | 4 | 5 | 6 | 7 | 8 | 9 | 10 | 11 | 12 | 13 | 14 |

56b ▶10 Manipulative control: aligning copy

half sheet; 50-space line

1. Exact vertical center; DS; set tab stops according to the KEY and the guides above the table. Tabs should be set to require the least forward and backward spacing.

2. Repeat problem if time permits.

margin ↓	tab ↓	tab ↓	tab ↓
apparent	TO:	495.67	I
rhyme	FROM:	45.00	II
rhythm	DATE:	5.50	III
signalize	SUBJECT:	93.56	IV

key | 9 | 8 | 8 | 8 | 6 | 8 | 3 |

56c ▶35 Problem typing: interoffice communications

1″ side margins; proofread; circle errors; address envelopes marked COMPANY MAIL [LM pp. 85-88]

Problem 1
Half-size interoffice memorandum

Read the information in Problem 2, page 113. Then type the memo shown at the right.

words

Hart Manufacturing Company   INTEROFFICE COMMUNICATION

TO: Phillip Morris, Personnel Department 7

FROM: Jerome Monke 10

DATE: March 21, 19-- 13

SUBJECT: Booklet on Fringe Benefits 18

Pages 1-10 of the booklet on fringe benefits for Hart employees 31
are enclosed. The printer promises that he will have the rest of 44
the booklet completed by the end of this week. I expect to receive 58
the copy early next week. 63

I would appreciate receiving any corrections or suggestions you 76
care to make on these first 10 pages as soon as possible. 87

xx 88

Enclosure 89

section

19

Employment communications

lessons 94–96

Learning goals

The lessons of this section are planned to help you achieve the following goals:

1. Increase awareness of employment communications.
2. Continue development and refinement of composition and communications skills.
3. Continue development and refinement of subskills required for typing on printed lines and applications.

Machine adjustments

1. Margins: 70-space line for drills and ¶s.
2. Follow directions outlined for each problem. In the absence of directions, use your best judgment to determine what should be done.
3. SS drills; DS ¶s.

94

94a ▶ 5

Preparatory practice

each line 3 times SS; DS between 3-line groups; retype selected lines as time permits

alphabet	The goofy clowns can make up a jovial and crazy exhibit when required.
fig/sym	The May 18 bill showed a credit of $253.90 and a balance of $1,476.14.
long number patterns	3,467; 134-56; #15880; 1995-2000; 300-20-5752; (401) 902-3845; 351,864
fluency	Title to both the land and the lake is held by their skeptic neighbor.

| 1 | 2 | 3 | 4 | 5 | 6 | 7 | 8 | 9 | 10 | 11 | 12 | 13 | 14 |

94b ▶ 45

Problem typing: personal data sheet

Problem 1
Data sheet

1. From the copy shown at the right, type the personal data sheet.
2. Use a 2″ top margin and 1″ side margins.

Problem 2
Constructing a data sheet

Construct and type a personal data sheet, using your own data arranged attractively on the page.

Margins 12-90

JOSEPH M. CRANE

TS

Permanent Address	Temporary Address
2200 Lafayette Avenue	P.O. Box 379
Kansas City, KS 66104	Lawrence, KS 66044
DS	
Telephone: (913) 834-0564	Tab 64 Telephone: (913) 792-2157

DS

Career Objective: Management position in the accounting department of a growing company. Eventual objective is to become an officer in a medium-size firm. 2 spaces

Tab 35 DS

Major Qualifications: University background in business administration. Experience in various aspects of accounting.

Education: College: BA, University of Kansas, June, 1980
Courses in Accounting: cost accounting, federal tax accounting, accounting-computer systems, auditing, financial accounting, accounting systems.

Courses in related fields: economics, marketing, law, statistics, communications, business policy, management.

High School: Central High School, Kansas City, Kansas. Valedictorian. Majors in mathematics and science.

Experience: Gayle & Gompers Insurance Agency, 1414 Junction Road, Kansas City, KS 66106. Summers 1978 and 1979. Duties: accounts receivable, payroll preparation, routine accounting, telephone sales, also wrote and edited technical manuals.

References: Available along with academic credentials at your request.

56c, continued

Problem 2
Interoffice memo on full sheet

Type the memo at the right. Address a COMPANY MAIL envelope to:
Mr. Ronald Hizer, Supervisor, Communications Center.

Assume that the cc for Elena Bolen will be prepared on a copy machine.

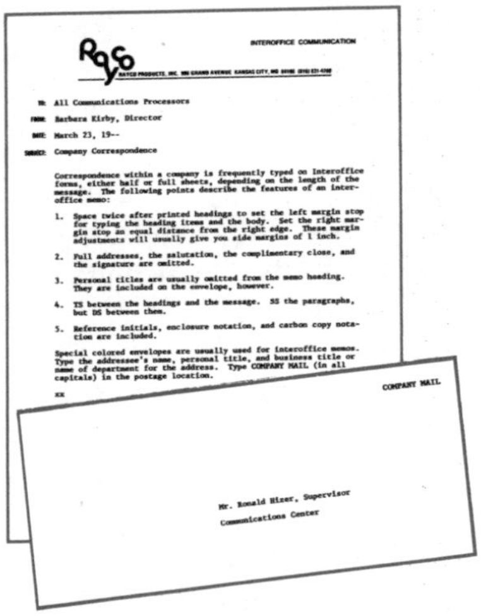

If a memorandum form is not available, use plain paper and follow the example illustration below.

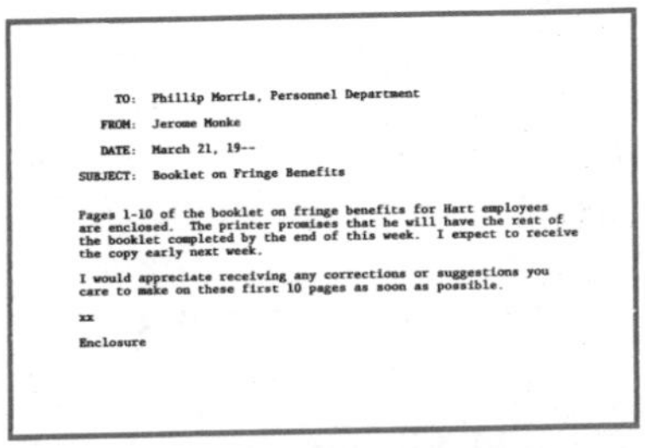

TO: Phillip Morris, Personnel Department

FROM: Jerome Monke

DATE: March 21, 19--

SUBJECT: Booklet on Fringe Benefits

Pages 1-10 of the booklet on fringe benefits for Hart employees are enclosed. The printer promises that he will have the rest of the booklet completed by the end of this week. I expect to receive the copy early next week.

I would appreciate receiving any corrections or suggestions you care to make on these first 10 pages as soon as possible.

xx

Enclosure

TO: All Communication Processors

FROM: Barbara Kirby, Director

DATE: March 23, 19--

SUBJECT: Company Correspondence

TS

Correspondence within a company is frequently typed on interoffice forms, either half or full sheets, depending on the length of the message. The following points describe the features of an interoffice memo:

1. Space twice after printed headings to set the left margin stop for typing the heading items and the body. Set the right margin stop an equal distance from the right edge. These margin adjustments will usually give you side margins of 1 inch.

2. Full addresses, the salutation, the complimentary close, and the signature are omitted.

3. Personal titles are usually omitted from the memo heading. They are included on the envelope, however.

4. TS between the headings and the message. SS the paragraphs, but DS between them.

5. Reference initials, enclosure notation, and carbon copy notation are included.

Special colored envelopes are usually used for interoffice memos. Type the addressee's name, personal title, and business title or name of department for the address. Type COMPANY MAIL (in all capitals) in the postage location.

xx

cc Elena Bolen, Assistant to the President

57

57a ▶5

Preparatory practice

as many times as possible in the time available

alphabet	Jacky requested that Elizabeth Wagner pay to fix their vacuum cleaner.
fig/sym	Invoice #46-851 lists credit terms of 2/10, n/30. She can save $7.49.
adjacent key	Bert Trapp named Polly Hamner as the trustee for the new opera season.
fluency	Take what I own that is valuable, but do not deprive me of my dignity.
	| 1 | 2 | 3 | 4 | 5 | 6 | 7 | 8 | 9 | 10 | 11 | 12 | 13 | 14 |

93b ▶ 45

Production measurement: reports and title page

Time schedule

Assembling materials ... 3′
Timed production ...... 35′
Final check; compute *n-pram* .... 7′

1. Arrange plain paper and supplies for easy handling.

2. When directed to begin, type for 35′ from the problems on this page. If you complete the problems in less than 35′, start over with Problem 1.

3. Correct errors neatly as you type.

4. Proofread and circle any uncorrected errors found in final check.

5. Compute *n–pram* (see p. 110).

Problem 1
Unbound report with reference citations

full sheets; DS; SS enumerated items in ¶ 2 but DS between them; indent enumerated items 5 spaces from left and right margins

Problem 2
Title page

Type a title page for Problem 1 above in an acceptable format from the following data:

EDUCATING
EXCEPTIONAL CHILDREN
Robert C. Allen
Syracuse City Public School
June 30, 19—

Problem 3
Leftbound report with reference citations

Follow the directions given for Problem 1 above except type the report in leftbound format.

words

THE EDUCATION FOR ALL HANDICAPPED CHILDREN ACT OF 1975 11

Selected Information Related to PL 94-142 19

The passage of Public Law 94-142 (The Education for all Handicapped 33
Children Act of 1975) signaled the beginning of a new era in both public and 48
private education. To assist you in implementing the full intent of Public Law 64
94-142, several key elements of the law are identified in this report. 79

Background. In the "Statement of Findings and Purpose," the EHC Act 95
presents several findings to support the rationale for the legislation: 1. More 111
than eight million handicapped children live in the United States today. 2. The 127
special education needs of such children are not being met. 3. More than half of 144
the handicapped children in the United States receive insufficient educational 160
services which result in their being deprived of equality of opportunity. 4. One 176
million of the handicapped children in the United States are excluded entirely 192
from the public school system and do not go through the educational process 207
with their peers. 211

Compliance. One major provision of the EHC Act is designed to insure 227
that all handicapped children receive "due process" when administrative deci- 242
sions are made. The areas of concern expressed in the Act relate to the fol- 258
lowing four areas in which decisions are made regarding the education of 272
handicapped children: (1) identification, (2) evaluation, (3) placement, and 288
(4) provision for a free appropriate public education (Barbocovi and Clelland, 304
1977, 41). 306

To comply with the Act, all states must submit an annual plan to the U.S. 321
Office of Education. The plan must include the goals, timetables, facilities, and 337
personnel required for providing full educational opportunity to all handi- 352
capped children. To assist with formulating the plans of the states, the Act calls 369
for the appointment of advisory panels to help identify unmet needs and to help 385
the state develop and implement future plans. "Membership of these panels 410
will include handicapped individuals and parents and guardians of handicapped 416
children" (Goodman, 1976, 7). 422

Summary. The objective of PL 94-142 is to insure that all handicapped 438
children within a community have available to them, within reasonable time 453
periods, education and related services designed to meet their unique needs. 468

REFERENCE LIST 471

Barbocovi, D. R., and R. W. Clelland. Public Law 94-142: Special Education in 495
Transition. Arlington, VA: American Association of School Adminis- 511
trators, 1977. 514

Goodman, L. V. "A Bill of Rights for the Handicapped." American Education 535
(July, 1976), pp. 6-8. 539

57b ▶45

Problem typing: communications

Problem 1
Report on terminal punctuation

plain paper; 2" top margin; 1" side margins; DS, but SS multiline rules and example sentences

1. Type each rule and example; compose and type a second sentence to illustrate further the rule.

2. Proofread; correct errors.

TERMINAL PUNCTUATION

1. A complete sentence has a period for terminal punctuation.

   Few of us are great enough to be modest.
   (Compose and type a sentence illustrating the rule.)

2. A request in the form of a question is usually punctuated with a period.

   Will you please send me a copy of your annual report.
   (Compose a sentence.)

3. Use a question mark after a direct question--not after an indirect question.

   When did you hire her? He asked how long she worked for you.
   (Compose a sentence.)

4. Use an exclamation point after a word, a phrase, or a sentence to indicate strong emotion or to carry sharp emphasis.

   Your sales met your quota! Congratulations!
   (Compose a sentence.)

Problem 2
Memo about the message/reply form

1. On a full-size interoffice memo form, type the memo at the right [LM p. 89].

2. Correct errors.

3. Address a COMPANY MAIL envelope.

TO: Ana Mendez, Supervisor
FROM: Carrie VanMeter, Director
DATE: March 24, 19--
SUBJECT: Message/Reply Forms

TS

A message/reply form is a two-way, within-company communication form in which the message and the reply are typed on the original copy of the multiple-copy form. The following procedure should be used in preparing them.

1. Sender types message in left-hand column, keeps the second copy (yellow), and forwards others (white and pink) to addressee.

2. Addressee types reply in right-hand column, keeps third copy (pink), and returns the original copy (white) to sender.

3. Signatures of both persons may be handwritten, or typed and then initialed.

4. The envelope address depends upon whether the message travels through the U.S. Postal Service or through COMPANY MAIL. Crease the message form at the center of the page to insert it in an envelope.

xx

Problem 3
Two-way communication on a message/reply form

1. On a message/reply form [LM p. 91], type the message and reply at the top of page 115.

2. Correct errors.

3. Address an envelope marked COMPANY MAIL.

▶ Although most message/reply forms come in sets of three to provide the necessary two carbon copies, the *Laboratory Materials* provide for only one carbon.

92c ▶ 25
Problem typing: bibliography and title page

Problem 1
Bibliography

full sheet; margins same as for unbound report

▶ Articles or news stories without a by-line are reported in a bibliography by the first word in the title, disregarding *A*, *An*, *The*.

Problem 2
Composing a title page

Compose and type a title page appropriate for the report that the bibliography in Problem 1 might be used. Use your name, your school, and the current date.

BIBLIOGRAPHY

Lecture notes and handouts	Baker, William H. "Report Evaluation Form." Class handout in Business Education 320, Omnibus University, 1980.
Government publication	General Services Administration. U.S. Government Correspondence Manual. Washington, DC: U.S. Government Printing Office, 1977.
Personal interview	Menard, Robert. Communication Supervisor, Plymouth Corporation, Boston, Massachusetts. Interviewed by Carol Valentino, March 31, 1980.
News story; no by-line	"New Options in Communications Methods." Modern Office Procedures (January, 1979), pp. 97, 100, 102, 104.
Four or more authors on a book	Robinson, Jerry W., et al. Typewriting: Learning and Instruction. Cincinnati: South-Western Publishing Co., 1979.
Unpublished report	Telfer, Terry A. "A Style Guide for the Preparation of Typewritten Reports." Ottenhaven College, 1980.
Three-author book and edition number	Wolf, Morris Philip, Dale F. Keyser, and Robert R. Aurner. Effective Communication in Business, 7th ed. Cincinnati: South-Western Publishing Co., 1979.
Magazine article	Woodcock, Barry E. "Characteristic Oral and Written Communication Problems of Selected Managerial Trainees." The Journal of Business Communication (Winter, 1979), pp. 43-48.

92d ▶ 10
Report on using quotation marks

plain paper; 2" top margin; 1" side margins; DS, but SS multiline rules and example sentences

1. For the heading, use QUOTATION MARKS.

2. Type each rule and example; compose and type a sentence to illustrate further the rule.

3. Proofread; correct errors.

4. If time permits, retype the third Communication aids checkup, page 102. Check your corrections with your instructor.

1. Enclose a direct quotation with quotation marks. When a quotation is broken, enclose both parts with quotation marks.

   "Great minds," Irving wrote, "have purposes; others have wishes."

2. Place periods or commas inside the closing quotation mark. Place semicolons or colons outside the closing quotation mark.

   She wrote, "Great joys, like griefs, are silent"; but does she believe it?

3. Place a question mark or exclamation point inside closing quotation marks when it is part of the quotation; place it outside when it refers to the entire sentence of which the quotation is a part.

   Did she say, "It is time to strike"? She said, "It's time to strike!"

4. Enclose in quotation marks the titles of articles, parts of publications, song titles, television programs, theses, and dissertations. (Underline or type in all capitals titles of books, magazines, and newspapers.)

   Chapter 5 of Corporate Systems is entitled "Communications."

93

93a ▶ 5
Preparatory practice

each line 3 times SS; DS between 3-line groups; retype selected lines as time permits

alphabet	My jolting blitz astounded few people except the visiting quarterback.
( ) and fig	My payments ($768) were taxes ($493), food ($210), and clothing ($65).
fig/sym	The latest bid of $13,495.72 was a 16% increase over the 1980 figures.
fluency	She may make a bicycle handle to fix it, or she may also dismantel it.

| 1 | 2 | 3 | 4 | 5 | 6 | 7 | 8 | 9 | 10 | 11 | 12 | 13 | 14 |

57b, continued

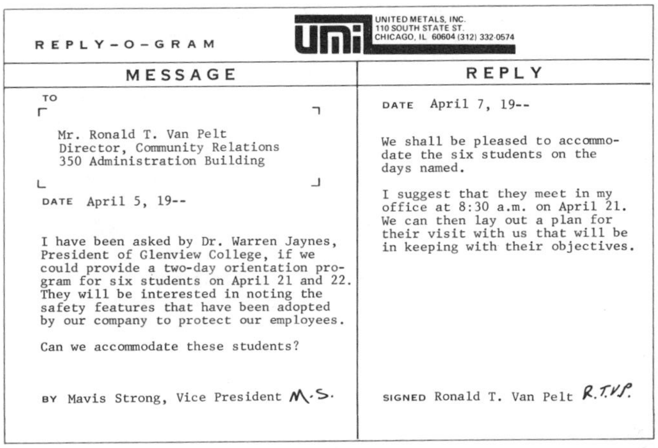

REPLY-O-GRAM — UMI — UNITED METALS, INC. 110 SOUTH STATE ST. CHICAGO, IL 60604 (312) 332-0574

MESSAGE	REPLY
TO Mr. Ronald T. Van Pelt Director, Community Relations 350 Administration Building DATE April 5, 19-- I have been asked by Dr. Warren Jaynes, President of Glenview College, if we could provide a two-day orientation program for six students on April 21 and 22. They will be interested in noting the safety features that have been adopted by our company to protect our employees. Can we accommodate these students? BY Mavis Strong, Vice President M.S.	DATE April 7, 19-- We shall be pleased to accommodate the six students on the days named. I suggest that they meet in my office at 8:30 a.m. on April 21. We can then lay out a plan for their visit with us that will be in keeping with their objectives. SIGNED Ronald T. Van Pelt R.T.V.P.

(Message for Problem 3)

TO: Mr. Ronald T. Van Pelt Director, Community Relations 350 Administration Building DATE: April 5, 19-- (¶ 1) I have been asked by Dr. Warren Jaynes, president of Glenview College, if we could provide a two-day orientation program for six students on April 21 and 22. They will be interested in noting the safety features that have been adopted by our company to protect our employees. (¶ 2) Can we accommodate these students?
BY: Mavis Strong, Vice President

(Reply for Problem 3)

DATE: April 7, 19-- (¶ 1) We shall be pleased to accommodate the six students on the days named. (¶ 2) I suggest that they meet in my office at 8:30 a.m. on April 21. We can then lay out a plan for their visit with us that will be in keeping with their objectives. SIGNED: Ronald T. Van Pelt

58

58a ▶5 Preparatory practice

as many times as possible in the time available

alphabet	Jack Fledger will accompany me when I visit the quaint, exotic bazaar.
fig/sym	Your Invoice #246-80 says, "Pay this total: $57.91." We paid $57.39.
1st row	Dexter and Zachary Buchmann carved many black candles from a wax ball.
fluency	You can see your skill grow when you use good form each time you type.
	| 1 | 2 | 3 | 4 | 5 | 6 | 7 | 8 | 9 | 10 | 11 | 12 | 13 | 14 |

58b ▶45 Problem typing

Problem 1
Report on using the semicolon and colon

plain paper; 2" top margin; 1" side margins; DS, but SS multiline items

1. Use SEMICOLON AND COLON for the heading.

2. Type each rule and example; compose and type a second sentence to illustrate further the rule.

Problem 2
AMS style letter

1. Type on plain paper the letter on page 116 in the style shown.

2. The body of the letter contains 173 words.

3. Correct errors as you type.

1. Use a semicolon between the independent clauses of a compound sentence when no conjunction is used.

   The report was not received today; it may come tomorrow.
   (Compose a sentence.)

2. Use a semicolon between the independent clauses of a compound sentence that are joined by a conjunctive adverb (however, therefore, etc.).

   His conclusions are sound; therefore, we shall accept his report.
   (Compose a sentence.)

3. Use a semicolon to separate independent clauses of a compound sentence if any of the clauses are punctuated with commas.

   He can take Sue, Hilda, and Joe; and the others will go by bus.
   (Compose a sentence.)

4. Use a colon to introduce an enumeration or listing.

   Please buy the following parts: fuse box, light, and switch.
   (Compose a sentence.)

5. Use a colon to introduce a question or long quotation.

   The question is this: Is she an experienced driver?
   (Compose a sentence.)

91c, continued

by someone aged 54 to 64, the husband is at the peak of his earning power, the wife has returned to work, the grown children are leaving home and the couple has the security of generous retirement plans, much research is being directed toward the middle-age market. Recent projections indicate that by the year 1985, nearly 40 percent of the middle-aged families will earn $25,000 or more annually and that by the year 2000, the "graying of America" will be nearly complete: "Americans aged 45 to 64 will make up 23% of the U.S. population"(Lublin, 1979, 1). The 1980s will present opportunities and chalenges to Managers in the make up of the market but also in the communications between sellers and buyer. One example is the potential use of cassetts for home television to provide mail-order catalog distributers and opportunity to use sound, lighting, and the persuasive words of professional representatives rather then by pictures along. The successful marketer is the one who is planning today.

References

Louis E. Boone, and David L. Kurtz. Contemporary Business, 2d ed. New York: Holt, Rinehart and Winston, 1979.

Lublin, Joann S. "Marketers Discover Free-Spending Group." The Wall Street Journal. April 16, 1979, p. 1.

Markin, Rom J. Marketing. New York: John Wiley & Sons, 1979.

92

92a ▶ 5
Preparatory practice
each line 3 times SS; DS between 3-line groups; retype selected lines as time permits

alphabet Six key groups have now vowed to join arms to quell the fumbling czar.

- and fig These 64 rooms house up-to-date files for a 127-year span (1853-1980).

fig/sym Please correct the discount on Invoice 936-45 (May 27) from 8% to 10%.

fluency The usual problem is the chaotic rush for the authentic antique works.

| 1 | 2 | 3 | 4 | 5 | 6 | 7 | 8 | 9 | 10 | 11 | 12 | 13 | 14 |

92b ▶ 10
Preapplication drill: bibliography

1. Use the same margins that you would use for page 1 of the manuscript (for this drill use margins for unbound report).
2. Start the first line of each entry at the left margin; indent the second and subsequent lines 5 spaces. SS each entry; DS between entries.

BIBLIOGRAPHY
TS

Clark, Charles T., and Lawrence L. Schkade. Statistical Analysis for Administrative Decisions, 3d ed. Cincinnati: South-Western Publishing Co., 1979.

Fischer, Paul M., William James Taylor, and J. Arthur Leer. Advanced Accounting. Cincinnati: South-Western Publishing Co., 1978.

Glueck, William F. Management. Hinsdale, IL: The Dryden Press, 1977.

Gordon, Robert J. Macroeconomics. Boston: Little, Brown and Company, 1978.

Business Communications, Inc.
850 Waukegan Road, Glenview, IL 60025 312 724 8111

		words in parts	total words
Begin all major lines at left margin	April 12, 19--	3	3
Begin address 3 blank line spaces below date	Mr. Dennis St. John, Manager	9	9
	The Pioneer Company	13	13
	Box 893	14	14
	Greenville, SC 29602	19	19
Omit salutation			
Subject line in all capital letters with a triple space above and below it	AMS SIMPLIFIED STYLE	23	23
	This letter is typed in the timesaving simplified style	34	34
	recommended by the Administrative Management Society.	45	45
	To type a letter in the AMS style, follow these steps:	56	56
Begin enumerated items at left margin; indent unnumbered items 5 spaces	1. Use block format.	5	61
	2. Omit the salutation and the complimentary close.	15	72
	3. Include a subject heading and type it in ALL CAPS a	27	83
	triple space below the address; triple-space from the	37	94
	subject line to the first line of the body.	46	103
	4. Type enumerated items at the left margin; indent	57	113
	unnumbered items five spaces.	63	119
	5. Type the writer's name and title in ALL CAPS on the	75	131
	4th line space below the last line of the letter body.	86	142
	6. Type the reference initials (typist's only) a double	97	154
	space below the writer's name.	104	160
	Correspondents in your company may like the AMS Simplified	12	172
	letter style not only for the eye appeal it gives letters	23	183
	but also for the resultant reduction in letter-writing	34	194
	costs.	36	196
Omit complimentary close	*B. Erma Sunkees*		
Writer's name and title in all caps at least 3 blank line spaces below letter body	B. ERMA SUNKEES, PRESIDENT	41	201
	xx	41	201
			216

Style letter 4: AMS Simplified

91c ▶ 35

Problem typing: report with reference citations

1. Type the rough-draft material at the right in unbound report form.

2. Make corrections indicated in the copy. Correct errors as you type.

3. Place references in an alphabetical list 3 spaces below the last line of the report on page 2.

~~THE CHANGING MIX OF~~ TOMORROW'S MARKETS — Center

One of the *major* objectives of *marketing* managers is to identify and serve potential markets. a market is rarely a homogeneous mass of people. Instead, the market ~~typically~~ consists of many sub segments made up of individuals with different needs *and wants*. Market segmentation is the purpose of *to* identify~~ing~~ and *to* evaluat~~ing~~*e* various *sub*segments of the total market.

~~There are~~ many population-related factors ~~that~~ effect market opportunities. The ~~total~~ number of persons, the mix among age groups, *the population* mobility, *and* location, and the number of households are all *important* indicators of market opportunities. ¶ Successfull market~~ing~~*ers* have learned that the characters of markets shift *s* over time with varying degrees of impact. Some drastic changes have been observed in the over all characters of the american market in the last 2000 years. We have seen faimly size dercease; we have become an *much* older mix within the population; we have become a wealthier and more educated ~~mass~~; and we have moved from farm to city and from city to suburbs *(markin, 1979)*. Each age group has different consumption patterns, and marketers must design their strategies accordingly. Food Distributors ~~will not~~ use ~~the same~~ *a different* promotional appeals for ~~diets of~~ *diet-conscious* young adults ~~as~~ *than* they ~~will~~ *do* for young children. An insurance company may stress income protection to a young adult and retirement planning to a middle-age*d* person (Boone andKurtz,1979). Major shifts among age groups have been noted recently and projected for the coming years.

~~A great deal of though~~ *t and pasts* ~~is being given to the middle-aged market since~~ *Because* in many of the 25 million u.s. households headed

¶ Age groups are one of the most important market characteristics studied by marketers because they are a good indicator of different degrees of buyer response.

(Continued on next page.)

59

59a ▶5

Preparatory practice

as many times as possible in the time available

alphabet	Major Forbes quickly recognized the power of an auxiliary naval force.
fig/sym	Hume & Odell collected $6,582, plus 4% interest, less $137.90 in fees.
long words	Punctuation, pronunciation, and enunciation show communication skills.
fluency	Training is learning the rules; experience is learning the exceptions.

| 1 | 2 | 3 | 4 | 5 | 6 | 7 | 8 | 9 | 10 | 11 | 12 | 13 | 14 |

59b ▶ 15

Straight-copy skill measurement

1. Two 1′ *speed* writings on each ¶; determine *gwam* on each.

2. One 5′ *control* writing on all ¶s combined; determine *gwam*; circle errors.

Difficulty index

all letters used | A | 1.5 si | 5.7 awl | 80% hfw |

	gwam 1′	5′	
Composing a friendly letter is at the top of the list of skills	13	3	50
that most business leaders would like to possess. The job of develop-	27	5	53
ing this skill is not very difficult for the person who is sincerely	41	8	55
willing to take the time to analyze the problem. First, be your humble	55	11	58
self. Remember that you are communicating with someone very much like	69	14	61
yourself. Assume that the person is as intelligent as you are. Do not	84	17	64
write down to him or her. It is an insulting, unfriendly practice.	97	19	67
Second, be genuine. Your letters will not gain friends if you try	13	22	69
to persuade your reader that you have Plato on one line, Aristotle on	27	25	72
another, and Demosthenes in the next room waiting to see you. No one is	42	28	75
that important. If you really want to write friendly letters, be honest	57	31	78
with yourself. A front of veneer never deceived anyone.	68	33	80
Finally, the kind of letter that is appreciated must be fresh and	13	36	83
lively. Select words that say exactly what you mean. Obscure general-	27	38	86
izations are out. They reflect a fuzzy mind. Further, repetition for	42	41	88
the sake of trying to make your letter clear is deadly. Say it right	56	44	91
the first time. Remember to compose the kind of letter you would like	70	47	94
to get.	71	47	94

gwam 1′ | 1 | 2 | 3 | 4 | 5 | 6 | 7 | 8 | 9 | 10 | 11 | 12 | 13 | 14 |
5′ | 1 | 2 | 3 |

59c ▶30

Production measurement: business communications

Time schedule

Assembling materials .... 3′
Timed production .... 20′
Final check; compute *n–pram* .... 7′

1. Follow time schedule shown at the left.

2. Arrange supplies (forms, letterheads, erasers, etc.) [LM pp. 93–96].

3. Correct errors neatly.

4. Address envelopes.

5. When directed to begin, type for 20′ from the problems given on page 118. If you complete the problems in less than 20′, start over on plain paper.

6. Proofread and circle uncorrected errors found in final check. Deduct 10 words from total words for each uncorrected error; divide remainder by 20 to compute *n–pram*.

90c, continued

Problem 3
Leftbound report
full sheet; DS

Problem 4
Composing leftbound report
If time permits, compose several ¶s outlining action being taken in your community to alleviate the problems discussed in the report typed as Problem 3.

words

ECOLOGY[3] 2

Prior to the 1960's, our nation and its popu- 11
lation showed little concern over "environmentalism." 22
Americans dumped polluting materials into lakes and 32
rivers; consumed goods with no thoughts for whether 42
the containers were biodegradable; and generated little 54
concern about their gasoline consumption. 62
Times have changed! The 1980's promise to be 71
a period of increased public awareness of the environ- 82
mental movement. One area that will receive a great 92
deal of attention in the future is solid-waste pollution. 104
The sight and smell of junkyards and garbage across 114
the country continues to plague our once beautiful 125
nation. In fact, each individual in the United States 136
generates about seven pounds of trash each day.[1] 145
The solid-waste problem, which has received 154
little attention in the past, may become our number 164
one pollution problem in the future unless new 174
solutions are found. 178

______________ 182

[1] Ferdinand F. Mauser and David J. Schwartz, 190
American Business (New York: Harcourt Brace 203
Jovanovich, Inc., 1978), p. 5. 209

91

91a ▶ 5 Preparatory practice

each line 3 times SS; DS between 3-line groups; retype selected lines as time permits

alphabet We have just finished making crazy but quality cards for export trade.
! and fig Stop! Think! We must find Check No. 2643 or deposit $10,953.87 cash!
fig/sym Last year, 75% of the 8,060 workers at Wise & Lee earned over $12,493.
fluency The town proviso is so rigid she may wish to halt or suspend the work.

| 1 | 2 | 3 | 4 | 5 | 6 | 7 | 8 | 9 | 10 | 11 | 12 | 13 | 14 |

91b ▶ 10 Preapplication information: reference citations

full sheet; DS; 1" side margins

1. Type the information at the right beginning on Line 13.

2. As time permits, study and analyze the content. Discuss the procedures with your instructor.

Instead of using standard footnotes, many modern authors and publishers reference articles and reports in other less-cumbersome ways.

In one of these styles, references are noted in the body of the report or article by placing the surname of the author, the year of the publications, and the page number (required only if the citation is a direct quotation) in parentheses within the text. Examples include: One experiment (Richards and Wiener, 1975) revealed that learning time was shortened; however, a more recent study (Kline, 1980, 234-35) indicates that "learning time depends heavily on the learner."

An alphabetical reference list by author names is then placed at the end of the report under the heading "REFERENCES" or "REFERENCE LIST."

59c, continued

Problem 1
AMS Simplified letter

words

April 20, 19-- | Mr. Henry Makimoto | 77390 Overmyer Drive | Jacksonville, 14
FL 32205 | LET THE OUTSIDE COME INSIDE (¶ 1) Our weather-protected 26
casement windows are a beautiful way to make the most of a free-spirited 40
life-style. Just open them all the way and let the outside come inside. 55
(¶ 2) Our customers tell us that their low maintenance makes them easy to 69
enjoy. Over their wood core is an exterior sheath of long-life, rigid vinyl. The 85
finish doesn't rust, pit, or corrode. It doesn't chip, crack, peel, or blister, 101
either. (¶ 3) Our casement windows are also easy on heating and cooling bills. 116
They are two times more weathertight than recognized standards. The 130
snug-fitting design and our use of a wood core as an insulator makes double- 145
panel insulating glass practical. (¶ 4) There's beauty in color, too. You have a 161
choice of several colors: white, off-white, yellow, blue--just about any color 177
you want. (¶ 5) Do you want to know more? See a Bowman dealer today. You 191
will find one in the Yellow Pages under "Windows." MS. SUSAN VANESTA, 205
SALES MANAGER | xx (168) 208

Problem 2
Interoffice memo

words

TO: Jay Rogers, General Manager FROM: Donald A. Bowers, President DATE: 11
April 20, 19-- SUBJECT: Attached Reprint of a Recent Editorial (¶ 1) The at- 24
tached editorial first appeared in Iron Age in the November 29, 1973, issue. It 40
was reprinted in the February 20, 1978, issue and for good reason. It is as 55
timely now as it was then, if not more so. (¶ 2) After reading the editorial, 70
will you please let me know how we can best implement the suggestions 84
made by the author, Gene Beaudet, among the department heads in our 97
company. | xx | Enclosure 102

Problem 3
Message/reply memo

words

(Message)

TO: Stanley M. Kaufman | Director of Customer Relations | 340 Administra- 13
tion Building DATE: April 20, 19-- (¶1) As you know, for a number of years we 27
have been giving some of our customers tickets to outstanding athletic events 42
in the community in appreciation of their patronage. (¶ 2) Should this practice 57
be continued? Why? or why not? BY: Jay Rogers, General Manager 69

(Reply)

DATE: April 23, 19-- (¶ 1) I definitely feel that the practice should be con- 82
tinued. It builds goodwill and helps finance athletic programs in our commu- 98
nity. (¶2) While I do not think we should attach any strings to our offer of 112
tickets to an event, I do think we might call the customer, offer the tickets, 128
and find out whether or not they can be used. The practice loses its value 143
if we appear to engage in an indiscriminate distribution of tickets. SIGNED: 157
Stanley M. Kaufman 161

90

90a ▶ 5
Preparatory practice
each line 3 times SS; DS between 3-line groups; retype selected lines as time permits

alphabet	We very quietly jumped ahead by organizing all six of the key factors.
, and fig	Matilda, Tom, Ronda, and I processed 3,064 orders on January 25, 1978.
fig/sym	The current market price ($74.50) would yield a return of 23% by 1986.
fluency	Is the town rigid with the bid or is the bid divisible by eight firms?
	| 1 | 2 | 3 | 4 | 5 | 6 | 7 | 8 | 9 | 10 | 11 | 12 | 13 | 14 |

90b ▶ 8
Preapplication drill: centering main headings in leftbound reports
plain paper; 2″ top margin

Read the material contained in the drill at the right. Then type the drill according to the directions in the report.

Drill

CENTERING MAIN HEADINGS IN LEFTBOUND REPORTS

Outlined below are basic guidelines used for centering main headings in leftbound reports. Read these guidelines and then apply them when typing this report.

1. Set the left margin 1 1/2″ from the left edge of the paper. Set the right margin 1″ from the right edge of the paper.
2. Add the scale numbers at both margin stops. Divide the sum by 2. The result is the horizontal center point for leftbound reports.
3. Backspace from center as you normally do for centering problems to center headings.

90c ▶ 37
Problem typing: title pages and reports

Problem 1
Title page for topbound report

On a full sheet, type the title page illustrated at the right for a topbound report. Center each line horizontally.

Problem 2
Title page for leftbound report

1. Type a title page for a leftbound report that deals with opportunities available to exceptional persons. Compose an appropriate title. Center each line over the line of writing used for a leftbound report.

2. The report was prepared by Ruth Fulton who works for the U. S. Office of Education. Use the current date.

3. Type according to spacing shown in the illustration at the right for leftbound report.

Problems 3 and 4 are given on page 184.

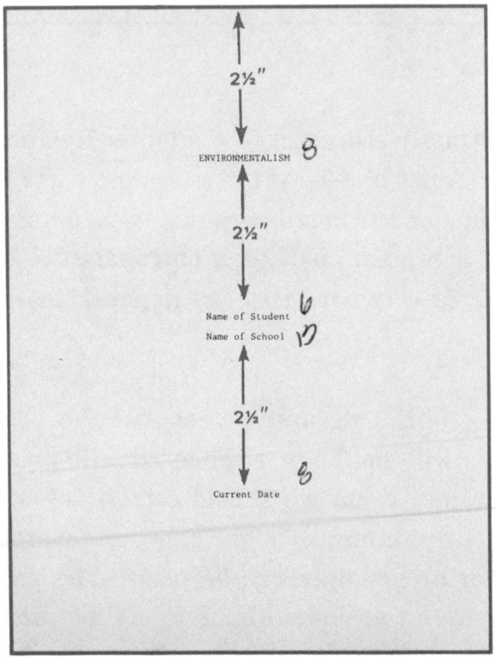

Title page for topbound report

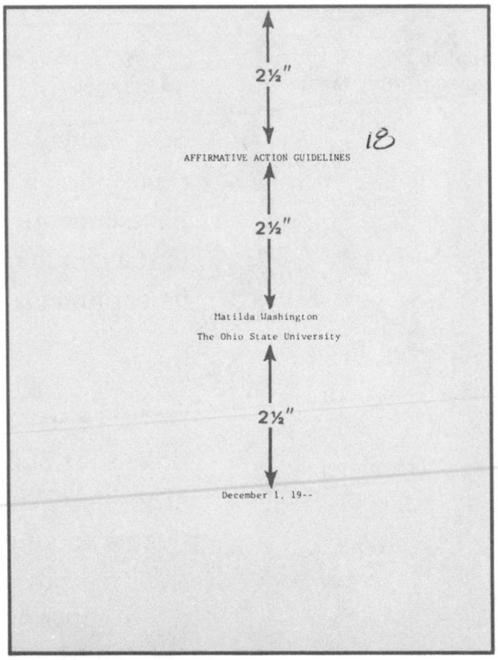

Title page for leftbound report

Supplemental skill-building practice

Technique improvement: direct reaches

a 1′ writing on each line for *control*

She can see an unexcelled musical program on any sunny day in Olympia.
Myrtle Cloony agreed to see the mundane aluminum monuments in Hungary.
She obtained a mystical symbol, an unknown object; and two tiny trays.
No doubt, Amy Humphrey will take my bronze grinder and hymns to Tracy.

| 1 | 2 | 3 | 4 | 5 | 6 | 7 | 8 | 9 | 10 | 11 | 12 | 13 | 14 |

Technique improvement: adjacent keys

a 1′ writing on each line for *control*

There were three points on Kili's eastern slope free of rough weather.
They were assured Polk Power Saws were proper saws to cut these sides.
Three tired wrens stopped on their return trip to the old poplar tree.
Bertha Roberts excelled in singing Yule hymns in Trenton and Stratton.

| 1 | 2 | 3 | 4 | 5 | 6 | 7 | 8 | 9 | 10 | 11 | 12 | 13 | 14 |

Building straight-copy skill

1. Two 1′ *speed* writings on each ¶; determine *gwam*.
2. One 5′ *control* writing on all ¶s combined; determine *gwam*; circle errors.

Difficulty index

all letters used | A | 1.5 si | 5.7 awl | 80% hfw |

	gwam 1′	5′	
A typical way to start the second article in this series on succeed-	14	3	55
ing on the job might be, "If you haven't been promoted yet, read on."	28	6	58
Appropriately enough, the first point to be explored is to recognize your	46	9	61
weaknesses. You can be certain that your co-workers have, so why not	57	11	64
you? It's good to have faith in your abilities, but it may be equally	71	14	67
desirable to know what shortcomings are blocking your road to success.	85	17	69
Take an inventory of yourself. Learn from the criticisms you get on your	100	20	72
work. Be sensitive to the things you do and say that irritate others.	114	23	75
On the plus side, be genuine; have a wholesome sense of humor. These are	129	26	78
among the qualities that give an otherwise listless person some character.	144	29	81
Continue to learn. Read as widely as possible: trade journals,	13	31	84
technical books in your field, well-written magazines. Join a club in	27	34	87
which you can exchange ideas with others engaged in the same field. At-	42	37	89
tend talks and exhibits that give you new insights into your job. Your	56	40	92
ability to create new markets for your firm's products or new ways of	70	43	95
making them depends to a great extent on how much knowledge you have	84	46	98
acquired. Also, expand the skills that will make you more promotable;	98	48	101
a working knowledge of the computer, for example, will probably make you	112	51	104
more valuable to your firm.	118	52	105

gwam 1′ | 1 | 2 | 3 | 4 | 5 | 6 | 7 | 8 | 9 | 10 | 11 | 12 | 13 | 14 |
5′ | 1 | 2 | 3 |

89

89a ▶ 5
Preparatory practice

each line 3 times SS; DS between 3-line groups; retype selected lines as time permits

alphabet Franz wanted to revoke extra wage requirements for many physical jobs.
. and fig Ms. T. E. Roe, Ph.D., addressed 6,178 of us at 9:45 a.m. and 2:30 p.m.
fig/sym Regal & Johnson received a 10% discount totaling $8,396.57 on June 24.
fluency They may make by the island dock a visual signal to them with a flame.
| 1 | 2 | 3 | 4 | 5 | 6 | 7 | 8 | 9 | 10 | 11 | 12 | 13 | 14 |

89b ▶ 15
Preapplication drill: footnotes

2 full sheets

1. Type the drill once beginning body of the report on Line 48 and using 1" side margins.

2. Retype the drill beginning body of report on Line 20 and placing the footnotes at the foot of the page.

Drill
If a page with footnotes is only partially filled, note the number of lines to be used for typing the footnotes, plus 2 lines for the divider line, and 6 lines for the margin at the bottom of the page. Count from bottom of page to determine placement of footnotes.

Drill

changes in the climate of work and the characteristics of the work force, these human resource approaches are all the more urgent.[3]

---

[1] Lawrence A. Wangler, "The Intensification of the Personnel Role," Personnel Journal, LVIII (February, 1979), p. 111.

[2] Robert L. Trewatha and M. Gene Newport, Management (Dallas: Business Publications, Inc., 1979), pp. 423-24.

[3] Elmer H. Burack and Robert D. Smith, Personnel Management (New York: West Publishing Company, 1977), p. 103.

89c ▶ 30
Problem typing: report with footnotes

Problem 1
2d page of leftbound report

1. Type the report at the right as page 2 of leftbound report. Page number is typed on 4th line space even with right margin from top edge of paper.

2. DS but SS multiline footnotes.

Problem 2
Unbound report

Retype Problem 1. Compose and type as ¶ 3 your ideas and comments on the values and purposes of footnotes.

Passim means here and there.

Ibid. means the reference just cited. Different pages may be cited.

Op. cit. means in the work cited but not the one immediately preceding.

Loc. cit. means in the exact passage cited.

words

2

Footnotes may be shortened somewhat by using Latin 11
terms or by abbreviating Latin terms. The following examples 23
represent acceptable applications of the terms passim, ibid., op. 39
cit., loc. cit.:[4] 46

DS

[1] Arthur R. Olsen and John W. Kennedy, Economics--Principles & Applications (9th ed.; Cincinnati: South-Western Publishing Co., 1978), passim, pp. 25-36. 58 76 86

DS

[2] Ibid. 88

[3] Thomas J. Adams, The Business of Business (San Francisco: Canfield Press, 1976), pp. 57-59. 104 112

[4] Ibid., p. 110. 117

[5] Olsen and Kennedy, op. cit., p. 47. 126

[6] Adams, The Business of Business, loc. cit. 142

Make use of an acceptable style manual any time you 152
question the proper format of a footnote. 161

SS

--- 164

DS

[4] Arno F. Knapper and Loda I. Newcomb, A Style for Communication (Columbus: Grid, Inc., 1974), p. 30. 178 190

Building statistical-copy skill

1. Two 1′ *speed* writings on each ¶; determine *gwam*.

2. One 5′ *control* writing on all ¶s combined; determine *gwam*; circle errors.

Difficulty index

all letters used | A | 1.5 si | 5.7 awl | 80% hfw

	gwam 1′	5′
Virtually the same principles apply to written communications. Note	14	3
how these principles are applied in this example. "A Super Bowl runs	29	6
approximately $20, a ticket to the World Series goes for $10, and a walk-	43	9
about at the Masters costs $30. The SPORTS MAGAZINE, on the other hand,	58	12
charges only $14 a year--75 cents a single copy if you buy it on the	72	14
newsstand. However, if you'll return the order form below (it's already	86	17
made out in your name), we'll send you SM for only 19 cents a week, for	101	20
36 weeks or more. Quite a saving! Send for SPORTS MAGAZINE now for the	115	23
week's most enjoyable reading. Join us for the stimulating activities	129	26
you can't find anywhere else--and at a price that's easily the best buy	144	29
in sports."	146	29
Here is a communication from a correspondent who had to admit an	13	32
error, explain it, and make a bid for the customer's future business.	27	35
"Thank you for taking the time to write us about your car rental. We	41	37
appreciate your giving us the opportunity to respond. The charges, in	55	40
U.S. currency, represent two weeks at our $85 unlimited mileage rate,	69	43
with three additional days at the rate of $12.55 a day. The supplemental	84	46
charge is for gasoline and the 11% tax in Germany. The new total comes to	99	49
$277.45. As you paid $305.91, I am sending you a refund draft for $28.45.	114	52
We appreciate your business; and the next time, we shall try harder to	129	55
give you an accurate billing as well as rapid, courteous service."	142	58

gwam 1′ | 1 | 2 | 3 | 4 | 5 | 6 | 7 | 8 | 9 | 10 | 11 | 12 | 13 | 14 |
5′ | 1 | 2 | 3 |

Improve speed/control paragraph

1. A 1′ writing on the ¶; determine *gwam*.

2. Add 4 *gwam* to your *gwam* in Step 1 for a goal rate. Type another 1′ writing on the ¶ trying to equal your goal rate.

3. Two 2′ writings for *speed*. Compute your *gwam*.

4. One 2′ writing at this new rate for *control*; circle errors.

Goal: no errors

Difficulty index

all letters used | A | 1.5 si | 5.7 awl | 80% hfw

	gwam 2′
Do you know what a family home in Mexico has in common with an (4, 8, 12)	6
office building in Quebec? Both use solar energy for heat and hot (16, 20, 24)	13
water. The age of solar energy is finally just over the horizon. Few (28, 32, 36, 40)	20
of us understand its outstanding potential. It promises clean air, (44, 48, 52)	27
power for industry, and even fuel for our cars. Solar energy is lim- (56, 60, 64)	34
ited, not by any inefficiency on the sun's part, but by our loss of (68, 72, 76, 80)	41
motivation. Some intelligence would probably help, too, as we are (84, 88, 92)	47
running dangerously low on oil and gas supplies. (96, 100, 104)	52

gwam 2′ | 1 | 2 | 3 | 4 | 5 | 6 | 7 |

88c, continued

Problem 2
Outline

2 plain sheets; top margin: 1½" for pica or 2" for elite; 1" side margins; at least 1" bottom margin

1. Space forward once from margin to type Roman numeral **I.** Reset margin 2 spaces to right of period in **I.** for subheadings **A.** and **B.**

2. Set 2 tab stops 4 spaces apart, beginning with left margin which is now set at **A.** Use margin release and backspace to type **II.**, **III.**, and **IV.**

3. Type page number for 2d page on Line 4 in upper right corner even with right margin. Begin typing copy on Line 7 for 2d page.

4. As a reminder to leave at least a 1" bottom margin, make a light pencil mark about 1½" from bottom edge. (Erase the mark later.)

TYPING MANUSCRIPTS OR REPORTS

2 spaces

I. MARGINS

DS

- A. Unbound Reports
  1. First page: top margin 1 1/2", pica; 2", elite; side and bottom margins, 1" for both pica and elite
  2. Subsequent pages: top and side margins, 1"; bottom margin at least 1"
- B. Bound Reports
  1. Topbound: top margin for first page 2" pica, 2 1/2" elite; subsequent pages 1 1/2" top margins for both pica and elite
  2. Leftbound: Same top and bottom margins as unbound; 1 1/2" left margin; 1" right margin

DS

II. SPACING

- A. Body
  1. Double-spaced with 5- or 10-space paragraph indentions (and at least 2 lines of paragraph at bottom and top of page)
  2. Quoted materials of 4 or more lines single-spaced and indented from both margins
- B. Footnotes
  1. Numbered consecutively throughout short reports and identified by superscript figures in body of report
  2. Separated from last line of body of text by a divider line approximately 1 1/2" long a single space below body of report (double-space below divider line)
  3. Typed superscript figures 1/2 space above the line of writing to identify footnoted references in the footnotes (type a footnote on the same page with its corresponding superscript figure)
  4. First line indented to paragraph point; single-spaced; double-spaced between footnotes

III. HEADINGS AND SUBHEADINGS

- A. Main Heading
  1. Centered in all capital letters over line of writing
  2. Followed by 1 blank line space and the secondary heading or 2 blank line spaces and first line of body if no secondary heading used
- B. Secondary Heading (Explains or Amplifies the Main Heading)
  1. Centered with all important words capitalized
  2. Preceded by 1 blank line space and followed by 2 blank line spaces
- C. Side Headings
  1. Typed even with left margin, no terminal punctuation, underlined
  2. Followed by 1 blank line space
- D. Paragraph Headings
  1. Indented to paragraph point, followed by period, underlined (text copy immediately follows this "run-in" heading)
  2. Usually first words only are capitalized

IV. PAGINATION (PAGE NUMBERING)

- A. Unbound and Leftbound Reports
  1. First page: folio centered on line of writing 1/2" from bottom of page (or omitted)
  2. Subsequent pages: folio on Line 4 at top right margin
- B. Topbound Reports
  1. First page: folio centered 1/2" from bottom of page (or omitted)
  2. Subsequent pages: folio centered 1/2" from bottom of page

Building script-copy skill

1. Two 1′ *speed* writings on each ¶; determine *gwam*.
2. One 5′ *control* writing on all ¶s combined; determine *gwam*; circle errors.

Difficulty index

all letters used	A	1.5 si	5.7 awl	80% hfw

	gwam 1′	5′	
Don't you wish you had a dollar for every	8	2	47
article you have read on being successful in your	18	4	49
occupation? These articles are as numerous as	28	6	51
the ones that tell you how to make millions	37	7	53
of dollars investing in the stock market.	45	9	55
Perhaps there are vast problems to be resolved	55	11	56
that are beyond the power of words to express--	64	13	58
or minds to grasp. If succeeding in your	72	14	60
occupation falls into this category, this	81	16	62
article may give you some direction on being	90	18	64
a noteworthy failure or at least a borderline	99	20	65
case. If so, that may be reason enough to	108	22	67
read another "success guaranteed" treatise on	117	23	69
the subject.	119	24	69
To advance in your occupation, you	7	25	71
must be an idea person. This is easier than	16	27	73
you may think. Still, it is sad to contemplate	26	29	75
how little imagination many workers give to	34	31	76
their jobs. You must be inquisitive--even	43	32	78
skeptical. Don't assume that the "tried and	52	34	80
true" way is always the best. It probably	61	36	82
isn't. Try to verbalize the problems or areas	70	38	83
of waste that confront you in your present	79	40	85
position. Then jot down as many solutions	87	41	87
as you can, keeping in mind that new	95	43	88
ideas are often adaptations of procedures	103	44	90
that worked in other fields.	109	46	91

Skill building: response patterns

A 1′ writing on each sentence; compare *gwam* on the three response levels

letter response
Seven prominent polio experts regularly attend those Toronto meetings.
Several inspectors hesitantly gestured toward certain rejected crates.

word response
A quantity of soap lay on the shelf visible to all entitled to use it.
They may make a right turn with no penalty to go downtown in the auto.

combination response
The civic center formed a trade panel to review all eligible opinions.
Such trade cases as the one stated in your brief make problems for us.

| 1 | 2 | 3 | 4 | 5 | 6 | 7 | 8 | 9 | 10 | 11 | 12 | 13 | 14 |

section

18

Technical and statistical reports

lessons 88–93

Learning goals
The lessons of this section are planned to help you achieve the following goals:

1. Develop your manuscript and report-typing skill.

2. Increase your speed and improve your accuracy.

3. Continue to refine your basic typing techniques.

Machine adjustments

1. Paper guide at *0*.

2. A 70-space line for drills.

3. Margins and spacing for manuscripts and reports as directed.

88

88a ▶ 5 Preparatory practice

each line 3 times SS; DS between 3-line groups; retype selected lines as time permits

alphabet Quite frankly, none of their publicized exhibits will get very jammed.

? Have you compared the cost of the item? quality? availability? design?

fig/sym On December 31, they reported sales of $19,546,082, up 7.3% this year.

fluency Lena may work with their ensign to rig a theory to fix their problems.

| 1 | 2 | 3 | 4 | 5 | 6 | 7 | 8 | 9 | 10 | 11 | 12 | 13 | 14 |

88b ▶ 10 Preapplication drill: superscripts and subscripts

70-space line; DS; repeat drill as many times as possible in time allotted

When typing a figure or symbol above the line (superscript), operate automatic line finder or turn platen *backward* (toward you). Type the figure or symbol, then return platen or automatic line finder to original position.

To type a figure or symbol below the line (subscript), use the same procedure given for superscript except turn the platen *forward* (away from you).

Drill Several theories of Herzberg,[39] Maslow,[40] and Argyris [41]were analyzed.

The footnotes included: [19] Ibid.; [22] Ibid., p. 87; and [54] Lee, loc. cit.

Did the Anderson Report [9] discuss the development of tolulene, $C_6H_5CH_3$?

88c ▶ 35 Problem typing: reports and outlines

Problem 1
Unbound report

full sheet; DS body; SS and indent numbered items 5 spaces from both margins; 5-space ¶ indention

Margins
top: pica 1½″
elite 2″
sides: 1″
bottom: 1″

center and use the following heading:

THE BUSINESS REPORT

Problem 2 is on the next page.

words

A report is any record that helps people understand their business envi- 18
ronment. The steady, complex flow of information down, up, and across organi- 34
zational lines has made clear, concise reports a necessity for the success of any 50
enterprise. 53

Reports vary in length, scope, and nature and include financial, sales, 67
personnel, informative, interpretive, and analytical reports. Regardless of 82
purpose or magnitude, the effectiveness of any report will be enhanced if the 98
originator: 101

1. defines and limits the purpose of the report to make sure it meets 115
a real need for information; 121
2. uses the proper format and directs the report to the willingness 134
and ability of the receiver to understand and respond; 145
3. stresses the need for accuracy and validity; and reports 159
must be factual, objective, and specific; 166
4. takes action to insure that the finished product is properly 180
coordinated and disseminated. 185

Building rough-draft skill

1. Two 1′ *speed* writings on each ¶; determine *gwam*.

2. One 5′ *control* writing on all ¶s combined; determine *gwam*; circle errors.

Difficulty index

all letters used	A	1.5 si	5.7 awl	80% hfw

gwam 1′ | 5′

, believing that their abilities can qualify them

in the final analyses sucess is secondary. To some it 11 | 2
seems to be a pleasant, challenging job with people they like, 23 | 5
anadequate salary, and time each summer for hunting, for fish- 35 | 7
ing, or travelling. Others want to move ahead for a better job. 58 | 12
If you will be satisfied with nothing less then a high job, be 70 | 14
at least prepared to pay the cost. You will forgo pleasures of 83 | 17
others enjoy, Such as foot ball game or tennis match to attend 97 | 19
a Committee meetings. Competition for top a jobs is keen; and 109 | 22
the road is steep. as you move the ladder, you will become res 121 | 24
responsible for the work of others. This means that your 134 | 27
DS supplement skills in your own field, with skills in handling people. 147 | 29

¶ Settling on the qualifications of a leader can be risky. Some 13 | 32
lack the sense to tie their own shoes; yet the enjoy the title. 29 | 35
Generally speaking, a successful leader is expert in the job 39 | 37
There are no exceptions to this principle.
that must be done. You must show thosewho work with your who 61 | 42
to handle their jobs. Often, you should work with them. You 75 | 44
just set goals, exaplain, and listen. You may be expert to 87 | 47
direct by example. Be patient, yet demanding and decisive. 103 | 50
DS You must build pride in the finished product by giving credit 116 | 53
to those who deserve it. You must realize that 125 | 55
without their help you would have no one 134 | 56
to lead. 135 | 56

Skill-transfer typing

a 1′ writing on each line; additional 1′ writings on each line for which your *gwam* was less than on Line 1

		words
straight copy	Most men can do better work with machines than without them.	12
script	A scientist knows that those fearing failure seldom succeed.	12
statistical	Paul Wilson ran the 100-yd. dash in reverse in 13.3 seconds.	12
rough draft	To many men stop looing for a job when we fnid a job to do.	12

87b, continued

words

Problem 3
Bill of lading
Type bill of lading shown at right. Make 1 cc.

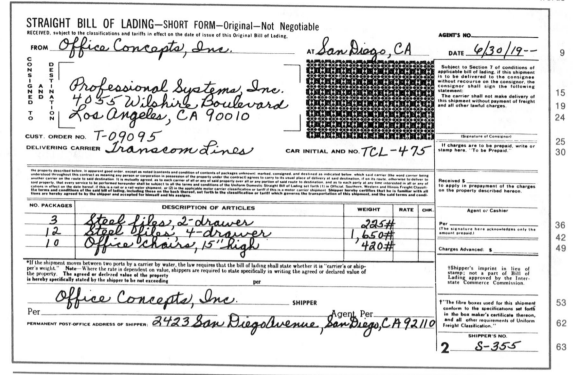

STRAIGHT BILL OF LADING—SHORT FORM—Original—Not Negotiable

RECEIVED, subject to the classifications and tariffs in effect on the date of issue of this Original Bill of Lading.

AGENT'S NO. ____

FROM Office Concepts, Inc. AT San Diego, CA DATE 6/30/19-- 9

CONSIGNED TO / AND DESTINATION:
Professional Systems, Inc. 15
4055 Wilshire Boulevard 19
Los Angeles, CA 90010 24

Subject to Section 7 of conditions of applicable bill of lading, if this shipment is to be delivered to the consignee without recourse on the consignor, the consignor shall sign the following statement:
The carrier shall not make delivery of this shipment without payment of freight and all other lawful charges.

(Signature of Consignor)

CUST. ORDER NO. T-09095 25
DELIVERING CARRIER Transcom Lines CAR INITIAL AND NO. TCL-475 30

If charges are to be prepaid, write or stamp here, "To be Prepaid."

the property described below, in apparent good order, except as noted (contents and condition of contents of packages unknown), marked, consigned, and destined as indicated below, which said carrier (the word carrier being understood throughout this contract as meaning any person or corporation in possession of the property under the contract) agrees to carry to its usual place of delivery at said destination, if on its route, otherwise to deliver to another carrier on the route to said destination. It is mutually agreed, as to each carrier of all or any of said property over all or any portion of said route to destination, and as to each party at any time interested in all or any of said property, that every service to be performed hereunder shall be subject to all the terms and conditions of the Uniform Domestic Straight Bill of Lading set forth (1) in Official, Southern, Western and Illinois Freight Classifications in effect on the date hereof, if this is a rail or a rail-water shipment, or (2) in the applicable motor carrier classification or tariff if this is a motor carrier shipment. Shipper hereby certifies that he is familiar with all the terms and conditions of the said bill of lading, including those on the back thereof, set forth in the classification or tariff which governs the transportation of this shipment, and the said terms and conditions are hereby agreed to by the shipper and accepted for himself and his assigns.

Received $ ____ to apply in prepayment of the charges on the property described hereon.

Agent or Cashier

NO. PACKAGES	DESCRIPTION OF ARTICLES	WEIGHT	RATE	CHK.	words
3	Steel files, 2-drawer	225#			36
12	Steel files, 4-drawer	1,650#			42
10	Office chairs, 15" high	420#			49

Per ____ (The signature here acknowledges only the amount prepaid.)

Charges Advanced: $ ____

*If the shipment moves between two ports by a carrier by water, the law requires that the bill of lading shall state whether it is "carrier's or shipper's weight." Note—Where the rate is dependent on value, shippers are required to state specifically in writing the agreed or declared value of the property. The agreed or declared value of the property is hereby specifically stated by the shipper to be not exceeding ____ per ____

†Shipper's imprint in lieu of stamp; not a part of Bill of Lading approved by the Interstate Commerce Commission.

Office Concepts, Inc. SHIPPER 53
Per ____ Agent, Per ____

†"The fibre boxes used for this shipment conform to the specifications set forth in the box maker's certificate thereon, and all other requirements of Uniform Freight Classification."

PERMANENT POST-OFFICE ADDRESS OF SHIPPER: 2423 San Diego Avenue, San Diego, CA 92110 62

SHIPPER'S NO. 2 S-355 63

words

Problem 4
Invoice
Type invoice at right. Make 1 cc.

DATE **January 30, 19--** 3

SOLD TO **Ace Publishing Co.** 7
1428 Brady Street OUR ORDER NO. **PO-3043-J** 13
Davenport, IA 52803 17

CUST. ORDER NO. **88460-T** 18

TERMS **2/10, n/30** SHIPPED VIA **Midstate Trucking** 24

QUANTITY	DESCRIPTION	UNIT PRICE	TOTAL	words
1	Checkwriter	63.95	63.95	29
6	Cork boards, 48" x 96"	67.95	407.70	37
3	Contemporary chair	120.00	360.00	44
3	Calculator, 10-digit	119.95	359.85	51
1	Single-pedestal desk	179.95	179.95	60
			1,371.45	62

words

Problem 5
Statement of account
Type statement of account at right. Make 1 cc.

DATE **July 30, 19--** 3
TO **Williamsport Systems, Inc.** 8
430 High Street 11
Scranton, PA 18508 15

DATE	ITEMS	DEBITS	CREDITS	BALANCE	words
July 1	Balance			549.50	20
8	Invoice T-7952	355.90		905.40	26
12	Invoice T-8004	125.50		1,030.90	33
18	Payment on account		549.50	481.40	40
22	Credit memo 866		81.19	400.21	46

section **13**

Typing letters with special features

lessons 60–65

Learning goals

1. To improve your basic, proofreading, and punctuation skills.
2. To improve skill in handling the materials needed for each job.
3. To develop skill in typing business letters containing special features.
4. To develop judgment skills in handling unusual problems in typing business letters.

Machine adjustments

1. Paper guide on 0.
2. Margins: 70-space line for drills and ¶s; as directed for problems.
3. SS drill sentences; DS ¶s and indent 5 spaces; space problems as directed.

60

60a ▶5 Preparatory practice

as many times as possible in the time available

alphabet	All of his money exhausted, lazy Jacques is now verging on bankruptcy.
fig/sym	By buying stock at 248 and selling it at 106, Juan Garcia lost $3,759.
adjacent key	Martha Yule appointed the reporter to buy a true story of the tragedy.
fluency	Be sure to vote; it is with our vote that we ensure and insure rights.

| 1 | 2 | 3 | 4 | 5 | 6 | 7 | 8 | 9 | 10 | 11 | 12 | 13 | 14 |

60b ▶5 Skill-transfer typing

first line once; remaining lines as many times as needed in time available to match speed and control of Line 1.

		words
straight copy	Hold the arms as quiet as you can and let your fingers type.	12
script	*The way you read what you type may control the way you type.*	12
statistical	They all typed 20, 35, 47, and 69 words a minute by June 18.	12
rough draft	the elament off injury onthis may riase our insuencerates. (corrections: e, danger, #, job, rp, #)	12

60c ▶15 Problem typing: communications

Report on using the comma

plain paper; 2" top margin; 1" side margins; DS, but SS multiline rules and example sentences

1. Use COMMA for the heading.
2. Type each rule and example; compose and type a second sentence to illustrate further the rule.
3. Proofread; correct errors.

1. In citing a date within a sentence, set off the year with commas.
   June 15, 1979, was the deadline set for the report.
   (Compose and type a sentence illustrating the rule.)
2. When two or more adjectives modify a noun, separate them by commas if they bear equal relationship to the noun.
   The literate, alert speaker gave a short interesting talk.
   (Compose a sentence.)
3. Words or phrases in a series are separated by commas.
   Their letters are short, clear, and friendly.
   (Compose a sentence.)
4. Use a comma after a dependent clause that precedes its principal clause.
   When the parts are completed, we shall send them to you.
   (Compose a sentence.)
5. Separate with a comma two consecutive, unrelated numbers.
   In 1978, 172 cars were sold. During 1979, 52 were repaired.
   (Compose a sentence.)
6. Use a comma to separate a city and a state name.
   The next meeting will be held in Dubuque, Iowa, on May 4.
   (Compose a sentence.)

87b ▶ 45

Production measurement: business forms

Time schedule

Assembling materials ..... 5′
Production ..... 30′
Final Check .... 10′
[LM pp. 199–208]

Problem 1
Purchase requisition

Type purchase requisition shown at right. Make 1 cc.

words

office-power TEMPORARIES, INC.

PURCHASE REQUISITION

Deliver to: Jerry Remington — Requisition No. 8-24-243 — 5
Location: Central Mailing — Date August 24, 19-- — 11
Job No. Central 33-X — Date Required October 1, 19-- — 17

Quantity	Description	words
25 reams	Onionskin, 8½" × 11", smooth	25
10 reams	Bond, 50% rag, 20 lb., 8½" × 11"	34
5 boxes	File folders, legal size	41
3 dozen	Permanent felt-tip markers, blue	49
1 dozen	Staple removers, tweezer type	56

Requisitioned by: ______________________

Problem 2
Purchase order

Type purchase order shown at right. Make 1 cc.

words

Century Supply Company
219 North Commerce
Fort Worth, TX 76102 (817) 871-5640

PURCHASE ORDER

Purchase order No. TV-359-J — 2
Date August 30, 19-- — 5
Terms 2/10, n/30
Ship Via American Express

Higbee Department Store — 10
1061 W. 35th Street — 16
Chicago, IL 60609 — 20
— 23

Quantity	Cat. No.	Description	Price	Total	words
12	N76R543	Lambert stereo	397.00	4,764.00	31
10	N76T380	Graft color television	298.00	2,980.00	41
20	N78E115	Clearway vacuum system	139.00	2,780.00	51
5	N93F301	Caldwell chain saw	99.00	495.00	60
6	N55L978	Minola camera	266.00	1,596.00	70
				12,615.00	71

By ______________________ Purchasing Agent

60d ▶ 25
Problem typing: mailing notation/attention line

1. Study the information and the illustration at the right.

2. Type Problems 1 and 2 below [LM pp. 97–100]. Make 1 carbon copy (cc) and address an envelope for each letter. Refer to RG p. xi for assembling a carbon pack.

3. Proofread and circle errors. Check correct placement of special features.

Mailing notation in letter: If a special mailing notation (REGISTERED, CERTIFIED, SPECIAL DELIVERY, etc.) is used in a letter, type it a double space below the dateline at the left margin of the letter in all capital letters.

Attention line in letter: Type an attention line a double space below city/state line of letter address, preferably at the left margin.

```
Current date
                  DS
SPECIAL DELIVERY
                  DS
Tyner Company, Incorporated
4790 McAlpin Street
Savannah, GA 31404
                  DS
Attention Mrs. Verna Dickson
                  DS
Ladies and Gentlemen
```

Problem 1
Letter with mailing notation and attention line
block; open punctuation

words

Current date SPECIAL DELIVERY Tyner Com- 5
pany, Incorporated 4790 McAlpin Street 13
Savannah, GA 31404 Attention Mrs. Verna 21
Dickson Ladies and Gentlemen (¶ 1) Think about 29
the impact a SKALD motor home would make if 38
it were to show up for a sales presentation! It 48
could do more than sell your product. It could 58
sell your company. In the end, it could say a 67
whole lot about the way you and your people do 76
business. (¶ 2) Your SKALD motor home can be 84
outfitted to display machinery and show movies 94
or slides. It can be a conference room, a hospi- 104
tality center, or both. It can be as luxurious as a 114
yacht; and in many cases, it's a lot handier than 124
a company plane. (¶ 3) All we want to do is have 133
you think about what a sound business tool a 142
SKALD motor home could be for your firm. Why 151
not join the firms who have already made this 160
smart investment? See your nearest SKALD 169
dealer. Let someone show you what a motor home 178
can do for you. Sincerely yours Jerome B. 187
Custer Sales Representative xx (155) **193/216**

Problem 2
Letter with attention line
modified block; indented ¶s;
mixed punctuation

words

Current date The Waco Corporation 999 5
Antoinette Lane Houston, TX 77015 Attention 14
Information Services Director Dear Sir or 22
Madam: (¶1) You've figured and figured long 30
enough. Now Southern lets you touch and 38
know. We offer a calculator that's easy to oper- 48
ate. It has as much or as little memory as you 58
need. It performs tasks like percentage and 67
proration automatically with special feature 76
keys. (¶2) Our calculator lets you store up to 515 85
program steps--all you do is enter the numbers 95
for each problem. Just touch and know. Your 104
programs are recorded on magnetic cards so 112
you can maintain a whole library of them if you 122
like. (¶3) Behind our calculators is a company 131
with trained representatives to help you select 140
just the machine you need--which may be less 149
than you think you need. There's a fully stocked 159
service center nearby to provide maintenance if 169
and when you need it. (¶4) For complete infor- 177
mation, write us; or call the Southern dealer in 187
your community. Sincerely yours, Miss Elaine 196
Ikada Assistant Sales Manager xx (165) **203/222**

61

61a ▶ 5
Preparatory practice

as many times as possible in time available

alphabet	Examine Herb's work; judge for quality; recognize needed improvements.
fig/sym	For $247.31 (plus tax), Ms. Starr can take UAL Flight 580 at 9:16 a.m.
1st row	Ancient, wizened men circled the bubbling mixture, exorcising a demon.
fluency	One step a day takes us on our way to the work we want to do some day.
	| 1 | 2 | 3 | 4 | 5 | 6 | 7 | 8 | 9 | 10 | 11 | 12 | 13 | 14 |

86c, continued

words

Problem 3
Type credit memo shown at right

A credit memorandum notifies a buyer that his or her account has been credited, usually for returned goods.

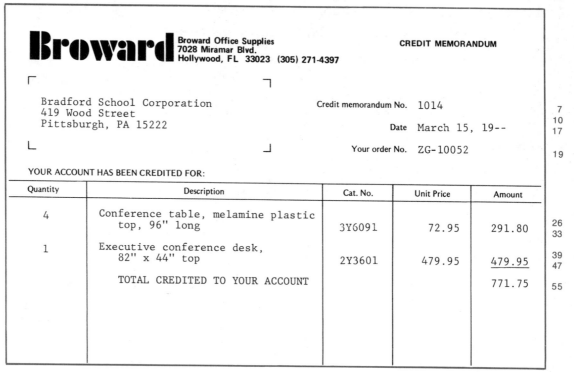

Broward Broward Office Supplies
7028 Miramar Blvd.
Hollywood, FL 33023 (305) 271-4397

CREDIT MEMORANDUM

Bradford School Corporation
419 Wood Street
Pittsburgh, PA 15222

Credit memorandum No. 1014 7
Date March 15, 19-- 10 17
Your order No. ZG-10052 19

YOUR ACCOUNT HAS BEEN CREDITED FOR:

Quantity	Description	Cat. No.	Unit Price	Amount	words
4	Conference table, melamine plastic top, 96" long	3Y6091	72.95	291.80	26 33
1	Executive conference desk, 82" x 44" top	2Y3601	479.95	479.95	39 47
	TOTAL CREDITED TO YOUR ACCOUNT			771.75	55

86d ▶ 13
Report on capitalization

plain paper; 2″ top margin; 1″ side margins; DS, but SS multiline rules and example sentences

1. Use CAPITALIZATION for the heading.
2. Type each rule and example; compose and type a second sentence to illustrate further the rule.
3. Proofread; correct errors.

1. Capitalize the first word of a sentence, the first word of every direct quotation, and the first word after a colon if the word begins a complete sentence.

   The sign read: No one is allowed in the cafeteria after hours.

2. Capitalize names and nicknames that designate particular persons, places, or things.

   The First Lady saw the Stars and Stripes from the White House.

3. Capitalize all official titles of honor and respect when they precede personal names.

   Governor Ellen T. Grassman and Rabbi Silverman spoke to us.

4. Capitalize the names of places, such as streets, buildings, parks, monuments, rivers, oceans, and mountains.

   I visited the World Trade Center and Central Park in New York.

5. Capitalize main words in titles of plays, poems, and so forth.

   I reviewed The King and I in the May issue of Theatre Magazine.

87

87a ▶ 5
Preparatory practice

each line 3 times SS; DS between 3-line groups; retype selected lines as time permits

alphabet Juicy new sap quietly oozed over the exposed bark forming a wet glaze.
figures The spry 76-year-old woman quit the 34-member board on April 25, 1980.
tab tow 10 quiz 10 top 10 many 10 pop 10 sax
fluency The rigidity of the body of the amendment is the work of a firm panel.
| 1 | 2 | 3 | 4 | 5 | 6 | 7 | 8 | 9 | 10 | 11 | 12 | 13 | 14 |

61b ▶ 5
Technique improvement: response patterns

1. Each line once SS.
2. A 1′ writing on Line 2, then on Line 4, then Line 6.
3. Determine *gwam* on each writing; compare speed scores.

letter response
Several inspectors hesitantly gestured toward certain rejected crates.
New concepts and techniques are being tested to deal with the project.

word response
If they know the way to do it, I do not think they should wait for us.
Sign the right form so the people on the panel may handle the problem.

combination response
Either you or I can go. Neither of us has a session during that hour.
A quick, light, easy stroke of the keys will make you a better typist.

| 1 | 2 | 3 | 4 | 5 | 6 | 7 | 8 | 9 | 10 | 11 | 12 | 13 | 14 |

61c ▶15
Report on using the comma

plain paper; 2″ top margin; 1″ side margins; DS, but SS multiline rules and example sentences

1. Use COMMA for heading.
2. Type each rule and example; compose and type a second sentence to illustrate further the rule.
3. Proofread; correct errors.

1. Use commas to set off nonrestrictive clauses or phrases.

   The trip, which is recommended in guide books, costs little.
   (Compose a sentence.)

2. Commas should not be used when clauses or phrases are restrictive.

   The girl who won the contest received an award.
   (Compose a sentence.)

3. Use commas to set off a nonrestrictive appositive, but do not set off a restrictive appositive.

   Mr. Charles, our art teacher, reviewed the book AUTUMN WIND.
   (Compose a sentence.)

4. Use a comma to separate contrasting and opposing phrases.

   Fred Adams, not I, prepared the report.
   (Compose a sentence.)

5. Use a comma before and after the etc. when it is used to complete items in a series.

   Paint, paper, brushes, etc., will be needed for the job.
   (Compose a sentence.)

61d ▶ 25
Problem typing: subject line/reply reference notation

1. Study the information and the illustrations at the right.
2. Type the three letters that follow [LM pp. 101–106]. Make 1 cc and address an envelope for each letter.
3. Proofread and circle errors. Check correct placement of special features.

Reply reference notation: Type the notation as you would a subject line. The word *Reference* or *Re* followed by a colon and 2 spaces may be typed before the notation.

Subject line in letter: Type a DS below salutation at left margin, at paragraph point, or centered. The word SUBJECT is typed in all caps or the *S* only is capped. A colon and 2 spaces follows *Subject*.

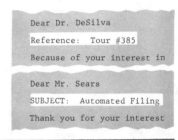

Dear Dr. DeSilva
Reference: Tour #385
Because of your interest in

Dear Mr. Sears
SUBJECT: Automated Filing
Thank you for your interest

Problem 1
Letter with reference line

modified block; block ¶s; open punctuation; blocked reply reference notation

words

July 31, 19-- Dr. Bernard DeSilva 7905 Waverly Avenue Dayton, OH 45405 14
Dear Dr. DeSilva Reference: Tour #385 (¶) Because of your interest in our 28
tour to Williamsburg, Virginia, this fall, I am sending to you in another mail- 44
ing our brochure and itinerary of the trip. I hope you decide to join us 59
in this visit to historic, colonial Virginia. Please refer to the tour 73
number above when writing to us about this particular tour. (¶) Thank you for 88
calling us; and if we can be of any service in the future concerning your 103
travel needs, please call or write us. Sincerely yours Henry Tseng, Agent 118
xx (87) 119/130

Problems 2 and 3 are on page 126.

86

86a ▶ 5
Preparatory practice

each line 3 times SS; DS between 3-line groups; retype selected lines as time permits

alphabet A complex fight could jeopardize quickly my earnest vows to keep busy.

figures Between now and 1985 the 23,476 workers must vote on the 10 proposals.

space bar All of the new ads may not be on the list if we do not do the job now.

fluency I may wish to own both an ox and a cow to work the land on the island.

| 1 | 2 | 3 | 4 | 5 | 6 | 7 | 8 | 9 | 10 | 11 | 12 | 13 | 14 |

86b ▶ 7
Preapplication drill: tabulating/figures

SS; set margins and tab stops according to key; repeat if time permits

12345	23456	34567	45678	56789	67890	78901
13579	24680	35791	46802	57913	68024	79135
01928	10293	37465	73645	56478	65743	92387
22999	77733	11100	66444	55588	99100	22133

key | 5 | 4 | 5 | 4 | 5 | 4 | 5 | 4 | 5 | 4 | 5 | 4 | 5 |

86c ▶ 25
Problem typing: statements of account/credit memorandum

[LM pp. 193–198]

Problem 1

Type statement of account shown at right. Make 1 cc.

Statements of account are sent to customers at the end of the month showing the month's transactions.

words

Statement of Account

MINUTEMAN products, inc.
280 MILK STREET
BOSTON, MA 02109
(617) 465-9900

Date June 30, 19-- 3

To

J. F. Smith Builders, Inc. 8
1780 Kenny Road 11
Columbus, OH 43212 15

Date	Items	Debits	Credits	Balance	words
June 1	Balance			1,549.78	20
5	Invoice T-5312	107.25		1,657.03	27
7	Credit memo 657		55.38	1,601.65	33
10	Invoice T-5538	973.25		2,574.90	40
12	Payment on account		1,549.78	1,025.12	48

Problem 2

Retype Problem 1 adding the information at the right. Determine balances.

15	Invoice T-6406	303.75
21	Payment on account	973.25
25	Credit memo 873	7.25

61d, continued

words

Problem 2
Letter with subject line
modified block; block ¶s; open punctuation; blocked subject line

Current date Mr. Daniel G. Sears Records Control Manager Utah Distributors, 13
Inc. 9774 Southwell Street Ogden, UT 84404 Dear Mr. Sears SUBJECT: Auto- 27
mated Filing (¶1) Thank you for your interest in Auto-File. I am pleased to tell 43
you how you can modernize your filing methods. (¶2) Auto-File brings total 57
automation to your files in the same way that the computer has brought auto- 72
mation to data processing. It uses digital filing and retrieval techniques to 88
solve large-scale filing problems. (¶3) If you think advanced methods of filing 103
are limited to archival storage with photographic images, consider these 118
dynamic capabilities brought to you by Auto-File. No document is ever out of 133
file. Auto-File updates, sorts, and purges automatically. Moreover, it cen- 149
tralizes files without limiting distribution. (¶4) Ms. Hilda Wilkie, our Utah rep- 164
resentative, will call to see if she can be of further service. Sincerely yours Ms. 181
June Mullican, Manager Advertising Department xx (146) **191/212**

words

Problem 3
Letter with subject line
modified block; indented ¶s; mixed punctuation; centered subject line

Current date Mr. Carlos Santiago Office Manager Pullman Products, Inc. 7894 13
Forbes Avenue San Diego, CA 92120 Dear Mr. Santiago: SUBJECT: The 26
Remarkable Secretary (¶1) Busy executives stay ahead of paperwork even 39
when they are out of the office. They do it with Fillmore's remarkable new 55
vest-pocket Secretary. (¶2) It's so small and light you can slip it into your pocket 71
and take it anywhere. Yet it packs a full hour of ideas, letters, memos, and 86
reports on a single microcassette. You can hear the recording with astonishing 102
clarity--all at the touch of a single button. (¶3) Fillmore products are sold just 118
about everywhere. See your Fillmore dealer for additional information or a 133
demonstration. Sincerely yours, Miss Jennifer Moresby Sales Manager xx **147/166**
(105)

62

62a ▶ 5 Preparatory practice

as many times as possible in the time available

alphabet	Excessive assignments will often quickly jeopardize both joy and zeal.
fig/sym	The height of the frames is 2'8"; length, 15'7"; code number, 29-4306.
left hand	Fears increased as westward breezes gave six vessels access to a reef.
fluency	Our neighbor and her visitor may take a dirigible to the ancient city.

| 1 | 2 | 3 | 4 | 5 | 6 | 7 | 8 | 9 | 10 | 11 | 12 | 13 | 14 |

62b ▶ 5 Technique improvement: keystroking

each line 3 times SS (slowly, top speed, in-between rate)

direct reaches	Type with minimum wrist movement: obtained, anyhow, unhurt, subtract.
adjacent keys	We hope to develop a trade policy based on these new position reports.
double letters	Will the official committee offer to supply the staff accounts needed?
long words	The conference participants were provided with adequate documentation.

| 1 | 2 | 3 | 4 | 5 | 6 | 7 | 8 | 9 | 10 | 11 | 12 | 13 | 14 |

85b ▶ 45
Problem typing: invoices

[LM p. 191]

Problem 1

Type invoice shown at right. Make 1 cc.

An invoice usually accompanies a shipment of merchandise. Words

CRAVER FURNITURE CO. 1709 Piedmont Avenue High Point, NC 27263 (919) 653-9042 *Invoice*

Date August 31, 19-- 3

Wolf Manufacturing Company 9
1020 South Road 14
Harrisburg, PA 17109 18

Our Order No. YO-53486

Cust. Order No. CU-83178 20

Terms 2/10, n/30 Shipped Via Hess Transport 25

Quantity	Description	Unit Price	Total	Words
5	Executive swivel chair	124.95	624.75	33
6	Armchair	69.95	419.70	37
10	Coffee table	74.75	747.50	43
6	Corner table	84.95	509.70	49
3	Conference desk	579.95	1,739.85	56
6	Telephone cabinet	139.95	839.70	64
			4,881.20	66

Problem 2
Constructing an invoice form

Using a full sheet of paper, follow Steps 1–5 outlined at the right and type a copy of the invoice form shown.

1. Set margin stops for an 80-space line. Carriage should lock after stroke eighty.

2. Beginning on Line 7, move the carriage to the extreme right margin and backspace to type INVOICE. DS and return the carriage to the left margin. Type "Sold to" (use 2 lines). Move the carriage to 60 for pica or 65 for elite and set a tab. Backspace from this point to type the following:

Date (DS)
Our Order No. (DS)
Cust. Order No. (DS)
Shipped Via

3. After typing "Shipped Via," move the carriage (without spacing) to the left margin and type "Terms". SS and type an 80-space horizontal line. TS and type another 80-space horizontal line.

4. Draw three 3" vertical lines 15, 50, and 65 spaces, respectively, from the left margin.

5. Center headings in the heading blocks: Quantity; Description; Unit Price; Total.

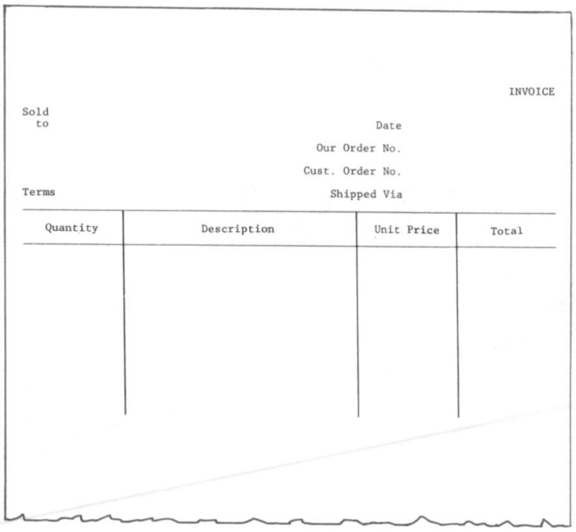
INVOICE

Sold
to

Date
Our Order No.
Cust. Order No.
Terms Shipped Via

Quantity	Description	Unit Price	Total

Problem 3
Invoice

Using the form typed in Problem 2 above, type an invoice from the copy and directions at the right.

SOLD TO Kingston Office Supply
1799 Raleigh Avenue
Lubbock, TX 79416
TERMS 2/10, n/30

DATE July 31, 19--
OUR ORDER NO. JY-873187
CUST. ORDER NO. T-509
SHIPPED VIA Interstate Trucking

(Use the quantity, description, unit price, and total listed in Problem 1 above.)

62c ▶15
Report on using the comma

plain paper; 2″ top margin; 1″ side margins; DS, but SS multiline rules and example sentences

1. For heading, use COMMA.

2. Type each rule and example; compose and type a second sentence to illustrate further the rule.

3. If time permits, retype the first Communication aids checkup, page 102. Check your corrections with your instructor.

1. Use commas to set off words of direct address.

   Thank you, Mrs. Harris, for your letter about the flowers.
   (Compose a sentence.)

2. Use a comma to set off an introductory phrase containing a verb.

   To qualify for this job, applicants must have good references.
   (Compose a sentence.)

3. Use commas to set off parenthetical words, phrases, or clauses.

   Learning to typewrite, for example, requires practice.
   (Compose a sentence.)

4. Use a comma between the members of a compound sentence connected by the conjunctions and, or, for, or whereas. The comma may be omitted if the compound sentence is short.

   He will collect the data, and she will write the report.

   Joyce sings and Joe plays the piano.
   (Compose a sentence.)

5. Use a comma before the conjunction but in a compound sentence whether it is long or short.

   Take the bus, but remember it is slow.
   (Compose a sentence.)

62d ▶ 25
Problem typing: company name in closing and enclosure notation

1. Study the information and the illustration at the right.

2. Type the letters that follow [LM pp. 107–110]. Make 1 cc and address an envelope for each letter.

3. Proofread and circle errors. Check correct placement of special features.

Company name in closing lines: When a company name is used in the closing lines, type it in ALL CAPS a DS below the complimentary close. The writer's name is then typed on the 4th line below the company name.

Enclosure notation: Type an enclosure notation a DS below the reference initials. If there is more than one enclosure, list them on succeeding lines, indented 3 spaces from left margin.

Sincerely yours

THE MILLS CORPORATION

June Mullican

Ms. June Mullican, Manager
Advertising Department

xx

Enclosures
   Sample table
   Reply card

Problem 1
Letter with company name in closing and enclosure notation

block style; open punctuation

▶ Because of the special lines in this letter, type the date 3 lines higher than usual.

words

Current date Mr. Waldo P. Waltz Office Manager Fairfax Corporation 2002 12
Magnolia Street Amarillo, TX 79107 Dear Mr. Waltz (¶ 1) Your professional 25
people have more creative work to do. Your clerical staff would probably quit if 42
asked to do just ten percent of the tabulations Quicktab performs; such as align- 54
ing, formating, and calculating automatically. (¶ 2) Quicktab produces decision- 69
making tables without help from programmers, calculators, or office personnel. 85
It puts data together the way decision-makers like it--graphically informative. 101
Quicktab works fast--error free. Feed it some changes, and it automatically 116
turns out a corrected table; then stores it for future use. (¶ 3) The input is in 132
simple everyday English so you don't have to be a programmer to use it. Maybe 148
the best decision you can make today is to get Quicktab working for you right 163
away in all those areas involving tables and numerical data. (¶ 4) It's available 179
on a rental, lease, or license basis. A sample table prepared by Quicktab is 194
enclosed--so is a card that will bring you additional information. Sincerely yours 211
THE MILLS CORPORATION Ms. June Mullican, Manager Advertising Depart- 225
ment xx Enclosures Sample table Reply card (189) 233/**252**

84c ▶ 35
Problem typing: bills of lading

[LM pp. 185–190]

Problem 1
Type bill of lading shown at right. Make 1 cc.

A bill of lading is a receipt listing the goods being shipped and is issued by the common carrier.

words

STRAIGHT BILL OF LADING—SHORT FORM—Original—Not Negotiable

RECEIVED, subject to the classifications and tariffs in effect on the date of issue of this Original Bill of Lading.

AGENT'S NO. ______

FROM General Supply Services, Inc. AT Boston, MA DATE 3/28/19-- 10

CONSIGNED TO AND DESTINATION

Promotional Services, Inc. 16
208 East Avenue 19
Norwalk, CT 06855 22

Subject to Section 7 of conditions of applicable bill of lading, if this shipment is to be delivered to the consignee without recourse on the consignor, the consignor shall sign the following statement:
The carrier shall not make delivery of this shipment without payment of freight and all other lawful charges.

(Signature of Consignor)

CUST. ORDER NO. U-18834 24

If charges are to be prepaid, write or stamp here, "To be Prepaid."

DELIVERING CARRIER National Transport, Inc. CAR INITIAL AND NO. Y-0165 30

the property described below, in apparent good order, except as noted (contents and condition of contents of packages unknown) marked, consigned, and destined as indicated below, which said carrier (the word carrier being understood throughout this contract as meaning any person or corporation in possession of the property under the contract) agrees to carry to its usual place of delivery at said destination, if on its route, otherwise to deliver to another carrier on the route to said destination. It is mutually agreed, as to each carrier of all or any of said property over all or any portion of said route to destination, and as to each party at any time interested in all or any of said property, that every service to be performed hereunder shall be subject to all the terms and conditions of the Uniform Domestic Straight Bill of Lading set forth (1) in Official, Southern, Western and Illinois Freight Classifications in effect on the date hereof, if this is a rail or a rail-water shipment, or (2) in the applicable motor carrier classification or tariff if this is a motor carrier shipment. Shipper hereby certifies that he is familiar with all the terms and conditions of the said bill of lading, including those on the back thereof, set forth in the classification or tariff which governs the transportation of this shipment, and the said terms and conditions are hereby agreed to by the shipper and accepted for himself and his assigns.

Received $ ______ to apply in prepayment of the charges on the property described hereon.

Agent or Cashier

NO. PACKAGES	DESCRIPTION OF ARTICLES	WEIGHT	RATE	CHK.	words
3	Executive conference desks	756#			37
2	Secretarial desks	454#			42
2	Credenzas	350#			46
3	Executive chairs	195#			50

Per ______
(The signature here acknowledges only the amount prepaid.)

Charges Advanced: $ ______

*If the shipment moves between two ports by a carrier by water, the law requires that the bill of lading shall state whether it is "carrier's or shipper's weight." Note—Where the rate is dependent on value, shippers are required to state specifically in writing the agreed or declared value of the property. **The agreed or declared value of the property is hereby specifically stated by the shipper to be not exceeding** ______ per ______

†Shipper's imprint in lieu of stamp; not a part of Bill of Lading approved by the Interstate Commerce Commission.

General Supply Services, Inc. SHIPPER 56

Per ______ ______ Agent, Per ______

†"The fibre boxes used for this shipment conform to the specifications set forth in the box maker's certificate thereon, and all other requirements of Uniform Freight Classification."

PERMANENT POST-OFFICE ADDRESS OF SHIPPER: 921 Boylston Street, Boston, MA 02185 64

SHIPPER'S NO.
2 Z-38954 65

Problem 2
Type bill of lading shown at right.

Problem 3
Retype Problem 1 above. For the section dealing with "Description of Articles," use the first four articles described in the purchase order on page 173, Problem 2. Estimate approximate weights.

words

FROM **Paramount Office Supply Co., Inc.** AT **Memphis, TN** DATE **6/17/19--** 11
CONSIGNED TO AND DESTINATION **Rumford Insurance Company 680 Bauman Drive** 20
Knoxville, TN 38108 CUST. ORDER NO. **T-6335** DELIVERING CARRIER **Road** 26
Runner, Inc. CAR INITIAL AND NO. **V-8732** 30

NO. PACKAGES	DESCRIPTION OF ARTICLES	WEIGHT	
6	Contemporary chairs	360#	36
6	Steel files	600#	39
2	Desks	400#	42
2	Collators	50#	45

SHIPPER **Paramount Office Supply Co., Inc.** PERMANENT POST OFFICE ADDRESS 52
OF SHIPPER **956 Monroe Avenue, Memphis, TN 38104** SHIPPER'S NO. **V-0074** 61

85

85a ▶ 5
Preparatory practice

each line 3 times SS; DS between 3-line groups; retype selected lines as time permits

alphabet They realize major pieces of gaudy work are not valuable or exquisite.
fig/sym The 16-unit mall and the 27-acre lot were reduced by 9% to $1,483,500.
shift lock Jane recently quit WSAR radio and WJAR-TV to work for ABC in New York.
fluency Their goal is to make the worn towpaths a bicycle path for their town.

| 1 | 2 | 3 | 4 | 5 | 6 | 7 | 8 | 9 | 10 | 11 | 12 | 13 | 14 |

62d, continued

Problem 2
Letter with attention line, subject line, company name in closing, and enclosure notation
modified block; block ¶s; open punctuation; blocked subject line; date on Line 15

	words
Current date Office Supplies Center 56 Fleetwood Street Bakersfield, CA 93306	16
Attention Mrs. Sarah L. Wilcox Ladies and Gentlemen SUBJECT: A Gift from	31
Outer Space (¶ 1) Not really, but the Space Pens were originally developed for	45
use in outer space. Realizing that there was no pen of any kind that would write	62
instantly in any position, in the blazing heat, the freezing cold, or the vacuum of	78
space, we developed the pressurized ball-point pen ink capsule. It is now used in	95
all manned space flights. (¶ 2) To work in space, the pen had to be different. To	111
please users on earth, it had to be better! I urge you to make Space Pens	126
available to your customers. They're more than a novelty; they really write!	142
(¶ 3) Order forms and price lists are enclosed. Your orders will be filled	156
promptly. Sincerely yours SPACE ORIENTED PRODUCTS, INC. Ms. Barbara F.	170
Troutman Advertising Manager xx Enclosures Order forms Price lists (124)	183/196

Problem 3
Letter from rough draft
plain paper; modified block; 1½" side margins; date on Line 17; indented ¶s; mixed punctuation; centered subject line

Note: See top of page 129 for directions for typing a postscript.

October 12th, 19-- [handwritten: delete "th", insert ","]

[handwritten: Mrs.] Veronica Summerville ← [handwritten: 4th line space]
768 Paxton St. [handwritten: spell out]
Apartment 35A
harrisburg, PN 11704

[handwritten: SUBJECT: We Need Your Answers]

Dear ~~Madam~~ [handwritten: Mrs. Summerville]:

may I ask your ~~assistance~~ [handwritten: help] ina Special Survey some of our long-time customers? In the next few days, I'll be senting you a very brief questionaire. It should take [handwritten: no] more then a few moments too fill out--yet you participation in this ~~little~~ survey is quite important us ~~to~~ [handwritten: to] and to the Validity of the study, itself. [handwritten: Naturally, your reply will be kept confidential.]

Thand you for your ~~corporation~~ [handwritten: cooperation]--and for your lasting interest in HARRISON's, your freindly nieghboorhood store.

Sincerely Yours,

[handwritten: 3 blank line spaces] →

(Mr.) Dino Sanchez, manager

xx [handwritten: DS]

[handwritten: The questionnaire will reach you in a few days.]

63

63a ▶ 5 Preparatory practice

as many times as possible in the time available

alphabet	Fred Zwik gave an excellent speech by quoting many famous journalists.
figures	Type 1 and 2 and 3 and 4 and 5 and 6 and 7 and 8 and 9 and 10 and 456.
direct reaches	Many bright nylon flags decorated the old aluminum bridge in Plymouth.
fluency	To do your best work, you must keep your eyes on the copy as you type.

| 1 | 2 | 3 | 4 | 5 | 6 | 7 | 8 | 9 | 10 | 11 | 12 | 13 | 14 |

83c, continued

Problem 2
Type purchase order shown at the right. Make 1 cc.

Problem 3
Retype Problem 2 making these changes:

1. Double the quantities of all items listed.
2. Determine new totals for each item and total column.
3. Send order to:

Ocean State, Inc.
228 Broad Street
Warwick, RI 02888

words

GREELEY CO., INC.
1836 N. Glenstone Springfield, MO 65803 Telephone: (417) 445-3260

PURCHASE ORDER

Purchase order No. *3546-0608* 2

R. W. Anderson & Son
312 Stanwix Street
Pittsburgh, PA 15222

Date *March 13, 19--* 5
Terms *Net* 9
Ship Via *Action Express* 14 18 21

Quantity	Cat. No.	Description	Price	Total	words
1 2	AX650L	Steel floor safe	180.00	180.00 360.00	29
2 4	AX3771	Checkwriter	84.53	169.06 338.12	36
6 12	3AX602	Cork boards, 18" x 24"	50.00	300.00 600.00	45
3 6	3AX606	Contemporary chair, gold	153.90	461.70 923.40	54
6 12	AX616J	Steel files, 4-drawer	130.00	780.00 1,560.00	63
1 2	AX776N	Single-pedestal desk	215.00	215.00 430.00	74
				2,105.76	76
				4,211.52	

By____________________ Purchasing Agent

84

84a ▶ 5
Preparatory practice
each line 3 times SS; DS between 3-line groups; retype selected lines as time permits

alphabet An explicit majority recognized the quality of his working vocabulary.
figures Joe gained 1,768 yards in 340 carries and scored 259 points this year.
tab totals 5 43,970 5 amount 5 8.215 5 terms 5 2/10, n/30 5 2%
fluency Pam may wish to make a rigid audit of these eight firms by the eighth.

| 1 | 2 | 3 | 4 | 5 | 6 | 7 | 8 | 9 | 10 | 11 | 12 | 13 | 14 |

84b ▶ 10
Preapplication drill: drawing/typing rules (lines); typing on printed lines
full sheet; 1" top margin

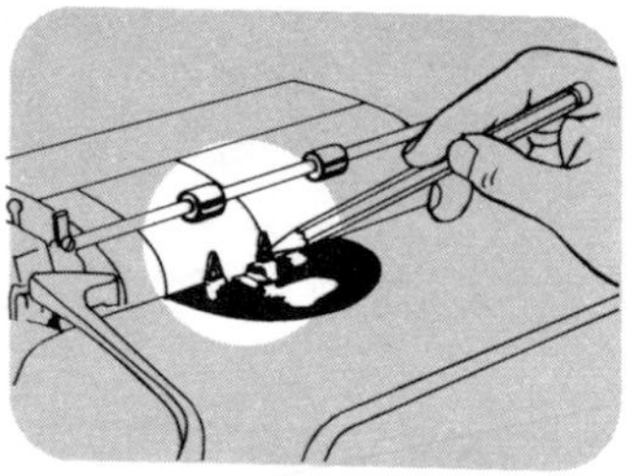

Typing horizontal rules
Depress the shift lock and use the underline key.

Drawing vertical rules
Operate the automatic line finder. Place the point of a pencil or pen through the cardholder (or on the typebar guide above the ribbon). Roll the paper up until you have a ruling of the desired length. Remove the pen or pencil and reset the line finder.

1. Type an approximate 5" horizontal rule. Remove the paper; reinsert it; align the typed line with the aligning scale; center and type the following sentence.

May my affirmative action group meet today?

2. Note the relationship of the letters to the line. The words should be close to the line, but letters with down stems should not cut it. Repeat No. 1 above.
3. Type two 4" horizontal lines 4" apart vertically. Connect the ends of the lines with vertical rules to create a 4" square. Center your name in the square.
4. Draw 2 vertical rules approximately 3" long and 6" apart. Between the rules, center and type these items leaving 4 spaces between columns:

13 65AUD Tubes $10.95 $142.35

63b ▶ 10
Problem skill building

1. Study the information at the right and the letter on page 130.

2. Type the opening parts of the letter on page 130, beginning with the date through the first line of the body. Leave proper spacing between parts.

3. Type the last 2 lines of the body and remaining letter parts, leaving proper spacing between them.

Carbon copy notation: Type a carbon copy notation (if any) a DS below the reference initials or enclosure notation (if any).

Blind carbon copy notation: When the carbon copy notation is to appear on only the carbon copy of the letter, type the notation on a piece of paper held between the typewriter ribbon and the original (top) sheet. Type the notation as: *bcc Mr. Floyd Kravatz.*

Postscript. Type the postscript a DS below item at end of the letter. Block or indent to agree with the letter style. Omit the letters *P.S.* at the beginning of the postscript.

63c ▶ 35
Problem typing: letters with special features

Problem 1 [LM p. 111]

Type the letter on page 130 illustrating special features. Because of the many extra lines in the letter, raise the dateline two or three lines and use 1" side margins. Address an envelope.

Problem 2 [LM p. 113]

Type the script letter below in block style with blocked subject line and open punctuation. Address an envelope.

words

October 12, 19-- | Fairview Manufacturing Co. | 94 9
Auwaiolimu Street | Honolulu, HI 96813 | Attention Miss 20
Beverly Lim | Ladies and Gentlemen | SUBJECT: Sometimes 30
the Truth Hurts (¶1) We are an independent testing 40
organization that tells you -- by brand name -- 49
if a product is likely to perform as promised. 58
We tell you, too, how a product compares with 67
competing makes, what are its good features, 76
and what are its bad features. (¶2) Purchasing 85
professionals in more than three thousand orga- 94
nizations turn to our test reports to find out 104
what we have to say about a product before 112
they buy. For a free sample report and infor- 122
mation on how our service can help you cut 130
costs, merely return the enclosed card. Sincerely 140
yours | Fred L. Cord, Manager | xx | Enclosure 148/**167**

64

64a ▶ 5
Preparatory practice

as many times as possible in the time available

alphabet	The five dozen quarts of blackberry and grape juice mixture were mine.
figures	Your 1978 edition of the book has 3 parts, 25 chapters, and 460 pages.
shift keys	Senator Neil Potts visited the United States Naval Academy in January.
fluency	Habits are like muscles--the more we use them, the stronger they grow.

| 1 | 2 | 3 | 4 | 5 | 6 | 7 | 8 | 9 | 10 | 11 | 12 | 13 | 14 |

83

83a ▶ 5
Preparatory practice
each line 3 times SS; DS between 3-line groups; retype selected lines as time permits

alphabet A key objective was to quell an exorbitant loss of highly prized gems.
fig/sym My 20 shares of stock ($43/share) have jumped 56% in value since 1978.
shift Ed, Joy, and Dot will visit Fort Wayne, Miami, St. Paul, and Gulfport.
fluency The quantity of work their dismal neighbor did to the dock is a laugh.

| 1 | 2 | 3 | 4 | 5 | 6 | 7 | 8 | 9 | 10 | 11 | 12 | 13 | 14 |

83b ▶ 15
Preapplication drill: tabulating
SS; DS between groups

10 ctns.	15%	$3.19	87AUG1	10:18	c.o.d.	25.4 mm
25 doz.	#63	$7.55	CP-2-M	12:46	fig.	2.54 cm
50 lbs.	*18	$6.00	AYC 10	1:39	a.m.	0.305 m
10 ea.	15"	$1.00	142/0D	11:36	ibid.	0.91 m
9 lbs.	12'	$9.22	14--6B	10:54	incl.	0.47 L
36 ctns.	(3)	$5.91	63/EZG	2:38	FIFO	0.45 kg
10 doz.	65*	$3.83	0B63Y1	4:49	dept.	1.61 km
60 lbs.	2/8	$9.83	18-1-5	5:07	U.S.A.	28.35 g

key | 8 | 4 | 3 | 4 | 5 | 4 | 6 | 4 | 5 | 4 | 6 | 4 | 8 |

83c ▶ 30
Problem typing: purchase orders
[LM pp. 179–184]

Problem 1
Type purchase order shown at the right. Make 1 cc.

A purchase order is completed by the purchasing department to order requisitioned supplies or equipment.

HORIZON PUBLISHERS, INC. 3850 El Camino Real • Palo Alto, CA 94306
(415) 631-2000

Tab **PURCHASE ORDER**

Purchase order No. B536-0058 2

Allstate Office Supply
1186 Main Street
Wakefield, RI 02879

Date July 18, 19-- 9 13
Terms 2/10, n/30 19
Ship Via Runner Express 22

Quantity	Tab Cat. No.	Tab 2 spaces from rule **Description**	Tab **Price**	Tab **Total**	
DS					
1	18-163	Heavy-duty portable cutter	210.00	210.00	32
2	71-711	Typewriter stand, 26"			38
	Indent 3 spaces →	adjustable	65.00	130.00	43
3	11-169	Time-date wheel	9.95	29.85	50
1	18-149	Power paper drill	250.00	250.00	58
12	18-129	Editors' shears, 9"	13.25	159.00	67
36	34-909	Cloth tapes, black	.44	15.84	75
6	15-221	Label maker, 1/2" tapes	21.20	127.20	85
Approximate center	Approximate center		Approximate center	DS 921.89	87

By ______________________ Purchasing Agent

Phillips and Johnson

(213) 221-5435
165 Howard Street Glendale, CA 91206

		words in parts	total words
	Current date	3	3
Mailing notation	SPECIAL DELIVERY	6	6
	Hillcrest Industries, Inc.	12	12
	9005 North Boyd Street	16	16
	Portland, ME 04101	20	20
Attention line	Attention Miss Jessica Lawrence	27	27
	Ladies and Gentlemen	31	31
Subject line or reply reference	SUBJECT: Special Features in Business Letters	40	40
	Mr. Floyd Kravatz asked me to send you a copy of our recently com-	53	53
	piled report, SPECIAL FEATURES IN BUSINESS LETTERS. This report	13	66
	illustrates many of the special features that may be used in modern	27	80
	business letters.	30	83
	The aim of these special features is to improve the efficiency of	43	97
	correspondence. The special features are presented in this letter	57	110
	in life-size format; however, the chance of using all these special	70	123
	features in a single letter is quite remote.	79	132
	There are variations to the style presented here. For example, the	92	146
	subject line may be blocked, indented to match the paragraph inden-	106	159
	tations, or centered. Attention lines, however, are preferably	119	172
	typed at the left margin.	124	177
	The purposes of the special features are limited. However, a good	137	190
	typist understands their functions and knows how and when to use	150	203
	them. I hope you will find the enclosed report interesting and	13	216
	useful.	14	217
	Sincerely yours	17	221
Company name	PHILLIPS AND JOHNSON	22	225
	Raymond Knapp	24	228
	Assistant Sales Manager	29	232
	xx	30	233
Enclosure notation	Enclosure	32	235
Carbon copy notation	cc Mr. Floyd Kravatz	36	239
Postscript	Additional free copies of the report are available.	46	249
			272

Style letter 5: modified block illustrating special features of a business letter

section

17

Business forms

lessons 82–87

Learning goals

The lessons of this section are planned to help you to:

1. Improve keystroking speed and control.
2. Develop greater facility with figure and symbol reaches.
3. Develop skill in processing business forms.
4. Develop greater tabulator control.

Machine adjustments

1. Paper guide at *0*.
2. 70-space line for drills.
3. Margins and spacing as directed for business forms.

82

82a ▶ 5

Preparatory practice

each line 3 times SS; DS between 3-line groups; retype selected lines as time permits

alphabet Pat realized the heavy backlog of new orders required many extra jobs.

figures In 34 days the 198-member band will log 3 756 kilometers to 20 cities.

tab after 5 added 5 hilly 5 onion 5 crest 5 pupil 5 devastated

fluency They may visit Japan when they go to the Orient on their leisure trip.

| 1 | 2 | 3 | 4 | 5 | 6 | 7 | 8 | 9 | 10 | 11 | 12 | 13 | 14 |

82b ▶ 15

Problem typing information

Study the forms below and on page 172 and the tips at the right before typing the business forms in this section.

1. Set left margin stop for address and first column; set tab stops for other "columnar" items.

2. SS the items in the description column if there are 4 or more lines. DS the items if there are 3 or fewer lines.

3. For single items of more than 1 line, indent the second and succeeding lines 3 spaces.

4. In *total* columns, underline the amount for the last item; then DS and type the total.

5. Center columns of figures under the headings. Begin the items in the description column about 2 spaces to the right of the vertical rule.

82c ▶ 30

Problem typing: purchase requisitions

[LM pp. 175–178]

Problem 1

Type the purchase requisition shown at the right. Make 1 cc.

Problem 2

Retype Problem 1 making these changes:

1. Use 635709 for the requisition number, March 19, 19— for the date, and 78–RAP–95 for the job number.

2. Delete the request for a typewriter stand.

3. Arrange the items alphabetically.

4. Double the quantities of all items.

A purchase requisition is completed by the company unit that needs the supplies or equipment.

words

HORIZON PUBLISHERS, INC. Tab PURCHASE REQUISITION

Deliver to: Viola Card — Requisition No. 63518 ~~635709~~ 3

Location: Editorial Department — Date July 15, 19-- March 19 10

Job No. 78-RAP-46 78-RAP-95 — Date Required As soon as possible 16

Quantity	Description (Tab 2 spaces from rule)	words
DS		
1 2	6 Power paper drill	20
12 24	2 Editors' shears, 9"	25
36 72	1 Cloth tapes, black	29
6 12	3 Label maker, 1/2" tapes	35
24 48	4 Label maker tapes, 1/2" x 144"	41
~~2~~	~~Typewriter stand, 26" adjustable~~	48

Approximate center

Requisitioned by: ______________________

64b ▶ 45
Problem typing: multipage letters

1. Study the information at the right and the illustrations below.

2. Type the problems that follow [LM p. 115]. Make 1 cc and address an envelope for Problem 1.

3. Proofread and circle errors. Check placement of second-page headings.

Second and subsequent pages of a letter: In typing a multipage letter, use plain paper of the same color and quality as the letter-head for the second and subsequent pages.

Do not end a page with a divided word. If possible, leave at least 2 lines of a paragraph at the foot of a page and carry at least two lines to the next page.

Type the first line of second and following page headings on the 7th line from top edge. TS, continue typing. Use the same side margins as for the first page.

If the *horizontal style* is used for the heading of the second page, center the page number and make sure the dateline ends at the right margin.

▶ Before typing the first page of any long letter, draw a light pencil line 1½"–2" from the bottom edge of the page as a page-end warning. You can then judge where to end the page if the letter is too long for the page.

1"

Orient Trade Center
Page 2
January 20, 19--
TS
greet you and to personally show you how work that formerly took
you tedious hours can be accomplished in mere seconds. Just let

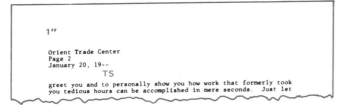

Block style heading for second page

1"

Orient Trade Center 2 January 20, 19--
TS
greet you and to personally show you how work that formerly took
you tedious hours can be accomplished in mere seconds. Just let
me know what time is most convenient for you. If you prefer to
have the demonstration in your offices instead of at the trade

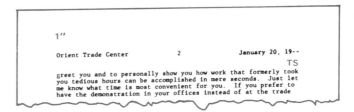

Horizontal style heading for second page

Problem 1
Two-page letter with block second-page heading

modified block; block ¶s; open punctuation; centered subject line

words

January 20, 19-- Orient Trade Center 6664 El Nido Avenue Pasadena, CA 91107 15
Ladies and Gentlemen SUBJECT: Harvey, the Manageable Minicomputer (¶1) 29
Let me introduce you to Harvey, the newest and most advanced minicomputer 43
on the market today. Harvey is just right for small businesses that want to 59
boost efficiency with something more manageable than a big computer--and all 74
at a surprisingly affordable price. Harvey is ideal for offices, warehouses, 90
manufacturing plants, contractors, and a host of other businesses--many of 105
them like yours. (¶2) Harvey gathers facts and figures geared to your specific 120
business because you tell him to do just what needs to be done. You provide the 136
information once--and Harvey never forgets it. You'll get help with your 151
periodic or ongoing evaluations and reports for controlling any facet of your 166
business. You can simplify your daily routine and make it more accurate. 181
What's more, Harvey can be programmed to schedule and route delivery 195
trucks, to check your inventory, to process product orders, to send and with- 211
draw information between departments, and do dozens of other jobs. In short, 226
Harvey handles all detail work in less time. (¶3) As a management aid, Harvey 241
will tell you if there is trouble ahead and how to avert it. You'll get a super-fast 258
overview of information needed for vital decision making. Moreover, Harvey 273
can grow with your business when required--with added units and components. 289
(¶4) You don't have to be some kind of programming whiz to make Harvey do all 303
these things for you. You simply work with the distributors who sell Harvey. 319
Tell them what kinds of problems you want Harvey to do and how your business 334
works, and leave the rest to these people. They are the programming experts, 350
and you get all the happy results. (¶5) Harvey is manageable in every sense of 365
the word. You control him. He's your brightest new employee. Work will be 380

(Continued on page 132)

Proofreading: identifying errors

1. Read the ¶; identify the errors; note corrections needed.
2. Type the ¶; make needed corrections as you type.
3. Mark your errors as your teacher reads the corrected ¶.

Your pen should had as much class has a suit or dress. Your cloths has beautiful lines, impeddible details, and absolutely know compromise in the way its made. Why should you seddle for any thing less in a pen? What you need as a knew pen with beau- tifull lanes, impeddible details, an no compromises in the say it's make. Try Star by Warner. You no your cloths are write when people ask who your tailor its. Star will made them ask who your pen company is.

Straight-copy skill measurement

two 5′ writings; determine *gwam*; proofread and circle errors

all letters used

Difficulty index

A	1.5 si	5.7 awl	80% hfw

	gwam 1′	5′	
A friendly person is one who uses certain signals when he or she	13	3	62
meets others as a means of making a good impression. Such people take	27	5	65
the initiative and try to make the first effort to develop a warm feel-	41	8	68
ing from which to work. For example, a person with a ready smile is	55	11	71
easily interpreted as a friendly person. The smile seems to handle many	70	14	73
psychological barriers that might exist in a meeting of strangers. Your	84	17	76
smile helps you to feel accepted by such individuals right from the start.	99	20	79
There are many other things you can do to help make a good first	13	22	82
impression. Simple words such as hello, good morning, and thank you are	28	25	85
examples of friendly verbal signals; shaking hands, nodding positively,	42	28	88
or opening a door for people are various types of nonverbal messages you	57	31	91
send that make it easier for individuals to get to know you. When you	71	34	93
send out such signals, others do not feel awkward about approaching you.	86	37	96
You have made it easy for them to communicate, and they like you for it.	100	40	99
People who reveal confidence by sending out signs of friendship make	14	43	102
good impressions, and they are able to build quickly many lasting, work-	28	45	105
ing, and personal ties. Have confidence in yourself and in your own abil-	43	48	108
ity to relay such signals. Take the initiative and use every chance to	57	51	111
recognize the presence and help of others. Just by sending out your own	72	54	114
brand of signals in your own style, you will be an easier person to meet.	87	57	117
And, you will be happy with the net results of your efforts.	99	60	119

gwam 1′	1	2	3	4	5	6	7	8	9	10	11	12	13	14
5′			1					2				3		

64b, continued

Problem 2
Second page of 2-page letter

Retype the second page of the letter you just typed using horizontal second–page heading.

done faster and cost about half the price. (¶6) The enclosed brochure gives you 396
additional details and invites you to a private demonstration at the Los Angeles 412
Convention Center any time suitable to you on February 15-17. Harvey will be 427
there to greet you and to show you personally how work that formerly took you 443
tedious hours can be accomplished in mere seconds. Just let me know what time 459
is most convenient for you. If you prefer to have the demonstration in your 474
offices instead of the trade center, we can arrange that, too. Arrangements can 490
be made to introduce you to Harvey at a time suitable to you on either February 506
14 or 18. Sincerely yours Ms. Tanya Danforth Assistant Sales Manager xx 521
Enclosure You'll receive a written warranty with Harvey backed by a 90-year- 536
old company. 538/**550**

65

65a ▶ 5 Preparatory practice

as many times as possible in the time available

alphabet	His proclivity to work explains his fine grade on a major botany quiz.
fig/sym	In 1978, storms delayed delivery of 4,630 tons (25% of all shipments).
adjacent keys	Polly Trammers opposed Rupert Hamner's proposal to buy the Yuen store.
fluency	Every worker is expected to do the work well enough to be proud of it.

| 1 | 2 | 3 | 4 | 5 | 6 | 7 | 8 | 9 | 10 | 11 | 12 | 13 | 14 |

65b ▶ 10 Measuring straight-copy skill

Difficulty index

all letters used | A | 1.5 si | 5.7 awl | 80% hfw |

	gwam 1'		5'
One of the most durable requirements of succeeding on a job is the	13	3	57
ability to communicate: speaking and writing. You must be able to pre-	28	6	60
sent your ideas in an organized, lively, forceful fashion. The average	42	8	63
person spends more than seventy percent of the time in face-to-face commu-	57	11	66
nication, either as a speaker or a listener. If you can communicate well	72	14	69
with your family and friends, you should be able to do so before a com-	86	17	72
mittee, a board meeting, or a large audience.	95	19	73
Speaking is basically the magical gift of persuasion. Your first job	14	22	76
is to convince your listeners that you and they share a common interest in	29	25	79
the topic you will examine. Once you do this, you will have an attentive	44	28	82
hearing. Beyond this, think in terms of ideas; don't memorize the presen-	59	31	85
tation. Have your ideas so well in mind that the words will spring from	73	34	88
that organization. Refer to notes or an outline if you must. In general,	88	37	91
do not read your presentation. Reading a talk stifles spontaneity.	101	39	94
Relax; get lost in your subject. Your listeners will know if you	13	42	96
are more interested in yourself than in your topic. People who are self-	28	45	99
centered are not good speakers. Interest in your subject must be openly	42	48	102
intense and genuine. Be specific; use a chart, a table, a picture, or an	57	51	105
occasional story to make your points. A sincere presentation is basic to	72	54	108
success in speaking.	76	54	109

gwam 1' | 1 | 2 | 3 | 4 | 5 | 6 | 7 | 8 | 9 | 10 | 11 | 12 | 13 | 14 |
5' | 1 | 2 | 3 |

Technique improvement: keystroking

each line 3 times SS (slowly, top speed, in-between rate)

one-hand	1	In my opinion, my best crew was tested by each regatta crew who raced.
direct reaches	2	Cecil Myerson tried to unlock a numbered gate near the old art museum.
left-hand	3	A brave barber was awarded a rare badge after he saved a bearded crew.
fluency	4	The rush by the panel to zone the town may risk a profit for the firm.
alphabet	5	Jim quickly analyzed all twelve pages of the fixed and variable costs.
figures	6	Pete May's policies, Nos. 83-1092 and 54-7736, are dated July 5 and 6.
1st row	7	Can Mr. Van Box, the banker, visualize our volume six months from now?
direct reaches	8	Lynn tried to decide just how much of the old junk might be destroyed.

Skill comparison: progressive straight copy

1. A 1′ writing on ¶ 1 to set base rate.

2. Two 1′ writings on ¶ 2. Work to meet or exceed ¶ 1 rate.

3. A 5′ writing on the *control* level on the two ¶s combined; determine *gwam*.

¶ 1 Difficulty index

E	1.2 si	5.1 awl	90% hfw

¶ 2 Difficulty index

HA	1.7 si	6.0 awl	75% hfw

	gwam 1′	5′	
As you know, there are thousands of business firms all over the	13	3	57
world. Each one of these firms must have competent workers in order to	27	5	60
stay in operation. That means there is a place for you in the business	42	8	63
world, if you want it. But before you can choose a job, you must first	56	11	66
know what types of jobs are open and just what kinds of duties are done	70	14	69
on different jobs. Then you need to know what education and training	84	17	71
are necessary to succeed. It will also help to know what kind of a	98	20	74
future there is for the work you have in mind. All firms need workers	112	22	77
to service customers, to sell goods, to type reports and letters, to	126	25	80
file business papers, and to do many other tasks.	136	27	82
On the other hand, you may be very interested in the long-range	13	30	84
and more complex goal of transforming a quite successful job into a	26	32	87
meaningful career. Statistics show that the fund of available knowledge	41	35	90
is doubling every decade, so it is not difficult to imagine how the	55	38	93
vastly changing scope of employment activities is affected. Opportuni-	69	41	95
ties exist today that were not even heard of a decade ago, and new jobs	83	44	98
will exist a decade from now that are not even being talked about today.	98	47	101
In every phase of your career planning, keep your mind open to new ex-	112	50	104
periences and opportunities. Major career direction may be properly	126	52	107
determined only after the entire map has been analyzed.	137	55	109

gwam 1′ | 1 | 2 | 3 | 4 | 5 | 6 | 7 | 8 | 9 | 10 | 11 | 12 | 13 | 14 |
5′ | 1 | 2 | 3 |

65c ▶ 35

Production measurement: business letters

Time schedule

Assembling materials .... 3′
Timed production .... 25′
Final check; compute
n-pram .... 7′

1. Follow time schedule shown at the left.
2. Arrange letterheads and envelopes [LM pp. 117–122], and supplies for easy handling.
3. Correct errors neatly as you type.
4. Address envelopes.
5. When directed to begin, type for 25′ from the problems below. If you complete the problems in less than 25′, start over on plain paper.
6. Proofread and circle uncorrected errors found in final check.
7. Compute *n-pram* (see p. 110).

words

Problem 1
Letter with subject line and cc notation
block style; open punctuation

October 10, 19-- Mr. David F. Dalbeck Production Manager Tappan Builders, 15
Inc. 7890 Ryerson Avenue Scranton, PA 18509 Dear Mr. Dalbeck Subject: 29
Your Letter Dated October 5, 19-- (¶1) Thank you for your letter asking for 43
information about two products: RES interior spackling compound and RES 58
panel and dry-wall adhesive. I am pleased to describe these products to you. 74
(¶2) RES interior spackling compound is ready-mixed for easy filling of fine- 88
line cracks or deep holes in walls or ceilings. It has a smooth-spreading 103
texture, dries quickly, and sands to a featheredge. It takes paint beautifully; 119
it contains no asbestos. (¶3) RES panel and dry-wall adhesive saves time and 134
work in paneling a room. It reduces the need for nailing and simplifies panel 150
alignment. Moreover, it fastens paneling and wallboard to studding and furring 166
with a tough, water-resistant bond. (¶4) A brochure describing RES products 180
further is enclosed. Both products are fully guaranteed. You can get them at 196
hardware stores and building supply houses just about everywhere. Ask for 211
them by the RES name. Sincerely yours George M. Mirsky Sales Corre- 224
spondent xx Enclosure cc Ms. Carol Jacobsen (178) 233/**253**

Problem 2
Letter with mailing notation, attention line, reply reference notation, cc notation, and postscript
modified block style; block ¶s; mixed punctuation; block reference line

February 23, 19-- REGISTERED Macko & Reynolds 3007 Montevideo Street 14
San Juan, PR 00921 Attention Purchasing Director Dear Sir or Madam: 28
Re: Your Order 56774 (¶1) Today, a second unsuccessful attempt was made to 42
deliver the above-listed order to your address. The goods are currently being 58
held at our warehouse at 2210 Mayaguez Street. (¶2) You may claim them there 72
during regular business hours if you will show your copy of the shipping order 88
to the person in charge. (¶3) We shall hold the goods there for 30 days. After 103
that time, they will be transferred to our warehouse at 79 Munoz Rivera 118
Avenue; and a rental charge will be assessed you for each day thereafter. Yours 134
very truly, Cesar L. Remon, Dispatcher xx cc Miss Marie Rodriguez Before 149
acceptance, please examine the shipment carefully for damages. (100) 161/**181**

Problem 3
Letter with reply reference notation and company name in closing
modified block style; indented ¶s; mixed punctuation; centered reference line

November 12, 19-- Ms. Helen Dewitty 2290 Hooper Street Norfolk, VA 23513 15
Dear Ms. Dewitty: Reference: Your Letter of November 4 (¶1) Thank you 28
for your letter about our repair policy. I am pleased to explain it to you. 44
(¶2) Because of the intricate workmanship involved in the manufacture of our 58
products, all merchandise must be returned to our factory for repair or re- 73
placement. Please place your camera in a sturdy box; wrap it carefully. Send it 89
to us at the above address. (¶3) Any unit which becomes defective within one 104
year from date of purchase is repaired or replaced at no charge to you under the 120
terms of our guarantee. All other repairs are done at nominal charge. (¶4) We 135
appreciate your business and look forward to serving you further. Sincerely 151
yours, WALTON, INCORPORATED Harvey L. Firestone Vice President xx (122) 164/**174**

Typing from edited copy

The ¶ at the right contains many errors commonly made by letter writers. Type the ¶ making the revisions. Note the guides at the left of the ¶ which explain the changes in the copy.

1 Use short word
2 Use more precise word
3 Use short word
4 Be direct
5 Clarify the idea
6 Arrange ideas logically
7 Use more precise word
8 Use parallel construction
9 Everybody . . . they
10 Makes more sense

As an employee of a business ~~organization,~~ firm, (1) you must ~~exude~~ project (2) a vigorous desire to serve. That is ~~fundamental~~ basic (3) to the growth and ~~ready acceptance~~ reputation (4) of your firm. ~~Selling is essential~~ You must practice the art of selling (5) to do this. Selling is not limited to people called salespersons, for everyone working for a firm must be interested in meeting the needs of customers. (6) When everybody sells, ~~you~~ they (9) create a mental and emotional climate of friendliness and goodwill that makes ~~selling~~ buying (10) a joyous, happy adventure. Selling is having a wholesome, friendly ~~feeling~~ attitude (7) toward people and a sincere desire to be helpful--whether you are answering the phone, writing a letter, ~~or~~ working behind the counter, or ringing (8) doorbells.

Statistical-copy skill building

1. Two 1′ *speed* writings on each ¶; determine *gwam*.
2. One 5′ *control* writing on all ¶s combined; determine *gwam*; circle errors.

Difficulty index

all letters used	A	1.5 si	5.7 awl	80% hfw

	gwam 1′	5′	
The Fair Labor Standards Act of 1938 set a minimum wage that cov-	13	3	49
ered most American workers. The Act set a minimum rate of 25 cents	27	5	52
per hour with raises that went to 40 cents per hour by 1945. Subsequent	42	8	55
changes have increased the minimum wage over the past years. In May,	56	11	57
1974, the minimum wage had reached $2.00 per hour and the January, 1981,	70	14	60
rate is set at $3.35 per hour. The 1981 minimum represents an increase	85	17	63
of over 1200 percent of the original minimum of 25 cents per hour. There	99	20	66
have been many arguments stated both pro and con each time increases in	114	23	69
the minimum wage have been suggested.	121	24	70
For example, organized labor fought hard recently for raises in	13	27	73
the minimum wage. At the same time, many opponents were after a lower	27	30	76
wage for teenage workers than for adult workers. This plan would enable	42	33	79
employers to pay persons from 16 to 19 years of age about 15 percent less	56	36	82
than the adult minimum. One reason for making this argument is the fact	71	38	85
that the postwar baby boom has swelled the supply of this age group to	85	41	87
about 9.5 percent of the total labor force. In the middle 1950's, the	99	44	90
labor pool for this age group was about 6.5 percent.	110	46	92

gwam 1′ | 1 | 2 | 3 | 4 | 5 | 6 | 7 | 8 | 9 | 10 | 11 | 12 | 13 | 14 |
5′ | 1 | 2 | 3

section

14

Typing administrative communications

lessons 66–71

Learning goals

1. To improve your basic, proofreading, punctuation, and composing skills.
2. To improve skill in organizing and handling the materials needed for each job.
3. To develop skill in typing administrative communications.
4. To produce usable copy under the pressure of time for an extended period.

Machine adjustments

1. Paper guide at *0*.
2. 70-space line for drills and timed writings.
3. SS drill sentences; DS ¶s and indent 5 spaces; space problems as directed.

66

66a ▶ 5 Preparatory practice

as many times as possible in time available

alphabet	The missile, its jets blazing, flew unswervingly; it exploded quickly.
fig/sym	About 17 2/3 percent of 16,450 persons have read George Orwell's 1984.
direct reach	Brett Drum tried to unlock the gate in front of the deserted bungalow.
fluency	They know that in the long run this project will yield useful results.

| 1 | 2 | 3 | 4 | 5 | 6 | 7 | 8 | 9 | 10 | 11 | 12 | 13 | 14 |

66b ▶ 10 Communication aid

full sheet; leftbound report margins; DS, but SS multiline rules and example sentences.

1. For the heading, use HYPHEN AND DASH.

2. Type each rule and example; compose and type a sentence to illustrate further the rule. Proofread; correct errors.

1. Use a hyphen in compound numbers from twenty-one to ninety-nine.

   Approximately thirty-seven of the forty-eight parents came.
   (Compose and type a sentence illustrating the rule.)

2. Retain the hyphen in a series of compounds with the same ending or beginning; this is called suspended hyphenation.

   All fifth-, sixth-, and seventh-floor rooms are closed.
   (Compose a sentence.)

3. Use the hyphen to join certain prefixes to words; but, when in doubt, check a dictionary.

   The ex-mayor and former vice-principal was self-conscious.
   (Compose a sentence.)

4. Use dashes to set off a clause that is an independent interpretation.

   Our football team--believe it or not--won the championship.
   (Compose a sentence.)

66c ▶ 35 Problem typing: interoffice communications

Problem 1
Two-page interoffice memorandum [LM p. 137]

1" side margins; proofread; circle errors; address COMPANY MAIL envelope

words

TO: Frederick Wood, Branch Manager 6
FROM: Domenica Rodriguez, Vice President 13
DATE: February 15, 19-- 17
SUBJECT: Impact of Privacy Laws on Personal Information 26

TS

Few legislative acts will exert greater influence on your sales proposals 41
to customers than the current and proposed privacy protection laws. 55
Designed to protect management employees, and others, these laws will 69
demand a thorough understanding of controls of the collection, mainte- 83
nance, and dissemination of an increasing variety of personal information. 98
Your understanding will need to include the control of source documents 112
now stored in conventional paper files, as well as the control of com- 126
puterized personal data files. 132

(Continued on the next page)

Technique improvement: keystroking

each line 3 times SS at a controlled rate

v/b Several vibrations became obvious, but seven brave boys never wavered.

m/n Many metropolitan managers meet annually in Milan to nominate members.

t/r Gert, it won't hurt to try a rinse on her hair; just don't try a tint.

c/e Cecil Cecchetti decided to descend to a lower level to check the cell.

| 1 | 2 | 3 | 4 | 5 | 6 | 7 | 8 | 9 | 10 | 11 | 12 | 13 | 14 |

Building/measuring rough-draft skill

1. Two 1' *speed* writings on each ¶; determine *gwam*.
2. One 5' *control* writing on all ¶s combined; determine *gwam*; circle errors.

Difficulty index

all letters used	A	1.5 si	5.7 awl	80% hfw

gwam 1' 5'

Your initial job could be the most valuable one you will ever have 14 3
and how you act and react to it can set you sailing smoothly up the 27 5
career ladders or floundering badly down the road to no where. Poor 40 8
evaluation can hurt you four years afterwar; good marks can make a 55 11
very big difference. But keep also in mind that your job is very 68 14
important for more reasons than job status or material purposes. 81 16
Merely by taking the right appraoch, youcan receive much more. 97 19

For instance firms of all sizes noramaly provide some type of 12 22
training for employees. Regardless of how well equipment you may 26 25
think you are for job, the training offered maybe just what you need 42 28
to smooth the rough edges of your academic back ground. Be alert too 56 31
such opportunities. Finally will you find that the more exposure you 70 33
have to a vast range of people and ideas, then the better you will be 84 36
able to evaluate the company and the job fit in to your career. 99 39

One final suggestoin about your first job: don't be afraid to 12 42
quit it. Because a first job can establish direction and motivation 26 45
to your carere, take corrective action any time you see it veering 40 47
off course. Observe the many signs and realization that let you know 55 50
it's time to exit and organization or to even change career direction. 69 53
The very words--first job--imply it won't be your last one. The trick 83 56
is to know when any job has lost its value and then do some- 95 58
thing about it. 98 59

66c, continued

▶ Second-page headings for memos are the same as second-page headings for letters (see p. 131). Use the block style heading for this memo.

Problem 2
Composing a memo

1. Compose for Frederick Wood a brief answer on a half-sheet memo [LM p. 139] to the memo in Problem 1.

2. Include a statement of appreciation for the information and request 10 additional copies of the brochure.

3. Use February 20, 19— for the date; devise your own subject line.

4. Address a COMPANY MAIL envelope; correct errors.

This memorandum is being sent to you with the hope that it will help you to 148
understand the three basic objectives of privacy laws. Moreover, I shall 162
point out how our System 900 equipment can provide the controls needed 177
to satisfy these basic objectives. The three basic objectives are as fol- 191
lows: (1) ready access to information; (2) protection against unauthorized 207
access; and (3) availability of accurate, up-to-date information. 220

TS

<u>1. Ready Access to Information</u> 232

DS

Under privacy protection statutes, our users will be required to provide 246
individuals having a need or right to personal information with ready 260
access to these records. Our users will also be required to furnish author- 275
ized individuals with a copy of pertinent information for their reference 290
and use. 292

Our System 900 can help satisfy both of these requirements by permitting 306
ready access to individual records as well as providing suitable file copies 322
without undue expense or effort on the user's part. 332

<u>2. Protection Against Unauthorized Access</u> 348

Privacy laws will also require record holders to safeguard source docu- 362
ments against privacy invasions, thus assuring complete security and 376
confidentiality. 379

Our System 900 can fulfill this requirement with built-in storage and re- 394
ferral controls that make it a highly effective, yet completely practical, 409
security screen. All records related to an individual file are recorded on a 425
master file film which never leaves the central file. Only authorized data 440
from an individual file may be made available--not the entire file. 453

<u>3. Availability of Accurate, Up-To-Date Information</u> 474

A further requirement of privacy laws will encompass the continuous 487
need to control the quality of information subject to referral by authorized 503
individuals. This means the maintenance of accurate, up-to-date records 517
which can be readily amended or voided for compliance with legal re- 531
quirements. 533

Our System 900 can be completely and quickly updated. It is already 547
being used to maintain up-to-date records in both public and private sec- 561
tors. To date, over 20 million records have been imaged and stored on 576
System 900 file film. 580

I am enclosing a brochure, <u>Management of Personal Information Records,</u> 603
that you may find helpful in promoting our System 900. Write for 616
additional copies if you want them. 623

xx 623

Enclosure 625

Script-copy skill building

1. Type two 2′ writings on the exploration level. Determine *gwam* and circle errors. Record the higher *gwam*.

2. Type two 2′ writings on the control level. Determine *gwam* and circle errors. Record the *gwam* for the writing with the fewer errors.

Exploration level: Try for a few more words a minute with each writing. Temporarily ignore errors.

Control level: When the purpose of your typing is to type with ease and control, drop back in rate and type on the *control level*.

Difficulty index

all letters used	A	1.5 si	5.7 awl	80% hfw

gwam 2′

Your ability to reason and your capacity to solve problems 6
are closely related to the quantity of words you know. Most 12
experts say, however, that just memorizing new words will 18
do little to add to your mental stature. If word knowledge 24
is retained, a large vocabulary will make it possible for 31
you to understand and assimilate more. Keep in mind, 36
though, that a person is not smart because of a huge 41
vocabulary. It is the other way around. 45

Script-copy skill inventory

two 5′ writings; determine *gwam*; proofread and circle errors

Difficulty index

all letters used	A	1.5 si	5.7 awl	80% hfw

gwam 1′ | 5′

To match the different ways in which typing errors are made, 12 | 2
a number of ways have been invented to correct them. While the 25 | 5
equation may be weak, the idea makes some sense. The old- 37 | 7
fashioned eraser is still available. With it, you can get rid 49 | 10
of an error by using the eraser to rub it off. Complete directions 63 | 13
for doing this are given in the reference section. 73 | 15

More modern methods are also available. When correction 11 | 17
paper or cards are used, you merely position the paper or 23 | 19
card behind the ribbon and type the same error. The error is 35 | 22
covered with a powder-like substance, and correct copy can 47 | 24
be entered. When opaquing fluid is used, you paint over 59 | 26
the error. In addition, a machine is available that literally 71 | 29
lifts the error off the paper just by operating a special 83 | 31
key and restriking the error. 89 | 32

Typewriting errors are as sure as death and taxes. 10 | 34
Fortunately, errors can be corrected; and you should take 22 | 37
the time needed to become proficient in using the 32 | 39
method that has been adopted to correct them. The clean, 44 | 41
clear appearance of a letter is a prize worth the effort. 55 | 43

67

67a ▶ 5
Preparatory practice
as many times as possible in time available

alphabet	This capital, Byzantium, was subjected to six very frightening quakes.
fig/sym	This year our profits may reach $9,461.05; last year they were $8,723.
3d row	Our pitcher, Marilyn, threw three powerful pitches and won the series.
fluency	No one, however, believes that we need to leave the outcome to chance.

| 1 | 2 | 3 | 4 | 5 | 6 | 7 | 8 | 9 | 10 | 11 | 12 | 13 | 14 |

67b ▶ 45
Problem typing

Problem 1
Minutes of meeting

1½" top margin; 1" side margins; SS; 5-space ¶ indentions

Indent list of members and resolutions 10 spaces from both margins.

words

MINUTES OF THE MEETING 5
OF THE BOARD OF DIRECTORS 10
DS
June 15, 19-- 13
TS

A regular meeting of the Board of Directors of Freedom Oil Company was 27
held in the Conference Room of the Corporation, 10783 Wilshire Blvd., Los 42
Angeles, on June 15, 19--, at 10 a.m. All members of the Board were present: 57
DS

Virginia C. Ford	Maxine A. Jacobs	64
Alice L. Garakian	Wesley T. La Belle	72
Harold Garfinkel	Marie Ann Saenz	78
Fred A. Gehringer	James L. Wilkins	85
E. Bruce Holcomb	Catherine Z. Young	92

DS

Mr. Harold Garfinkel, President of the Corporation, chaired the meeting, 107
and Miss Catherine Z. Young, Secretary, was recording secretary. 120

The minutes of the regular meeting of the Directors held on May 12, 19--, 135
were distributed and approved. 141

Mr. Garfinkel stated that a resolution concerning the dividend for the 156
third quarter of the fiscal year would be considered. On motion duly made, 171
seconded, and unanimously approved, the following resolution was adopted: 186
DS

RESOLVED, that the regular quarterly dividend of 25 196
cents per share on the common stock of this Corporation 207
be and it is hereby declared payable on the 15th day of 218
September, 19--, to stockholders of record at the close of 230
business on the 15th day of August, 19--. 239
DS

The reports about relocating administrative offices and the Aliso Project 254
were discussed, with action delayed until further information could be made 267
available. 271

Discussion of the proposal to submit a resolution to amend the Stock 285
Option Plan for corporate stockholders was postponed at the suggestion of Ms. 301
Jacobs. 302

There being no further business, the meeting was adjourned at 2 p.m. 316
DS

Respectfully submitted 321

3 blank line spaces

Secretary 323

Supplemental skill-building practice

Technique improvement: keystroking

each line 3 times SS (slowly, top speed, in-between rate)

direct reaches	1 Cecil Briggs unlocked the door of the cellar under the deserted house.
1st/2d fingers	2 Gary Fredericks informed them they might apply for the jobs on Monday.
3d/4th fingers	3 As Alex Azer pointed out in his paper, the essay quiz was quite short.
long reaches	4 I may prepare a summary of my lumber, linoleum, and plywood purchases.
1st row	5 My main economic concern is to maximize my move to the branch at once.
3d row	6 Polly Ritter may support you and your witty programs for saving trees.
home row	7 Sal had a salad; Dallas had hash. Ask Dad if Hal Lash had a sad saga.
double letters	8 A well written, attractive letter will need good grammar and spelling.
hyphen	9 They found this to be an up-to-date plan for out-of-town credit sales.
fluency	10 Any one of the six guides should be able to do a very good job for us.

| 1 | 2 | 3 | 4 | 5 | 6 | 7 | 8 | 9 | 10 | 11 | 12 | 13 | 14 |

Straight-copy skill building

1. Two 1′ *speed* writings on each ¶; determine *gwam*.
2. One 5′ *control* writing on all ¶s combined; determine *gwam*; circle errors.

Difficulty index

all letters used | A | 1.5 si | 5.7 awl | 80% hfw |

	gwam 1′	5′	
An enduring problem of management relates to workers who do not come	14	3	62
to work or who come to work late. Employers readily agree that fewer	28	6	64
and fewer people are taking pride in their attendance or on-time records.	43	9	67
And, as a result, problems of absenteeism and lateness are becoming more	57	11	70
and more serious. In the meantime, the company pays the price in loss	72	14	73
of efficiency, loss of sales, or loss of customer faith. In essence,	86	17	76
the absence of an employee costs the company in one way or another.	99	20	79
In addition to costing money, too much absenteeism or tardiness may	14	23	81
cause a credibility gap between labor and management. This may hurt a	28	25	84
worker's future chances, since those who are not dependable are seldom	42	28	87
promoted. Records that reflect heavy absenteeism and tardiness are kept	56	31	90
on file and may be sent to other firms upon request. You must realize	71	34	93
the record you are now building, both at school and at work, may either	85	37	96
help you or hurt you when you decide to seek a new line of work.	98	39	98
A solid record shows you have an interest in your job and the goals	14	42	101
of your company. It tells others that you are a motivated worker rather	28	45	104
than a reluctant one. In addition, it reveals a positive attitude about	43	48	107
your work and the way you do it. Build a good attendance record, and	57	51	110
you'll build a good reputation. Take pride in being a dependable worker,	71	54	112
and you'll build excellent rapport with co-workers and employers alike.	86	57	115
Put it all together, and you'll be a much happier person.	97	59	118

gwam 1′ | 1 | 2 | 3 | 4 | 5 | 6 | 7 | 8 | 9 | 10 | 11 | 12 | 13 | 14 |
5′ | 1 | 2 | 3 |

67b, continued

Problem 2
Letter on executive-size stationery (7¼″ × 10½″) [LM p. 141]

modified block; indented ¶s; mixed punctuation; 1″ side margins; date on Line 16; address large envelope

▶ When typing letters on stationery narrower than the standard 8½″ × 11″ paper, use 1″ or ¾″ side margins, depending on length of the letter. The date placement may vary from Line 10 to Line 16.

words

March 10, 19-- | Dr. William F. Stacy | 27 7
Goodland Park Road | Madison, WI 53711 | 15
Dear Dr. Stacy: (¶1) The annual John Adams 23
Award Breakfast will be held Saturday, 31
April 3, 19--, in the Garden Room of the 39
Hilton Hotel, from 7:30 to 9:15 a.m. You are 48
cordially invited to attend. (¶2) We are 55
eagerly anticipating your joining us this 64
year for breakfast and a brief period of 72
social and professional fellowship. Please 81
let us know that you will attend. Sin- 87
cerely yours, | Ms. Mary Helen Dublin | 96
Coordinator, Special Events | xx 102/**114**

Problem 3
Executive-size letter from rough-draft copy
[LM p. 143]

block; open punctuation; 1″ side margins; date on Line 16; address envelope

words

January 20~~th~~, 19-- (9) 3

← 3 blank line spaces here

Mr. ⓐ Mrs. Normen Shelton, (and; o; delete comma) 9
2893 Aguilar (wy.) Way 12
Los Angeles, (C.A.) CA 90065 17

Dear Mr. and Mrs. Shelton 22

[ ] Thanks, you most sincerely for your purchase of a new 32
Deluxe 400 television set. We were pleased to serve 43
you. We hope your set is bringing you many hours of 54
happy ~~pleasure.~~ entertainment. 58

DS → We appreciate your ~~patronage~~ business and pleged our continuing 69
efforts to please you. Your satisfaction with us and 80
with your Deluxe remains our constant goal. 89

We hope ~~hope~~ to ~~gain~~ merit your exprrssion of confidance in 99

SS → us. You can count (our/on) continuing effort s to main- 109
tain that confidence in the ~~days to come.~~ future. 117

Sincerely yours, (9) 120
DS → SCOLET-SERRANO TELEVISION CO. (T) 126

3 blank line spaces

Richard L. Scolett, Sales Manager 133

xx 133/**146**

Problem 4
Composing a letter
[LM p. 145]

plain executive-size paper; modified block; block ¶s; open punctuation; address envelope

Compose for Dr. Stacy a friendly, dignified acceptance to the letter in Problem 1 above from Ms. Dublin. Use March 15, 19— for the date.

Address the letter to:
Ms. Mary Helen Dublin
Coordinator, Special Events
Arnold Publications, Inc.
444 Belmont Avenue
Waterbury, CT 06708

81b, continued

Problem 3

full sheet; center vertically in reading position; DS body; 14 spaces between Columns 1 and 2; 6 spaces between Columns 2 and 3; insert rulings

words

COMPARISON OF ADVERTISING COST TO SALES 8

(Cost and Sales in 000) 13

Company	Costs	Sales	words
			35
			39
			51
Procter & Gamble	$445,000	$ 5,300,000	58
General Motors	287,000	47,181,000	65
General Food	275,000	3,641,600	71
Sears, Roebuck	245,000	12,535,000	78
Warner-Lambert	199,000	1,300,000	85
Bristol-Myers	189,000	1,986,370	91
Ford Motor	162,000	28,839,661	97
			108

Source: The World Almanac and Book of Facts 1978. 126

Problem 4

full sheet; exact center; DS body; determine spacing between columns

Review Drill 2 of 76b, page 155, before typing this table with exceptionally long lines.

words

ALL-TIME TOP TELEVISION PROGRAMS 7

(A. C. Nielsen Estimates of TV Households Tuned) 16

Program	Date	Percent	words
			25
Roots	January 30, 1977	51.1	30
Gone With the Wind,			34
Part 1	November 7, 1976	47.7	40
Gone With the Wind,			44
Part 2	November 8, 1976	47.4	50
Bob Hope			52
Christmas Show	January 15, 1970	46.6	59
Roots	January 28, 1977	45.9	65
The Fugitive	August 29, 1967	45.9	72
Roots	January 27, 1977	45.7	77
Bob Hope			79
Christmas Show	January 14, 1971	45.0	86
Roots	January 25, 1977	44.8	92
Ed Sullivan	February 9, 1964	44.6	97

68

68a ▶ 5 Preparatory practice

as many times as possible in time available

alphabet Woodrow may quiz eighty executives on kickbacks from false job prices.

figure On January 23, we moved from 56994 More Street to 7801 Johnson Avenue.

one-hand As Wade Carver asserted, Johnny was regarded as carefree and careless.

fluency Except for what is marked, they will be glad to accept their shipment.

| 1 | 2 | 3 | 4 | 5 | 6 | 7 | 8 | 9 | 10 | 11 | 12 | 13 | 14 |

68b ▶ 10 Proofreading: reading for meaning

1. Read the ¶; select meaningful words from the list at the left of the ¶ to fill in blank spaces.
2. Type the ¶ using appropriate words.
3. Mark your errors as your teacher reads the corrected ¶.

away
bearing
become
conscious
effort
English
express
habit
passive
precise
social
standard
status
television
valuable
write

Your use of correct _____, good grammar, and _____ word choice must _____automatic to be really useful. When it becomes a _____, this skill becomes a _____ business and social asset. It has a _____ on your _____ of living, your _____ in your occupation, and your _____ position. Your ability to speak and _____ well will improve as you listen, read, and _____ yourself. It can never be a _____ experience. You must make a _____, determined _____ to improve. So tear yourself _____ from _____ long enough to talk and write.

68c ▶ 15 Report on using the apostrophe

plain paper; 2″ top margin; 1″ side margins; DS, but SS multiline rules and example sentences

1. Use APOSTROPHE for the heading.
2. Type each rule and example; compose and type a second sentence to illustrate further the rule.
3. Proofread; correct errors.

1. To show possession, add the apostrophe and s to (a) a singular noun and (b) a plural noun which does not end in s.

   My employer's company will finance the children's trips.
   (Compose a sentence.)

2. To show possession, add only the apostrophe to plural nouns ending in s.

   The girls' rings and the officers' pins will be shipped soon.
   (Compose a sentence.)

3. To show possession, add the apostrophe and s after a proper name of one syllable which ends in s.

   Please reserve a room in the dormitory for the Grams's son.
   (Compose a sentence.)

4. To show possession, add only the apostrophe after a proper name of more than one syllable which ends in s or z.

   Mrs. Williams' niece got a ride in Mrs. Cortez' car.
   (Compose a sentence.)

5. When common possession is to be shown for two or more persons, add the apostrophe after the last name only. Separate possession is indicated by adding the possessive to each name.

   Sue and Fern's mother is here; Jan's and Pat's mothers left.
   (Compose a sentence.)

81

Preparatory practice

each line 3 times SS; DS between 3-line groups; retype selected lines as time permits

alphabet	Their experienced quarterback froze just viewing the enemy game films.
fig/sym	Send Check #479 for $522 ($580 less 10%) to 606 Ocean Drive by May 30.
direct reaches	Denny Brand hunted the zebra near the edge of the muddy, humid jungle.
fluency	The problem is with that firm, so she may sue to enrich the endowment.

| 1 | 2 | 3 | 4 | 5 | 6 | 7 | 8 | 9 | 10 | 11 | 12 | 13 | 14 |

81b ▶45 Production measurement: tables

Time schedule

Assembling materials .... 5′
Timed production .... 30′
Final check; compute *n*–pram .... 10′

Problem 1

half sheet, short side up; center vertically in reading position; DS body; 10 spaces between columns

SELECTED FAMOUS LEFT-HANDED PEOPLE		words
		7
Jimmy Connors	tennis player	13
Gerald Ford	former president	18
Judy Garland	actress and singer	25
Michelangelo	artist	29
Paul McCartney	composer and singer	36
Harry S. Truman	former president	42
______________		46
Source: The Book of Lists.		55

Problem 2

full sheet; center vertically in reading position; determine spacing between columns; DS body

PERSONAL STOCKHOLDINGS (5)
(Values at Close of Market May 5, 19--) (13)

Stock	Initial Cost	Current Value	words
			25
			29
			32
			45
Control Data	$ 8,900.17	$10,467.50	52
Delta Airlines	5,264.00	4,309.90	58
International Business Machines	6,322.75	12,839.40	69
Libbey-Owens Ford	857.60	938.62	75
Pennzoil	1,003.66	862.09	80
St. Regis Paper	2,305.22	3,476.08	87
			100
Totals	$24,653.40	$32,893.59	105

Problem 3 is on page 164.

68d ▶ 20
Problem typing

Problem 1
Telegraphic message

Type the message on a plain sheet; 2" top margin; 60-space line; DS message; proofread and correct errors.

words

PHONED TELEGRAM 3

TS

Telegram 5

DS

November 19, 19--, 10:15 a.m. 11

DS

Miss Diana Herrick, Manager 17
Home Industries, Inc. 21
5000 Sherman Avenue 25
Sioux City, IA 51106 29
Phone: (712) 876-2415 34

DS

Can offer you exclusive dealership on Rizzo greenhouses. Ideal 47
for hanging baskets, topiary trees, any plants requiring inside 59
environment. All-aluminum to fit any site and budget. All 71
parts prefit, glass precut. Easy to assemble; easy to maintain. 85
Urge prompt reply. 88

DS

Bruce Limbaugh, Vice President 94
Rizzo Greenhouses, Inc. 99

DS

xx 100

Problem 2
Night letter

Type the same message as a night letter, using the same day and 4:40 p.m. Substitute the words "Night letter" for "Telegram" at the left margin. Send to the following addressee:

Mr. Fred L. Case, Manager
Garden Center
2456 Mullen Road
Omaha, NE 68124
Phone: (402) 321-7889

Problem 3
Postal card

1. Type the message side of a postal card [LM p. 147] (or use paper cut to 5½" × 3½") as illustrated at the right.

2. Type the address and return address as shown at the right.

TS

April 21, 19--

4 spaces TS

Dear Miss Henry

DS

The Executive Committee will meet Tuesday, May 3, at 10 a.m. in the Board Room. Items to be discussed include the following:

DS

1. Employment of management consulting firm
2. Flexible hours for office employees

DS

Please let me know if you can attend.

DS

S. Charles Whitman, Executive Secretary

Problem 4
Composing a postal card response

1. Compose and type a message to Mr. Whitman (Problem 3) [LM p. 147] for Miss Henry. State that she will attend and add two additional items for discussion.

2. Mr. Whitman's address and Miss Henry's return address are found in Problem 3.

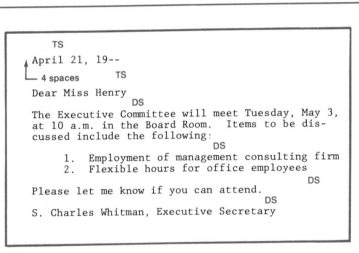

DS

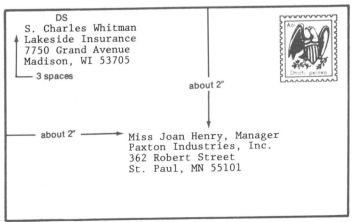

S. Charles Whitman
Lakeside Insurance
7750 Grand Avenue
Madison, WI 53705

3 spaces

about 2"

about 2" →

Miss Joan Henry, Manager
Paxton Industries, Inc.
362 Robert Street
St. Paul, MN 55101

80c ▶35
Problem typing: boxed tables

Problem 1

full sheet; center vertically in reading position; DS body; 8 spaces between columns; insert rulings

line: 18
b.5:30

words

FAIR LABOR STANDARDS ACT 5

(Dates and Sizes of Minimum Wage Increases Since 1967) 16

Date	Wage	Monetary Increase	Cumulative Percentage	words
				41
				45
				51
				63
February, 1967	$1.40	---	0	69
February, 1968	1.60	.20	14	74
May, 1974	2.00	.40	43	78
January, 1975	2.10	.10	50	84
January, 1976	2.30	.20	64	89
January, 1978	2.65	.35	89	94
January, 1979	2.90	.25	107	99
January, 1980	3.10	.20	121	105
January, 1981	3.35	.25	139	110
				122

Problem 2

full sheet, reading position; DS body; 6 spaces between columns; insert rulings

line 19
b.5.31

words

DEPRECIATION SCHEDULE 4

(Sum-of-the-Years'-Digits Method) 11

Year	Depreciation Expense	Accumulated Depreciation	Book Value	words
				32
				38
				45
				55
at acquisition	$ ---	$ ---	$42,000	62
1	12,000	12,000	30,000	67
2	10,000	22,000	20,000	72
3	8,000	30,000	12,000	76
4	6,000	36,000	6,000	80
5	4,000	40,000	2,000	84
6	2,000	42,000	---	88
				99
	$42,000			100
				111

69

69a ▶ 5
Preparatory practice
as many times as possible in time available

alphabet	Zeke Weber likes the piquancy of orange juice mixed with clover honey.
figure	During May, they sold 390 radios, 157 clocks, 48 tripods, and 26 pens.
direct reaches	My uncle, Jimmy Bricklin, mumbled sadly, "My TV must be broken again."
fluency	In addition, cartoons for today's edition are packed in those cartons.
	| 1 | 2 | 3 | 4 | 5 | 6 | 7 | 8 | 9 | 10 | 11 | 12 | 13 | 14 |

69b ▶ 10
Typing from edited copy

The ¶s at the right contain many errors commonly made by letter writers. Type the ¶s making the revisions. Note the guides at the left of the ¶s which explain the changes in the copy.

1 Unnecessary
2 Descriptive adjective needed
3 Use short word
4 Use of personal pronoun more effective
5 Be concise
6 Use right word
7 Redundant
8 Use short word
9 Be concise
10 Use of personal pronoun more effective
11 Be concise
12 Avoid split infinitive
13 Redundant
14 Use short word
15 Unnecessary
16 Write as you talk

(1) ~~Have you ever asked if~~ energy shortages are becoming a way of life? leaky (2) Gas lines, brownouts, curtailed power supplies--the warnings continue to grow. (3) ~~multiply.~~ We (4) ~~Our country~~ must realize (5) ~~face the fact~~ that our energy problem (6) ~~situation~~ is today's, not tomorrow's. Tough realistic (7) ~~and firm~~ decisions are needed (8) ~~a requirement.~~ Now! (9) ~~There is no better time than now.~~

We (10) ~~Our people~~ must be determined (11) ~~make a determination~~ to (12) fully develop every feasible energy source--whether it is nuclear, hydroelectric, (13) ~~water power,~~ solar or geothermal energy or coal, natural gas, or wind. We need them all, and we must use them wisely. (14) ~~prudently.~~ Despite our best efforts, (15) ~~along these lines,~~ we may still face an energy gap for two or more decades.

Energy shortages don't (16) ~~do not~~ have to be a way of life. We have the know-how and the resources to prevent them.

69c ▶ 20
Problem typing

Agenda for meeting

1. Type on a full sheet the Agenda for Meeting on page 141; center vertically and horizontally.

2. Use spaced leaders between columns.

3. Correct errors as you type.

Typing leaders: After the first item in a column, alternate a space and a period to a point 2 or 3 spaces short of the next column. Note whether you type the periods on odd or even line-of-writing scale numbers; align subsequent rows by starting them in like manner; end all rows at the same point.

79c, continued

Problem 2
Table with horizontal rulings

half sheet; center vertically; SS body; 6 spaces between columns; insert rulings

				words
TIME INTERVAL FOR PRODUCT PRODUCTION				7
(Years Between Conception and Realization)				16
				43
Product Classification	Conception	Realization	Years	53
				67
Heart pacemaker	1928	1960	32	72
Helicopter	1904	1941	37	77
Nylon	1927	1939	12	81
Photography	1782	1838	56	86
Radar	1904	1939	35	90
Videotape recorder	1950	1956	6	96
Zipper	1883	1913	30	100
				113
Source: New York Times, June 18, 1976.				125

80

80a ▶5
Preparatory practice

each line 3 times SS; DS between 3-line groups; retype selected lines as time permits

alphabet Jack explained some very tough questions about the bizarre town forum.

fig/sym Our Check #952 for $1,840.86, covering your Invoice #307, is enclosed.

adjacent keys I was positive a new revision of the entire report was here last week.

fluency The lame-duck panel may wish to signal an end to the work of the body.

| 1 | 2 | 3 | 4 | 5 | 6 | 7 | 8 | 9 | 10 | 11 | 12 | 13 | 14 |

80b ▶10
Preapplication drill: boxed tables

half sheet; 1½" top margin; DS; 8 spaces between columns; center and type the drill as directed below

Drill

Type the table in the normal way, including horizontal rules.

To insert vertical rules, remove the page and, using a ball-point pen (preferably black ink), draw vertical lines at the midpoint between columns.

POSSIBLE SOURCES OF TAX REVENUES

(Current Estimates)

Revenue Source	1980	1985
City Income Tax	$11,580,900	$13,850,736
Retail Sales Tax	17,433,240	22,469,981

69c, continued

FREEDOM OIL COMPANY 9
DS
Agenda for Meeting of the Board of Directors 22
DS
June 15, 19--
October 14, 1981 8
TS

1.	Call to Order	Harold Garfinkel
		DS
2.	Reading and Approval of Minutes	E. Bruce Holcomb
3.	Reports of Officers	
	President	Harold Garfinkel
	Vice President, Production	Alice L. Garakian
	Vice President, Finance	Marie Ann Saenz
	Vice President, Research	Wesley T. La Belle
4.	Report of Special Committees	
	Report on Relocating Administrative Offices	Fred A. Gehringer
	Report on Aliso Project	Virginia C. Ford
5.	Dividend Declaration	
6.	New Business	
	Presentation of Resolution to Amend Stock Option Plan	Maxine A. Jacobs
7.	Adjournment	

69d ▶ 15

Report on using the apostrophe

plain paper; 2″ top margin; 1″ side margins; DS, but SS multiline rules and example sentences

1. Use APOSTROPHE for the heading.

2. Type each rule and example; compose and type a second sentence to illustrate the rule further.

1. The possessive of initials, abbreviations, etc., is formed with apostrophe and s.

   Donald Wright, Jr.'s signature must appear on these checks.
   (Compose a sentence.)

2. It is better not to use the possessive form for inanimate objects; but business sanctions the possessive with day, month, year, etc.

   Eight years' work was wasted on the design of the airplane.
   (Compose a sentence.)

3. Use the apostrophe to indicate the omission of letters or figures.

   The '73 class portraits didn't arrive in today's mail.
   (Compose a sentence.)

4. Do not use an apostrophe with a possessive noun if a preposition follows it.

   Mary had five years of experience as manager of the studio.
   (Compose a sentence.)

79

79a ▶5 Preparatory practice

each line 3 times SS; DS between 3-line groups; retype selected lines as time permits

alphabet	Five executive managers jointly analyzed the proposed equal work bill.
fig/sym	Policy #52-806 is due April 19; the premium is $347.70, or 29% higher.
3d/4th fingers	Lana was looking at the six women who were walking past the west wall.
fluency	They may provoke big problems if both of them fight for the amendment.

| 1 | 2 | 3 | 4 | 5 | 6 | 7 | 8 | 9 | 10 | 11 | 12 | 13 | 14 |

79b ▶10 Preapplication drill: single and double rulings

half sheet; 1" top margin; 10 blank lines between Drill 1 and Drill 2; type according to instructions given at the right; 10 spaces between columns

Drill 1

DS after the centered heading; determine placement of the columns; set both left and right margin stops; type the first of the double rulings; then operate the variable line spacer and move the cylinder forward slightly; type the second ruling.

Drill 2

Type the last items in the columns; SS and type a single ruling. DS and type the footnote.

EMPLOYEE ROSTER

DS

═══════════════════════════

DS

Employee	Date Employed

SS

───────────────────────────

DS

Art Lake	June 17, 1980
Joan Lee*	April 3, 1967

SS

───────────────────────────

DS

*Includes military service time.

79c ▶35 Problem typing: tables

Problem 1
Table with horizontal rulings

full sheet; exact center; DS body; 6 spaces between columns; insert rulings

			words
RECENT PAST PRESIDENTS			5
(National Association of Business Teacher Education)			15
═══			43
Name	**Year**	**School**	47
───			61
T. James Crawford	1969-71	Indiana University	70
		Bloomington, IN 47401	74
Lawrence W. Erickson	1971-73	University of California	85
		Los Angeles, CA 90024	89
Z. S. Dickerson, Jr.	1973-75	Madison College	98
		Harrisonburg, VA 22801	103
Mearl R. Guthrie	1975-77	Bowling Green State University	114
		Bowling Green, OH 43403	119
Harry H. Jasinski	1977-79	Northern State College	129
		Aberdeen, SD 57401	132
Thomas E. Langford	1979-81	University of Rhode Island	143
		Kingston, RI 02881	147
───			161

70

70a ▶ 5
Preparatory practice
as many times as possible in time available

alphabet	They have excused a man who plagiarized quotes from books or journals.
fig/sym	Dotson & O'Dell's 7% discount ($27.50) reduced our 1980 total to $436.
double letters	Miss Poole, from Tallahassee, will see Tennessee and Mississippi soon.
fluency	If they have some time sometime this week, we can discuss their plans.

| 1 | 2 | 3 | 4 | 5 | 6 | 7 | 8 | 9 | 10 | 11 | 12 | 13 | 14 |

70b ▶ 10
Report on using the apostrophe
plain paper; 2" top margin; 1" side margins; DS, but SS multiline rules and example sentences

1. For the heading, use APOSTROPHE.

2. Type each rule and example; compose and type a second sentence to illustrate further the rule.

1. Company and organization names sometimes omit the apostrophe.

   She walked from Wilson's Shoe Store to Citizens State Bank.
   (Compose a sentence.)

2. Use the apostrophe and s to form the plural of most figures, letters, and words. Market quotations need only the s.

   His 3's look like 8's, and he has too many and's in the report.

   Alabama Power Company First Mortgage 8s are due in 1999.
   (Compose a sentence.)

3. Use 'd to form the past participle of coined words.

   She X'd out the last line; then she OK'd the cable.
   (Compose a sentence.)

4. Possessive pronouns do not take an apostrophe. (It's is the contraction of it is and thus requires an apostrophe.)

   The book is theirs. Its cover is torn, so wrap it with care.
   (Compose a sentence.)

70c ▶ 35
Problem typing
Problem 1
Itinerary

1. Type the itinerary (travel schedule) given at the right; full sheet; center horizontally and vertically; DS; 4 spaces between columns.

2. Make any necessary corrections as you type.

Problems 2 and 3 are on the next page.

ITINERARY FOR HAROLD GARFINKEL

August 16 to August 25

Date	From	Time	Flight	To	Arrive	Hotel
8/15	Los Angeles	9:30a	AA/184*	Chicago	3:16p	Ascot
8/17	Chicago	11:00a	AA/426	Cincinnati	12:20p	Hilton
8/19	Cincinnati	2:20p	DL/565	New Orleans	3:40p	Brent
8/22	New Orleans	9:27a	EA/907*	Mexico City	10:30a	Aristos
8/25	Mexico City	10:05a	MX/900**	Los Angeles	12:25p	

*Breakfast flight
**Luncheon flight

78c ▶ 30

Problem typing: tables

Problem 1
3-column table

half sheet, long side up; SS data; center vertically; 8 spaces between columns

			words
HIGHEST ALTITUDES IN SELECTED STATES			7
(Elevations are in Feet)			12
State	Name	Height	20
Alabama	Cheaha Mountain	2,407	26
Idaho	Borah Peak	12,662	31
Kansas	Mount Sunflower	4,039	36
Ohio	Campbell Hill	1,550	41
Rhode Island	Jerimoth Hill	812	48
SS			
______________			52
DS			
Source: Geological Survey, U.S. Department of			61
the Interior.			64

Problem 2
4-column table

full sheet; DS data and between footnotes; center in reading position; 4 spaces between columns

				words
Introduction to Business				5
(Grade reports For First Semesters)				12
Student Name	Participaiton	Exam Averages	Final Grade	14 / 29
Regina Bacon	averege	80	B	34
Chang, Lucy	below average	74	C	40
Jacobs, Ben	excellent	93	A	46
King, Laurel	poor	70	D	51 / 58 / 62
Hill, Henry	very poor	62*	F	
Lucas, Kraen	poor	65	D	67
Sissenwien, Roberta	above average	87	B	74
Zabik, Donald	poor	69	I**	79
Hartley, Williams	excellent	97	A	

____

*First examination is missing. 83

**Project Two has not been completed. 89 97

70c, continued

Problem 2
Letter on half-size stationery [LM p. 147]

block; open punctuation; ¾″ side margins; date on line 10; address envelope

▶ Half-size stationery (5½″ × 8½″) is suitable for short letters (130 words or fewer). Margins of 1″ or ¾″ are used; date placement may vary from Line 8 to 10.

words

June 20, 19-- Ms. Diane Bayliss 1410 Beckwith Avenue Los Angeles, CA 14
90049 Dear Ms. Bayliss (¶ 1) On behalf of its employees, officers, and Board of 28
Directors, I am happy to inform you of this Company's decision to donate the 44
amount of $5,000 toward the development of playground and park facilities in 59
the Brentwood area. (¶ 2) As a corporate resident of this city, we welcome this 74
opportunity to express our interest in and concern for Los Angeles. It is a great 91
city, and we take pride in the small part we have been able to play in its 106
development. (¶ 3) We await your instructions for the delivery of our check. 120
Very truly yours Harold Garfinkel, President xx (112) 129/**141**

Problem 3
Typing a speech from rough draft

The president of Freedom Oil company has made extensive changes in a talk he will deliver to the stockholders. This is the first part of his talk. Because the typed copy of the talk must be easy to read, follow these directions:

- 1½″ top and side margins
- DS the ¶s
- 2 DS between ¶s
- Indent ¶s 5 spaces

I am not going to review our record in great detail. However,

KEY ELEMENTS OF FREEDOM'S PERFORMANCE

do comment on elements led
I want to ~~talk about~~ some of the key ~~things~~ that ~~lead~~
during the past year
to our performance because it was a great year. for us.
(3 blank line spaces between ¶s) dedicated
¶ 3 We are proud of our record and are ~~committed~~ to maintain-
best and
ing Freedom as one of the most profitable companies in the
industry. In this regard,
~~United States.~~ Let me note our current set of financial objec-
of all, shall an of
tives. First, we continue to strife for annual average of 10
intend
per cent growth in earnings. We ~~hope~~ to maintain a prudent
m financial
structure and compare favorably with our copetitors.

the major share of
¶ 2 As in previous years, our budget was spent on finding and
developing
new reserves of crude oil and natural gas. Our North American
exploration and production
spending has more than tripled since 1970. This past year,
60 spending
~~sixty~~ percent of all domestic ~~effort~~ went to exploration and
operations.
development ~~activities.~~ In the United States, we have more
than 10 million producing acres. Last year, we completed 157
o
gross wildcats and 1,456 develpment wells.
acres in nonproducing leaseholds--and about
2 million net

77c, continued

Problem 2
4-column table

full sheet; DS; reading position; decide spaces between columns

Typist note: Place all last names first in Column 1.

Interim Sales Report

(Period ending June 15, 19--)

Salesworker	Department	Sales	Quotas
CONNORS, ROBERT	Clothing	$ 1,825.94	$ 2,500.00
Marc Goldstien	Hardware	3,647.50	3,875.00
Marci Helenski	Sportinggoods	3,250.00	2,596.36
Kathy plaisted	Clothing	1,509.00	1,815.00
Carol Penza	Infants	4,879.75	5,495.50
Mike Tirella	Plumbing/Heating	5,296.73	4,972.50
Willie Lincoln	Furniture	2,804.11	4,650.50
Wally Wrong	Automobiles	3,652.37	3,975.50
TOTALS		$26,900.25	$33,037.00

78

78a ▶5 Preparatory practice

each line 3 times SS; DS between 3-line groups; retype selected lines as time permits

alphabet	Viewed by many as lazy speech, excessive jargon shows lack of quality.
fig/sym	We sold the 16-acre lot in 1980 for $37,250 and realized a 24% profit.
adjacent keys	Several different ideas were proposed before we were really satisfied.
fluency	The pair, the visitor and a dog, also roam the island when they visit.

| 1 | 2 | 3 | 4 | 5 | 6 | 7 | 8 | 9 | 10 | 11 | 12 | 13 | 14 |

78b ▶15 Report on using the hyphen and dash

plain paper; 2″ top margin; 1″ side margins; DS, but SS multiline rules and example sentences

1. Use HYPHEN AND DASH for heading.

2. Type each rule and example; compose and type a second sentence to illustrate further the rule.

3. Proofread; correct errors.

1. Use a hyphen to join compound adjectives preceding a noun.

   The well-known judge served a four-year term.
   (Compose a sentence.)

2. Use a dash to indicate a sudden change in thought.

   The best way--maybe the only way--to have friends is to be one.
   (Compose a sentence.)

3. Use a dash before a summarizing statement.

   He got a job, bought a car, moved--all in one day.
   (Compose a sentence.)

4. Use a dash for emphasis to set off an appositive.

   These topics--profits, taxes, markets--will be discussed.
   (Compose a sentence.)

5. Use a dash for added emphasis or clarity.

   All companies--ours included--must offer this service.
   (Compose a sentence.)

71

71a ▶ 5
Preparatory practice

as many times as possible in time available

alphabet	The exact propinquity of the moving red object was quickly recognized.
fig/sym	Memo 538 says, "Bel & Bel's May 27 order ($1,694.50) is a cash order."
one-hand	In my opinion, the mill weavers should request oil for the extra loom.
fluency	If I am to profit from my work, I must give more than just time to it.

| 1 | 2 | 3 | 4 | 5 | 6 | 7 | 8 | 9 | 10 | 11 | 12 | 13 | 14 |

71b ▶ 10
Straight-copy skill measurement

a 5′ writing on control level; determine *gwam*; circle errors

all letters used

Difficulty index

A	1.5 si	5.7 awl	80% hfw

	gwam 1′	5′	
Almost every person is required to make a number of decisions--	13	3	60
every day. Making decisions is a luxury we can all enjoy. Each day's	27	5	63
activity presents alternatives and comparisons that demand a choice by	41	8	66
us. Such choices are rarely of equal value; that is, in most cases one	55	11	69
choice will lead to better consequences than the other. A wise choice	70	14	71
is based on logic taken from education and experience; and the better	84	17	74
decisions we make, the better judgment we are said to have.	95	19	77
Although our contemporary world surrounds us with a sense of ur-	13	22	79
gency, an important decision ought not to be made in haste. When we	27	24	82
confront such a decision, we need time to deliberate about our alter-	40	27	85
natives, to discriminate between this and that idea, to distinguish the	55	30	87
plausible from the unlikely, and to check carefully all of the facts.	69	33	90
What we store away in our minds becomes our "data bank," to which we	83	36	93
turn for solutions to problems. We can do this--or we can guess.	96	38	96
Other factors can, and should, be part of our deliberations. Each	13	41	98
of us, for instance, needs to develop and to use the personal touch of	28	44	101
beauty, of symmetry, and of compassion; for emotions, as well as logic,	42	47	104
are a vital part of making a decision. But we should avoid the hazard	56	49	107
of looking for absolutes, of believing that we must always decide one	70	52	110
way or another. When we face problems that involve people, a small com-	85	55	113
promise is often a better solution than a large decision.	96	57	115

gwam 1′ | 1 | 2 | 3 | 4 | 5 | 6 | 7 | 8 | 9 | 10 | 11 | 12 | 13 | 14 |
5′ | 1 | 2 | 3 |

71c ▶ 35
Production measurement: administrative communications

Time schedule

Assembling materials	3′
Timed production	25′
Final check; compute *n-pram*	7′

1. Arrange letterheads, envelopes [LM pp. 149–154], and supplies for easy handling.

2. 1 cc; address envelopes.

3. Correct errors neatly as you type.

4. When directed to begin, type for 25′ from the problems given on page 145. If you complete the problems in less than 25′, start over on plain paper.

5. Proofread and circle uncorrected errors found in final check.

6. Compute *n-pram* (see p. 110).

77

77a ▶5
Preparatory practice

each line 3 times SS; DS between 3-line groups; retype selected lines as time permits

alphabet Joey, the quick back, kicked five extra points to win a dazzling game.

fig/sym Your Invoice #5062 for $197.84 is subject to a 3% discount in 10 days.

direct reaches Many large organizations placed special orders for my trade brochures.

fluency This half of the map did provoke a problem for both us and the ensign.

| 1 | 2 | 3 | 4 | 5 | 6 | 7 | 8 | 9 | 10 | 11 | 12 | 13 | 14 |

77b ▶5
Preapplication drill: dollar signs

half sheet, long side up; 2" top margin; DS; center and type the drill according to instructions at the right; 10 spaces between columns

Drill

Type a dollar sign before the first amount in the column and before the total. Type the dollar sign before the first amount aligned 1 space to the left of the longest amount, which might be the total.

Totals are treated as a part of the column, and they are usually separated by a blank line from the last item in the column and indented 5 spaces.

Rental income	$ 5,891.76
Sales income	8,234.90
Interest income	3,076.42
Total	$17,203.08

77c ▶40
Problem typing: tables

Problem 1
4-column table

full sheet; DS; reading position; decide spaces between columns

ALLOCATED VERSUS EXPENDED BUDGET

(Includes Requisitions Through September 31, 19--)

Account	Allocated	Expended	Available	words
				7
				17
Account	Allocated	Expended	Available	31
Automobile	$ 3,000.00	$ 2,459.15	$ 540.85	42
Equipment rental	1,500.00	955.00	545.00	50
Insurance	600.00	600.00	---	56
Office salaries	16,000.00	12,000.00	4,000.00	65
Printing and stationery	800.00	356.92	443.08	74
Rent	18,000.00	13,500.00	4,500.00	82
Telephone	900.00	852.98	47.02	89
Other	500.00	254.67	245.33	101
Indent 5 ——→ Totals	$41,300.00	$30,978.72	$10,321.28	105

71c, continued

Problem 1
Interoffice memo

words

TO: Ms. Aline Bakewell, Office Manager FROM: Mrs. Linda Beattie, Vice Presi- 13
dent DATE: August 17, 19-- SUBJECT: Improving Paper Handling Efficiency 25
(¶ 1) While I was at a meeting of purchasing agents last week, I learned of a 39
company that makes a comprehensive analysis of paper handling operations. 54
The analysis is designed to detect and correct weak links in flow of paper, 69
involving copying, collating, folding, inserting, addressing, and mailing in such 86
areas as sales, accounts receivable, payroll, in-plant printing, shipping, and the 102
mail room--just about any operation dealing with the handling of paperwork. 118
(¶ 2) The survey and analysis are free and can be conducted in our office, at our 133
convenience, by an experienced representative. The name of the company 147
providing this service is the Harrison-Brown Corporation, 7788 Brightwood 162
Avenue, Boston, MA 01604. (¶ 3) Would you please look into this matter and let 177
me know what you think of it. xx 183/**193**

Problem 2
Executive-size letter

modified block; indented ¶s; mixed punctuation

words

October 19, 19-- Mrs. Mabel F. Christie 4789 El Rancho Avenue Santa Ana, CA 15
92708 Dear Mrs. Christie: (¶ 1) We are conducting a survey to evaluate the 29
performance of each of our branch offices. We are asking you to assist us 44
because you either are or recently have been a user of our investment service. 60
(¶ 2) Enclosed is a questionnaire designed to let us know what you like and what 75
you do not like, so we can continue to improve our service. Please take the time 92
to complete the form and return it to me in the envelope provided. All re- 106
sponses will remain confidential. (¶ 3) The purpose of conducting this survey is 122
to give you the kind of investment service you want when you want it. We are 137
counting on your help. If you require additional information or help in complet- 153
ing the survey sheet, please write to me. (¶ 4) Your assistance in conducting the 169
survey will be greatly appreciated. (¶ 5) Thank you. Sincerely, Ms. Gloria R. 184
Vazquez Vice President xx Enclosure 191/**204**

Problem 3
Half-size letter

block; open punctuation

words

February 23, 19-- Miss Bernice Y. Tobias 4142 Paradise Parkway Tacoma, WA 15
98466 Dear Miss Tobias (¶ 1) The retirement party for Ms. Myra Thompson 28
will be held on Tuesday, March 3, at 6:30 p.m. at the Fox and Hounds Restaurant 44
in Seattle. (¶ 2) I am attaching a flyer giving all the details. Let's make this an 60
occasion that Myra will not forget. She has served us well, and we want to show 76
our appreciation. (¶ 3) Let me know that you will be part of this great day! 91
Sincerely Miss Barbara S. Stratton xx Enclosure Please address your reply to 106
my home address: 45789 Caroline Avenue, N. Seattle, WA 98103. 119/**131**

Problem 4

If time permits, retype the letter in Problem 3 using the following address:

Mr. Tony Peveler
9680 Ainsworth Avenue
Tacoma, WA 98444

76c ▶30
Problem typing: tables

Problem 1
3-column table
full sheet; reading position; DS; 12 spaces between Columns 1 and 2, 6 spaces between Columns 2 and 3

▶ Style for metric measurement omits the comma and substitutes a space.

			words
DISTANCES BETWEEN NEW YORK AND SELECTED CITIES			9
(Approximate Air-Line Distances)			16
City	Kilometers	Miles	25
Berlin	6 632	3,979	29
Chicago	1 190	714	32
Honolulu	8 282	4,969	36
London	5 782	3,469	40
Montreal	3 483	2,090	44
Paris	6 060	3,636	48
Rome	7 155	4,293	51
San Francisco	4 287	2,572	57
Warsaw	7 117	4,270	60

Problem 2
full sheet; reading position; DS; 12 spaces between columns

Retype Problem 1 with the changes noted at the right.

Changes:

1. Rearrange cities in order of the greatest distance from New York.
2. Eliminate Column 3.
3. Insert the proper country following each city name in Column 1.
4. Change title of Column 1 to City and Country.

76d ▶ 10
Report on using parentheses

plain paper; 2″ top margin; 1″ side margins: DS, but SS multiline rules and example sentences

1. For the heading, use PARENTHESES.
2. Type each rule and example; compose and type a sentence to illustrate further the rule.
3. Proofread; correct errors.

1. Use parentheses to set off parenthetical or explanatory matter (commas or dashes may also be used).

   Grace (my cousin) is manager of the Pittsburg (Kansas) branch.
   (Compose a sentence.)

2. Use parentheses when an amount expressed in words is followed by the same amount in figures.

   She sold the lot for ten thousand (10,000) dollars.
   (Compose a sentence.)

3. Use parentheses to enclose identifying letters or figures in lists.

   We should work for (1) good form, (2) speed, and (3) control.
   (Compose a sentence.)

4. A punctuation mark is placed inside the closing parenthesis if it applies to the parenthetical material. It follows the closing parenthesis if it punctuates the sentence.

   The price quoted is too high ($17.45). (The price quoted last year was $10.45.)
   (Compose a sentence.)

section

15

Measuring basic/production skills

lessons 72–74

Measurement goals

1. To measure basic skill on straight, rough-draft, and statistical copy.
2. To measure skill and understanding in producing business letters, simplified communication forms, and administrative communications covered in Level 3 lessons.

Machine adjustments

1. Paper guide at *0*.
2. Margins: 70-space line for drills and timed writings; as directed for problems.
3. SS drill sentences; DS ¶s; as directed for problems.

72

72a ▶ 5 Preparatory practice

as many times as possible in the time available

alphabet Alex judged their zither performance quickly, boldly, and very wisely.

fig/sym The blue sedan (Model 950--315 hp) has a BLUE BOOK value of $2,786.40.

long reaches Many young people ate their lunch at Lenny Burgos' cafe in Huntsville.

fluency Four of us wish to work on the panel to amend the ancient city policy.

| 1 | 2 | 3 | 4 | 5 | 6 | 7 | 8 | 9 | 10 | 11 | 12 | 13 | 14 |

72b ▶ 10 Straight-copy skill measurement

a 5′ writing; determine *gwam*; circle errors

all letters used

Difficulty index

A	1.5 si	5.7 awl	80% hfw

	gwam 1′	5′	
Everybody knows the importance of a sound, basic education. We need	14	3	57
to be able to read, write, and figure. Our jobs require these essentials;	29	6	60
unemployment can be directly traced to a lack of this kind of education.	43	9	63
We must be intelligent buyers and users of the goods and services produced	58	12	66
for us if we wish to stretch our earnings to cover our needs. Moreover,	73	15	69
we must be able to conduct ourselves as responsible citizens. In short,	88	18	72
we must be able to do and to think.	95	19	73
The need for knowledge is essential to our form of government, too.	14	22	76
As citizens in a democracy, we must pass judgment on proposals that will	28	25	79
affect us, our families, and our country. Even when we select articles	43	27	82
in a store, we cast an economic vote in a free-enterprise system. When	57	30	85
we express political or economic preferences, we vote; and we must com-	71	33	88
prehend what we are doing. Our form of government can't flourish in	85	36	90
ignorance.	87	36	91
Finally, it might be said that the need for education is essential	13	39	93
to humanity. Knowledge is practical; it works for us. But beyond the	28	42	96
functional side of learning is the fact that the acquisition of knowledge	42	45	99
is an enriching endeavor. Simply to know, to get at truth, can be reward	57	48	102
enough, whether or not the information gained is useful. An active mind	72	51	105
looks for answers; and the time it takes to find them--hours or years--	86	54	108
is usually worth it.	90	54	109

gwam 1′ | 1 | 2 | 3 | 4 | 5 | 6 | 7 | 8 | 9 | 10 | 11 | 12 | 13 | 14 |
5′ | 1 | 2 | 3 |

75d, continued

Problem 2
2-column table
half sheet, long side up; exact vertical center; DS items in columns; 10 spaces between columns

		words
WINDIEST CITIES IN THE UNITED STATES	DS	7
(United States Weather Bureau Statistics)		16
	TS	
	Average	17
City and State	SS Wind Speed (mph)	30
Great Falls, Montana	13.1	35
Oklahoma City, Oklahoma	13.0	41
Boston, Massachusetts	12.9	47
Cheyenne, Wyoming	12.8	51
Wichita, Kansas	12.7	55
Buffalo, New York	12.4	60
Milwaukee, Wisconsin	11.8	65
Des Moines, Iowa	11.2	70

76

76a ▶5
Preparatory practice

each line 3 times SS; DS between 3-line groups; retype selected lines as time permits

alphabet	A jury asked puzzling questions of an expert about his views on music.
fig/sym	Riddley-Lowell's Order A-35245 (shipped 12/18) totals $1,790.66 C.O.D.
adjacent keys	Specific questions were answered shortly after I read her last report.
fluency	The town audit may also signal a dual problem for the firms to handle.

| 1 | 2 | 3 | 4 | 5 | 6 | 7 | 8 | 9 | 10 | 11 | 12 | 13 | 14 |

76b ▶5
Preapplication drill: centering

half sheet, long side up; 1" top margin; DS; type Drill 1 and Drill 2 on same paper with 4 blank lines between them; center according to instructions at the right

Drill 1
For eye appeal and ease of reading, leave a greater number of spaces between the description column and the first figure column than between the figure columns.

Drill 2
If a column consists of 1 or 2 exceptionally long items, break the long item into 2 or more lines and determine which line is the longest in the column. Then use the longest line to position the column in backspacing from center.

Drill 1

Marguerite Devereaux	(10 spaces)	86.4	(6 spaces)	3,098,077
Ira Jacobson		51.2		1,563,094

Drill 2

Pace University		New York, New York	(6 spaces)	1906
Illinois Institute of Technology	(6 spaces)	Chicago, Illinois		1892

72c ▶ 35

Production measurement: business letters

Time schedule

Assembling materials .... 3′
Timed production .... 25′
Final check; compute *n-pram* .... 7′

1. Follow time schedule shown at the left.
2. Arrange letterheads and envelopes [LM pp. 161–166] and supplies for easy handling.
3. Correct errors neatly as you type.
4. Address envelopes.
5. When directed to begin, type for 25′ from the problems below. If you complete the problems in less than 25′, start over on plain paper.
6. Proofread and circle uncorrected errors found in final check.
7. Compute *n-pram* (see p. 110).

Problem 1
Letter with attention line, subject line, company name in closing, and postscript
block style; open punctuation; blocked subject line; date on Line 15

words

May 10, 19-- Ruskin Business Products, Inc. 4478 Bowling Avenue Columbia, 15
SC 29203 Attention Miss Edith Sachs, Purchasing Agent Ladies and Gentlemen 30
Subject: If You Don't Need It, Why Pay for It? (¶ 1) That's the question we 44
asked ourselves when we designed the Eastside copier. The only features we 59
build into an Eastside are the kind you are most likely to need. (¶ 2) For exam- 74
ple: Our copier has manual two-sided copying instead of automatic. You save 90
yourself up to $60 a month. Our copier has manual document feed instead 105
of automatic. You save at least $40 a month. Our copier has reproduction 120
only--same size, no reduction. You save up to $300 a month. (¶ 3) Your monthly 135
bills for copy service will be lower. You will have fewer service calls because 151
there are fewer things to adjust or repair. So if you don't use it, why pay for it? 168
(¶ 4) Look for your Eastside dealer in the Yellow Pages. Call for a free demon- 183
stration. Sincerely yours EASTSIDE BUSINESS MACHINES, INC. Mrs. Ruth 197
McDougall, Sales Manager xx It's what our copier doesn't have that makes 211
it so good. (144) 214/**228**

Problem 2
Letter with mailing notation, reply reference notation, listed enclosures, and cc notation
modified block; block ¶s; open punctuation; block reply reference notation

words

March 15, 19-- SPECIAL DELIVERY Mr. Joseph M. Portola, Architect 90231 14
Mayflower Street San Antonio, TX 78209 Dear Mr. Portola Reference: Your 29
Letter About Clear-View Drawing Aids (¶ 1) Thank you for your letter. I am 43
pleased to describe our drawing aids. At a distance, and sometimes up close, 58
triangles, T squares, rulers, and other technical aids all look the same. This 74
apparent equality is not real. (¶ 2) The next time you buy one of these products, 90
examine it closely. Check the weight or gauge of the material. Is it sturdy, yet 106
flexible? How about the calibrations or printing? Are they laminated so they 122
can't wear off? Those edges--are they precise and smooth? (¶ 3) We wouldn't 137
ask you to do these things if we didn't believe we'd come out on top. Our catalog 153
and price list are enclosed. We'll be pleased to serve you. Yours very truly Ms. 170
Carol La Forge Technical Aids Division xx Enclosures Catalog Price list 185
cc Miss Jennifer Hicks (129) 161/**207**

Problem 3
Letter
modified block; indented ¶s; mixed punctuation

words

April 9, 19-- Mrs. Adelaide Willcox Sales Analyst Empire Manufacturing 14
Co. 1270 Avenue of the Americas New York, NY 10020 Dear Mrs. Willcox: 28
(¶ 1) "To be conscious that you are ignorant of the facts is a great step to 43
knowledge." This simple message was written by Benjamin Disraeli about a 57
hundred years ago. It's as true today as it was then. (¶ 2) A precautionary step 73
in the direction of knowledge for the company planning an international mar- 88
keting strategy is to get in touch with an organization that collects, sifts, and 104
makes available facts on foreign markets. We are such an organization. (¶ 3) 119
We can be helpful to you in supplying the facts needed to draw up a marketing 135
plan. We would be delighted to help. Write or call us for full details. Very truly 152
yours, Miss Carolyn Murgraff Sales Manager xx (121) 161/**182**

75

75a ▶5 Preparatory practice

each line 3 times SS; DS between 3-line groups; retype selected lines as time permits

alphabet	An extra thick and lazy fog just over the bay made a picturesque view.
fig/sym	Order #29308 (dated May 16) comes to $12,741.05 (with a 7% sales tax).
adjacent keys	I certainly remember preparing three short progress reports last week.
fluency	She did audit both the forms and the profit to make the problem right.

| 1 | 2 | 3 | 4 | 5 | 6 | 7 | 8 | 9 | 10 | 11 | 12 | 13 | 14 |

75b ▶5 Preapplication drill: centering

half sheet, long side up; 1" top margin; DS; type Drill 1 and Drill 2 on same paper with 4 blank lines between them; center according to instructions at the right; 8 spaces between columns

Drill 1
Centering columns
Backspace from center of paper once for each 2 letters, figures, or spaces of longest line of each column and then once for each 2 spaces between columns. Set left margin stop at this point. From left margin, space forward once for each character and space in longest line of first column plus each space to be left between first and second columns. Set tab stop at this point. Use this procedure for all columns.

Drill 2
Column headings
From point where column begins, space forward once for each 2 letters, figures, or spaces in longest line (heading or column). This is center point of column. From center of column, backspace once for each 2 letters in heading. Begin to type where backspacing ends.

Drill 1

Clearfield	Pennsylvania
Narragansett	Rhode Island
Syracuse	New York

Drill 2

City	Population
Denver	514,768

75c ▶15 Production typing information

1. Read page 153 noting the main points or ideas.

2. On a full sheet, center on Line 13 the heading:

KEY TERMS

3. Prepare a list of the key terms or words used on page 153, DS; center all terms typed.

75d ▶25 Problem typing: tables

Problem 1
2-column table
half sheet, long side up; exact vertical center; DS body of table; 8 spaces between columns

Problem 2 is on page 155.

		words
EXAMPLES OF JOB TITLE REVISIONS		6
DS		
(To Eliminate Sex and Age-Referent Language)		15
TS		
airline stewardesses	flight attendants	23
businessman	business person	29
congressmen	congressmen and women	36
firemen	fire fighters	40
housewife	homemaker	44
maid	houseworker	47
manpower	human resources	52
salesmen	sales workers	57
usherette	usher	60

73

73a ▶ 5 Preparatory practice

as many times as possible in the time available

alphabet	Zyma Jo expected her boats to be serviceable and equipped for working.
fig/sym	A & D Mine sold 8,764 tons of #10 coal (2,359 tons more than in June).
double letters	A committee will meet soon to discuss the differences between classes.
fluency	The auditor may work with the mayor to amend the city audit procedure.

| 1 | 2 | 3 | 4 | 5 | 6 | 7 | 8 | 9 | 10 | 11 | 12 | 13 | 14 |

73b ▶ 10 Rough-draft skill measurement

a 5′ writing; determine *gwam*; circle errors

Difficulty index

all letters used | A | 1.5 si | 5.7 awl | 80% hfw |

gwam 5′

Computers are now used to de sign air conditioning units 2
for homes. It's like having an uncle in the business who want 5
to do the very best for you for the lest money. The computer 7
calculates exactly what your home needs for efficient cooling. 10
It works with facts--not gesstimates. The computer draws upon a 14
hole range of compative units toput together a stystem that's 17
just just right for you home. You recieve a custom-job wih no 19
unnecessary parts no over size units. The computer informs 22
you what equipment you need; what size ducts, and where should 25
be located; and what insulation should be installed. The com- 28
puter is so intelligent that some hold it has brains. The com- 30
puter can do many things that poeple do. it adds, compares, 33
reads codes, follow directions (a job that many people can not 35
do), and hold facts in it memory to make them as needed. People 39
who do this must have some intelligence. An it be siad that 42
the computer also has intelligence? While the kinship is close, 44
there is important differences. The computer does these jobs 47
following a set of guides. Each job must have them. People 50
learn to do a job by observing, reading directions and prac- 53
ticing. They learn by doing. They can recall a process 55
without being reprogrammed. 56

73c ▶ 35 Production measurement: simplified communication forms

Time schedule

Assembling materials	3′
Timed production	25′
Final check; compute *n-pram*	7′

1. Arrange supplies (forms, letterheads, plain sheets) [LM pp. 167–172].
2. Correct errors neatly as you type.
3. Address envelopes.
4. When directed to begin, type for 25′ from the problems on page 149. If you complete the problems in less time than 25′, start over on plain paper.
5. Proofread and circle uncorrected errors found in final check.
6. Compute *n-pram* (see page 110).

Tabulation summary

Vertical placement of tables

Exact. Count total lines to be used, including any blank lines; subtract total from lines available; divide remainder by 2 (disregarding a fraction). Leave this number of blank lines in the top margin.

Reading position. Start the material 2 lines above the computed exact center.

Roll-back method. Insert the paper; roll it to the vertical center. Roll the cylinder back (toward you) once for every 2 lines in the table. This will place the copy in exact vertical center. For reading position, roll the cylinder back 2 additional lines.

Spacing after headings. Leave 1 blank line between a main and a secondary heading and between a column heading and its column. Leave 2 blank lines below a main heading, if a secondary heading is not used, or after a secondary heading when both a main and a secondary heading are used.

Horizontal placement of tables

Centered headings. After determining the top margin and spacing down to the starting line, center the main heading; DS and center a secondary heading, if used; then TS--as noted above.

Columns (backspace-from-center method). Note the longest item in each column. If a column heading is the longest item, count it as such unless judgment indicates otherwise. Decide the number of spaces to leave between columns (preferably an even number).

From center of paper, backspace once for each 2 characters and spaces in longest line of each column, then for each 2 spaces to be left between columns. Set the left margin stop at this point. If the longest line in one column has an extra letter or number, combine that letter or number with the first letter or number in the next column when backspacing by 2's. If in backspacing for columnar items 1 stroke is left over, disregard it.

From the left margin, space forward once for each letter, figure, symbol, and space in longest line in the first column and for each space to be left between first and second columns. Set tab stop at this point for second column. Follow this procedure to set tab stops for the remaining columns.

Column headings. Center column headings over the columns. When you have counted a column heading as the longest item in a column, you may need to reset the tab stop to center the *column* below the *heading*.

There are several methods of centering a column heading over a column, but probably the easiest is to add the cylinder-scale figures for the first and last strokes in the column. Dividing the sum by 2 will result in the center point of the column.

When using the forward-space-backspace method of centering a column, find the point at which the column begins and space forward once for each two letters, figures, or spaces in the longest line. This is the center of the column, backspace once for each 2 spaces in heading. Begin to type where backspacing ends. (In both steps disregard an extra space.)

Leaders. Alternate the period and the space to make leaders in a table. Leaders are sometimes used to connect typed material. When typing leaders, note from the line-of-writing scale whether you strike the first period on an odd or an even number; then strike all periods for additional lines on odd or on even numbers to align them. Use left first finger on space bar.

Horizontal rulings

Horizontal lines or *rulings* are often used in tables to set off the column headings. Usually, a full-width double ruling is typed above the column headings and a single ruling below them. A single ruling is also typed below the last line of the table.

To type rulings the exact width of the table, first determine the placement of the columns. After setting the tab stop for the last column, continue spacing forward once for each stroke in the last column. Immediately after spacing for the last stroke, set the right margin stop to lock the carriage at that point. You can then type rulings across the page until the carriage locks.

Double rulings. DS from the last line of the centered heading; type the first of the double rulings; then operate the variable line spacer and move the cylinder forward slightly; type the second ruling. DS between this double ruling and the column headings.

Single rulings. SS from the column headings; type a single ruling; DS and type the first items in the columns. After typing the last items in the columns, SS and type a single ruling.

Source note (if used). DS from the last single ruling; type the source note at the left margin or indent 3 to 5 spaces. If a table is not to be ruled, the source note is handled the same as footnote style in a report.

Tab stops for columns of figures

Uneven columns. When a column contains items uneven in length, set the tab stop at a point that will suit the greatest number of entries. After tabulating, backspace for longer items and space forward for shorter ones.

Dollar signs. In a money column, type a dollar sign before the first amount in the column and before the total, if one is shown. Type the dollar sign before the first amount aligned 1 space to the left of the longest amount in the column, which might be the total.

Totals. Totals are treated as a part of the column. For easier reading, totals are usually separated by a blank line from the last item in the column. The word "Total" is typed in the first column on a line with the total amount. It is usually indented either 3 or 5 spaces. In ruled tables, however, it may be typed at the left margin.

73c, continued

Problem 1
AMS Simplified letter

words

January 10, 19-- Miss Mary Hertz 2214 8
Shoreline Lane St. Paul, MN 55112 A SOLUTION 17
TO YOUR HEATING AND COOLING PROBLEMS 24
(¶ 1) Here's how to keep your home warm in 32
winter and cool in summer without spending a 41
fortune or draining the nation's energy re- 49
sources. (¶ 2) First, have your local Weston 57
dealer tell you about our new money-saving 66
heat pump that installs with your furnace to cut 76
your winter heating bills. A built-in computer 85
lets the heat pump keep you warm until extreme 95
outside cold tells it to turn on your furnace. 104
That means big wintertime savings! (¶ 3) Your 112
Weston dealer will also explain how the same 121
heat pump automatically becomes a highly 130
efficient air conditioner during the hot days 139
and nights of summer. (¶ 4) Second, send for 147
our new booklet <u>Cutting Your Energy Bills</u>. The 162
booklet gives you up-to-date information about 171
all types of energy. It gives you advice on 180
keeping your home comfortable--summer or 188
winter--while saving energy and operating 197
costs. (¶ 5) Use the coupon for your free copy 205
of the booklet. LOREN HENDERSON, ADVERTIS- 214
ING MANAGER xx Enclosure (179) 218/**229**

Problem 2
Interoffice memorandum
Address COMPANY MAIL envelope.

words

TO: All Travel Advisers and Agents FROM: 6
James Oliver DATE: June 5, 19-- SUBJECT: Im- 12
proving Slide Presentations (¶ 1) Many of our 20
travel advisers and agents are using slide pre- 29
sentations to sell tours and cruises to interested 39
travelers. To make your presentations more 48
effective, I should like to make the following 57
suggestions: (¶ 2) 1. Keep your viewers in mind. 67
You know what you like, but forget that for a 76
moment. Think of the people who will be look- 85
ing at your presentation. Avoid the hackneyed; 95
remember most people aren't interested in 103
seeing your mother-in-law in front of Old Faith- 113
ful. Why not use slides unlike any your viewers 122
have ever seen. (¶ 3) 2. Burn the bad ones. You 131
know an obvious failure when you see one; get 141
rid of it. Build your presentation with what's 150
left. (¶ 4) 3. One shot is not enough. Anything 159
worth one slide is probably worth two or three. 169
Let your viewers see the subject as you did-- 178
from more than one angle. (¶ 5) 4. Organize! 186
Give your presentation a beginning, a middle, 196
and an end. Keep related slides together. Fol- 205
low a time sequence or a logical outline. (¶ 6) 5. 215
Make your comments meaningful and interest- 223
ing. If you are at a loss for comments, study the 233
picture comments in HOLIDAY, NATIONAL 241
GEOGRAPHIC, and other magazines. Note that 250
they do not say the same thing that the picture 259
does. (¶ 7) 6. Save the best for last. There's noth- 269
ing worse than a presentation that runs down 278
at the end. Show your most breathtakingly 287
beautiful landscape or bit of human interest to- 296
ward the end. This makes your presentation 305
both humorous and colorful. (¶ 8) Good luck! xx 313
/322

Problem 3
Postal card (5½" × 3½")

words

RETURN ADDRESS: Maywood's Fashions 2350 5
Spruce Avenue Wilmington, DE 19808 AD- 12
DRESS: Ms. Millicent Stevens 7893 Stockton 19
Street Wilmington, DE 19801 November 14, 27
19--Dear Ms. Stevens (¶ 1) Thank you for shop- 36
ping at Maywood's. We hope the merchandise 44
you purchased measures up to your highest ex- 53
pectations. (¶ 2) We look forward to your return 62
visit and the opportunity to be of service again. 72
Miss Clara Knight, Manager 78/**90**

Problem 4
Second-page heading

Type a second–page heading (block style) on plain paper for the memo in Problem 2, followed by as much of the message as time permits.

level

4

Statistical communications

lessons 75–100

The primary objective of this level is to help you become proficient in typing a variety of statistical papers. These include tables with special features, frequently used business forms, statistical and technical reports, and employment communications.

A secondary, but important, objective is to help you improve your ability to type from straight-copy, script, rough-draft, and statistical paragraphs in preparation for employment testing.

If the time schedule given in each lesson is followed closely, over 65 percent of your classroom time will be devoted to production activities and just under 35 percent will be devoted to improving basic skills.

The mastery of typing processes presented in this level can be both a challenging and a rewarding experience. How well you succeed with the materials, however, will depend largely upon your attitude, your desire to learn, and your willingness to follow the learning/skill-building strategies that are given in the directions.

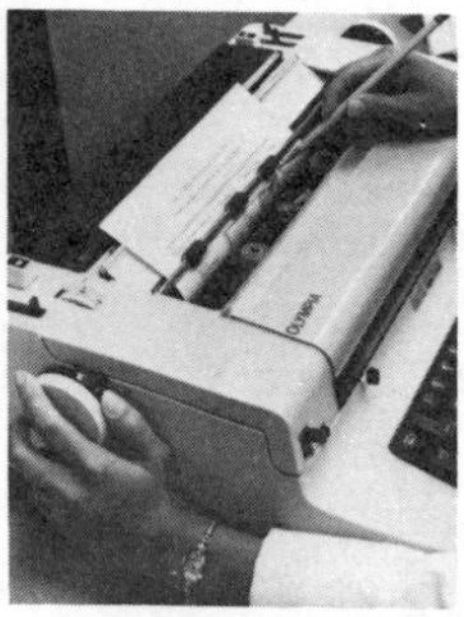

section

16

Tables with special features

lessons 75–81

Learning goals

The lessons of Section 16 are planned to help you achieve the following goals:

1. To improve your ability to arrange and type tables with special features.
2. To increase your skill in handling the subroutines (processes) required for table typing.
3. To increase your skill in typing tables shown in script and rough draft.

Machine adjustments

1. Set paper guide at *0* on most typewriters.
2. Set paper-bail rolls to divide paper into thirds.
3. Clear all tab sets at the beginning of each problem.
4. Use a 70-space line and SS for drill lines unless otherwise indicated.
5. TS after lesson parts.

74

74a ▶ 5
Preparatory practice

as many times as possible in the time available

alphabet	Five zebras will quietly make appearances in this dark, exotic jungle.
fig/sym	Cody & Dee's checks #381 ($176.89) and #407 ($154.72) are outstanding.
3d/4th fingers	Our annual contract renewal calls for adequate provisions for storage.
fluency	Any one of the six guides should be able to do a very good job for us.

| 1 | 2 | 3 | 4 | 5 | 6 | 7 | 8 | 9 | 10 | 11 | 12 | 13 | 14 |

74b ▶ 10
Statistical-copy skill measurement

a 5′ writing; determine *gwam*; circle errors

all letters/figures used

Difficulty index

A	1.5 si	5.7 awl	80% hfw

	gwam 1′	5′	
We are currently spending more on taxes than on food, clothing, and	14	3	59
housing combined. The average household pays more than 40% of its total	28	6	61
income in taxes. This increasing tax bill is only one part of the two-	42	8	64
way squeeze on incomes. The other is inflation, which takes a large	56	11	67
bite out of what is left after taxes. In 1977, for example, $1 bought	70	14	70
only 64% as much in goods and services as the same amount got in 1970;	85	17	73
and this disheartening deterioration of the dollar continues.	97	19	75
Federal taxes have climbed 105% in the last decade. State and	13	22	78
local taxes have jumped an unbelievable 152% during the same period.	27	25	81
The rapidly growing taxes are for social security--from 0.4% of total	41	27	83
personal earnings 30 years ago to more than 6% last year. Local personal	55	30	86
taxes advanced from 0.6% to almost 2.5% in the same time span. The total	70	33	89
tax bite for the ordinary household this year amounts to $9,600, which	84	36	92
is about half our income.	89	37	93
Rarely has the inflation rate been below 5% a year in the last 10	13	40	96
years. In 1978, it was over 8%; and in several years it actually reached	28	43	99
as high as 11%. In 1962, we had our first $100 billion federal budget.	43	46	102
Fifteen years later, it escalated to over $500 billion, with a deficit	57	49	104
of over $60 billion. This condition is a principal cause of inflation.	71	52	107
Because of deficit spending by our government, every baby born in the	85	54	110
United States is born $15,400 in debt.	93	56	112

gwam 1′ | 1 | 2 | 3 | 4 | 5 | 6 | 7 | 8 | 9 | 10 | 11 | 12 | 13 | 14 |
5′ | 1 | 2 | 3 |

74c ▶ 35

Production measurement: administrative communications

Time schedule

Assembling materials .... 3′
Timed production .... 25′
Final check; compute *n–pram* .... 7′

1. Follow time schedule shown at the left.
2. Arrange letterhead and envelope, plain paper and other supplies for easy handling [LM p. 173].
3. Correct errors neatly as you type.
4. Address envelope for letter.
5. When directed to begin, type for 25′ from the problems below. If you complete the problems in less than 25′, start over on plain paper.
6. Proofread and circle uncorrected errors found in final check.
7. Compute *n–pram* (see p. 110).

Problem 1
Minutes of meeting
1½″ top margin; 1″ side margins; SS; 5–space ¶ indentations
If necessary, see p. 136 for appropriate spacing.

words

MINUTES OF SPECIAL MEETING OF PLANNING 8
BOARD October 10, 19-- (¶ 1) A special meeting 16
of the Planning Board of Anatco, Inc., was held 25
in the office of the general manager at 2 p.m. on 35
Tuesday, October 9, 19--. Members present 44
were Lola Bird, Christine Murphy, Harold Solis, 53
Barbara Theus, and Alice Bottino, who presided. 63
(¶ 2) The purpose of the meeting was to reach a 71
decision on the question of permitting em- 80
ployees to use "flexitime" scheduling in arrang- 90
ing their working hours. (¶ 3) Miss Bird re- 97
ported that she checked the company policies 106
and found nothing pertaining to the matter in 116
them. (¶ 4) Mrs. Theus stated that, on the basis 124
of a number of published studies she had read, 134
she learned that productivity was signifi- 143
cantly increased when "flexitime" scheduling 152
was adopted. Turnover and absenteeism were 161
significantly decreased. (¶ 5) Mrs. Solis stated 169
that a poll of employees showed 60% favored 178
the plan, 25% opposed it, and 15% had no opin- 187
ion. (¶ 6) After a discussion of the matter, Miss 196
Bottino called for a vote on the issue. All 205
present approved the plan. (¶ 7) Miss Bottino 214
named Christine Murphy, Barbara Theus, and 222
Harold Solis to a committee, with Mr. Solis as 232
acting chairperson, to draft a detailed working 241
report of the plan for discussion and action by 251
the Board at a later meeting. (¶ 8) The meeting 259
adjourned at 3:30 p.m. Respectfully submitted 269
Secretary 271

Problem 2
Executive-size letter
modified block; block ¶s; open punctuation

words

January 10, 19-- Mr. Gardner L. Yates 8
Attorney-at-Law 3297 Elmerton Avenue Har- 16
risburg, PA 17110 Dear Mr. Yates (¶ 1) We have 24
a number of positions for promising young men 33
and women in our organization. We want intel- 42
ligent persons interested in excellent incomes. 52
They will be backed by our century-old national 62
reputation as a leader in the retail marketing 71
field. (¶ 2) Selection tests based on aptitudes 80
will be applied to help the candidate make a 89
realistic decision. Among those who might qual- 98
ify are your son or daughter, a friend (or his son 109
or daughter), a recent college graduate, or the 118
best salesperson who has called on you recently. 128
(¶ 3) If you know of two or three persons who 136
qualify, you can do them a real favor by sending 146
me their names and addresses. Cordially yours 155
Ms. Dorothy C. Bemis President xx 161/177

Problem 3
Agenda for meeting
full sheet; 20 spaces between columns; center vertically and horizontally
If necessary, see pp. 140-141 for appropriate spacing and typing of leaders.

words

SUNSET INDUSTRIES, INC. 5
Agenda for Board of Directors Meeting 12
August 10, 19-- 16

		words
1. Call to order	Orville Johnson	28
2. Approval of Minutes	Susan Kelly	40
3. Reports of Officers		44
4. Committee Reports		49
Asian Markets	Violet Pullman	60
Employee Pensions	Dolly Menges	70
5. New Business		74
Change Meeting Dates . .	Fred Gregory	84
6. Adjournment		87

Reference guide

▶ Capitalize

1 The first word of a sentence.

2 The first word of a complete direct quotation (but not of an interested or fragmented quote).

He said, "Say exactly what you mean."
"Doing it right," I said, "means doing it once."

3 The first word after a colon if that word begins a complete sentence.

Note: Our office closes promptly at five.
We need the following: boat, oars, and bait.

4 The first and all important words in titles or headings, but not words of four or fewer letters used in conjunctions, articles, or prepositions.

See "The Case for the Defense" in The News.

5 An official title when it precedes a name or when used elsewhere as a title of distinction.

See Doctor Cleve, our resident surgeon.
She met the Prime Minister in the hall.

6 All proper nouns and their derivatives.

We ate Mexican food in a Chicago restaurant.

7 Days of the week, months of the year, holidays, historic periods and events, and other items of specific identity.

On Monday, we begin our study of the Civil War.

8 Seasons of the year only if they are personified.

Soft voices of Spring told us winter was over.

9 Specific geographic regions, but not general directions or compass points.

Turn north and drive to Upper New York.

10 Brand names, but usually not the commodity they identify.

She installed a Twitone radio in her Dorset car.

11 Names of organizations, clubs, buildings, etc.

The Kiwanis Club meets at Lamar's Restaurant.

12 A noun preceding a figure (except the common nouns *line*, *page*, and *sentence*, which may be typed with or without capitalization).

Check line 9, Chapter 7, of Book 397.

13 Both parts of a hyphenated word if each part is ordinarily capitalized.

the North-South game   the Kellog-Briand pact
a Sino-Soviet agreement

▶ Type as words

1 Numbers from one to ten, except when used as part of a series of numbers, some of which are above ten and are typed as figures. **Note:** It is common business practice to use figures for all numbers except those that begin a sentence.

The child will be six in October.
Use 4 of the 24 bricks as a base.

2 A number beginning a sentence.

Five of the 35 members voted nay.

3 The shorter of two numbers used together.

7 one-ounce jars   two 5-gallon cans

4 Isolated fractions or indefinite amounts in a sentence.

Only about one third of the members voted on five or six of the resolutions.

5 Names of small-numbered streets (ten and under)

355 Seventh Avenue   161 First Street

▶ Type as figures

1 Dates and times, except in very formal writing.

June 17, 1980   11:15 a.m.
Fourth of May   nine o'clock

2 A series of fractions.

Type 3/4, 4/5, 9/10, and 2 1/2.

3 Numbers preceded by nouns.

Case 14   page 3   Flight 230   line 1

4 Measures, weights, and dimensions.

9′ x 12′   5 ft. 10 in.   118 pounds.

5 Definite numbers used with a percent sign (%), but type percent (spelled) with approximations and in formal writing.

The bank charged 9% interest.
Almost 75 percent of the oil is still here.

6 House numbers, except house number One.

2200 – 50th Street   One Park Avenue

7 Sums of money, except when spelled for emphasis or when the sum is an even number and very large (type even sums without a decimal).

$815.99 $.10 or 10 cents $100 million
twenty-five hundred dollars ($2,500)

8 Numbers with abbreviations.

100 lbs. $20 per sq. yd.   1 gal.

▶ Use an apostrophe

1 As a symbol for *feet* in billings or tabulations and as a symbol for *minutes*. Use the quotation mark as a symbol for *seconds* or *inches*.

2′ x 7′   7′2″   9′8″ x 9′5″

2 As a symbol to indicate the omission of letters or figures.

Rob't   sec'y   She's here.   Crash of '29.

3 With *s* to form the plural of most figures, figures written as words, and letters. In market quotations, form the plural of figures by the addition of *s* only.

2's   two's   A's   Boston Fund 4s

4 To show possession: Add the apostrophe and *s* to a singular noun not ending in *s*. If a singular noun ends in *s*, add *'s* to form the possessive if the *s* is to be pronounced as a syllable; add the apostrophe only if the ending *s* would be awkward to pronounce.

child's play   lady's glove   dog's bone
boss's office   species' characteristics

5 To show possession: Add the apostrophe and *s* to a plural noun that does not end in *s*.

men's ties   women's hats   children's toys

6 To show possession: Add the apostrophe and *s* to a proper name of one syllable that ends in *s*.

Jones's house   Jess's automobile

7 To show possession: Add the apostrophe *only* after (a) plural nouns ending in *s* and (b) a proper noun of more than one syllable ending in *s* or *z*.

ladies' gloves   Lopez' ideas   Doris' hat

8 To show possession: Add the apostrophe after the last noun in a series to indicate joint or common possession of two or more persons; however, indicate separate possession of two or more persons by adding the possessive to each of the nouns.

Lewis and Clark's expedition
Jo's and Dale's grades

▶ Use a colon

1 To introduce an enumeration or listing.

The following are my favorite authors:
Hemingway, Faulkner, and Gide.

2 To introduce a statement, question, or long quotation.

Important: Shake well before using.

▶ Use a comma (or commas)

1 After (a) introductory words, phrases, or clauses and (b) between words in a series.

If you can, bring my cap, skis, and sweater.

2 To set off direct quotations.

"You may borrow my typewriter," she said.

3 To set off explanatory and descriptive words, phrases, and clauses in a sentence.

Pie, my favorite dessert, was not served.
I loaned the book to Bob, my best friend.

4 To set off words used in direct address.

It is time, Laurie, to leave for the lake.
Pack your suitcase in my car, Mike.

5 To set off nonrestrictive adjective clauses (not necessary to the meaning of the sentence), but not restrictive clauses (necessary to meaning).

Your report, which is too long, was not read.
Your report that discussed taxation was read.

6 To set off (a) the year when it is used as part of a date and (b) the state when it follows a city.

I wrote you May 2, 1980, from Ames, Iowa.
We met in Miami, Florida, on June 5, 1975.

7 To separate two or more parallel adjectives (adjectives that could be separated by the word *and* instead of the comma). Do not use commas to separate adjectives so closely related that they appear to form a single element with the noun they modify.

My new boat has red, white, and blue stripes.
The big white tuba was in the large civic center.

8 To separate (a) unrelated groups of figures that come together and (b) whole numbers into groups of three digits each (however, policy, *year*, *page*, *room*, *telephone*, and most *serial numbers* are typed without commas).

In 1980, 1,205 autos were impounded under Law 4260.

9 To set off contrasting phrases and clauses.

Men, not machines, did the work.

10 Before and after *etc.*

All the books, papers, etc., were removed.

▶ Use an exclamation point

1 After exclamatory words.

She won! No! Look out!

2 After exclamatory sentences.

Something must be done now!

▶ Use a hyphen

1 To join numbers from twenty-one to ninety-nine when they are typed as words.

fifty-two   thirty-one   eighty-six

2 To join compound (two or more) adjectives written *before* a noun they modify as a unit.

first-class fare   up-to-the-minute schedule

3 After each word or figure in a series of words or figures that have a common ending (suspended hyphenation).

two-, three-, or four-day trips

▶ Use a dash

1 For dramatic emphasis or clarity.

The cliff—higher than Mt. Nebo—had been scaled.

2 To emphasize a sudden change of thought.

An orange—I thought Mary suggested it—was perfect.

3 To show the name of an author when it follows a direct quotation.

Use a dash to separate, a hyphen to join.—Duncan

4 To indicate in written form verbal pauses.

"Well—er—yes," he muttered.

▶ Use the parentheses

1 To enclose explanatory matter and added information where commas are inappropriate.

The list (Appendix A) is inclusive.

2 To enclose identifying letters or figures in lists.

List your (a) name, (b) address, and (c) age.

3 To enclose figures that follow spelled-out amounts to give clarity or emphasis.

It paid two hundred dollars ($200) in benefits.

▶ Use a question mark

At the end of a sentence that is a direct question (requests an answer); however, use a period after a requested action in the form of a question.

Have you seen that movie?
Will you please telephone me this evening.

▶ Use a semicolon

1 To separate two or more independent clauses in a compound sentence when the conjunction is omitted.

I tried it once; I shall not try it again.

2 To separate independent clauses when they are joined by a conjunctive adverb (however, therefore, furthermore, etc.).

She is here; I did not see her arrive.

3 To separate a series of word or figure groupings if one or more of the groupings contains a comma.

I wore a beige, brown, and tan sweater; brown slacks; and white deck shoes.

4 To precede an abbreviation or word(s) that introduces an explanatory statement.

He found my work; that is, the portion of it that I lost.

▶ Use an underline

1 With titles of complete works such as books, magazines, and newspapers. Such titles may alternatively be typed in ALL CAPS without the underline.

<u>College Typewriting</u>   <u>The Daily News</u>

2 To call attention to special words or phrases (or you may use quotation marks). Use a continuous underline unless each word is to be considered separately.

Simmer slowly <u>at least three minutes</u>.
Can you spell <u>chaos</u>, <u>separate</u>, and <u>quiver</u>?

▶ Use quotation marks

1 To enclose a direct quotation.

"The weather has been very warm," he said.

2 To enclose titles of articles and other parts of complete publications, poems, song titles, television programs, and unpublished works.

"The Star Spangled Banner"   "Trees"

3 To enclose special words, phrases, or coined words.

A program is the "brains" of the computer.

4 When quotation marks are used with other marks of punctuation, the quotation marks come after a comma or period; before a semicolon or colon; after a question mark if the quotation is a question, otherwise before the question mark.

"He is," I said, "a splendid actor."
He read "Invictus"; the applause was genuine.
She asked, "Who devised this formula?"
Do you know whether to use "its" or "it's"?

Word-division guides

1 Divide words between syllables only; therefore, do not divide one syllable words. **Note:** When in doubt, consult a dictionary or word–division manual.

pic-tures else-where im-por-tant
bridge caught straight

2 Do not divide words of five or fewer letters, even if they have two or more syllables

after copy every media ratio

3 Do not separate a one–letter syllable at the beginning of a word or a one–or two–letter syllable at the end of a word.

a-dored e-nough storm-y friend-ly

4 You may usually divide a word between double consonants; but, when adding a syllable to a word that ends in double letters, divide after the double letters of the root word.

sum-mers bag-gage excel-lent win-ner
call-ing stress-ing add-ing still-ness

5 When the final consonant is doubled by adding a suffix, divide between the double letters.

get-ting jog-ging sun-ning star-ring

6 Divide after a one–letter syllable within a word; but when two single–letter syllables occur together, divide between them.

emu-late impetu-ous
gradu-ation insinu-ation

7 When the single–letter syllable *a*, *i*, or *u* is followed by the ending *ly*, *ble*, *bly*, *cle*, or *cal*, divide before the single–letter syllable.

med-ical lik-able read-ily fam-ily

8 Do not divide figures; try to avoid dividing proper names and dates.

ZIP Code abbreviations

Alabama, AL
Alaska, AK
Arizona, AZ
Arkansas, AR
California, CA
Canal Zone, CZ
Colorado, CO
Connecticut, CT
Delaware, DE
District of Columbia, DC
Florida, FL
Georgia, GA
Guam, GU
Hawaii, HI
Idaho, ID
Illinois, IL
Indiana, IN
Iowa, IA
Kansas, KS
Kentucky, KY
Louisiana, LA
Maine, ME
Maryland, MD
Massachusetts, MA
Michigan, MI
Minnesota, MN
Mississippi, MS
Missouri, MO
Montana, MT
Nebraska, NE
Nevada, NV
New Hampshire, NH
New Jersey, NJ
New Mexico, NM
New York, NY
North Carolina, NC
North Dakota, ND
Ohio, OH
Oklahoma, OK
Oregon, OR
Pennsylvania, PA
Puerto Rico, PR
Rhode Island, RI
South Carolina, SC
South Dakota, SD
Tennessee, TN
Texas, TX
Utah, UT
Vermont, VT
Virgin Islands, VI
Virginia, VA
Washington, WA
West Virginia, WV
Wisconsin, WI
Wyoming, WY

Letter placement/special parts

Margins/Date Placement. The letter placement table below is a guide to be used only until experience has taught you to make quick mental judgments about the width of the margins and placement of the dateline.

5-stroke letters in letter body	Side Margins	Date-line
Up to 100	2″	20
101–250	1½″	14–17*
Over 250	1″	12

*Dateline is moved up 2 lines for each additional 50 words.

Horizontal placement of date varies according to letter style. In the block and AMS Simplified styles, type the date at the left margin. In the modified block style, begin the date at the center point.

Letter address. Type the first line of the address on the fourth line space below the date. Type an official title, when used, on either the first or second line—whichever gives better balance. A personal title (Mrs., Ms., etc.) should precede an individual's name.

Attention line. An attention line, when used, is typed at the left margin on the second line below the letter address and a double space above the salutation. (The salutation should correspond with the address and not with the attention line.)

Subject line. A subject line, when used, is typed on the second line below the salutation at the left margin. Type the word *Subject* in ALL CAPS, with only the first letter capitalized, or omit the word entirely.

Multiple pages. If a letter is too long for one page, at least 2 lines of the body of the letter should be carried to the second page. Start the heading of the second and subsequent pages on Line 7, and leave 2 blank line spaces below it.

Use the same side margins on all pages of a letter.

Company name in closing. When the company name is used in the closing lines, type it in ALL CAPS on the second line below the complimentary close.

Typewritten name/official title. Type the name and official title of the writer of a letter on the fourth line space below the complimentary close, or 4 lines below the typed company name when it is used. With the exception of the AMS Simplified style, the writer's title may either go on the same line as the name or on the line below it—whichever gives better balance.

Reference Initials. At the left margin a double space below the name and official title, type your initials in the lowercase letters. If there is some good reason for doing so, precede your initials with the writer's or dictator's initials typed in *ALL CAPS* and separated from your initials with a colon or a diagonal.

Enclosure notation. Type an enclosure notation (Enclosure, Enclosures: 2, or the like) a double space below the reference initials.

Carbon copy notation. A carbon copy notation (cc) indicates for whom copies of the letter were made. Type the cc notation a double space below the reference initials or the enclosure notation if one is used. If the notation is to appear on the carbon copy only (blind carbon copy), type the notation *bcc* and the recipient's name(s) on a piece of paper held between the typewriter ribbon and the original sheet.

Postscript. Type a postscript a double space below the last letter item. The letters P.S. need not be used. Type the postscript in the same style as was used for other paragraphs of the letter.

Second page headings

Block form

1″

Orient Trade Center
Page 2
January 20, 19--
TS
greet you and to personally show you how work that formerly took
you tedious hours can be accomplished in mere seconds. Just let

Horizontal form

1″

Orient Trade Center 2 January 20, 19--
TS
greet you and to personally show you how work that formerly took
you tedious hours can be accomplished in mere seconds. Just let
me know what time is most convenient for you. If you prefer to
have the demonstration in your offices instead of at the trade

sms
the society of management specialists
24 EAST BROADWAY
SALT LAKE CITY, UT 84111
(801) 221 3212

August 27, 19--

Clark Enterprises, Inc.
5N061 Wood Dale Road
Wood Dale, IL 60191

Attention Office Manager

Dear Sir or Madam

Please note that all lines in this block style letter begin at the left margin. The spacing between the top of the paper and the date depends on the length of the letter.

The spacing between letter parts is standard, regardless of the letter style or length. The first line of the letter address is typed on the fourth line space below the date. There is a double space above and below the salutation, between paragraphs, and above the complimentary close. The writer's name is typed on the fourth line space below the complimentary close. There is a double space below the writer's name or title, and the notations at the end of the letter are generally double-spaced.

Please accept the enclosed booklet with my compliments.

Sincerely yours

Martha Landon
Mrs. Martha Landon
Vice President

xx

Enclosure

cc Ms. Verna Dickson

1 Block, open

sms
the society of management specialists
24 EAST BROADWAY
SALT LAKE CITY, UT 84111
(801) 221 3212

April 30, 19--

SPECIAL DELIVERY

Miss Louise McCoy
Manager, Gretti Company
1313 S. Glendale
Sioux Falls, SD 57105

Dear Miss McCoy

The pamphlet about letter formats that you requested is enclosed. One of the styles described in the pamphlet is the modified block style. This letter illustrates that style.

A mailing notation is typed at the left margin, a double space below the date; however, the date, the complimentary close, and the name and official title of the dictator begin at the horizontal center of the paper. One tabulator setting works for all these lines.

We are using open punctuation, which omits punctuation after the salutation and complimentary close.

Although we do not usually use the company name in the closing lines, we do so here to illustrate the correct style. When the dictator's name is used in the closing lines, the reference notation consists of the typist's initials only. The dictator's initials, if used, precede those of the typist.

If we have more than one enclosure, we list them on succeeding lines, indented three spaces from the left margin.

We are enclosing a reply card that you can use to request additional copies of Styling Business Letters if you need them. After you have examined your copy, we would be pleased if you would send us your impressions of it.

Sincerely yours

THE SOCIETY OF MANAGEMENT SPECIALISTS

Deborah Telfer
Mrs. Deborah Telfer
Public Service Director

xx

Enclosures
   Pamphlet
   Reply card

2 Modified block, open

sms
the society of management specialists
24 EAST BROADWAY
SALT LAKE CITY, UT 84111
(801) 221 3212

October 16, 19--

Loughman Control Systems
Box 50598
Severn, MD 21144

Attention Mr. D. E. McGowan

Ladies and Gentlemen:

Subject: Modified Block Style Letter

I am pleased to answer your letter. We use the modified block style with indented paragraphs and mixed punctuation in all our correspondence. It is the style used in this letter.

The spacing from the top of the paper to the date varies with the length of the letter. All other spacing within the letter is standard. The date, complimentary close, and name and official title of the writer are begun at the horizontal center.

Please write again if I can be of any further help.

Sincerely yours,

Michael Besozzi
Michael Besozzi
General Manager

xx

Our new Communications Guide will be sent to you as soon as it comes from the printer.

3 Modified block, indented ¶s, mixed

sms
the society of management specialists
24 EAST BROADWAY
SALT LAKE CITY, UT 84111
(801) 221 3212

July 10, 19--

Mr. John Ketchum, Manager
Shelly & Rockford, Inc.
Box 9378
Zanesville, OH 43734

AMS SIMPLIFIED STYLE

This letter is typed in the timesaving simplified style recommended by the Administrative Management Society. To type a letter in the AMS style, follow these steps:

1. Use block format.
2. Omit the salutation and the complimentary close.
3. Include a subject heading and type it in ALL CAPS a triple space below the address; triple-space from the subject line to the first line of the body.
4. Type enumerated items at the left margin; indent unnumbered items five spaces.
5. Type the writer's name and title in ALL CAPS on the 4th line space below the last line of the letter body.
6. Type the reference initials (typist's only) a double space below the writer's name.

Correspondents in your company may like the AMS simplified letter style not only for the eye appeal it gives letters but also for the resultant reduction in letter-writing costs.

Hulda Heston
MRS. HULDA HESTON, PRESIDENT

xx

4 AMS Simplified

1 Addressing procedure

Envelope address

Set a tab stop (or margin stop if a number of envelopes are to be addressed) 2½" from the left edge for a small envelope or 4" from the left edge for a large envelope. Start the address here about 2" from the top edge of a small envelope and 2½" from the top edge of a large one.

Style

Type the address in *block style*, single–spaced, without punctuation at the ends of lines, except when an abbreviation ends a line. Type the city name, state name or abbreviation, and ZIP Code on the last address line. The ZIP Code is usually typed 1 space after the state name.

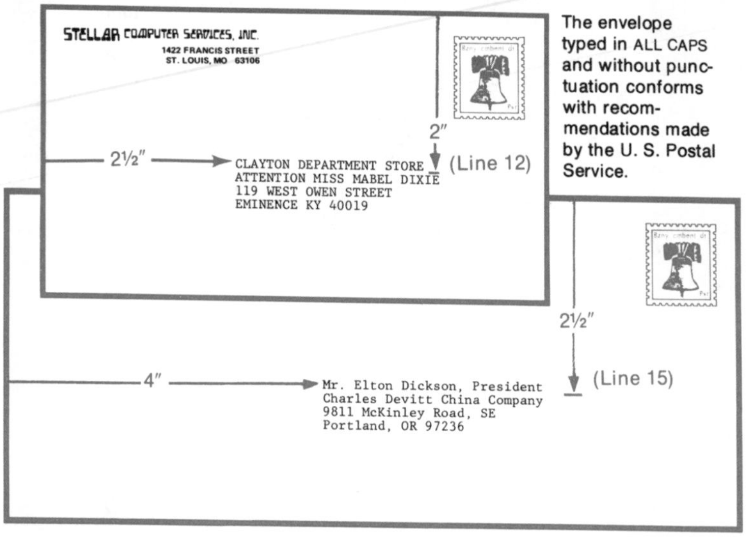

The envelope typed in ALL CAPS and without punctuation conforms with recommendations made by the U. S. Postal Service.

Addressee notations

Type addressee notations, such as *Hold for Arrival*, *Please Forward*, *Personal*, etc., a triple space below the return address and about 3 spaces from the left edge of the envelope. These notations may be underlined or typed in all capitals.

If an *attention line* is used, type it immediately below the company name in the address line.

Mailing notations

Type mailing notations, such as SPECIAL DELIVERY and REGISTERED, below the stamp and at least 3 line spaces above the envelope address. Type these notations in all capital letters.

2 Folding and inserting procedure

Small envelopes (No. 6¾, 6¼)

Step 1 With letter face up, fold bottom up to ½ inch from top.

Step 2 Fold right third to left.

Step 3 Fold left third to ½ inch from last crease.

Step 4 Insert last creased edge first.

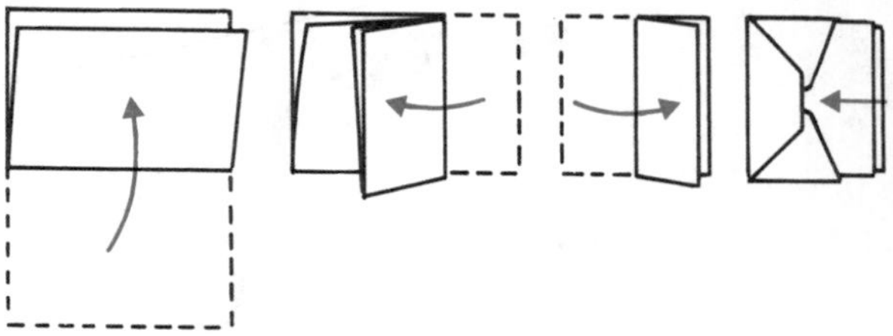

Large envelopes (No. 10, 9, 7¾)

Step 1 With letter face up, fold slightly less than ⅓ of sheet up toward top.

Step 2 Fold down top of sheet to within ½ inch of bottom fold.

Step 3 Insert letter into envelope with last crease toward bottom of envelope.

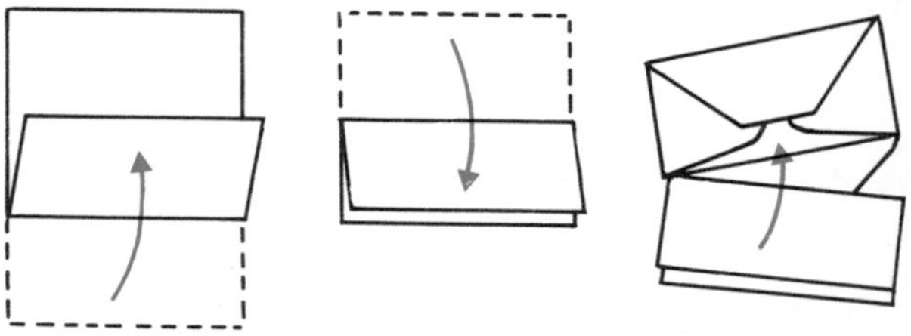

Window envelopes (letter)

Step 1 With sheet face down, top toward you, fold upper third down.

Step 2 Fold lower third up so address is showing.

Step 3 Insert sheet into envelope with last crease at bottom.

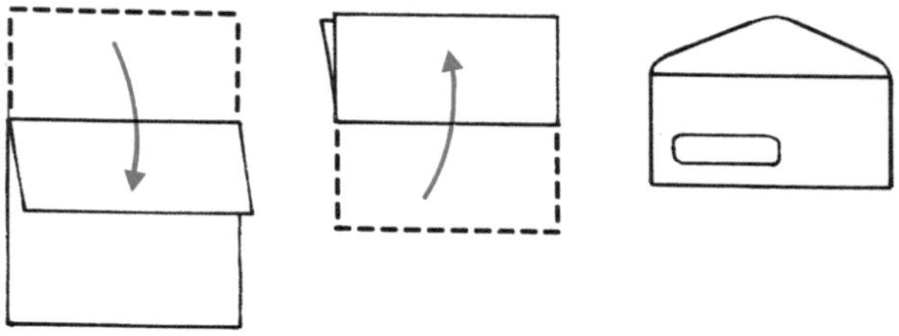

Window envelopes (invoices and other forms)

Step 1 Place sheet face down, top toward you.

Step 2 Fold back top so address shows.

Step 3 Insert into envelope with crease at bottom.

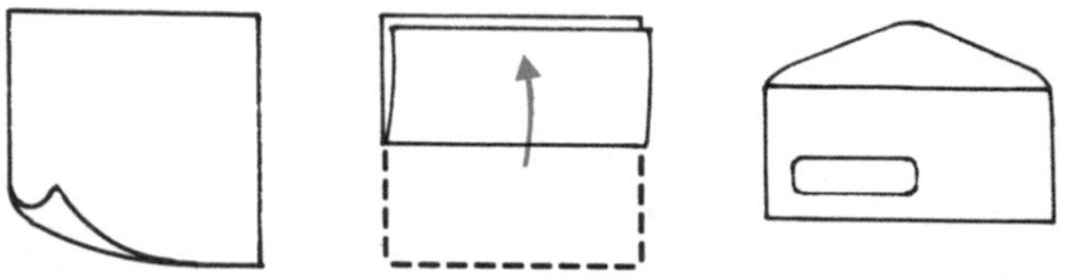

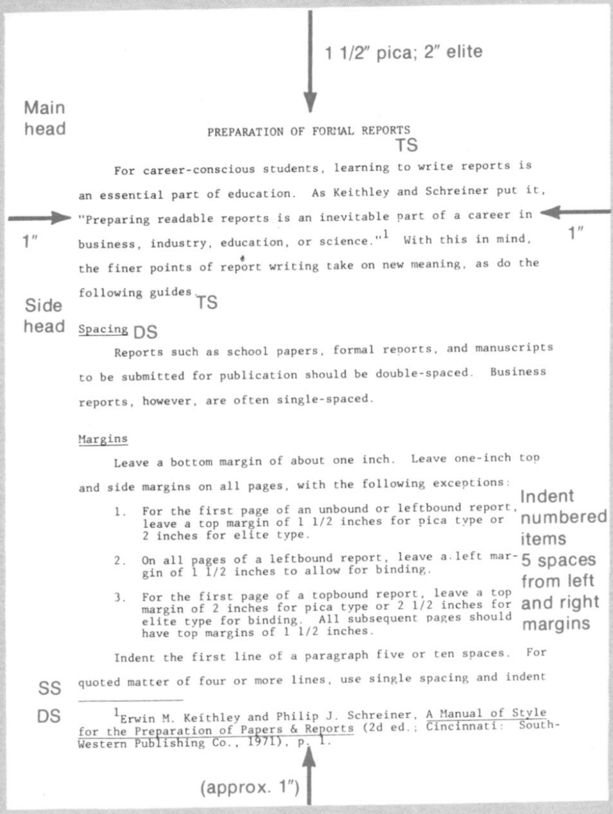

PREPARATION OF FORMAL REPORTS

For career-conscious students, learning to write reports is an essential part of education. As Keithley and Schreiner put it, "Preparing readable reports is an inevitable part of a career in business, industry, education, or science."[1] With this in mind, the finer points of report writing take on new meaning, as do the following guides.

Spacing

Reports such as school papers, formal reports, and manuscripts to be submitted for publication should be double-spaced. Business reports, however, are often single-spaced.

Margins

Leave a bottom margin of about one inch. Leave one-inch top and side margins on all pages, with the following exceptions:

1. For the first page of an unbound or leftbound report, leave a top margin of 1 1/2 inches for pica type or 2 inches for elite type.
2. On all pages of a leftbound report, leave a left margin of 1 1/2 inches to allow for binding.
3. For the first page of a topbound report, leave a top margin of 2 inches for pica type or 2 1/2 inches for elite type for binding. All subsequent pages should have top margins of 1 1/2 inches.

Indent the first line of a paragraph five or ten spaces. For quoted matter of four or more lines, use single spacing and indent

[1] Erwin M. Keithley and Philip J. Schreiner, A Manual of Style for the Preparation of Papers & Reports (2d ed.; Cincinnati: South-Western Publishing Co., 1971), p. 1.

1 Unbound, page 1

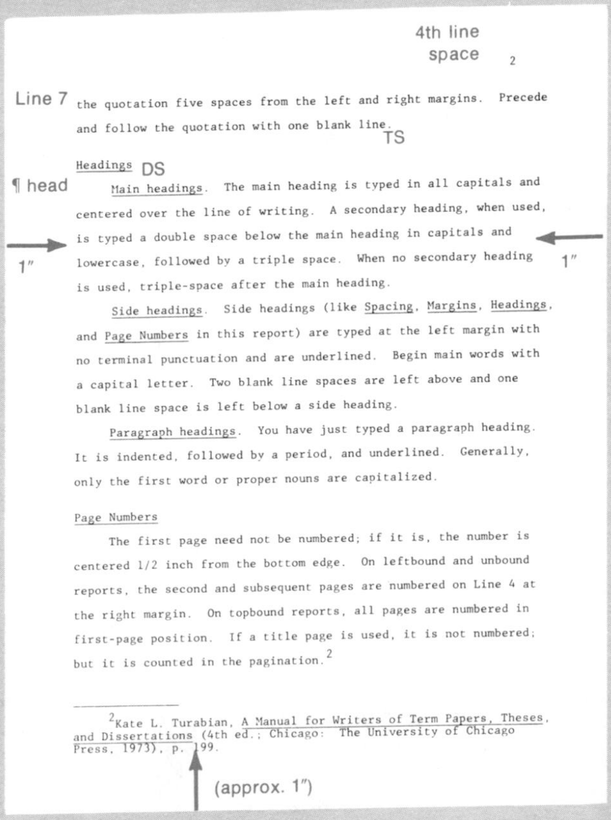

2

the quotation five spaces from the left and right margins. Precede and follow the quotation with one blank line.

Headings

Main headings. The main heading is typed in all capitals and centered over the line of writing. A secondary heading, when used, is typed a double space below the main heading in capitals and lowercase, followed by a triple space. When no secondary heading is used, triple-space after the main heading.

Side headings. Side headings (like Spacing, Margins, Headings, and Page Numbers in this report) are typed at the left margin with no terminal punctuation and are underlined. Begin main words with a capital letter. Two blank line spaces are left above and one blank line space is left below a side heading.

Paragraph headings. You have just typed a paragraph heading. It is indented, followed by a period, and underlined. Generally, only the first word or proper nouns are capitalized.

Page Numbers

The first page need not be numbered; if it is, the number is centered 1/2 inch from the bottom edge. On leftbound and unbound reports, the second and subsequent pages are numbered on Line 4 at the right margin. On topbound reports, all pages are numbered in first-page position. If a title page is used, it is not numbered; but it is counted in the pagination.[2]

[2] Kate L. Turabian, A Manual for Writers of Term Papers, Theses, and Dissertations (4th ed.; Chicago: The University of Chicago Press, 1973), p. 199.

2 Unbound, page 2

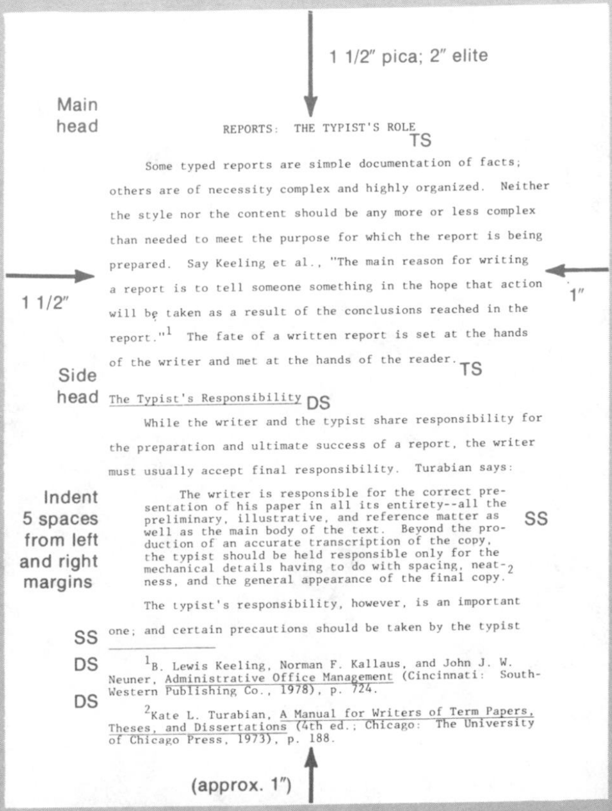

REPORTS: THE TYPIST'S ROLE

Some typed reports are simple documentation of facts; others are of necessity complex and highly organized. Neither the style nor the content should be any more or less complex than needed to meet the purpose for which the report is being prepared. Say Keeling et al., "The main reason for writing a report is to tell someone something in the hope that action will be taken as a result of the conclusions reached in the report."[1] The fate of a written report is set at the hands of the writer and met at the hands of the reader.

The Typist's Responsibility

While the writer and the typist share responsibility for the preparation and ultimate success of a report, the writer must usually accept final responsibility. Turabian says:

> The writer is responsible for the correct presentation of his paper in all its entirety--all the preliminary, illustrative, and reference matter as well as the main body of the text. Beyond the production of an accurate transcription of the copy, the typist should be held responsible only for the mechanical details having to do with spacing, neatness, and the general appearance of the final copy.[2]

The typist's responsibility, however, is an important one; and certain precautions should be taken by the typist

[1] B. Lewis Keeling, Norman F. Kallaus, and John J. W. Neuner, Administrative Office Management (Cincinnati: South-Western Publishing Co., 1978), p. 724.

[2] Kate L. Turabian, A Manual for Writers of Term Papers, Theses, and Dissertations (4th ed.; Chicago: The University of Chicago Press, 1973), p. 188.

3 Leftbound, page 1

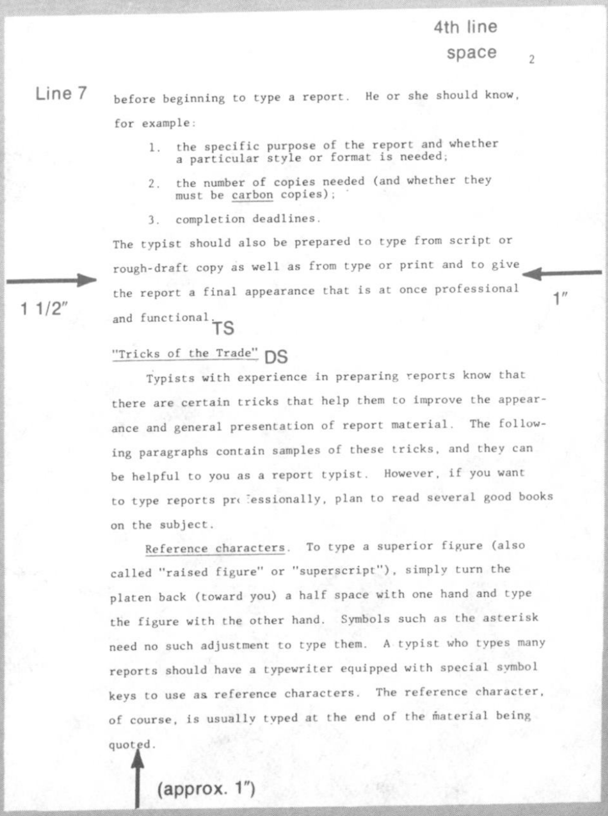

2

before beginning to type a report. He or she should know, for example:

1. the specific purpose of the report and whether a particular style or format is needed;
2. the number of copies needed (and whether they must be carbon copies);
3. completion deadlines.

The typist should also be prepared to type from script or rough-draft copy as well as from type or print and to give the report a final appearance that is at once professional and functional.

"Tricks of the Trade"

Typists with experience in preparing reports know that there are certain tricks that help them to improve the appearance and general presentation of report material. The following paragraphs contain samples of these tricks, and they can be helpful to you as a report typist. However, if you want to type reports professionally, plan to read several good books on the subject.

Reference characters. To type a superior figure (also called "raised figure" or "superscript"), simply turn the platen back (toward you) a half space with one hand and type the figure with the other hand. Symbols such as the asterisk need no such adjustment to type them. A typist who types many reports should have a typewriter equipped with special symbol keys to use as reference characters. The reference character, of course, is usually typed at the end of the material being quoted.

4 Leftbound, page 2

Report Styles

5 Leftbound, contents page

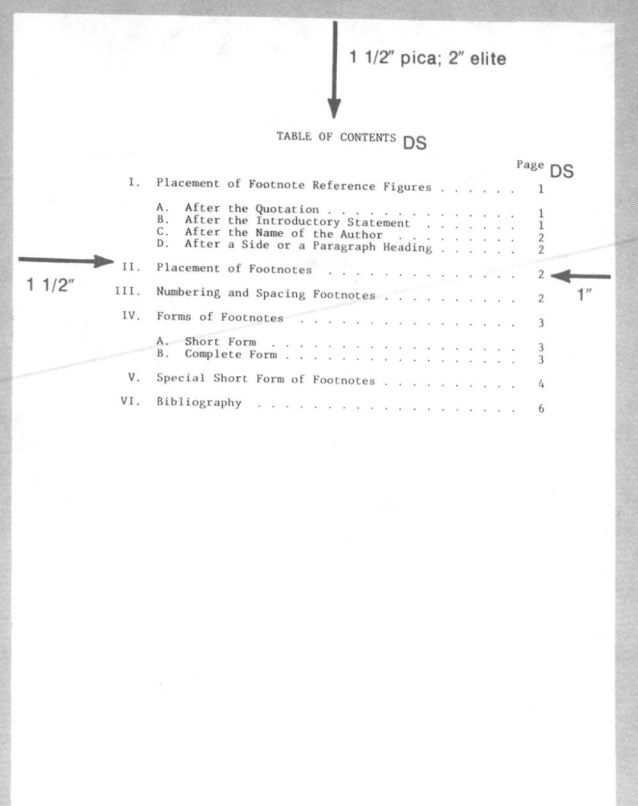

1 1/2" pica; 2" elite

TABLE OF CONTENTS DS

		Page DS
I.	Placement of Footnote Reference Figures	1
	A. After the Quotation	1
	B. After the Introductory Statement	1
	C. After the Name of the Author	2
	D. After a Side or a Paragraph Heading	2
II.	Placement of Footnotes	2
III.	Numbering and Spacing Footnotes	2
IV.	Forms of Footnotes	3
	A. Short Form	3
	B. Complete Form	3
V.	Special Short Form of Footnotes	4
VI.	Bibliography	6

1 1/2"

1"

6 Unbound, bibliography

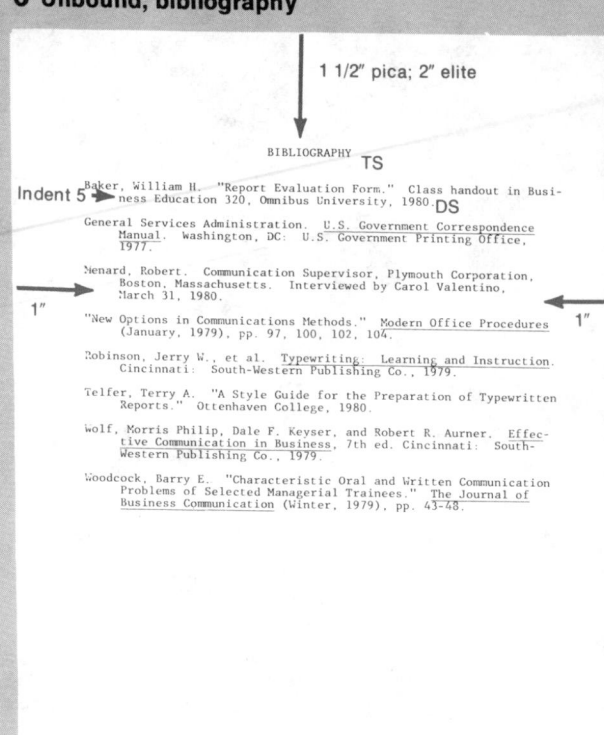

1 1/2" pica; 2" elite

BIBLIOGRAPHY TS

Indent 5

Baker, William H. "Report Evaluation Form." Class handout in Business Education 320, Omnibus University, 1980. DS

General Services Administration. U.S. Government Correspondence Manual. Washington, DC: U.S. Government Printing Office, 1977.

Menard, Robert. Communication Supervisor, Plymouth Corporation, Boston, Massachusetts. Interviewed by Carol Valentino, March 31, 1980.

"New Options in Communications Methods." Modern Office Procedures (January, 1979), pp. 97, 100, 102, 104.

Robinson, Jerry W., et al. Typewriting: Learning and Instruction. Cincinnati: South-Western Publishing Co., 1979.

Telfer, Terry A. "A Style Guide for the Preparation of Typewritten Reports." Ottenhaven College, 1980.

Wolf, Morris Philip, Dale F. Keyser, and Robert R. Aurner. Effective Communication in Business, 7th ed. Cincinnati: South-Western Publishing Co., 1979.

Woodcock, Barry E. "Characteristic Oral and Written Communication Problems of Selected Managerial Trainees." The Journal of Business Communication (Winter, 1979), pp. 43-48.

1" 1"

7 Topbound, page 1

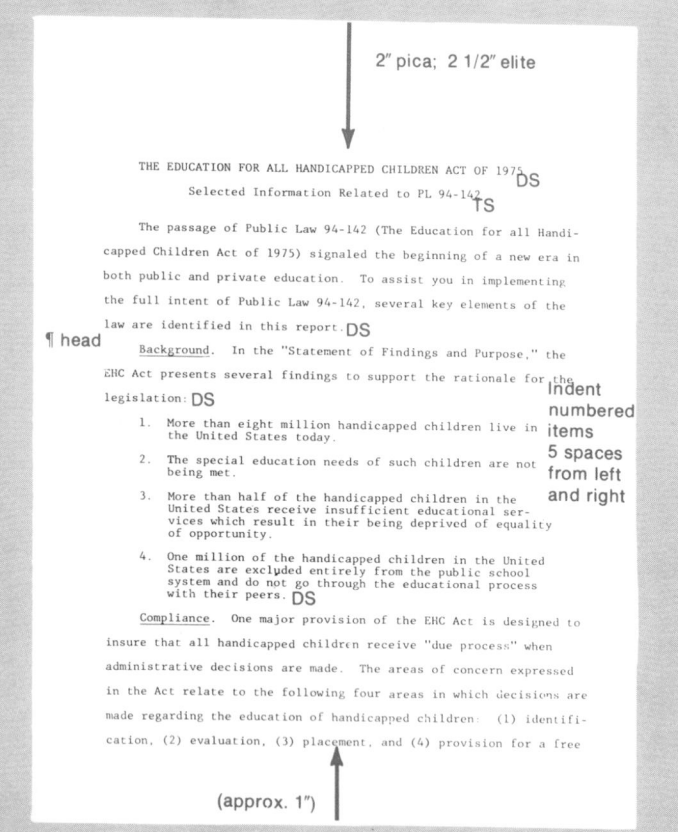

2" pica; 2 1/2" elite

THE EDUCATION FOR ALL HANDICAPPED CHILDREN ACT OF 1975 DS

Selected Information Related to PL 94-142 TS

The passage of Public Law 94-142 (The Education for all Handicapped Children Act of 1975) signaled the beginning of a new era in both public and private education. To assist you in implementing the full intent of Public Law 94-142, several key elements of the law are identified in this report. DS

¶ head

Background. In the "Statement of Findings and Purpose," the EHC Act presents several findings to support the rationale for the legislation: DS

Indent numbered items 5 spaces from left and right

1. More than eight million handicapped children live in the United States today.
2. The special education needs of such children are not being met.
3. More than half of the handicapped children in the United States receive insufficient educational services which result in their being deprived of equality of opportunity.
4. One million of the handicapped children in the United States are excluded entirely from the public school system and do not go through the educational process with their peers. DS

Compliance. One major provision of the EHC Act is designed to insure that all handicapped children receive "due process" when administrative decisions are made. The areas of concern expressed in the Act relate to the following four areas in which decisions are made regarding the education of handicapped children: (1) identification, (2) evaluation, (3) placement, and (4) provision for a free

(approx. 1")

8 Interoffice memorandum

Rayco

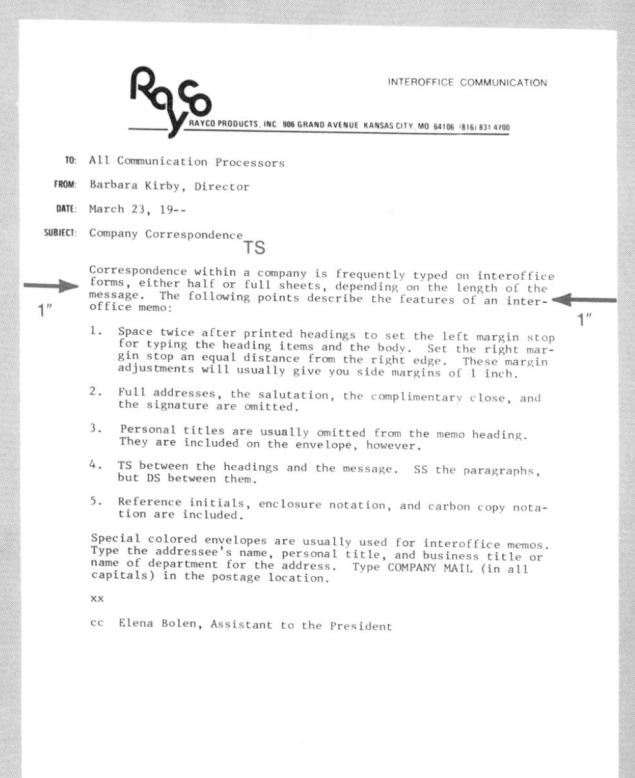

INTEROFFICE COMMUNICATION

RAYCO PRODUCTS, INC. 906 GRAND AVENUE KANSAS CITY, MO 64106 (816) 831-4700

TO: All Communication Processors

FROM: Barbara Kirby, Director

DATE: March 23, 19--

SUBJECT: Company Correspondence TS

Correspondence within a company is frequently typed on interoffice forms, either half or full sheets, depending on the length of the message. The following points describe the features of an interoffice memo:

1" 1"

1. Space twice after printed headings to set the left margin stop for typing the heading items and the body. Set the right margin stop an equal distance from the right edge. These margin adjustments will usually give you side margins of 1 inch.
2. Full addresses, the salutation, the complimentary close, and the signature are omitted.
3. Personal titles are usually omitted from the memo heading. They are included on the envelope, however.
4. TS between the headings and the message. SS the paragraphs, but DS between them.
5. Reference initials, enclosure notation, and carbon copy notation are included.

Special colored envelopes are usually used for interoffice memos. Type the addressee's name, personal title, and business title or name of department for the address. Type COMPANY MAIL (in all capitals) in the postage location.

xx

cc Elena Bolen, Assistant to the President

- Capitalize
- Close up
- Delete
- Insert
- Insert comma
- Insert space
- Insert apostrophe
- Insert quotation marks
- Move right
- Move left
- Move down; lower
- Move up; raise
- Set in lowercase
- Paragraph
- No new paragraph
- Set flush; align type
- Spell out
- Let it stand; ignore correction
- Transpose
- Underline or Italics

Proofreader's marks

Sometimes typed or printed copy may be corrected with proofreader's marks. The typist must be able to interpret correctly these marks in retyping the corrected copy or *rough draft* as it may be called. The most commonly used proofreader's marks are shown above.

1 Horizontal centering

1 Move margin stops to extreme ends of scale.

2 Clear tab stops; then set a tab stop at center of paper.

3 Tabulate to center of paper.

4 From center, backspace *once* for each 2 letters, spaces, figures, or punctuation marks in the line.

5 Do not backspace for an odd or leftover stroke at the end of the line.

6 Begin to type where backspacing ends.

Formula for finding horizontal center of paper

	Example
Scale reading at left edge of paper	0
+Scale reading at right edge of paper	102
Total ÷ 2 = Center Point	102 ÷ 2 = 51

2 Spread headings

1 Backspace from center once for each letter, character, and space *except the last letter or character* in the heading. Begin to type where the backspacing ends.

2 In typing a spread heading, space once after each letter or character and 3 times between words.

3 Vertical centering

Backspace-from-center method
Basic rule

From vertical center of paper, roll platen (cylinder) back once for each 2 lines, 2 blank line spaces, or line and blank line space. Ignore odd or leftover line.

Steps to follow:

1 To move paper to vertical center, start spacing down from top edge of paper.

a half sheet
down 6 TS (triple spaces)
− 1 SS (Line 17)

b full sheet
down 11 TS
+ 1 SS (Line 34)

2 From vertical center

a half sheet, SS or DS: follow basic rule, back 1 for 2.

b full sheet, SS or DS: follow basic rule, back 1 for 2; then back 2 SS for *reading position*.

Mathematical method

1 Count lines and blank line spaces needed to type problem.

2 Subtract *lines to be used* from *lines available* (66 for full sheet and 33 for half sheet).

3 Divide by 2 to get top and bottom margins. If fraction results, disregard it. Space down from top edge of paper *1 more than number of lines to be left in top margin.*

For *reading position*, which is above exact vertical center, subtract 2 from exact top margin.

Formula for vertical mathematical placement

$$\frac{\text{Lines available} - \text{lines used}}{2} = \text{top margin}$$

Prepare

1 Insert and align paper.

2 Clear margin stops by moving them to extreme ends of the scale.

3 Clear all tab stops.

4 Decide the number of spaces to be left between columns (for intercolumns).

1 Plan vertical placement

Follow either of the vertical centering methods explained on page ix.

Report headings. Double–space (count 1 blank line space) between main and secondary headings, when both are used. Triple–space (count 2 blank line spaces) between the last report heading (either main or secondary) and the first horizontal line of column items or column headings. Double–space between column headings (when used) and the first line of the columns.

2 Plan horizontal placement

Backspace from center of paper 1 space for each 2 letters, figures, symbols, and spaces in *longest item* of each column and for each 2 spaces between columns. Set left margin stop at this point. If an extra space occurs at the end of the longest item when backspacing, carry it forward to the next column. Ignore an extra space at the end of the last column. (See illustration below.)

An easy alternate method is to backspace for the longest item in each column first, *then* for the spaces to the left between columns.

Note. If a column heading is longer than the longest item in the column, it may be treated as the longest item in determining placement. The longest column item must then be centered under the heading, and the tab stop set accordingly.

Set tab stops. From the left margin stop, space forward 1 space for each letter, figure, symbol, and space in the longest item in the first column and for each space in the first intercolumn. Set a tab stop at this point for the second column. Follow this procedure for each additional column to be typed.

3 To center column headings

Backspace-from-column-center method

From point at which column begins (tab or margin stop), space forward (→) once for each 2 letters, figures, or spaces in the longest item in the column. This leads to the column center point; from it, backspace (←) once for each 2 spaces in column heading. Ignore an odd or leftover space. Type the heading at this point; it will be centered over the column.

Mathematical method

1 To the number of the cylinder (platen) or line–of–writing scale immediately under the first letter, figure, or symbol of the longest item of the column, add the number shown under the space following the last stroke of the item. Divide this sum by 2; the result will be the center point of the column. From this point on the scale, backspace to center the column heading.

2 From the number of spaces in the longest item, subtract the number of spaces in the heading. Divide this number by 2; ignore fractions. Space forward this number from the tab or margin stop and type the heading.

4 To type horizontal lines

Depress shift lock; strike underline key.

5 To draw vertical lines

Operate the automatic line finder. Place a pencil or pen point through the cardholder (or the type bar guide above the ribbon or carrier). Roll the paper up until you have a line of the desired length. Remove the pencil or pen and reset the line finder.

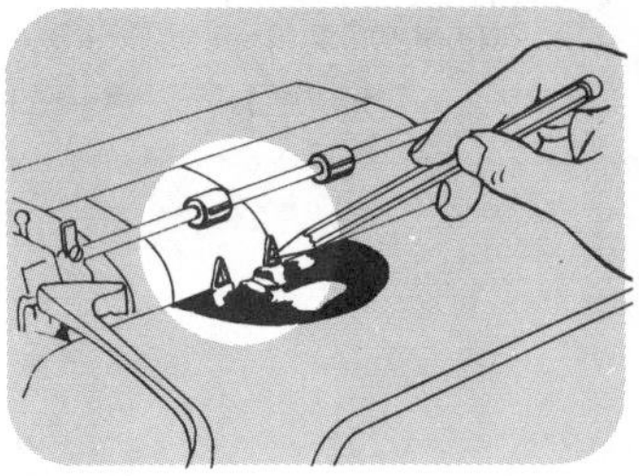

MAIN HEADING

Secondary Heading

These	Are	Column	Heads
xxxxxx	*longest*	xxxx	xxxxx
xxxx	*item*	*longest*	xxx
xxxxx	xxxxx	*item*	*longest*
longest	xxxxxx	xxxxx	*item*
item	xxxx	xxx	xxx

lo ng es t1 23 4l on ge st 12 34 lo ng es t1 23 4l on ge st

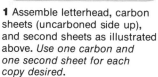

1 Desk-top assembly method

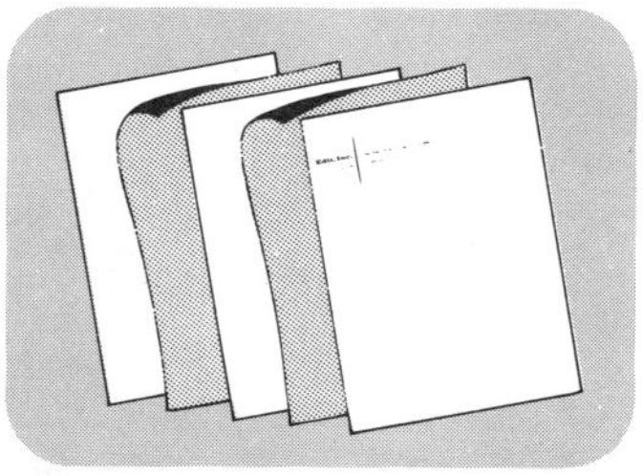

1 Assemble letterhead, carbon sheets (uncarboned side up), and second sheets as illustrated above. *Use one carbon and one second sheet for each copy desired.*

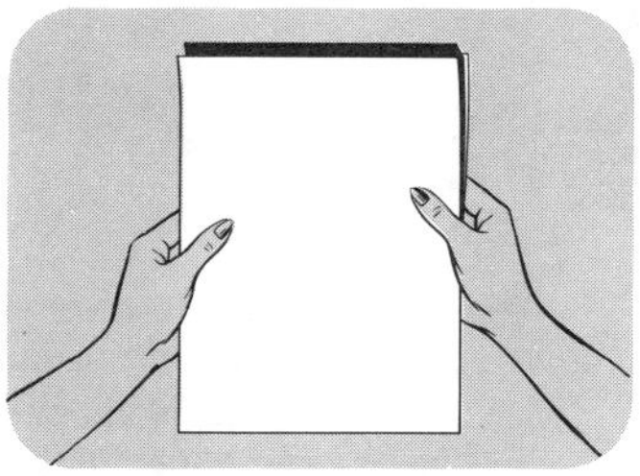

2 Grasp the carbon pack at the sides, turn it so that the *letterhead faces away from you, the carbon side of the carbon paper is toward you, and the top edge of the pack is face down.* Tap the sheets gently on the desk to straighten.

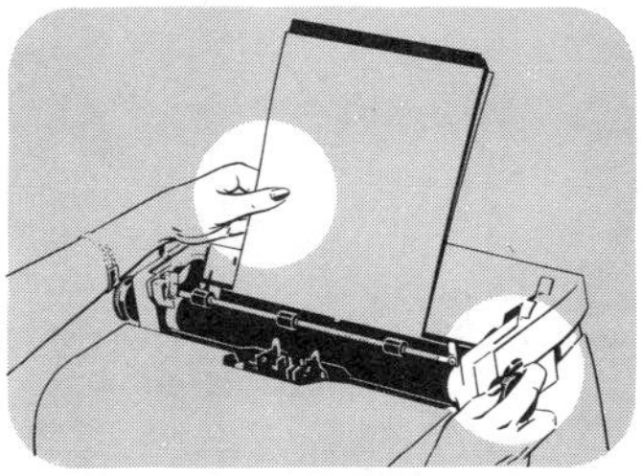

3 Hold the sheets firmly to prevent slipping; insert pack into type-writer. Hold pack with one hand; turn platen with the other.

Tips for wrinkle-free assembly

Start pack into typewriter with paper-release lever forward; then reset the paper-release lever and turn pack into the machine.

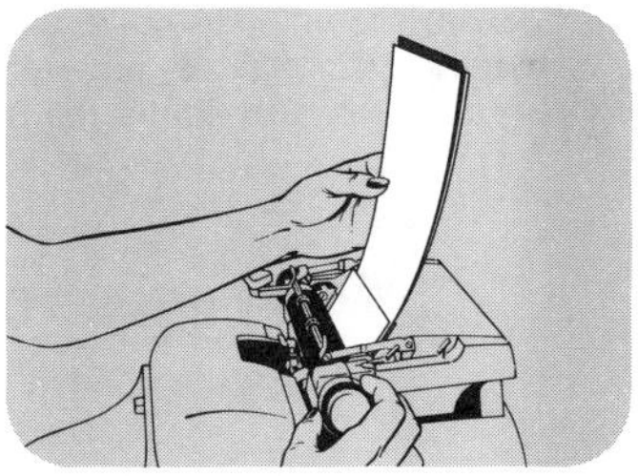

2 Inserting the pack with a trough

To keep the carbon pack straight when feeding it into the typewriter, place the pack in the fold of a plain sheet of paper (paper trough) or under the flap of an envelope. Remove the trough or envelope when the pack is in place.

3 Removing carbon sheets

Hold the left edge of the letterhead and second sheets; remove all carbons at one time with the right hand.

4 Machine assembly method

1 Assemble paper for insertion (original on top; second sheets beneath). Turn the "pack" so *original faces away from you* and *the top edge faces down.*

2 Insert sheets until the tops are gripped by the feed rolls; then pull the bottom of all sheets except the last over the top (front) of the typewriter.

3 Place carbon paper between sheets, *carboned side toward you.* Flip each sheet back (away from you) as you add each carbon sheet.

4 Roll pack into typing position.

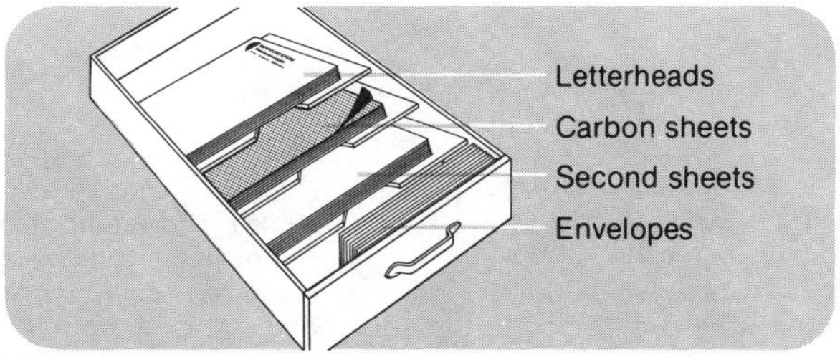

5 Slotted drawer assembly method

1 With sheets correctly arranged in slotted drawer, pick up a let-terhead with left hand, a sheet of carbon paper with right hand; pull sheets slightly forward; grasp both sheets with left hand as right hand reaches and pulls second sheet into position.

2 Pull sheets from slots. Straighten pack by tapping gently on desk as the sides of the sheets are held loosely by both hands.

3 Add extra sheets (a second sheet and a carbon) for any addi-tional copies that may be needed.

4 Insert into typewriter as with desk-top assembly method.

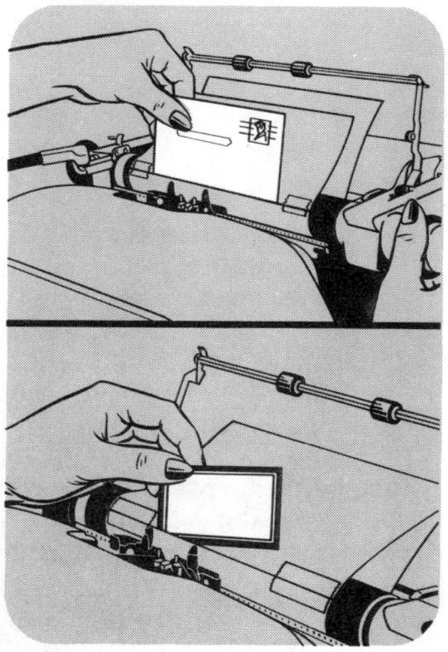

Front feeding small cards and labels

1 Changing a typewriter ribbon

The technique for changing a typewriter ribbon is not the same for all machines. In no case, however, is it a difficult operation; but the following suggestions may be helpful.

If you are working with a fabric ribbon, wind it onto one spool (usually the one containing the less ribbon) before beginning the procedure.

Observe carefully the winding path of the ribbon in the machine before you remove it. Make pencil notes if necessary. Reverse the procedure to install the new ribbon.

Consult the machine manufacturer's manual for their recommendations for changing ribbons.

In case of unusual difficulty, consult with the manufacturer's representative or the retailer from whom the typewriter was purchased.

2 Correcting errors

Rubber eraser

Move the carriage or carrier to the right or left to prevent bits of rubber from damaging the type mechanism.

To avoid disturbing the alignment of the typed copy, turn over the cylinder forward if the erasure is to be made on the upper ⅔ of the paper; backward, on the lower ⅓ of the paper.

To erase on the original sheet, lift the paper bail out of the way, place a 5″ x 3″ card or other heavy paper in front of the first carbon sheet. Use a special typing erasure and an eraser shield to protect the typing that is not to be erased. Brush eraser bits away from the type mechanism.

If more than one copy is involved, move the protective card in front of the second sheet of carbon paper. Erase errors on carbon copies with a soft (pencil) eraser; then, if necessary, use the hard typing eraser used to erase original copies.

When the error has been erased on all copies, remove the protective card, position the carriage or carrier to the paper point, and type the necessary correction.

Correction paper

Backspace to the error. Place the correction paper in front of the error, coated side toward the paper.

Special correction paper is available for use in correcting carbon copies. Turn the cylinder forward if the correction is to be made on the upper ⅔ of the paper; backward, on the lower ½ of the paper. Place a piece of the special correction paper between the carbon and the copy, coated side toward the copy. Then place the correction paper in front of the error on the original.

Retype the error. The substance on the correction paper will obliterate the error.

Correction fluid

Be sure the color of the fluid matches the color of the paper.

Turn the paper forward or backward to ease the correction procedure.

Brush the fluid on sparingly. Cover only the error—and it lightly—on the original and all carbon copies.

Wait a few seconds for the fluid to dry. Return to typing position and type the correction.

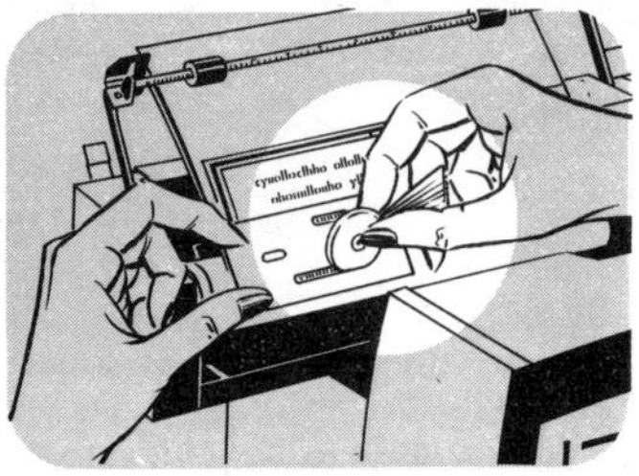

3 Squeezing/spreading of letters

In correcting errors, it is often possible to "squeeze" omitted letters into half spaces or to "spread" letters to fill out spaces.

Error	Correction
an omitte letter	an omitted letter
a leter within	a letter within
a lettter within	a letter within

1 An omitted letter at the beginning or end of a word

Corrective steps

a Move carriage to the letter *e*.

b Depress and hold down the space bar; strike the letter *d*.

Note: On an electric typewriter, it may be necessary to hold the carriage by hand at the half-space point, or to use the half-space mechanism.

2 An omitted letter within a word

Corrective steps

a Erase the incorrect word.

b Position the carriage at the space after the letter *a*.

c Press down and hold the space bar; strike the letter *l*.

d Release the space bar, then press it down again and hold it; strike the next letter.

e Repeat the process for any additional letters.

Note: On the Selectric and some other electrics, use the half-space mechanism.

3 Addition of a letter within a word

Corrective steps

a Erase the incorrect word.

b Position the carriage as if you were going to type the letter *l* in its regular position following the space.

c Press down and hold the space bar; strike the letter *l*.

d Release the space bar; then repeat the process for each remaining letter.

Note: On the Selectric and some other electrics, use the half-space mechanism.